The Travels and Adventures of *Our Pleasure*

A Family's Nine-Year Sailing Adventure Around 95 Percent of the World
Sept. 3, 1997 to June 4, 2006

Richard L. Bennett

For Mona,
With best wishes.
Dick Bennett
Cortez, Fl '13

Strategic Book Publishing and Rights Co.

Strategic Book Publishing and Rights Co.
12620 FM 1960, Suite A4-507
Houston TX 77065
www.sbpra.com

U.S. Library of Congress-in-Publication Data
Bennett, Richard L.
December 9, 2011
The Travels and Adventures of ***Our Pleasure***/Richard L. Bennett
Copyright, I Title
Registration Number: TXu 1-785-085

ISBN: 978-1-60693-175-2

DEDICATION

For Pat

Best friend, seaman and wife, who made this journey possible; and, to our children, David, Marjorie and Leslie, who gave us their full support, time and talents.

TABLE OF CONTENTS

ACKNOWLEDGEMENTS

I give my family a lot of credit for support of and encouragement for this 9-year journey of a lifetime. The task of finding a secure and reliable vessel that could take a crew safely around the world was formidable. However, even more difficult for any family are the time and resources needed for the preparation.

We purchased ***Our Pleasure*** second hand, but she was virtually a new boat with only 50 hours of engine time, and all sails had been stored on land. Being unused, she had virtually no electronics or equipment that would be needed for years of cruising miles away from marine services. She had no porthole coverings for storms or cockpit protection from the weather, all of her mattresses and cushion foam had to be replaced and her sails and handling equipment were basic. The original electronics consisted of only a VHF radio, depth sounder, and knot meter/log.

On the plus side, even though the boat was three years old when we purchased her, she had almost no prior use. The big Ford-Lehman Diesel was still gleaming in its factory-red paint. The four sails, previously used once or twice, were in new condition. It took several years to add the necessary electronics, hardware, spare parts, tools, cockpit electronics/protection, and interior decorating to turn ***Our Pleasure*** into a comfortable, well-equipped sailing vessel. Many weekends and evenings of time away from home, family and friends, were necessary to make this vessel ready for the world's oceans.

For their time and support, I gratefully acknowledge my wife, Pat, and three children: David, Marjorie (and husband, Gary) and, Leslie (and husband, Bob). Everyone helped with such things as bottom painting, hardware installation, and sailing excursions. David, Marjorie, and Gary contributed to our CD and movie collection. Marjorie did a fantastic job of taking care of mail, forwarding messages and filing important papers. Leslie and Bob were great crewmembers for the first year and a half, helping with everything and even painting the masts from a boatswain's chair.

Two of The Boeing Company's most highly regarded engineers, Chuck Goggio and Lloyd Crabtree, helped install the generator, new hardware, and miles of wiring. Chuck Goggio, Clay Eals, Marjorie, Pat, along with friends and family, contributed many hours proofreading the text and encouraged me to put our story into words.

Lastly, I need to thank many of our cruising friends mentioned in this book for their valuable friendship, resources, and help during our journey.

INTRODUCTION

This book is the true story of a family sailing adventure around 95 percent of the world over a nine-year period from Sept. 1997 to June 2006. Our youngest daughter Leslie and husband Bob were married only two weeks before we left Seattle and their honeymoon became a one-and-a-half-years-long sailing odyssey with my wife Pat and me. Our sailing took us down the U.S. coast into Mexico, through the Pacific Ocean, through the Indian Ocean, around Africa and through the Atlantic Ocean into Florida.

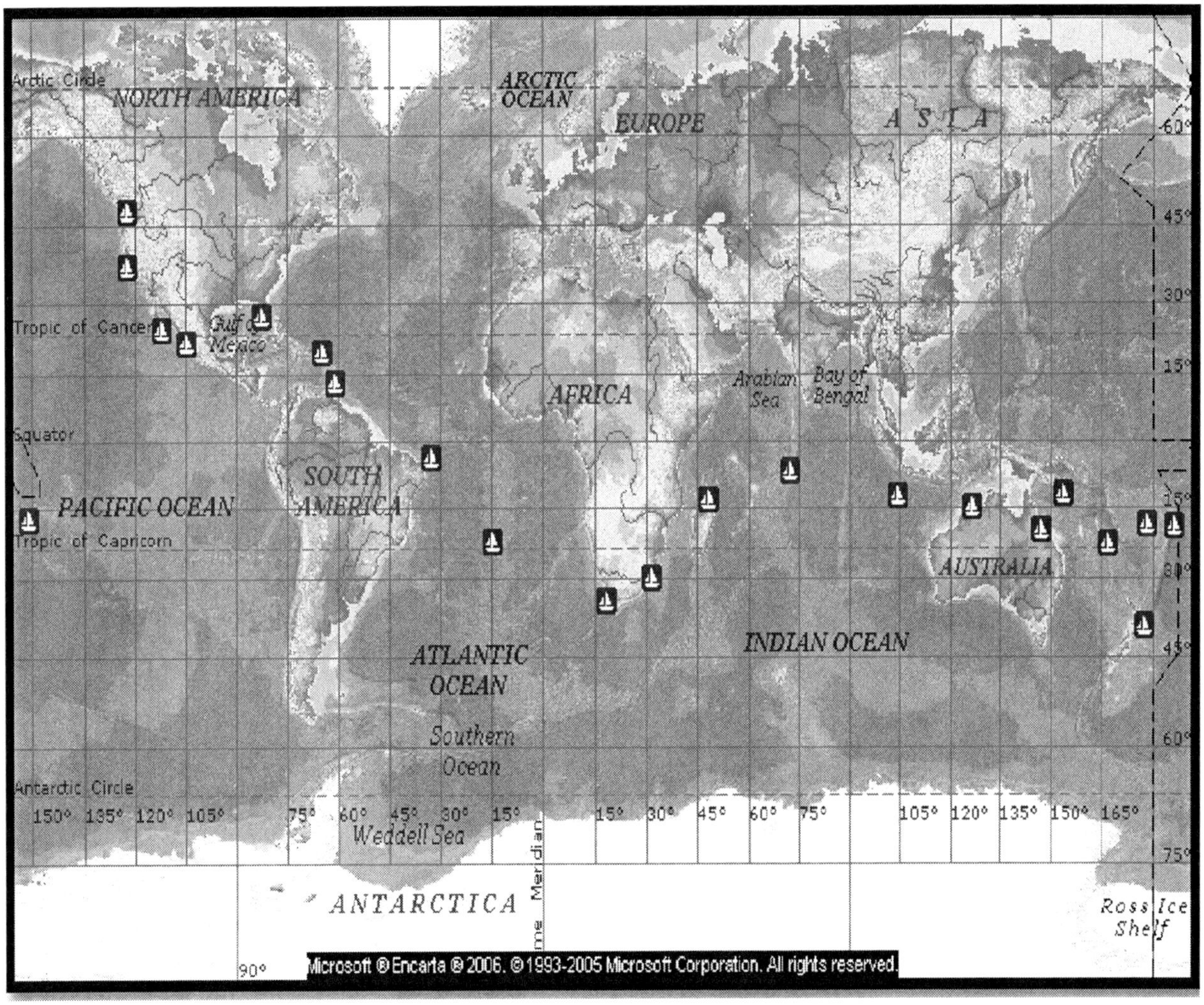

ROUTE OF *OUR PLEASURE*

We weathered one horrific storm on the way to New Zealand where lives were lost and we survived several minor storms. Along the way, we picked up varied crewmembers and visited some remote places. We met many people who love life and are happy to share what they have, yet their material possessions are almost non-existent. The sailing life can be extremely rewarding and joyous, but also frustrating, difficult and sometimes sad. At sea, problems are solved with just the resources on hand, so preparedness and farsightedness play a big role in comfort and safety. If a reader of this book is thinking of offshore cruising, please approach it as a serious endeavor. Offshore sailing is a risky business, but it is also truly rewarding.

First, Pat, Leslie, Bob, and I thank everyone who attended the blessing of ***Our Pleasure*** by Father Ibar Lynch on Sunday, Aug. 31, 1997. That day was special, a beautiful way to start our journey. We think of Father Ibar as our own family priest. He helped us in all family matters, through thick and thin, for the past 45 years. It was a beautiful day at Shilshole Bay Marina, Seattle, Washington. I think that about half of St. Anne's parish from Queen Anne Hill and almost all our Seattle friends were there to wish us well – quite a day!

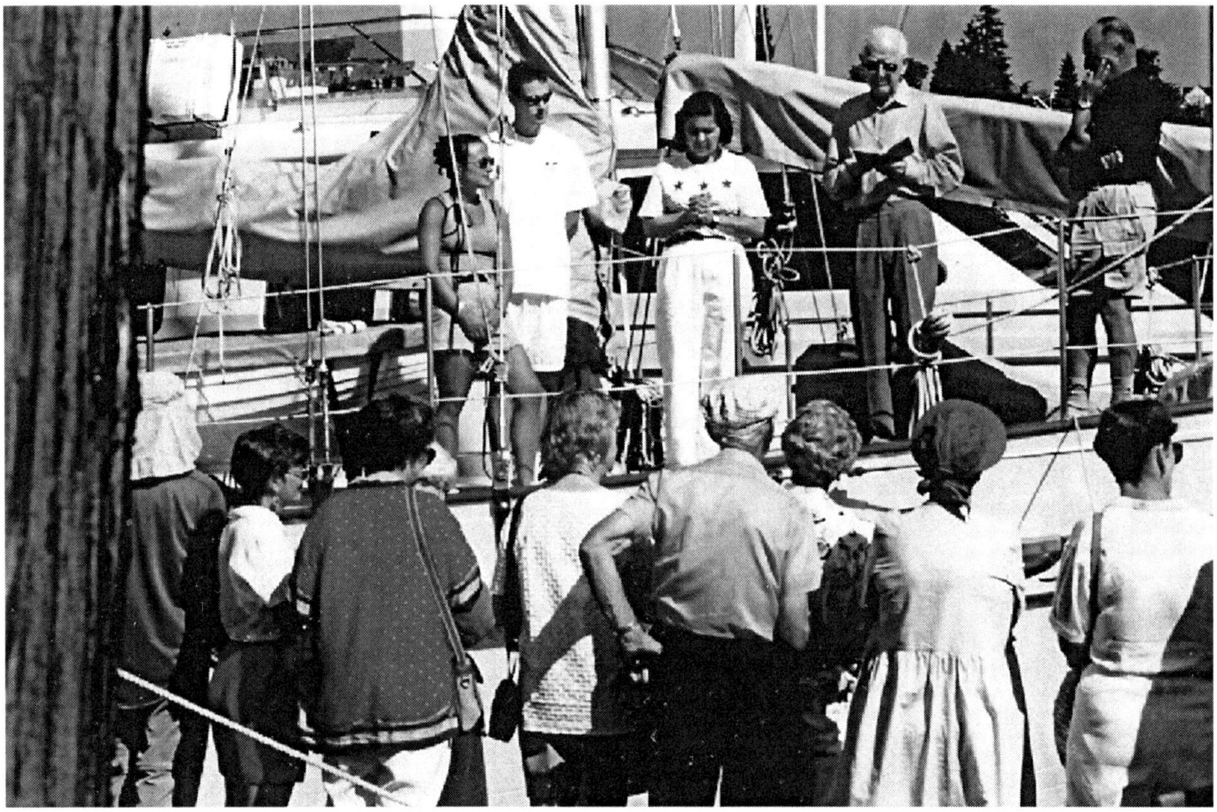

REV. IBAR LYNCH BLESSING *OUR PLEASURE* & CREW,
Aug. 31, 1997, SHILSHOLE BAY MARINA, SEATTLE, WASHINGTON

Reverend Ibar Lynch's blessing prayer for ***Our Pleasure*** and her crew:

May St. Nicolas and St. Brendan bless this craft
May the angels dance above its deck

To ward off dangers fore and aft
From wind and wave and sunken wrecks
All who sail it may they protect
May all who cruise this mighty ocean
Treat it always with wise respect
And no foolish risks ever take
May Jesus who preached from a boat
Bless and protect this boat
Together with the Father and the Son and the Holy Spirit. Amen.

Father Ibar joined our youngest daughter Leslie and Bob Fischer in marriage on Aug. 23, 1997. The wedding took place just one and a half weeks before we began our sailing adventure of a lifetime. Pat and I were busy with boat and food preparations, so daughter Marjorie and other family members worked on the wedding planning. Little did anyone realize the newly married couple was about to embark on an 18 month seafaring adventure. Thus started a wonderful new twist to cruising — a year-and-a-half honeymoon with parents and in-laws.

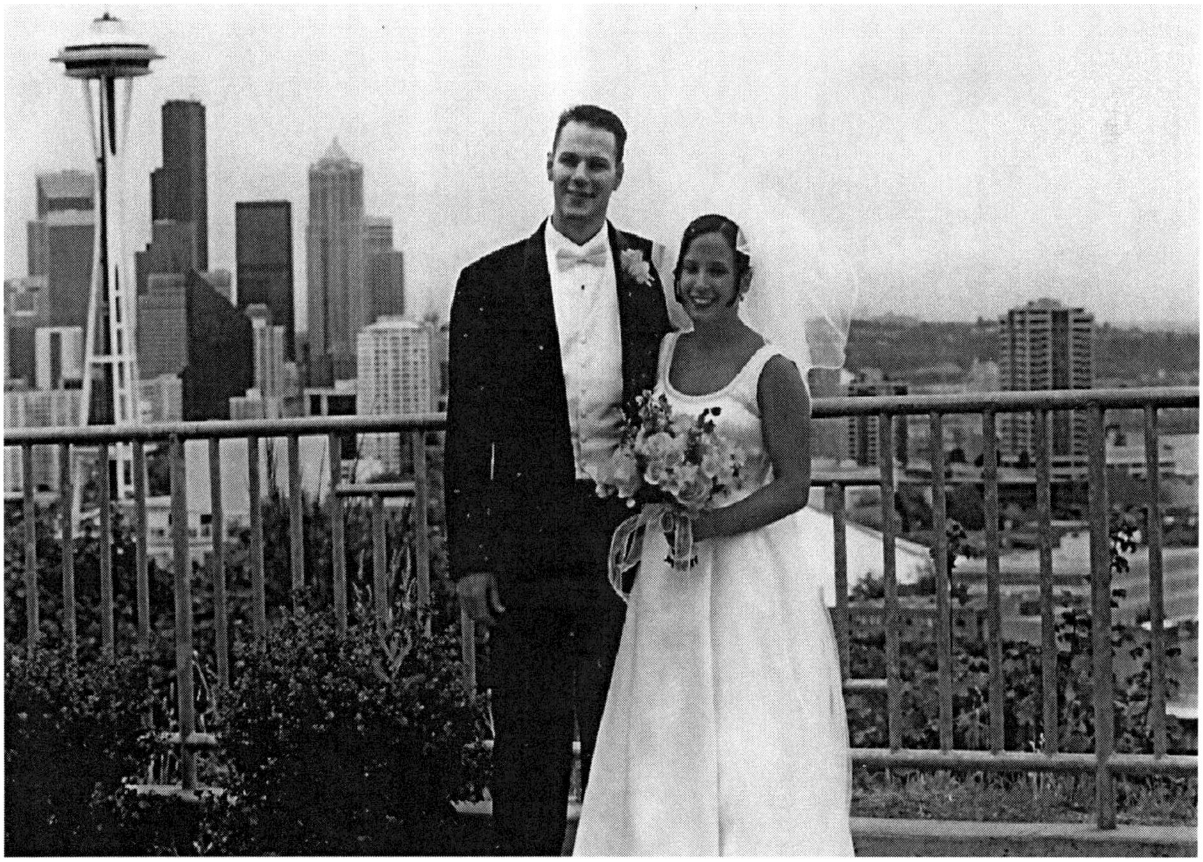

BOB & LESLIE'S, WEDDING DAY, QUEEN ANNE HILL, SEATTLE, Aug. 23, 1997

Three days after our dock party and blessing, we managed a deep breath and slipped our dock lines on Wednesday, Sept. 3, 1997. We caught the early morning ebb tide at 6:25 a.m. to help us out of Puget Sound. Among those who braved the wee hours of the dawn to wave us good-bye were Arlen McGregor, a long time friend; Bill and Diane, sailing buddies from the yacht *Golden Ring*, Dr. Ken Kelly, who worked out our complete medical chest; and, Bob's father, Jace, mother, Nancy, and brother, Zach.

Chapter 1

SEATTLE TO MAZATLAN

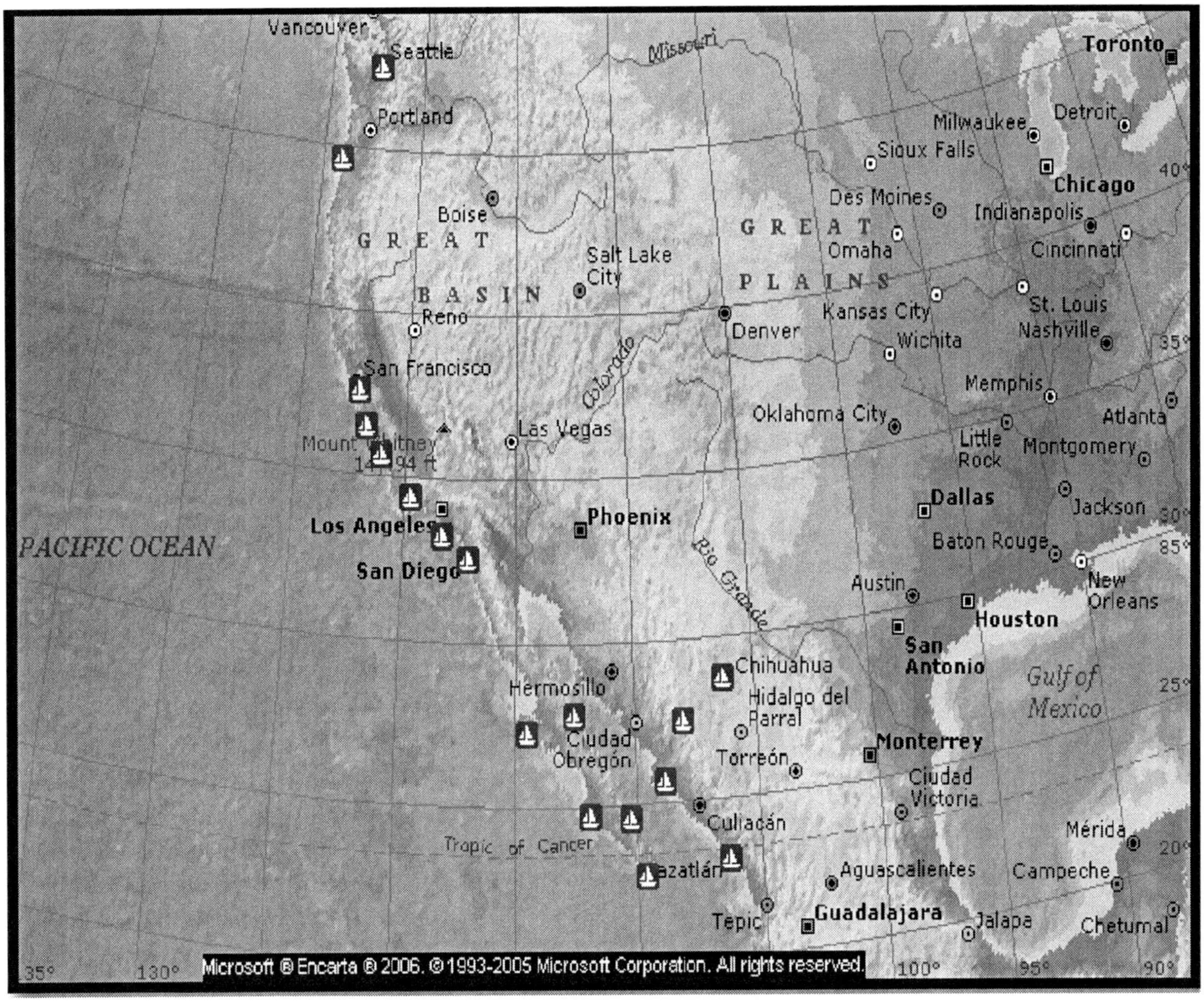

WEST COAST PORTS AND SIDE TRIPS, SEATTLE TO MEXICO

After we left Puget Sound and the Strait of Juan de Fuca to reach the Pacific Ocean, our first port of call and an exciting night entry, was Newport, Oregon. We were confused about just where the outer channel markers were located. The channel lights that we visually located were not, where the chart placed them. The problem may have been a combination of bright city lights in the background and inoperative channel lights, but with the help of radar, electronic charts and the GPS, we managed just fine.

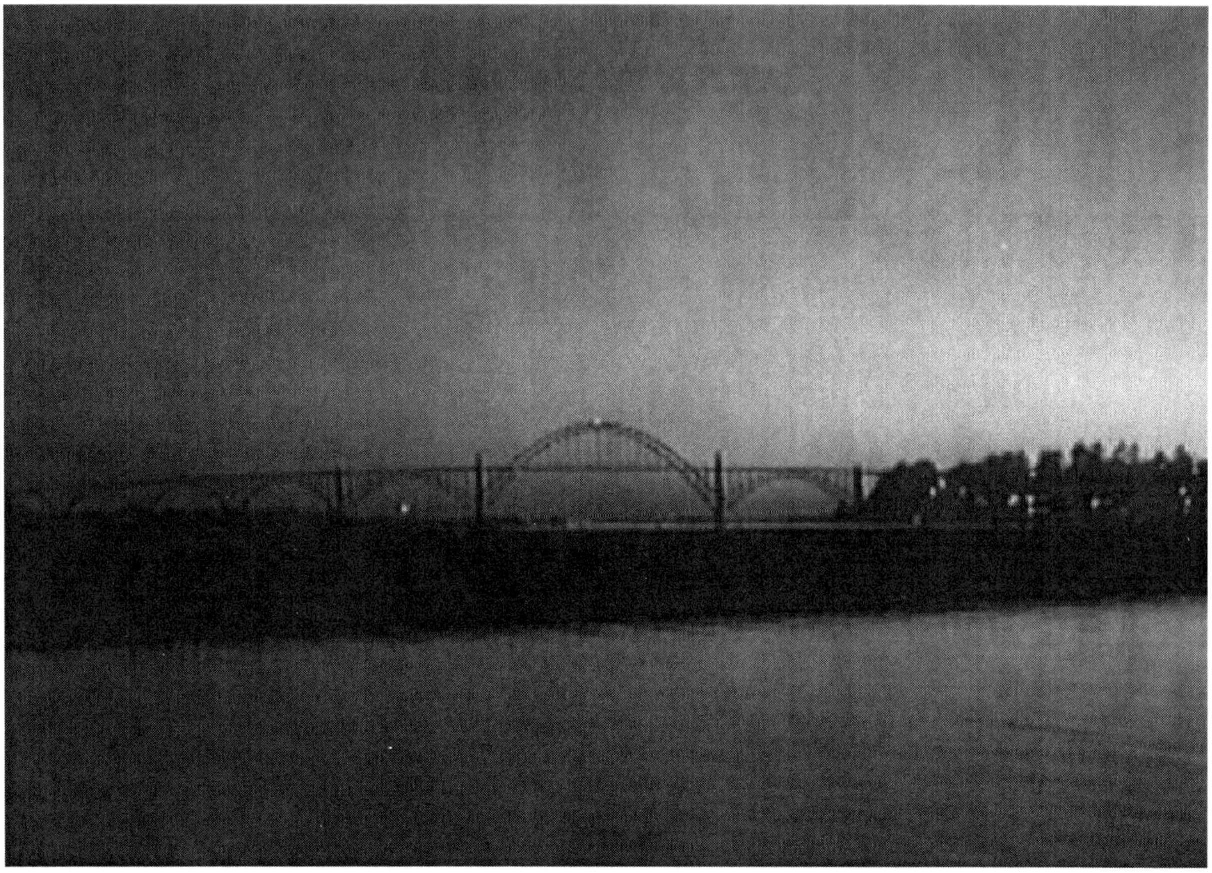

SUNSET, NEWPORT, OREGON

The next morning, Bill and Diane surprised us when they knocked on our hull. They had driven down from Seattle to greet us and see how things were going. Bill and Diane were our neighbors on "G" dock back in Seattle. Our boats were similar; both designed by Bill Garden. We always have helped each other with boat projects. That made Bill a perfect choice to help with any needed repairs. No repairs were required however, as the boat was in good shape. Just the captain and crew were a bit tired from sleep deprivation.

We had a good time talking about our trip. Soon another couple, Dick and Betsy Russell, longtime friends from Lincoln City, Oregon, were knocking on our hull. They arrived with a meal fit for a king: freshly caught Dungeones crab, fresh-baked bread and homemade pie, a wonderful treat for 4 bleary-eyed sailors.

Oregon ports are not friendly to boaters who lack firsthand knowledge of the ports' channels, tide flow and currents. To negotiate their bars safely, you must wait for the right tide and current. We chose to play it conservatively and bypass the rest of the Oregon coast. Our next ports were along the west coast of California, including San Simeon, Morrow Bay, Pier 39 (San Francisco), Sausalito (across from San

Francisco), Benicia (up the Sacramento River), Santa Barbara, Long Beach and Avalon (Santa Catalina Island).

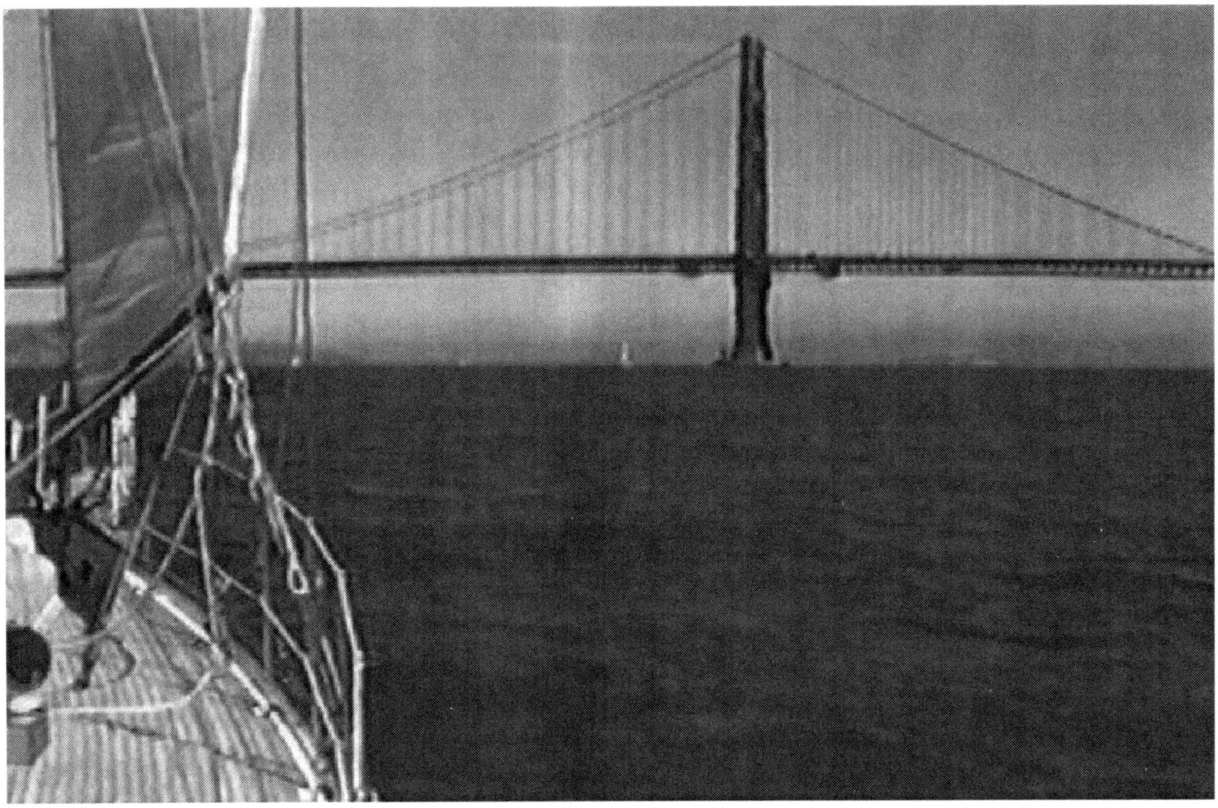

GOLDEN GATE BRIDGE, SAN FRANCISCO

We arrived at Sun Road Marina in San Diego on Oct. 6, 1997, to prepare ***Our Pleasure*** for the "Baja Ha Ha" rally. "Marina" is somewhat of a misnomer, as this place was like a resort with a heated pool, large spa, small store, grassy, park-like areas, and nice restrooms. The whole marina was spotless. The staff even hosed off the docks every morning — seagull poop was not allowed. We had plenty of time to check all the boat systems and do the routine oil-filter changes on the engine and generator. We tied down everything securely, finished the outfitting and filled all nooks and crannies with our favorite foods.

Our daughter Marjorie, and her husband, Gary, flew from Seattle to spend time with us before we left for Mexico. They stayed at a nearby motel and invited Bob and Leslie to stay at the motel so they could luxuriate a little before starting the real part of ***Our Pleasure's*** big adventure.

We became acquainted with a California family on *Albion* moored at the next dock, which would also be in the rally. At 10 a.m. on Oct. 28, we left San Diego with an amazing rally fleet of 108 boats. The "Baja Ha Ha" rally was off to a perfect start under warm, sunny skies and light north winds. It was quite a sight. Colorful spinnakers dotted the horizon and every type of sailboat imaginable started to move along smartly. Helicopters, press boats and sightseeing boats sent us off properly. We put up our spinnaker at the start and didn't have to change a thing for the next three days.

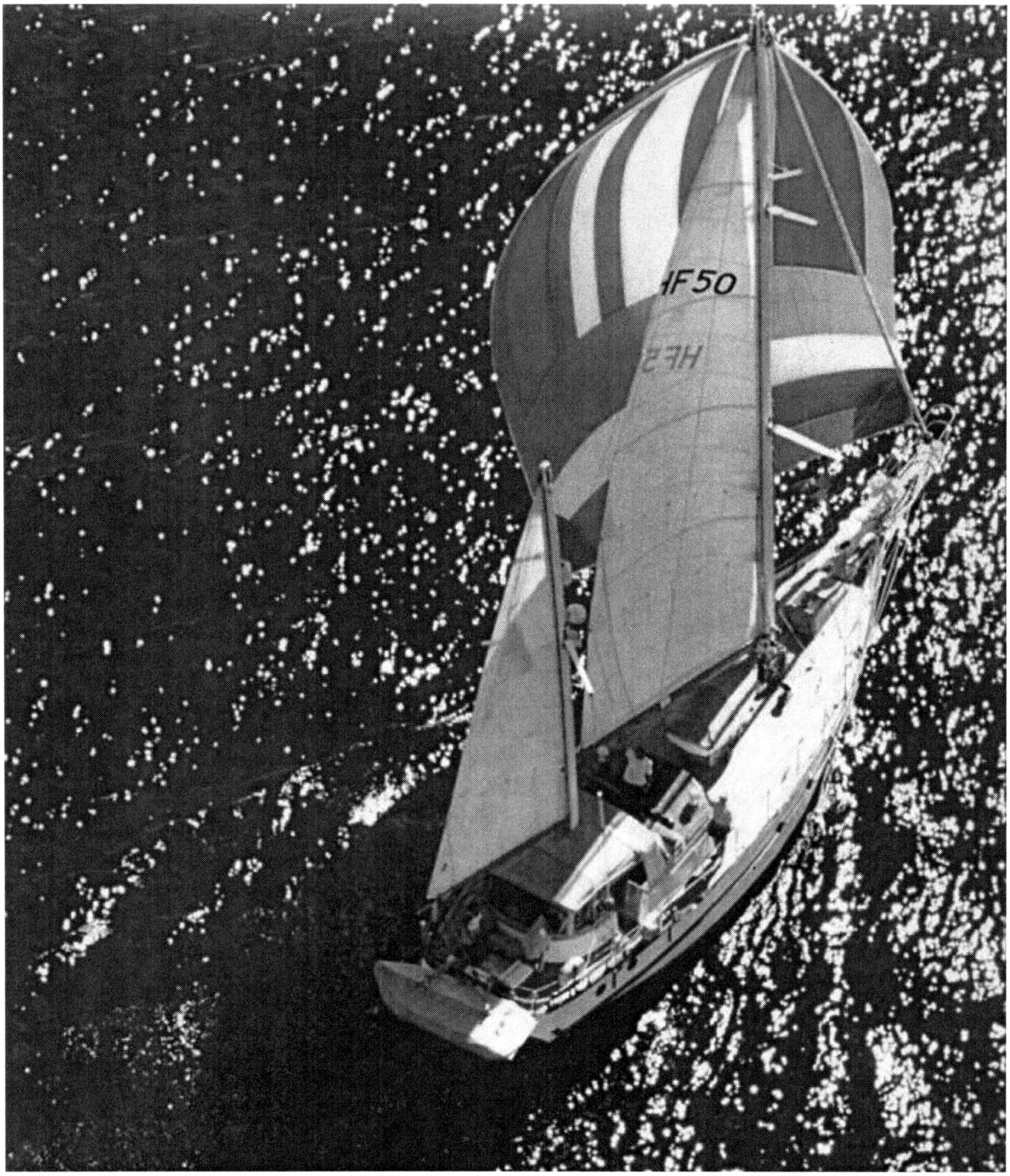

Baja Ha Ha photo courtesy of Tom Lyon
***OUR PLEASURE*, LEAVING SAN DIEGO, Oct. 10, 1997**

Our first stop in Mexico was Turtle Bay. Many of the boaters had gifts for the children of the village, school supplies for teachers and medical supplies for the hospital. The *Albion* crew called us on the VHF radio just outside the bay's entrance, saying they couldn't get its engine started. Bob and I put our dinghy in the water and towed the *Albion* into the bay. Once she was alongside ***Our Pleasure***, it didn't take much time for us to get the *Albion* engine back in working order.

Jorge came by our boat in an outboard-powered Panga and sold us 7 live lobsters for $10. Since *Albion* was still alongside, we turned it into a special occasion for both our families, opening a bottle of champagne to have with our lobster. Two young Mexicans took away our garbage for $2.

Our second stop was the big, beautiful and picturesque Mexican bay, Bahia Santa Maria. The stopover in this bay was to be the saddest of the rally, but not of our journey. Little did we know how cruel seas and storms would dampen our adventure in the future by taking away friends and boats?

Here, Joan Kelly, a crewmember on the 44 foot motor trawler, *Song of San Francisco*, suffered a fatal heart attack. When Joan first collapsed about 1:30 p.m., every medically trained person in the rally fleet rushed to her boat. Dianne Foster, a registered nurse we had met in Sausalito, was visiting on our boat. When she heard the call for help on the VHF radio, she jumped into her dinghy and left in a flash, with no hesitation what so-ever. It turned out that, the fleet had more doctors, nurses, emergency medical personnel and medical supplies than the nearest Mexican hospital.

Their combined efforts were valiant and lasted well into the late afternoon, but Joan's attack was too severe. The only medical equipment not available in the fleet was a heart defibrillator. However, most members of her emergency team thought Joan's attack too severe for a defibrillator to make a difference. The medical team of boaters worked without letup to restore her heartbeat, but it was not to be. They continued to work on her as a high-speed boat and later an ambulance took her to the nearest Mexican hospital. Everyone hoped the Mexican doctors would work miracles, but the ambulance was just an open pickup truck with no medical equipment. The truck pretending to be an ambulance did not even contain a first-aid kit.

The hospital, to everyone's amazement, had almost no medical equipment and no defibrillator. Everyone in the fleet felt so disheartened that Joan had passed away despite everyone's best efforts and prayers. Her husband was with her on the *Song of San Francisco*, and I can only imagine how depressed he must have felt. Chatter on the VHF radios became quite somber as the fleet and the *Song of San Francisco* continued on to Cabo San Lucas.

So far, the sailing part of the rally had gone well, but we began encountering light sailing winds as we neared Cabo San Lucas. Bobby and Leslie caught two tuna, each about a foot long, our first fish. I ran our water maker — taking advantage of the calm seas to make water from the sea.

Then one evening around 8 p.m. just north of Cabo San Lucas and 17 miles from shore, thousands of flying earwigs invaded our serene evening with unmatched fury. It was like a horrible horror movie — eerie and frightening. Pat and I were on watch at the time and we looked at each other in angst and astonishment. The air was so thick with earwigs, akin to a heavy snowstorm, we were afraid to open our mouths. These elongated slender insects are ugly things with pincers that protrude from their abdomens. They were about an inch and a half long. This variety had two pairs of wings; the front pair were small and leathery. The large second pair consisted of a clear membrane that folded beneath the first pair in a complicated manner.

The earwig's scientific name comes from the Greek, Dermaptera (dermatos means: skin, and pteron means: wing). For unknown reasons, they must have lost their bearings because they were flying west away from land. The nearest land west of our boat was thousands of miles away with nothing but ocean in between. This event was doubly odd because earwigs normally like warm, humid crevices such as between leaves and under rocks and bark. Living in crevices provides the association with their popular name, "earwig." Therefore, the idea that they might crawl into a warm ear cavity could have merit. However, the myth that they might enter your ear and penetrate into your brain to lay eggs is unfounded.

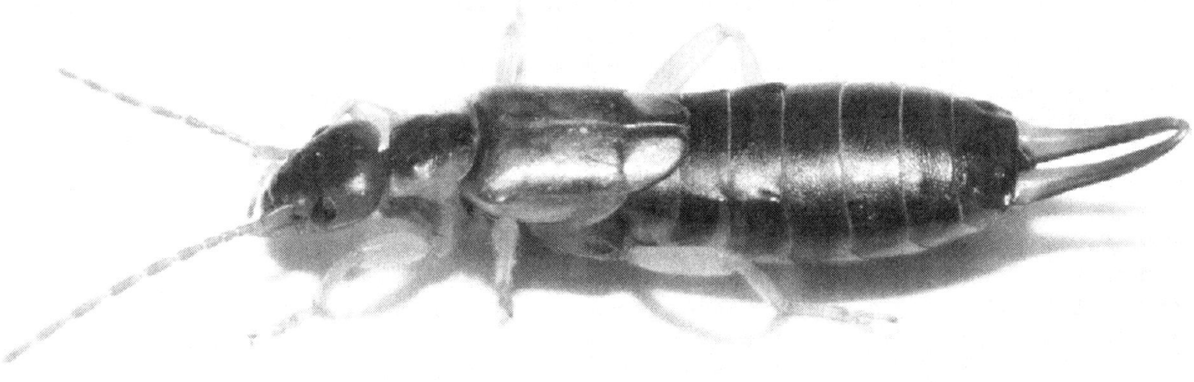

Photo courtesy of Wikipedia©

EARWIG, SCIENTIFIC NAME: DERMAPTERA, THE FORICULINA SPECIES

We thought the earwigs were attracted to our running lights, so we turned them off. I don't think the lights had much of an effect, because they kept coming even with all the lights off. What a mess! The air, decks and water surrounding our boat were thick with them. The majority of the earwigs were exhausted and not moving smartly. Those that landed, we washed off the decks with buckets of salt water or killed by stomping hard on them. They have a hard shell, so the stomping worked only with shoes, which by this time into our trip we were not wearing. We had to go into our cabins to find our shoes.

If the sheer number of earwigs was not dispiriting enough, they managed to stink to high heaven. When we crushed them, they exuded a semi-sweet smell that was nauseating.

The earwigs that still had a fair amount of life, seemed to sense the danger from us humans. They scattered and crawled into every conceivable hiding place. The earwigs that landed in the water tried to find their way into the boat from openings near the waterline. They did this by crawling into the sink drains, which connect through tubing to the hull's drain fittings at the waterline. We managed to close off the drains after realizing how they were getting inside, but not in time to get all of them. We could see the speedy ones crawling under the coverings of hatches, the dinghy and other on deck gear, but we had to concentrate on the larger earwig groups on the deck.

After we arrived in Cabo San Lucas on Nov. 6, no slips were available so we anchored in the inner harbor to wait for a slip. Slip K4 at the Cabo Isle Marina finally became available after 5 days of anxiety. The dock berth provided the needed stable platform to fight the remaining earwigs that were hiding in the bowels of the ship. We needed strong chemicals, as seeking them out to squash them was inefficient and difficult. Who knows how many eggs they had laid already?

Rumor had it, that Mexican hardware stores had potent insect weapons with chemicals now outlawed in the States. War was declared. Leslie and I went off in search of the weapons we needed at the local hardware store. Walking up and down the aisles, we couldn't find anything resembling insect bombs. Now we were faced with the dreaded problem of trying to communicate with the hardware clerks in Spanish. After about 15 minutes of slow English and a few words of poor Spanish, we were not getting through. Leslie then put on a brilliant pantomime imitating flying insects, throat choking and dying on the floor. It was quite a performance, but success looked as though it would elude us. The store clerks looked at each other and we knew they thought us to be just another couple of crazy Americans.

Just as we were about to give up and walk out the door, one of the clerks arose out of the darkness and into the light. Our message had seemed simple to me, but I guess the clerks were on a different wavelength. They had what we needed; insect bombs with warning labels and symbols like a skull and crossbones. We just didn't know where to look. However, the bombs were so potent that they would have done us in if we had not moved off the boat. We put all our dishes, silverware and pillows in plastic bags. While the bombs were doing their thing, we found a nice bed-and-breakfast, The Bungalows, about a mile's walk from town. We stayed in a two-bedroom unit with an efficiency kitchen and living room for $109. We were pleased by the wonderful breakfast prepared by our cordial host, Estella.

The earwigs were just an unusual phenomenon. Their navigation system had failed them and we just happened to be in their way. We were not the only victims, however. The earwigs also landed on three or four other boats near us. The earwigs were not seen by other boats that sailed through the area earlier in the day or after us — we were just the lucky ones. No one could suggest a good reason, so we just blamed it on El Nino or a weird electro-magnetic disturbance. Who knows?

Back to the rally, we crossed the finish line in Cabo San Lucas at 6 p.m. on Nov. 6. The rally's Grand Pooh-Bah hosted an awards ceremony on Nov. 8. We were awarded the third-place finish out of the 12 boats in our rally class. I believe ***Our Pleasure*** did actually win the third-place slot, although each of the remaining nine boats in our class also were awarded third place. We will never know for sure, but it really doesn't matter, since the rally was a lot of fun and a worthwhile effort.

An unusual event happened along the Mexican coast involving two, 30 foot gray whales. They swam past the bow of our boat, missing us by a matter of a few feet. Seeing these beautiful whales swimming so gracefully and up close was an emotional experience that I can't adequately describe.

The paperwork required by the port captain and immigration offices to make our way into or out of Cabo was tedious, as each bureaucratic stop took about 20 minutes. Their offices are spread out and the walk takes one over deeply rutted, windblown dirt roads. The walking itself took close to an hour in the hot afternoon sun.

One of our dock neighbors owned a big and expensive Sport Fisherman powerboat. I asked him if he was familiar with the quality of the drinking water in Cabo, as I needed to fill our tanks before we left. He had made several previous trips to Cabo for their annual deep sea-fishing contest — looking around, he was just one of many U.S. sport fishermen in Cabo for the contest. I guess he wasn't too impressed with their water because he brought out his own high-tech, portable, water purification systems. It contained several large mechanical filters as well as a final stage of ultra violet light. He told us to use it as long as we wanted. We filled our tanks to the brim without further worry about water quality.

We headed for La Paz on Nov. 12 and sailed 43 nautical miles[1] (NM) overnight to Los Fralies, a beautiful bay in the Sea of Cortez. On shore, was the Los Fralies Hotel, consisting of 6, two-bedroom bungalows that looked attractive from the water. Also on the beach was an area for recreational vehicles. We took our dinghy ashore to see if one of the RVs belonged to Al and Rosemary Adams. For the last 30 years, they have driven to the tip of Baja for their vacation. We had met Al while obtaining our fishing license in San Diego, and he invited us to stop by. They just happened to be there, and we had a nice visit while trading travel stories over coffee. Mike and Lillian, two young people whom Bob and Leslie had met, also were camping at the bay. We

1 One nautical mile or sea mile is equal to 6,076 feet and a statute mile or land mile is equal to 5,280 feet.

stayed another day so Bob and Leslie could snorkel at the next bay, Cabo Pulmo. That bay has the only live reef in North America and is full of beautiful coral and sea life.

The day after we left Los Fralies, the wind started gusting to 35 knots, and the seas were building to a height of around 4 feet. It was uncomfortable sailing into the wind, which reduced our speed to about 3.5 knots. The head winds doubled our time to reach La Paz to 12 hours. We knew the weather was about to worsen, and we could have avoided the head winds by leaving a day earlier, but the crew wanted to stay one more day. We were so relieved when Marina Palmira answered our radio call and said a reserved moorage spot was awaiting our arrival. We did not understand the "reserved moorage," but who was to argue with a reserved moorage?

As we checked in at the marina office, the staff invited us to their party. We hadn't heard anything about a party, so that evening we were all pleasantly surprised. The party had been planned for marina guests and boaters arriving from the "Baja Ha Ha" rally. We were treated to a dinner of grilled steak fajitas, homemade guacamole and fresh salsa. Unbeknownst to us, Marina Palmira had planned an informal race from Cabo to La Paz. The idea, of course, was to encourage the Baja'ers to come to Marina Palmira. We were surprised to find out that we arrived in fourth place and had won 3 days of free moorage. During the course of the evening, the staff held several drawings, and Bob won a sport shirt he thought was pretty nice. What a nice welcome to La Paz, Mexico's "City of Peace."

La Paz, the capital of the Baja California Sur, has a population of 160,000. I've been told that there are more than 20 churches in La Paz, most of them Catholic. The church we attended had an English Mass at noon every Saturday. The church was a bit of a walk, though, about 50 minutes if we couldn't find someone going that way. Smokey and Sonja, two cruisers from California, showed us where the department stores, grocery stores, and churches were located. At Thanksgiving, Chris and Gordon joined several other boaters and us for a wonderful turkey dinner at a nearby restaurant, Club Marlin. The entire city was beautifully decorated for Christmas, and Christmas Carols were played through public speakers everywhere. Many festivities were going on, all centered on the feast of Our Lady of Guadeloupe, patroness of Mexico. Her feast day is Dec. 12. The boating community initiated several fund raising events to help children in the orphanage and the poor children on the streets. Boaters also distributed gift bags with Christmas presents for individual children.

We were able to find almost everything we needed in La Paz. The main sources of food were two large "CCC" grocery stores that were stocked with familiar U.S. products. We were fortunate to know a few boaters with cars who offered to carry our groceries back to the marina. I also played bridge one afternoon and was amazed that I could still remember the game, although not all that well, after 15 years.

Glissade, a local 42 foot Swan sailboat helmed by Leo Haanpaa and dive instructor Ken Hogal, took Bob, Leslie and Dianne Foster to the islands of Espiritu Santo and Bolanda for scuba diving. Leslie obtained her scuba certification, and Bob obtained his advanced certification.

We left La Paz on Dec. 23 and headed for Galeta Partida to spend Christmas Eve and Day at the Espiritu Santo anchorage. We were delighted to see Jim and Helen, on their boat *Go West*, anchored there. We invited them over for hot dogs and chili and they brought the wine. While we were there, Gordon's brother, Buzz, flying back to San Diego, dropped us a small package on a parachute. Our crew was excited to dinghy out to the floating package to see what was in it. It turned out to have been sent by Seattle friends and dock neighbors, the Robertson's, on the yacht *Charisma*. We met them while sailing in Mexico and they must have also met Buzz. There was a couple of novelty items and candy in the package — what a treat.

On Christmas morning, Jim came over with his floating scuba air pump and with Bob and Leslie scrubbed the slime off the bottom of ***Our Pleasure***. Our crew reciprocated and cleaned the bottom of *Go West*. Later that day, we sat down for a wonderful Christmas dinner and opened presents.

Pat, I, and the honeymoon couple, Bobby and Leslie, were becoming good friends and finally turning into an experienced sailing team. Bob and Leslie cooked delicious dinners when taking their turn in the galley, which was a real treat for Pat. We stayed in La Paz until the middle of Jan. After that time, we made trips further up north into the Sea of Cortez. There are many beautiful bays to explore up there with good snorkeling. Pat and I did the snorkeling, while Bob and Leslie went scuba diving. They were so in love and almost weekly replayed the video of their wedding. Eventually, we planned to sail southeast over to the mainland for our Mexican departure, sometime in early April.

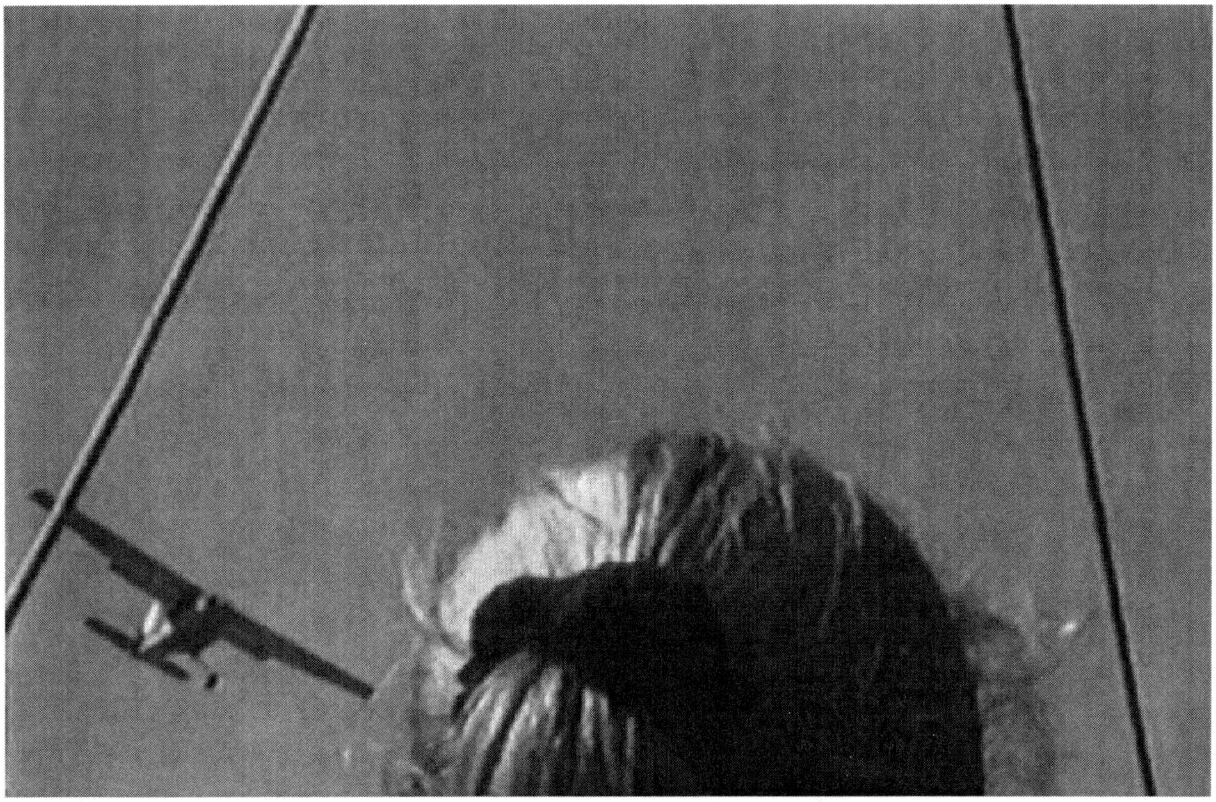

CARE PACKAGE DROP FROM *CHARISMA*, AT ESPIRITU SANTO

During the Christmas holidays, friendly Mexicans were always greeting us with "*¡Felices Pascuas*!" (Merry Christmas!), and "*feliz año*!" (Happy New Year!). La Paz is an unusual city for Mexico, as it is middle-class, with few tourists. Marina Palmira was a pleasant marina. The marina property also contained a five-star hotel, swimming pool, spa, tennis courts and three restaurants. The walkways were decorated with lights and palm trees, which always swayed in light breezes. Soft Christmas music was played at night. La Paz even put on a boat parade, but only 8 boats participated — much smaller than Seattle's big Opening Day parade of several hundred boats.

New Year's Eve is quite different when celebrated Mexican style. The music was so loud that no one could talk above it without shouting. The Mexicans danced with every song and drank brandy mixed with cola or soda, not a combination we liked, but included in the price of admission. On New Year's Day, we sadly watched Washington State University (Bob's and Leslie's alma mater) get defeated in the Rose Bowl. We found a local horseracing and sport-betting bar where we could watch the game. We could tell it was likely to show the game because the roof sported five huge satellite dishes.

Pat and I, along with Chris and Gordon (*Fuzzy Logic*), did a touristy thing and flew over to the mainland at Los Mochis to tour the Copper Canyon. There, we hopped on the far from elegant but functional, Chihuahua Pacifico Railroad. This railroad was built for travel through the middle of the Sierra Madre mountain range to Chihuahua. The views of the beautiful Copper Canyon were striking. The line, completed in 1961, is a marvelous feat of engineering for its time. It runs from sea level to 8,000 feet across 37 bridges and through 86 tunnels for 406 miles. With the opportunity to get off or on the train at any town, we chose three towns for overnight stays. We took tours of each town and boarded the train on the following day. The towns were El Fuerte, (or fort, for the big Spanish fort there), Divisadaro (lookout) and Creel (named after an early American ambassador to Mexico). The last two towns are both over 7,000 feet above sea level and are cold in both the morning and night.

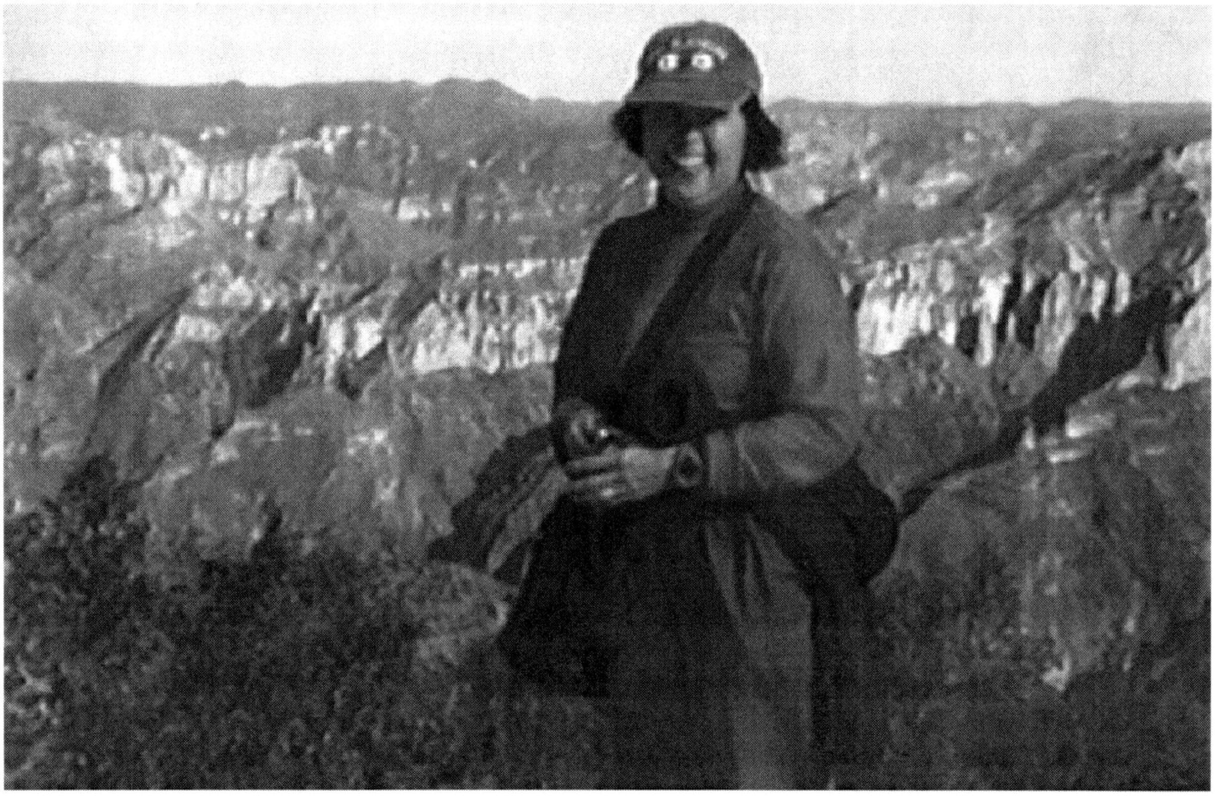

PAT ENJOYING THE VIEWS AT MEXICO'S COPPER CANYON

The days were not bad. With the sun shining, we could get by with a warm jacket and normal clothes. Besides the wonderful scenery (there are six major canyons four times the size of the Grand Canyon), we learned that the wonderful and reclusive Tarahumara Indians live in these canyons. The Spanish discovered the Indians in 1564, but their origins are unclear. Guides said scholarly folks think they may have settled the area as far back as 1,300 BC. The Indians have found notoriety in news articles because of their long-range running ability. They can run 50 to 100 miles while kicking a small wooden ball. Somehow, they have managed to preserve their customs, dress and culture. They number about 50,000 and live in small groups all over the mountains in this region, with no electricity or running water. They raise corn and beans for their needs and sell their crafts to the tourists. The villages communicate with each other by sending runners with messages. Mexican law requires the children to go to school, but no one enforces the law, so most do not.

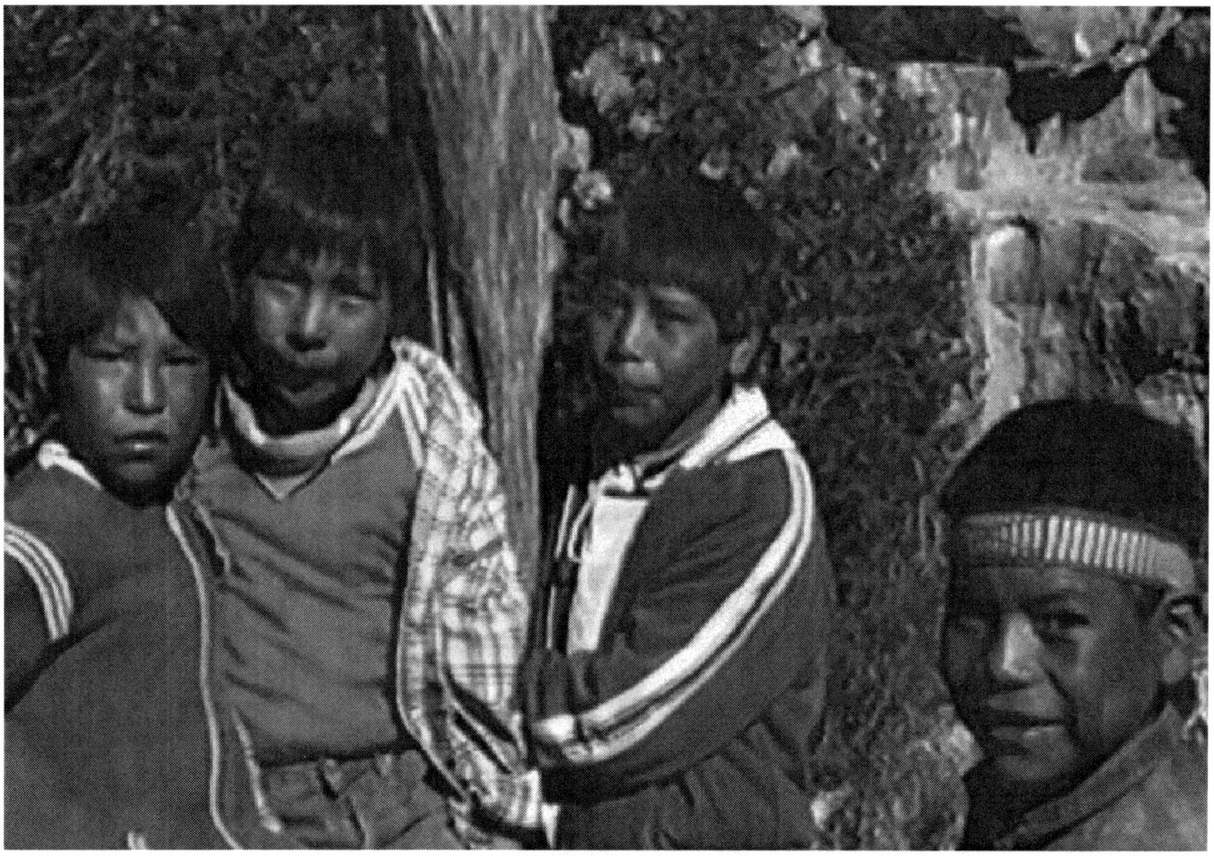

TARAHUMARA INDIAN BOYS LEAD US ON THE HIKING TRAILS

We left La Paz on Jan. 22, 1998, and headed north to explore the Sea of Cortez past Aqua Verde to Loreto. Except for fishing villages, the coast was rather deserted. The fishermen were always willing to sell their fish — a real treat. The Sea of Cortez was full of deserted islands with beautiful but dry anchorages. If this area were moved to Seattle, with its weather and warm water, you would have to leave your car at home and walk because Seattle would be over grown with wall-to-wall people. We sailed across to Mazatlan on Feb. 7, covering 285 miles in two days. This sail was exceptionally beautiful with gentle breezes, 2 to 4 foot high seas and a nearly full moon every night.

We sailed into Marina Mazatlan, on Feb. 9, 1998. The marina was about 6 miles from downtown in the Estero del Sabalo waterway. Good bus service provided a bus every 15 minutes for 16 cents. Buses were not air-conditioned, so effective deodorant and antiperspirant is important. Actually, we could ride for about 20 miles for just 16 cents — quite a bargain. We ran out of rum in Mazatlan, but at the Mexican government store, a 1.7 liter bottle costs only $9. We had a hard time finding the store by bus, as it was several miles from the marina.

We were not sure, but we think the government stores were supposed to be for low-income Mexicans. No one said anything to us, but we did receive odd stares.

Marina Mazatlan arranged a special viewing platform for the Mazatlan Carnival just celebrating its 100th anniversary. Workers built the platform over most of the entry stairs to a downtown hotel. It was probably 6 feet off the ground and large. The platform, designed to seat 200 people, easily accommodated the yachties from the marina with good views of the parade. I was sure the platform would not pass any kind of stress analysis, but it did make it through the parade without collapsing.

The whole affair was wonderful, and I have never been closer to any parade in my life. The fee of $30 included a served dinner and 5 drinks of our choice from an open bar. They made money on us as our crew managed to average only 2.5 drinks. By newspaper accounts, two million people watched the parade. In comparison to the parades, we have seen in Seattle, this got the best ranking by far. The Spanish queens and their princesses were beautiful with their dark and sparkling eyes, justly described in the song "Spanish Eyes." Pat and I also went to several other carnival activities that week. Each time, the talents and enthusiasm of the Mexican people surprised us. Mexico was truly wonderful experience for all of us.

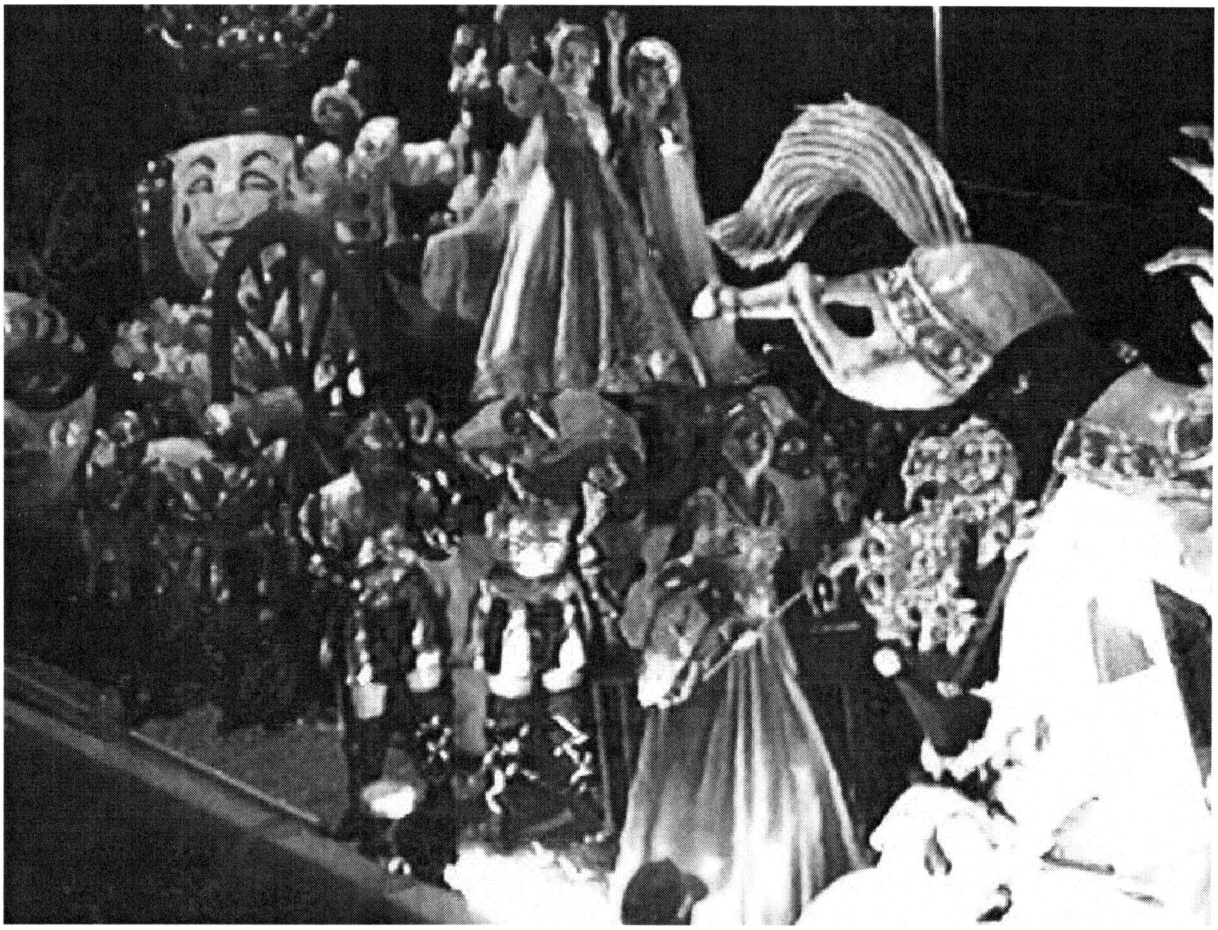

CARNIVAL PARADE FLOAT WITH PRETTY WOMEN

Mazatlan showed itself to be a wonderful city for Americans, as it has a helpful and friendly group of native Mexicans. They often went out of their way to help answer our questions. Most Mexicans here seemed to be well educated and many spoke limited English. Mazatlan seemed to thrive on cultural activity like the opera, theater, symphony and dancing and it also has bullfights and baseball. Movie theaters showed unaltered American movies for $2 — first-run films in English were a wonderful treat. We even found American music on one radio station and old American movies on one of the TV stations. American brand food was available at most grocery stores easing, the chore of shopping. Eating was a bargain, as the four of us ate well for about $75 per week. Even at those prices, I believe it was cheaper to eat at Mexican restaurants than to cook on the boat. At the restaurant, Panama's, Pat and I could eat a big breakfast for under $4 each, including a huge omelet with bacon, ham, cheese and tomatoes, two pastries, and brewed coffee.

On St. Patrick's Day, the marina hosted a Mass at 10 a.m., followed by a blessing of the fleet. The priest blessed the fleet from a Mexican Panga going up and down the waterway. Quite a few boaters followed behind him in their dinghies. There was a sailing dinghy race at 1 p.m. The beer tent opened at 3 p.m. and a pig was roasted and ready to eat by 4 p.m. — fun day.

Pat and I flew to Seattle on Mar. 25 to visit family and file our federal taxes. We got back on April 18, 1998, and found the crew working hard to get ***Our Pleasure*** ready for our next voyage. We had planned to sail to Puerto Vallarta in March, but because of grandson Vincent's baptism and the tax filing in Seattle, we had to ditch that plan. Our return from Seattle was timely since Bob's mother, Nancy, and his Aunt Barbara took their vacation time to see Mazatlan. Bob and Leslie stayed at their hotel for a couple of days, complements of Nancy and Barbara, so they were delighted to have them in Mazatlan. For our next leg, we planned to sail from Mazatlan and visit the islands of French Polynesia, Cook Islands, Tonga and Fiji and recuperate in New Zealand. Assuming all would go well, we were to arrive in Whangarei, New Zealand about mid-Nov. 1998.

The first port of call after leaving Mazatlan was to be the island of Nuka Hiva in the Marquises. This island lies about 3,000 miles to the southwest, across the equator, and will take anywhere from 21 to 30 days of sailing, depending on the wind speed, direction and currents.

Provisioning for six months was quite a task. Ellie, one of the yachties we met in Mazatlan became a good friend. Peruvian-born, she spoke perfect Spanish. With her ability speak to the Mexicans; she helped negotiate the fresh fruits and veggies. She was able to get across that we needed different degrees of varying ripeness to maximize longevity. However, the major problem was washing and storing with the right wrapping or container. Air circulation was important, but finding space for the stuff was the real challenge. Most of the veggies arrived in crates. Not realizing how large the volume would be, we just stared at each other in amazement. One of our successful storage methods was to put the onions in panty hose. Knots above and below each onion separated them in the stocking. Simply cutting the knot below the lowest onion set it free from the stocking.

Most of the 33 boats making the same crossing to Nuka Hiva left Mexico before us and were now scattered across the Pacific. We kept in contact via single sideband (SSB) and high frequency (HF) radio every day. We called our radio communication system "The Westbound Net." Each boat checked in with the net control boat *Cristal Blue,* twice a day on the frequency of 8.104 megahertz (MHz). This net was ideal for understanding approaching weather from the boats sailing ahead of us. It also helped us to know each of the skippers and crews a little better. For boaters with ham licenses, there was also the "Seafarer's Marine Net." This HF communication system operated everyday at 15:00 universal coordinated time (UTC) on a frequency of 14.313 MHz, upper side band. Volunteers operated this net, which reached the entire Pacific Ocean from Washington State to New Zealand. The volunteers provided a great service with phone calls to families back home, medical help and weather information.

While we were in Seattle for taxes and the baptism of Vincent and his mother, Jennifer Bennett, we purchased an electronic modem from the SGC Company in Bellevue. This modem and a computer were supposed to provide the link at sea for e-mail service. In Mazatlan, we worked several hours with a software designer off *Mimosa*. We found the operating software was still in development and not fully operational. That was a disappointing finding and meant no e-mail for our boat yet.

The day we tried to leave Mexico, we found we didn't have the right exit papers to get our passports stamped. The officials were so helpful and tried to work it so we would not have to go back, but that effort was futile and we couldn't finish our paper work until Monday, April 20. This became a good delay, since the harbor entrance still had waves breaking over the break-wall and huge surf running outside. The 35 knots of wind that had been blowing for several days was just starting to diminish.

With a good weather report for moderate winds for the next seven days, our close friends gave us a going away dock party on Thursday. It was quite a surprise, as they used devious devices to keep it a secret. The hors d'oeuvres were wonderful, and one of the boats, *Mimosa*, brought five pounds of big fresh shrimp that are always a taste treat in Mexico.

Leaving port is always a sad, as people to whom we have become close, go different ways on their journey. Sharing similar problems and experiences breaks down barriers and makes it easy to develop good friendships. For instance, it is usually late at night or early in the morning when everyone has fallen asleep in a beautiful anchorage. That is when the wind pipes up, and you have to go on deck to check your anchor. If a boat's anchor is dragging, everyone will get involved until the problem boat is re-anchored and secure. Everyone in the boating community here was so supportive of each other.

Mexico was a wonderful experience for the crew of ***Our Pleasure***, with its slow pace of living, good food, low cost of living and friendly, helpful Mexicans. Nightlife with jazz concerts, birthday parties, classical-music concerts, and gala concerts to help orphanages will always be wonderful memories.

Chapter 2

THE FRENCH ISLANDS, *ÎLES MARQUISES*

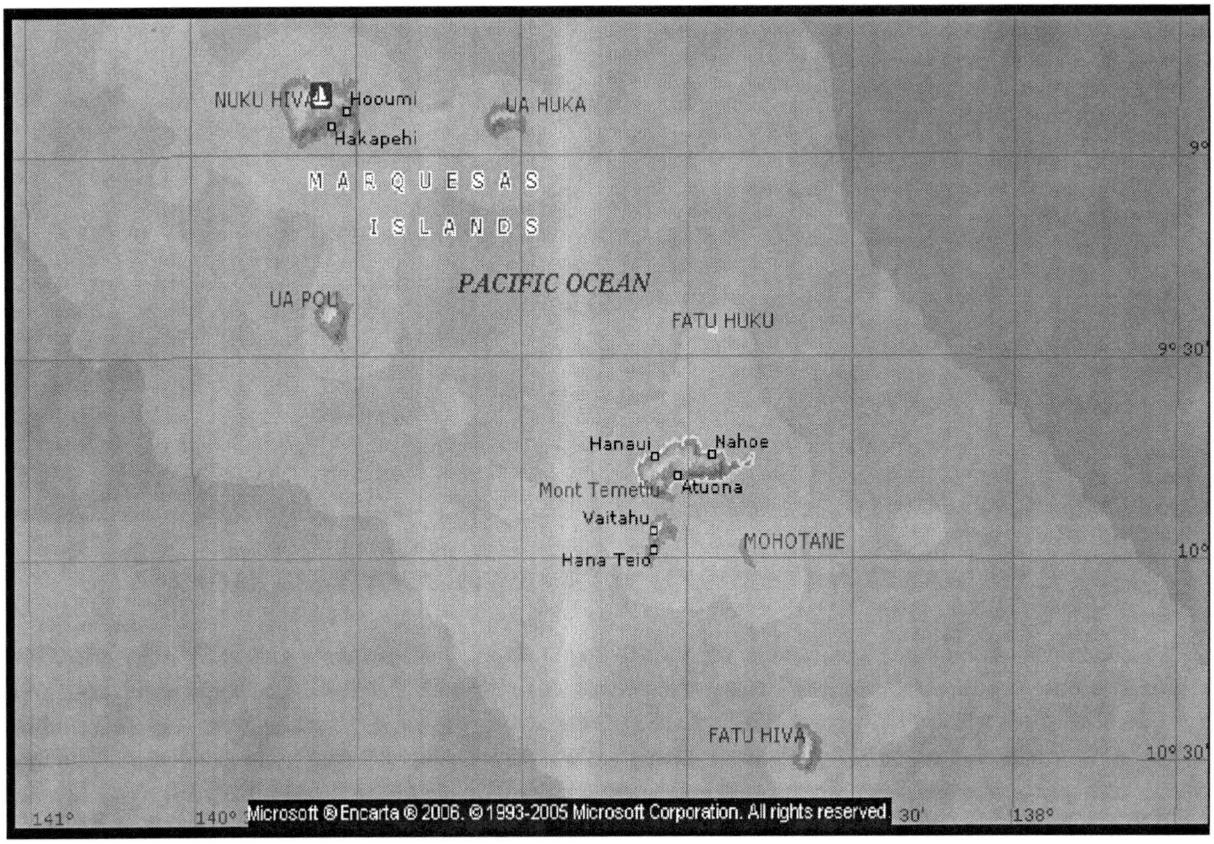

NUKU HIVA, MARQUESAS ISLANDS, FRENCH POLYNESIA May 17, 1998

We left Mazatlan, Mexico, on April 21, 1998, at 9 a.m. We had to make our way through the Estro Del Sabalo channel to the Pacific Ocean. The ocean end of the channel was reduced to about 20 feet in width (we need 14 feet) by a dredge. The dredge was removing the silt on which we had momentarily grounded when going into Mazatlan Marina about two months prior. The first day out, winds were light, and we could make only three knots with our working sails. We rolled up the genoa and put up our 1,750-square-foot spinnaker, immediately adding two knots to our speed. The effort to get the spinnaker to fill and work properly, though, took about an hour. It went up twisted from its last use along the Baja coast, and two months of sitting in

Mazatlan did not help our sail-handling abilities. We had a wonderful spaghetti dinner that night using a sauce that Dar from the sailboat *Mimosa* had given us. I checked-in with the amateur Seafarers Marine Net that kept track of boats sailing the Pacific, and we were on our way.

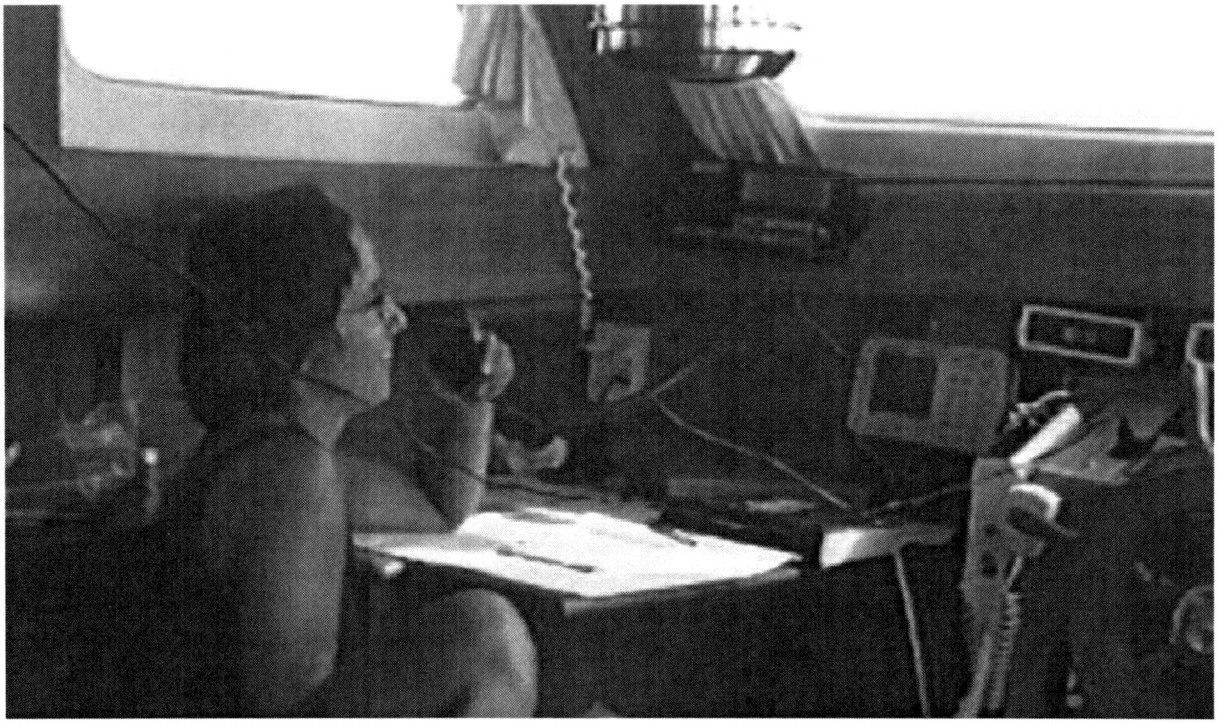

LESLIE KEEPING IN TOUCH WITH THE FLEET VIA SSB RADIO

Our next destination was Nuka Hiva in the French Archipelago, Des Marquises, and 3,000 miles away. The Marquises are the northern most islands forming the western part of French Polynesia. The island group has a total population of about 6,000. This route also took us to a point that was the longest distance from any other land on the globe. We arrived at Taiohae Bay (the port of entry), Nuka Hiva at 2 p.m. on May 17. These volcanically formed islands were spectacular, with high, rugged peaks and green valleys. The islands become visible from about 20 miles at sea — a navigator's dream landfall. It took us 27 days to travel those 3,000 miles at an average speed of 4.5 knots.

I used a computer program to plan our sailing route. This program predicted an average value of wind speed, wind direction, current speed and direction for each season of the year. It used data collected over decades throughout the world from ships at sea and weather satellites. By adding our boat's design parameters, we received a prediction of our passage times. The computer program predicted 18 days, nine hours, with an average boat speed of 5.9 knots. Of course, the predictions were just estimates and proved optimistic.

The crossing was an event of many emotions. There were good days with perfect weather, and there were long days with rough weather. After crossing the equator into the Southern Hemisphere, we ran into many squalls, a few were quite fierce — not the level seen in the movie *White Squall* but close.

Off in the distance, a squall appeared as a dark cloud connected to the water (rain between the cloud and water). As the squall approached, the wind picked up and we had to reduce the sail area quickly, as wind velocity could approach 45 knots in a few seconds. The resulting rain reduced visibility to nearly zero — it was usually that intense. After 15 to 45 minutes on average, the squall moved on and the sun returned. Sometimes we had squalls five to six times a day. It was hard to stay dry.

At night, you could not see a squall approaching unless the moon was providing light or we were tracking the squalls on radar. There were frequent lightning storms forcing us to turn off and disconnect all our electrical equipment to avoid damage. One night while I was sleeping, the boat found itself under a heavy discharge of sheet lightning. It caused our voltage regulator to lose its capability to regulate and over charged the active battery bank at 16 volts instead of 13.8 volts. The battery bank over heated so much that it took two days for it to cool down. We were lucky it didn't explode. Other nights were filled with moon lit skies and bright stars or just inky blackness.

We celebrated my birthday on April 27 with a great pasta dinner and marshmallow squares for dessert. Bob and Leslie gave me a pair of red shorts and cinnamon toothpicks. Pat gave me a good pair of BUM® sunglasses, a T-shirt from Mazatlan and a box of chocolates.

As we sailed closer to the equator, the air temperature and humidity moved higher and higher until it was extremely hot. We lived and slept in our bathing suits and stayed in the shade of the boat's awning. Sleeping at night required a fan directed over one's body and no covers.

On May 1, with the wind blowing at 12 knots out of the north/northeast, I managed to put two minor cracks in the wooden main boom. This was the result of too much pressure on the boom's down haul preventer system, which used blocks and tackles to connect the boom to the deck. Luckily, I had long wood screws and lengths of wood to reinforce the boom.

The best day on this leg was crossing the equator. The day was just beautiful. We arrived at the equator at 21:20 UTC (3:20 p.m., equator time) on May 10, 1998. We dropped the sails, and everyone jumped in to swim across the equator. Of course, Bobby was first and swam across the imaginary line full-Monty. We had to follow his lead, but in swimsuits. We toasted King Neptune with Wild Turkey shots and mimosas (orange juice and vodka). Bob and Leslie opened a can of Cougar Gold cheese they had saved just for my birthday. This outstanding extra sharp cheddar cheese is a product of Washington State University and a favorite of everyone in our family. It originally made it onto our boat as a Christmas present from Bobby's parents. When it was Leslies turn swim across the equator she thought the water temperature was like a bathtub, but she worried about sharks and was anxious to get out quickly — no dilly-dallying in the ocean for Leslie.

The crossing also occurred on Mother's Day so we had more celebrating to get out of the way. We had a celebration for Pat and Leslie, although Leslie wasn't to become a mother for a few more years. Bob and Leslie gave Pat a Polo shirt from Mazatlan, and Bob gave Leslie a pair of silver Aztec calendar earrings. To top all that off, I was able to call Seattle on the ham net so Bob could wish his mother a happy Mother's Day. Of course, once we had crossed the equator, we now had four new "shellbacks" aboard ***Our Pleasure***, no more pollywogs!

On the evening of May 14, we experienced three squalls in a row, but the last one was the strongest we had experienced during the whole trip. We had the full main sail up and the staysail in 35 knots of wind. A huge wave broke over our stern and dumped about a gallon of salt water on my head. Believe me this is not a good way to wake up. It was a good lesson — close all hatches.

We anchored in Taiohae Bay on the island of Nuku Hiva on May 17, 1998. While still at sea, we could smell the island's lush green hills and the exotic flowers. Land has never smelled so good. We checked in with the Gendarmerie (French equivalent to the state police or national police) and purchased 30 day visa stamps.

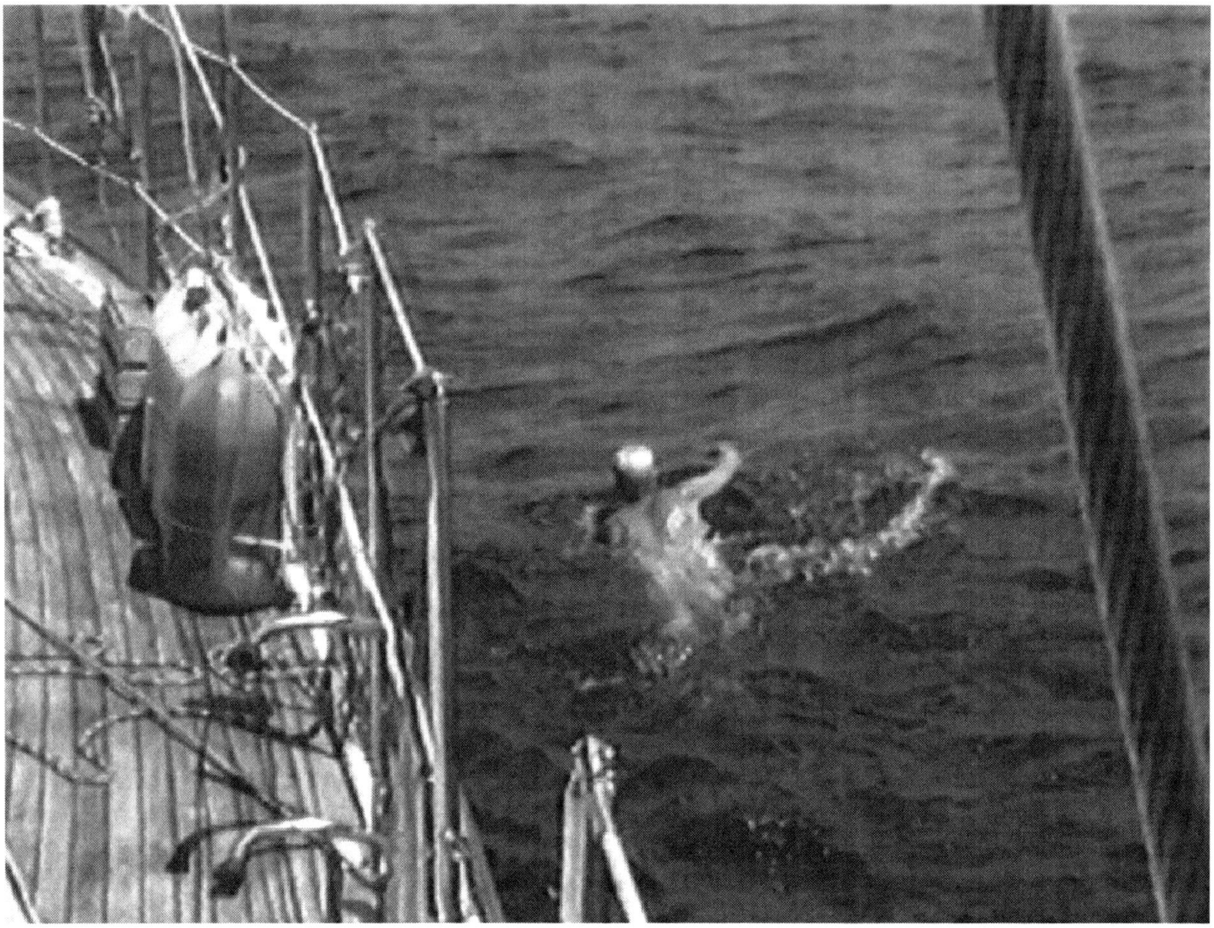

BOB SWIMMING ACROSS THE EQUATOR, May 10. 1998

Nuku Hiva is the second largest of the 10 volcanic Marquesas Islands and contains the administrative seat at Hakapehi. The largest island, Hiva Oa is the burial site of Paul Gauguin. While we were there roosters crowed 24 hours a day, goats ran free, and islanders rode their horses through town. Every tree had an exotic flower or a tropical fruit: bananas, papayas, lemons, limes, breadfruit, coconut, or pamplemousse (a gigantic grapefruit the size of a football). However, we found out that none of the small grocery stores sold fresh fruit or vegetables. Pat was able to find four cucumbers at an unusually high price. In fact, everything was pricey and in limited supply.

Bobby and Leslie went on excellent hikes to waterfalls and enjoyed swimming and exploring different parts of the island. One afternoon, Pat and I went to Rose's Keikahanui Hotel for happy hour with a bunch of other cruising boaters and stayed for dinner. Rose and her husband anchored their sailboat in Taiohae Bay about 20 years ago and decided to stay. They built a small hotel and restaurant overlooking the bay. Flying in fresh food daily, she confided, made running the restaurant difficult. Her husband worked hard at making a go of the restaurant, but since his death, she was on her own.

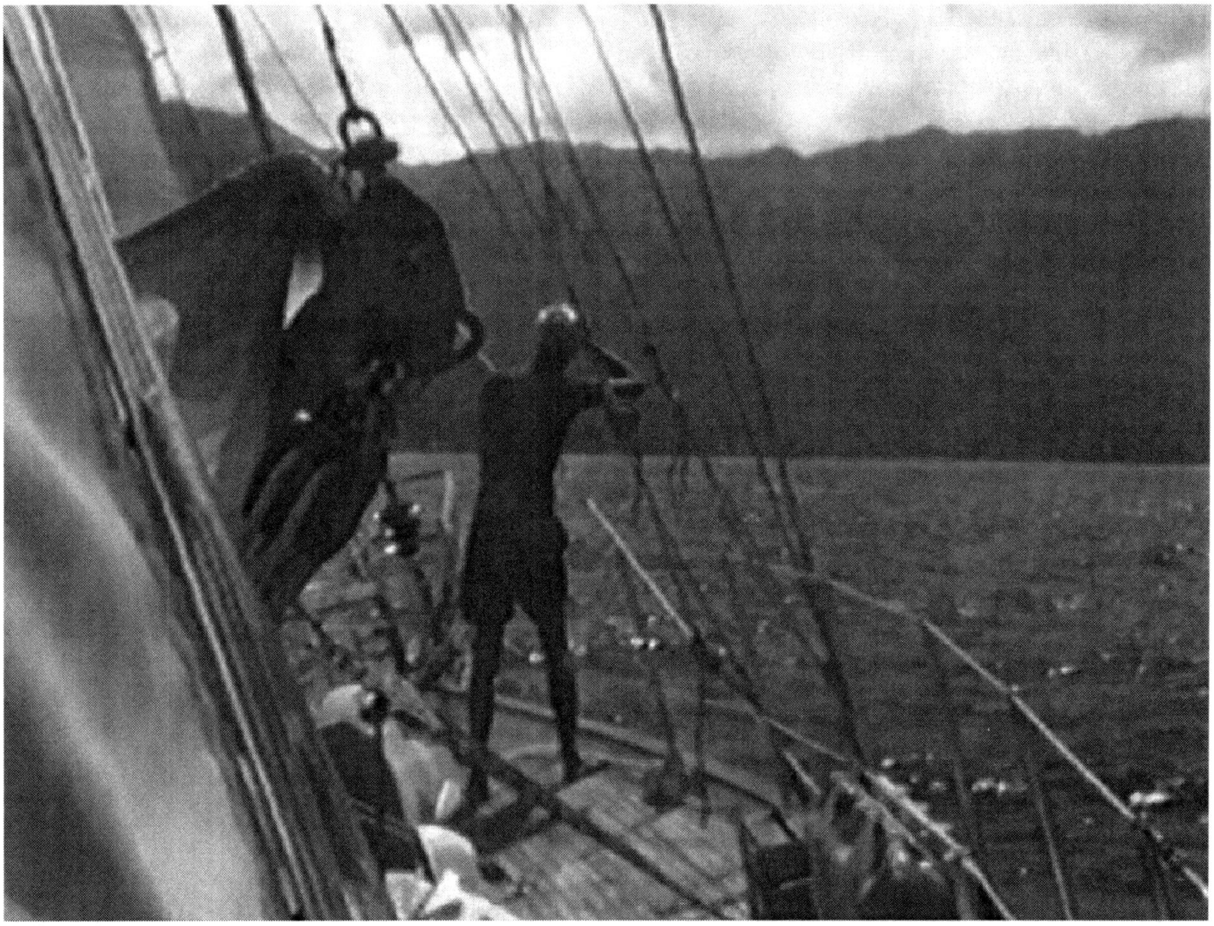

ENTERING TAIOHAE BAY, NUKU HIVA, May 17, 1998

While Pat and I were at the restaurant one night, Rose brought out her collection of tapa cloths. She claimed that tapa artwork originated on the island of Fatu Hiva in the Marquesas. The natives on these islands produced tapa cloths using traditional methods. Mulberry trees produce the inner bark used to make tapa cloth. The bark is first made pliable by constant pounding and working by hand. That process turns the bark into a paper like cloth used by natives on which to draw and paint their art. Sometimes they use stencils to decorate the cloth, which can be fashioned into mats, clothing, and wall hangings. They make their own dyes that produce mostly black colors in an ink-like fluid. We could not resist buying a two-foot-by-two-foot tapa depicting a beautiful Polynesian woman at work making a tapa. We hung it on a bulkhead in our main saloon.

Unfortunately, Nuku Hiva was infested with no-no flies. Their common name is "midge," the smallest bloodsucking insect known. Each of these nasty insects is packed into a body that is as small as one millimeter long. Also known as sand flies, punkies and no-see-ums, they swarm in the early spring and late fall. In addition, of course, their bigger cousins, the mosquitoes, also were there in great numbers, and we all had welts to prove it.

Itching from the bites finally reached a point where we did not want to go ashore anymore. So after a week, we headed to the other side of the island to the beautiful and serene, Anaho Bay. This was an even more picturesque and well-protected anchorage, surrounded by coral reefs and coconut palms. We could swim and snorkel here in clear water. We swam every day instead of going ashore. On our last evening, an islander paddled his outrigger canoe out to trade fresh fruit: 12 pamplemousse, a stalk of bananas and 4 papayas for 10 fishing hooks. We were delighted to have fresh fruit, and he was happy with the hooks. He was a delightful person who could speak four languages and gave us a good rundown on his background and the island. He had worked at a hotel his uncle owned in Tahiti and had to learn English to help English-speaking guests. After several years of experiencing life in the big city, he longed to return to the peace and tranquility of his native island.

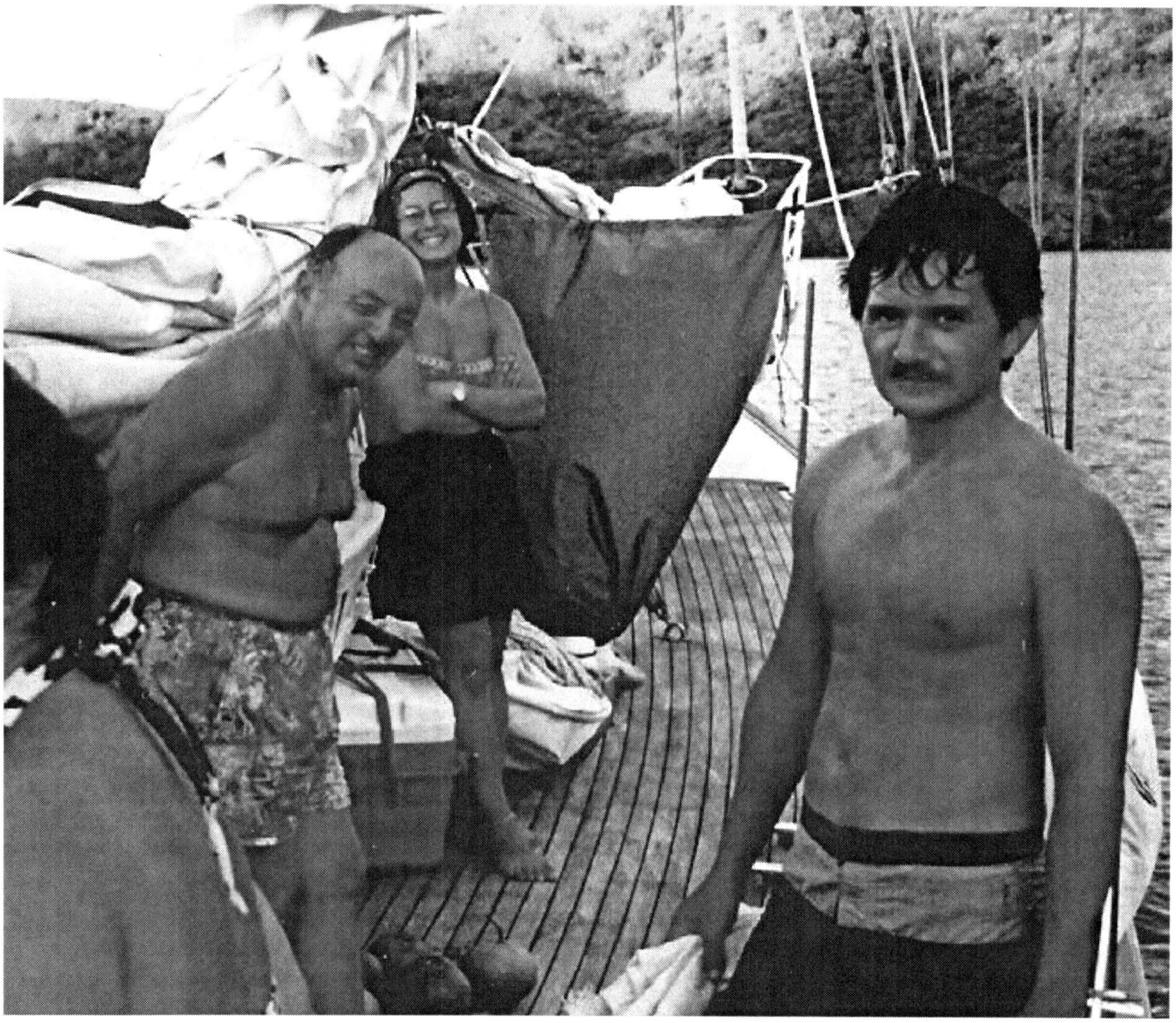

NEW FOUND TRADING PARTNER AT ANAHO BAY, MARQUISES

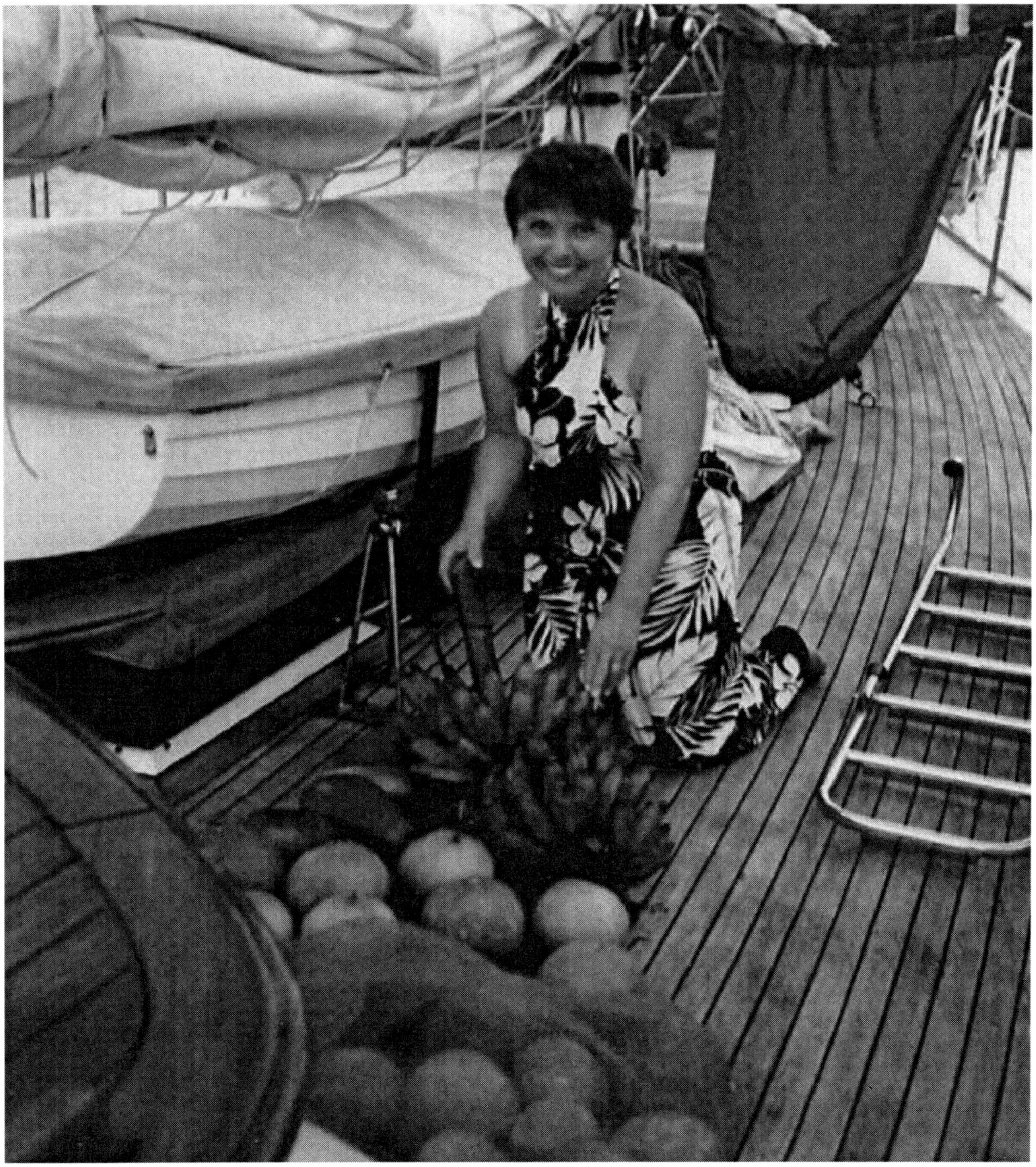

PAT, HAPPY OVER HER NEW FRESH PRODUCE

Chapter 3

MARQUISES TO THE TUAMOTUS

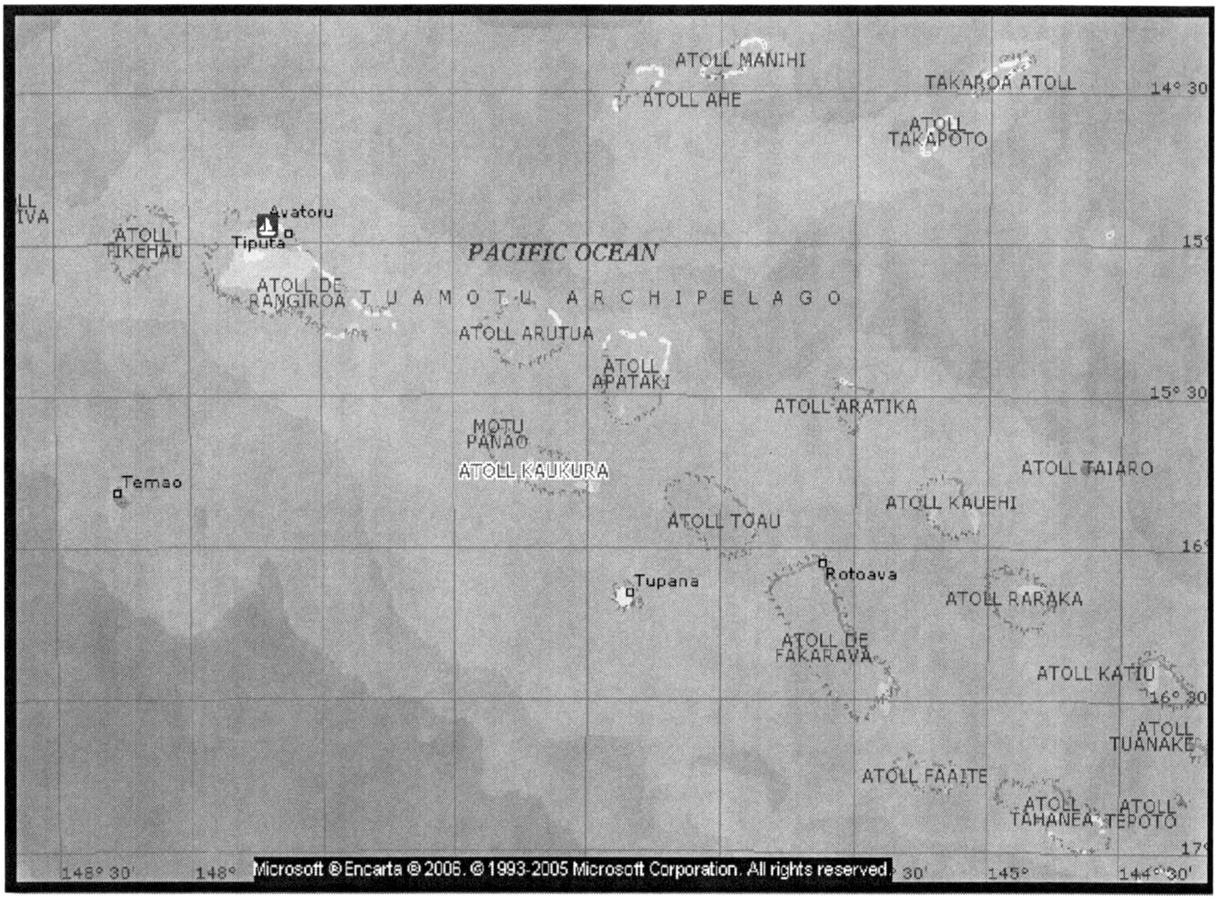

RANGIROA ATOLL, TUAMOTU-ARCHIPELAGO, FRENCH POLYNESIA, May 31, 1998

We left Anaho Bay and headed to the Tuamotu Islands, discovered by the Spanish in 1606 and annexed to the French in 1881. This chain of 78 atolls extends almost 900 nautical miles in a northwest-southeast direction across 15 degrees of south longitude. The largest islands are Rangiroa, Fakarava, Hao and Makemo. The southernmost atolls were the site of the unpopular French nuclear tests. The French test program started in the late 1960s and ended in 1996 after riots almost destroyed downtown Papeete.

Atolls are lagoons surrounded by coral reefs. Usually, reefs have an opening for entry into their calm waters. The openings are formed naturally, or sometimes they receive a little help from man. Most reefs are white sand and coconut palm trees. The land is low, and old-growth palm trees grow to only about 70 feet. Therefore, a good image return cannot be expected on small-boat radars until the atolls are within two to four miles.

Because of all the low-lying reefs, boaters consider this area one of the most dangerous places in the world. The charts are full of icons indicating boats that have grounded on reefs. Reefs are hard, with sharp edges that can slice open a fiberglass hull quickly. Steel hulls can resist a bit longer but usually succumb. A gash in the hull fills the interior with sand and saltwater, making it close to impossible to remove and repair the boat. Most stricken boats cannot be removed and are left to disintegrate in the harsh elements.

Good visibility also brought out visual remnants of grounded boats that could not be salvaged. One boat, whose owner we did not know, had struck a reef a few months prior, and the accident ended their journey. We proceeded with extreme caution, double-checking our position continuously. GPS navigation and the latest charts provided the best information for wind and current effects on the boat's real location. A cautious approach to locating reefs while sailing is with a watch on deck or up the mast. Together, both methods help to reduce the anxiety of navigating around reefs.

Heading to Ahe, the most northwest of all the atolls, we figured, would take five days. During this time, the wind was 5 to 30 knots, and the seas were 10 to 15 feet. These conditions were wearing on our crew. Just as we neared Ahe, four squalls hit us back-to-back with gale-force winds and seas. We were unable to make our course to the entrance so we gave up on Ahe and continued on to the next atoll, Rangiroa.

Naturally, we arrived at Rangiroa in the dark of night and had to hang out about three miles from the entrance to wait for the sun to shed light on the pass. The pass into Rangiroa at Tiputa can be quite dangerous without local knowledge. Therefore, we waited all night for the 9 a.m. slack tide. There was a previous slack tide at 2 a.m., but attempting an entry in the rain and blackness would have been too risky.

By morning, we were exhausted-but excited to be there. We anchored in front of the Kia Ora ("greetings") Resort in 40 feet of clear blue water. This beautiful resort was a conglomerate of over-the-water bungalows ($490 a night) and on-shore bungalows ($320 a night). The resort restaurant featured a lounge and bar built over the water with thick, glass floors. We found it striking to view sea life swimming under our feet. Comfortable lounge chairs were placed to watch the fish swim by in the crystal clear water over white sand. The scene below and the décor of the lounge mesmerized us all. It was the kind of place that invited everyone to stay and enjoy the moment.

The majority of the resort guests seemed to be young Japanese or French honeymooners — amazing that they could afford the resort's overly high prices. Loot from the weddings and the generosity of their parents must have must have been the ticket. The water was bathtub-warm and the blue of our dreams. The beaches were white and covered with tiny coral remnants. This place was a true paradise, with no welts from the no-no flies.

Rangiroa is world-renowned as one of the top five scuba- diving locations in the world. Not wasting any time, Bobby and Leslie went diving with a French diving club and guides Bernard and Floent. They met several French couples and became fast friends while sipping tea after dives. Bobby and Leslie had never experienced a better dive. They all dove three times, and Bobby managed a fourth with the guides. They dove several more times on their own after learning the locations of the good spots.

Leslie's favorite dive was in an area the guides called the "Deep Blue." They started out on a 25 foot Zodiac® inflatable and headed through the channel into the six-to-nine foot ocean swells. This was where Leslie began getting nervous. As they flew from swell to swell, they were holding on just to stay in the boat while attempting to put on their gear. Once they were ready, Bernard pointed out the importance of submerging below the gigantic wave crests as soon as possible so as to sink fast. Once they were down under, it was fine.

Okay, back to "Deep Blue," Flo (pronounced Flu), dropped them away from shore and they sat at 60 feet below the surface. The gray reef sharks and the silver-tipped reef sharks came up from the depths circling between them. The water looked like a blue movie screen full of sharks. After the wild boat ride, the sharks seemed comforting. They reached depths of 105 feet with visibility between 150 and 200 ft. The last dive that Bobby went on was a drift dive in which the current moved him along at five-plus knots through the channel. He went in caves with sharks and came face-to-face with a moray eel that had a head the size of a soccer ball. He guessed there were 200-250 sharks at one time; a few were up to 10 feet long. Leslie kicked herself that she did not go on that dive. I however was glad that she didn't go.

We rented bikes at Kia Ora to explore Rangiroa and the villages. The women all wore flowers in their hair and sarongs in colorful fabrics called pareus. The men wore surf shorts, tank tops and flip-flops, and everyone moved at a slow pace. We found a good, black pearl farm and could not resist buying several, rare black pearls. They are so unusual and beautiful. Bobby made friends with Patrick, the owner, who showed him how to knock down coconuts and hack them open with a dull machete.

On Sunday, we went to church, and although the mass was in a combination of French and Tahitian (we could not understand a thing), we felt right at home, as always, in a Catholic church. The singing was truly amazing. The women harmonized perfectly and sang the entire mass without musical accompaniment or amplification. They sang every part of the mass except the readings and homily with such warmth and strength that we went away with goose bumps.

We left Rangiroa after the best week yet to head for Papeete, Tahiti. We left the Tiputa channel several hours before slack water on advice that, "the channel looked good." However, the ebb current was still flowing fast and pulled our boat into three standing waves that I tried to avoid but couldn't. We were trapped in the 9 knot ebb current. The deck hatches were open, as we were not expecting water to come over our bow. Water poured over our deck after the bow dug into the standing waves. The water on our deck was at least 12 inches high and moving fast. The dorade vents filled with water and soaked the interior, including Bob and Leslie's cabin, with saltwater. The carpeting was soaked in saltwater — what a mess!

Although Tahiti was only 190 miles away from Rangiroa, it proved to take longer to reach than we expected. After the first 24 hours, we sailed into a "tropical disturbance," as reported by weather information from Hawaii. I would hate to be in a real storm if this was only a disturbance. At one point, Bobby, Leslie and I went out to double-reef the main. The wind drove big waves against our hull and over the dodger and soaked us so much that my automatic life vest inflated. It's not supposed to inflate unless actually submerged in water, so that event was quite a surprise, but at least it let me know that it works.

While on deck, we were securely clipped to the boat with our safety harnesses and tethers. When the rain started, it was so dark that we couldn't make out the sails in front of us. Bobby described it as "sailing in an ink blotter." Pat started calling on the VHF to our friends in Papeete harbor when we were 20 miles out. At about 15 miles offshore, we finally got a response from our friends on *Go West* and *Canick*. *Go West*, offered to wait and guide us in. We made it a rule never to enter a harbor at night after several hairy experiences, but we were exhausted, and *Go West* assured us it was doable.

When we were about 2 miles out from Tahiti, the wind, rain, and waves subsided, and *Go West* guided us into a perfect anchorage. Here, we had to anchor on about 250 feet of chain, run two stern lines into shore and tie them to huge bollards near the sidewalk. It is a European method, so it was new to us. Jim and Helen were a great help in telling us where to drop the anchor and taking the lines ashore in their dinghy.

When the engine was finally turned off, everyone was overcome with this wonderful feeling of serenity and security. Actually, sailing from port-to-port can be quite difficult and often requires a great deal of resourcefulness. Continual sail changes and other disruptive problems can make sailing downright unpleasant.

Chapter 4

PAPEETE, TAHITI AND THE SOCIETY ISLANDS

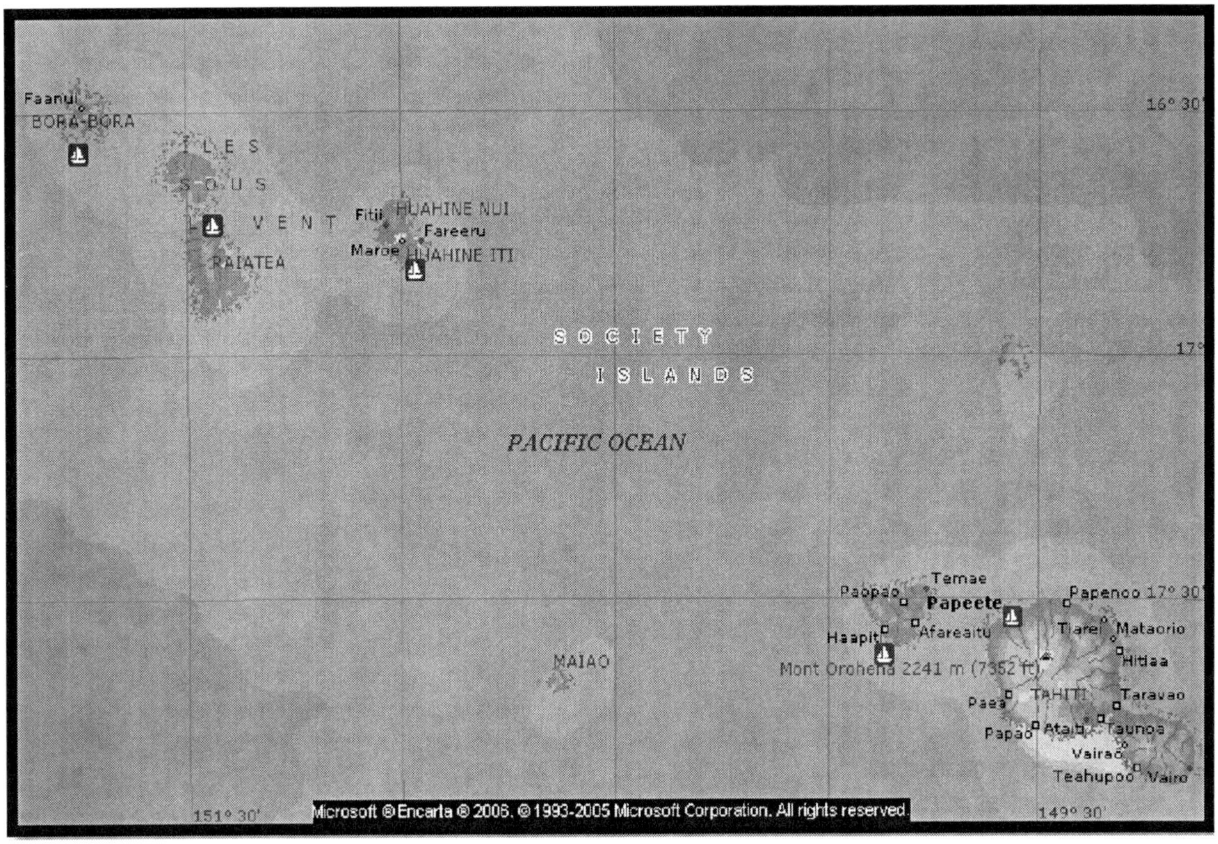

TAHITI, MOOREA, HUAHINE, RAIATEA & BORA BORA, June 10, 1998

"Ia Orana" — hello in Tahitian was the phrase we heard repeatedly in Tahiti. Papeete is a bustling port city and the territories capital. The road traffic was always heavy, like Seattle's, but the population is only about 150,000 people — the first real city since Mazatlan. Tahiti, at 402 square miles, is the largest of the 118 islands and atolls that comprise French Polynesia. Although there are reefs around the island, it is also mountainous. Technically, it is a "high reef-rimmed volcanic Island." The highest peak, 7,353 feet, is on Mount Orphan. Each non-French citizen entering here for longer than 30 days must post a $850 bond plus the bank's processing fee of about 40 dollars. This is the only country in the world with such an extreme bond requirement — very unfair! Note: We did get most of the money back when we left except the processing and commission fees.

Most of the French boats in the harbor were unkempt and derelict looking compared to the visiting foreign boats. The French boats looked as though their owners tied them up years ago and left them to rust and grow seaweed below the water line. The rust comes from steel — the French favor building their boats in steel.

The stores had fresh produce, a real treat, so we ate salads every day. You do not realize how the U.S. is the land of plenty until you travel to faraway places and see that other people are not so fortunate. The city was expensive however; one gallon of fuel was $3.50 as compared to $1.50 at home and most other costs were high as well so, we did not live high-on-the-hog as we did in Mexico.

We heard that working with the French would be more difficult than working with the easy-going Mexicans. The Tahitians, we found, do tilt toward the lazy side, but they are friendly. Our perspective did change when we learned to make our way around the French customs and language a little better. Tahiti is often compared to the French Riviera because of its beauty, but the population comprises a large Chinese influence. In addition, the hard working Chinese own most of the businesses and drive the most expensive cars.

We found it difficult to drop our Mexican Spanish for French and spoke Spanish often by mistake. Bobby, Leslie, and I tried to remember our high school French, but too many years had passed.

We kept busy getting the boat in order and walking around town to learn about its services and resources. It actually felt good to be in a big city that had real marine stores, grocery stores, restaurants, and sidewalk cafés with espresso coffee. There were several boater friends in town from the U.S., Canada, Australia and Mexico plus new ones we have made along the way. It's almost "Mazatlan Southwest"; there were so many boating friends in Tahiti. We all got busy writing postcards and letters and managed to send that mail with people traveling back to the states to save on postage. We would have mailed many more, but the cost of stamps ($1 just for post cards) was a bit outrageous.

Leslie polished our boats stainless steel and Bobby was hoisted up *Go West's* mast helping to put on a new Pro Furler®. Furlers are a big help, their design allows them to roll up a sail in a similar action to a window shade, but with control lines in the cockpit. Jim, on *Go West,* hates heights while Bobby is just the opposite; he has to talk himself out of unclipping his safety line and jumping off Jim's spreaders into the water. Jumping would have been even more attractive if the water was cleaner. As a small reward, Jim paid for Leslie, Bobby and himself to go on a charted dive to one of the nearby islands. They had a great time and no sharks to hamper the exploration of an old sunken wooden passenger ship. They also found a sunken seaplane in about 40 feet of water.

We moored in front of an area where the local Polynesians store outrigger canoes called pirogues. Paddling these canoes is a national sport to Tahitians and they do it with great fervor every day. The outriggers come in 1, 2, 3, 5, 6, 12 and 16 person versions. The women are also involved, but not like the men. Several men actually practiced in the morning before work and at lunchtime for the 2 hours when all businesses are closed. After work, they sometimes race each other. We had a perfect moorage spot to watch this fun sport. Most men were beautiful specimens with developed muscles, dark skin and good looks. Many of the women looked like they should be featured in magazines and on postcards.

We jumped on a bus June 20, ($1.70 each way) and went to a beautiful park to see a contest for young Tahitian men. The park was on the ocean but protected by a reef that keeps the water in the lagoon calm, clear, and green. The grounds were manicured and clean with a restaurant, snack bar and lounge chairs. Yes, as on most French beaches, there were a few women sun bathing topless. Anyway, back to the contest. The contest turned out to be timed athletic events for young men in their prime, similar to a decathlon, but nothing like we had ever seen before.

There were eight contestants, all muscular, all tattooed like early day warriors, but not so extreme. Tattoos are fairly common among Tahitian men or more correctly, among Polynesian men and a few Polynesian women. The women's tattoos seem to be more ornamental than functional. While the men's tattoo styles, body location and the number of tattoos relate to their age, past achievements and village of birth.

All the men dressed in the native dress of their village (which means, not much in the way of clothing). In the first contest task, they had to climb up a tall coconut tree. In the second task, they each had to open up 10 coconuts on a sharp stick and separate the husk from the interior. Third, they had to lift a rock weighing 180 pounds off the ground and onto their shoulder (which they all could do). The fourth task was to carry 80 pounds of fruits on their shoulders and demonstrate a little personality.

They had a lot of latitude in the forth task; one of the contestants had a small pig, 2 hens and a bunch of fruit tied to his pole that was about 6 feet long and carried across his shoulders. The last and fifth task required them to row a pirogue out to a buoy and back (probably 200 yards).

We were all impressed with their skill, speed, and agility. We were commenting on the skill of the contestants when one of the judges actually asked me if I'd like to try breaking open a coconut. Being only one of four Americans, and not wanting to embarrass the U.S., or myself I gratefully declined. At the time, I had this vision of stabbing myself on the sharp stick. The sticks would be difficult to use for any inexperienced person as they are not placed deeply in the ground and can deflect off the husk.

One night, while wondering around, we found a great place near the waterfront to eat — self-contained restaurants in a van. I don't know what the locals call them, but we made up a name of our own, "Le Trucks." They were in an area by the large commercial wharf. Local enterprising chefs cook their specialty foods in customized vans complete with lights, awnings, stools, footrests and fold down tables. Everything folds into or onto the trucks so they can be driven on the roads. Most are decorated in good taste; they made good use of varnish, hardwoods and Formica®.

The average price of a dinner varied from $8 to $10 with generous portions. The surprising thing was that there were about 50 of those trucks and serving everything from pizza to chicken chow mien to crêpes and banana splits. They are there every night and draw many of the locals because of their reasonable costs (for Tahiti). Pat and I liked their dessert crêpes. We especially liked to split the crêpe filled with chocolate, hazelnuts and banana; and, topped with ice cream, whipped cream and Grand Marnier ($8.00) – crème de la crème!

On June 24, I experienced a second sharp pain from a new kidney stone. This one first showed up in Rangiroa and confirmed by a nurse crewmember on, *Cristal Blue.* It is working its way down the left side urinary track and hopefully out. This is about the fifth or sixth one I've had so I know the symptoms well. It's a good thing we have strong painkillers aboard as it usually takes about half a day for a stone to make it through each narrow restriction in the canal.

I applied for and received a temporary French Amateur license. My new French call sign was "FO0BEN." The French have a few odd radio rules, i.e., to make a phone call to friends or family through another amateur in the states, I had to be 12 miles away from their islands. I guess this protects their phone company revenues that run about $1.50 a minute to the U.S.

We just happened to be there for the Bastille Day festivities. The celebrations began on June 29 and ran through July 14. We were not sure of what to expect, but knew there would be parades, dancing and exhibitions. We had good seats for the parades, as the boat was moored only 150 feet from the parade route. We also received a letter from the Port Captain asking us to dress up our ship, whatever that meant.

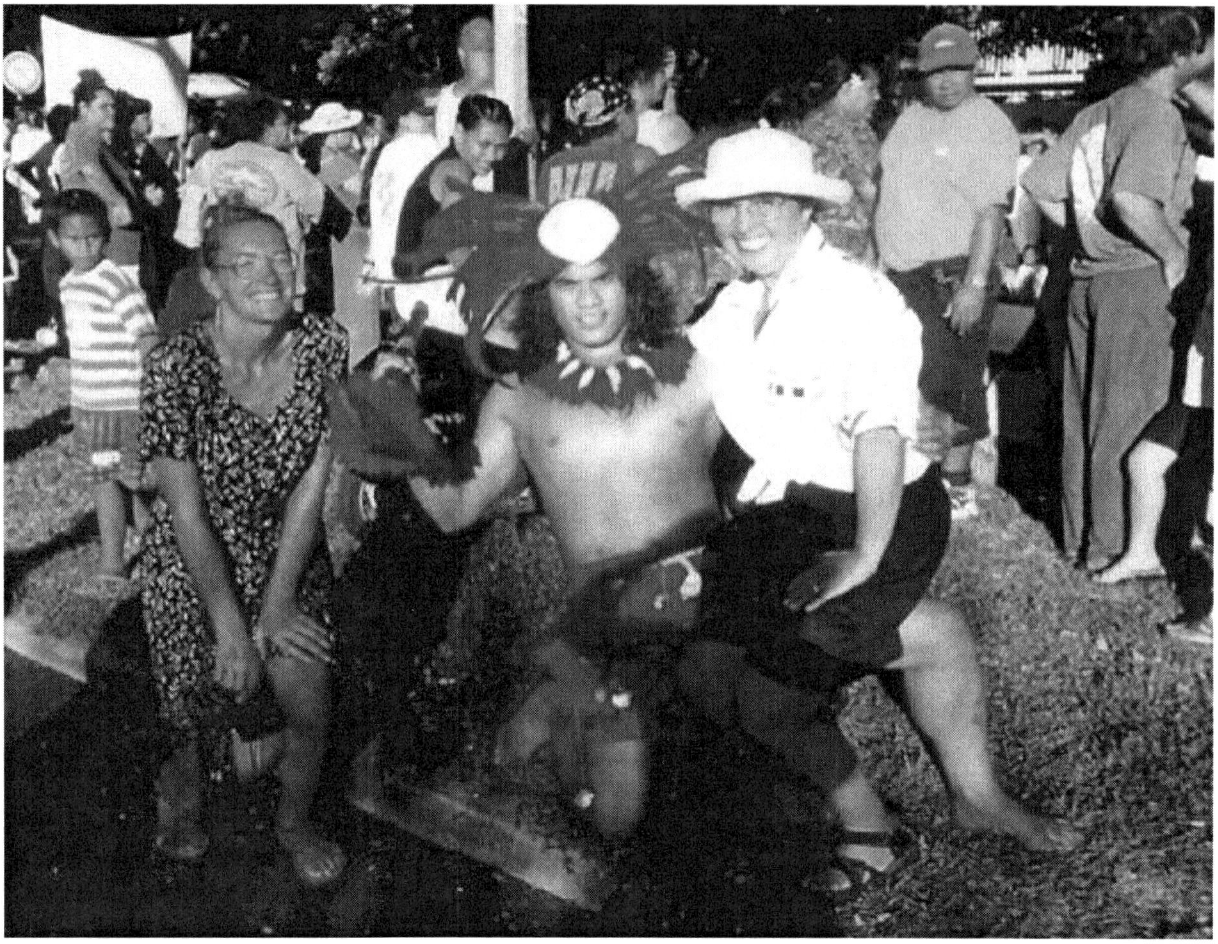

BOBBI (*Cristal Blue*) AND PAT, BASTILLE PARADE

Bobby and Leslie rented a teeny tiny car (US $75 a day, plus gas) to explore Tahiti and camp over night. They went to the other side of the island, it rained all night, and the next day — bad timing since it had not rained in two weeks. They then decided to try camping on Moorea with a young couple from an Australian boat, *Giselle* — they never sit still. David and Gay, the owners of *Giselle*, were former owners of a pizza restaurant in Australia so last night we had a big pizza party using their recipes. The women spent half a day shopping for all the fresh pizza ingredients. They made 4 different types that each had 6 to 10 toppings, enough for 10 diners to have 4 pieces. They gave their now non-secret dough recipe to us and we were anxious to give it a whirl.

Last Friday Pat, Joe and Bobbi from *Cristal Blue* and I went to the Beachcomber Hotel for happy hour. This hotel is probably the most luxurious hotel in all of French Polynesia. The dinner buffet cost a mere $57 per person so we opted to luxuriate in the lounge to watch the floorshow. This is one advantage of knowing many boaters; someone has gone before us and figured out the most inexpensive way to enjoy each city's offerings. In this case, the lounge has nearly the same view of the stage as the dining room, but much less expensive. The floorshow was 100% Polynesian with beautiful young women and handsome young men. The billing for the show claimed it was authentic native dancing, but it looked a bit Hollywood theatrical to me. The costumes were too perfect with brilliant colors. The various pieces of each costume were color coordinated with precisely matching hues. The exception was the coconut halters that are always dark brown or black. The men were always slapping their hands against their legs, thighs, arms and chest — reminded me of the Broadway musical "Grease." We just can't figure how the women can move their hips like that, what great fun.

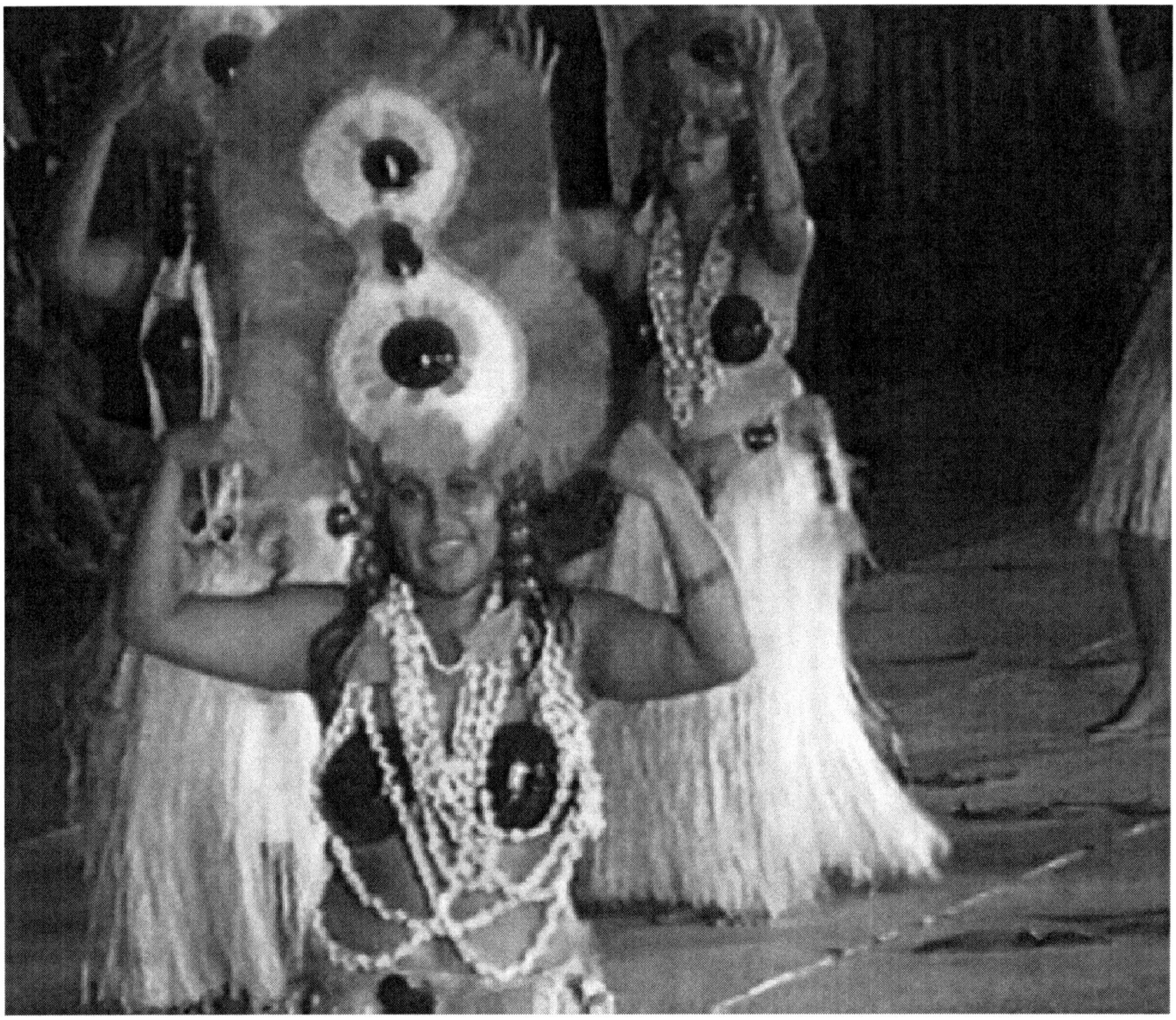

LOVELY NATIVE DANCERS DURING THE BASTILLE DAY CELEBRATIONS

When Leslie and Bobby got back from camping, they had many stories to tell: They stopped a young Polynesian man to ask directions to a campsite. He got so excited; he wouldn't just point out the road to them, but insisted on taking them in his small truck. After dropping them off, he said he'd be back with his guitar and they would sing songs. When he came back he had cold beers for everyone, but his cousin had borrowed his guitar so he brought his boom box instead. His music was taped Polynesian music that his family of brothers, sisters, uncles, aunts and cousins had recorded. The harmony and the songs were of wonderful quality. He gave Bobby and Leslie his favorite tape — that they liked to play during dinner. Then they met an extremely large Tahitian who told them in poor English he loved them and would be their security guard (he actually was a security guard at the airport). Well, he brought them beers also, and insisted on sleeping on the ground near their tent to provide security. He told Leslie and Bobby that a few people camping nearby might not be quite right in the head. He did not have a tent or anything to sleep on; claiming the natural way to sleep was directly on the ground.

They returned on June 29 for the parade that started Bastille Day celebrations. This parade went on for 4 hours and was strictly an affair for Polynesian families as every island group or organization was represented. There were Boy Scouts, Girl Scouts, Cub Scouts, soccer teams, tennis teams, basketball teams, church groups, cycle groups, canoe teams, body builders, surfers, singers, dancers, etc., etc. That night there was a torch light parade on the water. Six man canoes accompanying a double-hulled canoe that was about 100 feet long. It had two large lateen type sails, a Diesel engine, and drummers playing their drums loudly. The drums provided the rhythm for the rowers in the canoes. The final ending of a fun day was an evening display of excellent fireworks right at our anchorage.

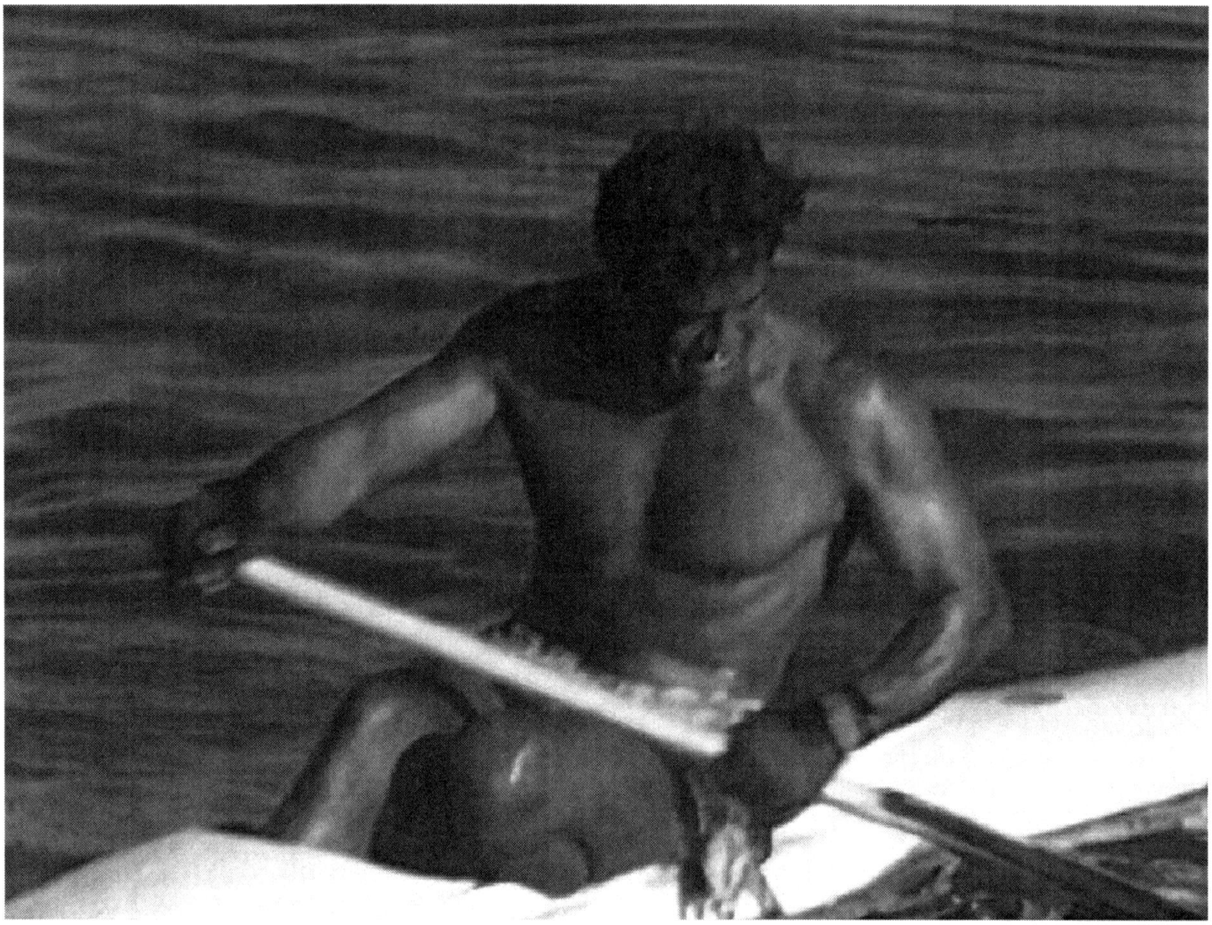

BEAUTIFUL SCULPTURED TAHITIAN PADDLING AN OUTRIGGER CANOE

Friday and Saturday, they held outrigger canoe races right off our stern. It looked like there were teams from all over French Polynesia. In the men's singles, there were 230 participants. The course was across the harbor and back, about 4 miles. These canoes are lightweight, about 12 feet long, and constructed something like a rowing shell except the seats are stationary. They row using one paddle, which is slightly curved and has a large blade. Saturday night, one of the champions in the men's singles ended up celebrating at our potluck dinner. He brought his personal paddle and demonstrated to anyone who would listen, the correct way to paddle. He was quite a character, but I think he did too much celebrating before he arrived at our party. It must be quite an honor here to win a contest like this with so many competitors. As part of Bastille Day celebrations which goes on for 15 days, there is a show every night at the stadium. Each village puts on a show that includes dancing, singing and music. The participants are judged on their performances.

Tuesday and again a week later, our friends on *Cristal Blue* dragged their anchor. This means the anchor was not set hard and did not hold their big sailboat in place. Their boat weighs 110,000 pounds and the winds were gusting to 40 knots. It's a hairy situation since everyone's stern line is tied to shore; the boat that is dragging can't maneuver with its engine until the stern lines are free. Unless quick action is taken, a heavy boat may move into their neighbor and dislodge and/or damage them. In this case, lots of people came to help. We used dinghies to push their boat away from the nearby boats. Bobby and Leslie cast off the stern lines from the bollards on shore while making sure the lines couldn't foul the props. The first time it happened their anchor windless was not working and the anchor had to be pulled up by hand — not much fun. Joe had just picked up the new anchor windless motor from New Zealand that morning. After getting him re-anchored in the harbor and away from other boats, Joe and I worked for three hours to assemble the windless so he could re-anchor.

The second time *Cristal Blue* dragged we were touring the Island. It was quite a shock when Joe saw his boat anchored in the harbor instead of where he had left it. Bobby and Leslie came to the forefront once again to help move *Cristal Blue* safely away from its closely anchored neighbors. We all worked hard to move them back to the quay and get them well anchored. Joe and Bobbi had a party for all those who helped and it was a blast. They arranged to have a onetime professional guitar player from England (he and his wife were cruising this area on their boat *Cracker*) play and sing Beetle songs as well as other songs from the sixties.

The *Cristal Blue* folks were not happy with all the unexpected excitement. They decided to ship their boat back to the states on a freighter. This was not uncommon, as we knew six other couples that decided not to continue sailing because the enjoyment was overshadowed by frustration and difficulty. Many of the boats, after sailing this far, have sustained some rather significant damage to their sails, rigging, transmissions, engines, or hulls, etc. We put about 8,000 miles on ***Our Pleasure*** at this point, which is more than we would have on Puget Sound in a lifetime of sailing. So far, ***Our Pleasure*** has done well and kept us safe.

Some of the people we have met along the way are true Jimmy Buffett fans to the point of being a so-called "Parrot Head." This means when they go to his concerts their dress code is taken to the absolute limit of tastelessness. Gary, my son-in-law, sent me four of his CD's that we enjoy playing during sunset — seems to go well with happy hours and sunset. Buffett's music is like a fantasy to find a perfect town by the ocean where the air is warm, the sea is crystal clear and the locals are legendary characters who wile away the hours mixing margaritas — Margarita Ville. His music is great fun and can be classified into four categories: Boats, Beaches, Bars and Ballads.

You just never know what will happen next around here. One day an extremely large Tahitian woman weighing close to 500 pounds was walking along the sidewalk when she decided to go swimming. She removed her top and splashed around for about 30 minutes right behind our boat. Leslie said she had the biggest boobs she has ever seen. I guess it must be okay here because no one paid any attention and the police never came.

One day Pat and I were carrying 300 feet of new 5/8 inch diameter line back to the boat from a local marine store and it was heavy. A good-looking, well-dressed Tahitian, Valentine Cowan, pulled up alongside and asked, "Where are you going"? We said, "The Park next to the Quay." She said, "Get in." At first, we said, "No, we we're okay," but boy was she insistent, she practically dragged us into her car. It did not take long for our two families to develop a close friendship. Her husband was educated in the U.S. and now runs the company that unloads cargo ships that call in Tahiti. His grandfather started the company after moving to Tahiti from the Netherlands. Their 20-year-old daughter also studied in the U.S. She and her boy friend quickly became friends with Leslie and Bob.

Since meeting, we had several dinners together both at their house and on our boat. One night when they stopped by for happy hour, they brought a cousin carrying a 15-month-old girl and an executive from the bank of Tahiti. They also brought enough Tahitian food to feed an army. Pat had cooked a leg of lamb, mashed potatoes and invited some close American friends over who brought a salad. We had a wonderful time together until the wee hours of the evening. Valentine told us several stories about her grandmother who became one of Paul Gauguin's mistresses.

Gauguin was born into a liberal, middle-class Paris family in 1848. During that part of his life, he became a successful Paris stockbroker. He had five children and a wife, but his interest in impressionist painting around 1874 changed everything. Deeply in debt by 1891, he sailed to the South Seas without his family, to escape, "everything that is artificial and conventional[2]." He stayed in Tahiti and later in the Marquesas until his death in 1903.

The family had so many interesting stories about their culture. Valentine showed us around Papeete and even insisted on taking our laundry to her house. The people we meet on our travels more than balance out the difficulties of crossing mighty oceans and dangerous storms in small boats. Some sailors have compared ocean sailing to locking yourself in a dark closet and continuously throwing water over your head — a good description.

We moved our boat to an area in Papeete's harbor known by everyone as "The Quay." The quay is in a park like setting where boats tie their sterns to a massive concrete break-wall. We moved to the quay to take advantage of placing our stern only 5 feet away from the concrete wall and park, a bit more civilized. We now can reach land over a gangplank instead of a wet dinghy ride. We did lose some privacy as tourists and locals are always strolling by and like to ask questions about our travels. The good news is we are in the heart of Papeete and much closer to everything. I had intended to moor at the quay originally, but a friend told Pat that giant sized cockroaches infested the area — not a good joke. We did see one cockroach, but they seem to be a way of life in every country we have been in since leaving the U.S. I think we have seen cockroaches in every tropical home we visited. People learned to live with them, ignoring their presence as if they don't exist.

We had planned to leave Papeete about July 2, a little behind our original intentions, but still with time to visit other islands before heading to New Zealand. We planned to visit Moorea next, which is only 11 miles away, then Bora Bora, which is probably the most beautiful island in the South Pacific.

Well, things do not usually go as planned, so we delayed leaving Papeete to help *Cristal Blue*, our friends from Portland. They decided to ship their boat on a yacht transport ship bound for Vancouver, BC. This extra time also allowed us to run all the systems on ***Our Pleasure*** one more time to make sure everything was in working order. This environment is tremendously hard on equipment and sometimes on people. To illustrate this, the following items failed and needed our attention before we could leave Papeete.

- On July 25, 1998, the new engine driven refrigeration compressor froze from insufficient internal lubricant and I had to reinstall our old one, which also failed a few days later. Loss of this system meant we could only refrigerate using the 120 volt AC system powered from the generator or the engine using the 12 volt DC to 120 volt AC inverter.

2 Microsoft® Encarta® 2006. © 1993-2005 Microsoft Corporation. All rights reserved

- The next day, I discovered the generator would only run for about 10 to 45 minutes and then turn itself off. I replaced the water pump impellers, reset the valves and tested the thermostat in boiling water. The boiling water test indicated the thermostat switched off at about 150° F instead of 185° F. When it switches off it interrupts the fuel flow to the generator's engine. I called the generator manufacturer in Portland and they shipped me a new thermostat in 5 days — good for Tahiti. With the new thermostat installed, the generator was back and running.
- On August 2, 1998, the forward head stopped working. Bob took it apart and installed a rebuild kit to get it working again. This job ranks high on the list of worst possible jobs on any boat.
- Bob has gotten good at splicing and keeping the lines in good working order. When he discovered the snubber line connected to our anchor chain had frayed to a single strand, he reworked it back to health in no time.
- The next day, a young man on a motor scooter ran into Pat when she crossed the street at the post office. At the time, road congestion had stopped vehicle traffic and the driver of the motor scooter was running fast in between stopped cars. She suffered a bruised hip and ankle along with some minor scrapes. This cruising life must have hardened her up because she was fine in a couple of days to the great relief of the crew.

On the fifth, the crew of ***Our Pleasure*** helped our good friends on *Cristal Blue*, pull up their 80 pound anchor. The anchoring system consisted of a 1 inch diameter by 400 foot line with 80 feet of half-inch chain at the anchor end. This system bypassed the ships hawse-pipe system and therefore negated using the anchor windless. Now retrieving the anchor relied on manual labor. After the anchor was up, we motored over to the transport ship.

The exposed cargo deck was well below sea level and we entered through the opened stern. This transport freighter was at least 600 feet long. Constructed with chambers that flood (or can be pumped out), the entire freighter settles down in the water until the freight deck is 12 feet below sea level. Divers secure each yacht to heavy steel cradles. Pumping the chambers out restores the transport ship's normal water line. The yachts inside are high and dry. The yacht cradles are then welded to the freighter's deck and inspected by the ship's insurance provider. For the 10 day trip to Vancouver, BC, Joe and Bobbi will eat all their meals with the ship's officers and sleep on *Cristal Blue*. The ship's engineers connected all the yachts to power and water.

Crews traveling with the transport can work on their yachts, e.g., put new bottom paint on the hull. The cost for their boat was $25,000, which they viewed as a worthwhile cost since it saved the wear and tear and problems of ocean sailing for the 5,000 miles or so. It took from 6:45 a.m. to 4:30 p.m. to get their boat and 12 others, safely secured.

The next day we paid the French port captain our port bill for staying in Papeete 58 days, $796. Expensive for 1998 and he was sort of a curmudgeon type person or maybe he just didn't like Americans.

Pulling up our anchor, we found that the yacht next to us the 108 foot ketch *Gleam*, had dropped their anchor chain over ours and we could not break our chain lose. *Gleam* is a yacht with five professional crewmembers. Two of the crew put on scuba gear and to our relief, unsnarled the two anchor systems.

The anchor fouling delayed our fuel dock appointment, but the fuel dock crew took pity on us and let us fuel anyway. Fuel was the only bargain in French Polynesia. When you leave it is duty free, but there are a bunch of hoops to jump through. We needed 159 gallons to fill our 300 gallon tanks. Their duty-free rate was $1.39 per gallon, a bargain compared to the retail rate of $4 per gallon.

We left Papeete about 9 a.m. put up the yankee and staysail and headed for Moorea. It felt good to be under sail again after our long stay on land. The weather was perfect with a 12 to 15 knot wind out of the NE.

We arrived at Oponohu Bay at 11 a.m. and anchored near *Esprit*, *Endurance* and *Bandit*, all boats we knew from Mexico. This bay is the nicer of the two major bays in Moorea. The other bay is known as Cook's Bay, but we later learned that this famous sea captain actually anchored his ship in Oponohu and not in Cook's Bay.

Pat and I hitched-hiked over to see Cook's Bay where there is a small town. The driver could not speak any English and let us off by the Catholic Church where he was working. Actually, this is just were we wanted to go to find out what times Mass would be celebrated. Being curious, we were peeking in the windows when Father Jean Claude walked up and introduced himself. He spoke good English and had a wonderful sense of humor. He had been on Moorea for ten years and was responsible for the four churches on the island. The Pope started sending his order of priests to Tahiti 150 years ago. For the first time in all those years, he now has several young men studying to be priests or brothers. He was proud of this accomplishment and his order sent him another priest who specialized in teaching seminarians. He then showed us the original Catholic Church that he is restoring as a chapel. Above the old altar is a beautiful oil painting depicting the flight to Egypt of the Holy Family: Mary, Joseph and the baby Jesus. A white angel is watching over them. The family obviously looked Tahitian in the large 10 foot by 10 foot oil painting. However, wooden planks provided the medium for the painting and termites have been feasting on the wood for many years. They have developed a plan to save the painting that sounded logical and we wished him luck. We invited Father Jean Claude back to our boat and spent a wonderful afternoon drinking beer left over from Mexico and solving the worlds' problems.

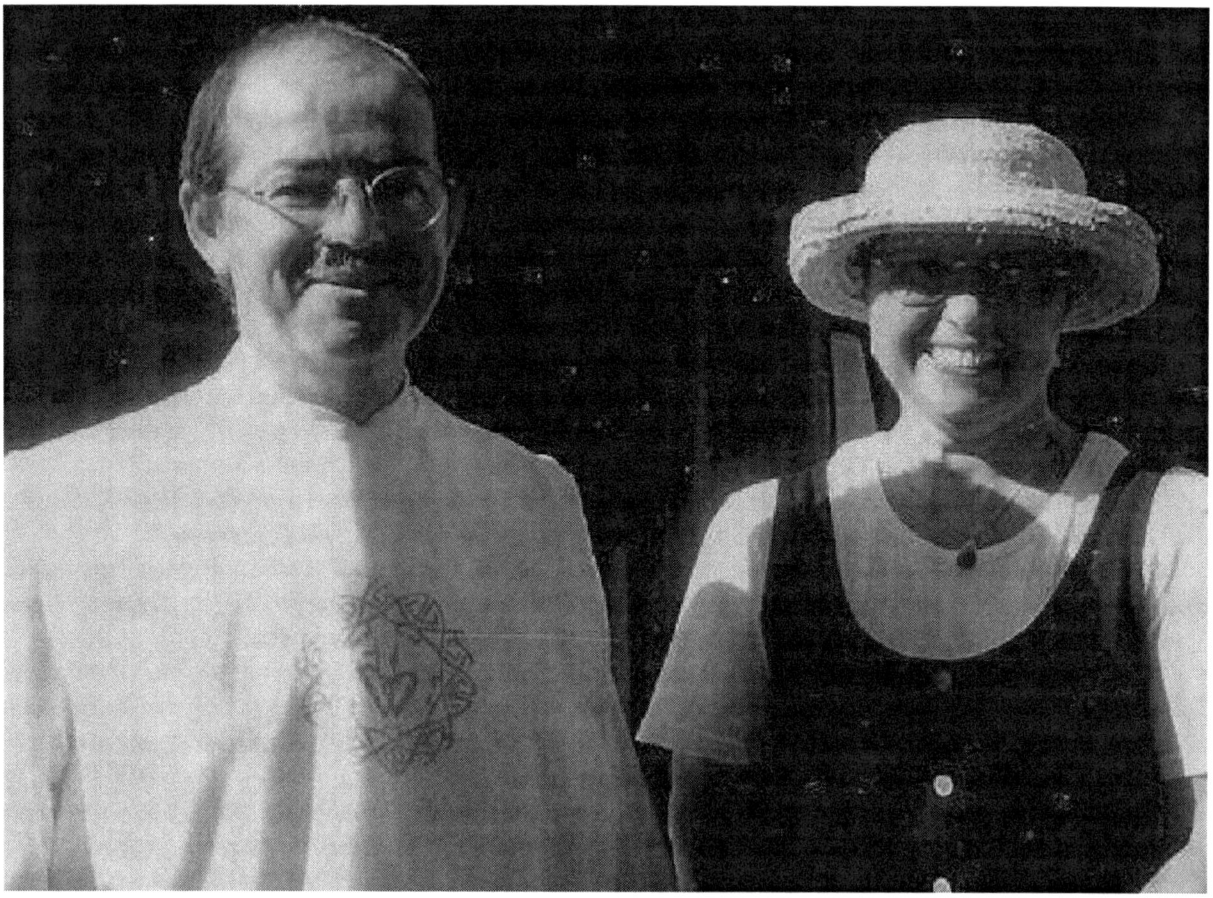

FATHER JEAN CLAUDE AND PAT

Bob and Leslie were off climbing a mountain near our bay to a viewpoint called Belvedere, which looks into both Cook's Bay and Oponohu Bay, quite a sight. Also at the head of our bay are two mountains Tohiea and Mouaroa. Mt. Mouaroa stands out because of its rugged and multi-tiered spire that appears on post cards of the island. These two mountains form the backdrop for several scenes in the Hawaiian filmed movie *South Pacific*.

On Sunday, to get to Father Jean Claude's closest church, St. Michael's, we managed to stumble out of our bunks around 6:30 a.m. Island car traffic that early on Sunday mornings is almost non-existent. Patience paid off just as we thought about putting our thumbs away. A nice Tahitian woman named Adora picked us up in her truck. We pointed to her rosary beads hanging from the rearview mirror and that was the only destination clue she needed. Off she went to St. Michael's and a good thing since we could not have found it on our own. It was located in the tiny town of Papetoai, off the main road and looked like a small store, no cross. We were slightly late for the 8:30 a.m. Mass and when we walked in everyone turned to stare at the only white people in the church. However, they made us feel us right at home when an elderly Tahitian woman with obvious authority, made a row of people move over so we could sit down. They must build the roof of these churches extra strong to contain the beautiful singing — I am sure the Lord was pleased.

All the readings were in Tahitian, but Father said his homily in French. He explained later, while driving us back to our boat, the great difficulty in speaking Tahitian correctly. He felt he could not express himself well unless he used French (not long ago, the French language was the only permissible language in Tahitian schools). There was no doubt that he was getting through because they were all laughing and smiling and enjoyed the whole homily. He used so much body language with hand and eye movements that if I hadn't known better, I would have thought him Italian. Pat asked him what he said (understanding French as well as we do) and he explained that he was commenting on people carrying too much baggage throughout their lives. He used an analogy of people packing for a vacation. They were not able to decide what items would be needed so they pack everything. The resulting burden is so heavy that walking with the baggage becomes extremely difficult. Pat laughed and said she understood the "packing too much, real well!" We wanted to spend more time with Father Jean Claude and invited him for breakfast, but he had other Masses to say.

We were stuck on the boat for several days because of 40 knot winds roaring through the bay and heavy rain. When it finally calmed down, we enjoyed an evening happy hour on *Endurance*. The next day we made arrangements to tour the island with a guide. Our guide showed up driving a 4X4. His name was Blanc-Blanc (White-White) because he had light colored blond hair (Tahitian mother, Swedish father). We shared the 4X4 with a young couple from San Diego on their honeymoon. The honeymooner's names were Andrea, a 23-year-old graduate student and Steve, a 37-year-old Catholic youth minister. Andrea's English was excellent though she grew-up in Germany. German schools must do a fine job teaching English. It was quite a tour. Blanc-Blanc left no road or stream untouched. We saw their pineapple fields, juice factories, experimental forest of mahogany trees, a 300 foot waterfall, Belvedere lookout, and several other minor sites.

On Aug. 15, we left Moorea early in the morning for an overnight sail and arrived at Fare Village on the island of Huahine about 11 a.m. the next day. The sea during this passage was extremely sloppy and made the boat roll in an uncomfortable motion. It even made Pat feel queasy, which is unusual. The wind was blowing about 15 knots most of the way so we had to reduce sail to time our arrival at the island at first light. The anchorage at Fare Village is poor as it exposed us to winds from the north, south, and west. We were lucky, this time of year the wind blows steadily from the east, but speeds up in the anchorage due to the venturi effect of the mountains. The holding was poor where we dropped our anchor. We had to try four times before it finally snaked its way around some coral heads and held. The first place we dropped anchor was a deep 80 feet, but the port captain asked us to move. The inter-island ferry was arriving that night and he was afraid our location might hinder their maneuvering capability we gladly moved.

The next day, a rather old-fashioned sailing ship came in and anchored next to us — *Barbarossa*. She had sailed from England with Rob, Sue, and their two teenage children aboard. It was not long before they called us over to share half of a huge Mahi-Mahi they had just caught. Rob left professional fishing in England when the government bought his fishing boat. The decline in fish forced many fishermen out of the industry. Money from the sale of his fishing boat built *Barbarossa* and allowed the family to sail away.

There wasn't much to see on Huahine, so we just bought some fresh food in town (Craigmont pop was only $12 a case, good price for this part of the world), did a few loads of wash in ***Our Pleasure's*** washing machine and left for Raiatea.

We planned to sail past Raiatea on our way to Bora Bora, but since we arrived about mid-day, we decided to anchor overnight and leave the next day for Bora Bora. There was confusion over channel markers, but we were able to sort out the channel we wanted and anchored in front of the Raiatea Carnage (boat yard). Daryl and Marlene from *Rumplesteelskin* rowed over to greet us. They are from northern British Columbia and were leaving their steel (of course) sailboat in the Raiatea boat yard for the hurricane season. They stayed for happy hour and dinner and rowed back to their boat after dark. We left Raiatea the next morning at 10 a.m. to head for Bora Bora just 23 nautical miles away.

The sailing was beautiful as the island of Raiatea provided good protection from the ocean swells, which gave us a smooth ride to Bora Bora in about 12 knots of wind. Approaching Bora Bora from the ocean is quite spectacular. The tremendous force of ocean waves crash against the island's fringing reef, which forces water, spray and mist at least 15 feet into the air. Behind the reef the water is calm, but takes on many varied hues of blue and green — a wondrous sight. Since the reef calms the water inside the lagoon, the entrance pass, Teavanui, is generally easy to navigate. However, water is always flowing out the pass and when we entered the opposing current slowed us to 2 knots even at full engine power.

We dropped our anchor in 74 feet of water in front of the Bora Bora Hotel. The most famous restaurant on the island, *Bloody Mary's* was just around the point. Unbeknownst to Pat and me, Leslie had planned her twenty-eighth birthday celebration around dinner at this iconic restaurant. Pat and I decided to stay on the boat though because of strong winds in the anchorage. We needed more confidence in the anchor set before we could leave the boat unattended. While they were gone, Pat baked a cake and wrapped their present, a hand crafted cup and plate she bought in Mexico. When Bob and Leslie got back, the real celebration started.

The two confirmed that *Bloody Mary's* was everything they imagined or heard about. The floor was fine white sand. Hand crafted furnishings of varnished palm tree woods established a pleasant, soft atmosphere. The patrons and staff were all barefooted. Incidentally, bare feet and bathing suits or light clothing has been our norm since leaving San Diego. The exception is when native townspeople have a strict dress code. A glass-covered case with layers of ice inside the entry displayed all the main entrées. You simply pick out which lobster, fresh fish, or aged New Zealand beef you want and the chefs will grill it to perfection.

When Pat and I went, several days later, we noticed two large name boards posted at the entrance to *Bloody Mary's*. The boards listed every famous person that had ever visited the restaurant. The list was impressive and included most of Hollywood's movie stars. Of course, the list included Jimmy Buffett whose songs describe such enchanting and romantic places as Bora Bora.

We found an unusual snorkel spot only 45 minutes by dinghy from our anchorage. You get in the water at the north end of the coral area and drift in the 3 knot current for about 1,000 yards. The beautiful coral was teaming with sea life. Large clamshells, with slightly open purple lips, closed quickly whenever I pointed my finger at them. I did not see any eyes so I have no idea how they knew I was reaching out. There were no sharks or rays, just brightly colored fish of every description. We did that drift snorkel twice since it was so interesting. We spent the rest of the day exploring small islands inside the reef in our dinghy.

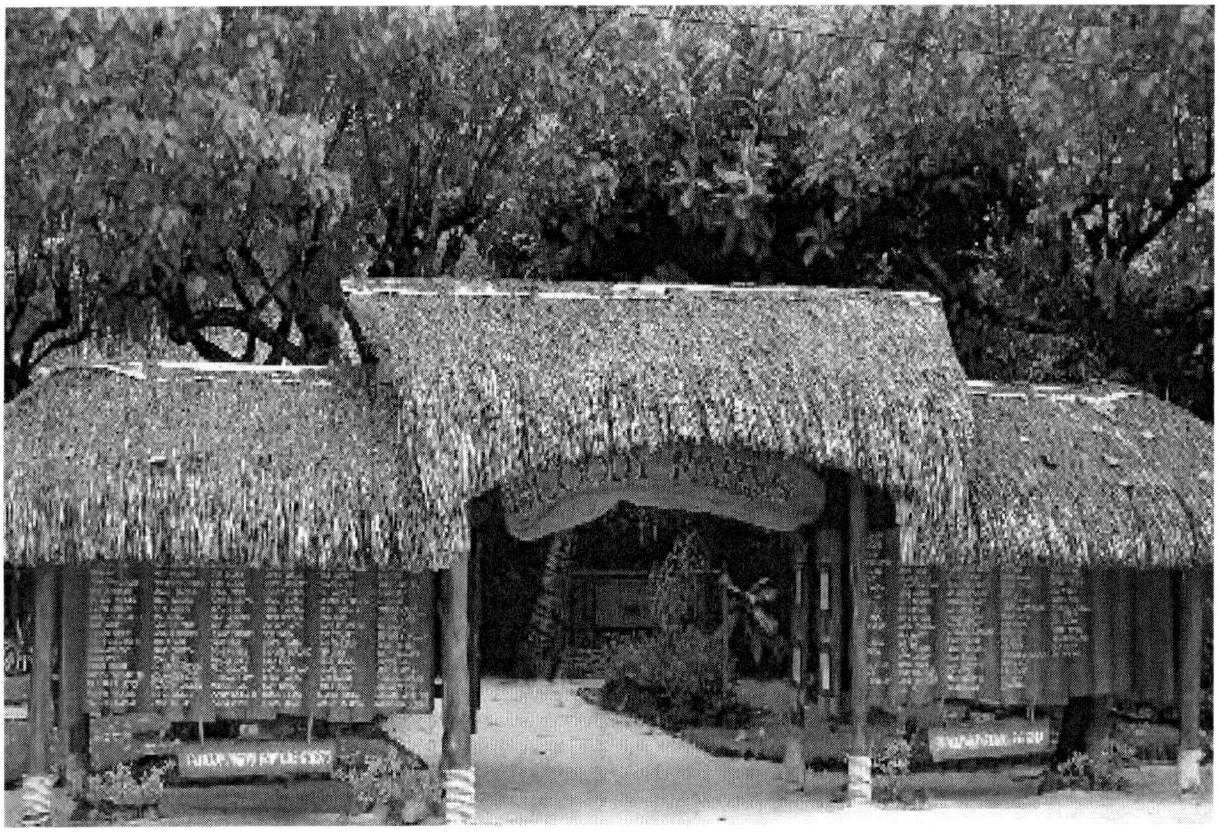

BLOODY MARY'S, BORA BORA

On Aug. 23, we had another celebration for Bob and Leslie, their first wedding anniversary. Pat made everyone Swedish pancakes for breakfast. The family on the sailboat *Hoptoad* (also from Seattle) invited us over for happy hour. Margie made Leslie a set of pearl earrings and Shawn, one of their teenage sons, made her a small gecko out of brightly colored beads. Information about their wedding anniversary had not made the rounds yet; these presents were for Leslie's birthday.

The next day we spent about 30 minutes untangling our anchor chain from coral heads and moved our boat over to a mooring buoy at the Bora Bora Yacht Club. Using moorage buoys is a much better way to secure the boat, as it does not damage coral. A previous April storm had badly damaged the yacht club. The repair process was moving slowly since funds were limited. The roof had many plywood patches and waterside bungalows were in sad shape. They had an open-air restaurant on the water serving American type food and with other yachties there, it was great fun.

During our first night on their mooring, the club's mooring line failed only we were sleeping and didn't know it. Bob and I both woke at the same time when we realized things did not sound right, it was 11:30 p.m., and we were drifting on the outgoing current. We were only three quarters of a mile from wrecking ***Our Pleasure*** on the islands fringing reef — not good! At first, we did not know our location as it was dark and everything looked strange. After calming down, using a little logic and radar, we found the club and motored slowly back watching our sonar for coral heads. Our sonar is high tech; its sound waves penetrate the water in front and below the boat in continuous ninety-degree sweeps. Our monitor in the cockpit displays the seabed beneath the boat and any objects in its path. Everyone was relieved when we dropped our anchor back at the club and could go back to sleep.

The next day Bob and Leslie rented a pair of worn 21 speed bikes. Each bike had only one operational speed and by a stroke of luck, they took some tools along allowing them to keep the bikes going. The road around the island is almost flat so it was easy going. One hillside had a couple of leftover American, WWII cannons that had provided protection to the lagoon's entrance. The next day they went off to scuba dive from a local dive boat while Pat and I lunched with John, from the yacht, *Not Yet.*

On Sunday, Pat and I took a 15 minute dinghy ride into town for the 8:30 a.m. Mass. The church was beautiful with tile floors and the entire wall behind the altar depicted religious scenes in brightly colored stained glass. The scenes included the seven sacraments, the four gospel writings and the fruits and flowers of Polynesia. After Mass, we found a great French bakery that served pastries and espresso coffee. When we got back to the boat, we used our marine VHF radio to say our goodbyes. We headed out the pass toward the Cook Islands.

Chapter 5

BORA BORA TO THE COOK ISLANDS

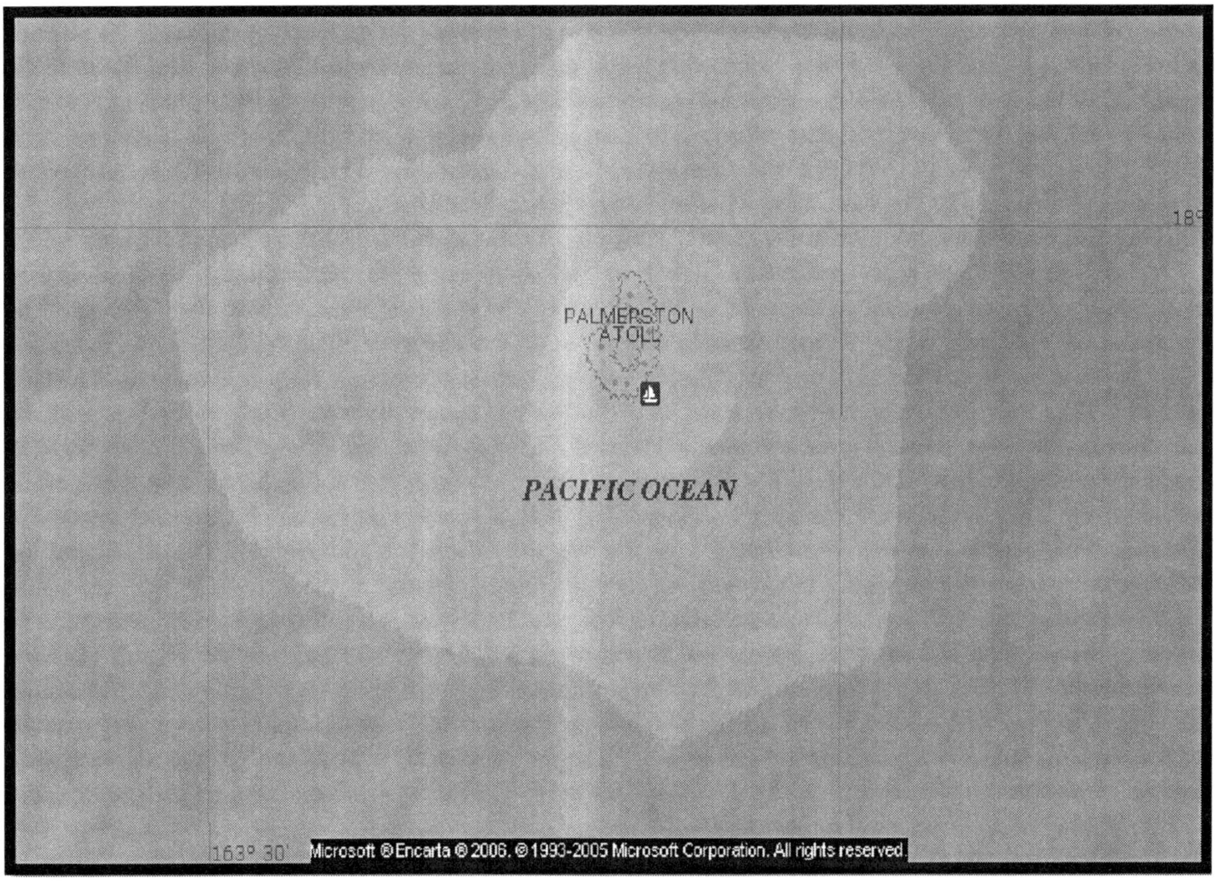

PALMERSTON ATOLL, COOK ISLANDS, Sept. 6, 1998

Before *Cristal Blue* left for Vancouver, Joe gave us a big bucket filled with fishing gear for trolling behind the boat. Bob brought the bucket on deck to sort out something appropriate to troll behind the boat. We were all happily surprised to find an extensive collection of lures and line with bungee cords already attached. There were 12 large, top quality lures of make believe squids with brightly colored tail feathers and big eyes. An assortment of fish hooks, small squid lures and lead weights. Around 5 p.m., we managed to catch a large yellow fin tuna that fed the four of us for two days. I am sure Joe and Bobbi heard us thanking them.

It took us a little over six days in moderate sailing conditions to sail the 800 nautical miles to Palmerston Atoll in the Cook Islands. The Cook Islands, a former colony of New Zealand, has been self-governing since 1965. The land mass of the 15 islands is small at about 90 square miles, but spread out over 900 nautical miles across the Pacific Ocean. Customs and Immigration are located on Rarotonga, the main island of the Cooks. However, sailing to Rarotonga would take us 200 miles south of our rhumb line course to our next islands, Niue and Tonga. Therefore, we kept our west heading to Palmerston Atoll in the northern part of the Cooks.

During this sail, we reached our one-year anniversary date of leaving Seattle, Sept. 3, 1997. When we arrived at Palmerston Atoll, it was close to midnight, dark with no lights on shore and no lighted buoys. Radar images were indicating strong squalls all around us, which blocked out the islands fringing reef. Before we left Seattle, our son David gave us an infrared night vision scope and this was the perfect night to use it. From prior radio contacts, we knew there were five or six other boats anchored outside the reef that encircles the atoll. We could not see them on radar or with our marine binoculars. The night vision scope was truly amazing; it turned night into day and the illusive sail boats popped into view. I also spotted a dim light from a flashlight in a small dinghy. The dinghy looked as though it was leaving the island and headed our way. When the dinghy reached us, we found it contained two brothers, Edward Marsters and Simon Marsters.

They had been out fishing when they saw our masthead running lights and came out to show us where to drop our anchor. There is no entrance through these reefs deep enough to accommodate our boat so they explained where to drop anchor in about 40 feet of water and let the wind blow us back from the reef. The reef drops off extremely fast so with our anchor dropped at 40 feet and with 300 feet of chain out, the depth below the boat was now 140 feet. The prevailing trade winds blew our boat away from the reef until the chain tightened. Then the catenary of the chain pulled us back towards the reef until the boat's position was steady. Just when it looked like we were good and secure it started raining so we invited Edward and Simon aboard to escape the rain and to have a little chat. The two brothers informed us that they would be our host family while at Palmerston. They left us sometime after 1 a.m., guiding their 14 foot aluminum dinghy through the reefs in light rain. We looked at each other wondering what the brothers meant by "host family"? This island and the Marsters were to be our most extraordinary experience since leaving Seattle.

Sometime around 8:30 a.m. on the same morning and after little sleep, two officials from Palmerston were knocking on our hull. Bill Marsters represented Immigration and David Marsters was the Health Minister. They motored out through the reefs in their 14 foot aluminum dinghy to check us officially into Palmerston. This island, as they told us, was not an official check-in station for the Cook Islands. However, they were so welcoming and glad of our visit; they told us how to fill in the paperwork to justify our visit as an emergency because of equipment problems. Actually, our generator stopped running again that day, so it all worked out with no fibbing or finger crossing required.

The island was unusual as it is actually an atoll made up of seven small islands scattered along the coral reef surrounding the lagoon. Coconut palms cover all the islands, yet the overall height of the atoll is barely over 50 feet. There are some small boat passages into the lagoon, but they are only 4 feet deep at the most. All inhabitants are descendants of a patriarchal figure, William Marsters, a Lancashire (Northwestern England) man who settled there with three Polynesian wives from another Cook island, Penrhyn. The year was 1862 and over time, he managed to father 26 children. He divided the islands into three sections for each of the three families and established strict rules for intermarriage. His descendants, like Edward, Simon, Bill, and David are all Marsters and still control the island while the majority of the descendants have settled in New Zealand.

The islanders live a basic and simple lifestyle with few changes over the years. They have one large community generator that runs between 4 p.m. and 10 p.m. every day. Some lucky families also have their own Diesel generator they can use if needed. The New Zealand Government does provide assistance like the generators and dinghies, but obtaining money comes from either their labors or relatives. Relatives working and living mostly in New Zealand do send some money back to the islanders. The labor comes from catching and preserving fish and supplying copra, the dried white flesh of coconuts. An interisland supply vessel stops about once a month to buy their goods, provide mail service, and brings ordered supplies. Nature supplies all their food needs from the water surrounding the islands and items that grow or graze on their land. However, on the atolls, poor soils restrict what vegetation that can be grown. Watering vegetation can also be a serious problem as it must come from rain or collected rainwater.

Ordering supplies for delivery to the island takes a lot of early planning, sometimes months. Visiting yachts help in a small way by donating items islanders cannot obtain easily or would not have the money to buy. We always figured, if we have it and they need it, it's theirs and we'll replace it later.

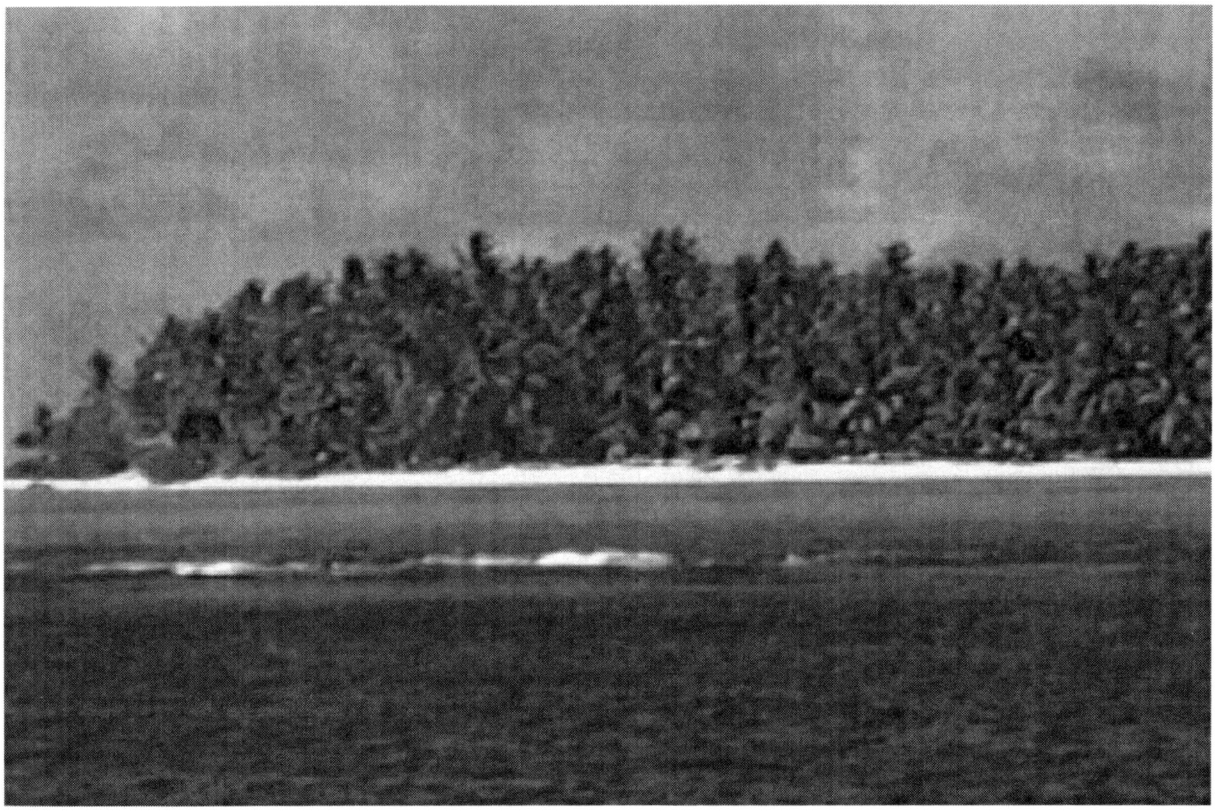

PALMERSTON ATOLL, COOK ISLANDS

That afternoon, Edward came out in his dinghy to invite us to his home for dinner. We had no idea what to expect or even what to wear, which was a concern of Pats. The path through reef was tricky with coral heads sticking out or just below the water all over the place. They marked the really bad places with sticks of ironwood. Some sticks had strips of reflective tape to help reflect light from flashlights at night. They seemed to manage these shallow channels with ease, but a stranger would find navigating the channels extremely difficult. Small white shells cover the ground of the island, little dirt or grass was visible and closely planted coconut palm trees covered most of the island. The path to the house or family complex was just a short walk from their beach. The main house was all concrete block for hurricane protection, complements of New Zealand. Window frames existed, but the glass was absent; there was a big front porch with chairs, two beds and many family pictures hanging on the walls. The area in front of the house was set-up for family and guest eating. There was a large canvas tarp stretched between two trees. The tarp covered tables and chairs that could seat twenty people, picnic style. Other family member homes and buildings in the compound fronted along a path about 30 feet wide and 100 feet long. This road like area was cleared of palm trees and made use of the small white shells. The family raked the area to keep it neat and clean.

Buildings included an open-air work area for preparing fish, crabs, lobsters, birds, and butchering pigs. A building with open sides provided a shelter for cooking food in the belowground rock oven. There was a building to house the generator away from the family area and a carport like structure with a small farm tractor. They built a sturdy structure using palm trees in the form of a log cabin to house their pigs. White flesh from coconuts feeds the wild pigs and boy were they wild, fat and mean. We helped feed them one day and we got the distinct impression they would voraciously devour us if given the chance. The biggest fellow was at least 600 pounds and sat quietly in his mud until we approached. We could see his beady eyes watching us and when we were about 10 feet away, he tried to tear his pen apart.

Nature also provides drinking water in the form of rainwater. All the roofs have large gutters to direct rainwater into to a cistern. They have a well, but the water quality is poor. Boiling is necessary, but the smell will not go away. Dry spells in past years have required the use of well water. To circumvent using well water, the family is building a huge buried cistern. The cistern construction consisted of manually mixing concrete for the foundation and mortar for concrete blocks. It looked huge, about 1,700 cubic feet.

Burning coconut shells in a rock-lined, underground oven, cooked our dinner. We heard Edward started the lunch process, like heating the cooking rocks sometime around three in the morning — big effort, little sleep. Only the older family members, like their widowed mother, Tuaine (originally from the Gilbert Islands), Simon and Edward ate with us. The women who did the cooking and the children had to wait until we left the table before they could eat. That afternoon, the family also hosted two other boats *Hio Avae* and *Lisa Rae*. This feast centered on two types of fish, Parrot and Wahoo. Side dishes included rice, lamb, pancakes, dumplings, shortbread, juices, coffee, and tea. When we finally managed to stand up, Edward took us for a walk. He showed us the Marsters cemetery that contained many of the original family members in above ground vaults. The artisanship of the tombstones impressed all of us. Some of those dates made me feel like a baby, figuratively, of course.

The original Marsters house is by far the strongest wooden building I have ever seen. The home took advantage of timbers salvaged from an old sailing ship driven up on their reef during a ferocious storm. The floor space was small about 20 by 20 feet. The floor, wall, and ceiling timbers were constructed from 14 by 10 inch ruff- sawn, knotless beams that were clear oak and straight. The corner and main vertical supports were from the same wood, but with 20 inch sides as were the major roof beams. Heavy wooden shutters closed off the window openings and the wooden doors, were about 4 inches thick. The timbers we saw are rare and probably no longer available at any price. This building was about the only thing that withstood a hurricane in 1929. That mean storm blew away almost all the palm trees and everything standing. Some natives survived by tying themselves to strong trees. It took several years to replant all the palm trees.

Edward introduced us to several other island families and left us with Bill Marsters, the fellow who handles immigration. He is an enterprising person probably in his late forties. He showed us a building he is putting together as a yacht club for visiting yachts. A place to hang out, do laundry, buy limited supplies and have a few beers imported from New Zealand. We bought a few of his Palmerston Yacht Club tee shirts and gave him a

Tacoma Yacht Club burgee to hang up when the club is finished. He thought it would be finished in time for the seasonal yacht migration to New Zealand and Australia.

When a fire destroyed the island's schoolhouse, he assumed the rebuilding task. The school effort delayed the clubhouse build as he added long missing amenities like running water and toilets — high tech for this part of the world. They were looking for a new schoolteacher — what a tough call that would be. That teacher would be giving up most creature comforts to lead an extremely austere life. They brought us back to the boat in time for happy hour and we had a great time discussing the day.

That evening our generator stopped running after about 45 minutes. I spent most of the next day trouble shooting the generator while the rest of the family spent the day on Palmerston. I found the engine driving the generator did not have any compression. The intake valve was not seating as air was coming out of the air intake during the compression stroke. To compensate for the loss of the generator I had to run the main engine with its high output alternator (200 amps) driving our 2,800 watt inverter. With this system, I can run all the 120 volt AC equipment except it will only run the water maker at about half its normal output capacity of 22 gallons per hour. This was a huge relief, as I was not sure the inverter would drive the one horsepower water maker motor.

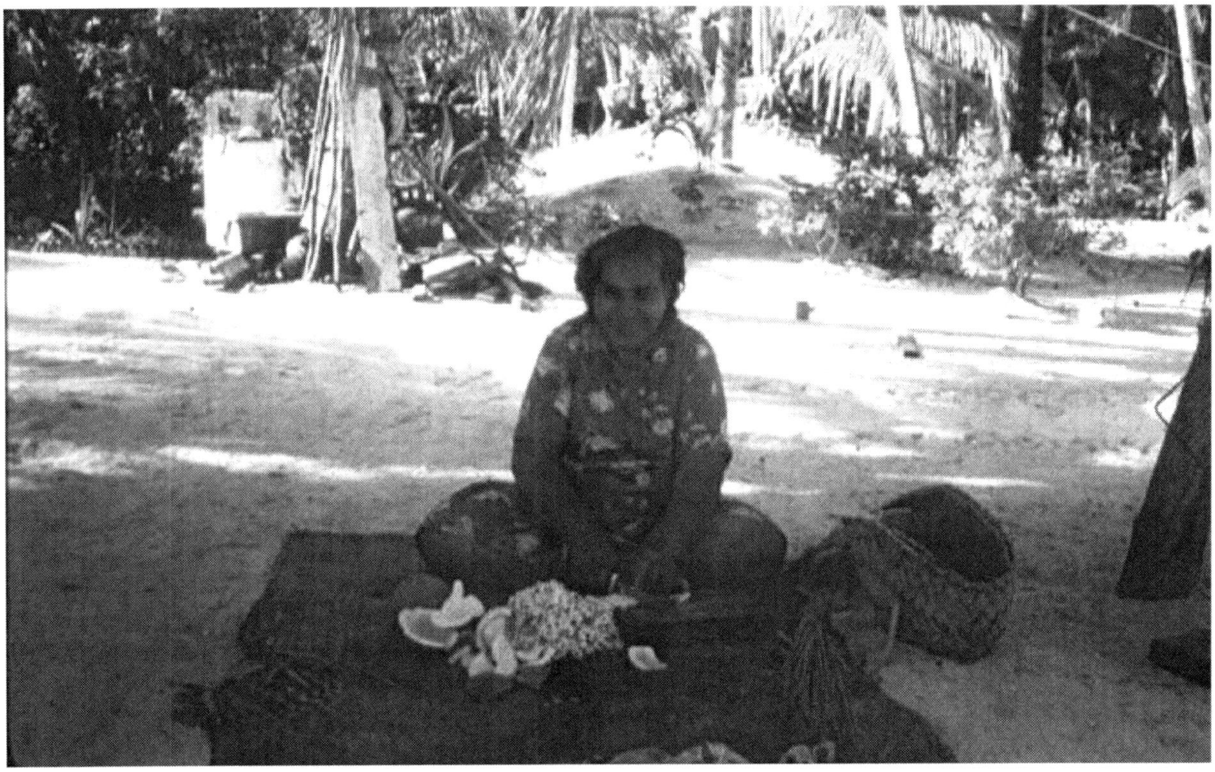

TUAINE MARSTERS WITH COCONUT MEAT TO FEED THE CHICKENS

The next morning Peter Marsters sent over one of his relatives to take us whale watching. We saw one large whale, but he or she was determined to keep its distance. We spent the rest of the day chasing him or her all over the bay.

The day before we left Palmerston, they came to get us early in the morning. All the families have 14 foot aluminum boats with Evenrude outboards, gifts from New Zealand. They are one of the few cultures that still fish with fervor for their subsistence. Pat and I spent most of the day with the mother, Tuaine who was 68, but appeared to be at least 10 years older than that. We walked around the island first while the younger adults went out with the natives looking for crabs. We had a wonderful time just listening to stories from her childhood, when her mother and an aunt taught her to weave hats. I got the feeling that the yachties they have hosted did not take the time to sit and talk to her on a one-on-one basis like Pat and I did because of the way she cried and hugged Pat that evening when we left.

We left Palmerston Sept. 9, 1998 at 10:30 a.m. Before leaving, five members of our host family came out to say good-bye. They were Simon, Edward, Rangi, little David, and Kori. Rangi and Kori, two teenagers brought us two giant lobsters they dove for late last night. We felt like giving them everything on the boat and had already given them many useful items. We gave them all but one gallon of gas we had for the outboard as a last gesture of friendship. They were all on our deck wanting to do anything to help like haul up the anchor, but our anchor windless was in good working order. There was a lot of hugging and a few tears shed before we could pull out, it was sad to say good-bye to these wonderful happy people and their wonderful island. I think we learned an important lesson on Palmerston, material possessions and wealth do not equate to happiness. These island people had almost no material possessions, but they were happy to share what little they had with complete strangers.

Chapter 6

PALMERSTON ATOLL TO NIUE

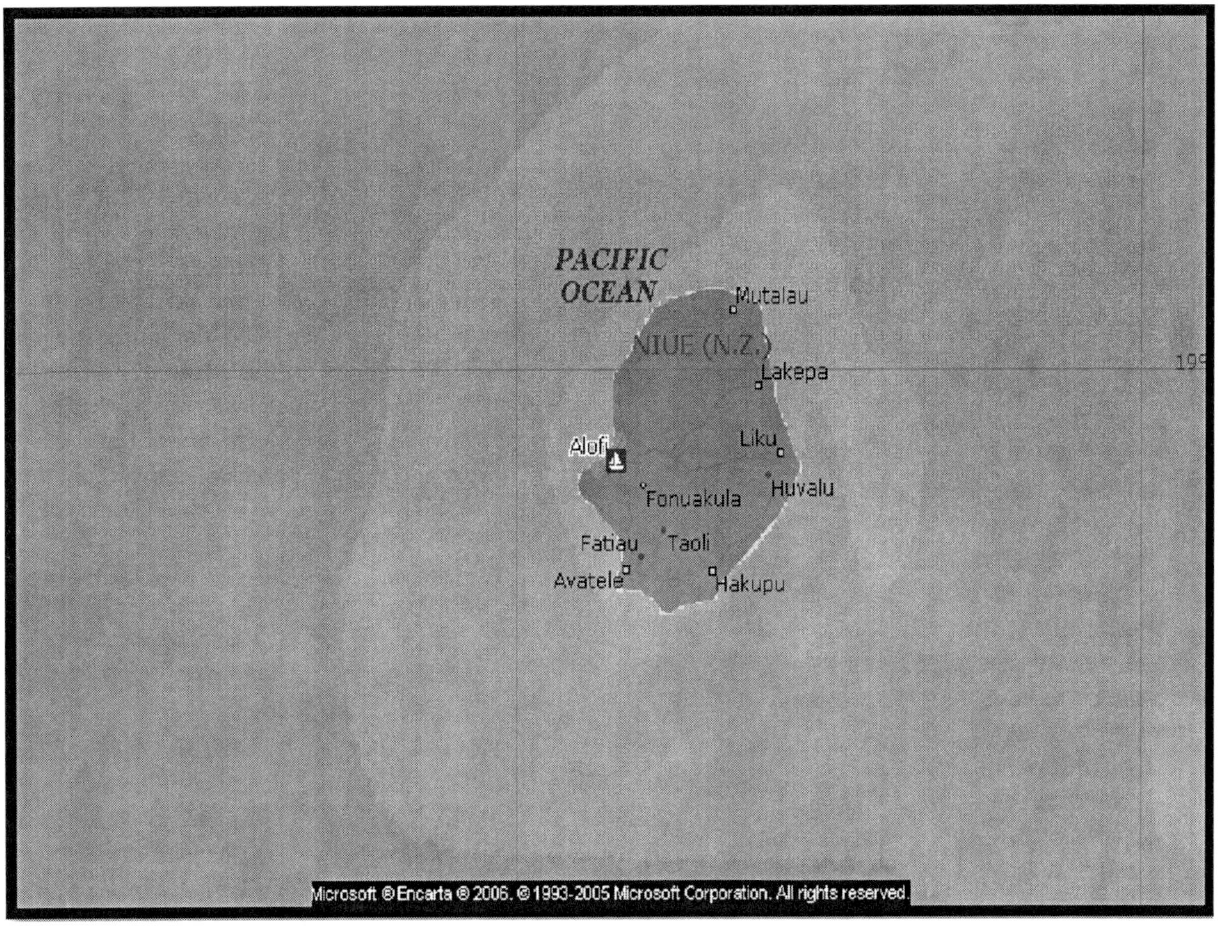

FROM PALMERSTON TO NIUE, A RAISED CORAL IS. Sept. 12, 1998

We arrived at our next port, Alofi on the island of Niue, in three good sailing days. The sail was ordinary except that we tore an 8 foot hole in our mainsail while reefing it. It was not because of high winds, it was a combination of poor communications and improper use of the mainsail reefing lines — a costly mistake. Niue does not have a harbor, so the local business people got together and put in 17 moorage buoys for visiting yachts. The bottom is all coral and 80 or more feet deep making anchoring a risky business without their buoys. We called the Niue Yacht Club on VHF channel 16 and heard a nice English female voice with a New Zealand accent greet us in return. She acknowledged our tie to buoy number 6 and scheduled our check-in for 10 a.m.

Two items surprised us after arriving at their big, solid concrete wharf in our dinghy: First, there was no facility to tie our dinghy to the wharf and second; U.S. Seabees were at work to extend the wharf another 40 feet. If we had left our dinghy alongside the wharf, ocean swells would damage our inflatable. The Seabees designed the wharf extension so large ships could tie-up at the end of the wharf in calmer water. The islands customary method was to anchor supply ships out beyond the wharf. Offloading supply ships requires two time consuming processes. First, the supply ship offloads its supplies to a barge using the ship's cranes. The barge then moves to the wharf for offloading by the wharf's crane. Bob and Leslie had to drop me off so Bob could go back to the boat and make a lifting sling for the dinghy. There is a huge Diesel/electric crane on the wharf to lift dinghies, boats, and supplies. The crane's lifting capacity is several tons.

Some of the Seabees came over, introduced themselves and explained how to operate the crane. They keep their construction services well honed with non-wartime projects like the wharf — U.S. tax dollars of course. They were full of information about the island and knew all the good dive spots and places to eat. All the women yachties were abuzz about these guys as they exercised every ten minutes, had perfect hard bodies, and were truly nice young men. They even brought their own doctor with them.

Check-in was the easiest of the trip. We arrived on Saturday (a non-work day) and the customs agent was off working on his "ranch" where he grows his own vegetables. We learned on this island, "Saturday" is synonymous with ranch work. "Ranch," loosely described everything between a small backyard garden to an authentic farm or cattle ranch. The friendly customs agent drove to the wharf, introduced himself and drove us to his office for ten minutes of paperwork. We found a store nearby and tried to purchase supplies, but they only accepted New Zealand dollars. Not a problem, they drove us to the Niue Hotel so we could convert U.S. dollars to New Zealand dollars.

On Sunday, a clean looking Niuean named Motu, met Pat and me at the wharf and took us to the 9 a.m. Mass at the Catholic Mission church. I had met Motu on Saturday while talking to the Seabees. He was operating a mobile crane for them and his clothes at that time were grimy. The island people were super friendly, interested in talking to us, and had many questions. This was the first time since leaving the U.S. that everyone spoke good English.

The Mass was long as all the readings, the gospel and homely, were said in both Niuean and English. The singing was beautiful and unusual because the children took the lead and sang with such gusto. The priest was an import from Tonga and with a beautiful voice sang the whole Mass. I was to find out later in the trip that singing is important in the Tongan culture. A woman behind us tapped me on the shoulder to loan me her songbook. The songbook was in both English and Niuean and had many songs that were popular at our church in Seattle. However, singing of Niuean songs surpassed singing the English songs in enthusiasm.

Several people and father Sari came approached us after Mass to invite us to their tea party. Father Sari asked Pat and me to sit next to him and explained the party was to welcome a new doctor from the Philippines. He explained that he had been a priest on this island for 30 years, but always enjoyed going back to Tonga to visit with his friends. Again, we stood out, as there were only six white people. One young man working in the Peace-Corps from Minnesota, a couple from Melbourne, Australia on vacation, Emanuela Benetti Sabatini a local restaurant owner and us.

Emanuela is an attractive young Italian woman who owned the Italian café, "Ciao" (chow). We talked about what spelling my original Italian family name might have been in Italy. She thought, in Italy, my family name, and her maiden name to be the same, "Benetti." My father was actually a second generation Bennett born in the U.S. I had asked him several times about changes to our original family name, but he had no records of any other spelling. Anyway, Emanuela said she would reserve a table for us on Wednesday night. Eating at one of the three Niue restaurants requires reservations, as seating is limited and the Seabees usually got there first. Meanwhile at the party, so many baked goods covered the 20 foot long table, I thought they were having a baked-goods' sale. The president of their parish council introduced Pat, me, and the visitors from Melbourne before leading the parish in prayer. One reason I liked Niue so much is that the men ate first (best choice of desserts), and then the women and the children eat last. I had visions of children in the states screaming, yelling, and causing general mayhem standing last in line.

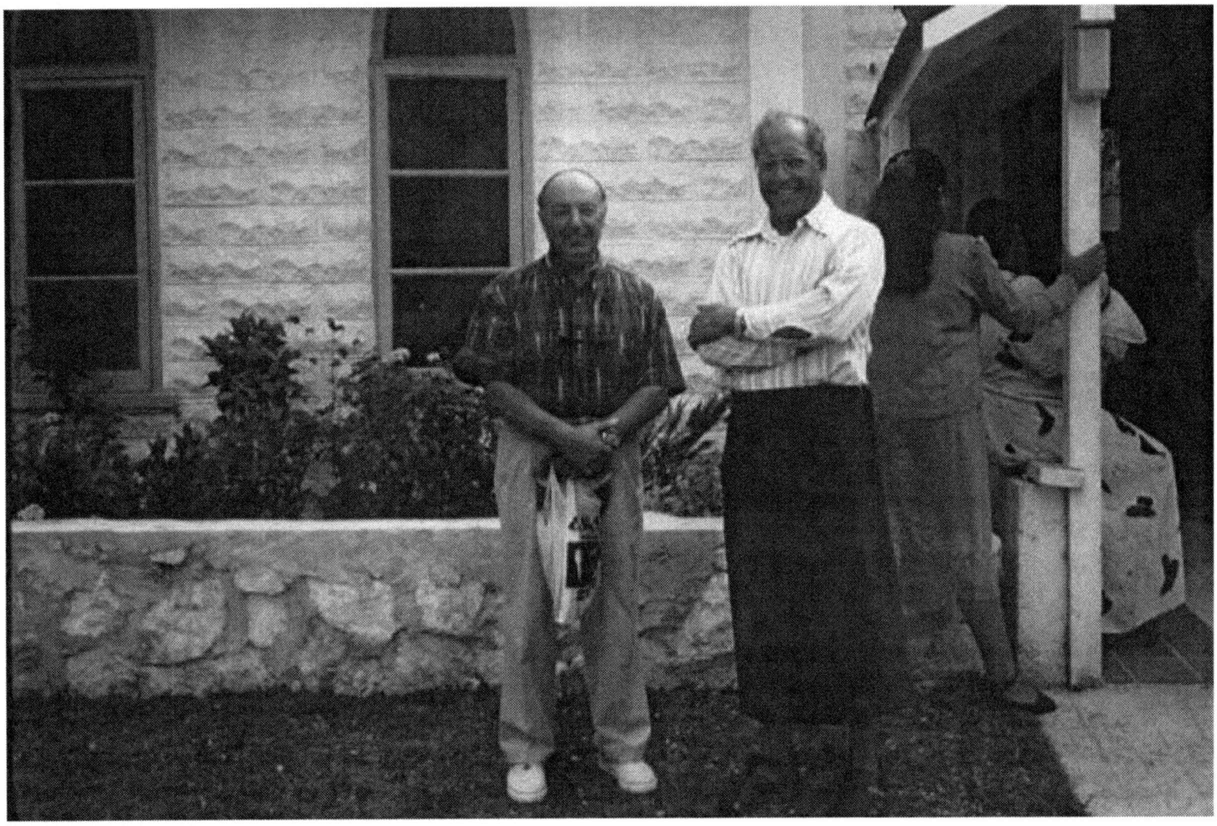

FATHER SARI & MYSELF, CATHOLIC MISSION CHURCH, NIUE

Many Pacific Island Nations follow the same pecking order of men, women and then children. Several people offered to drive us back to the wharf, but Motu had left his car with his teenage son who waited patiently for more than an hour to drive us back. This young man wore a white shirt, a tie and long pants on a hot Sunday afternoon.

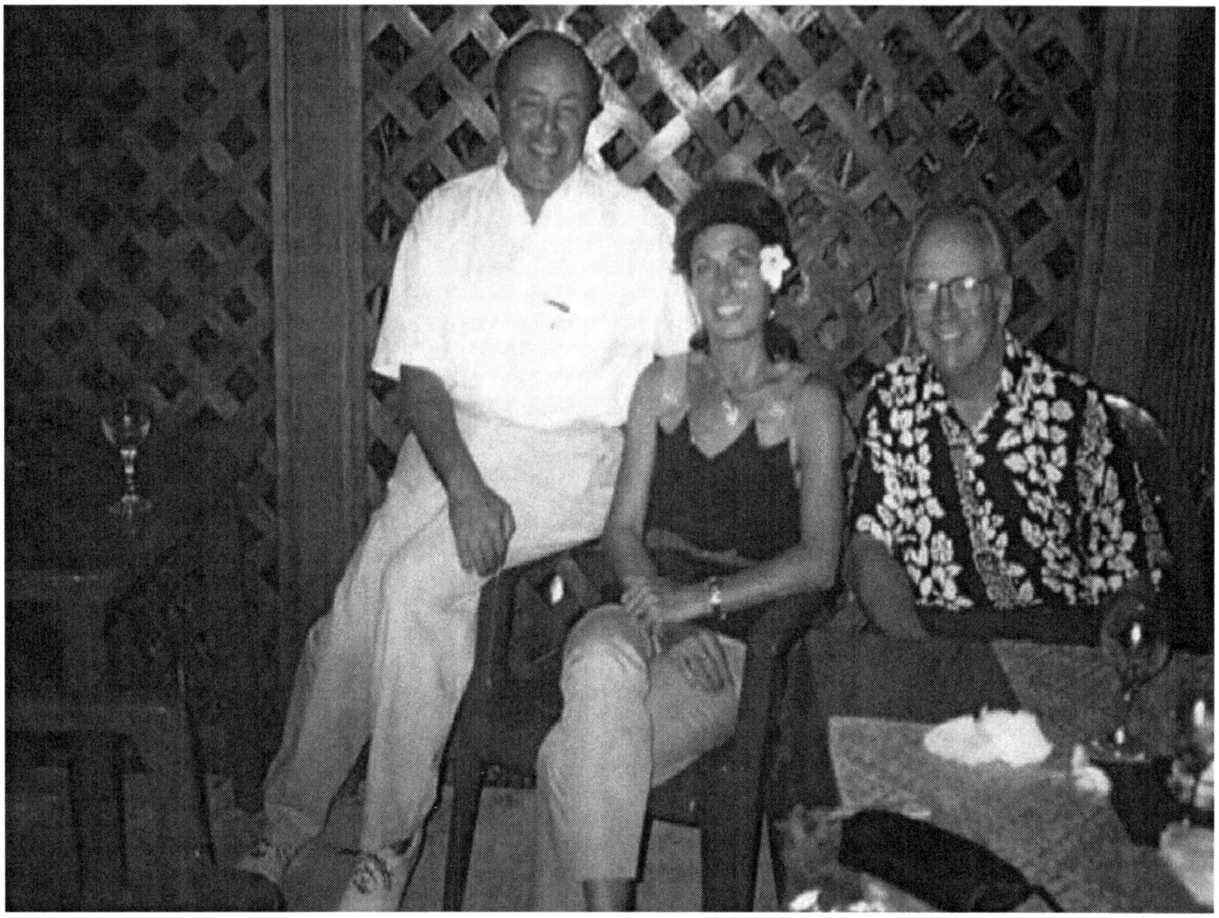

DICK, EMANUELA BENETTI SABATINI AND JOHN (*KNOT YET*) AT "CIAO"

Niue is known as the world's largest *upraised coral atoll*, which means it has not sunk to form the typical lagoon surrounded by a reef. The land is mostly rock, but it has the appearance of Swiss cheese, not solid. The distance around the island is about 40 miles on a 200 foot high, flat plateau. About 2,000 people still live on Niue; they are proud of their island and keep it neat and clean. Residents are mostly Polynesian with a few Europeans, Samoans and Tongans thrown-in. They once were part of the Cook Islands, but since 1994 have governed themselves in free association with New Zealand. We were told that New Zealand throws in about NZ $6 million a year to keep everything going. About 18,000 Niuean natives have moved to New Zealand looking for a better living as they enjoy dual citizenship with New Zealand. As in many of the islands, they send money back to relatives in Niue. The island's average temperature is 81° F and is close to the International Date Line at minus 11 hours UTC time.

We had heard from other boaters that the island had some of the greatest diving opportunities in the world, but could not imagine how great it really was. The entire coastline is full of caves and chasms. The visibility through the water was close to 200 feet, the best clear water we had seen. Bob and Leslie have wonderful tales about the abundant sea life, sharks, eels and some of most poisonous snakes in the world.

The snakes live in the caves, but their mouths are too small bite humans, which they mostly ignore anyway — thank goodness.

We stayed in Niue for 6 days, rented a car, toured all their parks, tried all their restaurants and thoroughly enjoyed ourselves. Niue has around 140 miles of roads (some not so good), but the most interesting part of our drive were family gravesites. Most of the families bury their deceased members between their home and the road. So even if the real property owners have all moved to New Zealand and boarded up their homes, the gravestones uniquely identify the real property owners.

Pat and I stayed at the only resort on the island called "Matavi," which I loosely think means eye of the sea. We understand the New Zealand government has invested a lot of money in this resort in hopes it would draw vacationers. Making Niue a desirable tourist destination would certainly help the economy. The rooms and location of the resort were beautiful with sweeping views of the ocean and decks built out over steep cliffs. The staff was friendly, the food was great, but the resort lacked vacationers. The only other guests were two couples from Australia on a scuba diving holiday. It has only been open for a couple of years, but the high cost of flying to Niue discourages vacationers. Flights into, and out of Niue, were limited to once a week, which just adds another level of difficulty for travelers. London vacations cost close to the same dollar amount as a Niue vacation so London draws the majority of vacationers from that part of the world. Many people living south of the equator also have relatives in London and like to visit there.

When we got back to the boat, we received news via the mariner's amateur radio net, that our daughter Marjorie needed a serious operation in Seattle. Of course, she wanted her mother to be there. Reviewing flight schedules and routes to the U.S., we decided it best to leave for Tonga right away. We put the torn mainsail away and moved the 550 square foot mizzen sail up to replace it. Tonga was only two and a half days away.

Chapter 7

NIUE TO THE KINGDOM OF TONGA

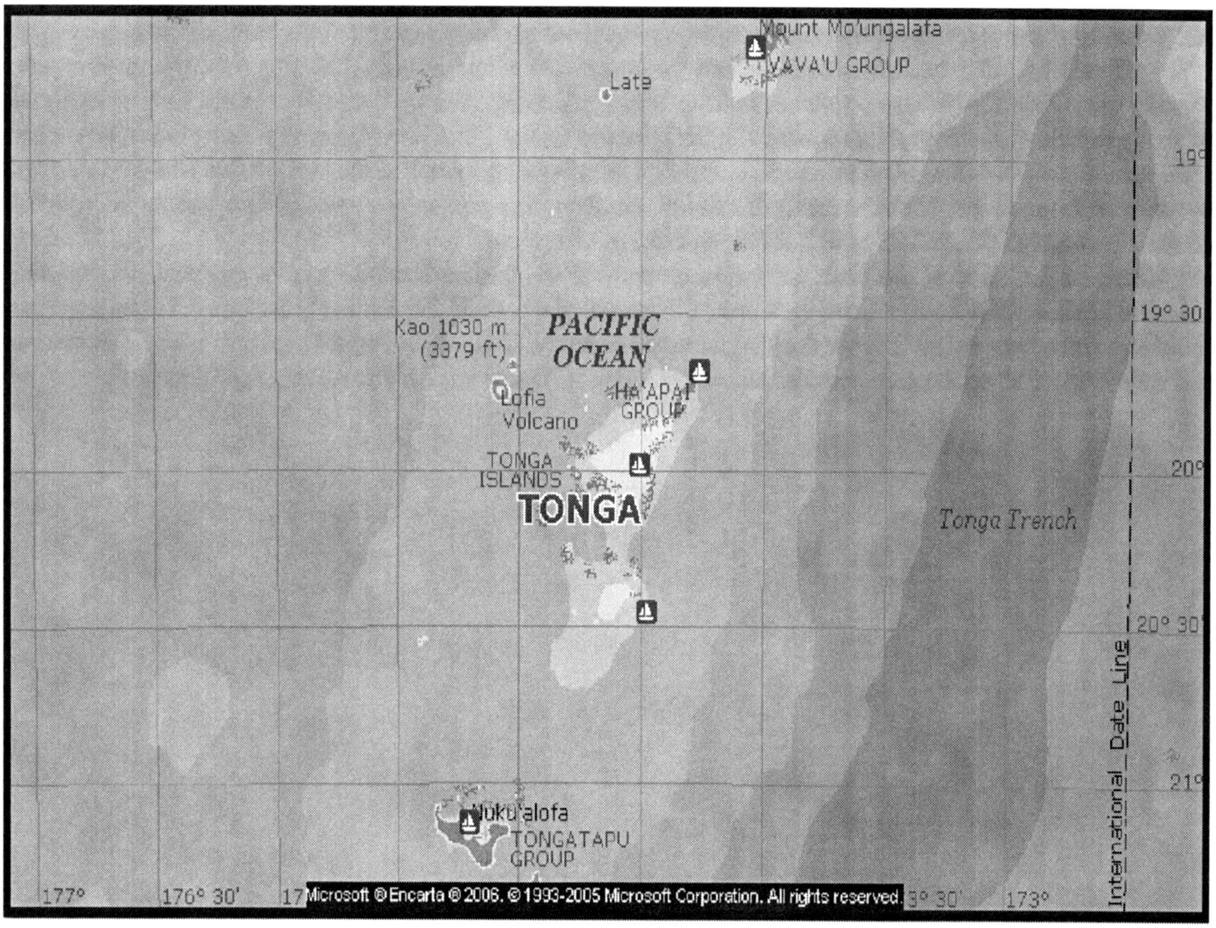

THE KINGDOM OF TONGA, Sept. 22, 1998

We arrived in the city of Neiafu, Vava'u group of islands, Kingdom of Tonga on Sept. 22, 1998. Tonga moved the International Date Line to jog around them making it Sept. 23 in Tonga time. Checking in with local officialdom did not go well. First, we broke a two foot section of our teak rub-rail on their pier. The steel cofferdam pier, under construction to hold back the land, had no cap or protective bumpers for yachts.

The strong winds and current and limited maneuvering room forced us into a protruding steel beam before Pat could get a fender in place. Second, the officials all took an early lunch break that lasted for two and a half hours while we waited on their unfriendly pier. When they finally staggered back from lunch, they jumped off a high mound of mud onto our deck in their heavy work boots. It was obvious they had too much to drink at lunch and whatever they ate was causing them to fart all over the cabin. They were not embarrassed, but instead, giggled and smiled broadly as each official contributed to the obnoxious odors. Running all the fans helped clear the air. Of course, they wanted to see how much beer we had on board so they could continue drinking. Luckily, we were down to one lonely beer in the refrigerator, which they insisted on seeing just to make sure. They ended up being content with water, which also got them off the boat faster.

To worsen matters, they said we could not keep our 25 pound sack of New Zealand onions. Bob's face dropped as he and Leslie are crazy about onions and add them to most dishes. So they took our onions and then had the nerve to charge us for their disposal. Of course, onions of that quality were not available in Tonga (they import them from the same place, New Zealand) so we were sure they did not end up in the garbage dump. Entering foreign countries is always an unknown enterprise of a questionable nature.

We found a mooring buoy in the harbor placed there by two Americans. They rent their buoys for $4.80 a day, a reasonable price. Andy and Sandy have lived at this harbor for 8 years aboard their custom Sparkman and Steven's 55 foot sailboat, *Jacaranda* (named after a flowering tree that grows in tropical areas of the Americas). Andy, a professional sail maker, had all the materials needed to patch our main sail. The next day Pat flew to Seattle for Marjorie's surgery. We were all praying this would finally relieve the pain she had been enduring for several years.

Tonga is similar to the San Juan Islands in Washington State as there are about 150 islands scattered over 120 miles. However, there are several substantial, but beneficial dissimilarities like clear warm water, white sandy beaches and palm trees. On the negative side, Tonga is home to an abundance of nasty reefs, which keeps skippers on their tippy toes.

The following day we joined a group of 11 other boats on a nearby island to help celebrate Jim Boswell's fortieth birthday (yacht *Go West*). We had quite a potluck party on the beach. Bob built a small bonfire and Leslie made a spinach dish with melted cheese that was so delicious the yachties gobbled it up as if they had never eaten good food before.

The following day we sailed back to town and enjoyed a nice dinner with friends at a restaurant run by an Englishman. The next day, Sunday, I was able to call Pat to check on Marjorie. The doctors were pleased with the operation and Marjorie was doing well, but would stay in the hospital for several days. The phone service is something else. It was clear, but it has some automatic circuitry that thinks the other person is going to talk. If the person talking briefly hesitates, some of the following conversation will disappear into cyber space. We learned to say "over" when it was the other person's time to talk, which did help.

After talking to Pat, I went to the local Catholic Church, "St. Joseph's The Worker." What a wonderful experience. The church seating filled up fast with probably upwards of 350 people. An additional 100 children filled the altar with boys on the left, girls on the right. I thought the altar looked crowded, but then a procession of five altar boys and eighteen adults moved to the altar to assist the priest. I arrived at church about a half hour early and sat in the front on the left side. Before ten o'clock, a bunch of men came in and sat all around me without their families. It turned out I was in the middle of the men's choir section. However, the whole church was actually the choir section. With no music or songbooks, but with a director, everyone sang 15 to 20 songs during the Mass. All songs where sung in parts or in harmony. Truly, the best singing I have ever heard in a church including the Mormon Tabernacle Choir. Mass took an hour and a half, but time flew by. All the singing was in Tongan as were the readings, but the priest said some parts and the gospel in English. These people go to church every day and must practice their music every day. In the harbor, if we were quiet, we could hear church music being sung early every morning.

Les Ball, one of our radio amateur contacts near Seattle, called me via short wave radio a few days later. He had been telephoning Pat at Marjorie's house to inquire about the recovery, but this time Marjorie surprised him by answering the phone. We were so excited to hear she was doing well. The world is still full of loving caring people. Les Ball is in his eighties, has lost his vision, not a wealthy person and made long distance calls to find out how Marjorie was doing — pretty darn nice!

I took the engine that drives the generator apart to find out why it lost its compression. Found the inlet valve had a small piece that broke off and banged back and forth between the head and piston. The broken piece imbedded itself in the head, which it then cracked. Pat is in the process of rounding up replacement parts in Seattle and will cross her fingers going through Tongan customs.

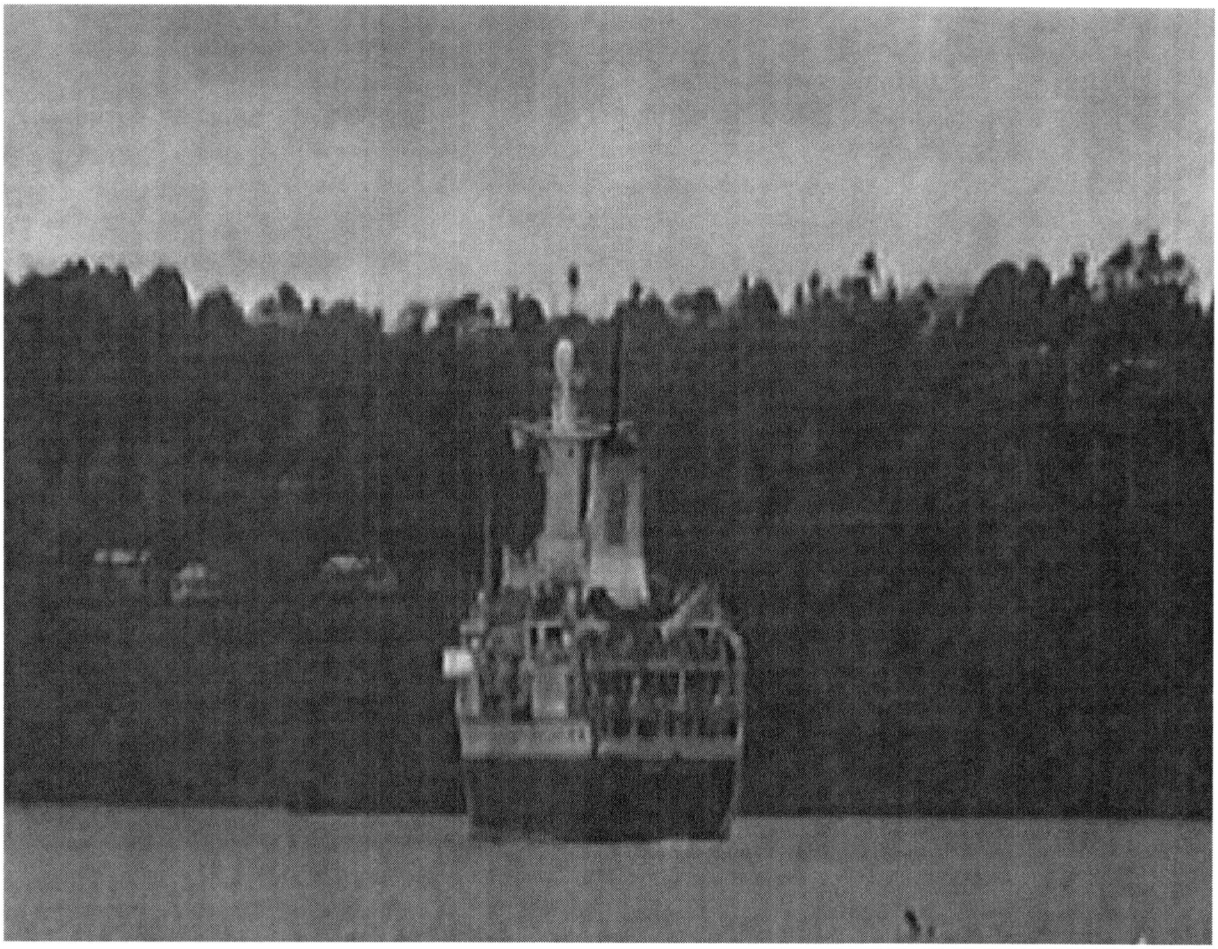

***WORLD DISCOVERER* LEAVING NEIAFU WITH DICK AND BETSY RUSSELL**

On Oct. 3 the cruise ship, *World Discoverer*, pulled into the harbor at Neiafu, Tonga. We knew our good Seattle friends, Dick and Betsey Russell, were vacationing on this ship, but I didn't know Neiafu was a scheduled stop. I called the ship on channel 16 via VHF radio to ask the captain if the Russell's were on the passenger list. He found their names were on the list, found them at the ship's barbeque and asked them to come up to the bridge. We talked on the radio and the captain agreed to bring them over to our boat via one of the ships large inflatable dinghies.

What a wonderful surprise to meet unexpectedly with close Seattle friends on the other side of the world. They were able to stay with us for an hour and a half before the ship called them back. For Neiafu, an hour and a half is more time than passengers need to look at all the town's woodcarvings, chickens, pigs and woven baskets. I thought this was an odd stop for a passenger ship because the town is small. There are only two small stores with limited supplies, but there are lots of dogs, pigs, and chickens running through the streets. These people are poor in material things and have almost no opportunity to earn money except through their crafts or government jobs — no welfare.

I found out, *Annapurna*, one of the U.S. boats here had a spare, but used refrigeration compressor they were willing to sell. It was slightly larger than my broken compressor and had a higher capacity. I rummaged around and managed to come up with the right spacers to make it fit my existing mount. Success, it worked like a champ. The increased compressor capacity reduced the operating time of the refrigerator/freezer to just a half hour twice a day. Whereas, when the generator is used to run the 120 volt AC system, it requires 1.5 hours running time twice a day. Saving two hours of engine running time a day is a big deal. Now the only equipment not working is the generator.

Leslie and I went into town and bought all the groceries and fresh vegetables we could for our 120 mile trip through the islands of Tonga to Nuku'alofa where we had arranged to meet Pat's return plane from Seattle.

Our first anchorage was Kapa Island. There is a large cave there with an entry big enough for a dinghy, called "Swallow's Cave." The entry is about 12 feet wide and 20 feet high in 10 feet of water. Once inside, the cave opens into a huge chamber with two adjoining chambers. One of the smaller chambers had a small opening in its 50 foot ceiling that allowed the sun to enter. With sunlight coming in the opening, the water inside turned into a beautiful green color. This place had such a spiritual feeling; everyone became inclined to talk in whispers. The ceiling was home to hundreds of swallows that lived in little nests resembling dirt mounds. The amazing thing was the number of small fish in the water. They must have numbered several thousand, as they were so thick, the bottom was not visible in 10 feet of clear water.

We got back to the boat at happy hour time and lit the barbecue for a chicken leg dinner. The rest of dinner consisted of canned corn, brown rice, and chocolate cookies. Leslie's recipe for chocolate cookies does not require baking. The anchorage was in a bay that had a beautiful white sand beach, quiet and peaceful, no pigs, only a couple of roosters and a couple cows mooing on the beach.

We stopped at two more islands and then stopped at an island called Hunga. This island is unique because land surrounds its big interior bay. There is a narrow entrance, but the channel is only 20 feet wide and 9 feet deep. To increase any skipper's apprehension, big sharp rocks are plainly visible on each side of the channel. We were close enough to slack water to make it through without difficulty. We picked-up a moorage buoy near some buildings masquerading as a resort — "Club Hunga."

A misplaced New Zealander, Pete, owns this resort with his fourth wife, a Tongan named Hapi. Like many Tongans, she is big, about the size of a Seattle, Seahawk linebacker. Hapi's relatives are Tongan royals, but beware; she is a black belt in karate. When we first met Pete, we noticed a slightly swollen face and one black and blue eye. We learned later that Pete and his wife really get into their auguring and she always wins. In addition, only Tongans can own land so Pete married the landowner.

We were at Club Hunga to celebrate the birthday of Leslie and Bob's friends, Christine (29) and Stephanie (30). The party was a great success and even the food turned out to be good. It was a good thing the bar included a can of bug spray, as the mosquitoes were also Tongan size. About ten other boats made it to the party and we made new friends. Pete was great fun and quite the character. He had overnight guests staying at the resort the week before we arrived. They checked-out before their week was up because the island's roosters kept them from sleeping. Pete found an unconventional solution; he shot every rooster he could find with his 30-06 rifle.

From Hunga Island, we headed south for the Ha'apai Islands. We stopped at several interesting islands in this group, but Uiha was probably the most fun. At Uiha, we picked our way through the coral and anchored off the small village of Felemea. We had just decided not to visit the village when two young Americans changed our minds. Smoky and Kim, two teachers on a one-year sabbatical, barrowed a leaky dugout canoe and paddled out to greet us. They were staying on Uiha Island for 8 days at a resort and invited us to dinner.

When we rowed ashore and looked around at the poor excuse for a resort, we had to give them huge amounts of credit. The "resort" was three native huts made of palm fronds, including the floor, a kitchen (same construction), and a 20 by 20 foot open eating area covered by palm fronds. A small plywood shack, not much bigger than an outhouse, supplied the cold-water shower/salt water toilet. A 25 gallon drum on top of the shack supplied gravity fed water after hand-pumping water into the drum. The resort owners, doubled as hosts, chefs and waiters.

We were early for the fresh lobster dinner, but no worries, the beer was cold and the air was calm as we watched the sun disappear below the horizon. Dinner was ready at 7 p.m., as always, native portions are more than we can eat. There were several kinds of fish and vegetables cooked in a sweet/sour sauce, baked bananas and breadfruit, fried octopus, raw fish in a marinate and the lobsters — maybe this resort was okay. The two teachers were both 32 and there was a young Japanese girl of 22 also staying there, which we found rather implausible. We listened to their stories well into the evening.

The village of Felemea was neat and clean, but small. The people are religious and happy. There were three churches, a meeting hall, and lots of pigs, chickens, and roosters. They go to church every day and three times on Sunday. Some young men were playing tennis and were laughing in hysterics most of the time. They had no concept of being competitive, only having a good time and laughing at each other's mistakes. They laughed so hard, they had us smiling from ear-to-ear. The young men and women thinking about marriage have a courtship of only three days under their parent's supervision. Following the courtship, if they decide to marry, it is permanent, as their culture does not recognize divorce. Smoky, in talking to the young men, found out they had no interest in marrying women for their looks or bodies, just what is in their heads — what a concept.

After visiting several other islands, we did the remaining 40 miles to Nuku'alofa with four other boats. This city is the capital of Tonga and 80% of their population lives here. Everyone speaks good English and the grocery stores are the best we have seen since Papeete. We hung out waiting for Pat to return and hopefully a good weather window for our trip to Auckland.

Pat arrived in Nuku'alofa on Nov. 4 after a month long stay in Seattle. Her trip to Seattle for Marjorie's surgery went well. Marjorie was glad for her help and support and it gave Pat a chance to see the rest of our family and her friends. Everyone is keeping Marjorie in his or her prayers in hopes that this operation will get rid of the source of her endometriosis. It will take quite a while though, maybe up to a year, before the doctors will know if the operation was successful.

Pat brought back about $2,000 worth of spare parts including a new head, valves, injector, and piston with rings for the generator. Gary, our son-in-law, packed all the parts in bubble wrap inside a heavy-duty aluminum suitcase that ended up weighing a little over 94 pounds. I was worried what Tongan customs would say at the airport because even with wheels, Pat was straining to maneuver that monster suitcase. No worries, they did not even ask what the suitcase contained. Believe me; it is extremely unusual for customs in a foreign country to miss an opportunity for collecting import duty!

The next day I put the generator back together and pushed the starter: smoke, backfiring, but no joy. The one thing not covered in the English translation of the German shop manual is which push rod is the intake and which one is exhaust. I had a fifty-fifty chance of getting it right, but naturally, I flunked on the first guess. I was lucky nothing was damaged. Once they were positioned correctly, the beast roared to life and once again, our lives became more civilized.

We had planned to top off our fuel tanks in Nuku'alofa at the one and only fuel dock. However, on the scheduled day we found two broken-down Tongan fishing boats tied to the fuel dock. Both boats had serious propulsion problems and we could see they would be immobile for a long time. I am surprised they managed to keep those two relics floating! So, for the first time on our voyage, Bob and I moved about 112 gallons of Diesel fuel by filling 5 and 6 gallon plastic jugs and rowing them back and forth between the fuel dock and our boat. This little treat took most of the day and became extremely messy for it was impossible not to spill fuel no matter how hard we tried. Our inflatable dinghy was slick with fuel as was the parts of our deck near the fuel ports. We try very hard to keep the water clean and it really bothers me to spill fuel into the water. We were fortunate that no one in Tonga monitors fuel spills.

We cleared with Immigration on Nov. 10, 1998 and were out of Egeria Channel, Tongatapu Island by 12:45 p.m. Our plan was to sail a direct rhumb line course toward Auckland, New Zealand some 1,000 nautical miles away.

Chapter 8

KINGDOM OF TONGA TO NEW ZEALAND
...OUR MOST DANGEROUS STORM

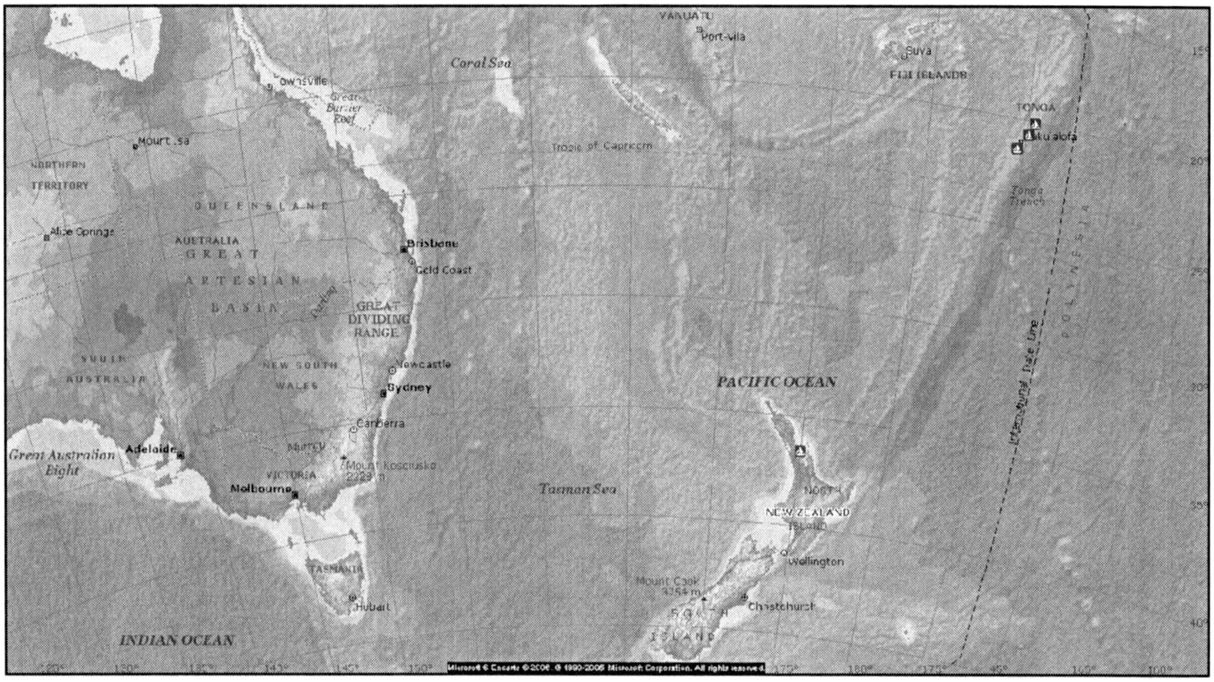

TONGA TO AUCKLAND, NEW ZEALAND; Nov. 10, 1998 TO Nov. 20, 1998

The first 24 hours found us motoring at 4.5 knots in glassy seas; we, not the wind, made the only ripples on the water. The next day around noon, the wind started blowing 15 knots from the southeast. We put up all our sails, turned off the engine and moved comfortably along at 6.5 half knots. By Nov. 11, the wind had picked up to around 20 knots, the wave height went from 3 to 5 feet, and the barometric pressure dropped two millibars overnight. There was a small fleet of about 21 cruising boats between Tonga and New Zealand. Twelve boats had gone to Minerva Reef to wait for good weather.

This reef is approximately 200 miles from Tonga and provides good protection from waves, but not the wind. It is rather unusual with a fringing reef that is under water at high tide and steaming with sea life. There are no trees at Minerva Reef, but inside the reef, the water is about 50 feet deep with good anchoring in sand. Pete on *Max Grody* and Buddy on *Annapurna* called us on their SSB radios with invitations to the reef. They claimed they needed help to eat all the giant lobsters they caught. Minerva (Roman goddess of handicrafts) Reef was about 100 miles west of our position when they contacted us. We were sailing a rhumb line course to Auckland so the reef was out of our way. Most boats at Minerva Reef were sailing to the north islands of New Zealand, a more direct path from the reef.

I contacted Des on SSB radio to see what might be brewing in the weather department. He operates a volunteer weather service on the northern tip of New Zealand in the city of Russell. Cruisers worldwide know his station as **Russell Radio**. He advised me that a low-pressure area was forming, but did not see it as a threat to our position. With this information, I decided not to make the out-of-the-way diversion to Minerva Reef, but continued on our direct course to Auckland.

On Nov. 13, the pressure dropped 5 millibars and for some reason the wind also dropped, so we started motoring. Overnight the weather had deteriorated drastically. On the morning of the 14th Des advised us that the low-pressure system was now moving toward our position at 10 knots. The wave crests had been slowly increasing and were now around 10 feet. The wind noise was another sure indication we were in for a rough ride as it had risen to a steady 20 knots with higher gusts. By nightfall, we lashed our main and mizzen sails to their booms and we were flying along under just a storm staysail and partially furled yankee. Our total sail area was a minimal 200 square feet. Des was now predicting winds as high as 50 knots — not good, so much for the early good weather predictions.

That night, three major lightning storms surrounded us, banged, and flashed with fervor for six hours. Lightning is not nice and it's unpredictable. We disconnected all electronics, turned off power to everything except the compass light, and steered by hand. We put a great amount of faith in our autopilot for its accurate course keeping abilities so steering by hand seemed unnatural and more difficult. One wave in about forty had enough power to roll our boat about 35 degrees to starboard and bury the lee rail.

These waves came from our aft port side and rolled the boat as they passed under the keel. When the boat righted, many gallons of seawater rushed along the starboard deck, reflected off the aft bulkhead and tried to pass through the companionway doors into the pilothouse.

We tried several different methods to seal the companionway with large rubber mats, tape, plastic sheet, and towels, but seawater still managed to force its way past each barrier we devised. The water hits hard against the barriers, flowed down the companionway stairs and onto the pilothouse sole. From there it made its way to the aft cabin sole and slowly drained into the bilge. We have four high capacity bilge pumps so the amount of water was never a concern. However, no one likes to go inside the rolling boat to check the bilge water level and run a pump.

A smaller boat, *Never Monday*, closer to the center of the storm and riding badly, made a good decision to launch their sea anchor. The two adult couples on board, put out the sea anchor hoping to minimize the wild motion their boat was experiencing. Everything went well for several hours. They had to keep replacing the chafing gear on the anchor's heavy line, but the motion on their boat became more comfortable. Sadly, the powerful forces exerted on the hull by the sea anchor, wind and waves caused the deck cleat holding the sea anchor to fail. Then the sea anchor, along with several hundred feet of line disappeared into the raging sea. Before they could get the boat directed properly to the waves, a large wave rolled *Never Monday*.

Their boat encountered a knockdown where the wind and sea combine to rotate the boat's mast at least 90 degrees from vertical to below the water's surface. Luckily, the mast came back up, but their steering system was damaged along with their navigation system. I offered to try a rendezvous with them to send over a portable GPS, but they managed to restore the navigation system. They had the good fortune to have prepared their boat with an emergency steering system that worked. They were able to make New Zealand without further incident.

Hearing their plight and valiant efforts was not a morale boaster for the rest of the fleet in the middle of heavy weather and uncertain of what decisions they should make.

We slowed our boat speed down to 3.5 knots as Des was now predicting the low-pressure system would pass by to our west and the wind would moderate. However, the low stalled late in the afternoon of the 14th because of an intense high-pressure system of 1024 millibars located over the south island of New Zealand. This high of extraordinary size and power, stretched all the way to Australia over the Tasman Sea. We are still looking at New Zealand and an arduous 500 mile effort of mental and emotional strength. By 4 p.m. the wind was gusting past 40 knots, we were only doing 2.5 knots in heavy rain and the barometer was down another two millibars — bummer!

Early the next morning, the low stalled and the center was at a new low of 991 millibars, just 180 miles west of our position. Conditions on the boat were terrible with little sleep and no one felt much like eating. Leslie was always able to go into the galley no matter what the conditions were like and put some good meals together. I decided to make an all out run for Auckland, as the conditions were so poor and not likely to change. With Bob and Leslie's help, we added sail area, increased our boat speed to 7 knots and high-tailed-it for Auckland.

The New Zealand met service called this area we stumbled into, "A squash zone." A squash zone definition is loosely the area between two intense pressure systems where the isobars converge extremely close together. We sailed in this mess for the next 4 days until the 18th when the seas finally started moderate to 8 feet. The winds blew at 25 knots, but the barometer rose to 1016 millibars. On the 19th the sun came out, the seas dropped to 6 feet, the winds were kind at 15 to 20 knots and we were making 7.5 knots — perfect. Everyone was happy to get out of the worst gale of our voyage as another high/low pressure system was in process of forming in a similar fashion.

Our Pleasure held up beautifully through all these stressful conditions. I was glad the construction process produced a boat with, thick, solid layers of fiberglass. On the heavy side at 52,000 pounds, our little boat is solid and strong.

The heel angle of the boat and its rolling motion combined to keep the water maker inlet out of the water such that it lost its prime so we could not make water. The electric water pump for fresh water stopped working about three days from New Zealand. We switched to our hand pump for fresh water, but that also stopped working one day out. When we arrived, our only water source was a 5 gallon emergency jug. I still have no idea why the pumps stopped working, but after two days, they started working by themselves. I guess they also have an aversion to bad weather, but it points out the importance of redundancy.

Chapter 9

NEW ZEALAND

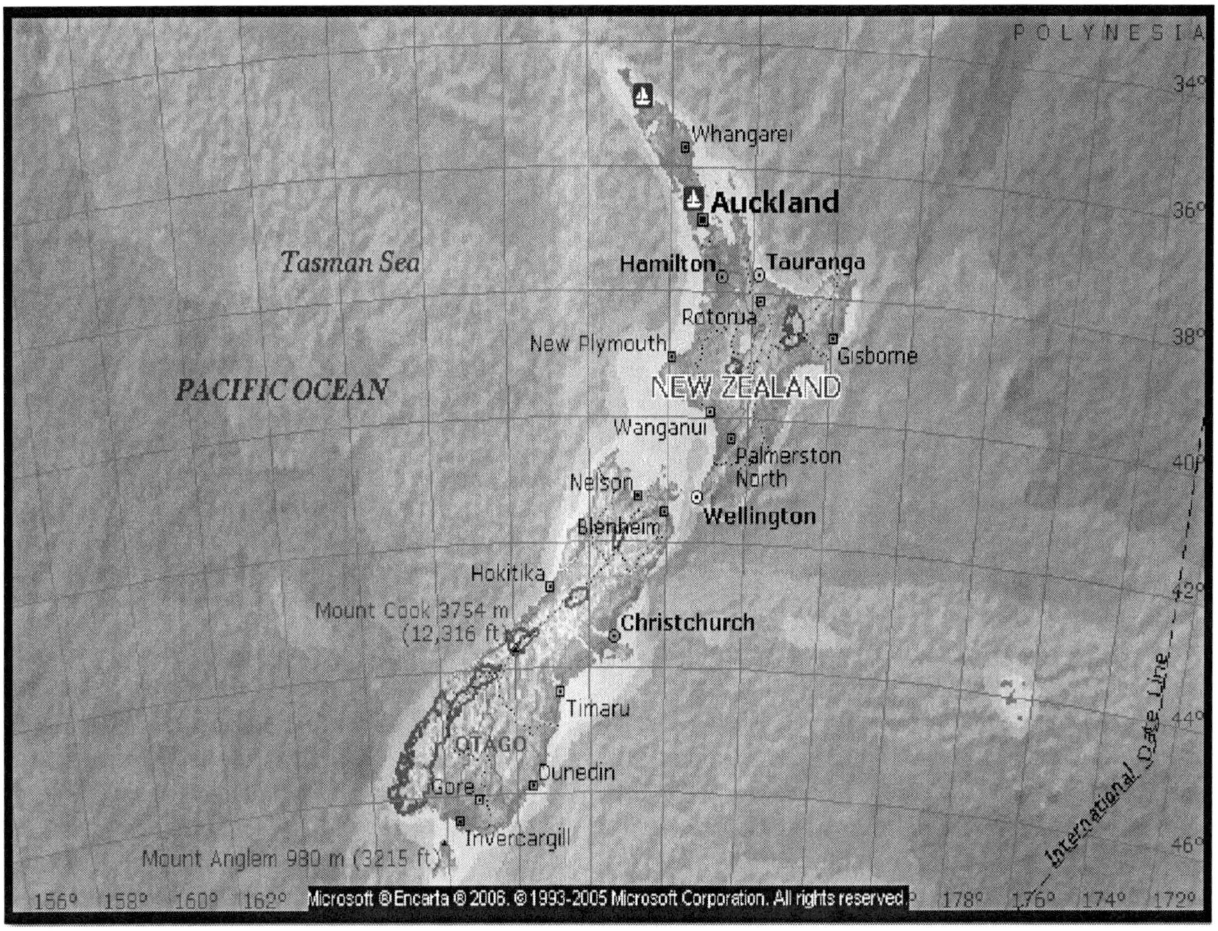

NEW ZEALAND AND PORT OF ENTRY, AUCKLAND, NOV. 20, 1998

We sailed into Auckland harbor at 4:30 p.m., Nov. 20, 1998, a Friday afternoon, right in the middle of their weekly rum race series. The Auckland harbor is a busy place with sailboats everywhere, along with ferries, tour boats, fishing boats, sailboards, tugs, and ocean going freighters. An extremely polite Harbor Control person watched us from his vantage point on a hilltop. He radioed instructions guiding us all the way to the Customs and

Immigration dock. The customs dock or "Admiralty Steps," are long concrete steps, like an entrance to a church. The steps go into the water and disappear beyond sight. There is no way to get into or out of a boat from these steps without getting wet — guess New Zealanders were not fond of admirals. We decided to moor alongside four pilings instead, but the pilings were tricky because of the swell running into the area. It took all four of us using fenders and a 2 by 8 foot plywood board to keep us from banging against the pilings. The officials were so nice, the best of all the countries except probably Niue. The check-in took until 8 p.m. as one of the officials was at the commercial docks to clear a freighter. The unusual part of the check-in was that no money was required, a new first. They did take away some food that was on their list, but we were forewarned and were not surprised.

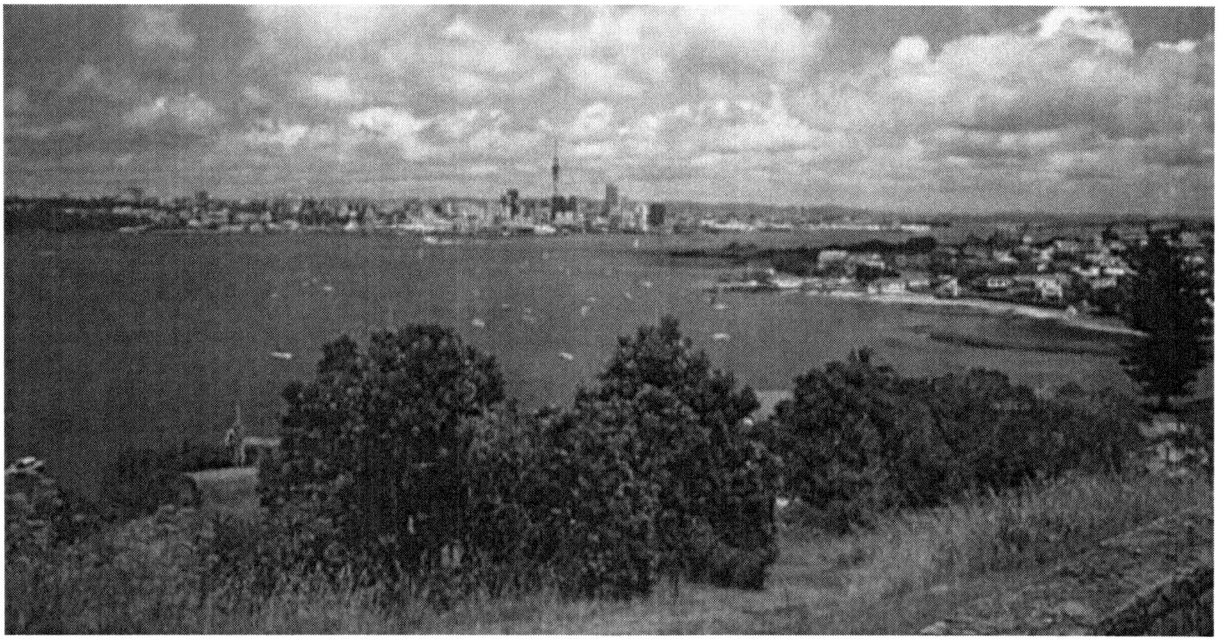

THE CITY OF AUCKLAND FROM ACROSS THE HARBOR

By the time we arrived at Westhaven Marina it was pitch black, still windy and we had no idea of where to go. The customs official told us this marina is the biggest in the world with about 3,600 berths. We were able to raise the marina's security guard, Tara, on the VHF radio, but his Maori accent and expressions were difficult to understand, which added some anxiety to deciphering his directions. The wind was now blowing 25 knots and he did not have access to marina slip assignments. He guided us to a temporary slip on pier "**X**," a large end slip with plenty of maneuvering room. The next day the wind was still blowing hard and trying to move into our narrow assigned slip looked like trouble with a capital "T." Therefore, we democratically decided to leave the boat on pier "**X**" and check-in at a beautiful downtown hotel. The hotel, especially for the women, was a dream come true, plenty of hot water and real bathtubs! Naturally, we all luxuriated in a bathtub for a long time. I thought I had a good tan, but after looking at the ring I left in the bathtub, I knew it was not all from the sun — no one cares much about bathing in stormy weather. We ordered three trays of snacks and opened the bottle of Dom Pérignon that John and JoAnn Poysky gave us before leaving Seattle. It was a wonderful treat! We toasted them and everyone we could think of. We all felt good! Here we were, moored to a real dock with power and water, quite civilized and looking forward to exploring NZ — by car of course.

We made our way back to the boat on Sunday afternoon and were amazed at how damp everything in the boat smelled. The wind had died down to about 10 knots so we moved the boat into its slip, B-17. The wind direction was good for backing into our slip and that went okay, but not perfectly. Bob was pushing hard to keep us from wrapping ourselves around a piling at the end of the slip when James Davern showed up. He helped with the pushing and welcomed us to NZ. He is one of our neighbors on this dock and owns a beautiful, custom 60 foot sailboat named *Cobalt.* He just retired, sold his house-moving business and was just starting to relax. He invited us to meet some friends and have dinner with him at the Royal New Zealand Yacht Club that night. "Very informal," he said, "just dress casually and no worries, it will be good that you all look rather salty."

Auckland, "The City of Sails," a motto and reputation well deserved. Westhaven Marina is about a mile from downtown Auckland, New Zealand's largest city at over one million people. The marina brochure indicates that they have many restrictive rules about everything. We were not quite sure what it all meant, but one rule jumped out clearly, "Living on board a visiting foreign yacht is limited to three months." This was a bit of a shock as we intended to stay for at least 6 months. NZ Immigration and Customs actually allowed us to import our boat and us for 18 months. To encourage foreign yachts to visit NZ during the year 2000 America's Cup racing, the NZ government temporarily relaxed some entry laws. I pointed this out to the marina staff, but a perceived imaginary wall seemed to get in the way, "Three months, period, no exceptions"! Officialdom is about the same all over the world, no flexibility and they love to assert their assumed authority with jubilant delight.

The yacht club is beautiful, the 137-year-old club just moved into a new waterfront building near our dock. The team sponsored by the yacht club won the last America's Cup race and therefore, proudly possessed the America's Cup. Bulletproof glass encased the cup's display and two beefy guards watched over it continually. Previously, without much security watching the cup, some crazy New Zealander battered the 149-year-old silver cup to smithereens with an axe. However, the British have a worse hoard-itis than I do because the original molds were still available. The repaired cup looked the same, but the silver had a beautiful luster.

We had a great time at the club and met many nice people, but Pat was mortified, dress was not casual. The women were all in gowns and many of the men dressed in formal yacht club blue blazer, white shirt, and tie. Pat was embarrassed as we stood out like the proverbial sore thumbs. The occasion turned out to be a celebration dedicating the new clubhouse. James was rather casual though so it was not only us. James introduced me to his friends as a "space scientist" from America, a reference to my design work on the Minuteman missile program. He is a real kick with a great sense of humor and a million friends. He started racing at the club at age twelve, remaining an active racer who gradually transitioned into big boat racing all over the world. Many people gave us their business cards and wanted to help us get situated, it was overwhelming. People even offered to do our laundry. We easily refused that offer, as most of our clothes are now getting pretty worn and needed replacing — too embarrassing. The next day, Cathy Knowles, good to her word, came down to our boat to show us around the area. She took Pat and Leslie to the laundry. The laundry bill totaled NZ $75 (about $40) for the initial load of dirty clothes. Cathy and her family have since become lifelong friends.

Next stops, the super market, post office and sightseeing all around town. The suburb of Ponsonby is nearest to the marina. It is quite an up-scale neighborhood with lots of coffee shops, restaurants, fresh food specialty stores and expensive homes. We opened a banking account there and bought ourselves a 1985 Toyota Corona five-door sedan at a car fair, $1,272. The sellers pay NZ $12 to show their cars and can set the selling price. There is a mechanic on hand to establish the car's condition for the buyer, NZ $80. Ours checked out with some minor rust problems and a broken motor mount. He fixed the mount on the spot for NZ $50, what a deal. There is no bus service to the marina so owning a car is important. The city of Auckland, about one mile from the marina, is blessed with marine stores, services, and restaurants. This small country completely remodeled the Auckland waterfront to accommodate the America Cup Races and visiting mega-yachts. Competing teams were busy building their team camps for the competition. Around town, excitement was clearly building in the newspapers, TV programs, and NZ visitors. Bob and Leslie also bought a used 1981 Toyota van for $300 — we are all loving this place.

Cathy and her husband Andy are both avid sailboat racers and Cathy's brother is the tactician for the New Zealand team. They wanted to show us the wonderful old house they are restoring and invited us to dinner. We had no idea what a New Zealand dinner would be like, but it turned out to be quite conventional. Following hors d'oeuvres' and cocktails it was roast lamb, four vegetables (only one of which I never had before), salad, white wine (New Zealand white wines are generally quite outstanding), and homemade Macadamia nut ice cream — an extraordinary dinner and dessert.

After dinner, Cathy said the TV news reported two yachts had sunk in the storm we were in, *Salacia* and *Freya*. We were shocked since we knew both boats, but were not aware of the unfortunate circumstances. We told her we would look into the circumstances and sinking's tomorrow. Their mansion is on a hillside in Ponsonby overlooking the marina and the city.

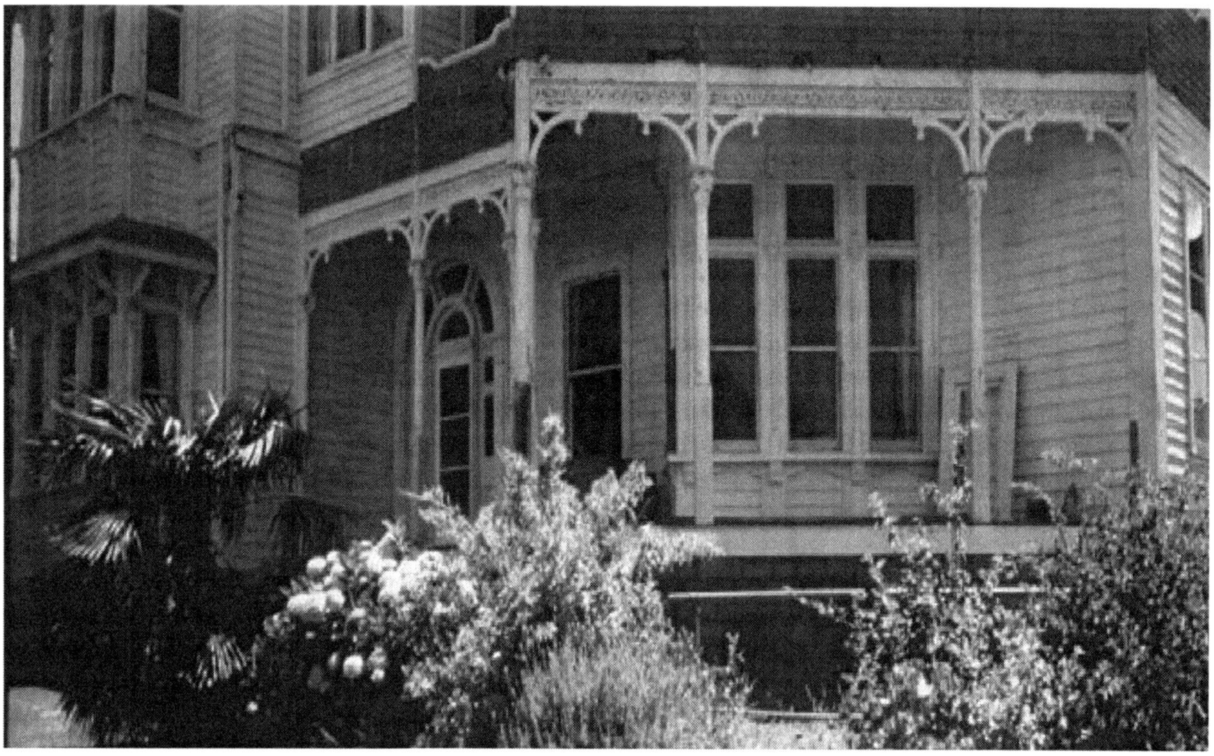

ANDY AND CATHY KNOWLES' MANSION, PONSOBY, NZ

Auckland is quite hilly and looks a lot like Seattle and Ponsonby looks like the Seattle suburb of Queen Anne. The mansion restoration is a slow process, as they work on each room when they have enough money saved for that room. Room counting is a question mark, I lost track after counting six bedrooms and some with adjoining studies and offices. The dining and living rooms were the combined size of our entire home in Seattle, but their ceilings are 12 feet high. Needless to say, they shop all the antique shops and auction houses. Actually, large antique furniture can get lost in the dining and living rooms. They also rent a large apartment that adjoins the main house. Cathy's parents operate a B&B near Katikati, a beautiful and fertile area in the Bay of Plenty region. Cathy and Andy have planned their restoration around an eventual B&B, but they are a few years away from that goal.

Monday morning, Nov. 30, Leslie was able to locate Mike Fritz at the American Embassy. We invited Mike to stay aboard ***Our Pleasure*** to help him recover somewhat from his pain. Mike lost his best friend Julie Ann Black, (42), and his sailboat *Salacia* when the container ship *Direct Kookaburra*, crushed their sailboat during a rescue attempt at sea. This tragedy occurred within 15 miles from the north coast of New Zealand in a major storm, which followed our storm. This time the high and low pressure systems created a storm with more intensity then the famous Queen's Day Storm of a few years ago, where several boats sank and four people died. In this storm, *Salacia* was under reduced sail in winds recorded at 70 knots and waves of 30 feet. Their sailboat suffered minor damage when a large breaking wave rolled the boat. Mike thought their mast dipped about 10 degrees below the water before the boat righted. The knock down locked up their steering system for a while and they lost their VHF radio antenna. They managed to get the boat sailing slowly toward NZ, but they could not restore communications and found their new hand held VHF radio would not work either. They were making about 3.5 knots under sail when the 600 foot *Direct Kookaburra* came along side at about 3 am and crashed into them. Mike said they had not sent out a **MAYDAY** or asked for help, but the ship could not contact them without a radio. There was a conflict here because the NZ search and rescue service said they did hear a **MAYDAY** from *Salacia* and directed the freighter to rescue them. The freighter and sailboat banged and scrapped along the whole 600 feet. Poor seamanship and bad weather destroyed *Salacia's* stanchions, lifelines, standing rigging, mast, dodger, and solar panels. At this point, debris from the impacts became dangerous objects flying all over the place and they prepared to jump into the water. On the third pass, the freighter threw them life rings that were heavy, hard, and too large to hold with a firm grip. At this point, the sailboat was sinking and they had to leave. Mike and Julie tied themselves together inside one life ring on the first attempt to haul them up. The freighter crew, however, said they were too heavy to haul together and they had to separate. They could not understand the crew's problem as together they only weighed 200 pounds. Anyway, they separated and grabbed different life rings. It was still dark and both boats were rolling wildly. The crew hauled Mike up to the rail, but after banging against the hull several times, he lost his grip and fell at least 30 feet back into the water. He did not think he could swim back to the life ring as he had boots on and heavy clothes to keep warm, but a big wave carried him back to the life ring. He made it on the second try, but during his fight for life and the confusion, he lost track of Julie's efforts. No one on the freighter's deck kept track of Julie and the crew was at a loss to tell mike what happened to her. Mike believes Julie did not have the strength to hold on to the life ring and was lost when she fell into the sea. They searched the area in a grid pattern until daylight, but no joy. A NZ search plane also joined in the search using heat sensors. They did spot Julie while she was on the bow of *Salacia*, but on the next fly around could not find her again — what a tragedy. While Mike stayed with us, the New Zealand government thoroughly investigated the tragedy. Mike was reluctant to talk about the findings of the investigation, so we never heard the official findings.

Mike only met Julie when he was in Moorea, the same time we were. They met at a resort when mike went in to look for someone who could carry his mail back to the states. They became instant friends and she went back home to pack clothes for sailing with Mike. The sad part for Julie was she had just recently accepted a managerial job in Seattle and had to turn it down. Her father was not pleased with her decision to leave everything and sail with Mike. He pleaded with Julie and asked her to rethink her decision and not to go with Mike, but to no avail — how sad.

Meanwhile, James Davern had some ideas he wanted to discuss with the yacht club to modify these types of rescues. He claimed yachts and freighters were not compatible and the yacht always sustains heavy damage and usually sinks in these rescue attempts. During the same storm, but a day earlier, than *Salacia*, another American yacht, *Freya*, was damaged beyond repair and sunk. Her skipper thought she was rolled completely over as many as four times. The knockdowns tore off the main hatch, broke several portholes, and removed everything off the deck including the mast. *Freya* was taking on water and sinking. They activated their 406 MHz emergency locator beacon (EPIRB) and were extremely lucky to be within the range of a helicopter rescue. I understand the water level inside their boat was above their knees and they saw it sink from the helicopter. It was almost dark and the rescue copter, low on fuel, could not have made another pass or searched for Mike and Julie. At the time, *Salacia* and *Freya* were separated by around 30 miles. We briefly saw this family in Tonga and said hello, but did not know them. They had a 13-year-old son on board who we understand did a remarkable job in trying to cover up the storm caused openings into the boat. They reduced the flow of water, but could not keep enough water out. Their emergency locating beacon is the same type we carry and it saved their lives. It only took a couple of hours for the National Coordination Center in Wellington to get a rescue copter on the scene. At the time of the rescue, they were about 90 miles off the north coast of NZ. The people we know who have talked to them tell us they were doing fine, happy to have made it safely, and the boat was insured; *Salacia* was not insured.

The crew of ***Our Pleasure*** found Auckland to be a beautiful city full of new excitements. We found their restaurants to be friendly, clean, more than enough selections to choose from, generous quantities and best of all, excellent quality. We went to their maritime museum, and enjoyed an Italian Festival complete with several opera stars singing well-known songs from several operas. I was invited to race with one of the yacht clubs on Thursday nights that "match race" (all boats are the same), for a bottle of rum; overall, we are feeling right at home!

New Zealand's population is just under four million, but their sheep population is close to 40 million. The people mostly live in urban areas on the north island. Europeans make up around 73% of the population, Maoris make up 12%, and the rest are divided between Pacific Islanders, Asian, and all other ethnic divisions. The total land area is only 104.4 thousand square miles, a little smaller than the state of Nevada. Therefore, the people have plenty of room to spread out with a population density of around 35 persons per square mile. However, in the largest cities the density is close to 10,000 persons per square mile. Their gross domestic product is around $54 billion of which 70% comes from services, 26% from industry and the rest from agriculture.

I found myself almost comfortable driving on the wrong side of the road, but not 100%. In traffic, keeping the car on the left side of the road is easy as I can follow the cars in front. Quite a few roads also have direction arrows painted in the roads and at "roundabouts" — probably put there after Yank drivers before us crashed all over their highways. When driving on roads without other cars it is hard to shake the tendency to drive on the right side. One thing that is always certain, if you see someone heading directly toward you, on the same side of the road, you had better move over. Not all insurance companies will sell auto insurance to Yanks. One insurance company turned us down, but two companies were okay with American drivers. New Zealand drivers are generally overly courteous. Horn blowing is somewhat of a rarity unless you do something requiring quick defensive action to avoid an accident. This happened to us one night while lost in Auckland. I pulled out in front of a car and did not leave him much room to stop. He honked his horn gently, at the next stoplight, rolled his window down and politely told me to be more careful when pulling out into traffic — can anyone imagine that happening in any big U.S. city? Pat apologized (I was mumbling some dumb male thing like drop dead) and told him we were lost. Well, he could not do enough to help us. He gave us explicit directions and stopped traffic so we could get in front of him and drive in his lane that was a left hand turn lane. I felt a little stupid as these people continue to amaze all of us with their friendliness and generosity. Although they are supposed to speak English, the words they choose are quite different from what Americans would use. For example, a sailboat is a yacht in Kiwi (New Zealanders), and a cruiser is a launch. One of our American friends keeps telling us he is going to go to Kiwi school so he can decipher their English. When they talk fast it is easy to miss communicate even if you listen carefully. This seems to be most prevalent when the men are speaking. We love listening to the NZ children speak as they use an English form that sounds so formal compared to American children.

We are amazed at the influence our American culture has in NZ. We thought NZ would be British; it is not. Sure, when the royal family gets in the spotlight the NZ news will cover it and some TV programs originate in England. In general, they do not seem to pay much attention to England. American influence is strong in music, movies, TV and sports clothing (expensive — a pair of Reeboks or Nikes goes for around NZ $200). I was embarrassed to find TV shows that badly reflect U.S. values, e.g., Jerry Springer, are exported to NZ. Naturally, our cigarettes are exported to NZ and smoking is big. The newspapers and newsreaders (TV news anchors are known as "news readers") are starting to talk negatively about the tobacco industry and are providing information on health problems. Anything pertaining to President Bill Clinton and American politics usually was found in their major newspaper, The NZ Herald. The American dollar is always compared against the NZ dollar in articles pertaining to money and the New York stock exchange news and trends are reported every day. Many American products are imported here including food, but imports are always priced higher than NZ products. However, women's clothing seems to lag the latest trends. It was difficult for Pat to find cotton clothes, but polyester seemed to be popular — I could not find cotton boxer shorts. At night, the women dress in black and usually in layers with over-blouses of fine net, all polyester of course — not American type styles.

Our U.S. TV and video player use a different format than NZ and most of the world for that matter, so we cannot watch their programs or rent their videos — bummer! We had to buy a new Sony combo TV/VCR that will play in any country format, voltage, or frequency.

NZ seems to have plenty of problems, but with a population approaching 4 million and many square miles, their resources are stretched thin. One of the more difficult problems is dealing with the "Pacific Islanders." Many people originating in the Cook Islands, Niue, Tonga, Samoa, and Fiji all migrate here looking for work, good health care, and just a better life. We understand that only a few years ago, crime was almost unheard of, but has increased within the last five years. The islanders; bringing no skills, low levels of education, bad habits and no family structure; seem to be the main culprits. Unemployment is also at an all time high, which hurts everyone. The police do not carry guns here and so far, that works. Until last year, medical care was free and that offered a big attraction to live here. The attraction still exists since medical care is still mostly subsidized by the government, although small fees are now required. They realize they cannot take care of everyone and are making great strides in getting away from socialistic medical care. Some surgical procedures, like angioplasty, may require a two-year wait. Private medical care is available for unheard of low fees, like NZ $35 a visit. So, most people who work and have good incomes, seek out private care for serious problems. Waiting for government care can be a frustrating process and the diagnosis, as reported in newspapers, is sometimes way off the mark. The tendency is cut laboratory tests in order to reduce time with patients and save money. It sounds like the GP's are quite over worked and required to work under stressful conditions to see their quota of patients. Difficult surgical procedures like brain surgery had to be done in England. This happened to Cathy Knowles when it was discovered she had a tumor around her optic nerve. The surgical skill was not available in NZ so she was sent to England for this delicate operation. NZ paid the operation's cost.

We moved ***Our Pleasure*** to a new marina, Gulf Harbour (English spelling) Marina in Whangaparaoa, NZ. It is a new 969-berth marina about 16 miles north from Auckland. It comes complete with everything: a country club, condominiums, town houses, and homes, boat yard, marine stores, deli, marine services, etc., etc. It was up-scale, something you would expect to see in Florida. Our slip A-63 was almost at the end of "A" dock and provided great views of all the boat traffic going in and out of the marina. We also had great views of the city of Auckland. The race area for the America's Cup was on the Hauraki Gulf, between Auckland and our marina.

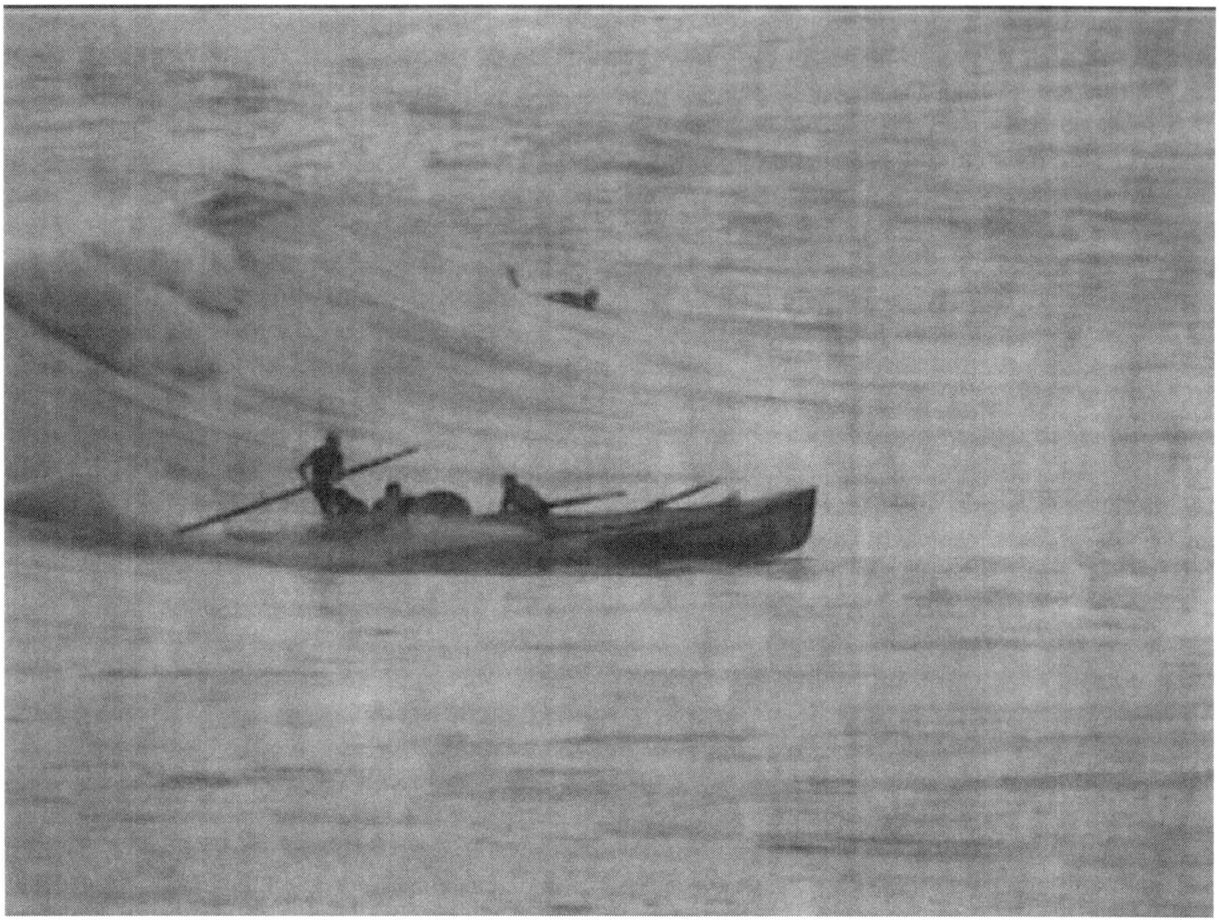

NEW ZEALAND RESCUE BOAT CREW PRACTICING IN BIG SURF

We had to leave West Haven marina, as their rules are set in concrete, three months period! Besides that problem, they were almost doubling rates for non-New Zealanders and commercial boats that moor there — rather discriminatory I thought. Moorage rates at Gulf Harbour were a much better value at $9.27/day for 60 feet. Costs aside, the staff welcomed us warmly and made us feel right at home. Comparing moorage rates at Gulf Harbour to Seattle would be like getting a big pay raise (1/3 the cost). However, the dock power throughout NZ is antiquated for power consuming newer boats. The dock outlet is 240 volts, 50 Hertz, and 10 amps. They call this a "casual" outlet for portable electrical equipment like a vacuum cleaner or battery charger. Equipment you would use an extension cord for and disconnect when finished. The 16 amp power outlets are available for boats that are wired permanently for 240 volt power with NZ type connectors. For foreign boats, the marina charges NZ $600 to install the NZ power connector and inspect the boat wiring for correctness. Foreign boats wired already for 240 volts still have to buy their unique connector that uses round pins and sockets. Since American power connectors made by Marinco or Hubbell are not approved for use in NZ, I installed a NZ approved connector and ran new boat wiring. Then the boat installation had to be inspected before a NZ "Warrant-of-Fitness" could be issued. After much fooling around, I bought a 2,000 watt isolation transformer that operates on 240 volts input and steps down to 120 volts. My U.S. battery charger made by Heart in Seattle would not work on their 50 Hertz frequency and 240 volts so I bought a new charger that would. Since the battery charger and transformer both have power cords with plugs, they are considered portable, allowing me to use their casual connector on the dock. It turns out that almost everything on the boat that runs on 60 Hertz will run on 50 Hertz with minor differences. All the clocks run about 17% slower and so do the ac motors, but the motors are conservative to begin with so, they all run without overheating and the microwave takes longer to cook. The TV and stereo have their own power supplies and they work fine on 50 or 60 Hertz. The only thing that would not work was the Heart inverter/battery charger so I bought a 40 amp charger that will work on both frequencies. The small chargers on the toothbrush and razor, etc. are probably not charging their batteries fully, but they did fine. I was now able to plug into all countries power with these changes, but will have to buy different power connectors, as each country is different. Our lap top computer, made by Toshiba, will operate on any voltage from 100 to 250 volts and 50 or 60 Hertz. Japanese designers solved these potential problems years ago. One boat from Sweden that has been sailing for over 6 years showed me their large collection box of connectors and adapters required by the countries they visited.

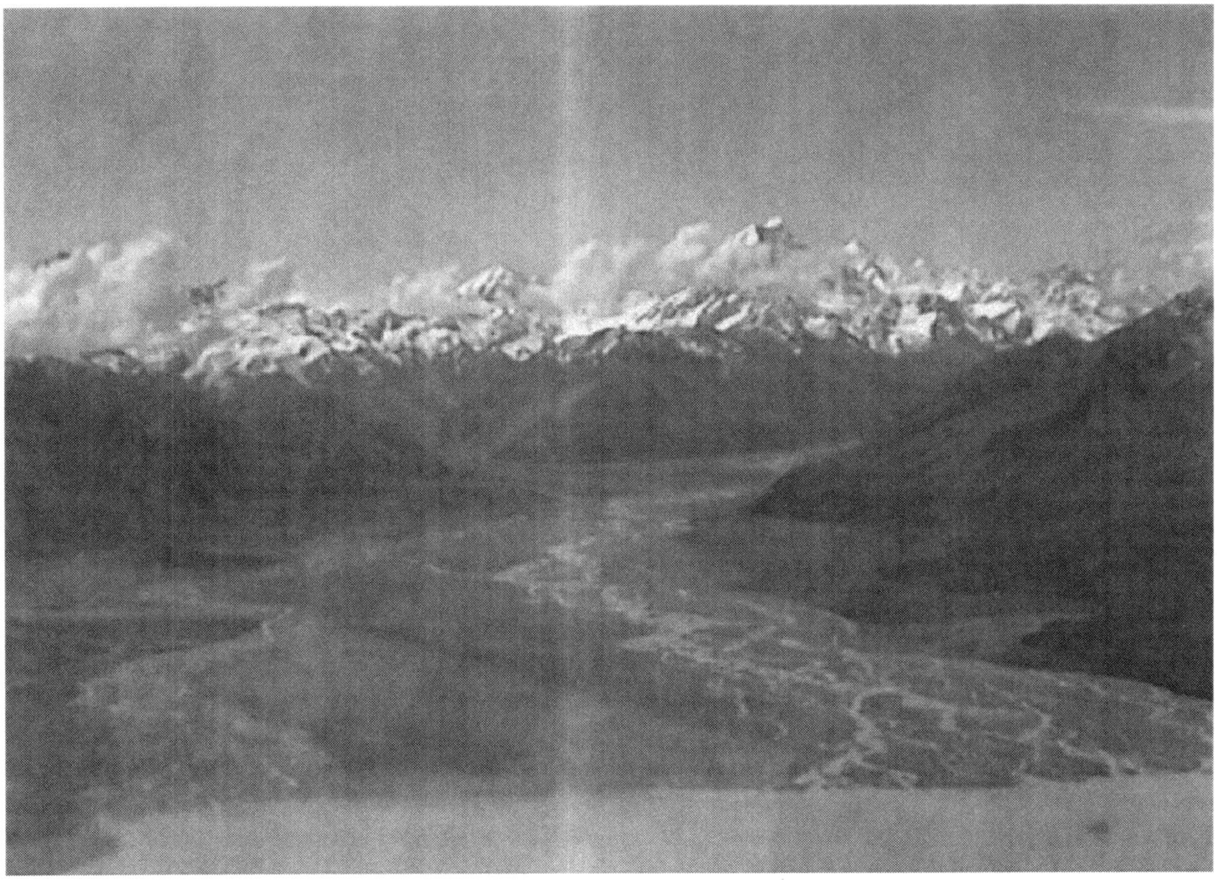

HELICOPTER TOUR, LAKE TEKAPO AND MOUNTAINS, SOUTH ISLAND, NZ

For the first two months in NZ, we saw quite a bit of the North Island, but none of the South Island. The locals are keen on their South Island and tell us we must see it, as we will find all of natures wonder there, pristine and unspoiled by humans.

Bob and Leslie started exploring the South Island on Jan. 29, with Bob's mother, father, and brother, Zach. Bob's parents brought their bicycles from Seattle to tour NZ by bike. His parents live to explore everything from their bikes and have actually biked across the U.S. Zach arrived here on Christmas Day and spent a couple of weeks with Bob and Leslie exploring the North Island.

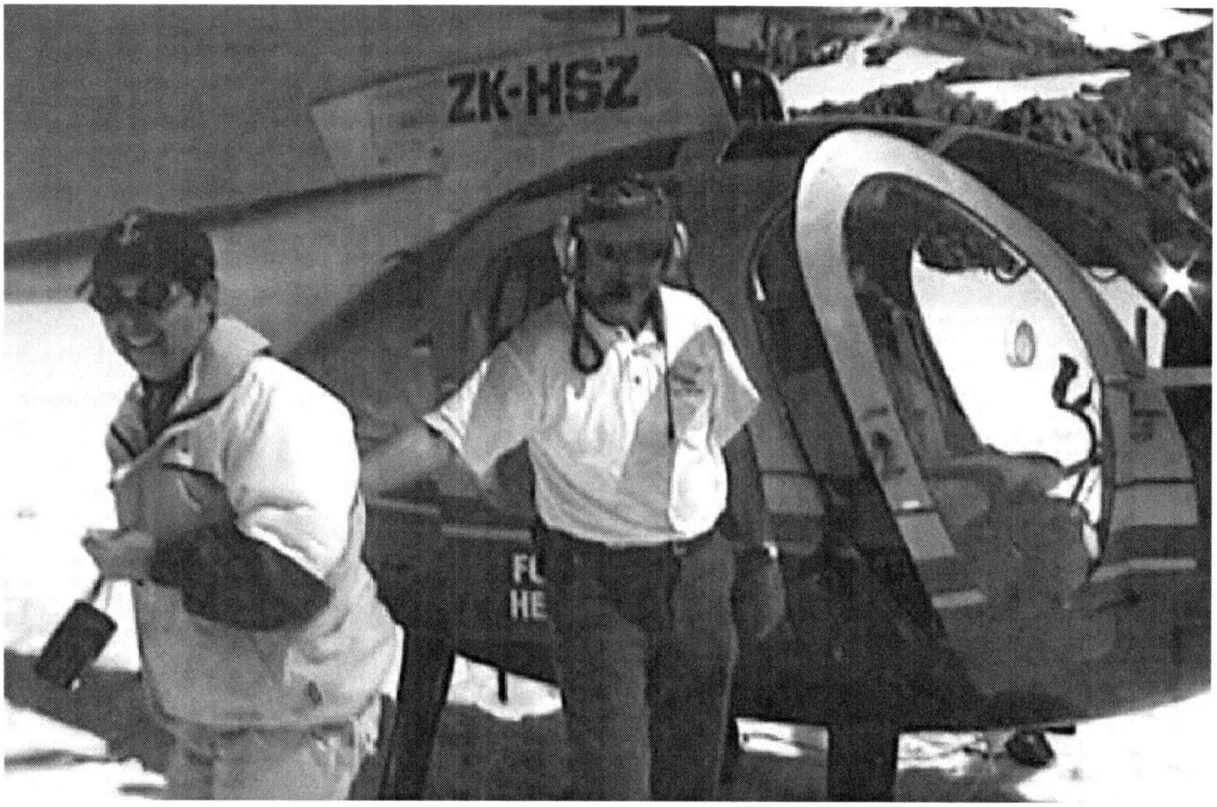

THE 11,500 FOOT TASMAN GLACIER, SOUTH ISLAND, NEW ZEALAND

For the last few weeks of Zach's visit, he helped the crew of ***Our Pleasure*** get the outside woodwork back in shape. A job made difficult by rain and marina restrictions to keep noise down and sanding dust off the docks and water. Our electric sanders remained in the tool locker and all the sanding was done by hand with tarps taped along the hull to catch the dust. After 10,000 miles, the exterior varnish had taken quite a beating as the force of the water literally peeled big sections of varnish off the wood. The epoxy paint on the two masts was starting to chalk, that means sanding and painting. Bob went up on the boson's chair for 4 days, sanded both masts and primed the main mast in epoxy, but sprained his wrist skate boarding with Zach. Leslie, bless her brave heart, finished the job the day before Bob's parents arrived.

Pat and I were waiting for one more estimate from a local boat yard to make several modifications to ***Our Pleasure*** before we can do any more NZ exploring. We wanted to make major changes to the anchor deployment system, the anchor, the mid and aft hatches and water proofing the main companionway.

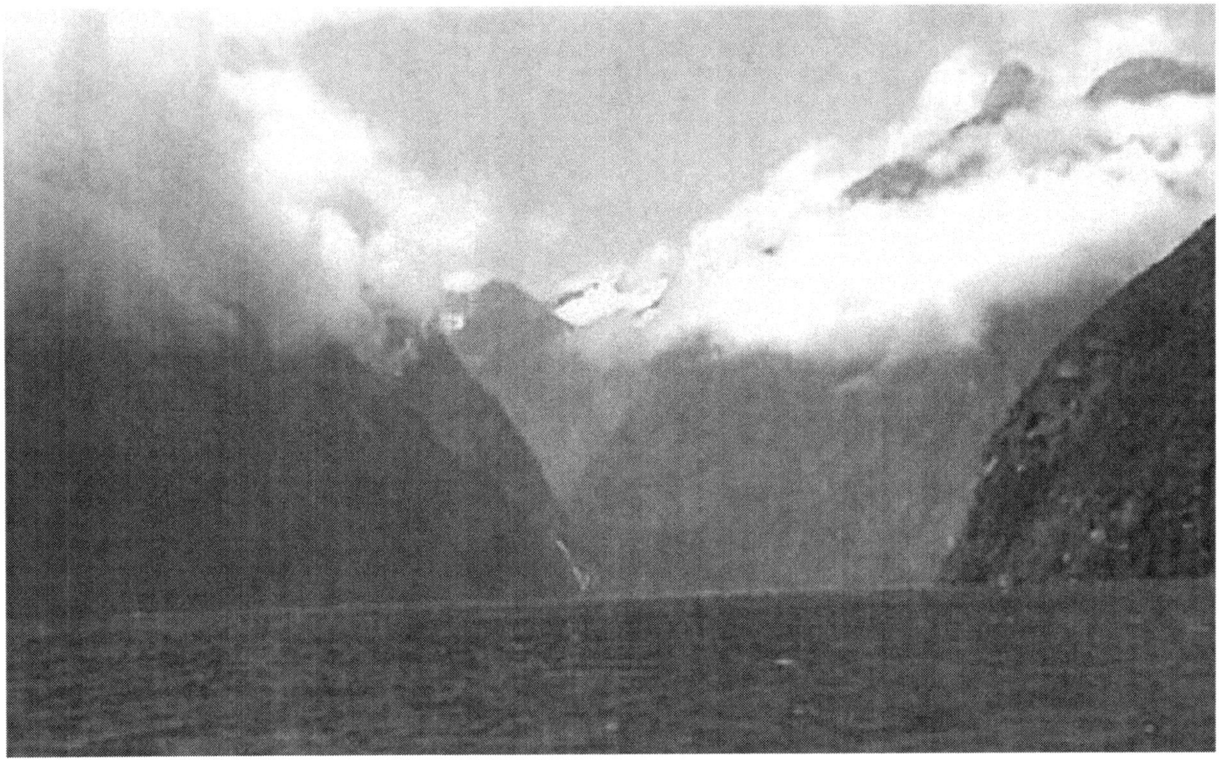

EXPLORING MILFORD SOUND, SW SOUTH ISLAND, NZ

On advice from local boaters, we moved ***Our Pleasure*** a few miles north to Robertson's Boat Yard at Warkworth, NZ for a makeover. With labor rates at a mere $20/hour and the highly skilled tradesmen that apprenticed in marine work, I could not pass up the opportunity. The passage from Tonga turned out to be quite hard on ***Our Pleasure*** as we found several problems related to storms that needed correction. The big honking stainless steel plate connecting the bow to the bowsprit broke at a weld. The plate provides the fastening point for a through bolt that helps to hold the bowsprit in place. Another weld that broke was on the base of the staysail stanchion plate. This load point took a beating from the staysail boom when the storm staysail drove the boat in heavy weather. Another interesting failure was the upper rudder bushing/packing gland. This big bronze plate was loose in spite of the six large bolts holding it in place. One bolt actually broke and the others had caused lightly elongated holes in the plate. Any force against the rudder would cause the bushing to move about $1/32^{nd}$ of an inch. Luckily, the bedding compound between the plate and the hull did not leak, but the packing seal did leak allowing small amounts of water to enter the bilge. I wondered where the extra water found in the bilge came from. I assumed it was water that passed through the closed companionway doors and other hatches — not entirely true. The boat yard's fix spread the load from the rudder shaft over eight bolts, 50% larger in diameter than the old ones. The new holes drilled in the plate, matched the bolt diameters in an extremely close tolerance fit. Before any work started, the yard agreed to provide me with a computer printout every 3 days of each person's time charge and material bought/dollars spent. A job number is assigned for each job to help with tracking. Even with good hourly rates, five people working nine hours a day can spend a lot of money quickly.

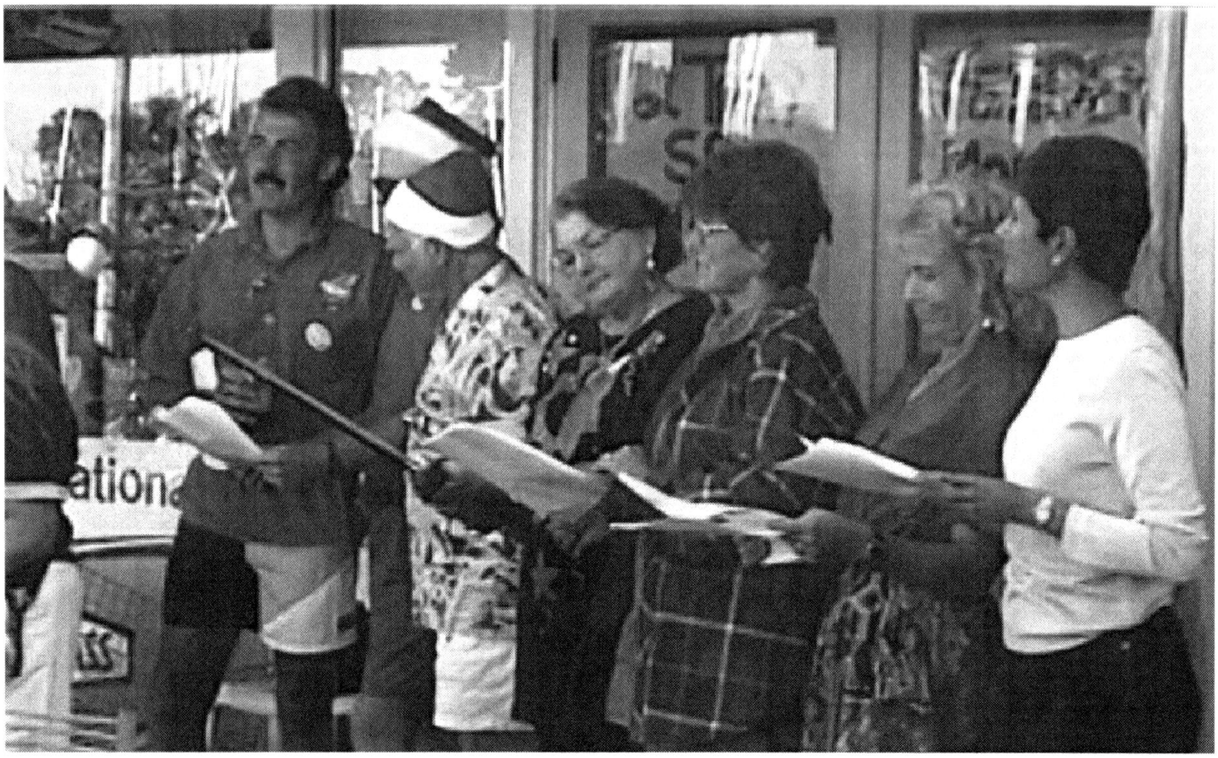

YACHTIE CHRISTMAS ENTERTAINMENT, GULF HARBOUR MARINA, 1998

One good thing though, our good NZ friends Andy and Cathy have loaned us their beach house on Algies Bay which is a short 10 minute drive to the boat yard. Their beach house has three bedrooms, three baths, is only two blocks from the beach and on a hill with beautiful views of the Hauraki Gulf, Kawau Island and the Barrier Islands. Walks were pleasant as we fed donkeys at a nature preserve and walked along the beaches. The area is hilly and an hour walk stretches many muscles used long ago — have to find a way to exercise more while sailing.

Bobby, Leslie, Bob's brother Zach, and parents came to visit after their bike tour of the south island. We listened with interest as they told us about the South Island. Bob and Leslie planned to visit some friends they met from Australia before heading back to the U.S. All their friends are buying homes now and starting families and I think they want to reenter the American dream competition.

Working at the yard was a rude awakening; I was there every day at 7:30 a.m. after rising at 6:30 a.m. and driving the 10 to 15 minutes to Warkworth. However, the drive was pleasant through pristine countryside. The yard itself is on the pretty Mahurangi River whose headwaters start at Warkworth. This is the first time since retiring from Boeing that I've had to get up every day and put in a full day of work. The work was mostly physical and all those long unused muscles were sore by the end of the day. Cathy's beach house came equipped with a spa in one of the bathrooms, but I didn't use it enough.

I worked mostly from scaffolding around the boat removing old varnish, sanding, scraping, and varnishing. I also did a lot of sanding on the bottom and put on 7 gallons of antifouling paint by roller and brush. I was continually impressed with the yard's woodworkers; they did some beautiful work using simple hand tools. I had them fill in a hole in the salon floor where a four inch diameter table support used to be. They made up teak strips to match the existing parquet flooring. They used chisels to remove the existing pieces around the hole and glued in the new pieces with no trace of the old hole. They used a sharp drawknife as a scraper to remove millimeters of the top surface that were uneven until the old and the new matched — pretty neat.

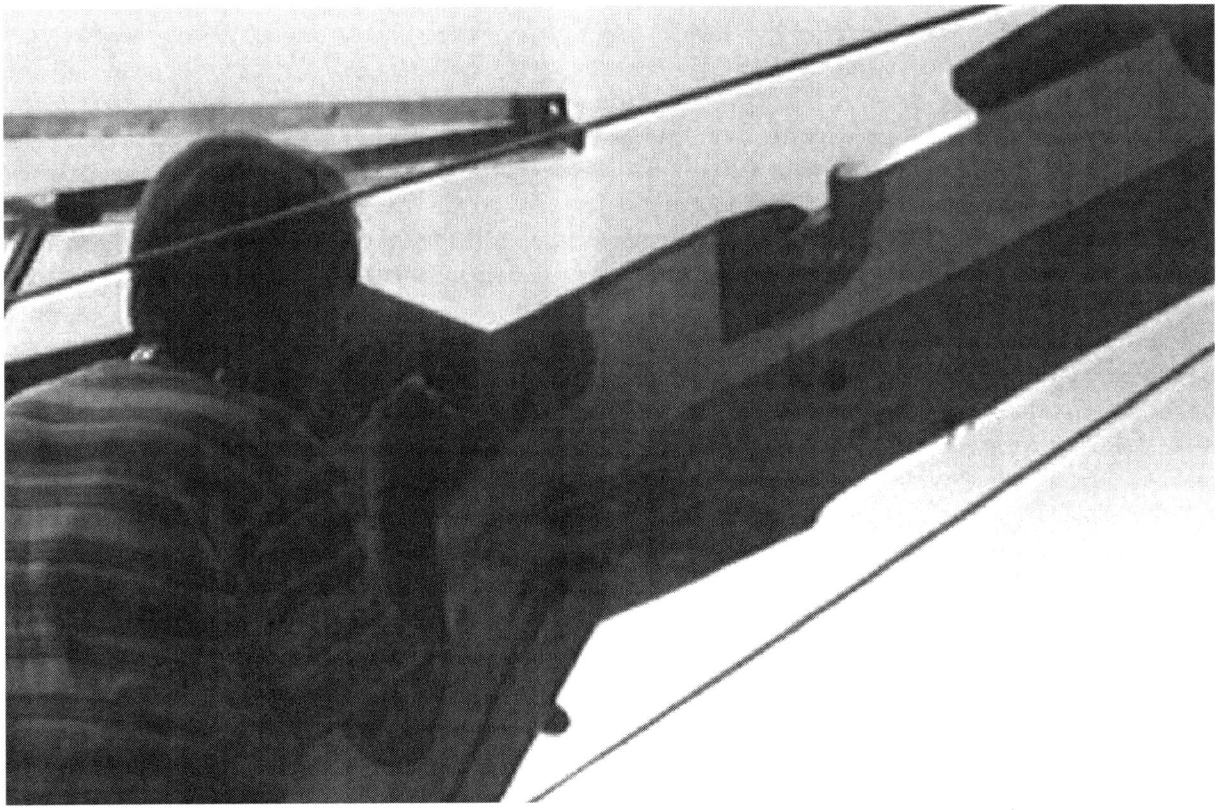

ROBERTSON'S YARD, BOWSPRIT MODS FOR NEW ANCHOR SYSTEM

It was good that I was there every day to help with decisions on how to implement changes, etc. One change that turned out really well was the new anchoring system. The old system used a 60 pound CQR anchor. The anchor shank required manhandling to move it off and onto the bow roller. If the wind blew over 25 knots, it meant another sleepless night in the anchorage since 60 pounds is light for ***Our Pleasure***. The new system uses a 120 pound Manson CQR anchor built in NZ that I had tested to Lloyds' requirements. The surface area of the new anchor is double that of the original anchor and is expected to do its job in winds up to 40 knots. Accomplishing these changes meant reworking the bowsprit, its teak platform, and the roller system. To move this big brute off its rollers without touching it meant a lot of stainless steel fabrication and welding using 3/8 inch stainless plates. Two rollers positioned 45 degrees from the vertical, allows the chain on the anchor shank to come into the rollers at 45°. This way the windless can pull the weight of the anchor at an easy angle. Before, the anchor shank came in at 90° to the windless and it could not pull the anchor shank around the roller. The new roller required fabrication of a new 4 inch thick block, machined to a diameter of 6 inches and with a grove in the center to match the thickness and shape of the anchor shank. It rotates on a 5/8 inch diameter stainless pin between two, 12 inch diameter by 3/8 inch stainless plates. The plates also act as a guide and keeper for the flukes. The flukes will not move once the anchor is in place. The anchor-to-chain shackle is designed not to catch on the roller or its plates because there are no pin protrusions outside the shackle body. In order for the big anchor flukes to clear the bobstay, several inches of new platform teak moved the rollers outboard the right amount. The platform was modified to match the new anchor and rollers.

The 375 feet of high tensile strength 3/8 inch chain were regalvanized. The original chain galvanizing did quite well until we anchored in areas with large amounts of coral. The coral acted like sand paper and wore the galvanizing off. When we arrived in NZ, the chain was rusty.

The windless gypsy that pulls up the chain had never matched the chain links well. The pawls that were supposed to capture the chain links were too far apart, which caused the chain to jump out of the gypsy when it was under pressure. Sometimes Bob had to use foot pressure on the chain to keep it from jumping — not good. Robertson called Maxwell, the NZ windless manufacturer, and sent them a small piece of the chain. They agreed it was not a good match and are casting a new gypsy to match the chain — at my cost of course. That is the story on the anchor modifications.

It was a bargain at about $1,300 for parts and $1,340 for labor. These costs also included taking the bowsprit apart, fixing some dry rot, rebuilding the bow chain plate, bonding and sealing everything with epoxy or bedding compound, sanding and painting. The same work in the U.S. would have cost three times as much or more just based on hourly rates. Based on the knowledge that the boat and its occupants will be safer at anchor and that the anchor will not require manhandling, I think convinced me that we got a bargain.

Our Pleasure arrived at the yard with a list of 31 work items. Most of the items were design improvements, some changes helped the boats performance, and a few were repairs. One of the best changes removed two wooden deck hatches and replaced them with aluminum hatches made in NZ. The wooden hatches were a delight to look at with their bright varnish, beautiful joints, and craftsmanship. However, the tightness of fit between mating surfaces was not good enough to keep out water. Water breaking on deck would force its way through the mating surfaces even when their canvas covers were in place. The aluminum hatches on the other hand are strong, lock in two different open positions for air circulation and have four locking levers in the fully down locked position. They do not leak under full pressure from a water hosing — the wooden hatches could never pass that test.

Another item, which turned out really well, was a 1¼ inch diameter, stainless-steel tube welded across the top of the rear stanchions starting at the entry gates (about 40 ft long). This tube, replacing the existing wire lifeline, provides strength for the dinghy davits and a safe handhold when walking around the aft deck. Additional tubing connected the upper part of the davits and the new rail to keep the dinghy from moving left or right. I almost had this tubing added in Mexico, but I am glad I didn't. It would have cost more, plus, they would not have electro-polished it and the workmanship would not have been as good.

The yard also made 44 chrome plated brass standoff fittings to mount Lexan® storm boards over the pilothouse windows. There are ten glass windows, eight in the pilothouse and two in the stern, which all use safety glass. I brought the Lexan® panels from Seattle already cut to size for all the glass windows. Since these panels are bulletproof, they provide a big safety margin as an additional benefit.

The yard also fitted a Lexan® plate between the pilothouse and the cockpit entry to block water entry into the companionway. Three additional deck drains and a through-hull valve facilitated draining the deck in the area of the plate. The yard also fabricated chrome plated brass locks, of our design, to lock all the interior hatches in the cabin soles. Some of the boats that made the crossing from Tonga to NZ had to duck loose floor hatches when knocked down ninety degrees or so. One boat that had a combination stove/oven, found their stove flying around the cabin after a knock down. The stove probably weighed 60 pounds and became a lethal object careening uncontrollably around the cabin. They managed to subdue it by moving it to a quarter berth and stuffing it in with blankets. We all found sailing to be full of daily surprises, events that seldom were planned, conditions that were often dangerous and frequently risky.

On Mar. 4, we moved ***Our Pleasure*** out of Robertson's Boat Yard after three and a half weeks of nine-hour days and I was exhausted. Bobby, Leslie, and I motored ***Our Pleasure*** down the Mahurangi River and back to Gulf Harbor. This river twists and turns for about 6 miles. It's quite a unique river, narrow with colored plastic bottles on sticks marking the channel. We left at high tide so the depth varied from 13 feet to 7 feet and we draw about 6.5 feet. The river bottom is mostly mud, which allows the locals living along the river to moor their boats in front of their homes. Most of these boats have flat bottoms so they sit on the mud when the tide goes out. There were many catamaran type boats, a tugboat, and a nice steam powered launch. We were lucky that the weather was picture perfect and fairly calm since all our sails were in storage. Without sails, the motion would not have been good if the wind and waves were up.

The Australian government produced a documentary of the 630 mile race from Sidney, Australia to Hobart (Tasmania), Australia that started on Dec. 26, 1998. When they reached the Bass Strait between Australia and Tasmania, they ran into 85 knot winds and some waves were estimated at 80 feet. Australia mounted the largest air/sea rescue ever attempted. As I remember, the fleet started with 115 boats and only 43 boats finished. Many boats pulled out early as they saw the weather deteriorate. The weather was predicted to have gusts around 45 knots — so much for predicting weather. Fifty-five planes and several ships were used to rescue 50 sailors from their broken and sinking boats in unbelievable conditions. Six sailors died and two were reported as missing, but never found. It was also interesting that the larger boats were able to sail fast ahead of the major portions of the storm where the conditions were slightly better. An American boat, the 80 foot *Sayonara*, owned by Oracle Corporation CEO Larry Ellison, was first-to-finish and the owner said he would never sail in that race again — in my opinion he was demonstrating good logical thinking.

Chapter 10

FRENCH POLYNESIA TO NZ AS TOLD BY BOB AND LESLIE

INTRODUCTION:

Our newlyweds, Bob and Leslie (our daughter) express some of their thoughts while sailing on ***Our Pleasure***. They pickup their story just before leaving Tahiti in French Polynesia and end in Auckland, New Zealand, before returning to Seattle. Their journal is presented for their different experiences and humorous involvements while they cruised with us for the first year and a half. Bob Fischer wrote the following paragraphs.

TAHITI (8.5.98)

Our final days in Papeete were spent getting supplies and going through the tedious checkout procedures that many countries require of traveling yachts. Our friends on *Cristal Blue* were throwing in the towel and shipping their boat home on a freighter. We spent a day helping them load it on the yacht transport ship and saw them off the next day. It was sad to see them go but a real experience seeing how these transport ships operate. They only paid $25,000 for the trip to Vancouver — what a bargain.

MOOREA, FRENCH POLYNESIA (8.7.98)

The next day we were set to leave Papeete and found that the 108 foot yacht *Gleam* had anchored with one of their anchor chains on top of ours. No way could our windless move chain and anchor the size of theirs. Happily, for me, they dove on it to unsnarl the mess. The harbor isn't exactly the cleanest and I had been in it before doing favors for people. Therefore, I was not looking forward to pulling out the dive gear and diving right before our departure. We left on our 14 mile trip to Moorea. Back in the saddle again and it did feel strange. Good thing it was a short trip. Les and I had been to the island a few times before to go camping. We stayed at a friend's cabin and got ankle tattoos. The Tahitian artist didn't speak any English, but he knew exactly what we wanted, tattoos that would tell our story. He did not use any drawings or templates, but did everything freehand. His girl friend was able to bridge the language gap between us whenever we had any questions. My tattoo and Leslie's are similar and describe our sailing adventure. On Leslie's, there is a Tiki that indicates she is female, a lizard which represents the meaning of the word *Moorea*, a shark to represent danger and adventure and a turtle for fertility and future children. Around the base are waves all around her ankle to represent sailing around the world and mountains that represent our first landfall. My tattoo is a little bigger with the same symbols except they indicate I'm a male, no turtle and a flag indicating a diver is under the water, pretty cool. It would be great to be back, explore more, and see our friends.

We had our choice of two bays and chose Oponohu over Cook's Bay. Oponohu Bay was less crowded and Cook never went into Cook's Bay, he sailed into Oponohu Bay. Majestic green velvet jagged mountainous peaks surround the bay with plantations in fertile soil leading up to them. There is only a small village with one little store where we could buy a few supplies and our fresh baguettes daily. It is really a beautiful bay with only four boats whereas Cook's Bay had 25 boats, go figure.

One of the first things we did was to have happy hour with our two good friends already in the bay, *Endurance* and *Esprit*. They were also kind enough to have fresh bread for us when we arrived. You need to order bread in advance and pick it up, which requires a high-speed dink ride across the bay. It rained and blew pretty hard some of the days we were there so with any good weather breaks Les and I jumped off the boat. One day we headed up to Belvedere Peak, which overlooked both bays. Some ancient ruins were on the way so we checked all those out. One was a royal archery platform where the kings held contests. They realized the potential threat of long-range flying arrows so archery was only for the elite and royals, smart. On our way up the road, this dog started trotting up in front of us and looking back as if he was leading us. We were like, okay, I guess he knows where he is going, cool. At one point, he got a ways up in front of us and we just looked at each other and started jogging after the dog, flip-flops or not. We caught up with him and he stayed close the rest of the day, through all the ruins and to the top of the lookout. We loved having our little adopted friend, served him water out of a homemade leaf bowl, and tried to interest him in our hummus sandwiches. He wasn't going for the hummus. The view was great; the mountains looked even more incredible up close. On the way down some Tahitians offered us a ride and we hopped in dog and all. They thought he was ours, but we dropped him off where he picked us up. We hitched a ride with them to Cook's Bay to hang out with our tattoo artist and his girl friend for the rest of the day. The rest of the time we just swam, snorkeled, cruised the reef, and watched the rain. One day we watched a huge mudslide on one of the peaks. We did more hiking through the pineapple and papaya plantations. *Endurance* has quite the movie selection so we had ample videos to watch at night. The time went fast and soon as a good weather break came, we made that move to Huahine, no more 40 knot winds.

The sail over to Huahine was the first real sail in months — it rather sucked. Confused seas made the should-have-been-nice-sail lame and uncomfortable. We had some confusion with the other boats as to what bay we were going to and we were headed to the wrong one. We had to change course and take a longer way around. Once in the right bay we found the wind was howling down the mountains, which made the anchorage less than desirable. We finally settled on a spot and after repeated tries to stay hooked, we were secured. Then the authorities told us to move because of the ferries and freighters that would be coming in. We were ho-humming around when a small cargo ship came through the channel and came close enough that we could have shook hands. The anchor came up quickly and we moved fast.

HUAHINE, FRENCH POLYNESIA (8.15.98)

I don't think Huahine was all that cool. There was a reef break to surf, but the locals had been threatening people with spear guns to rule over their territory and I'm not too keen on reef breaks at this stage of my surfing career. Overall, the locals were not too friendly and the best thing about the place was the topless thong sporting women who hung out on the beach in front of our boat. A lot of the island had been trashed by a cyclone that had passed by the area in April and I'm not surprised tourists didn't excite them. I'm sure they got along fine without us.

RAIATEA, FRENCH POLYNESIA (8.19.98)

On our way to Bora Bora, we had engine trouble, stopped at Raiatea to rest, and check it out. We just needed to adjust the valves. The bays were pretty and the land had many leafless trees from the cyclone. There were boat yards here that sustained lost roofs and dozens of boats that had crashed down in dry-dock during the cyclone.

BORA BORA, FRENCH POLYNESIA (8.20.98)

The next day we headed through the small channel with huge swells towards the famous Bora Bora. It was Leslie's birthday and some time ago, we had the idea of celebrating at a famous restaurant called "Bloody Mary's." We had a great sail and a killer view of Mt. Otemanu and Mt. Pa'ihia. A fringe reef surrounds the island and during our sail, we had long looks at swells breaking over the reefs and the turquoise water behind them. The Teavanui Pass that we would enter through had a strong current coming out and the process was slow. I swear we were hardly moving. Once finally through came happiness and a big sigh of relief. It's always a little hairy going through new passes with the swell, reef and current all around you.

We anchored down close to "Bloody Mary's" in about 100 feet of water. With not much scope and the wind howling, Les and I headed to dinner. Dick and Pat stayed on the boat to make sure we were secure. By time we got dressed and showered, it was dark, the swells and chop were up with the wind blowing. It was only about a quarter to a half-mile dink ride, but there was a large reef to navigate around and we couldn't see it. We stood in the dink so we wouldn't get wet and just swung wide to miss the reef. Just one of many things while cruising that keeps you on your toes.

The restaurant was way cool. Lots of famous actors and musicians had visited, but tonight Leslie was the only celebrity. The food was all displayed on ice and you just pick what you want and it is grilled right there. The floor was white sand and everything else was tropical woods and palm trees. Little geckos ran across the floor and up the walls. The bar and table seats were all tree stumps — pretty neat. We had a romantic dinner and cocktails and were happy just to enjoy each other's company in such a nice elegant tropical setting. It was like a movie set. Les was looking mighty fine on her 28th birthday (Aug. 20, 1998). Back on the boat there was a birthday cake for dessert.

The next week was fun filled, windy, sunny, rainy, and pretty cool. I know I say cool a lot, but that's how it is, COOL. Bora Bora is pretty big with lots of anchorages. We stayed put for a couple days and Les and I dinked around in the wind and chop getting soaked and filling the dink with buckets of water. We talked to dive shop guys and found some spots to dive. One pass we dove, we didn't find many fish, but lots of coral that went down a valley looking like melted mushrooms. After our dive, we cleaned the hull; previously we had gone snorkeling at the "Golden Reef." Tons of stag horn coral with a 3 to 5 knot current, so you just float down with the current then walk up the beach and do it again. Somehow, on the long ride over I ripped the butt of my shorts so I couldn't really walk up the beach without hanging it all out. So everyone else walked and I fought the upstream current.

Another day Les and I climbed a little hill to check out the cannons left from WWII that guarded the entrance to the lagoon and to see the view. There is a long road to the site or a family there will let you go straight up the hill behind their house. We chose the hill and had a great time trying to pick the path. The same family also rents bikes so we made a plan and spent a day touring around the island. Now they were not really bikes, but death cycles. I brought along some tools, which proved to be a wise decision. The bikes were 21 speeds with one gear that maybe worked. Les's crank bearings were stripped and sometimes just spun free. My rear derailleur was all bent and the rear hub was loose. Sometimes the tire would just stop turning throwing me into a skid. The island was flat, which is good because the bike didn't work. We found a beer hut about three-quarters the way around, ate lunch, and had a cold one. Not having been able to ride bikes for a while took a toll on our butts. We adopted a few dogs to share lunch and soon had a couple of cats as well.

One day we planned a dive to see manta rays that were 20 to 24 feet across. We were so excited when the dive boat showed up. However, they said they had tried to call us to say they were doing a shark dive in the pass instead. Needless to say, a French guy calling "the pleasure boat" at 7:30 in the morning just wouldn't register as a call for us. We wouldn't have gone if we had received the message, but since we were all set to go, we went anyway. We saw plenty of sharks, but no mantas. The dive was pretty cool though. We were immediately surrounded by a school of black tip sharks, fins down and looking aggressive. The guide, Philippe, starts pulling huge fish heads and tails out of his buoyancy compensator vest. The sharks go crazy, rushing and tearing at them and each other. I'm like, is this guy nuts? The sharks were more interested in the fish than him or us, so it was cool. They swarmed around us the whole dive only a few feet away. So many of them had hooks and lures sticking out the sides of their mouths, I was cracking up. It was so funny to see where many of our lures and hooks ended up. Another fun thing about this dive was the moray eels. Apparently, they used to feed them, so when divers come around they stick their big ugly snouts out looking for food. A guide at the dive shop just had one latch onto his finger the day before when he turned his head away. A big chunk was missing and it wasn't pretty.

So we finish the dive and start talking to the people on the dive boat. They're all interested in us and we're interested in how it is staying in the $500 a night bungalows. They did the manta dive the day before and said it was the ultimate. We felt okay about missing that one.

On Aug. 23, 1998, we spent our one-year anniversary hanging out with our buddies on *Hoptoad*, a cool couple from Shilshole Bay Marina in Seattle and their two teenage sons. We've been hooking up since Mexico and the boys are my best wrestling partners. They keep getting bigger as the trip goes on so they become a little more challenging our every meeting — I miss them a lot. We just missed them in Tonga. We spent the day snorkeling and looking for schools of spotted eagle rays, checked out a underwater black pearl farm and then had happy hour watching the sun set on their boat — awesome day.

Some more exciting events happened during our stay at Bora Bora once we moved over to the mooring buoys in front of the Bora Bora Yacht Club. Sunday morning Dick and Pat got gussied up for church and had lowered the dink, which becomes untied and drifts away. Dick comes to the honeymoon coffin and asks for me. Something that rarely happens, must be important? "The dink came untied and is floating away." No thought involved, just over the stern in my boxers before it gets too far away. It's only 8 feet to the water, but I lose my shorts and give myself a twanger in the process. Rescue complete and later that day I was rewarded with chocolate croissants Pat bought especially for me — it's the small things.

Another night I was reading, late as usual and started getting suspicious of the wave action. I was out of bed and heading to check it out when I ran into Dick at the companionway. Where are we and where are all the boats? Our mooring line broke and we floated three-quarters of a mile towards the outer reef — pretty lucky. We found our way back and anchored. Guardian angels protected us that night for sure.

Les, Pat, and I went out to the reef to see the spotted eagle rays that the tourist boats were feeding. There was a school of about twenty of them in about four feet of water so we snorkeled with them for about an hour. What can I say, cool!

Somehow, on the day we planned to leave we heard my parents were trying to get hold of us. Les and I sat at the yacht club all day trying to get hold of them. They were off bike riding, imagine that. Once we finally got through to them, they said they wanted to sport us a hotel room for a couple of nights as an anniversary present. Too bad we were leaving, but we'd take a rain check. About time to cash in on that one, this boat keeps getting smaller. We left the next day and had finally talked Dick out of going to American Samoa. We decided to sail to Palmerston Island in the Cook Island group, then off to Niue. We were ready to leave Bora Bora and get out of French Polynesia. Our stay there would dominate most of our south pacific traveling, most of it stuck in Papeete. Les and I were pretty excited, another country with cooler people. This would be the best leg of our trip by far. Skip everything previously talked about and head straight to Palmerston and Niue.

PALMERSTON ATOLL, COOK ISLANDS (9.6.98)

The trip to Palmerston was slow. The first day out, however, we caught a 30 inch yellow fin tuna. Our biggest catch yet and by far the best. This passage was uneventful, not much wind, a lot of slow motoring and a 4 day trip that took 6. We arrived at midnight at another fringe-reefed island. The moon was full though and instead of slugging about all night and waiting for daybreak, we would go in and radio the islanders for a guide to get us to the anchor spot. I was on deck enjoying the night air and what stars I could see. I saw something and I said to Les, what is that? Is it a whale? It turns out to be Simon and Eddie Marsters. We were a few miles off the island and they came out to get us, no call needed. They would be our host family and there was a lot of competition to get yachts among the three branches of the Marsters family living there. One Scottish guy with three wives created three different families all with the same father on the island. He established strict intermarrying rules — some life huh? They showed us where to drop the hook off the reef in about 30 to 40 feet of water. Then it drops off to around 200 feet. I was tired enough to turn the clutch the wrong way while letting chain out and couldn't figure out why it wouldn't stop. Zip, there goes all the chain. Fortunately, we have a safety line so it was still attached to the boat. I don't think I'll be doing that again. The rain started pouring so we had the brothers on board for beer and coffee. They weren't supposed to be on board until we checked through customs, but who's going to know and who's going to care? It's just all one big family but apparently, there is quite a bit of tension. The island is small; you can walk around it in 20 to 25 minutes.

Since we were anchored on the outside of the reef, we had to be careful of wind changes that would blow us into the reef. To get inside the reef you need to go through a narrow channel with a strong current and then weave your way through tons of coral heads — if you're cool you call them "bommies" — to get to the beach. The guys came out and always picked us up and drove us through the maze even at night. I wondered how they did it so well at night; no markers accept some sticks sticking out. Sometimes the wind was howling, the current was moving and the water was shallow. I was always impressed, even if we were stuck and hit a few things late one night.

So you have these three family branches competing with each other for yachts to feed, show around, do their laundry and taxi about. It was like grown up summer camp on a tropical island paradise. Nature walks, collecting coconuts (a major staple), crabbing, lobstering, scuba diving, snorkeling, a big volleyball court, and white sand beaches all hosted by the friendliest and most giving people.

In addition, they spoke English with a cool accent. We spent days doing all of the above-mentioned things, learning about the family history and travel tales. We fed the pigs and chickens. About 100 at least chickens would come clucking up when mama Marsters called them to their 5p.m. feeding. It was so funny. They roam free and sleep in the trees at night. All the many hermit crabs are way too big for their shells, they stick out inches sometimes. I think a good shell is seriously valued real estate. It cracks you up though. They climb trees too and you see like 15 to 20 hermit crabs "chill-in" in a palm tree.

The only dive we did here was one of the coolest yet. Before we hopped in, whales had been breaching in the vicinity and Leslie and I hopped in to see if we could snorkel with them. I could hear them, but not see them. We then dove the 200 foot wall, but only down to about 120 feet. On the way down, we found a chimney that went down through the reef from about 90 feet to 50 feet. We went up and loved it. On top, we traversed the reef and headed up the finger channels. One particular channel I turned to find an 8 foot white tip shark nipping at our heels. He was pretty territorial so we left his channel fast.

There were several boats anchored with us on the island, *Hio Avae*, *Mangoe* and *Lisa Rae* to name a few. We came to know them rather well on our field trips and at dinner hosted by our family on the island every day. Until we arrived in New Zealand, we would spend most of our time with these people. All people our age and very cool.

When it came time to leave, we were all pretty upset. This small island had been our best experience yet and such a wonderful change from French Poly. It had only been 4 or 5 days, but when the fellas came out to see us off, they brought two big fat lobsters with them. They were so great and hugging these five guys goodbye brought tears to our eyes. They were wonderful simple people there on their own island paradise that may have been a prison to them as well. Many of the family had gone to New Zealand and besides the cargo ship every four to five months; the yachties were their only visitors. This is only during the couple of months the weather allows yachties to cruise the area. As I said, it was hard to go; they were magical people who we will never forget. Upon our departure, I gave them some shirts and shorts and Pat had several T-shirts. Dick gave them the rest of our unleaded gas for their outboard. They don't have much money for material things and live simply. We were happy to give them anything we could like food and toys.

NIUE ISLAND (9.12.98)

The sail to Niue wasn't as slow and boring as it was to Palmerston, large seas, and winds of 30 to 35 knots. While reefing the main, Dick and I weren't too coordinated and ended up blowing out two of the reef points and had some tearing — quite a bummer. He was raising and I was tying down, but the reef line wasn't tight, so too much pressure on the points, too much wind, and "boom" in an instant it was shredding.

We arrived in Alofa, the main city of the largest coral island in the world, Niue. They had mooring buoys to protect the coral so we just tied up and we were there. High coral and limestone cliffs surround the island, so to go ashore you have to use a lift on the wharf to haul up your dink. There was a bunch of military guys working on the wharf to extend it. Les said those guys couldn't be U.S. because their shorts are too short. I said you'd be surprised. They were all cut, lying around doing pushups, pull-ups and leg exercises while at work. We talked to some of them and it turns out they were Seabees doing construction work down here to finish the wharf. Since they were all divers, we had lots to talk about, the states, how lame the French are all the island hot spots, our trip, and their stay and so on. We were able to get to know several of them over our stay, hang out and go to dinner and stuff — they were cool. I asked them the reason for wearing such (short) shorts. That was because somebody thought they should feel confident in boots and (short) shorts and that's it. I can't believe the gear we tax payers buy for them, nice. So our friends *Hio Avae*, *Mangoe*, and *Megot* were all there and we just kicked it live. This place was dam cool. Cheap, friendly and the terrain was amazing. If Peter Pan lived some place, this was it. New Zealand controlled, Niue is clean and quiet with superstitious natives. On land, there were caves above and below ground, limestone chasms, and valleys. There were arches and blowholes, fresh water springs, tunnels, rivers hidden nooks and crannies and all beautiful, unique and oh so cool. We went on several underground cave tours, checked out the caves on the ocean, chasms, and the arches with caves and tunnels surrounding them. Our time was limited so we did as much as possible, hanging with our young friends, ending each day in exhaustion.

The diving was indescribable. I had only dreamed of such cool formations and terrain. The visibility was unlimited, the coral insane and the water was filled with one of the world's most poisonous snakes. Les wasn't as anxious to dive as I was, so I did most of it with Todd and his buddy Mark Kistler who was visiting for a few weeks from the states. We set up an arrangement with the one and only dive guide for a two-tank dive day. On the first day out, once we were all picked up from our boats and heading to the dive spot, we saw several whales breaching in the harbor. Kevin, our guide, had an underwater listening system, but we were already in the water and didn't know what his system was picking up. They look so smooth, graceful, and big. They just slowly swim off until they're out of sight. What a rush to start the day off. The island is filled with underwater valleys, chasms, tunnels, chimneys and caves. Our first dive was called the "toilet bowl." You drop in from above, down through a chimney into two caves that exit into the big blue. The sun pours through the opening and lights up the water, it's almost spiritual. Kevin's wife, Carrie, did reprimand us for not staying close together and for walking up side down in the caves. The next dive was "coral valley." We saw tons of every kind of coral, parrotfish and some hard to spot turtles.

Les went on the next set of dives to the "sea fans" and "snake gully." The sea fans are about 8 feet tall, down about 130 feet and very green. The dive master never really dove with us, just pointed and said, "It's down there." He did venture down on this one though and a good thing. David, a cat with us, started chasing this turtle while we were at about 140 feet. The dive master pointed back to the wall meaning let's go. Decompression comes quickly at that depth. Meanwhile the cat keeps chasing the turtle deeper and I point him out to Kevin who goes after him. We all met at the wall and finished the dive. David, the cat, runs out of air sooner than the rest of us at that depth.

Our next dive was snake gully. You guessed it, massive amounts of snakes. They have real small mouths so the chance of being bit is pretty low, and most of them are pretty shy. We see them on every dive and I wore leather gloves so I could hold them. They just sit in your grasp and try to swim off. There you guessed it, pretty cool. The only problem is they curl up in nooks and crannies so when you're in a dark cave you don't want to touch anything you can't see; you might find a not so cool surprise. After the snakes, we swam behind the reef through a channel and found more caves, tunnels, and chasms. These caves all had lobsters in them. The rules don't allow you to catch them while scuba diving though.

Our last dive was unexplored territory. Kevin just said, "Go see what's out there." We found tunnels, chasms, and lots of surge and huge schools of parrotfish. Mark had a medical problem in the morning that turned out to be nothing serious, but missed my discovery of a tunnel that led into a fresh water cave. The water gets all blurry so you know its fresh water mixing with salt water. We surfaced in the cave and it was freaky. The surge sucked us in and out of most places so timing was important if you wanted to move without a lot of effort and keep from slamming into coral and rocks. Once we surfaced, Kevin wanted to know everything we saw and where it was…oh pretty good! Mark really missed out on our last dive. However, on that last dive there was a cute Japanese girl with some Aussies that were all staying at the resort. Todd and I were doing our thing, so we didn't spend any time with them down under, but Mark met the girl later that night and they hit it off well. He doesn't speak Japanese and she doesn't speak much English, but they found common ground in the universal language of love. After going to Tonga, Mark took a little trip to Tokyo. Mom and Dad e-mailed us with the news from his post card. Amazing how things like that happen when you're traveling.

I know if you don't dive you may not really care, but it was like a dream. Cool island, good friends, and just the best time. We received a message that Leslie's sister Marjorie needed to have surgery and she wanted her mother to be with her. Our time was cut short and we headed for Tonga so Pat could catch a plane out. It was hard to say goodbye to everyone, but we knew we'd see them soon enough. I can't wait to get back to Niue some day.

THE KINGDOM OF TONGA (9.22.98)

The sail to Tonga was uneventful except for our whale watching. We put the mizzen on the main mast and that worked like a triple reefed main, but moved us along despite the small canvas area. Several humped back whales greeted us upon our arrival at the Vava'u Island group on the northern edge of the Kingdom of Tonga, the last kingdom in the world. It's beautiful. It reminds me of a tropical San Juan Island group in Washington State, tons of islands and 60 or 70 anchorages. We head into the main town of Neiafu to check in and Pat needs to leave the next day for her Seattle flight. We have crossed a distorted international dateline that juts out to the east some because Tonga wanted to be on the same time zone as New Zealand. I think they may have planned well ahead to be the first country to celebrate the start of the 21st century. New Zealand people are claiming that Tonga really isn't first since the date line is moved for them. New Zealand would then be first since they're actually the first country in the eastern hemisphere past the 180°, international dateline. You can tell I'm really getting into this world politics thing. Stuff like this is really important.

So we have one of our biggest mishaps at the rickety old steel and dirt check-in wharf. The wind was blowing briskly and some other boats tied there didn't leave much room. We end up coming in at a bad angle too fast, smack the corner of the wharf with one of our rub rails, and chewed it all up. We are all in shock wondering how we could have done such a poor job. I think it hurt our ego's a little bit too since we all think after all this time we have our routine down much better. So let's just say it was some freak accident and certainly would never happen again. We checked in and hit the bank then tied up to a mooring. Our mooring in the bay looked up at the small town with a beautiful church dominating the skyline. That night we just chilled and talked to some of our friends who were already there.

The next day Pat headed for the airport so she could get home for Marjorie's major surgery. We were sad to see her go and sent our prayers with her. We thought a lot about Marjorie and hoped everything would work out for the best and she would have a smooth operation and a speedy recovery.

Pat's departure left Les and me with the task of doing all the grocery shopping and cooking. No easy task, shopping in such a small place like this. You need to go to at least five different places to get what you're looking for, depending on if they have it or not and if they want to sell it to you. Lots of old wilted vegetables, mystery meat, and canned goods.

Our best buddies were only two days behind us out of Niue so they arrived shortly and the fun began. Les and I did some serious kicking in Tonga. Jim from *Go West* fortieth birthday party started things off at an anchorage just out and around the corner of the bay.

We befriended the crew of the 100 foot charter boat *Markson*, and did some surfboard skittering and water-skiing behind their large 70 horsepower dink. Later Les and I hooked up with Dan off *Oasis* who had a real wakeboard for more glassy water nights of fun. Les was up on her first try and all that snowboarding has made her a natural wake boarder. She rips it up with a smile on her face. I wasn't used to having so much power at my fingertips and once while driving for Dan he went down and I whipped a sharp turn to pick him up and just flung myself clear out of the dink so fast you couldn't believe it. Les was shocked and I was just a little embarrassed. Good thing I was wearing the wrist kill switch. It was so fun and we played like this several nights, such a rush flying around the corners at top speed and dragging the dink all over the place.

We were staying in the harbor a couple of weeks to have semi easy communication with Pat. We were happy to hear the surgery went well and Marjorie was doing well. Les and I took off with Kristin and Nikki off *Hio Avae*, with the additional crew of Gunner and Cary. *Mangoe* came out as well and we planned some diving, cave exploration, anchorage hopping and a Tongan feast.

The first day we went to a small rock island and anchored off it to go diving. There was a small cave to explore. The surge was so bad that when Mark and I surfaced inside, the surge came up spewing white water and threw us up onto the rock ledge inside. I immediately went down thinking to get out of there. When Mark tried to follow, he forgot about taking his mask off and regulator out of his mouth, pretty funny when you think about it. After the cave, we headed over to Nitrogen Narcosis Valley and hit about a 160 feet, checking out coral and the likes, no narcosis though.

We pulled anchor after our dive and headed to another anchorage where a Tongan feast was to be served. We were going to be late so we anchored in another spot and planned to hike across land to have *Markson* pick us up in their big dink. *Mangoe* tried to take a short cut, but it was low tide and ended up going aground, so they pulled out. All of us were sort of stranded, but Markson" saves the day and comes to pick us up. Then we pick up the guys on *Mangoe*, this is where things get interesting — mini drama anyways; stick with me if you can. Dave on *Markson* likes Kristin. He picked us up because of this and was expecting to see Nikki, Les and I, not Gunner and Cary. So he's thinking, what's up with these two guys and am I missing something? Then since *Mangoe* is on the way, we ask if we can pick up the three of them? Yea sure, he said. So now, there are 12 of us in the dink and the chop is up. We travel quite a ways and the Captain of *Markson* sees his dink go by with all those people. After dropping us off, the *Markson* crew gets yelled at. The feast doesn't start for a while and we actually had plenty of time to sail around.

There are crafts, ladies selling goods and I swear Mark bought everything. He had to leave in a few days so he just cleaned them out. The feast finally gets served and it's dark. No real lights just pop cans burning with kerosene and coral. We sit on mats on the ground and eat off palm trays with no utensils or napkins. Some Germans are sitting across from us and eating off our tray. They weren't too sharing and hogged all the good stuff. It's so dark you can't see what you're eating. At one point one of the guys ended up gnawing on a hoof. We totally don't get enough to eat and it's so crowded you can't even sit comfortably. I'd eaten more at cocktail parties — not much of a "feast" for $20 a person. Moreover, we were stranded quite far from the boats and *Markson's* captain is so pissed that we over crowded the dink he won't talk to us. Dave is talking about how he planned on us guys staying on the luxury yacht *Markson*, but now that's not possible. So here we are 9 of us stranded a good 30 to 45 minutes from our boats, it's dark and the winds up. I'm looking at the palm leaf mats wondering how comfy they'll be with no blanket. Finally, Talua, our Tongan buddy who works on *Markson* talks a Tongan into using a Mooring's Charter Company dink and taking us all back. We're the last people to leave the feast. In addition, Peter and Eileen on *Max Grody* will take the *Mangoe* crew to their boat that is much closer. It was a wet, hairy, dark ride. Very real threat of capsizing and we actually took a large wave over the bow that filled the boat and really soaked Cary. We were so happy to get back we all gave our driver 5 bucks each.

The next day the boats all had different agendas. They stayed and went to Swallows Cave. We left and went to Mariners Cave, named after Will Mariner. I'll save the history lesson. It's an underwater cave that surfaces into a large cavern that's above water level. It has two underwater entrances one at about 12 feet and another at about 50. Les and I were on scuba and Nikki and Kristin snorkeled in. Gunner stayed onboard because there is no place to anchor. Inside the cave, the cavern is about 20 wide and 15 feet tall. The sun shines through the underwater opening and gives light. The surge makes the pressure inside crazy so your ears are freaking out, plus there is a crazy mist. It's awesome. Les and I finished our dive by going through the lower entrance/exit and hit the outside wall.

That night we went to another anchorage and hung out. The next day we headed back to Neiafu. Gunner had to leave for Fiji and Nikki and Mark were flying back to the states in a day or two. So many things happened in these couple of days of crazy mishaps and adventures we decided if we opened up our own tour group, we'd call it Surprise Adventures. Our motto would be Starvation, Dehydration, and Strandation.

Mark and Nikki's departure had us pretty bummed out. Losing two such cool people was going to be lame. Plus, with Nikki gone Kristen would be single-handed. The morning of their flight, we fellas sat on *Mangoe* and sipped tequila and rum talking about how much fun the last couple of weeks have been. I rubbed it into Mark about our upcoming wreak dive hoping he would stay longer, but he had already extended his stay by several weeks. We miss those two, but life did go on.

In the harbor, there was also a sunken copra ship that had caught fire at the wharf. The captain took her out to the middle of the bay to sink. Rumor has it he and the first mate went down with the ship. I find this hard to believe though because it's so close to shore. We made a plan to dive it with the *Max Grody* crew. It was sunk in 80 to 120 feet of water. We started at the stern and worked our way up along the decks and sometimes through some of the various cabins. The visibility was closer to Puget Sound and not at all what we had been used to. We saw lots of huge clams, sediment to kick up, coral, fish, and other plant growth. I kept expecting to see one of those huge sharks in one of the dark cabins like in the movies, but no luck. The 460 foot ship sank in 1917 and was rumored to be made by the same company that made the *Titanic*. The bow was the coolest part of the wreck. Since the ship was resting on its keel, the deck was level. It did look like the *Titanic* and the plant and coral growth gave it a surreal look. Maybe like something from outer space. After the dive, we all agreed it was like being in an IMAX® movie. Les and I would do it again on our own.

The next weeks were spent hanging out, going to the nightclub, and staying out late. We spent so much money our first week that we were taking things pretty easy so we just went out to visit and be out. We had a local cruiser, Andy and Sandy on *Jacaranda* repair the main sail; I borrowed some knot books and tied knots for a week. Then I read a book on how to get your captains license.

Kristin sailed with *Markson* back to Niue and then to Beverage Reef with a charter group of scuba guys and photographers. We were a little jealous since we didn't stop at Beverage Reef a reef in the middle of nowhere. The reef is full of fish that don't know what people are. Plus, Niue is so cool and she'll get to hang with our Seabee buddies. She did bring me back a sea snake T-shirt that I couldn't find so I was pretty happy. Dave blew the moves, got no action, so he became cranky. The drama continues. When Kristin came back, her birthday was only days away, as was Stephanie's off *Mangoe* — 29 and 30 years respectively. We planned a big party at Club Hunga, anchorage #13 on Moorings Charter chart of Tonga. Dick, Les, and I hit some anchorages on our way out there, all beautiful, peaceful, and great snorkeling. We also went to Swallows' Cave. This cave is big enough to drive your dink into and then climb into another section with a huge, dry cavern with a skylight. The hole in the roof was about 45 feet above our heads with the sun shining in — total caveman hangout. I guess places like this gives Disneyland their ideas — so cool. Les and I snorkeled inside the cave, which was pretty big. There was millions and millions of tiny silver fish swimming in a huge school. You could swim through the middle of them and be surrounded 360 degrees with a wall of silver sparkles. I swam deep underneath and couldn't see Leslie at the surface through them. There was so many seeking refuge in this nice calm cave with the sun shining in — I would live in that cave it was so cool.

Once we hit Club Hunga there was only us and two other boats. By the end of the day there were over 20 — party time. First, we all went snorkeling outside the narrow pass that leads into the ancient volcano harbor. The current through the pass was swift with lots of coral and colorful fish. The highlight was a school of squid that looked like alien spaceships. Then we all hung out together and funked out on *Bosinova*, a super nice catamaran. Then we all went to the club for potluck with music, good food and everyone having a blast. We spent the time talking and dancing and some of us were actually up until 4 a.m. — some B-party. I had made some gifts for the girls out of coconut shells. A ladle and a hanging bowl with the "30" made from beach glass. It's so nice to celebrate their special days with them.

The next day we did absolutely nothing, but chill and talk. The day after that we snorkeled more. Then we had to leave to start our journey south to Nuku'alofa the main island on Tonga. On our way, we would stop at several amazing islands.

It's an overnight trip so we left at dusk making it out the narrow pass before dark. Once out and on our way we saw *Salacia* with Mike and Julie on board. We were all going to the same island, Foa, so we kept in touch throughout the night. The entrance was a little tricky going through the narrow pass surrounded by reef with bommies in the middle.

The beach was golden sand and looked fabulous. Les and I snorkeled along the reef, which had many overhangs and channels. That night and the next morning, some weather blew through. Then the sun came out and all was calm. Les and I hit the beach and talked with Mike and Julie looking for shells. That night they came over for happy hour. Our semi first since Pat had left. Les and I had people over, but usually only when Dick was out on the town.

The next day we headed further south and would see many wonderful places and anchorages. We would bump against the bottom, anchor with 24 hour anchor watch in an area surrounded by exposed reef. We had to weave our way through bommies in shallow water, eat lobster, and hang with traveling friends we had met at the feast that wasn't a feast. We would drag anchor with reef all around us, stop at an uninhabited island and best of all catch the largest fish of our lives.

The first time we had a Wahoo on the line it got away. This was only a day after our yellow fin tuna so no biggie. The problem was we had on a catch and release hook and the fish was so big (54 inches at least), it wouldn't fit in the net. We don't have a gaff so what's a fella to do? Well, when this baby hopped on the line we weren't making the same mistake. I still had the same hook on and hadn't changed it because of sheer laziness. Besides, I like the challenge. So since I had this monster up to the boat and saw he was as big as the last guy. I decided to heave ho and pull him up about 8 feet to the deck. Les had instructions to jump on him once he hit the deck. Surprisingly, this worked and he slammed on the deck and didn't move, saving Les from having to throw some moves on him.

I decided to just lash him down and do the filleting and all that once we anchored. I had to use a hacksaw to get his head off. We had tons of fish, beautiful thick white meat. The guts and head all went into the water and I figured some sharks would be around pretty soon. Sure enough in about an hour, Dick spotted some fins. I jumped in, but didn't ever end up seeing anything. The water was somewhat hazy and that started me to freak out. I don't like not having good visibility any more — spoiled rotten. Besides, just getting in the water anymore is somewhat freaky. We've seen so many sharks, but to jump in the water and put on a mask can be too time consuming. I want to see quickly what may be making a move on me, plus you're always checking your back. They just come out of nowhere.

We ate fish for days because we didn't really have anyone to share it with. We ate it raw, barbequed it with lemon, butter and garlic; marinated it and made sun dried jerky — that was the super grub. We were all just sad Pat missed these island groups of Hapi and Nomuka plus all this fresh fish. It was some of the most beautiful scenery we had seen yet.

We leapfrogged our way down to Nuku'alofa racing from Kalelfesi Island to Nuku'alofa with *Annapurna* and *Aquabi* in the 1998 Race for Space. There may not have been enough room for all of us to tie up at the quay. We were a respectable second until *Aquabi* said, "Don't cut the last buoy," then he wheezed in front of us. He has a fast, custom designed, steel sloop. Later at the bar, he couldn't wait to ask us if we had our engine on. Of course we did. There was plenty of room so no big deal. Nuku'alofa was the biggest city we've been in since Papeete and it was nice to find markets, grocery stores an Internet café and all the trimmings. All our buddies ended up here waiting to make that final jump to New Zealand. We pot-lucked, went to the movies and saw Armageddon and the Big Hit. We watched movies on each other's boats and just had a nice time getting mentally ready for our final leap. Pat returned with lots of boat parts and good news about Marjorie. All the other boater woman thought Pat was crazy for coming back to this leg of the trip. I would tell them, "she's not crazy, she's hardcore."

We worked a deal with the local bar "The Bullfish" and had a costume party on Halloween. Everyone dressed up and we had a blast. Leslie was Pocahontas and I was the South Pacific Avenger. Amazing what you can do with a cape.

Everyone took off a few days before us and headed for Minerva Reef. We were held up checking out and a broken down boat was blocking the fuel dock. The day before we left, we ended up jerry jugging 185 gallons of fuel. That night I dropped our favorite bucket overboard and just couldn't leave without it. I went after it with snorkel gear and my light and couldn't see a thing the bottom was so silted. Finally, I found it using Braille and it kind of made my day. It's the little things.

The next day we headed out to no wind and glassy flat seas. We motored all day long. The next day we had some decent wind and had all the sails up. The day after that, things began to deteriorate. That's when we realized we were not going to Minerva Reef to wait out the weather with all our friends and see what was coming our way. Everyone had been paying close attention to the weather with projected reports and multiple day updates. A big low was coming in and was going to do some damage. Our option at this point was to sail on through and hope for the best. That night I woke for my trick at the helm to 360° sheet lightning. We had a close call with this sort of thing before so we turned off all power including the auto helm and I hand steered through my shift. The lightning was so close sometimes I could see the bolts shrieking across the sky and down to the water. I was sure I was going to be electrocuted. The wind had picked up earlier and we had dropped all sails and double reefed the main. I made my peace with God that night and hoped I was covered for the rest of the passage. The lightning didn't stop until 6:30 a.m. I hope everyone else made his or her peace too.

Everyday just got worse. The wind howled, the seas were black with white froth and the weather reports kept getting more and more depressing. This went on for 4 or 5 days. We had news of boats that had been knocked down, storm anchors out and the weather still getting worse. To top this off we're hearing about the lobster feast everyone at Minerva is having. The wind would hold steady at 40 knots with gusts well into the fifties; the seas just kept getting larger every day. We were on a port tack and had the toe rail in the water more often than not, sometimes the lifelines. The heel angle was so high for the clinometer; aka, heel-a-monster, to read, even though it goes up to 45 degrees. I was constantly afraid of a knock down. You heard a lot of "hold on" and "oh my god." I always thought the next wave was going to be the one.

Everyone was tired; it was hard to sleep even though you were exhausted because of the thrashing of the boat in the waves. Cooking was almost impossible and boiling water was a challenge until even that proved too hard. Stand up to take a pee? Forget about it. It was like mortal combat. A battle I usually got the worst of, finally I got smart. None of us showered for the entire crossing of 11 days.

We found all the hatches leaked, our cabin dorade vent leaked and with the rail in the water, we constantly took water through the companionway doors. Did I mention it was hard to sleep? Wet carpets? How about a wet bed? If you were Spiderman and could sleep on the wall, you would have been fine. The bilge kept filling with water and pushed up the floorboards pinching the hose from our 5,000 gallon an hour bilge pump. Dick also had to unclog the bilge pumps twice. The fresh water pump quit working and the hand pump quit working. We had only 5 gallons of jug water the last 3 days — it was almost impossible to pour. It was good water though from Niue.

So it pretty much sucked. I think everyone prayed a lot and everyone made the best of things. At one point, our ham contact told us to slow down and the low would pass in front of us. Well then, a super big high moved in and stalled the low adding time to our agony. So here, we are caught in between a 1,033 high and a 992 low (we're talking millibars here). That's known as a squash zone — Ooooh pretty good.

So we had a storm jib up and nothing, else still doing 5 to 9 knots. A storm jib is about the size of a fat boys pair of Levi's®. Not a lot of canvas. Wave height was 12 to18 feet. Slamming us as we had all the wind forward of the beam and were close hauled most of the way. The current was blowing us so far west I was starting to wonder if we were ever going to see New Zealand or just head for Australia. Yes, our friends are still hanging at Minerva Reef.

Well after many days of high wind, lightning, rain, sloppy huge waves, poor visibility, general discomfort and fear, things started to let up. Someone on the radio asked how we liked our gift. What gift? Then Dick remembered the tapa cloth Kristin had given to him to give to us at our half waypoint, better late than never. It was a tapa Leslie and Kristin unbeknownst to either until later had both seen in Niue and liked. Kristin bought it for us on her last trip back there — special.

We did have one casualty; a wave jumped into the cockpit and grabbed one of Leslie's Tevas (flip-flops). It tottered on the toe rail daring her to come and get it, tough decision. Before she had a chance to react, Poseidon claimed it as his own. Have you ever noticed when you're walking on the beach you usually see a number of single shoes? Well it's by my experience that at home I always count more left shoes than right ones. That's in the northern hemisphere. My logic tells me there must be more right shoes in the southern hemisphere, since that's how things tend to work. My guess is since it was her left shoe it's coming your way so be on the lookout.

The last two days of sailing was great. All sails were now up, reefs shook out and trying to bust a move to beat the next crappy weather coming in. Pat was even able to make some great eggs and we saw some sun. So, to sum it up: 2 days to start — a good 7 days of crap — a bad 2 days to the end — good. Not good odds if you're a betting man. Our friends at Minerva had to move fast to beat the next system. Some made it fine and others had no wind and had to motor a lot.

AUCKLAND, NEW ZEALAND (11.11.98)

We sailed into Auckland at about 6 p.m. and were surprised by all the traffic. We sailed right through a racecourse on our way to the Admiralty Steps to see the Customs and Immigration fellas — nice guys no problem. We headed to Westhaven Marina and tied up at the guest dock because we didn't know which slip was reserved for us — real happy to be here. The next day the wind was blowing like crazy. It was so bad and our slip was so tight we couldn't move. Well we all headed to a nice hotel instead. The hotel had the best hot showers, warm baths, room service, and TV. We brought along a bottle of Dom Pérignon that we had been saving. A fat dry bed and all the comforts we so desperately needed.

We moved into our slip that day and found out we can only live aboard for three months, then the boat can stay, we can't. They're not too friendly to live aboards — lots of money here. We have met some great people who have been taking care of us with a loaner car and lots of good info. The "America's Cup" trophy is about 200 yards away at the Royal New Zealand Yacht Club.

Well, at long last we're at a major port city with plans to stick around here for a while. It feels great to know we're to be someplace for an extended period of time. We should have reliable access to communication systems, grocery stores, shopping centers, and just good ole city traffic. I think we're all looking forward to the change of pace, but no doubt will be missing the South Pacific in no time. The weather change from the tropics to Auckland has been a little nippy. We've spent several days cleaning up the boat, which was filthy and wet and pretty much a disaster. We're still working on it two weeks later.

The city is great and it feels good to be alive. We've been making our way around town and have bought two cars. Leslie and I have a blue bomber Toyota Liteace Van. Dick and Pat have a Toyota Corona. Les's and my van is pretty worked, but it should get us around, into the mountains, and away from this boat for a while. I'm really looking forward to doing some land traveling and getting up north to where all our friends' boats are. The people are all so friendly I can't believe it. I really like this place. When we arrived, we imported the boat for 18 months. They're allowing us to do this for the America's Cup. What our actual plans are we don't have a clue. I think things are up in the air for all of us for the long term. Right now, I'm just ready to get off this boat for some fresh mountain air and see some of this wonderful country. Zach will be down on Christmas day and my parents will arrive at end of Jan. I hope to have things pretty well dialed in by then.

The weather since we've gotten here reminds us all of Seattle. Spells rain doesn't it? The last week has been rainy with extremely high winds. Eighty plus knots an hour or something like that. Some of the posse really had to hurry to beat the storm in. Some didn't make it. Most everyone we know is safe with the exception of two. One boat, *Freya*, ended up caught in the worst of it and rolled several times. They thought it might have been as many as 7 times, but who's counting after the first few rollovers. Their hatches were ripped off and they were taking on water. A New Zealand search and rescue helicopter luckily rescued them after being in waist deep water. Rescued were, mom, dad, and their 13-year-old son.

Our friends on *Salacia*, who left with us in Nuku'alofa and hung out with the Minerva yacht club group, just didn't sail fast enough. They left the day after the rest of the reef group and were caught in the same storm as *Freya*. They were in radio contact with *Freya* that is until their first knock down took their VHF antenna and tri-light navigation lights. This knockdown also speared their prop into the rudder and they had no helm. They were also hove-to with a sea anchor out and the knockdown shredded the sea anchor. Nothing was left, but the shackle and some bits of fabric. *Freya*, we believed was on their way to try to tow *Salacia* before their dire problems and air evacuation.

We heard about two boats in distress and about *Freya* being rescued. We were going crazy to know who the other boat was. At a dinner party at the local home of Andy and Cathy Knowles, we get the bad news. *Salacia*! Are they okay? "The woman didn't make it." I was floored. Les was listening to Cathy's two young children talk about their toys when I told her. She felt sick. I just wanted to cry. How could this be? We just left them two and a half weeks ago. It was hard to talk to little kids and be guests at some nice people's house after this devastating news. Where is Mike?

We learned he had come in on the freighter that had sunk his boat. It was in Auckland, but it was leaving at 7 a.m. and Mike had to be off. Leslie called the American Embassy and found him. We went to pick him up and brought him to our boat. The news people are looking for him; he gave a statement to the maritime board, the police, and others. He had been busy answering questions and piecing together the sequence of events. He lost all his belongings, his boat and his best friend. I can't imagine how that could feel. He had no insurance.

Julie and he had met on Moorea. She was visiting with girl friends, recently laid off with a severance package. She met Mike, they hit it off, and she decided to sail the world with him. She flew home to California, shut down her life, turned down a great job offer in Seattle, and headed back to Moorea. She was going to begin a new adventure. She was outgoing, cute, funny and a pleasure to be around. You couldn't help to fall in love with her. We all thought she was so brave to take off like that. Her father though wasn't speaking to her.

Salacia had seen a search and rescue plane monitoring them. They had earlier made a distress call, but not a MAYDAY call. All shipping traffic in the area was diverted in the direction of the two boats. Mike and Julie then had another knockdown that freed the rudder and they were able to sail under a storm jib. They had lost radio contact with *Freya* who was by this time through with their trouble and rescued.

Now the wind is blowing like a banshee, the seas are up to 30, maybe 40 feet. They're okay and resting down below and Mike gets a weird feeling. He steps on deck to be faced with 80 feet of black steel — a 600 foot freighter. The freighter is too close and *Salacia's* standing rigging scrapes along the side of its hull. Sparks are shooting everywhere as the boats skip against one another in pounding waves. The mast catches something and comes off snapping the stanchions and everything in its way. The freighter turns to make another pass. Apparently, it's there to rescue them even though they didn't need it until it slammed them and dismasted them.

Mike and Julie grab some belongings and wait to be rescued. It's dark with large sea and crazy wind. It's also 3 a.m. Mike and Julie get into the life ring that lands on deck and wait to be rescued. The freighter crew won't lift them up together. Mike leaves Julie in the ring ready to be pulled up to safety. She's panicking, but should be safe enough. He tries for another life ring that is on the bow. The boats are pulling farther apart. On the way up the 80 feet, the pitching and rolling is swinging him out over the waves and then bringing him crashing back into the cold steel hull. At the top, they have no way of pulling him over the edge. He falls. Another ring is thrown 50 to 60 feet away. Swimming with wool pants, knapsack and foul weather coat on, he finally makes it through the rough cold waves to the life ring. Another trip up, Mike uses all his strength just to hang on.

Mike had been with us several days now and is trying to get a grip and figure out his next move. He's a professional photographer and all his gear is gone. It's so sad to hear him talk about things on his boat, Julie, what they were going to do and what they had done. It breaks my heart and brings tears to my eyes just to think about it. She was so cool.

There will be some sort of investigation. Why did the freighter do what it did at 3 a.m. when *Salacia* was making way just fine? People here are pretty upset about this. It has happened before. Untrained rescue personnel carrying out night rescues at a moment's notice. It's too early to tell what will happen. Today is the first day Mike didn't have to talk to anybody so we just chilled, went to a bookstore, had Turkish coffee at a café and had a great dinner. Here I am trying to finish this and not cry. That could have been anyone of us out there. I suppose that's the chance you take.

Several other boats also had problems. Other people have died. Boats have broken away from their moorings and washed ashore. In one area of Auckland, this happened to about 35 boats. This had been the worst storm down here since the Queen's Day Storm. It's raining now.

There is so much we have left out about food, church and the native people we met along the way. Native customs and culture and all that is important, but I focused our story mostly on our experiences and what we did.

The sun finally struck his/her head out today so the carpets are happy from the hand scrubbing and sun tanning I've been letting them enjoy. Mike has gone up north to find the *Freya* folks and talk to them about the sequence of events. They are planning to fly back to Bellingham, Washington in a few days. Mike has some lawyers to talk to and the pilot of the plane that spotted them. After we sightsee around the south island, Les and I will be going back to Seattle. We expect life in the big city will be hard on us. All our friends are buying homes and starting their families, so we have to make our way back into the grind of everyday living and back into society.

BOB, LESLIE AND FAMILY TODAY

Bob and Leslie have now integrated themselves back into American society and added Mitchell and Mia to their family along with two cats, Coal and Trixie and a golden retriever, Max. They all live in a nice craftsman type home in the Seattle suburb of West Seattle. Bob is enjoying his work in service to others as a firefighter in Pierce County, WA and Leslie is doing well in a marketing firm, Catalyst Marketing.

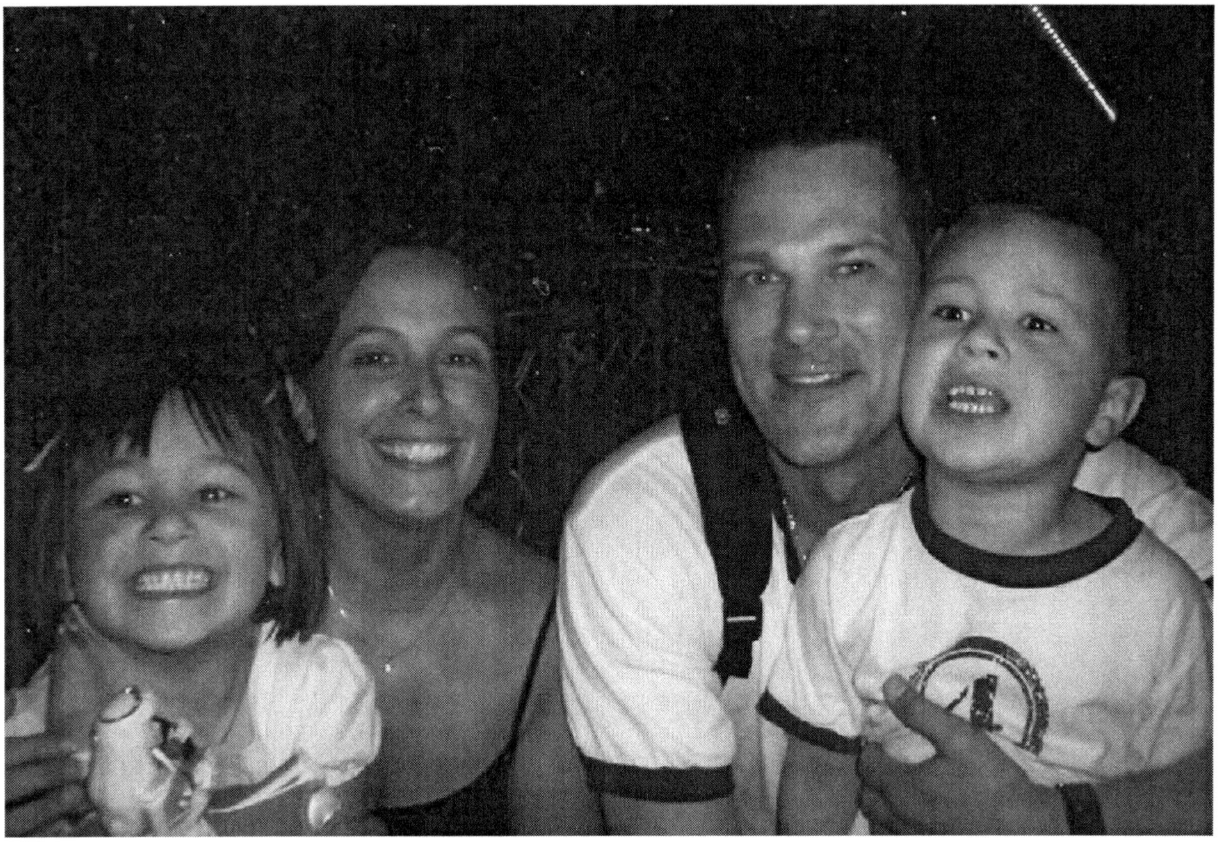

THE FISCHER FAMILY, MIA (3) LESLIE, BOB AND MITCHELL (4)

Chapter 11

OUR TRIPS TO SEATTLE, BUFFALO AND FLORIDA

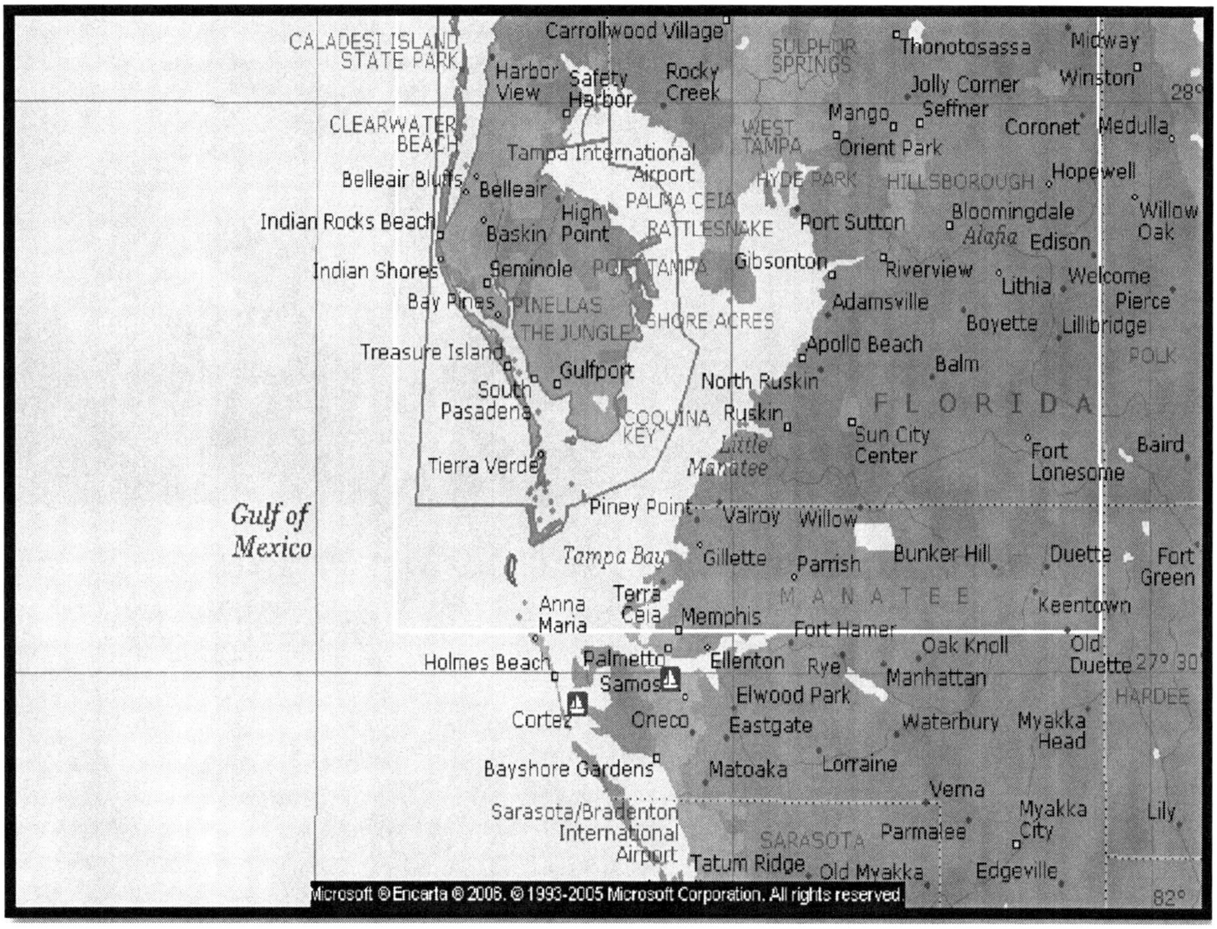

VISIT TO CORTEZ, ON FLORIDA'S WEST COAST AND THE GULF OF MEXICO

The first time we left New Zealand for the states it was mid-Mar. 1999. The idea was to file our federal taxes, spend time in Seattle, and visit my sister in Florida. Pat and I enjoyed our time back in the states visiting with both family and friends. Our family in Seattle seems to get along fine without us so we took a side trip to Florida. Whenever we go to Florida, it seems we usually spend part of the time looking for a more permanent place to hang out. We have been close to buying there a few times, but could never find a place we both could agree on — mostly Pat's fault of course. My sister, Barbara, has always insisted that if we bought a home there it had better be near her and her husband Jack. She is family oriented and would like our family to live closer together. This time, with the least time of any previous vacation, we bought a new condominium just starting construction. It is only a short block from her condo so we were all delighted. It has three bedrooms, about 2,200 square feet and comes complete with a 40 foot dock right in front. The slip is 23 feet too short for ***Our Pleasure***, but that's okay, as we don't know what we are going to do with the condo for several years anyway.

The location is on a nice canal that connects with the intercostals waterway and raising one drawbridge will connect us to the Gulf of Mexico. The postal address is Cortez, Florida. Cortez is a village on the mainland side of the intercostals waterway across from the barrier islands of Bradenton Beach, Holmes Beach, and Anna Maria. Sarasota is about 15 miles to the south. If we ever move in, family and friends will have a place to visit in the winter, spring or fall when the weather is usually warm and sunny and the humidity is in a comfortable range.

We picked out tiles, cabinets, carpeting, fixtures, and counter tops; and made many interior design changes. The time in Florida flew-by as most of the decorating shops were in Sarasota and we only gave ourselves ten days to put everything together. We probably could not have put it altogether without Barbara's help as she has a near perfect eye for color and knows the right places to shop. The construction was moving rather slowly and they moved up the completion date out to mid-Feb. 2000 from Thanksgiving 1999.

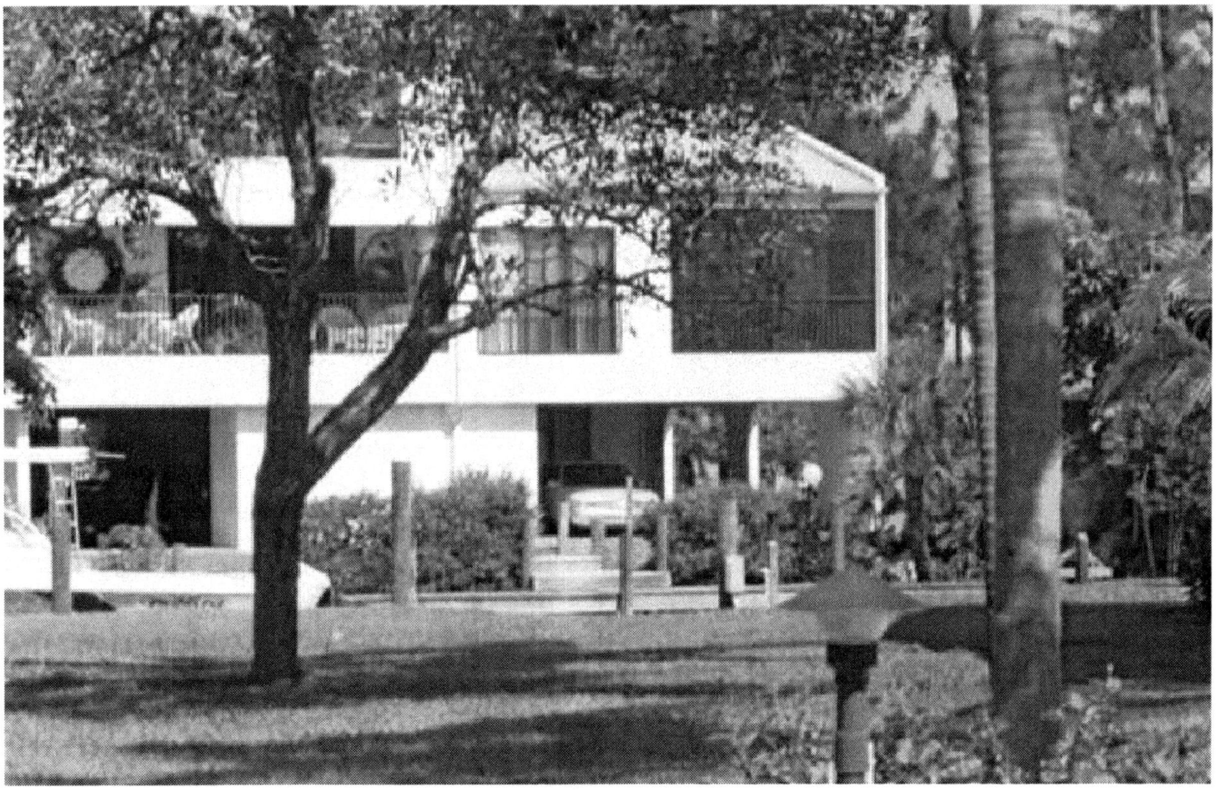

NEW CONDO AT SMUGGLER'S LANDING, GULF SIDE, CORTEZ, FLORIDA

We were rather tired upon arrival since the plane trip to NZ from Florida with a stopover in Seattle, took two full days. The NZ arrival time was a sleep deprived five o'clock in the morning. We waited at the airport for another hour before taking a taxi to Cathy Knowles's house. We left our car at their house, but did not want to disturb them so early in the morning. Pat picked up a bug on the plane, which took a couple of weeks to get over. The fridge on the boat was on the blink, but after fixing a leaky connector and adding new Freon, it ran better than new.

I checked-in with my young, talented, NZ GP doctor for the results of my physical and lab tests taken before we left for the states. The test results were good, but the amazing thing is the two doctor visits, blood samples and lab fees amounted to a total unheard of cost of $24 — I was loving New Zealand!

We volunteered to watch Cathy and Andy's two boys, Ben 6 and Chris 7, in their Ponsonby home. We are fond of this couple as they went out of their way so often with all sorts of help while we were in NZ. Cathy went to London for her extremely serious brain surgery to remove a tumor near her optic nerve. Cathy is only 43 and her husband, Andy, who was about the same age, stayed with her in England. Everyone was concerned and worried about the operation scheduled for Jun. 9 1999.

We watched Ben and Chris for 7 days and lest we forget, please remind us never to do that again. For us, they were completely undisciplined, refused to do anything we asked, fought with each other and fussed (as you cannot imagine) about everything. They do not even like the same foods except for chicken, so almost everything had to be prepared separately — Pat was a bit frustrated. The first day of school the oldest boy, Chris, refused to go to school. I took Ben to school and told the principal about Chris's refusal. She was quite firm that he would not stay home and was being "very naughty."

She drove me back to their house so she could bring him back to school. During the drive she injected a thought that the boy's poor behavior was probably tied to their mother's pending brain operation. Well, their mansion is large with rooms and hiding places everywhere. When we got back, he had hidden himself somewhere in the vast recesses of the house so well we could not find him. We looked everywhere for thirty minutes and could not find him. The principal was calm about the whole thing and said he would eventually come out and when he did to call her and she would come to "fetch him." He came out from somewhere upstairs about 10 a.m. He looked quite proud of himself and I wanted to wring his neck. We took him to school after lunch and the principal gave him a good lecture. He went to school the rest of the week without any pain or suffering on our part and so it went. We took them to the zoo, to McDonald's (food selection was perfect for them) and all over the place to keep them busy, but it did not improve the situation much. Well, now granny and gramps (both in their seventies) are taking their turn and we wished them luck, but were afraid to call to see how things were doing.

Before we left granny and gramps with Ben and Chris, they invited us to use their bed and breakfast facilities near Katikati, NZ. Katikati is close to the Pacific Ocean on the eastern side of NZ's north island. The drive from Auckland is southeast about 170 kilometers (105 miles) over beautiful green rolling hills and farmlands. Captain Cook named this area as the Bay of Plenty because of the abundance of food and water he found there. Today it is mostly citrus and fruit crops with a few wineries thrown in. Anyway, granny and gramps, Trevor and Thora Jones, (their son Murray Jones was the tactician on the NZ America's cup defender that year) have retired to a beautiful home, high on a hill looking out toward the Pacific Ocean. Their B&B is actually (what New Zealanders call a "flat") — a complete small home — attached to the main house with the same spectacular views. Their 2 acres used to be part of a dairy farm, but they landscaped the fertile property with flowers of bright colors, neatly mowed lawns, and green stuff found in Seattle like rhododendrons and magnolia trees. They also have about 100 fruit trees including limes, lemons, mandarin oranges, kiwi, bananas, and six varieties of apples. The down side was, last weekend was a three day holiday, the Queen's Birthday. The roads were crowded and granny and gramps decided it would be a good weekend for Ben and Chris to visit. Actually, the boys were well behaved and only popped in on Monday morning when we were getting ready to leave.

Katikati is a well laid out, nice small town. Artists colorfully painted scenes on the sides of buildings depicting the town's early history. They borrowed this idea from a town in British Columbia that we had sailed to on many vacations, Chamanis, British Columbia, Canada. We were also surprised to hear that they had people from 32 different cultures living in this small town. In our travels near Katikati, we found a great white sand beach and hot springs' spa at Mount Maunganui. This mountain (actually a high hill) borders the Pacific Ocean, is about 600 feet high and has been transformed into a nice resort and hiking area. Natural hot springs seemed to be all over NZ and some farms even have their own natural private spas. The spas at Mount Maunganui have several pools at different temperatures with separate pools for children and adults. Pat and I rented a private spa that could hold about six people for NZ $3.50 per person per half hour — quite a bargain.

The winters on the North Island are fairly mild with nighttime lows around 57° to 60° F and day times close to 70° F. Throw in a little wind once in a while, a slight shower every few days and the weather is similar to Seattle's spring time. I went to the boat show in Auckland and was quite surprised at all the quality small boats they build for fishing, especially in aluminum. Few NZ boats find their way to the states and that is too bad because their craftsmanship is outstanding. Since the U.S. dollar is so strong here, boats seem to be about half the price of U.S. boats. NZ is a great country for boating, as there is water everywhere and the fishing is still good. Everyone seems to own some kind of boat.

In late April, Bob Warner, yacht *Mariah*, and a NZ friend, Stew, helped me move ***Our Pleasure*** to Half Moon Bay to install a 10 horsepower bow thruster. During our 4 hour sail we had an opportunity to try reefing our newly installed main sail and Rife-Rite furling boom. The wind was blowing 31 knots on our starboard beam, too much wind for a full main. I was pleasantly surprised to see the sail roll itself into the boom without changing course. Wendy, Bob's wife, drove Bob and Stew back to Gulf Harbor and Pat and I stayed at Half Moon Bay until the bow thruster was installed. The yard crew did a fine job of installing all the mechanical/electrical hardware. They covered the thruster motor underneath a custom-made teak box that was like a piece of furniture. The total cost, including all hardware, was around $6,000, what a bargain compared to the $18,000 quote I received before leaving the U.S.

Bob and Leslie jumped ship in April and flew back to Seattle to put their lives back together in a more normal way. Leslie is working with her older sister Marjorie at a company called Waterways Cruises. They own three large cruisers, 85 ft to 135 ft for weddings, conferences, etc., and a water front building with commercial kitchens and large rooms for the same kinds of affairs on land. Leslie is one of their sales persons, gets to go out on the water quite often, likes her job, and is doing well. Bobby is back catering for Palisade's, an upscale Seattle restaurant he worked at before leaving Seattle. He was also taking exams for the Seattle Fire Department. He had been able to stay in the upper 20% of the tests so far, which I understand is quite difficult. They had over 2,500 applicants applying for a limited number of openings making competition fierce. Bob and Leslie found it hard to leave the cruising life and move back into American society. They are now doing those "normal" things like buying cars and looking for a house to buy, etc — how awful.

Pat had been receiving e-mail messages that her mother is not doing well. She had a lung infection that had adversely affected her breathing. Her lung capacity has diminished to a point where the doctors think they are working at only 30% capacity. She is now out of the hospital and was able to move back to her home. Pat's sister, Mona, has moved in with her to help with her daily care.

Pat got on a plane again and left NZ on Jun. 8 to fly to Buffalo, NY with a short stop in Seattle on the way. Pat planned to stay with her mother for about 3 weeks, as her mom was requiring constant care at her home. Pat let me know that her mother was suffering from a lung deficiency that kept the lungs from processing oxygen. They were at a point where they worked at about 70% below their normal capacity. Her doctor said the lung problem would not improve so her life expectancy was looking rather grim. She was on oxygen full time and needs help just moving a few steps — aging with medical problems is not a fun time.

Pat originally was going to have one of her knee joints replaced in Seattle, which had been giving her problems for a long time. She had been getting by with shots of a natural lubricating fluid that has worked for a couple of years. Her body rejected the last series of shots though so it was time for alternatives. But, while in Buffalo with her mother, she met with a surgeon/engineer who had perfected a low friction mechanical device he inserts between one of the knee joints. This is a day surgery procedure and a lot less intrusive in comparison to full knee replacement. Therefore, she scheduled that surgery instead of the knee replacement for late August in Buffalo. Following surgery, she stayed with her brother for several days of recuperation in Buffalo.

The Gulf Harbor Marina is about 16 miles north of Auckland right on the Hauraki Gulf. A little off the beaten path, which provides a quiet background for live aboards. A family runs the marina restaurant and lounge as a place for boaters to gather and tell stories. The father runs the lounge and the mother and their two grown daughters run the restaurant. After our first visit they knew our names and made us welcome. Their wonderful lattes came piping hot in a large bowl that could substitute for breakfast.

Well, it was quiet in Gulf Harbour and somewhat lonely without Pat and the two lovebirds around. I did get to work on boat projects at my own pace quite undisturbed. I rated Gulf Harbor Marina at a **10** on a scale of **1** to **10**, whereas Shilshole Bay Marina in Seattle was probably a **4** in comparison. The Gulf Harbour marina is maintained in new condition, nicely laid out and clean. The staff is super friendly; they express a genuine care about boat problems and respond to boat owners concerns. The staff knows us by our names and will often stop and chat. The management and security here, know they are running a marina and their customers come first. In Seattle, the marina visitors, strollers and sightseers came first and marina customers were endured by the staff. We moored boats at Shilshole for about 15 years and none of the staff knew who we were and were not friendly — The Port of Seattle, a King County entity, operates the marina.

For myself, I enjoyed the life of a bachelor in NZ: cooking with some of Pat's recipes, working on boat projects, going to movies and reading — not exciting, but restful. One of the better books I read was *The Memoirs of Cleopatra*. It came to us via daughter Marjorie and now I know how Marjorie's cat "Cleo" got her name. She is an awful cat, the worst, the real Cleopatra probably turned over in her grave. Margaret George wrote it in the first person after years of research. It is a fictional tale of Cleopatra's everyday life, thoughts, and feelings matched with as much accurate historical information as she could find. Since I never studied history from that period, I found the book stimulating and a revelation of a world and culture unknown to me. The Ancient World and the famous people of those times (Cleopatra died 20 BC) became more understandable. It depicts Cleopatra as intelligent, a women of surpassing beauty, multi-lingual, a charming voice and the power to subjugate everyone. An ancient historian Dio Cassius also echoes that appraisal. Some of her enemies were writers and poets the caliber of Cicero, Virgil and Horace. Their biased writings of that period became widely known and Cleopatra's life story became officially suppressed. So, according to George, much of what the general public knows about Cleopatra comes from the invectiveness of her enemies. The novel was a wonderful read, but digesting 1,000 pages of information, facts, and imaginative creation requires a lot of time. I have often thought it would be interesting to research a novel like that. Margaret George made hundreds of visits to many of the world's oldest libraries to find ancient manuscripts and references tying little bits of information together.

Meanwhile, Cathy got back to New Zealand on July 27, 1999 from England and was doing fine, but needed many hours of therapy. Because of the operation to remove the tumor, her right side motor functions were greatly impaired, but she was determined to get back to her normal self.

When Pat's surgery allowed her to fly, she flew to Seattle where I met her and helped her with the physical therapy part of the recuperation process. I caught up with Pat on Sept. 5 in Seattle and we stayed with our son David at his home while she recovered from her knee operation. David's house was in Monroe, Washington at that time and because it takes an hour and a half to drive into Seattle in traffic, we only made that trip a few times. We flew back together to NZ in early October.

I had to take Pat to a local NZ hospital to find out what was causing her leg to swell and why she was in so much pain after returning to NZ. I now know firsthand what their health care system is like. We first went to a local GP who thought she might have a blood clot, but did not have the right equipment to do an investigation. He arranged testing at a hospital about 45minutes from Auckland. When we arrived all the paper work, wrist tags, etc., were in place and a private room was waiting for Pat. Two nurses (both RNs) assigned to take care of Pat introduced themselves as did the woman doctor who was assigned to the case. I was quite impressed with their professionalism and their friendliness. They took a lot of time to talk to us, find out what was going on, what we were doing, were we were from and made us feel comfortable. They gave Pat pain medication through an IV and tested her oxygen level in the blood, etc., before they did an ultra sound on her leg. They spent 30 minutes doing the ultra sound on her leg — extremely thorough (the pain in her leg was in the area near the new knee joint implant). However, the hospital was overly busy and we ended up spending six hours there. Pat was offered two meals and of course tea, in between meal times. They were willing to feed me also, but I said "no" as everything looked overcooked as in our hospitals a few years ago — I hoped they were better now. The doctor was a junior doctor — not out of medical school very long.

Several teleconferences were set-up so Pat's doctor could confer with an orthopedic specialist in Auckland as our hospital was lacking in that skill. They found three problems: a small blood clot in between leg tissue, but not serious since it was not in a vein or artery; a Baker cyst behind her knee that had burst and some torn leg muscle. They said Pat could go home, but had to keep off her leg and should keep her leg higher than her hip joint for two weeks. This should allow the muscle to heal and the body will absorb the extra fluids. They asked me if I had medical insurance, which we did, but that is as far as it went, as we were not billed — amazing! These problems were apparently not a result of her knee surgery.

Three days later the GP doctor called to find out how things were going and to schedule an appointment to check on Pat's condition — good follow-through. We have to pay him for each visit, NZ $38 or about $20. Doctors, every government and private service wholesale or retail accepts a NZ bank issued credit card. We have only run into two businesses that required a NZ bank check or cash. Visa or Master cards can be used at most major businesses, but not minor restaurants, gas stations or the corner grocery.

Last Friday, the marina launch towed in Ferro cement, junk rigged schooner with engine problems. The owner, an 81-year old NZ doctor, failed on his second attempt to sail to Australia. Fierce winds blew him back to NZ on both attempts. He is quite a character and the NZ Herald wrote an article about him last weekend. He apparently is a well-known NZ adventurer. He told me he was waiting for additional "victims" that wanted to crew with him on his next attempt. He left on Wednesday morning aiming for Australia once more. I hope they are okay, as it has been blowing up to 50 knots since they left.

We went to the small Catholic Church in the town of Manly, NZ this morning, which is where we usually go for Sunday mass. Manly is near the Gulf Harbour Marina on the Whangaparaoa peninsula. The priest there is Irish, Father Manus Lyons. Our family has always had a particular fondness for Irish priests, as they all seem to have inherited many wonderful and loving qualities from their Irish culture. Well, this Sunday Father Manus shared his prayer for New Zealanders:

O God, so far today I've done all right.
I haven't gossiped, I haven't lost my temper.
I haven't been greedy, grumpy, nasty, selfish or over indulgent.
I am very thankful for that.
But in a few minutes I'm going to get out of bed.
And from then on, I'll need a lot more help.

After church, we went for a walk through Shakespear (English spelling of Shakespeare) Park. Shakespear is another beautiful NZ park near the end of the Whangaparaoa peninsula. From the viewpoint there, you can see all the way to Auckland in the south and the Great Barrier Island in the north — amazing view of one of God's gift to us; I had to sit down to regain my composure.

Pat and I stayed at Cathy's beach house until Pat was able to manage on-and-off the boat, etc. The house has some neat construction features, besides the water saving toilets that have two push buttons that allow selection of a half flush or full flush. All aluminum window frames, have a special channel to allow outside air to enter through a 1/2 by 12 inch screened, waterproof opening. The channel has a sliding plastic door to close it off when outside air is not wanted. The three bathrooms have skylights that allow inside air to vent out through a waterproof, screened opening in between the skylight and the roof. They ventilate the bathrooms without the need for exhaust fans, but they also allow outside air to enter the bathrooms at night, which can be quite cool. Also, the water control in the shower has a control knob that allows the user to dial in the water temperature, very cool.

No one had lived there since last fall and the place needed quite a cleaning. There were thousands of tiny, black, dead ants all over the place. We found the ants on the floors, carpeting, drapes, windowsills, bathtub and shower — quite a mess. The previous window cleaning must have used a chemical that encouraged mold growth because the windows were full of black mold and so were the window frames. All the bedding, dishes, glassware, pots and pans had to be washed. Since Pat was not supposed to stand on her leg, I pulled all the housemaid chores: cooking, cleaning, shopping, and washing. Almost everyone in NZ hangs their wash outside to dry because electricity is expensive. The clothes sure smell good in NZ's clean air, but the extra effort is time consuming.

Most homes are built on an acre of land and retired couples or non-working moms; spend many hours outside working in their gardens. The gardens all seem to have many varieties of flowers and large amounts of vegetables for their owner's consumption. The land and homes are what the New Zealanders refer to as "tidy" — neat and clean, everything is in place and they work hard at it. Once you get away from the city, most people spend a lot of time working outside on their property.

Cathy made it through a minor stroke and made a wonderful recovery. Physical therapy has greatly restored her leg and face muscles and some of her arm muscles. She was working super hard to get back into shape. The bad news was the doctors are concerned that the infection from her brain tumor operation may still be active — not good.

You probably have not heard of the New Zealand "All Blacks" Rugby Team. They were expecting to be rugby world champions that year (2000), but lost to France in an upset. They still had to beat Australia for the cup, but the whole country is already in mourning. The NZ people love rugby and go out of their way to support it; they were planning a ticker-tape style parade in Auckland with money from local businesses. Rugby games can always be found on NZ TV, but what a rough sport. It is strictly a game for young men in good physical condition and cannot be played for too many years. It is extremely physical, no padding, no protection to the reproductive parts of the anatomy and they take pride in inflicting pain on their opponents like gouging their eyes. Eye gouging is illegal, but happens under the shield of big body pile-ups when the referees cannot see inside the pile. It is an interesting game and for teams to excel, every member has to be an exceptional athlete.

The second round of the year 2000 America's Cup racing starts tomorrow, but since we are not on the boat, we can only follow it on TV. Italy at this point, was the only team that had not lost a race.

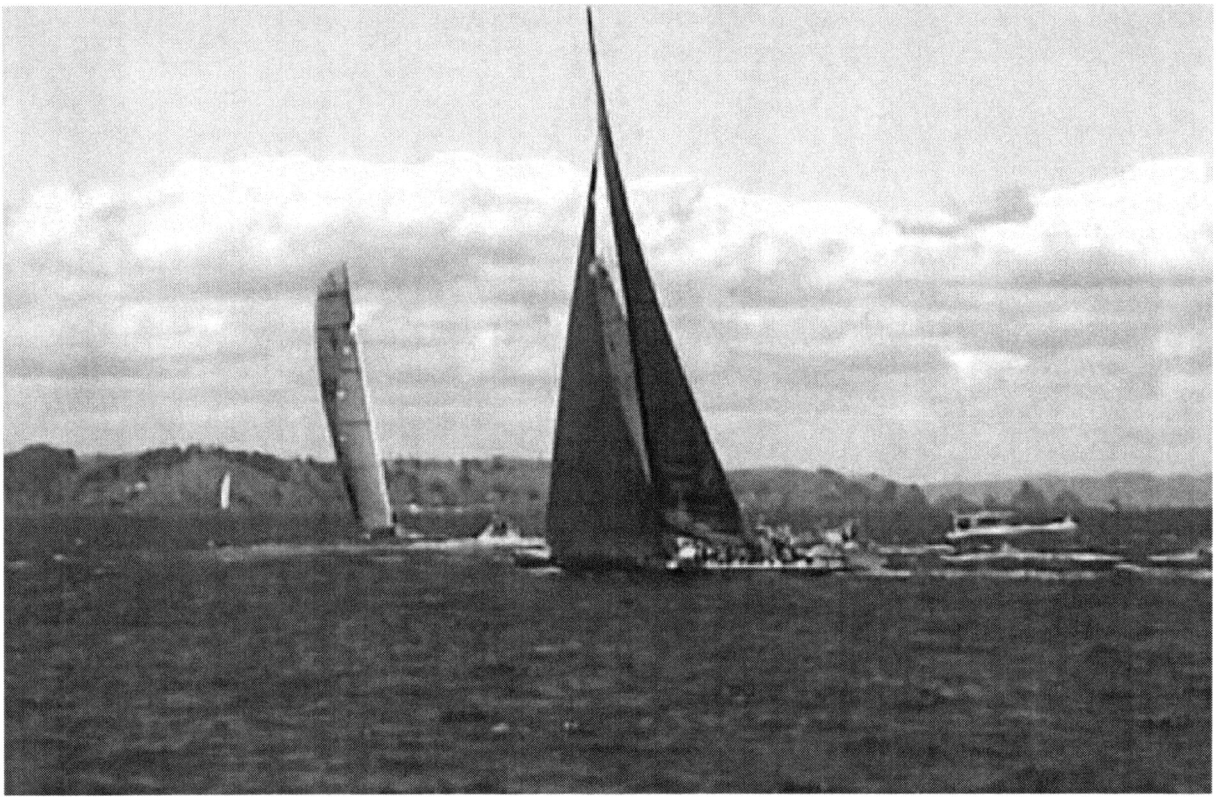

YEAR 2000, AMERICA'S CUP RACING, HAURAKI GULF, NEW ZEALAND

Pat and I had to make a quick trip to Florida to say our good-byes to my father, Vincent J. Bennett who died on a cruise ship just before docking in Clearwater, Florida on May 23, 2000. Dad was 93 and doing his favorite thing, traveling on a cruise ship with his close friend Esther. He was a wonderful father, sensitive, thoughtful, and intelligent. He left me with a legacy of wonderful spiritual and character traits that would make great goals for anyone, but hard to fully follow. He was the last person in my family of that generation, which left me with a sense of great loss and loneliness. He never pushed me to pursue lofty goals, but was always there to offer congratulations on the achievements I did manage to make.

Dad managed to keep good financial records on his computer, which helped immensely in understanding what he owned and where to find it. He left a fairly simple will, which helped us settle the estate easily. My sister Barbara and I managed, in a few days, to put his condominium in order for future selling. At one time, he owned two other condominiums — thank goodness he sold those beforehand. We were able to agree peacefully on all the difficult disposition decisions about the personal items Dad left behind, so that also worked out well.

However, the paper work completion in Florida was slow and took a little more than a year. Bob, Leslie and our oldest daughter Marjorie met us in Florida for the funeral. We stayed for a week on Bradenton Beach; it was a good time to be with family and talk about our family's story. Dad had worked as an executive for 45 years at American Telephone and Telegraph. Early in his career, he became the youngest member of the Long Lines Division promoted to management at the Manhattan, NY office of American Telephone and Telegraph. He was always active in swimming, baseball, tennis and played golf 2 and 3 times a week until he died.

Chapter 12

ANOTHER FIERCE NEW ZEALAND STORM

We arrived back in NZ on Jun. 15, 2000 from Florida and in two days, we left Gulf Harbor to head north to our NZ departure port, Opua. The boat had been prepared to leave before Dad's funeral so there was not a lot to do before leaving Gulf Harbor. Opua is located in northern NZ about 100 miles up the east coast along beautiful and rugged coastline. The wind was blowing out of the southwest at 12 knots and with 1 to 2 foot seas; we were doing some fine sailing at six plus knots under full sail. The new sails on the main and mizzen were pulling us along just fine. Our three furling systems are now operated from an electric winch in the cockpit. What a great treat and safety improvement to easily raise or lower sails from the cockpit without venturing out on the decks. Both the main and the mizzen have full-length battens and maintain a beautiful airfoil shape, which helps our 52,000 pound boat move a little faster. The new sails and booms were all made in NZ, but the sailcloth was made in the U.S.

Our destination for the night was the protected harbor at the small town of Tutukaka about 80 miles from Gulf Harbor. Later in the afternoon, we added about 1,200 revolutions, via the engine, to aid the sail power, which brought our hull speed up 8 knots. The theory was to make Tutukaka inlet while there was light left. Being winter here though, sunlight is gone by 6 p.m. unless the moon is shining. We arrived at the entrance to the channel behind schedule, naturally, at 7:30 p.m. The moon had not risen yet so it was black. With the help of NZ electronic charts that the folks from *Endurance* had given us, we found the entrance and their range lights easily. Further, up the channel though, Pat had to stand on the bow to locate their red channel pilings, which are not lit, do not have reflectors and are hard to spot until you practically run into them. By 8:30 p.m., we were safely tucked away into a nice quiet berth. Our newly installed bow thruster allows us great piece of mind. We now can maneuver in small channels with limited space. In the past, poking our bow into unknown spaces could develop into a hair-raising adventure. This marina and most of the other NZ marinas use concrete floating docks developed in Bellingham, Washington, USA. By 8:30 a.m. the next day, we had paid our NZ $25 overnight moorage bill for 60 feet — quite a bargain when compared to outlandish U.S. prices.

The next morning we fixed our course for Cape Brett about 28 miles north of Tutukaka. There was no wind so we motored at 6 knots the rest of the way to the cape, which is the turning point into the beautiful Bay of Islands. This area is home to quiet sleepy towns like Russell and Opua. Instead of taking the direct route to Opua, we decided to try a picturesque channel through the islands called Waewaetorea Passage. The chart indicated plenty of water and we slowed the boat speed down to about 3.5 knots because the channel was unknown to us. Pat and I were engaged in a serious conversation just as our depth sounder started indicating no terra firma beneath the keel and we managed to lightly go aground — this phenomenon seems to be a general occurrence whenever ***Our Pleasure*** gets a new coat of bottom paint. This does not bother the boat much as the bottom is one long continuous piece of thick fiberglass with no obstructions. I am sure the fiberglass has scratches, but grounding smoothly brought us to a smooth stop. Our next haul out and survey will be done in Australia at which time we can fix any scrapes. Our next intended port, Fiji, is supposed to be fraught with shallow channels, reefs and coral, which may cause further scrapes. At 5:30 p.m., we tied up to our berth, A8, at the brand new marina at Opua. This marina also uses concrete floating docks from Bellingham, Washington, but has more dock power, 32 amps at 240 volts (7,680 watts), than any marina in the South Pacific.

The next day, June 21, Katrina and Hugh, our newly recruited Kiwi crew to Fiji, came down with their gear. Katrina also brought her parents, as they were anxious to see what their daughter might be getting herself into. Katrina owns a sailboat, makes and repairs her sails and races sailboats with her father. Hugh is a homebuilder with quite a bit of sailing experience. They are both in their early thirties, pleasant to be with and as we found out, had excellent judgment for working out problems. After a brief rundown of our boat's systems, we checked out through NZ Customs, topped-off the fuel tanks, and headed out for Savusavu, Fiji at 12:30 p.m., June 23. Leaving port on Thursday is supposed to be a good omen for boaters. So many bad things have happened to boats leaving port on a Friday that leaving any port on Friday has become out-of-the-question.

We paid a NZ weatherman, Bob McDavitt of the NZ Met Service, $50 to look into future weather for the next 5 days. McDavitt said the weather patterns indicated good conditions for leaving NZ. In his forecast (faxed to me in Opua), he used computer modeling to predict long-range weather patterns. He has a good reputation among many of the cruising boaters and Pat was insistent that we get his blessings at least for 5 days before leaving. Let me quote his weather predictions before I tell you what actually happened:

- Thursday June 22:
  Southeast winds at 15 knots, cloudy, Easterly swell four feet.
- Friday June 23:
  Southerly winds at 10 to 15 knots, cloudy and fine periods, easterly swell three feet, occasionally four.
- Saturday June 24:
  Southerly winds at 10 knots, some areas no wind, mix of cloudy and fine, easterly swell three feet occasionally four.
- Sunday June 25:
  Southeast winds at 15 to 20 knots, cloudy periods, and a few brief showers, southeast swell three feet occasionally four.
- Monday June 26:
  East/Southeast winds at 15 to 20 knots, cloudy a few showers, easterly swell three feet occasionally four.
- Tuesday June 27:
  East/Southeast winds at 15 knots, mix of cloudy and fine periods, easterly swell three feet.

If you are thinking these predictions probably are going to be grossly in error you would be right, read on. A direct course from Opua to Fiji would be 358 degrees magnetic so any winds blowing from the East, South, West, or any combination from those directions would be in our favor. Winds between Northeast and Northwest would be against us, make for uncomfortable sailing and would make our forward progress slow since we would be sailing into the wind. When we reached the open ocean, the wind was blowing 17 knots from the East. This was a good wind direction; the boat was making good forward progress in 3 foot waves, but with some easting of our rhumb line course. On Jun. 24, we averaged 6.7 knots and traveled 174 nautical miles in 24 hours. This is a good average for ***Our Pleasure***. However, the wind was starting to blow more northward now and from the east-northeast at 25 to 30 knots. The waves were probably about six feet high (judging wave height is always an educated guess). We were heeling now on our port side between fifteen and twenty degrees.

The sailing is now getting uncomfortable, Pat and Katrina were both under the weather. Two problems popped up around this time:

1. The sink in the forward head, at this heel angle and boat speed, will force seawater up the sink drain, which fills up the sink with salt water and spills it onto the carpet. This has happened before so I installed a valve on the drain tube, which once turned off, corrects the problem, but takes the sink out of use. Of course, you have to remember to shut the drain off.
2. The rubber choker valve in the aft head was not sealing properly, which allowed gallons of salt water to enter the boat through the toilet. The toilet through hull valve had to be turned off to correct this problem. However, that valve is in an area, which restricts ones hand strength. Taking the head apart under these conditions is a formidable task, but by changing course, the boat sailed more upright and helped get the task done.

The third day out the wind was blowing directly from northeast at a powerful 30 knots. The wave height increased to about 9 feet. The wind direction was forcing us west and the best course we could sail was now 330 degrees, our boat speed was 5.5 knots. Usually before 30 knots of wind, the sail area on ***Our Pleasure*** has to be reduced to limit the heel angle and reduce the loads on the rigging. These adjustments will reduce the boat speed and forward progress will suffer. When we talked to Des on our single side band radio (NZ radio operator in Kerikeri), he thought the next day would be about the same. There was a big high-pressure system in the southwest that would bring relief, but moving east slowly. That night the wind had picked up to 35 knots, gusting to 40. Our boat speed was down to 4.3 knots.

We carry four bilge pumps, one 12 volt pump (15 gallons per minute), and one 120 volt AC pump (84 gallons per minute), one manual diaphragm pump (half a gallon per stroke) and one manual diaphragm pump (one gallon per stroke). The manual pumps were working okay, but the 12 volt pump kept clogging with debris and wood chips that were being flushed from inaccessible places into the bilge by the boats rolling action. Hugh and I cleaned the small inlet filter on that pump, but the pump kept clogging. Hugh suggested that the 15 feet of 1 inch hose to the bilge pump might also be a contributor. We figured out a way to disconnect the suction hose at the pump and blow clear the hose using the air pump from the inflatable dinghy. We were working on this problem at night using a flashlight deep inside a rear locker while on our ears — no sane person would volunteer to do this job. By the time we finished getting this pump to operate properly we had changed to a spare pump, replaced the hose coupling and replaced the inlet filter with a bigger filter that unscrews by hand. The old filter needed a screwdriver to remove the filter for cleaning. Around this time, we found the big 120 volt pump would not operate. I removed the cover to see if the shaft was stuck, but it wasn't, it just hummed when powered up. This pump had to have its motor rewound.

The wind continued to blow 35 to 40 knots and Des told us the latest weather predictions were showing increased winds up to 50 knots. I had a meeting with the crew and decided the smart thing would be to return to Opua until the weather settled. I hated the thought of going back, it was like giving up, but it was the right choice. We had been sailing more easterly to make up the 70 miles or so we had been blown off course to the west, but after 24 hours we were only able to gain about 12 miles toward Fiji. Pat had been doing well with meals, making sure everyone had at least two good meals a day, but it was increasingly difficult to cook or work in the galley in those conditions. With four crewmembers, we were doing 2 hours on and 6 hours off watch. Generally, this gave everyone enough time to sleep, but the wild boat motion and seas crashing into the boat near the bow did not let anyone sleep for 6 hours straight.

While we still had daylight left, Hugh and I put up our storm sail; furled in the genny, furled the mizzen and reduced the main down to two battens while Katrina watched the helm. This time the Des was right and the wind did go to 50 knots and higher. The steady wind range was between 47 and 54 knots. When we about 100 miles from the rugged NZ coastline we turned on the engine to make up the 8 miles we were being blown west and closer to the coast instead of running down the rhumb line. As we closed with the coast, the highest wind speed Hugh saw on the anemometer was an incredible 69 knots.

We were literally bashing our way back to Opua when the engine quit. It was early in the morning and I was exhausted. Hugh and Katrina were on watch and making repairs in the cockpit. The wind force had blown apart the heavy-duty zippers holding the Plexiglas® panels together on the port side. So Hugh and Katrina rigged up a light line to keep the panels somewhat together and the driving rain out of the cockpit.

There were two capes that we had to clear before we could turn into Opua Bay and I had to get the engine going or we would lose ***Our Pleasure*** on the rocky and rugged coast. Pat got in touch with the NZ Coast Guard every 15 minutes to keep them apprised of our position. I found the starboard tank was out of fuel and it shouldn't have been and I didn't know why, but the logical failure would have been a ruptured fuel tank. Looking into the bilge there appeared to be about 100 gallons of fuel sloshing around. It wasn't high enough to set off the high water alarms, but it must have been close.

To turn on the port fuel tank and bleed the engine fuel line under these conditions is not a happy circumstance. I had to unbolt the dinette seat, remove the carpeting, and open the engine room hatches to get at the fuel line valves. I was really lucky that I installed an electric fuel pump in Seattle, so I just had to change some fuel line valves, open the bleed screws on the engine injector pump, and run the electric fuel pump until the lines and fuel filters were full again. There is a manual fuel pump on the engine that does the same thing, but it's slow and in a low, awkward position on the engine where it is easy to burn your hand on the exhaust manifold.

By fixing the rudder angle at about 15 degrees to port and running the engine at 2,200 RPM, I was able to reduce the set toward the coast. We cleared the first cape, which stuck out the furthest, by only 4 miles as we clawed our way along the coast. Any failure of the engine, sail or the rigging and we would have to resort to our last backup, the sea anchor. Our sea anchor is a custom-built heavy-duty anchor similar to a parachute, but specifically designed for severe storms at sea. It is 12 feet in diameter and set out from the bow on a specially woven 600 foot line, 3/4 inches in diameter. The patented design of the sea anchor prevents it from rotating under pressure thereby reducing any tendency to rotate and tangle its support lines. The weave of the line also prevents it turning under the enormous tensile loads of the sea anchor holding the boat in position. I've never tried to set this anchor, but the published drift rates in those winds could have been as low as one tenth mile per hour, giving us about 40 hours of additional time to sort out problems. As I looked at the mean green water crashing over our bow, I seriously wondered if it would be possible to launch the sea anchor over the bow without being washed overboard or hurt. Looking back, this was the closest I've ever come to issuing a "**mayday**" and possibly losing ***Our Pleasure***.

Our last hurdle, after clearing the final cape, was to sail into the bay at first light, but in heavy rain and poor visibility. Even the bright range lights were not visible and we could not see the Cape Brett lighthouse. Visibility was down to about 50 yards. Katrina said she knew all the rocks, reefs, and islands in this bay from childhood and I turned the wheel over to her. Boy were we blest to have Katrina with us — God watches over us in unknown ways. She steered us through an extremely difficult entry into the bay with confidence and seemingly with ease, but I'll bet there was a lot of worry going on in her mind. The GPS began acting up right at this crucial point and turned itself off, but I was able to get it started in about 15 minutes by reprogramming the start-up menu. The GPS problem is not entirely unusual, in extreme situations the odds seem to be against all mechanical/electrical equipment working without a hiccup. We cleared Ninepin Rock at the entrance to Opua at 9 a.m. on June 28, 2000.

Back in the marina, I found the fuel tubing had worked its way out of the hose clamped fitting on the generator. This in turn siphoned off the 100 gallons of fuel into the bilge, starving the main engine of fuel. Also, the teak platform on top of the bowsprit had broken loose from the force of oversized waves hitting the platform from underneath. It was still in place, but two of the platforms hefty support beams were broken. We didn't want to pump the fuel overboard at sea so we brought it back with us. Luckily, we were able to find someone to pump out the fuel in the bilge and carry it away.

Pat and Katrina worked for 3 days to clean out the lower compartments that were contaminated with Diesel fuel. Lots of our clothing and bedding had to be washed as the driving wind and rain made everything inside damp. Hugh and I removed the framework and teak platform off the bowsprit to allow the local marine yard to weld on stainless steel plates to help hold things together in future storms. I cut some of the teak grating away to lower the resistance to water when the bow digs into waves. The fuel line connector on the gen-set engine was made without a barb that allowed the tubing to slip off the connector under pressure. This problem was corrected by welding a doughnut shaped plate to the end of the fuel line to create a barb. I also found the staysail stanchion had loosened during the storm. To correct this problem in the future, the yard welded two stainless plates to the stanchion so it could be bolted to the side of the bowsprit.

Sunday, July 2, Pat, I, and the crew had been staying at a B&B until the boat was livable again. The crew ran out of their vacation time and had to go back to work so Pat and I moved to the Opua Motel. ***Our Pleasure*** would be ready to sail again in about a week, but the crew is in question, as Pat has said she is flying to Fiji. The bilge pump motor came back from McQuinn Pumps rewound and with a new seal. They did not test it however, since their shop was equipped with only New Zealand's 240-volt power. Naturally it did not work. It would start spinning, but stop after a few minutes when the shaft froze. It was Saturday when I found this out so I took it apart to see if I could find the problem. It turned out to be a tolerance problem between the shaft, seal and retaining bolts. I was able to make a spacer to keep the shaft from freezing while turning, so it was back in business.

Meanwhile, Opua is a small town near the tip of New Zealand's north island with a one-person post office, one restaurant, one grocery store and several marine type businesses to support yachties. The restaurant, "Ferryman's," needs special mention. The owner is a Maori woman, Reawyn Wendy Raeber better known as Wendy. She is quite a bundle of personality and knowledge. Her excellent menu is a reflection of her world travels and she also claims to speak 11 languages. The restaurant is decorated like an old sailing ship, situated on a wharf supported on pilings next to a small car ferry — the kind of atmosphere I like. The first time we went there to make reservations she showed us around the restaurant and let us pick the table we wanted to sit at. At dinner, she came over to sit and chat about some of her adventures and brought a good bottle of wine — that was a first for any restaurant we have ever been in. There was live music with an Englishman playing an electronic keyboard accompanied by a young and talented Maori female singer, soon almost everyone was singing. It made for a wonderful atmosphere — it certainly lifted the spirits of our crew.

On Sunday, July 23, Jill and Jeff owners of the Opua Motel came down to the boat with going away presents of cakes and an insulating blanket for our coffee press. Our new crewmembers, Clint and Dave were there with their parents to look over the boat and say goodbye. Clint and I were introduced by members of the Opua Yacht Club. When I first met him, I was a bit taken aback by his dreadlock hair styling. For a 20 something New Zealander, dreadlocks were unusual. I was trying to figure out what kind of a statement he was saying about himself. He came well recommended from the local boat yard I had worked with and after talking together for an hour or so; I decided he was an all right kind of guy. He said he did not have a lot of sailing experience, but was knowledgeable about boats. Dave worked for a local sail maker and had some foredeck experience in local boat racing. This time of the year was slow for both of their businesses so they were glad to get offshore sailing experience.

One more problem to deal with before leaving: a glitch at my e-mail provider, AOL, caused the loss of all saved mail and e-mail addresses. I could not restore the lost data even after spending 2.5 hours on the phone with their "technical help experts." Anyway, I had to reload AOL and start all over again. We topped off the fuel tanks and left Opua for the second time on Monday, July 24, 2000, for Port-Vila, Vanuatu 1,080 miles away.

PAT'S THOUGHTS ON OUR STORM EXPERIENCE

"I would not say that I am feeling cheerful at all, but thankful to God for saving us. As I prayed during that time, I felt a sense of peace come over me and I knew we would make it. Frightening and rough out there, still we would be all right.

The clean up was horrendous. I went through the storage lockers, to remove all the contents, and wipe them out. In all the lower storage compartments, we had a mixture of fuel and water that seemed to penetrate into everything stored there regardless of how well they were packaged. Extra sheets had to be thrown away as they were saturated with the Diesel mixture and cannot be washed in the washing machines. All paper products stored there had to be thrown away as well as Christmas decorations, books, puzzles and even the foil insulation against the walls had to be removed and thrown out. We were hit by a couple of huge waves that sent water rushing through cockpit doors into the galley area and into the large storage compartment next to the stairs, which at the time contained all our fresh veggies and eggs. Even the carpeting in the galley had to be thrown out.

I do not know how I would have tackled this job by myself. Katrina stayed on and was a tremendous help. Hugh, in the meantime, was assisting Dick. It still took me the better part of a week to finish wiping out each compartment. Many items still needed washing even after a week of cleaning. At the end of the first week, Katrina took me shopping to replenish our food supplies. Yes, I am planning on flying to Fiji. I am not ready emotionally to tackle another long crossing at this time."

Chapter 13

NEW ZEALAND TO PORT VILA, VANUATU

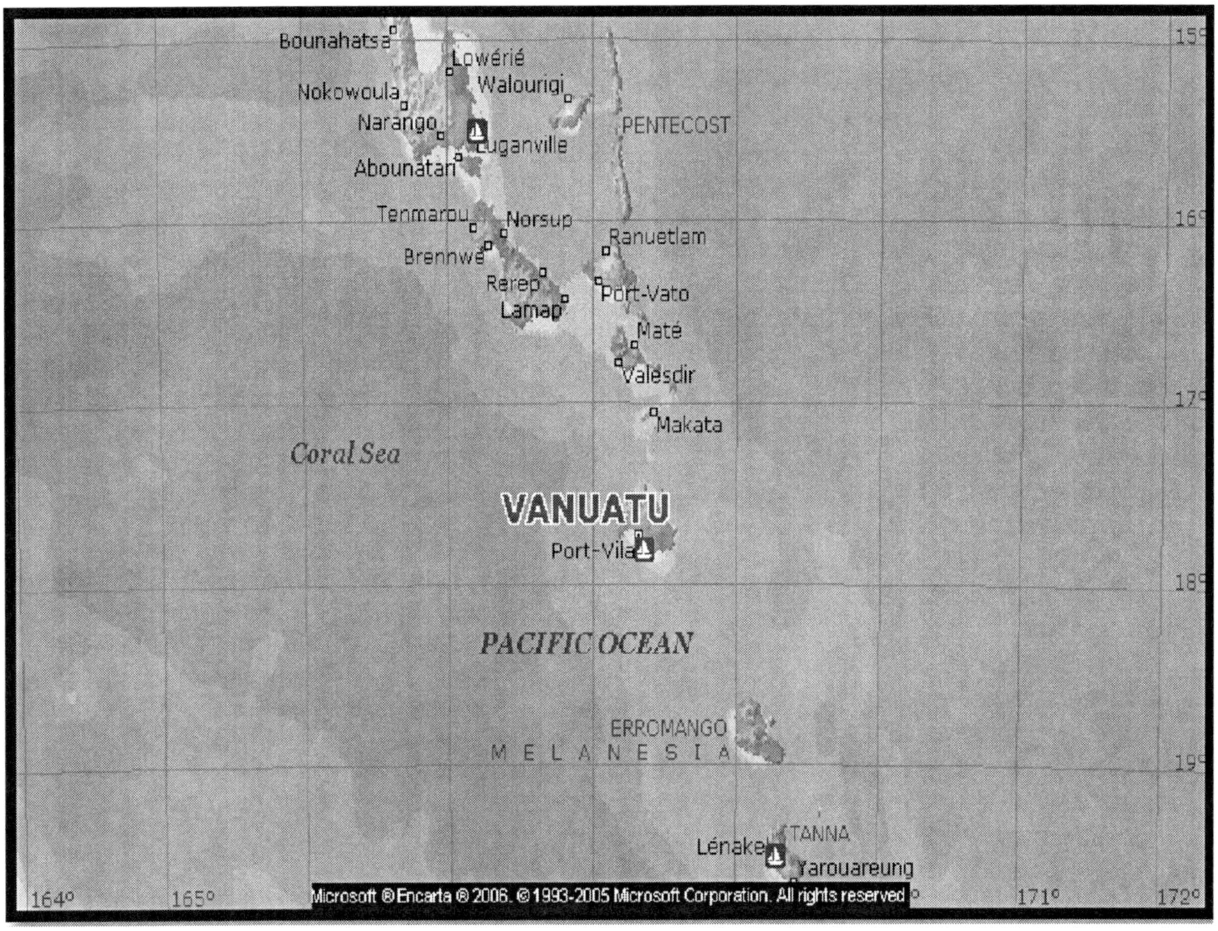

ARRIVED PORT VILA, ISLAND OF ÉFATÉ, REPUBLIC OF VANUATU, Aug. 4, 2000

We decided to sail to Vanuatu instead of Fiji for two reasons. One, the delays leaving NZ put us late into the sailing season and two; on May 19, 2000, seven masked, armed men stormed the Fiji parliament and took the Prime Minister, Mahendra Chaudhry and the entire cabinet hostage. The gunmen fired at least two shots from an AK-47 inside the new parliament building before locking up Chaudhry, his cabinet ministers and lawmakers of the ruling coalition. The 50 hostages reported no injuries. Chaudhry was the first ethnic Indian elected to the highest position in their government, **prime minister**. This caused hard feelings and angered many indigenous Fijians. The coup leader, George Speight, claimed he seized power on behalf of all ethnic Fijians and appointed himself prime minister. In Suva, Fiji's capital, rioting, looting and widespread damage took place causing the president, Mara (head of state), to declare a state of emergency. He deployed about 300 troops, but taking control of the streets was not easy.

The various news organizations put together minor profiles of Mr. Speight and this is what I gleamed from their releases. He is an indigenous Fijian with a bachelor degree in commerce from Australia and a Masters degree from Andrews University in the U.S. Andrews University founded in 1784 is in Berrien Springs, Michigan, and is a Seventh-day Adventist Church sponsored college. He had no military experience. By profession, he was a financial consultant with aspirations for a political career. He previously owned a number of failed businesses and misuse of funds got him fired from one of his positions. When the previous government lost their power, Speight lost his good government connections. His cause seemed to have a lot of support from the native Fijian population.

Two days later, the coup leaders released nine members of parliament, the prime minister's bodyguards, and 20 parliamentary workers. The released ministers said they were forced to sign an agreement to resign their positions in the government. Many tourists quickly left Fiji fearing the powder keg might erupt any minute. Soldiers walking the city streets with automatic weapons took up positions behind sand bags, established roadblocks, and checkpoints. Some East Indian people were harassed, forced from their homes, and fled violent areas to live with family or friends in safer neighborhoods. A week later, the Great Council of Indigenous Chiefs (14 members of the highest-ranking chiefs in Fiji's Islands) voted to accept the demands of the coup leaders. This included, removal of Prime Minister Chaudhry, amending the constitution to ensure top political positions only go to indigenous Fijians and immediate release of all hostages. They also urged president Mara to pardon George Speight. Into the second week, the president announced that he fired the country's democratically elected government and that Speight and his gunmen would probably be immune from prosecution.

This announcement caused a violent reaction outside parliament between troops and supporters of the coup. A TV cameraman and two soldiers were wounded. On May 29, Fiji's army declared martial law and the president was dismissed. Gunmen loyal to Speight killed a police officer — usually the Fiji police do not carry guns. Meanwhile negations stalled and the hostages were threatened with death if the army attacked the parliament compound. The Australian and New Zealand unions imposed a trade ban with Fiji because of the coup causing economic impact. Tourists were giving Fiji a wide berth and within 4 weeks over 4,000 jobs were lost. On July 27, coup leader George Speight was arrested at a military checkpoint and 350 of his followers were attacked at a Suva school. One man was killed and 39 others were injured. Speight and his cohorts were imprisoned on the Fiji island of Nucleus. During his trial Speight accused the Chaudhry administration was slowly stripping away the rights of Fiji's indigenous majority. Speight was sentenced to life imprisonment on Feb. 18, 2002 after pleading guilty to treason. Ten of the other gunmen were sentenced to a minimum of 10 years in prison.

The coup lasted for 56 days before the remaining hostages were freed. Apparently, most of the guns used were stolen from the military police. An irony of the coup is that the gunmen were members of an elite military counter-revolutionary unit established after a coup in 1987. The real leader was rumored to be a former British, SAS (British army *Special Air Service*) trained, Colonel Ligairi. It was rumored that Colonel Ligairi set up Speight as his front man because of his speaking ability and charisma. A claim the colonel denied. In essence, the coup may have been a military coup. It was estimated that the coup caused a financial loss of around $100 million.

The population of Fiji is about 650,000 with 51% indigenous Fijian and 44% Indian Fijian. When the British left Fiji independent in 1970, they also left with the non-indigenous population not well integrated. The Fijians lived side by side with the non-indigenous population for over 100 years. Their cultures are different and their values remained distinct. This is not an isolated case as it is familiar with former British and other European colonies all over the world. It is a shame they did not foresee the problems they created. If we had sailed to Fiji, the coup would have voided our boat insurance. Insurance companies do not like locations of civil unrest with warring factions shooting at each other and I cannot fault them for that. However, boats there at the time said that in locations outside the capital of Suva, the coup went mostly unnoticed.

Sailing progress to Port-Villa, Vanuatu was on the slow side as winds were mostly light from 7 to 15 knots out of the north. Clint had a slight mishap one day while walking past the table in the main salon. The boat lurched in a wind shift and threw his 200 plus pounds into the table. That accident pulled up the 8 hold-down, wood screws. No problem, I found 8 bolts, nuts and washers and Clint took care of putting it all back together. Clint was a little embarrassed and had a slight bruise, but otherwise he was ok.

On August 2, we were about 230 NM from Port-Vila when we had a close encounter with a freighter. It was 10:20 p.m. and dark, we were making about 6 knots when this freighter came into radar view on our 12 mile range marker. I followed his progress, which indicated he was coming directly down our electronic bearing line at about 12 knots. He did not change course, so if something did not happen soon, collision was imminent. As he got closer, I blew the danger signal on our long-range air horn, no reply. I next tried the radio and did get the captain to acknowledge the potential problem. He agreed to make a course change and we were to maintain our course and speed. In some of these potential collisions, it seems the crews are not keeping a good watch or they have to wake someone who speaks English (usually the captain) to respond to inquiries. There are captains I have talked to on the radio, like this one, who sound like they are not fully awake.

The next day, Clint caught a 4 foot long mahi-mahi with bright beautiful coloring. He was holding him down on deck with his knee to remove the hook. The fish was watching him closely with one eye. The instant the hook came out, this smart fish made one strong flip with his tail and back into the water he went. It seems to be well known among fishermen that mahi-mahi mate for life, therefore her mate swimming nearby was undoubtedly teary-eyed. So we felt both happy that the two mates could get back together, but sad that we lost several days of great eating.

I talked to *Endurance* on the SSB radio a couple of times as we neared Port-Vila. *Endurance* and *Esprit*, already anchored, had passed on some good advice about the check-in procedures. We anchored near the port's big yellow quarantine buoy in 74 feet of water. Health and immigration representatives came out to the boat, they were polite, and there were no problems. A local company named "Yachting World," arranged our moorage at their number 9 buoy. They sent out "Moses" in a small outboard boat to guide us into the harbor and help us tie to the buoy. Before 1980, the world knew these islands as the New Hebrides Islands; New Hebrides became Vanuatu following independence from France and England. Port-Vila is the capital city of Vanuatu located on the island of Éfaté. The city's population is about 34,000 and the total country population is around 193,000. This republic's ethnic divisions are loosely 94% Melanesian, 4% European and the remainder are Chinese, Pacific Islander and Vietnamese. English, French, and Bislama are the official languages, but there are several indigenous dialects. *Endurance* and *Esprit* had not been planning to stop at Vanuatu, but Marv had been experiencing stomach pain after leaving Fiji and sailed in seeking medical advice. The health authorities met him at the harbor with an ambulance and took him immediately to the hospital. They treated his symptoms with antibiotics and the pain diminished, disappeared, and did not return.

Our two Kiwi crewmembers worked out well so it was a happy trip to Vanuatu with much food consumed. We had only two and a half days of 40 knot winds on the nose, which limited forward progress on those days to around 40 nautical miles. Strong head winds required lots of tacking back and forth — frustrating. The rest of the 10 day trip provided good sailing winds and weather. Pat flew in from NZ and stayed on *Endurance* for a few days until we arrived. She had the town well scouted out by the time we arrived. Port-Vila is a quaint city with a good protected anchorage and friendly natives. The infrastructure has suffered badly since their independence, but the French and English influence was clearly visible in the architecture. It seemed that the locals mostly spoke French or Pidgin English (Bislama), but English was well understood. When I hear Bislama I have no idea of what they are saying, but seeing it written almost makes sense. For example, "What is your name"? In Bislama the question would sound like, "Wanem nem blong you"? They also speak so fast that there is not enough time to understand what they are saying.

The schools do teach French and English so anyone that deals with tourists can speak in the only language I understand. My 2 years of French was almost a waste of time — mostly my fault. I know basic greetings and can read some it fairly well, but I cannot really understand when they speak it. There is a nice market in town where we picked up a basket of grapefruit. The laundry in town cost us about $40 for 4 loads. Pat and I always try to go to the local Catholic Church when possible. We located the Catholic cathedral and were entertained by about 50 beautiful young children singing mostly in French, their voices sounded fabulous. Of course, we only had a vague idea of the songs meanings. The bishop's homily was said in three languages (one being English), but that sure lengthened the mass. About 15% of the population is Catholic, 15% are Anglican, but Presbyterian is the majority religion (35%).

Several of our yachting friends were anchored in the harbor here so it was like old home week. So far, we have spent our time catching up with old friends, doing laundry and trying out the French restaurants. We took the small passenger ferry over to the Iriki Resort on Ifira Island for lunch with Marv, Chieko, Dennis, and Martina. We had a hard time connecting to AOL at the only Internet cafe in Port-Vila. The French telephone system is a monopoly and you have to use their Internet service provider, "Naviti." The help at the cafe did not know how to connect either, but luckily, a young computer troubleshooter was there from Australia and showed me how to access the Internet using my AOL software.

The professional crew off the American yacht *Freedom*, asked us over for happy hour one evening. We met this crew, Greg and Jan, in NZ at the Gulf Harbor Marina. An American relative of *Freedom's* owner owned the end slip at our Gulf Harbor dock. *Freedom's* 80 foot length, deep keel, and high mast were too big for her to anchor in the inner harbor. We took our inflatable dingy out to their boat near the quarantine buoy. On the trip back our Honda outboard started acting up and quit, forcing us to row the half-mile or so back. This outboard became more and more temperamental after servicing in NZ. It was quite annoying when it would run only in short bursts. Usually we could coax it back to life by removing the cowling or cleaning the carburetor. It acted like a fuel or air problem, but all our fixes were short lived.

We arranged to fly to the island of Tanna to see the active Yasur Volcano and a coffee plantation. This island is quite primitive with no town or paved roads. The roads were once paved, but after the French and English left, they have fallen into such disrepair that they are now teeth and brain jarring roads that have no rivals except maybe the Burma Road of WWII fame. We stayed at the Tanna Evergreen Resort, which was not world class, but it was comfortable. The resort owners met us at the modern Tanna airport that was built for them by the French, but was starting to suffer from lack of maintenance. To bounce us across the potholes, ruts, rocks mud and muddy rivers, our tour guide had a Mitsubishi 4 wheel drive vehicle similar to a WWII jeep. We had to stop about every 10 minutes so the six of us could trade seats. The back two seats were just benches with 2 inches of foam rubber that did not cushion anything. The ride to the volcano was about 2 hours of misery each way. The volcano was rather spectacular, but safety issues left us a bit concerned. The Yasur Volcano is supposed to be the only active volcano in the world where you can stand on the rim and look in.

There are no fence shelters to stand behind or warning signs of any kind. We were standing among big rocks and boulders from previous volcano belching, bursts of fire and rock slinging. The volcano seemed to come to life about every 30 minutes. Our guide reassured our concerns for safety with, "Only a couple of people have been killed by boulders hurled up to the rim by the volcano." That sure made us a lot more comfortable and put our fears to rest. We were treated to a few bursts of volcano power as molten rocks were flying around inside the rim and loud rumblings were ever present, but nothing dangerous. We stayed until the light faded to get a better view of the volcano's fiery interior. Staying well into the night darkness would provide a much better view of the fireworks, but walking down the mountainside to the jeep in the dark was a big challenge.

The coffee plantation is high in the hilly countryside and interesting. The local native families receive about 2.5 acres per family of coffee plants to nurture and cultivate and they share the profits. The factory is small, about the size of a large barn. A large generator supplies all the power, but only during processing. The operation uses modern roasters and grinders and packaging equipment to process the coffee beans. The coffee label is "Tanna Coffee" and is quite good so we bought enough to keep us going for some time. We noticed hundreds of burlap bags full of processed beans destined for New Jersey, USA, Australia, and NZ.

The natives on this island live in huts made out of pandanus leaves, which are surprisingly dry inside during heavy rain. There is no electricity except for the few tourist resorts, which have generators. The rest of the island uses kerosene lamps or candles. We stopped at a native village about an hour and a half into our head-banging ride. The men wore grass skirts for the dancing, which consisted of a lot of chanting and hard ground stomping with their bare feet. The women of the village did not dance. They also demonstrated their use of a bow and arrow, which uses a blunt tip of about one inch in diameter. The intent of this weapon was to kill enemies with a sharp blow to the head. Following the battles, all the dead victims were eaten. Now the arrows are used to kill pigs. Alternately, the pigs are whacked over the head with a mean looking, long handled, wooden hammer. The hammer has a spike on one side and a blunt surface on the other. On some of the more remote islands, the women still wear grass skirts. The men only wear a "nambas," a sort of sheath for the penis made out of pandanus leaves. If you want one you have to tell the natives what length you need. However, the natives are quite fussy and do not want anyone to exaggerate and look to the wives to see if they agree with their husbands size estimates, which makes for a good laugh.

Pentecost Island in Vanuatu is the place where the men and boys jump off platforms from a 100 foot wooden tower lashed together with vines. For young men it provides the transition into manhood. They tie a vine to each ankle, which is similar to bungee jumping except vines have limited stretch characteristics. The length of the vines has to be quite precise as the men actually touch the ground at the end of the jump. If the vines were long enough to allow the jumpers head to hit the ground, the injury would be serious. However, we could not watch this amazing event as they only jump during April and May. The real purpose of the jumping is a spiritual one, to ensure a good yam harvest.

We were hoping to visit some of the other Vanuatu Islands before leaving for New Caledonia, but the weather has not been good for going north the hundred or so miles. One of the northern islands, Espiritu Santo, was a staging area for about 100,000 U.S. troops during WWII at Luganville. Our troops left a lot of rusting Quonset huts, concrete slabs and the luxury liner *SS President Coolidge* (converted to a troop ship for the war). The ship sank when it tangled with two U.S. laid mines in the harbor. There was apparent confusion over the actual location of the mines compared to the captain's information. Besides the *Coolidge*, another well-known dive site is at **Million Dollar Point.** Million Dollar Point is where the U.S. Army dumped hundreds of tons of war equipment after the war. The country of Vanuatu could have bought everything for eight cents on the dollar, but thought they would have it for nothing when the troops left. This did not sit well with the U.S. especially considering the American lives that were lost protecting the Pacific nations. So, rather than give it away the U.S. pushed it all into the ocean. I say, "Good on ya mate," if I had any say in the matter, I would have done the same. One of our former crewmembers, Clint, said he could not believe all the dozers, cranes, trucks, crates of equipment, etc., left behind. A lot of it was still in crates, never used and in new condition. He also dove on the *Coolidge*, which has become one of the world's must-do dives for the real scuba enthusiasts. Some of the grand decorations and paintings are still a visual pleasure to look at mostly in disbelief and amazement.

With the rain so prevalent, I had fun catching rainwater on our "sun" awning and using a siphon to get the water to the tanks. It only takes a few minutes to catch about 6 or so gallons in the awnings and 1 minute to move it to one of the water tanks, efficient and wonderful pure water. Our water maker makes about 20 gallons an hour, but I have to run the generator. The water maker, at that time, had developed a leak in the salt-water side that could not be reached without removing the unit. The leak had to wait until New Caledonia.

On Sept. 7, the clouds finally disappeared and the temperature rose with lots of sunshine. We had to move ***Our Pleasure*** to the quay (from our harbor moorage) where there is water and electricity because our fresh water pump on the generator was leaking water faster than I could replace it. Without the generator, I would have to run the main engine to make water and operate the AC refrigerator. That is not a good use of the main engine. If we are not motoring, I want to keep the main engine as reliable as possible by restricting its use. The generator water pump is a custom assembly with the fresh and salt-water pumps on one shaft. Johnson Pumps custom built this pump for the generator manufacturer, Entec in Portland, Oregon — good luck in finding a replacement anywhere else, right.

So, after a couple of faxes to Entec and problems with the fax number here, the parts finally arrived via DHL on Tuesday, Sept. 5, 2000. It took 2 days to fully service the generator and replace the pumps. It now seems to be working just fine. The generator only has 972 hours on it so it did seem a little early for the seal to fail. This can be compared to driving a car about 60,000 miles and having the water pump fail. It is not all that bad, but I thought I would get another 1,000 hours on the pump before replacing it. The freight to get it here was a rather big-ticket item at $166 for a 4 pound box. If I was not in a hurry, I am sure the U.S. mail would have been a lot less expensive, but maybe not.

Well, Pat and I used the down time to visit a young women's hostel run by French nuns to drop off some clothes. They were both delighted and grateful to get the clothing. A good day's wages here is about $7.50. We had quite a chat with a French nun who came to Vanuatu from Italy in 1952 and her English was about as good as our French — not good. We found a young woman there to help the both of us get through the language problems. The nun, sister Angelica, was just delightful and had a happy disposition in spite of only making one visit to Italy in all the time she has been here. If we were to change places, that would have made me quite unhappy. We also were able to do some site seeing on this island, including a visit to a high jungle waterfall and a few resorts.

We had intended to sail to Espiritu Santo, to catch up with two friends who have given up sailing to become land barons. The remaining sailing season has become limited so we decided to fly over instead. Jim and Hellen (she is Danish and spells her name with two l's) Boswell (formally of the sailboat *Go West*) have bought a fifth share in an 800 acre copra plantation. Copra is the dried white flesh of the coconut used to extract coconut oil. They have just moved into a new waterfront home on Aore Island, which faces the main city of Luganville across the water. The house is probably about 800 square feet and is quite modern compared to the native homes on the island. Their house uses mostly native hardwoods, has a metal roof and running water that comes from a rainwater catchment system. Electricity is supplied from 8 solar panels, a Trace® 3,300 watt inverter, batteries and a gasoline-powered generator. Hot water on demand and cooking, come from bottled gas. All the windows open via jealousy type windows and mosquito netting covers the beds — Vanuatu is a risk area for malaria.

After taking a bus into town from the airport, Jim and Hellen met us at the BP Wharf in their new aluminum dinghy with a 25-horse Yamaha outboard — a good find at an Australian boat show. It is a good thing the driver knew where the wharf was because there were no signs. It happened to be a leftover WWII, U.S. built, concrete pier with several old Quonset huts nearby. The boat ride across Segond Channel took about 5 minutes on flat water. They live close to the sunken *SS President Coolidge* and Million Dollar Point. Their investment group has leased the plantation land for 75 years. The lease is with a local chief and changes to the contract require the chief's permission — not always an easy task.

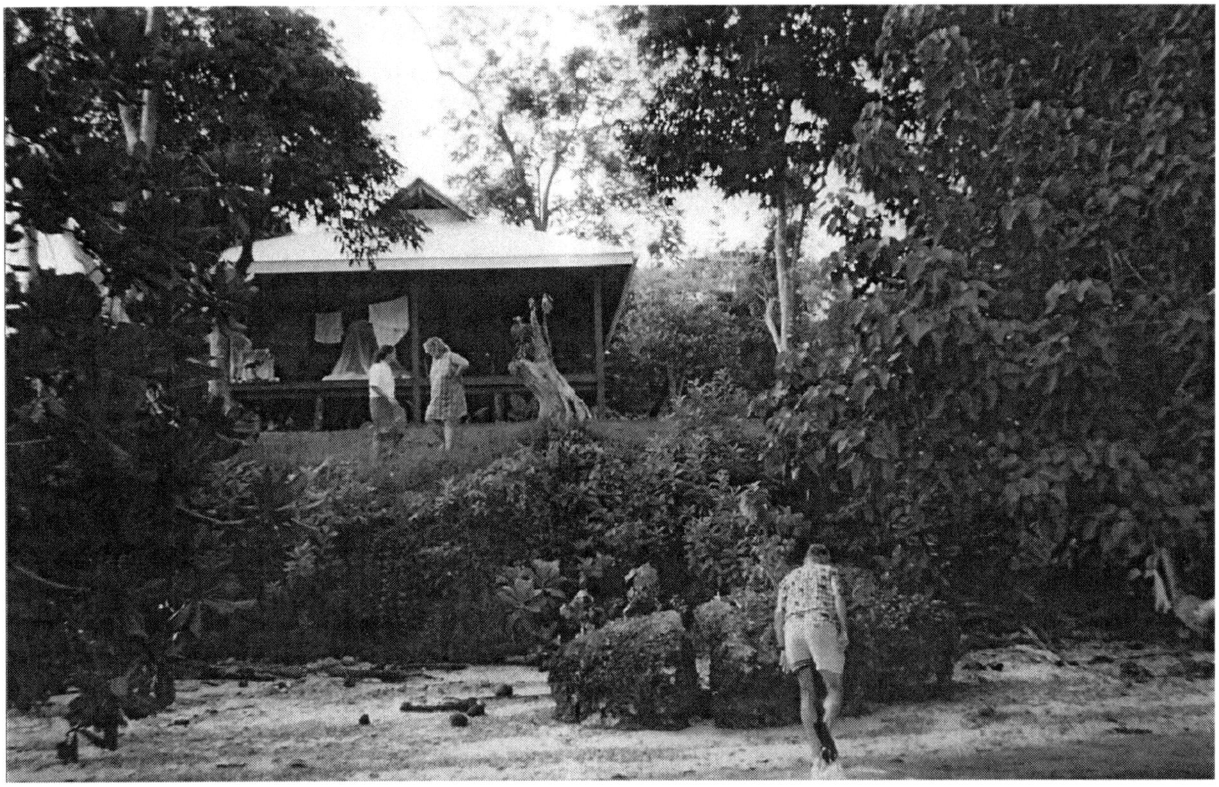

JIM & HELLEN'S HOUSE, AORE ISLAND, VANUATU

Saturday night, the islands residents hosted a big barbecue to honor Aore Island's newest residents, Jim and Hellen Boswell. A young steer was killed and all the native plantation workers and their families were invited. Pat made a big hit with the children when she passed out lots of candy. The price of copra is so low at this time, that it is not practical to go through the harvesting process. So, they are raising cattle and looking for other opportunities for their 800 acres.

Sunday we were invited to another plantation and a barbecue hosted by an Australian named Kevin. His plantation covers several thousand acres and he is raising pigs, cattle and a breed of sheep that has little hair. Normal sheep cannot survive in the hot climate of Vanuatu. These sheep are known as hairless sheep, imported from Africa and are raised just for their meat. He only lives on the island a few days a month as he has other business interests in Australia. He was a great host and generous. When the natives were cutting up the meat, he kept the tenderloin for us and grilled our pieces inside his house, because the natives like their meat over cooked. His house is attractive and nicely furnished with a large deck and an in-the-ground swimming pool. The interesting thing though is the size of his front lawn, which converts to a regulation soccer field. If he is living there on a Sunday, he invites all the natives over for a barbecue and a soccer game. He provides the uniforms and food. His workers have red uniforms and usually beat any visiting team. No air-conditioning made the 90 degree temperatures almost unbearable and it is wintertime.

Leaving Vanuatu means checking out through Customs and then you can take advantage of duty-free shopping, which everyone manages quite nicely. Back on the boat, the sun-awning was stowed and we stocked up on groceries. We planned a one-day stop at a place called Hideaway Island, which is only a couple of miles from Port-Vila. The island is known for outstanding snorkeling. We thought Vanuatu, was a unique place.

We checked out of Port-Vila, Vanuatu on Friday, Sept. 8, 2000. For the 1 month, plus a few days, the port charges were $50 and our moorage bill was $150 — all-in-all, pretty reasonable. A number of boaters griped at the charges though and didn't think they received much in the way of services. Some boaters are really penny pinchers, are hard to please and I think, enjoy complaining. We spent the rest of the day shopping in the many duty-free stores. I ended up with a new, really nice Swiss Tissot® watch. Pat added two more gold charms to her collection and found a jewelry designer who made her a rather unique setting for one of her black pearls from the Tuamotus. We also bought a painting of native girls from a well-known South Pacific artist, Pilioko, for our Florida condominium — there goes the kid's inheritance. The rest of the chores included filling the water tanks, adding 3 cases of soft drinks, and filling our freezer with many vacuum packed and frozen meats from the local Italian butcher. Vanuatu has a reputation for having some of the finest meats in the world because of their fine grazing land. They do not add chemicals to the soil or any of the feed. I really don't know much about organic farming, but the results speak for themselves, tender and flavorful.

On our way out of Vanuatu, we stopped at picturesque Mélé Bay on Hideaway Island. Coral reefs surround most of this bay making an ideal environment for snorkeling. We took under water pictures with a throwaway camera, but the camera was misplaced and we never saw the pictures. Several of our boating friends were also enjoying the bay: *Destiny* (U.S.), *Paraná* (Australia), *Crimson Tide* (New Zealand), *Wanderlust* (U.S.), and *Wega* (Czechoslovakia). I spent time on Sunday, Sept. 10, free diving on ***Our Pleasure*** to clean the prop and remove the light scum off the bottom (I sure miss Leslie and Bob at times like this). We left Mélé Bay at 4 p.m. and motored southwest in light winds towards New Caledonia.

Chapter 14

VANUATU TO NEW CALEDONIA

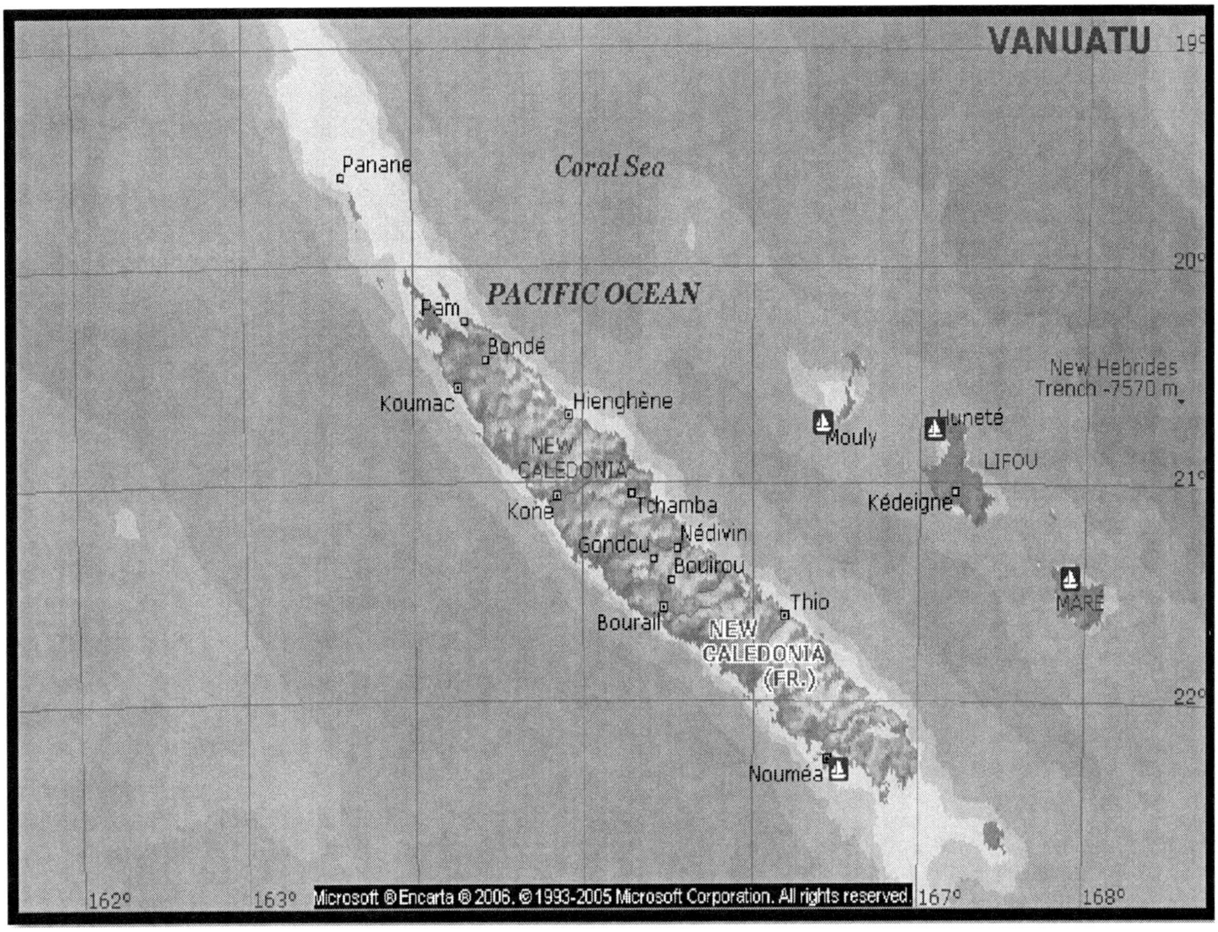

ARRIVED NEW CALEDONIA AND THE LOYALTY ISLANDS, Sept. 13, 2000

Pat and I tried 6 hour watches for this trip to see if longer sleeping times would work better us. We found it quite difficult at first, especially trying to fall asleep at 8 p.m. with the engine running and not really tired. By the third night, our watch system was working well as we were both getting enough sleep. We motored the 300 miles to New Caledonia with winds on the nose, but they were generally light and not much of a problem. The main entrance at the south end of New Caledonia requires navigating through a pass called Havannah Pass. This pass is similar to Deception Pass in Washington State's San Juan Islands. The water in the pass is fast moving, but dissimilarly, many reefs. Our friends on *Endurance* gave us a computer program for tides around the world so we were able to time our entry properly on the start of the flood tide.

There is only one port of entry for foreign yachts in New Caledonia and that is at Port Moselle, Nouméa. We called the marina at Port Moselle on VHF channel 67, they assigned us slip 37 at the visitors dock, and two dockhands were waiting to help with dock lines. They also arranged for Customs, Immigration and Agriculture agents to meet us at our boat — the most efficient and friendly check-in in all of the South Pacific. The sail to the island of Nouméa territory of New Caledonia, took about 4 days. New Caledonia is still governed by the French, quite beautiful and like anything French, expensive.

New Caledonia has been an overseas territory of France for 150 years and therefore mostly French speaking. The local Melanesian population, known as Kanaks, is seeking independence from France. From what we have seen, these small countries achieving independence, cannot manage themselves without the help of nations with large pockets and resources. However, this region is fortunate to have a major share of the worlds nickel deposits. Thus, the territory is prosperous and France would like to keep it. Of course, the nickel would become an important asset in independence.

The Kanak tribal customs are still strong among the natives and so are the French traditions, which have resulted in quite a few political problems through the years. The original men and women sent here by France starting in 1864 were some 21,000 convicts. They were deported for various felonies and political convictions. Many of them decided to settle here and therefore there are many French families with origins dating back several generations. The capital city of Nouméa is located on the largest of their islands, Grande Terre. Grande Terre is shaped like a cigar, mountainous with a rugged interior and dense vegetation. It's about 240 miles long by 35 miles wide. The highest mountain, Mount Pané, is 5,340 feet above sea level. There is an extensive barrier reef at Grande Terre second only to Australia's Great Barrier Reef.

We were surprised to hear about the American occupation of New Caledonia during WWII. The majority of the French people here chose to support President de Gaulle and the free French Forces as opposed to the Vichy regime. This allowed the U.S. allies to establish a military base on Grand Terre, the main island, in 1942. Soon 40,000 Americans and a smaller number of New Zealanders arrived under the leadership of Admiral Halsey — a well-known name for Americans my age. Attacks were launched from here against the Japanese in the Philippines and in the battle of the Coral Sea. The Kanaks have good memories of the U.S. presence. For the first time they received good wages for their labor. There is a beautiful monument in the park near the marina commemorating the presence here of some 200,000 U.S. troops. The troops built the airfield, which is now Nouméa's International Airport, and four hospitals that had a total of 2,000 beds. We met a French surgeon over lattes one day, who works at one of the hospitals the U.S. built. Now, of course, it is quite updated and modernized. The hospital now has only 400 beds to serve the population of 80,000 people living in Nouméa. He was also quite eager to tell me about the excellent quality of surgical tools they buy from the U.S. along with a number of high quality manufactured goods. He knew of a U.S. fighter plane that was found just a few years ago. It had crashed in the mountains during WWII, but the engine and associated parts had survived all this time in near perfect condition with no rust. Finding no rust in this climate is quite extraordinary.

New Caledonia's status was changed after WWII from a colony to a French overseas territory. The Kanak chief, Naisseline of the Island of Maré, proposed a native bill at that time asserting that the Kanaks were entitled to French citizenship. He successfully argued that they fought and died for France in both world wars and those efforts entitled them to citizenship. The French agreed and awarded citizenship to the Kanaks in 1946. The higher-ranking Kanaks like the chiefs, priests and former soldiers were allowed to vote. In 1957, all

Kanaks were allowed to vote. The Kanaks represent about 43% of the total population while the European community stands at close to 37% and the rest are Vietnamese, Polynesians, and Indonesians.

The nickel boom of the 1950's and 60's brought prosperity, but it caused an imbalance to the countries way of life. Farmers became miners and Kanaks left their villages to work in the mines. By the late 60s, there was a new wave of immigration from the islands of Vanuatu, Wallis, and Tahiti. Housing boomed, but the villages still were without running water or electricity. Schools and public offices were now open to Kanaks, but segregation and discrimination still flourished. The boom caused some bitter feuds. The Kanaks wanted their land back and the Caledonians wanted to be free of a state administration they did not know. Thus, the stage was set for violent political struggles for the next 20 years.

Nouméa's population is around 40% of the total population of New Caledonia (including the Loyalty Islands). The climate is temperate as it sits on the edge of the tropics just north of the Tropic of Capricorn. This city is probably the most sophisticated city in the South Pacific. The food available in restaurants is such high quality with so many choices that dining out was a real enjoyable treat. Many of the restaurants will serve a 3-course dinner for one price, about $19. The choices generally will include about 10 appetizers, 10 entrées accompanied by a selection of 2 vegetables and salads from a list of about 10. However, the most amazing part of dinner was always dessert. Here you just cannot make a mistake — they are all out-of-this-world.

Speaking of out-of-this-world, I have to mention my observations of the French women in Nouméa (and all my male friends will back me up on this). Sure, they mostly bathe topless at the beautiful beaches here, but the most notable part of the women is their appearance when dressed for work or going out for the evening. A great deal of their time must go into exercising, diet, grooming, dressing and clothes shopping as the majority of the women here look like they just stepped out of a fashion magazine. It is not that they are beautiful, actually, they are ordinary looking, but they dress in a simple, elegant way that is pleasing to the eye. They all seem to possess girlish figures and their hair, makeup, lipstick and nails always look fresh and in good taste. Their line of work did not seem important or their position, or their age; they always look well groomed and smartly dressed.

Needless to say, for a small, out-of-the-way country, we were impressed. The French-speaking people were friendly and they went out of way to help us. Our limited French did not seem to deter their willingness to help. We have heard a rumor that more French people speak English here than in France! I don't know if that's true, but we found that most of the French people could speak enough English to answer our questions. Grocery shopping in is a unique experience. Anyone who has shopped with Pat in a grocery store in the U.S. will appreciate how much time it takes to shop here. Not only does she like to read the contents of every label, now she takes an inordinate amount of time deciphering French labels. It is quite an experience with the French dictionary in hand, slowly sounding English words and a liberal use of sign language. However, the effort usually finds significant rewards in the wonderful French cheeses and wines that are available — simply outstanding.

The day after we arrived in Nouméa, Bob Warner pulled in next to us in his newly launched sailboat *Mariah*. He had sailed directly from NZ to Nouméa just a few months after launching his Greg Elliot designed fast cruising sailboat. He had already been in the area for over a month and gave us a lot of helpful information. He took us out to one of those outstanding French restaurants the next evening and we were happily impressed. His wife Wendy was back in the U.S. for a few more weeks so he invited Pat and me to explore the four Loyalty Islands of New Caledonia on *Mariah*. It was supposed to be a 10 day trip, but it turned into 14 days.

One of the trip's highlights was Fred, his French chef. Fred lost his crew position on another boat, *Flying Wings*, so Bob offered him a bunk on *Mariah* for helping with the chores. At the time, Bob did not know Fred had served in the French Navy and was an experienced chef in Nouvelle Cuisine. Fred did most of the shopping and made the menu decisions for each day, Pat loved it. He put together some wonderful meals that were healthy and beautifully presented. The way he cut up the vegetables and arranged the colors was extraordinary and Pat could relax only asking cooking questions of Fred as he did all the fancy work.

The majority of the cruising boats do not go to the Loyalty Islands because you cannot visit them until you first check-in at Nouméa. Once you enter Nouméa, it means backtracking a few hundred miles, usually against the wind, to visit the Loyalties. However, *Mariah's* design incorporates the latest technology in hull shape, keel/rudder design and sail handling to allow her to sail or motor fast to within 20 degrees of the apparent wind direction. Usually we were sailing along at 8 to 11 knots in winds that were not much higher. After sailing through Havannah Pass at slack water we arrived at the Bay Of Gaatcha on the island of Lifou by happy hour (we had sailed about 120 miles). We anchored in front of a Catholic mission (New Caledonia is mostly Catholic) and a nice sandy beach.

That night the local village people built huge barn fires along the beach, played loud music, danced and sang all night long until the roosters started crowing early in the morning. We joked that they were getting the water in the pots hot enough to boil us for a nice tender meal. The next morning we took the dinghy ashore and presented some gifts to the chief's wife. When venturing ashore here or even anchoring in their waters, it is customary to find the village chief first and offer him gifts before exploring his land. Fred found out for us that the chief was in bed suffering from a bad hangover. It seems the locals had been celebrating for 3 days the completion of a new "Grand Case," the traditional conical shaped home of a Kanak chief. The rest of the villagers also live in "Cases" that have a similar look, but the word "grand" is not in their description.

The next stop was Ouvea Island, an unusual coral atoll of two limestone masses joined by a thin natural causeway. The southern end includes an enormous green water lagoon with a beautiful, fine grain (no stones), white sandy beach that is about 8 miles long. The northern part is a fringing reef and coral cliffs that reduce the Pacific's swell in the lagoon to tiny waves. The cliffs were the scenes of a bloody massacre in 1988. France's elite antiterrorist squad killed a group of young Kanaks there. The young men were staging a miss-guided independence movement. The Kanaks managed to capture 27 gendarmerie (French military type police) stationed on the island and held them hostage in the caves. Their intent was to use the hostages as bargaining chips in negotiating independence from France.

The story told to me by a local Englishman in Nouméa was that the Kanaks had beheaded 4 of the gendarmerie — gruesome. They released 11 of the hostages during the crises and surrendered when 300 French troops surrounded the caves. However, there were no prisoners taken or trials. The French troops stormed their cave and machined gunned all the Kanak terrorists. The courts accused the army of torturing civilians in Ouvea for information, some of whom died from the ordeal. The story goes on with trials in France and suspensions in the army. As you can imagine the Kanaks in Ouvea are still carrying a lot of resentment against the French. The Kanaks believe their treatment was unfair and contrary to law, but when you lop off heads, the French uproar and response is not going to be subdued.

One day when Fred, *Mariah's* French cook, went to the store, he spoke French to some young Kanak fishermen. His polite message was that their fishing nets should have floats so boaters can see them. He was told in a malevolent manner that, "This was their land and they could fish anyway they wanted." Fred had no trouble seeing their anger and figured he had better leave before things turned ugly. He got back in the dinghy and left in a hurry without going to the store. Speaking English and broken French at the store, we were eyed suspiciously, but had no problems. We did not see any French people on this island except at the fenced, gendarmerie compound. After the fact, we got the message to fly only the American flag and not the French courtesy flag. Anyway, we anchored in several places along that beautiful stretch of beach.

At Mouly, Fred, Pat, and Bob set out to find a factory they heard about. It was supposed to be a native Kanak factory that made sturdy ropes from coconut fibers, what they found was a beat-up old building with rusty hand cranked machinery. Three women were sitting on mats and three men were nearby talking with each other. The women were working on a big pile of coconuts (the norm for the South Pacific where women do all the work) and the men were doing nothing but talking, also normal. Fred asked if some of their rope was available to look at. The women replied that there was none at the factory, but one woman took them to a nearby house to see examples of their rope. We told the women we would like to buy some rope, but it was not for sale because they manufactured it only for building native structures. Is this another case of a potential moneymaker and employment opportunity lost to laziness and deficient common sense or what?

Moving further down the beach we anchored in front of a new resort built with Japanese money and managed by the French. We thought it would be a great place to try some French food and wines. First, we saw what appeared to be a great island for snorkeling with the surf breaking over some coral. When we tried to dinghy to the area, local Kanaks called to us and said we needed permission from the island chief to be in those waters. We told them we would gladly get permission, but the only route to the island was through the water. They just shrugged their shoulders and said the surrounding water was a fish preserve and it was taboo to be in that tribe's water — we gave up on that endeavor.

The resort had not officially opened yet, but their world-renowned chef could prepare a meal for us at about $60 dollars each not including the wine, so said the manager. When the manager saw our surprised looks, he explained quickly that it would be a four-course meal with caviar. Since we are not fond of caviar and his prices were over the top, I said I would come back tomorrow morning to negotiate a better meal sans the caviar. He agreed, but the next day the wind started blowing and it was too difficult to take the dinghy into the beach. There were only two young Japanese couples staying there, probably on their honeymoon paid for by their parents. So, at this point in its young life, the resort must have been in bright red ink. The wind in our anchorage was a bit uncomfortable so we moved further down the beach to a more protected area.

At this time, we met two other boats, *Kama Lua* (U.S.) and *Southern Cross* (Australia). *Southern Cross* was a custom-built 63 foot motor sailor, ketch rigged, built of heavy wood construction in Scotland several years ago. Martin, his wife Mieka, their children Ammi 14, Joel 12, twins, Marina and Grace (two-years-old), take 6 months every year to go sailing from their homeport, Hobart, Australia. This boat was built the old-fashioned way with two big 160 HP Gardner Diesels (the Rolls Royce of Diesel engines, but no longer in production). They typically turn 800 revolutions per minute at cruising speed, less than half of what my engine turns. Another huge Gardner Diesel powered a 12 KVA generator and another 12 KVA generator was belted to one of the propulsion engines. There was a big four-foot-by-four-foot electrical control panel with lots of big analog meters and heavy-duty switches. The motors on Southern Cross were all 110 volts DC; the AC system is 240 volts at 50 Hz. The lights and electrical communication gear operated on 24 volts DC. The engine room also had pipes, tanks and valves everywhere — altogether an engineer's dream or nightmare depending on how things are working. We had coffee and coffee cake on their boat one morning and became immediate friends with the family. Martin fished commercially for 15 years in Tasmania — some of the worst and moat dangerous weather in the world, until he bought a commercial office building in downtown Hobart.

Next we dinghied into the town of Fayaoue to look for the only grocery store for miles, this turned out to be quite an experience. At first, we walked right by the store because it was closed for lunch (12 noon to 3 p.m.) and there were no signs to indicate that it was a store. We finally figured it out by asking the locals, but it was a good thing Fred was there, as you could not help yourself. All the food was displayed on floor to ceiling shelves, but behind a counter that was obviously a barrier. Everyone was expected to ask for what you wanted in French. You could also point which we tried, but the clerk had to touch several items in the general vicinity and look back for approval before he got it right. *Mariah's* rum supply was starting to run low and we thought it would be nice to buy more. However, they wanted $48 for a pint-sized bottle — a bit of a rip-off. We actually had a whole case of rum back on ***Our Pleasure*** and figured we could survive okay until we got back to Nouméa.

We left the beach area and headed north across the lagoon to the Pleiades Islands on *Mariah* with the yacht *Kama Lua* sailing close by. We put out a fishing line on this sail and caught a large white fish on a lure that Martin's son Joel had setup. It was putting up quite a fight at first and then the line went limp. When we pulled it up to *Mariah* we found out why, the bottom half of the fish was gone, probably eaten by a shark. Fred said he left us the best part though and we enjoyed a wonderful fish dinner that night. We anchored between two small, uninhabited islands with lots of bommies (coral outcrops), but well protected from the wind and waves. Fred was hoisted up to the first set of spreaders to guide us through the bommies. The weather being ideal, we had a fine picnic on a small, isolated, sandy beach — it was a wondrous evening.

Sailing back to Nouméa we stopped at a small village and one town on Lifou. The town was named "We" the capital of Lifou, but the anchorage was unprotected from weather. The village is a different story. It is known as Jokin or Doking in French. It is the most northern village in Lifou and sits high on limestone cliffs. The bay is spectacular with crystal clear water and beautifully colored coral. Our anchor was in 55 feet of water and we could see it on the bottom. Walking up the cliffs to the village was like walking up the 500 feet of Queen Anne Hill in Seattle only steeper. I did not count the number of concrete steps, but I would guess they numbered about 400. When we finally made it to the village, we all needed a rest.

We met Chief George and his wife and presented them with some gifts of material for dressmaking, fishing line and Frisbees for their children. The chief and his pretty wife were probably around 30 and well educated. He had a degree in architecture and spoke good English. He apologized for not greeting us when we first got to the village as they were in their "grand case" watching the Olympic Games on TV. The day was gloomy so he couldn't do what he wanted outside. He was quite proud of his satellite dish and the 13 channels he receives. He is a progressive chief and spent about an hour talking with us. He built what he referred to as a miniature Club Med with two bungalows overlooking the bay and a small restaurant serving mostly fish he catches while free diving — I don't think he's getting rich on his Club Med resort. He can free dive to 60 feet and uses a spear gun to catch fish.

The village has a nice primary school full of kids who were on break playing soccer. There was a nearby store where we bought ice cream bars, but we had to wait for the owner to wake up from his nap. On the way back to the boat, we found two young girls not in school. Their eyes got as big as saucers when I gave them each a balloon and lollipop. After saying our goodbyes, we sailed back to Nouméa and into Port Moselle with one more stop in a small, protected bay.

On Oct. 18, 2000 we moved ***Our Pleasure*** in light rain, but a warm 80 degrees to the CNC Yacht Club in Nouméa. We pushed our stay at the Port Moselle marina to the limit and had to move to make room for new arrivals. We found another good slip at the yacht club to wait for the Pacific Arts Festival. The festival was about to start in a few days and we were getting the boat prepared to sail to Australia. The generator has not been putting out enough power to start the 120 volt ac refrigeration system. It took about two days to get the right technical information from the manufacturer to reset the governor to correct the RPM, but now it is working fine. The arts festival only takes place every 4 years and draws tribes from all the Pacific Nations. One of the highlights is their native dancing and colorful costumes as the festival features the best in arts and dancing from all over the South Pacific: Palau, Wallis and Futuna, Norfolk, Tokelau, Marshall, Tuvalu, Vanuatu, Tonga, Guam, Mariana Islands, Cook, Niue, Hawaii, U.S. Samoa, Fiji, New Zealand, Australia and New Caledonia.

Pat and I were quite impressed as it was quite extraordinary and great fun. I was out bid on a beautiful wood sculpture from a Maori (New Zealand native) artist. The beautiful wood carving depicted the original discovery of NZ by six Maori men paddling a canoe. They were decorated in full body tattoos related to their lives and duties on the voyage, such as navigator. In their culture, tattoos contain information about the person's life, his accomplishments, and his tribe, something akin to an autobiography in pictures. I asked him how much he would like for the carving, but he would not establish a selling price. I made a couple of offers on different days with no success. My final offer was $800, but the winning offer was an impressive $2,000. There never was an auction; he just waited until he heard a number that he liked. Pat however did find some good artwork.

Chapter 15

NOUMÉA TO BUNDABERG, AUSTRALIA

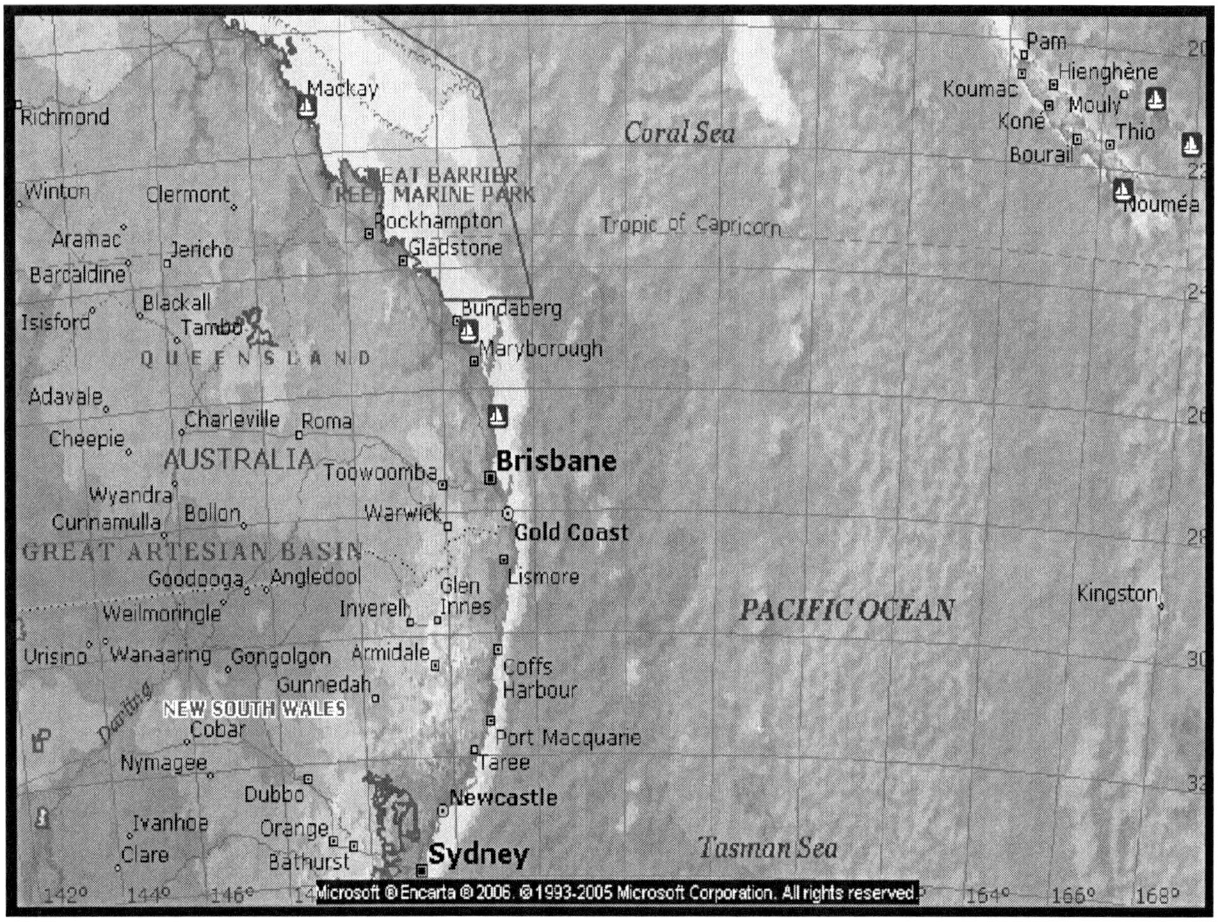

NOUMÉA TO BUNDABERG ON AUSTRALIA'S EAST COAST, Nov. 16, 2000

The weather finally became favorable to head for Australia on Nov. 11 at 8 a.m. With just Pat and me sailing, ***Our Pleasure*** we cleared Dumbea Pass at 10:01 a.m. and entered the Coral Sea in 15 knots of wind from the South East. We left Nouméa along with the yacht *Southern Cross*. Martin's keen weather sense correctly predicted when the good weather would arrive. About 10 other yachts left two days before us after researching weather forecasts and getting tired of waiting. The question of when to leave became quite an obsession with all the skippers. They talked with the weather guys at the Nouméa airport every day and discussed NOAA weather predictions sent by e-mail. The day they all decided to leave, Martin looked at the sky and said, "The weather isn't right yet we need two more days." He was so right; nothing can replace experience at sea. The boats that left early were stuck in head winds making little progress and rolled in uncomfortable seas for two days.

Southern Cross was on a different course than we were as they were going to Tasmania, Australia about 2,000 miles away. We kept in radio contact for several days, but Martin likes to motor sail at 8.5 knots keeping one engine going all the time. He can feather his props so he alternately uses either the port or starboard engine each day. We sailed the 809 miles to Bundaberg, Australia in just 5 days 7 hours at an average speed of 6.4 knots. This was probably the best crossing we have had so far with the wind mostly on our port quarter, which makes for fast (for a heavy displacement sailboat) and generally comfortable sailing. The trip was mostly without incident except for the Australian Navy. Early in the morning (12:15 a.m.) of Nov. 12, Pat woke me because of a large return blip on radar that was on a direct collision course with ***Our Pleasure***. She tried to call the ship, but there was no response. I also tried to call on the VHF radio, but received no response. When the radar blip was about two miles from us, I sent 5 long blasts from our powerful air horn, the marine signal for danger. The air horn on ***Our Pleasure*** uses the same system and air pressure used on Foss tugboats in Seattle and can be easily heard at two miles. The captain came back immediately on the VHF radio and announced that he was in command of an Australian Warship and asked for our position and several other pertinent questions relating to our presence in Australian waters. Satisfied with our answers we could now see this naval vessel's deck guns as they turned around and steamed out of sight.

We later theorized they were looking for illegal immigrants that are always trying to sneak into Australia. The illegal immigrants come from all over the world to Indonesia where clandestine people traders try sneaking them into Australia. It has become is a lucrative business as the illegal immigrants may be charged around $10,000. The island continent of Australia is big with a coast line of well over 8,000 miles. It must be a daunting task to patrol, but Immigration works hard at it with spotter planes to assist the Navy in fouling illegal immigration. Unlike the U.S. Coast Guard, Australia's Coast Guard is made up of volunteers and is not an armed service with ocean going ships.

Bundaberg is one of the several East coast ports of entry for Australia, neat and clean. It was voted the "Most Tidy" city in Queens Land (one of 6 states in Australia). We stayed in Bundaberg for half a month as the locals made us feel welcome. The restaurant at the marina "The Baltimore," served good food and became the meeting place for all the yachties entering Australia there. After we signed their guest book and glued in our picture, the owner carved the name ***Our Pleasure*** into one of the wooden chairs so if you ever visit Bundaberg look for our chair.

The area around Bundaberg is Australia's main sugar cane growing area and the city's claim to fame is their big Bundaberg Rum Factory. We went on a factory tour with several other yachties and learned a lot of good stuff about rum making. They had several varieties of their rums for sale at the factory store, so we bought a few of their most popular dark rums and one of their high-end rums. I am fond of Puerto Rico white rums so I didn't like the flavoring of Bundaberg's dark rums. Most yachties like dark rums and favor rums from the Caribbean, but they didn't like Bundaberg's dark rum either, it must be an acquired Australian taste. We decided it would be okay to keep it aboard for emergencies.

After leaving Bundaberg on Nov. 29, we sailed south down Australia's East coast toward Mooloolaba, a resort city on the Sunshine Coast of Australia. We had reserved moorage there months in advance by fax. As we were passing the Kingfisher Bay Resort on Fraser Island, *Gold Eagle* hailed us on the radio. *Gold Eagle* is a 42 foot trimaran owned by Dr. Andy and his wife June. He is a retired country doctor from a small city in southern Illinois. At the time, I didn't know that Fraser Island is the largest sand island in the world and I'm so glad they asked us to stop and visit. The island is 70 miles long and 14 miles wide at its widest point with sand hills as high as 800 feet. The sand hills are thousands of years old, pure white and soft. Many areas of the island are covered in dense vegetation, including kauri, palm and blackbutt trees and a rain forest that grows in the sand. The island does not have dirt, rocks or clay. One of the great evenings we had at the resort was a wine tasting party of Australian wines. After the wine, we enjoyed a wonderful dinner with Dr. Andy, June and another American couple Harry and Laura off the catamaran *Bresis*. The dinner came with a bottle of wine for each couple and after drinking all that wine, I had a hard time walking a straight line. I did not want to see another bottle of wine for a long time — good thing I didn't have to drive home. In addition, between wine tasting and dinner, an Australian yachtie found us in the resort bar to tell us he thought ***Our Pleasure*** was dragging on her anchor. I never thought to ask how he distinguished three American couples from all the Australians that were there. So, the three under the weather guys jumped in Dr. Andy's dinghy and motored around in the starless dark night looking for ***Our Pleasure***.

Sure enough, she was moved about 100 yards by the swift current. We think the current, when it changed direction, wrapped the chain around the anchor shank, and pulled it out. Although Pat thought it didn't sound right when the anchor was set, we were in a hurry to get ashore and party with our friends so the usual time consuming, anchor setting procedure was shortened. Even when the anchor doesn't dig in properly, the 120 pounds of the anchor, plus the chains weight will sit on the bottom and provide good security in minor currents and wind. I pulled up the anchor on its 200 feet of chain and reset the system letting the swift current set the anchor — problem solved. We went back to the resort and enjoyed our dinner without further incident. We found the Australian and his mate at one of the resort bars and bought them drinks to say "thank you."

Having recovered from the night's excitement Pat and I rented a Range Rover vehicle the next day. This baby is a British designed four-wheel drive vehicle made for difficult road challenges. The challenge on Fraser Island is to drive over the one lane, narrow, sand roads without getting stuck in the soft sand. The driving technique required is similar to driving in deep snow and the rental agency asked us to watch a video on sand driving techniques. The main driving focus is to recognize when the ruts may be deep enough to cause the cars undercarriage to drag on the sand where it may stop all forward motion. Without good wheel traction, you will need to call the rental company for a tow truck to get unstuck. So, the idea is to speed up through deep ruts enough to make it through to better parts of the road where the ruts aren't so deep.

When walking around the resort we noticed some unusual four-wheel drive buses that looked like they were designed for a Star Wars movie. Their axles were 3 feet off the ground and they had huge diameter tires with deep, wide treads. Well, we understood their purpose when we saw them drive large groups of people on tours over the deep sandy roads. We managed to tour the island and get back without getting stuck in the deep sand ruts. We guessed the powerful tour buses were probably responsible for many of the ruts when powering their way through the sand.

Along the way, we found some unusual, clean, clear, fresh water lakes: Wabby Lake and Lake Mackenzie. These lakes all had bottoms of only clean white sand that makes the water crystal clear throughout the entire lake. In trying to keep the water as pristine as possible there were signs asking bathers not to use sunscreen or any bug repellant. The repellant part was tough to follow as the picnic areas have the largest, biting, black flies we have ever seen. They fly slowly probably because of their weight and the high temperatures, which must drain their energy as it did ours. Lumbering along, the flies are easy to swat, but they try hard to bite tourists and swarm on exposed food on the picnic tables. We had to give up on the picnic in the park and finish eating in our car. There are more than 40 fresh water lakes on the island and the largest, Lake Boemingen, covers about 500 acres.

One unusual thing happened while we were driving along an isolated stretch. We picked up a back packer hitchhiking, which is unusual for us as we never pick-up hitchhikers. Well, this young man turned out to be a firefighter from Black Diamond, Washington a small town just southeast of Seattle. He was on his first vacation ever away from the U.S. — small world!

We left Fraser Island on Dec. 2 and crossed the Great Sandy Strait bar at the islands south entrance at 5:30 a.m. sailing with the wind. The weather reports said to expect light head winds by afternoon. About 9 a.m., the wind started building directly against our southerly course. Around 10:30 a.m., the wind was blowing constant at 35 knots, gusting to 45 and the waves were about 6 feet high. I called the Australian Coast Guard station at Noosa Head for weather info. They were surprised at the winds we were experiencing, but had no explanation as their latest weather report was for 15 knot winds. They suggested we duck in behind Noosa Head and anchor off the beach. The Australian charts indicated several large hills to block winds from the south, but anchoring at this resort required approval from the Coast Guard. Noosa Head was only 15 miles away, but in those building headwinds it took 7 hours before we could find shelter. We dropped anchor at 7:30 p.m. just after dark and the Coast Guard, via radio, guided us around the uncharted shark nets that help protect the swimming beach there. We anchored in 15 feet of water about 300 yards off the swimming beach in the heart of this up-scale resort town.

In the morning, visitors on everything that floats and swimmers stopped to see the American yacht anchored off their beach. They asked the usual questions about where we were from and welcomed us to their town. Even the lifeguards came out in their unusual (to us) 5 man, rowed, lifeboat to talk to us. One person named Ray, who looked to be around 60, swam over on his way to examine the shark nets. The nets are located about ¼ mile offshore and trap sharks that swim into them. He told us he has been doing this every day for many years — I guess he doesn't worry about the sharks. We took the dinghy into shore and did some shopping in shops that reminded us of Rodeo Drive in Beverly Hills. As we walked along the waterfront, we noticed quite a few people taking pictures of ***Our Pleasure***, a sight they don't usually see off their beach. It took 3 days for the weather to moderate and the wind finally moved around to the north making the remaining 15 miles to Mooloolaba an easy sail.

Mooloolaba is a nice resort town about an hour drive north of Brisbane with lots of restaurants, shops, and white, sandy ocean beaches. The "Sunshine Coast" aptly describes this part of Australia's east coast, which is in the Australian state of Queensland. It seems like many boating friends stopped by when we first arrived making it difficult to work on boat projects. After settling in, we bought a nice used '93 Mitsubishi to see more of Australia by land instead of by sea.

For Christmas, we drove down to stay with our good friends Marv and Chieko on their boat *Endurance*. For New Years, 2001, we packed the car and drove south 800 miles to Sydney. We stayed at the Park Royal Hotel in a nice beach town called Manly that is on one of Sydney's many bays. It is easier to drive to Manly, which is north of Sydney and only has 18,000 people as compared to Sydney with a population of 4 million. Sydney is a 30 minute ferry ride from Manly and with an all day pass; the cost is a bargain at $5. The pass also allows you to ride on any of their 29 high speed, catamaran ferries, buses or electric rail system all day long.

The city of Sydney has developed their waterfront into a wonderful area for people. The Sydney harbor contains several large protected bays and islands connected by the fast passenger ferries, walkways and walking bridges. It is probably one of the most protected natural ocean harbors in the world and quite beautiful. It was Pat's dream to celebrate New Year's Eve in Sydney and we did it in grand style. We managed to buy the last two available seats at the Sydney Opera House, which was featuring music from several of Verdi's operas. We were worried about the location of our seats since they were behind the orchestra in a semicircular seating area looking directly at the conductor. The seats turned out to be good with splendid close-up views of the orchestra, conductor, choir, and artists. The conductor was a woman with a lot of charisma and showed so much enthusiasm in her conducting with wonderful facial expressions.

During the intermission, we walked to one of the opera house terraces to view the 9 p.m. fireworks. The terrace has a wonderful view of the fireworks as they blast off and light up from the Sydney Harbor Bridge. After the concert was over, all the people on stage opened bottles of champagne, threw out streamers and enjoyed themselves immensely. After those celebrations, we went out to the terrace again to watch the fireworks at midnight. If you managed to catch them on TV, you know they are spectacular fireworks, at least Pat and I have never seen anything like them. The estimated crowd of 800,000 watching these fireworks was oohing and aahing the whole time, truly our best New Years Eve ever. While they fired off some 8,000 shells of fireworks from the harbor bridge, city building rooftops and harbor barges, Pat and I shared a bottle of champagne — quite a celebration!

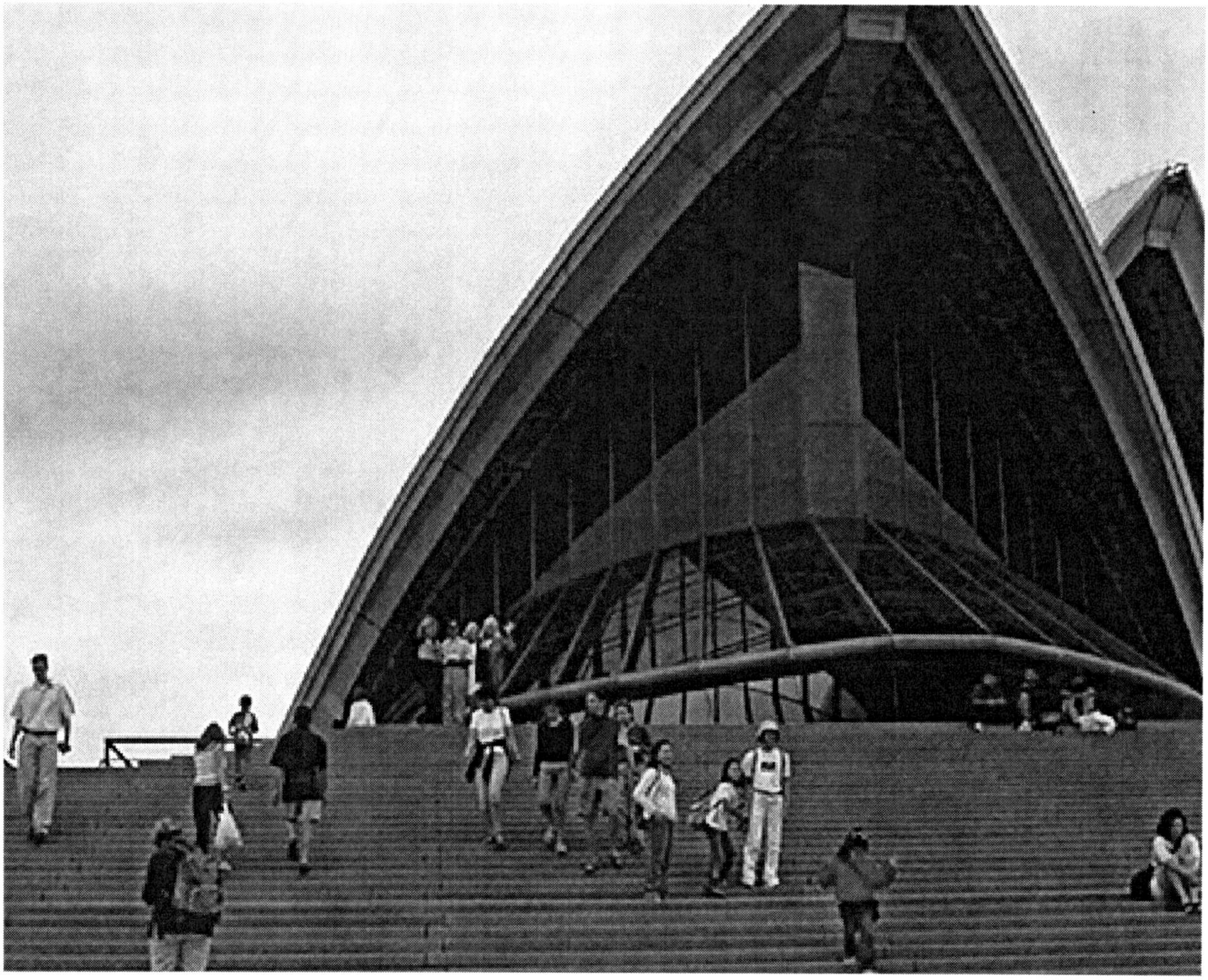

THE SYDNEY OPERA HOUSE, SYDNEY, AUSTRALIA

We managed to spend 7 days in Sydney and thoroughly enjoyed ourselves. Sydney is full of fine shops, restaurants, tall modern buildings and beautifully restored old buildings. One restored building, the Victoria Building, had two restored clock towers hanging from the fourth floor, down into the building's enclosed center courtyard. Each of the towers took 4 years to hand make. The sides of the towers were about 4 feet across and they stood 20 feet high. Technically, each tower is a marvel of ingenuity. They came to life on the half-hour with statues blowing trumpets from turrets and bells sounded the time. One of the tower clocks displayed 6 large scenes from England's history with animated characters. The other tower clock had several animated scenes from Australia's history. Both tower clocks showed local time from big clocks on each of their 4 sides. One clock showed the time in 9 major cities around the world on small clocks and the local time and date on 3 horizontal bands that moved clockwise around the clock. The talent and craftsmanship that went into the tower clocks is quite remarkable.

Dr. Andy, June and a friend Mickey, who was visiting them from the states, were also in Sydney for New Years and one afternoon we met them at a waterfront restaurant called "Nick's." They had just opened a bottle of real French champagne and that was the beginning of a wonderful 3 hour lunch. Our waitress was from Los Angles, but is now divorced from her Australian spouse, so of course, there was some conversation about that. Pat had the lobster salad that was a cooked, half lobster about the size of a small salmon and I had a huge piece of outstanding sirloin cooked to perfection. We had one more bottle of champagne and enjoyed everything. It was difficult to leave, but the bill startled us back to reality in no time.

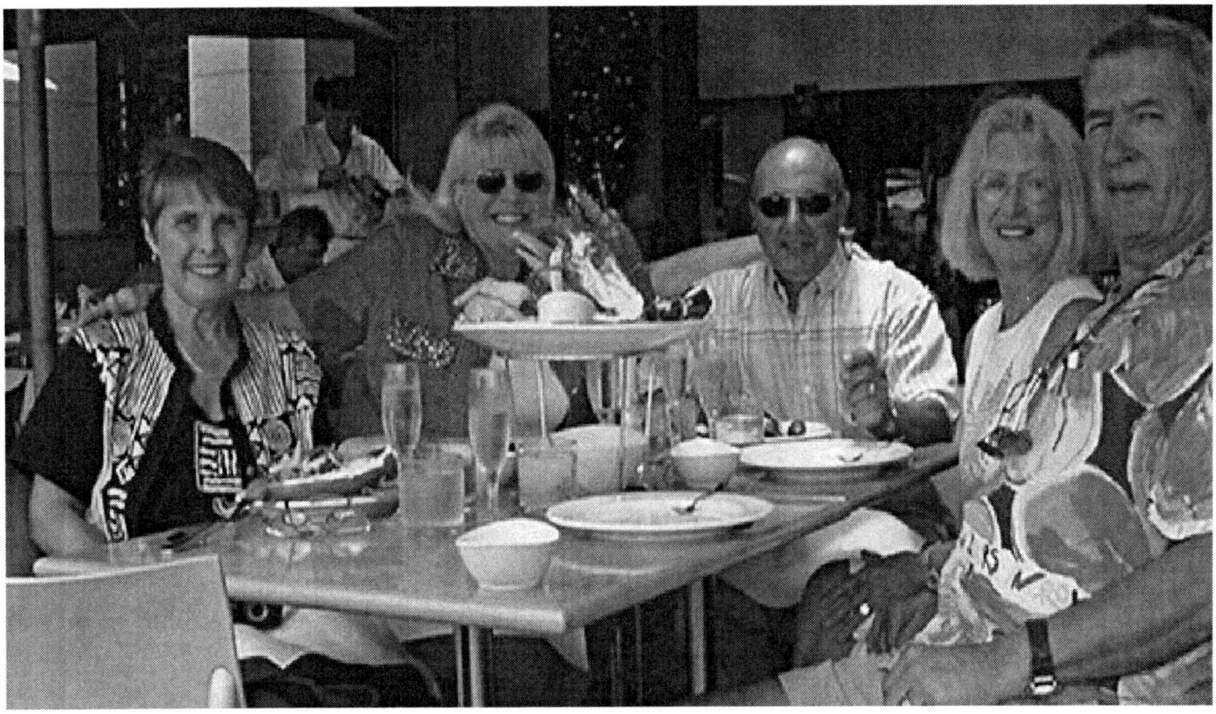

PAT, MICKEY, CAPTAIN DICK, JUNE AND DR. ANDY AT "NICK'S"

We took two days to drive back to Mooloolaba and stopped to have dinner with Dr. Andy and June at Bellina, Australia where they moored their trimaran. The road system in Australia is good, much better than New Zealand's, but you must watch your speed since the police have installed speed cameras everywhere. The cameras prime purpose supposedly is to reduce highway deaths from speedsters. However, the death toll was tittering on 70 already and that was only since the holidays started. Newspaper articles often cited big money sums the police raked in from speeding motorists, but they speed anyway. They also can give double demerits on weekends so driving can be a little disconcerting if you're trying to make time. This country has no mountains only hills so the roads are mostly flat and straight, perfect for speeding. One morning we were one of three cars pulled over for breath testing in random sampling that I understand from the newspapers is common. We were lucky, as we had planned to stop for wine tasting at a winery just a few more miles up the road. If the police had placed their random stop after the winery, we might have not been so lucky.

Pat and I decided to fly to Hobart, Tasmania to visit our newfound friends Martin and Mieka, from the ketch *Southern Cross*. We drove to Brisbane on Feb. 9, 2001, and waited at the airport hoping to pull-off our preplanned meeting with New Zealanders Tom and Fran Sager off the yacht *Dagon*. They were traveling to Australia for Fran's mother's 80th birthday and Tom's business. We had enough time to socialize while throwing down some cappuccinos at the airport. They also brought along some new tungsten-coated scrapers that are only available in New Zealand, but important for woodworking. The tungsten provides a hard strong blade that stays sharp when working with hardwoods like teak. We became good friends with Tom and Fran in NZ as we both moored our boats at the Gulf Harbor Marina. When the sun was setting in the west, we enjoyed quite few memorable happy hours on their boat and ours.

On arriving in Hobart, we followed Martin's advice and booked at the Oakford Hotel on Elizabeth Pier. The pier was once the site of an old wharf, but some good architects and a bundle of money transformed the pier into a beautiful hotel overlooking the Hobart harbor. The first floor was restaurants and coffee shops, floors two and three were hotel rooms. Our room was a suite with a full kitchen, bathroom, large living room and a stairway up to a large loft bedroom. Our balcony overlooked the major wooden sailing ships on display at the show including Martin's 63 foot wooden ketch, *Southern Cross*. Right in front of our balcony, we could look directly down on the deck of the finely detailed replica of Captain Cook's ship *Endeavor*.

We never appreciated the extent of Cook's navigation and sailing skills until our own trip. There probably are just a handful of islands in the South Pacific that do not have a placard or some kind of statue attesting to the fact that Cook had visited this particular bay, port or island — I cannot imagine how they sailed so extensively with the limited primitive equipment available at that time. We can make our own water; carry enough food for several months based on modern packaging/refrigeration; make extensive use of computers, satellite navigation, electronic charts, modern weather predictions, worldwide tidal/current predictions, and navigation is still a skill that challenges us every day we are at sea!

Anyway, the wooden boats on display were a great deal of fun to go through. Sailing ships with one just recently completed and several replicas of yesteryears ships, lined the pier. Some government grants helped build a few outstanding examples of boat building using a native Tasmanian pine. There was one American yawl *Astor*, homeport, California, on display. *Astor* is about 80 feet long sailed by a family of 4 and I think one crewmember. The boat had been beautifully restored and was quite impressive with glossy varnish on the teak cabins and cap-rails. Martin had met them in Nouméa and talked them into sailing the 2,000 miles to Hobart.

After 3 days of visiting all the boats on display at the boat show we were invited to "have a meal" (Australian for being invited to one's home to dine) at Martin and Mieka's home on Frederick Henry Bay (the entrance to Hobart's harbor). Their home is high on a hill overlooking the bay — beautiful view. Martin served us blue trevally, a favorite with Australians and always fresh in their best restaurants. Blue trevally may be related to the skipjack with a texture similar to halibut, but with a unique taste. Some of the best dining in Tassie included the fish, blue trevally, barramundi, and large crayfish (like a lobster, but without claws). The food that comes out of the sea here is incredible probably because of the clear clean water coming up from Antarctica. After a few more days in the harbor, I think we ate at every restaurant within walking distance and tried all the coffee shops. We packed the car again and left the busy city of Hobart to explore some more of Tasmania.

The first European to see Tasmania was a Dutch navigator, Able Tasman in 1642. Other early visitors included Baudin, Bligh and of course, Cook, however, they never realized it was an island until 1798. Roughly, the population of Tassie stands at just under 500,000 and is not much closer to the equator than Seattle is. This equates to a temperature similar to Seattle, except with no mountains to block the wind, it can be windy. Antarctica is only 1,500 miles away so some of the hardy adventurers try that trip. We discussed sailing to Antarctica, but ***Our Pleasure*** is not insulated well enough and icebergs could damage our fiberglass hull. We are used to warm weather and warm water now, and the thought of icebergs and freezing weather didn't sound all that appealing.

We first traveled south to one of the original penal colonies for England and Ireland located at Port Arthur. Port Arthur is a beautiful serene area on a southern Tassie peninsular. The only connection to the mainland is a 300 foot wide strip of land called Eaglehawk Neck. During its operative years, 1830 to 1877, ferocious guard dogs along the isthmus guarded this only route to and from the prison. Mean spirited dogs and the rumor that sharks infested the Tasman Sea, deterred escapes. Since many of the prisoners were skilled in building trades, the prison town became a thriving industry for lumber milling, shipbuilding, coal mining, brick and nail production and shoemaking. The prison buildings are in a setting that is mindful of a peaceful park. The buildings (some are restored and some were left in ruins) include a hospital (you would probably kill yourself rather than go there), commandant's house, guardhouse, the four-story penitentiary, church and several typical homes of staff members.

The prisoners became the construction workers of Tassie and constructed roads, bridges, churches and homes. We found many good examples of their handy work during our travels. The test of time has been kind to their stonework and it remains as a wonderful tribute to their skill. Some 12,500 prisoners served their time at Port Arthur for crimes that seemed so minor to us, e.g., the smallest sentence, 7 years, was the usual punishment for stealing food like one loaf of bread. During that period in Europe, many normally honest people had no work and stole food so their families could eat. The middle and upper class complained to the Queen because of the high incidence of stealing. Her response was the penal colony.

Eventually prisoners earned farm land grants for serving out their sentences with good behavior. Many present day Australians can trace their heritage back to the early penal colony days. Of course, the land given to the Europeans displaced more and more native Aboriginal people. The history of Aborigines in Tasmania is a tragic story. Some Europeans openly hunted the natives and often shot them on sight. The natives fought back and killed many of the European settlers, but superior numbers and weapons overwhelmed the Aborigines. Marshall Law was declared in 1828 and eventually they were completely forced off the island onto other small isolated islands in the north where they did not fare well.

Before we left the Port Arthur area Martin told us to be sure to visit their family farm purchased just a few years earlier. We found the farm down a long dirt road in a wonderful setting near a protected bay where the family anchors their boat. The farm, neglected by previous owners, needed a lot of work, but Martin, working in small increments, restored the house to a habitable point. We walked over to the huge barn where some workers were in the process of installing a new steel roof. They do not have any written records of the farm's history, but the bricks and construction methods probably date back to penal colony days. One of the workers thought women or boy prisoners originally worked the farm, but that is purely speculation. Martin was hoping to meet us at their farm and check out the work progress, but he had to move *Southern Cross* after the boat show closed to its normal berth and could not make the trip.

Leaving Port Arthur, we drove north along the east coast up toward Devonport. Devonport is the northern terminus for ferry traffic crossing the treacherous Bass Strait to mainland Australia. The next major city we stopped at was Launceston in the agricultural heartland of Tassie. This city of 68,000 has some beautiful parks.

It is near the headwaters of the Tamar River, which winds its way north up to the Bass Strait. Launceston is the third oldest city in Australia and the commercial center for northern Tassie. Commerce on the river appeared to be quite subdued from what it must have been during its glory days. One of the nice things to do here is to take the steamboat ride up the headwaters of the Tamar through the Cataract Gorge. Later we walked the trail that follows the gorge until we were blocked by waterfalls (about a 45 minute walk). At the end of the trail, we took a chair lift that crossed the gorge to the Gorge Restaurant and of course a souvenir shop.

We stayed in Launceston for two days and then continued the drive north through the Tamar Valley. In the valley, we came across the St. Mathias Winery. It was such a beautiful day and St. Mathias was probably such an all right person, we could not resist the urge to just sit and enjoy the wine and countryside. The winery sits on a hill overlooking the Tamar River with a large wrap around deck to enjoy the scenery. I think our mistake was to order the cheese plate that was so large we had to invite another couple over to help eat all the cheese and fruits. When the sun disappeared over the roof of the winery and we had overdone the wine drinking, it was time to find a nearby motel.

This part of the world is not populated and so the pace is slow and easy. The country is mostly flat with small hills and populated with large farms — the views are easy on the eyes. We were continually amazed at all the wallabies flattened by car and truck traffic along Tassie highways. I think we drove by a wallaby road kill every 100 yards or so. A wallaby is a small to medium size kangaroo and was a popular food of early day natives and settlers. They thrive in Tassie, multiplying so fast that their population is now a serious problem. The next stop was Devonport at the northern top of Tasmania. We found a nice B&B to stay at called the River View Lodge. It is across the street from a well-manicured park that fronts the Mersey River. This river handles all the mainland ferry traffic as well as commercial traffic. The family that owns the B&B was so friendly we felt like part of their family. The next morning we had a nice cooked breakfast that was included in the cost of staying overnight, AUS $70.

The drive back to Hobart was especially memorable for the scenery, but even better was the great tour of the three stories of the British candy factory, Cadbury. This tour included chocolate samples on every floor of the tour and we were encouraged to sample everything. I was quite lucky, with my limited willpower I miraculously managed to avoid over indulging to the point of sickness. The last part of the tour was their large store where everything was on sale. It looked like most people were stocking up for a lifetime of chocolate binging. Big plastic bags close to their breaking point were going out the door carried by people with big smiles. We called Martin and Mieka from the Hobart airport to say our goodbyes, a little while later Martin and their two twin girls Grace and Marina came to the airport to say goodbye. We enjoyed the company of this family, including their teenagers, Joel and Ammi since our first meeting in the Loyalty Islands. The two teenagers were so nice, well mannered and amazingly at ease when talking with adults. The family is a beautiful example of the warm and sincere Australians we have met in our travels.

Pat and I flew into Brisbane, Australia from Hobart and picked up our car at a nearby airport-parking garage. The drive back to Mooloolaba was going well until we had driven about half the distance when the cell phone rang. The parking garage was sorry, but they had not transferred one of our suitcases from the airport shuttle to our trunk and could we drive back to pick it up? It was a nice day and Highway 1 is a nice divided four-lane highway so we added an hour and twenty minutes to the normal drive time of an hour and twenty minutes. The added time gave Pat and me plenty of time to discuss our trip to Tasmania.

We arrived back at the boat in Mooloolaba on Feb. 20, 2001, just in time to pack for our annual trip back to Seattle. Getting the boat ready for its 3 month stay in the water at the marina and packing was quite a chore. We worked out last minute details with Mike Buky who would recaulk our teak decks while we are in Seattle. Packing, washing travel clothes, closing valves, and cleaning the boat took a good 7 days and we were ready to leave by Mar. 4. Air travel to the states required a shuttle to the Brisbane airport from Mooloolaba and a domestic two-hour flight on Ansett Airlines (no longer in business) to Sydney. In Sydney, a bus transferred us to the international United Airlines flight terminal. The United Airlines mileage program is more generous then the down under airlines so we usually fly on UA. However, the service, politeness, and food on the down under airlines, in my opinion, are a big leap above U.S. airlines.

Our flight time to LA was 16 hours, three full-featured movies and not much sleep. In LA Pat flew to Palm Springs, CA to visit with her long time friends Anne, Deane, Jean, and Sarah who were staying at a condominium annually rented by Jean. While Pat spent 7 days catching up with a year's worth of missed camaraderie, I kept on flying to Seattle to stay with Bobbie and Leslie. Leslie met me at the airport. The familiar drive through Seattle and the conversation with Leslie gave me the feeling that I was comfortably at home again.

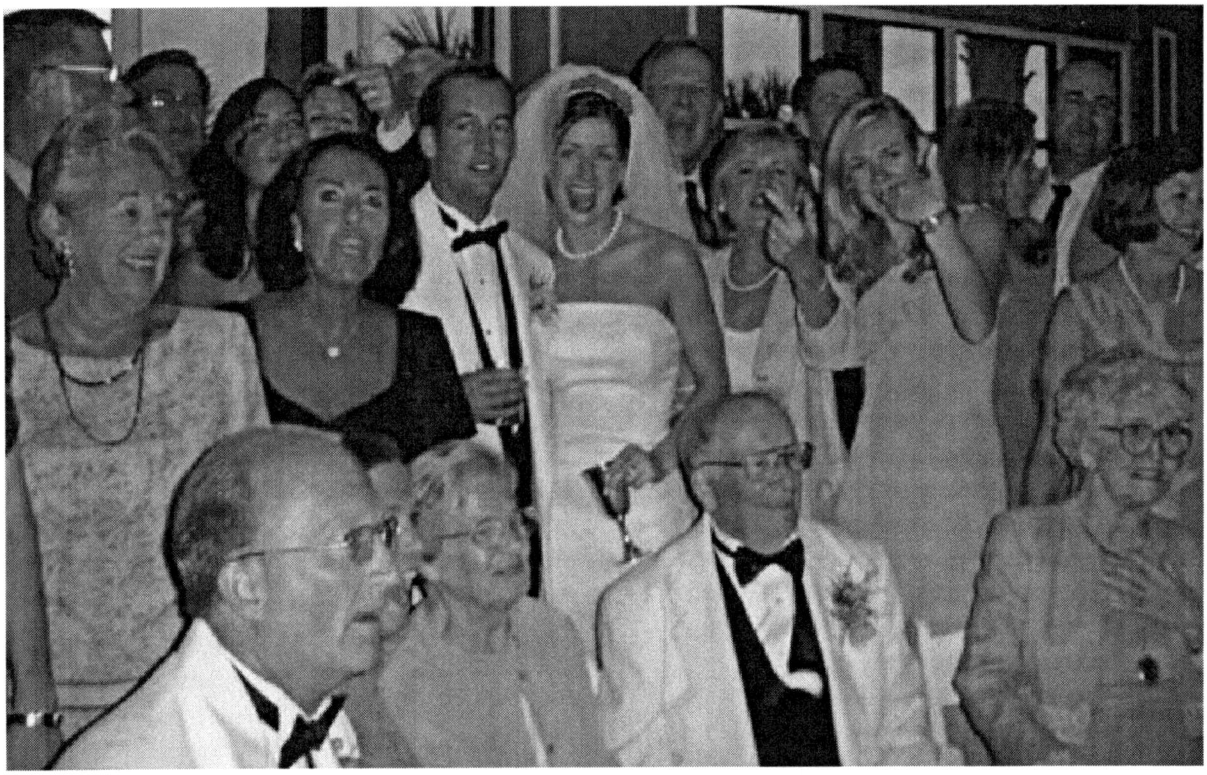

FAMILY WEDDING IN NORTH CAROLINA, SISTER BARBARA FAR LEFT, MY MOTHER'S SISTER EVE AND BROTHER JOE ARE SEATED IN THE MIDDLE

The time in Seattle, as always, flew by, but we managed to complete many important tasks. I bought a new customized Dell 8000 laptop as our 5 year-old Toshiba was out of hard drive space, had inadequate memory and could not handle any more software downloads. We also bought a Sony digital camera from Marjorie and Gary that will store up to 1,700 high-resolution photographs — as Bob would say, "very cool"! We bought enough miscellaneous items for to Australia to fill a large suitcase. Of course, we went through the dreaded yearly ritual of gathering financial records and loaning Uncle Sam some more money. The IRS extended our filing time an extra 15 days this time because of a Seattle earthquake (no loss of life) which occurred just before we arrived. A lot of paperwork type stuff always comes due at this time like renewing driver's licenses, Coast Guard boat registration, satellite emergency beacon registration, and yearly medical doctor/dentist visits. This time urologist, Dr. Tremann, removed 3 kidney stones. They must have loved were they lived because they did not budge for at least two years. Pat had her gall bladder removed as a single stone caused a lot of pain just prior to leaving Australia. Both our procedures were efficient day surgeries. I went to Florida for two weeks to visit my sister and brother-in-law. Pat took the same two weeks to fly to Buffalo, NY to visit her mother and family.

The weather in Florida was perfect and life seemed to revolve mostly around country clubs, cocktail parties, dining out and good conversations around the pool with Barbara. One of the trip highlights was driving across Florida to Amelia Island on the Atlantic Ocean for a family wedding. A cousin, Jane on my mother's side of the family, invited us to the marriage of her son. Jane's father, Joe Ragone was my mother's brother. Jane and her sister Gunnel are cousins whom I have not seen for probably 40 years. My good-looking cousins, blessed with great personalities, made us all welcome and everyone had such a good time. The way families have to separate these days' sure removes the closeness families once enjoyed when the pace was slower and jobs seldom took people out of the city.

On the other hand, Pat spent her time mostly visiting her mother and sister. Her mother at that time was not mobile with various health problems, which kept her close to home. Her condition had not changed from last year so we assumed she would not improve from this point in her life. They did manage to visit other family members and dine out a few times, but Pat was glad she could spend those two weeks with her mother. Pat and I managed to arrive back in Seattle within an hour of each other on May 14 so Leslie picked us both up at the same time.

Since David announced plans to sell or rent his large home on top of Summerset Hill, we faced losing a lot of our storage space. Pat managed to get United Airlines to extend our Seattle time two more weeks, but only after two phone calls to Australia and two to United Airlines. The Seattle clothes we did not give to St. Vincent de Paul were happy to stay with Leslie and Bob packed in suitcases. Most of the 4 file cabinet drawers of old paper records from previous tax returns, etc. dating back to 1977 met their end in the paper shredder. Of course, we should have managed our long-term storage items better, but putting them off is easier.

The 3 months we spent in Seattle gave us plenty of time to catch up with friends. Some of that time included: Dinner at Palisades with Karl and Deane; An afternoon at Lake Lawrence with Tom, Skip and Jackie and seeing Skip's collection of beautifully restored classic cars; Breakfast with Tom and Judith Challoner; Dinner with Father Ibar, Susan and John Ebel; A day with Bobby and Joe Kurka (ex owners of the yacht *Cristal Blue*). Of course, plenty of time was spent with our family over home cooked meals and at various restaurants around Seattle. We had a memorable 40th birthday party for Marjorie on one of the Waterways Cruise boats cruising around Lake Washington. My birthday also occurs in April, as does our wedding anniversary. It's hard to believe we have been married 42 years already, but true. So Pat and I spent a couple of days in Port Townsend at the Monresa Castle. This castle dates back to the late 1800's, has an interesting history and a first class restaurant. Seattle neighbors, Bev and Ole, paid us a surprise visit the second night and we found a good Italian restaurant in town to renew friendships.

I even managed several Friday lunches with my retired Boeing engineering friends, Al, Don, Chuck, Ralph, Senn, Bert, and Wes. Lloyd also made one lunch, but had to drive all the way from Cowiche, Washington. Cowiche is in Eastern Washington on the eastern side of the Cascade Mountain Range. One of the sadder days we had to face was visiting Debby Duffy at her bedside as Father Bob, pastor from St. Anne's church, gave her the last rites of the Catholic Church. Father Bob did a wonderful job in talking with Debby and administering the last rites. A small group of St. Anne's parishioners was there at her bedside including her mother; Pat and me, Judith Challoner, and Kathleen Cramer who had been helping Debby's mother care for Debby. Debby had been fighting cancer on and off for several years, but it reared its ugly head from remission. She wanted to spend her last days in Sun City, Arizona at her mother's home where she died a few weeks later.

We arrived back in Mooloolaba, Australia and ***Our Pleasure***, on June 5. It took several days to get rid of the sanding dust from Mike's fine deck work. In about two weeks, we had oiled some of the interior woodwork and managed to unpack our suitcases. Pat had purchased tickets for a ballet in Brisbane, inspired by aboriginal culture. On June 22, we loaded up the car for a two day stay and headed for Brisbane. Now, I'm not well versed in ballet dancing, but the Corroboree Ballet, in my opinion, was so far out it could have been anything they said it was. The artistic director, Stephen Page called it "vivid creativity," maybe, but to me it just looked like people hopping, jumping, twisting, twirling, and sliding on sand mixed with water in all sorts of contorted shapes.

The Corroboree was supposed to represent three ancient dreams of the Aboriginal people. The first dream called "Brolga," a sacred land of the Brolga tribe where the sprits dwelled. Here the sprits guide a young girl on her journey to womanhood. The name of the second dream was "ROO." Here the dancers tried to look like Red Kangaroos and the dance had something to do with the good old hunting days instead of modern times where they lose their identity. The name of the last dance was "Turtle." Now the third scene opens with three dancers lying on top of each other (a mother turtle?) while sand is poured on them from the ceiling for about 5 minutes. The mother turtle then goes to her sacred territory and lays her eggs, more sand. Then the baby turtles (crawling dancers) simulate the race to the water with all the dancers sliding around the stage on sand and water. Some people apparently liked it and Pat liked it, I guess I just wasn't in the right mood.

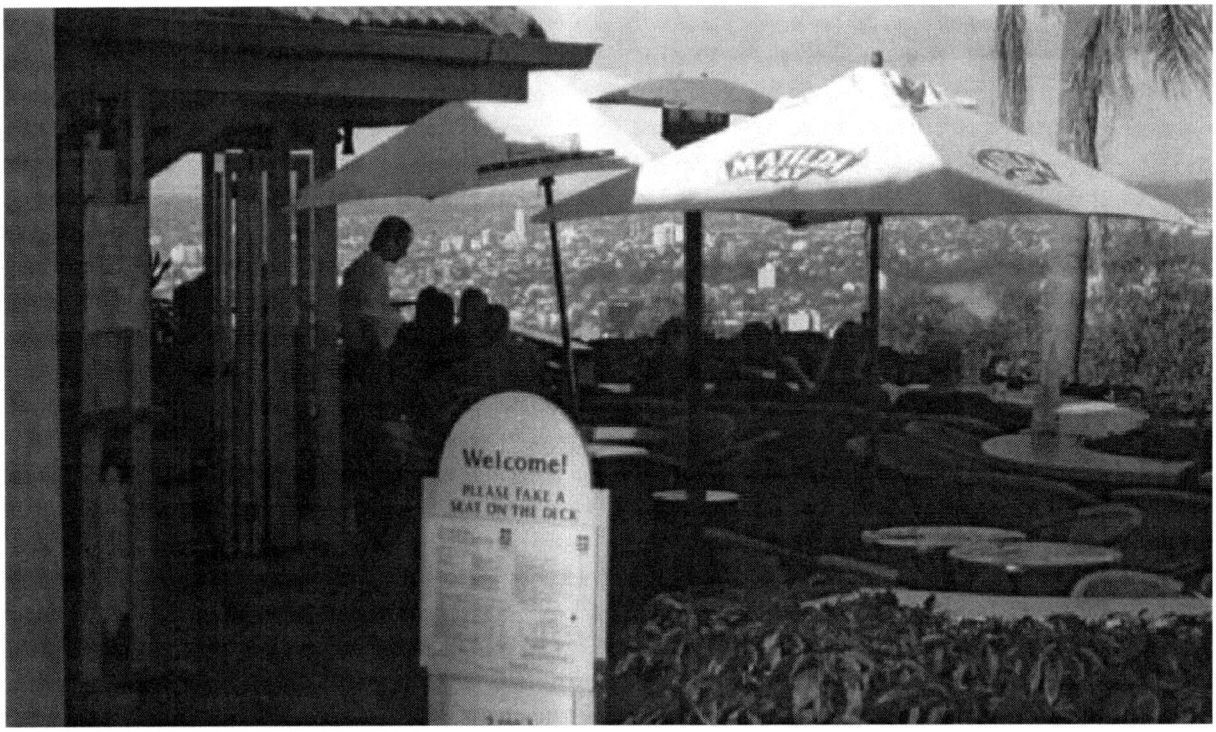

"SUMMIT" RESTAURANT OVERLOOKING THE CITY OF BRISBANE

Well, the rest of the time spent in Brisbane was good. Pat found a nice motel only 3 blocks from the cultural center. The motel room was just great and about $35. We did two other things in Brisbane that I thought were nice: Ride the high-speed city ferries along the Brisbane River and have lunch at the Summit Restaurant high above the city at the Mount Coot-tha Lookout. The passenger ferries are modern catamarans that alternate between terminals on opposite banks of the river as they travel upstream and downstream for several miles. They travel between 15, 30 knots, and the total loop takes 2 hours for about $8. They go right through the heart of the city, close to the commercial shipping terminals at the entrance to the river and through the major suburbs upstream. It is an efficient system as the terminals are close to: downtown buildings, University of Queensland, State Library, arts centers, Art Museum, Maritime Museum, Queens Street Mall, Botanic Gardens, Queensland's Parliament building, City Hall, Convention Center, some commercial areas and many suburbs. There is only a 15 minute wait between ferries, which encourages students, workers, and visitors to use them. There is no noticeable effort to move people on and off, but the time at the terminals is miniscule.

The Summit Restaurant and Lookout was memorable because it was probably the longest lunch we have ever had. Somehow the kitchen staff lost our docket (Australian for food order), which delayed our food by about 45 minutes. However, the wine didn't get lost and after a few glasses, we were doing just fine. They were so apologetic and insisted on giving us cappuccinos after lunch — okay. Actually, it was such a beautiful day, the spectacular view of the city of Brisbane all the way to Morton Bay and the Tasman Sea, made the food delay unnoticed. A somewhat interesting sidelight is that bread or rolls are never served at down under restaurants unless ordered as an entrée. Usually we don't order bread because the food portions in Australia are so large, but this time, bread would have made sense.

On July 8, 2001 when Pat and I were walking the beach at Mooloolaba, we were treated to a wonderful sight — huge waves rolling in from the ocean (the Tasman Sea). These waves were approximately 12 to 15 feet high. Aside from watching these goliaths crash onto the beach, the best part was watching crafts of every description trying to ride them into shore. The riders positioned themselves on the front slope of the largest waves and rode them the half mile to the beach. They included many single person kayaks and several 7 place outrigger canoes, but the most exhilarating rides must have been the life saving boats. These guys are about 30 feet long; open rowing boats, with 4 husky rowers pulling oars that are about 12 feet long. There is one man standing at the stern (coxswain) steering with an oar that must be close to 20 feet long. He gives the rowing commands and controls the whole effort while steering. These boats sport a pointy bow, rounded bilges, a bottom like a canoe and flat transom. For a heavy boat, they can move rather smartly. These boats look like speedboats racing down the front of the waves with foam flying everywhere. Once on the wave and moving, the rowers pull up their oars and the coxswain controls the boat. The ride back must make the effort of getting out there worthwhile as rowing against the surf takes a Herculean effort from the whole crew.

Last week Pat and I attended a renewal program at the local Catholic Church in Mooloolaba, Stella Maris. Three Dominican preachers from the Thomas More Center conducted the renewal or mission. Their center for preaching is located in Webster, Wisconsin USA. The team consisted of Fr. Michael Champlin OP, Sr. Joan Bukrey OSF, and Fr. Nicholas Punch OP. Their biographies are impressive with strong strengths in lecturing and religious education. Sr. Joan was the youngest at 52 while the two priests were both 62.

Before the mission and while attending church here for several months, we became quite impressed with the pastor of Stella Maris, Fr. Joe Duffy, but not overly impressed with the parishioners. He is friendly, warm, kind, charming and speaks in a manner that has everyone listening at quiet attention. When he heard we were living on our boat at the Wharf Marina, about 10 miles from the church, he offered to find us a lift. Of course, when he made the offer he thought we taxied or bussed and didn't know we owned a car. Then he said he wants to visit our boat because he has some special blessings and wants to hear about our adventures. When we decided to join the parish officially and ask for envelopes, he was so pleased that we offered to help support the parish that he sent us a nice personal letter thanking us — that's class.

The parishioners however are a different story as not one person even ventured to say hello or introduce themselves during the several months we attended the 9 a.m. Sunday Mass there. This may in part be a result of their culture, which seems to keep strangers at a distance unless they know you. As an example, during the prayer, *Our Father*, every church we have been to, except in NZ and Australia holds hands. Compared to the other churches we have visited on our travels, I would say they are 180 degrees out of phase. In Tonga, they squeeze your hand hard and sway back and forth while they sing the *Our Father*. The Sign of Peace sees some hand shaking, but forget about hugging or kissing.

Anyway, back to the story, Fr. Joe was so positive about the mission and the Dominican preachers that I agreed to give at least one evening session a go. We did not think many parishioners would support the mission, but we were wrong, they filled the church at every morning and evening session for four days. We actually met several parishioners during the tea time of the mission so there may be some hope yet. The mission team spoke and lectured like a well-oiled machine. They are probably the most well rounded, accomplished speakers I have heard since the Jesuit lectures in my early college days at the University of Detroit. I would say they did their homework and possessed superior knowledge of Catholic Church doctrine, history, customs, laws, myths, and superstitions.

After each lecture, which covered a wide range of interesting subjects, they opened up an hour-long question period on any subject people were curious about — how is that for confidence! I thought the questions were cogitative, the answers were always presented with remarkable depth, and terms that were understandable. The team often received a great deal of well-deserved applause. This mission team sure had it all together, but they must spend every waking hour studying as they could even quote the great philosophers of Catholic dogma. Anyway, I was glad I made four of the sessions, as it is always good to hear positive thoughts about religion and the church from informed sources,

One nearby neighbor on our dock at Mooloolaba is a Dutchman named **Iris**. He lives on a 34 foot steel sailboat and sort of takes care of it himself. He is somewhere close to 80 and speaks poorly because of a stroke a year ago and quite a few missing teeth. He lost his wife about two years ago and now is facing significant health problems. His dog of 16 years also just died and he is having a difficult time getting over his death. Whenever he stops by our boat, with tears in his eyes, the conversation will revolve around his deceased dog. The dog was a little Kelpie with plenty of health problems of his own. The poor dog had an artificial leg and walking challenged his balance causing a lot of sideways walking. Those two problems caused him to walk off the dock into the water a few times. Luckily, Iris was close enough to pull him back on the dock. Then the dog suffered an apparent heart attack a while back, but Iris was able get his heart going again with mouth-to-mouth and massaging. This effort gave the dog another two weeks, but when he stopped breathing a second time, Iris could not bring him back.

Poor Iris, now the doctors want to replace Iris's right arm and one of his legs with artificial limbs. His right arm is turning dark from an apparent lack of circulation and is not a healthy sight. His doctor had Iris buy an electric cart to help keep him off the bad leg. The marina manager went way out of his way to search for a storage area within easy walking distance to the docks. That enabled Iris to lock up his cart and keep it out of bad weather — aging with health problems is a serious problem. At his age, the task of keeping the batteries charged is a challenge and I have had to push his cart over to an outlet that had power when his usual outlet failed. Pat is always taking him something to eat and dog biscuits for his other Kelpie of six years, but the bond with this dog is not quite as strong.

Pat and I have always thought that one of the benefits from this lifestyle is staying in one place long enough to meet the local people on a personal basis and become involved in their lives. We slowly made more Australian friends, but the going is slow. Unless you see them quite often and make the first effort to talk with them not much happens, as they are quite reserved.

They had an offshore power boat race off the beach at Mooloolaba one Sunday, but there were only three boats competing in the big boat category. These boats are about 40 feet long and powered by three 2.5 liter Mercury outboards. After a few laps out in the ocean and back, only one boat was still running. This did not deter the on-lookers lining the shore though as several hundred people watched from the beach. It certainly was a far cry from the unlimited hydroplane races we watch during Seafair Week in Seattle, but with a beautiful, warm, sunshiny day, who cares?

Pat and I have been working on boat projects everyday now to get all the hardware in good operating condition in anticipation of leaving OZ. One of the things that surprised me was a cadmium plated lock washer on a bow thruster solenoid. This washer had rusted which in turn raised its contact resistance high enough that it fused itself to the nut. There are over 300 amps going through this connection each time the thruster is operated so the contacts have to be kept clean and tightly fastened. Cleaned out the primary fuel filters and their sumps; a job that is always messy as some Diesel fuel always manages to leak into the boat. The switch on the fuel manifold that selects between the primary fuel filters was stuck; the fix required dismantling to free the internal valves.

I polished all the interior brass, which had not been done since NZ. That chore took almost 3 days. A day's work is never a full 8 hours though as the morning walk, cappuccinos with breakfast at the Muffin Break (café overlooking the ocean), showering, and reading the morning paper usually takes us up to 10 a.m. Then we have to leave enough time to put project activities away, clean up and watch the sunset during happy hour, so that only leaves about four hours to work on projects — the cruising life can be demanding sometimes.

Thanks to some boating friends, Pam and Bruce on *Aquabi*, we were put in touch with a filtration firm that services water makers. I took our membrane in for cleaning, but tests determined it would not live past its advertised five-year life and needed replacing. The membrane is the heart of water makers, the part that removes salts, bacteria and almost every bad thing known to man. The result, when working right, is extremely pure drinking water. They also found a broken pressure switch that was badly leaking and needed replacement so we lucked out on that maintenance task. This company was only an hour drive from our marina, but so removed from populated areas, we had to buy a road atlas to find it. This firm does all the repair and service work related to drinking and filtered water for mines in Australia so they are well equipped to service water makers.

Since the water maker was disconnected, I decided to change its plumbing to make it simpler to add membrane preservative when it will not be used for more than a month. Buying hoses, three way valves, tubing adaptors to match American standards is not real simple in Australia. Their marine stores only stock a limited number of items in a limited number of sizes. This means a visit to several stores as compared to one in the states and ordering some parts from larger cities like Brisbane. In addition, I finally installed the new 120 volt bilge pump we brought back from our last trip to the states. The old one was not reliable even after rebuilding it in NZ as the impeller liked to bind on the bushing and seal. The new pump will pump about 4,000 gallons an hour — an important pump in case of minor flooding.

Docks seem to live a life of their own, quite different from city neighborhoods, at times exciting. On Friday afternoon, Aug. 17, I was sitting at our dinette table and saw the massive rigging of a 60 foot fishing trawler approaching the stern of the two yachts adjacent to us. The trawler *Valdon* was trying to back into their slip when a strong wind from the west southwest blew her down the narrow marina channel with her throttle stuck in reverse. She smacked, with a loud crunching noise, into the aft port quarter of the sailboat *Artameca*, right next to ***Our Pleasure***. The stern of the next sailboat, *Wanjina I*. *Wanjina I* was a 50 foot sailboat with a rusting steel hull in need of work. But *Artameca* was a beautiful, 63 foot, custom, Sparkman and Stevens aluminum sailboat freshly painted and for sale for $900,000. *Artameca* has a professional skipper and first mate that were off the boat at the time. They only moored at that slip a few days and if that slip were still empty, *Valdon* surely would have hit ***Our Pleasure***. The damage to the stainless steel railings, radar mast, boarding ladder, and paint job was extensive. The damage estimate came in at AUS $20,000, but some enclosed areas in the stern were not fully investigated. The story gets worse as the only yard with water deep enough to handle *Artameca's* draft is in Brisbane, where she was just painted. They were planning to head north in a few days for the Great Barrier Reef, but now will have to back track for 60 nautical miles. Waiting for good weather and a place in the paint-shed schedule could delay their trip several months. *Valdon* dropped her anchor just before hitting the two yachts, but it did not catch in time to prevent the accident. After they shut down the engine, she drifted across the channel on her anchor. A massive 85 foot aluminum catamaran fishing boat stopped her, but lightly enough so as not to cause any damage. A couple of guys with dinghy powered outboards tried to move *Valdon*, but the wind was blowing so hard that the effort was futile. The crew was eventually able to gain control of *Valdon* and move her back to her slip. The problem turned out to be loose screw on the throttle cable. The skipper said he recently replaced the throttle cable, but the 50-cent screw was not tightened properly — sad. I was told the fishing boats are required to have insurance so I hope that is true because the *Valdon* did not look like a prosperous fishing vessel.

Damage update: *Valdon* was insured and the damage estimate for *Artameca* was AUS $36,000.

Sunday, Sept. 1, is Father's day in Australia and the first day of spring. Each day the temperature slowly creeps up. The days will now run around 76 degrees and the nights around 60 degrees. Last week Andy and Cathy Knowles came to visit from Auckland, NZ so Andy could attend a law conference at the Gold Coast near Brisbane. This is the first Kiwi couple to befriend us when we arrived in Auckland back in late 1998 and we have kept in touch through e-mail. We had a good five days exploring the Sunshine Coast and nearby towns using ***Our Pleasure*** as home base. Since they have both sailed and raced sailboats most of their lives they were quite comfortable staying with us. Cathy has recovered remarkably well since her brain surgery a few years back with only a slight limp in her right leg. In the mental department, her faculties are working just fine with a lot of overtime activity.

She used her spare time obtaining heaps of information about the resorts around here so she could return during a future school holiday with their two boys Christopher now 10 and Ben 8. Her planning was detailed with regards to how close the boys should be living in relation to the ocean beaches, the Mooloolah River, the room floor level and what nearby activities would keep them busy. They were good company for us, they like to walk in the morning, and we enjoy similar tastes in food, coffee, and wine. Andy has a wonderful wine collection at home and is knowledgeable about wines. Pat did most of the evening meals on the boat, but on their last evening with us, they invited us to dine at Mooloolaba's finest restaurant located in the Outrigger Resort Hotel — superb!

Our 4 year Australian visitor's visa requires that Pat and I leave Australia every 6 months to have our visa stamped by a country outside of Australia. For us to leave the continent for a day so we can obtain another six month visa seemed silly, but those are their rules. Since we had not been able to see Fiji last year because of the fierce storm we encountered when leaving New Zealand and boat insurance problems during the Fiji coup, we decided to fly over to see what we missed. We drove to Brisbane on Sept. 11, 2001 and flew on Fiji's international airline, Air Pacific. The four-hour flight took us directly to the city of Nadi, Viti Levu. This island is large at about 4,000 square miles and it took an hour plus to drive the narrow two lane road from the Nadi airport to the Outrigger Reef Fiji Resort. The resort is located on the south west coast of Viti Levu on what they call their Coral Coast.

The resort faces the ocean and has a fringing reef where heavy surf breaks constantly about 100 yards from the beach. The water depth out to the reef is about knee height so walking out to the reef is easy, but there is a lot of old dead coral along the way and not much sand. This coral appears as large dark spots in the water and distracts from the natural beauty of the scene. It is a beautiful sight to see the ocean breaking over the reef, but the watercolors of the ocean and the lagoon are not as spectacular as the colors we saw in Bora Bora. The resort is only about a year old so everything is new and well cared for. Our room was on the seventh floor of the hotel that has 207 guest rooms. Each room is air-conditioned with private lanais and 150 degree views of the resort and the ocean breaking over the reefs.

There are also 47 bures, bungalows that are modern versions of native huts — with every modern convenience, vaulted ceilings, decorated with hand painted tapa cloth, but no air-conditioning only ceiling fans. Daytime temperatures were pushing 90 degrees so we opted not to stay in a bure. Most of the bures do not have views of the water, but their beautiful landscaping of native trees and flowers make up for the lack of views. Six of the bures faced the ocean near the sea wall, but the walkway passes close to their entries and windows reducing privacy for the people staying in these overly priced units. Many of the resort bures in the South Pacific actually extend out over the water. Private stairways face the water and enter into the water of the lagoon with a nice deck to sunbathe — real class.

There were two fine restaurants, three bars, a wee hour's nightclub if your ears could stand the pain of their megawatt sound system and a swimming pool about the same area as a football field. The atmosphere of the pool design was pleasant with waterfalls, clever use of shapes, palm trees, umbrellas and boulders designed to separate the shallow children areas alongside the adult areas. Sitting on our lanai watching the palm trees sway and the white water breaking over the outer reef was a relaxing, soothing experience.

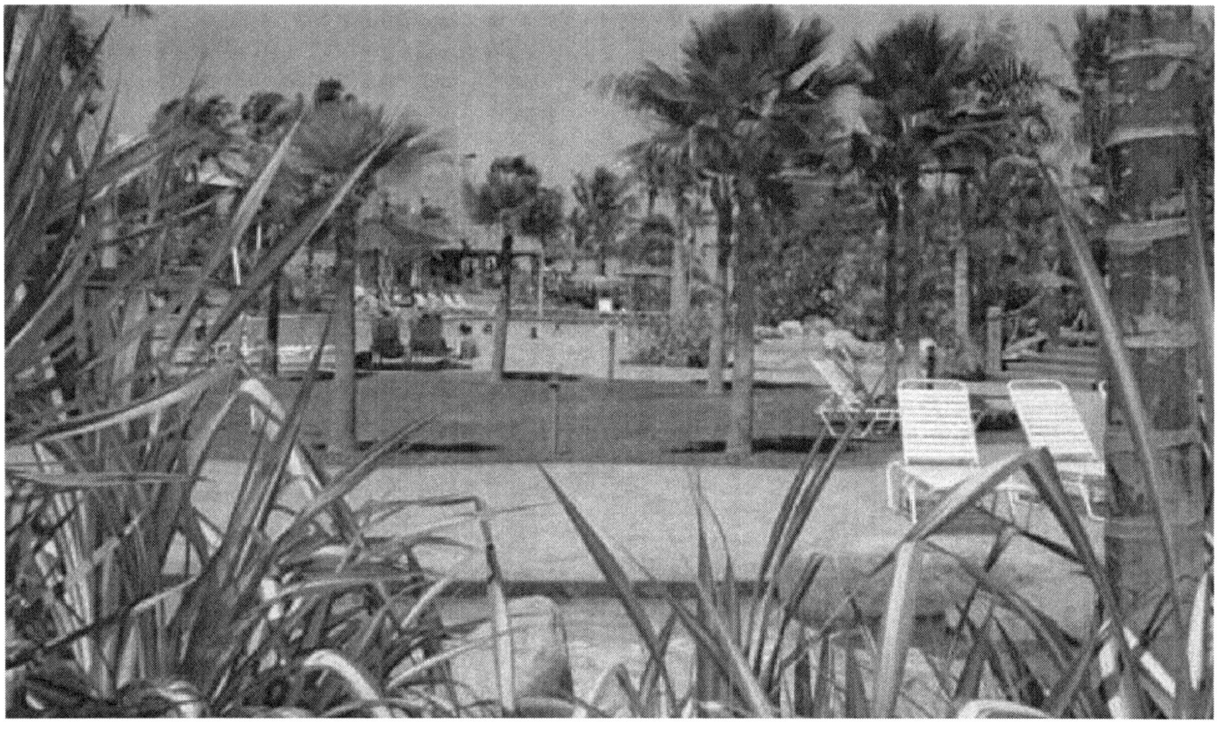

SWIMMING POOL, OUTRIGGER REEF HOTEL, FIJI

The next morning, Sept. 12 (Sept. 11 in the states), Pat was drinking coffee while watching the morning unfold from the lanai and I turned on the TV curious to see Fijian television. There are two channels, one

Fijian channel and one resort channel from Sky TV — South Pacific satellite television. Sky TV was showing American cartoons, but the Fijian channel had BBC coverage of the terrorist attacks on the Trade Center Twin Towers in New York. Up to this point, we knew nothing of the attacks and could only watch in disbelief, shock and horror to the unbelievable pictures of the carnage to one of our finest cities. We could not move for the rest of the news coverage that only lasted about three hours and then went back to normal programming.

The day became a blur for us almost as if it was non-existent and we lost the strength to do anything except release our tearful emotions. We felt quite cutoff from up-to-date information from the U.S. as their TV news contained limited information for about five minutes twice a day. That same day the Fijian government was swearing in a newly elected prime minister, president and cabinet in response to agreements from last year's coup. The election news became Fiji's focus for the rest of our weeklong stay. Several elected officials from the Fijian Indian labor party did not receive cabinet appointments. Those officials threatened to argue their case in court. Their problems seemed rather petty and trivial in comparison to world problems, but we found the Fiji Times from Suva was reprinting news releases from most of the world's important newspapers.

I must say that many of the resort's staff and other vacationers went out of their way to express their sympathies to us when they learned we were from the U.S. One amazing event we watched on TV was the Fijian fire department two days later joining together to hold a time of silence and prayer for the firemen who died in New York during the rescue efforts. It seems the firefighters around the world regard their counterparts as brothers no matter where they are from — what a great expression of closeness and empathy for that profession!

Pat and I cancelled our plans to visit some other parts of Fiji like the Musket Cove Resort on Malolo Lailai Island. The Musket Cove Marina has become the rendezvous place for all the cruising yachts that stop in Fiji. We found ourselves in a state similar to suspended animation, we were breathing, but moving about was an effort and enjoying ourselves seemed just plain intolerable. We did watch a group of Fijians from a local tribe perform a fire walk ritual one night, but it was a quiet peaceful ceremony presided over by their high priest. The rocks had been in a fire for several hours so they were hot. After the walkers had left, a few onlookers tried to touch those rocks and were shocked at just how hot the rocks were even after a cooling down period.

On Saturday, we went for a long walk on a road that parallels the ocean and ran into an Australian and his family. Ron, who has lived in Fiji for fourteen years, married a Fijian Indian woman and adopted her two children. He showed us his property and his two homes in what he called his "compound." He also owned a home and property in Australia and they were excited about going there the next day. His family recently received their Australian citizenship papers and was anxious to put them into play. He was quite proud of his son who is 28, trained as a chef, did not smoke, do drugs or drink and was looking forward to working in Australia. His two-year old grandson offered up his arms for us to bounce him off the ground and into the air. His six-year old granddaughter can already speak three languages. Fijian people are definitely a happy culture.

On Sunday, we called a taxi and went to St. Joan of Arc Catholic Church in the nearby town of Sigatoka. The church was an ordinary wooden structure, but the singing was extraordinary. In a manner similar to Tonga, everyone sang in parts with no music sheets to read, no music playing and without a director. Half the songs were in English and were the same songs we sing in Seattle, the other half were in Fijian. The 4 altar boys were dressed in white and red cassocks like those that I wore as an altar boy at St. Paul's Church in Kenmore, New York. There was one significant difference; the boys at St. Joan of Arc were barefoot.

After church, we talked to the Irish pastor who had served in Fiji for forty-four years. I told him of our fondness for Irish priests, but he considered himself not a typical Irish priest because his personality leaned more toward the feisty side, but mellowing with age. He probably should be retired at this stage in his life, but I am sure the diocese is too poor to pay retirement benefits. We complemented him on the singing during the

Mass, but with a grimace said: "It should have been much better." They were supposed to sing the "Our Father" and "The Gloria" but he claimed they get lazy and sing whatever suits their mood. This seems somewhat typical of the island people we have met during our sailing experiences in the South Pacific. The indigenous natives are quite happy to lease their lands to people of other cultures whom are more willing to put in the required physical effort. Whereas, the island people are quite happy to practice their time honored traditions of dancing, singing, art crafts and fishing — the path to happiness and contentment?

When we got back to Mooloolaba and the boat, we found six letters plus phone messages from the women's prayer group at the local Catholic Church, Stella Maris. They were all thoughtful messages expressing their sorrow and sympathies for us and the U.S. over the Sept. 11 terrorist's attacks. Our feelings were deeply affected by near strangers taking time to share their feelings of compassion. They demonstrated great insight on what our feelings would be like and the prayers they were saying for everyone — so uplifting to know caring people during such a sad time in our history.

Back in Seattle, one of our dearest and closest friends from St. Anne's Church, Judith Challoner, died on Oct. 14 after losing a short battle with leukemia. She had only been diagnosed with the disease a month before, but the cancer was already so widespread that she declined to go through the treatment process. She elected not to put herself or her family through an ordeal with a low probability of success and was sure to degrade her quality of life. She died at home surrounded by her husband Tom, some of her family, her nurse and close friends who were visiting at the time. The people who saw her after she died all witnessed that her wrinkles disappeared, her skin turned clear and smooth and her facial expression turned serene.

Carol Ford from St. Anne's and our daughter, Marjorie, were keeping us informed almost daily via e-mail of her condition. Their information explained the prayer service, what readings were read and songs that were sung. St. Anne's is a pretty close-knit community and Judith's friends needed a method to share their love for her. They surely gave Judith a strong understanding of everyone's love for her. Judith was blest with a deep spirituality and a truly wonderful mind. She and Tom were involved in everything at St. Anne's and always had us over or invited us out whenever we were in town. Her knowledge, wit and spirituality usually came up with some profound answers to any questions I saved for her — St. Anne's will just not be the same!

It is now Oct. 14, 2001 and Chris, the canvas guy who will build a new dodger for us, is trying to finish up some of his smaller jobs before he tackles ours so we have at least one week to do some exploring by car. Pat has been keen to explore more of Australia for quite some time. We had planned to do an October road trip with Bill and Dianne, but they decided to cancel their trip from the states after the Sept. 11 problems. Allen, who finally finished the stainless steel frame for the dodger, managed to spread out our job over two months as he only worked on our job in between his other work. His delays threw off Chris's dodger schedules and although Allen does beautiful work, he lacks a good work ethic, a common problem in the Australian marine trades.

Anyway, we finally packed the car for one week, but took two. We drove north from Mooloolaba along the east coast of Australia (The Great Barrier Reef area) until we almost ran out of paved road. We stopped at every major town and every major marina along the beautiful east coast. We also traveled into what is referred to as the "bush" which is that part of the country before you get to the "outback" (nothingness). We put about two thousand miles on our reliable Mitsubishi with only two minor problems. The first was a piece of metal went through our front tire during the twenty-five mile trip over dirt and gravel roads from Carnarvon Gorge. The second was driving over a dead kangaroo that was in the middle of the highway. With no shoulder and oncoming traffic, there was no room to drive around the dead kangaroo. I thought we would have enough clearance if we passed over him in between the tires — no such luck. He was bigger than I thought and made some terrible noises hitting various parts of our undercarriage as we passed over him at 70 miles an hour.

After running over the roo, I noticed a slight noise in our exhaust system, but it sounded rather minor. The poor dead kangaroos are a common sight alongside the highways further north. I can see why all trucks and many cars have heavy-duty tubular bars (bully bars) protecting their front ends. There were many signs warning of kangaroo crossings, koala crossings (did not see any of these guys) and cassowary crossings. Cassowaries are large flightless birds about the same size as an emu. We have not seen any cassowaries in the wild, but the bird life is incredible. In the areas we traveled, there are 257 known species of birds and they can be heard singing everywhere. Some of the common birds we have seen in the wild and can identify include the cockatoo, eagle, magpie, kookaburra, lorikeet, pelican, egret, ibis and osprey. We have seen all sorts of beautiful birds and heard some incredible singing, but cannot always identify the birds.

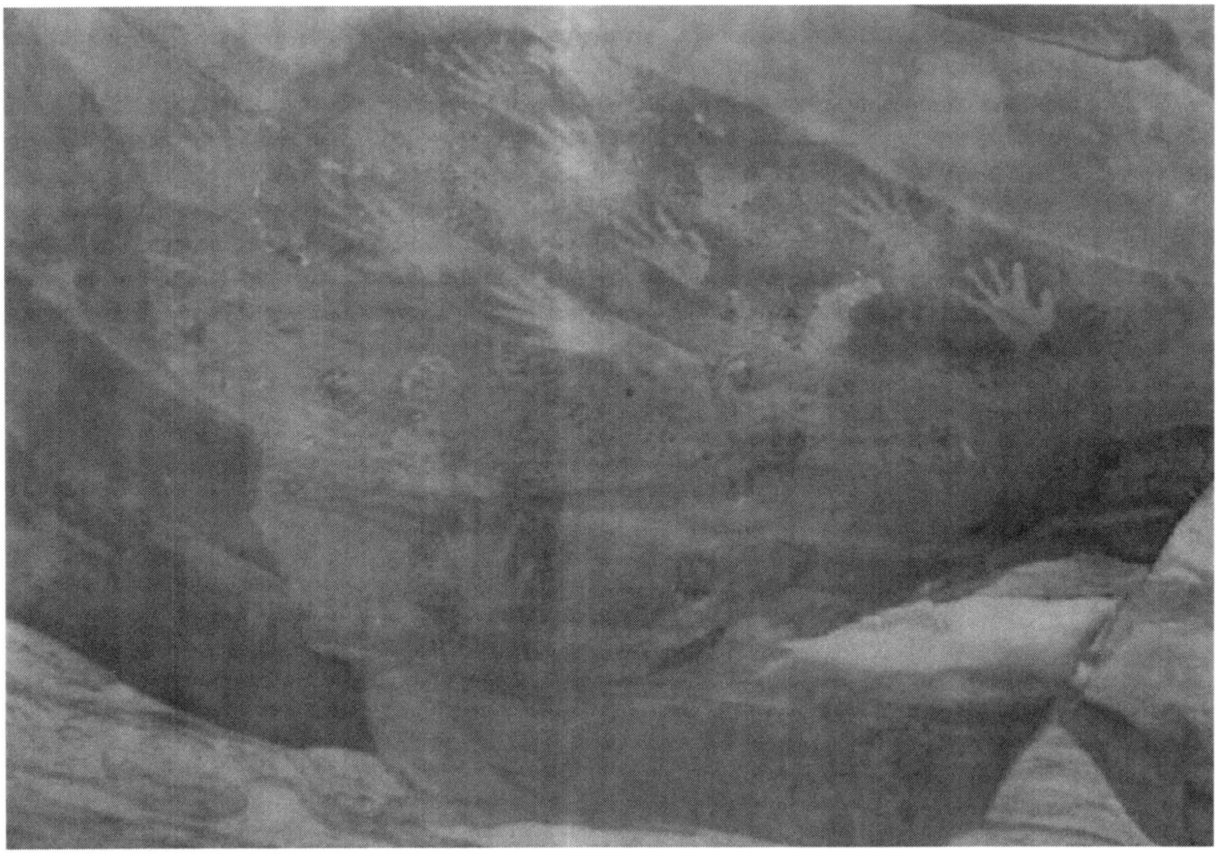

STENCIL CAVE ART, CARNARVON GORGE, QUEENSLAND, AUSTRALIA

Driving around this country gives one a good idea of just how vast Australia is and how rich the country is in minerals and precious gems. Part of our trip to the bush included the largest sapphire fields in the world in the towns of Rubyvale and Sapphire Ville. Pat managed to find a rare, golden yellow sapphire in Rubyvale so she considers the trip a complete success. To get there you have to drive along the Capricorn Highway, which is the same latitude as the Tropic of Capricorn. We took a private guided tour through the Heritage underground sapphire mine that was interesting. Most of the mines are only about 45 feet below the surface and maintain a natural mild temperature that is consistent all year long. It is spring here now and the temperature in this area was about 86 degrees, but inside the mine, the temperature was about 72 degrees. The miners usually do their mining in the summer when the outside temperatures are well over a hundred and visitors are scarce because of the heat.

From the sapphire fields we drove to Carnarvon Gorge National Park. The entry to the park requires a 30 minute drive over dirt and gravel roads. Pat liked the gorge, but I could have skipped it without much love loss. They are trying to maintain this park in its natural state, which translated means; you have to walk to all the sites. To visit the most difficult site would have required us to become mountain goats. We did manage to visit the three nearest sites, which gave us a good idea of what the park and gorge were like. I think the best site in the park was a cave only 1,500-feet from our cabin that contained old art work from the aboriginals who once lived in the area. The art is called stencil art formed by spitting a red paste (okra) around an object (usually a hand) pressed against the cave wall. Since this stuff is thousands of years old, no one knows if it has any significance. Some experts think they are communicating via a sign language since the hands and fingers are shown in different patterns.

We also went on a conducted tour through a gorge with a young women guide who was taking time off from her real profession of veterinary medicine. She was a super guide, knowledgeable. However, walking through the bottom of an 8 foot wide gorge, with sheer 60 foot canyon walls and walking in cold water was not pleasant.

The major cities we visited and did some exploring included: Gladstone, Rockhampton, Emerald, Rubyvale, Sapphire, McKay, Arlie Beach, Townsville, Cairns, Mission Beach, Halfmoon Bay at Yorkey's Knob, Port Douglas, Kuranda, Bowen and Barney Beach. Of course, my main thrust along the coast was to visit as many marinas as possible since we will pass this way when leaving Australia, whereas Pat wanted to see all the cultural centers, parks, aquariums, etc.

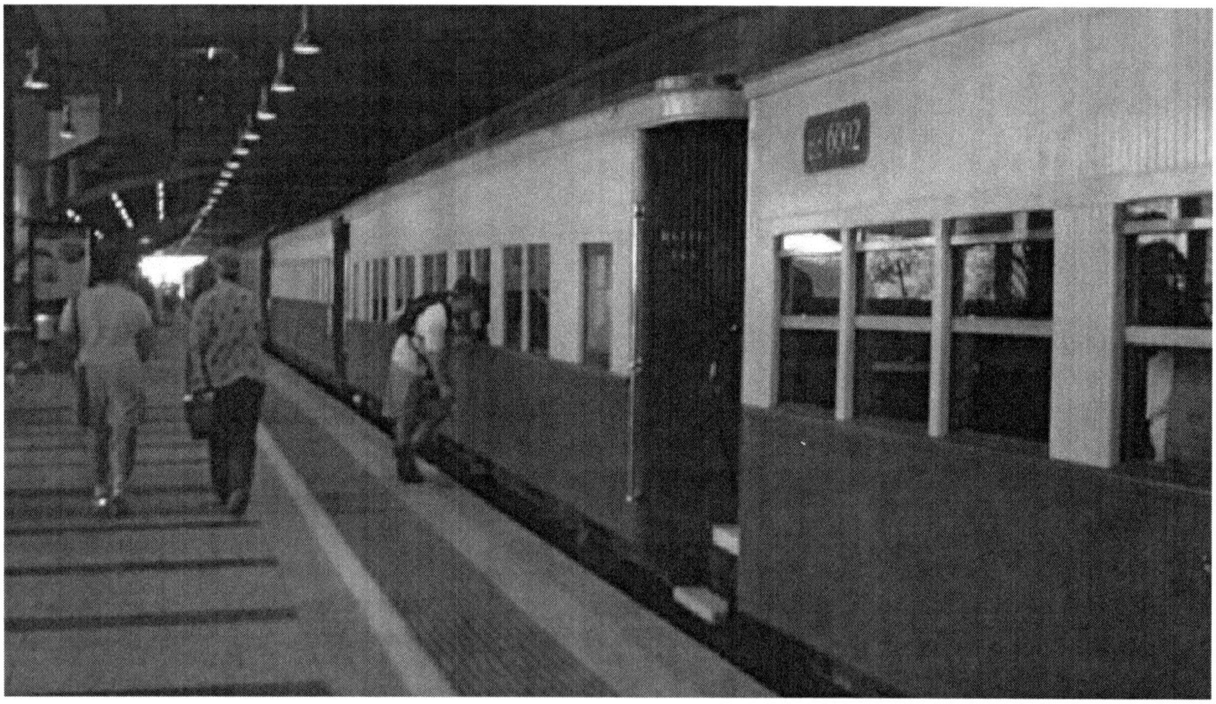

KURANDA RAILWAY TRAIN AND STATION, CAIRNS, AUSTRALIA

Port Douglas is near the northeastern tip of Australia and close to the end of paved roads along the east coast. This town is a big tourist destination for its closeness to islands and reefs of the Great Barrier Reef system. Townsville is a large city with an aquarium called "Reef HQ." Their reef display is the largest living reef display in the world and simulates the Great Barrier Reef. It is similar in size to two tennis courts enclosed in glass to a depth of twenty feet. Tour information claimed it was quite a feat to duplicate the wave action, salinity, temperature, plants and sea life so the reef and its thousands of inhabitants could exist in a natural environment. We found Cairns to be an interesting city with lots of attractions. One was the Kuranda Scenic Railway ride through the rain forest. The train's tracks were laid in 1882 when everything was done with manual labor including the tunnels, bridges and the path clearing through dense vegetation. The engine is now Diesel, but the passenger cars have been restored to their original functionality and charm.

The train trip took almost two hours and at the Kuranda terminal, you can take the train back to Cairns or take the cable car, "Sky Rail," to the bottom of the mountain and visit the Tiapukai Aboriginal Center. We had arranged to have a tour bus meet us at the center so we took the Sky Rail down. The Sky Rail trip is quite long as it makes three stops along its 40 minute route.

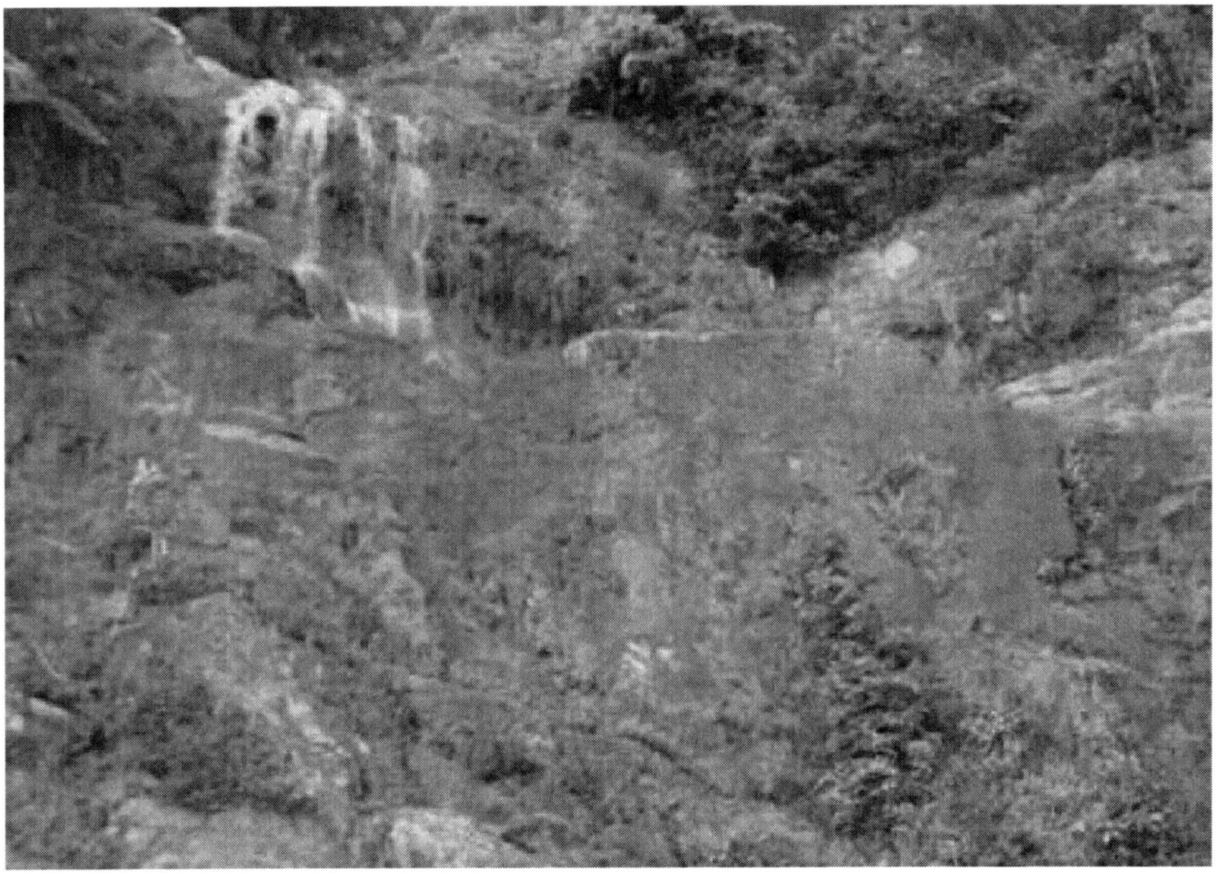

RAIN FOREST WATERFALL FROM THE TRAIN

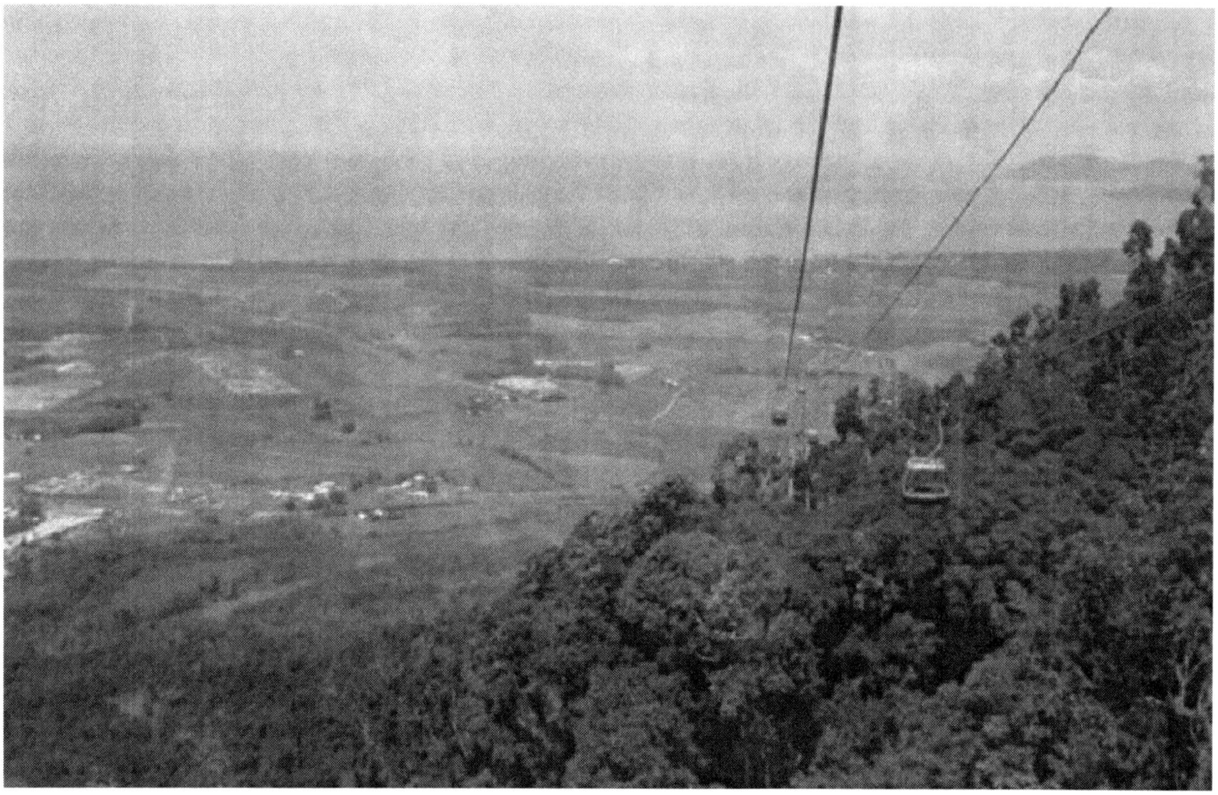

"SKY RAIL" TO THE TIAPUKAI ABORIGINAL CENTER

The accommodations when traveling in Australia are similar to those in New Zealand: home stays, B&B's, motels, hotels, resorts, campgrounds and caravan parks. You can expect well maintained rooms that are clean and fresh. All rooms except expensive hotels are setup with a small kitchen, as most people here will carry their own food to save on traveling costs. Caravan Parks (trailer parks) are a good place to stay while traveling. The lands where the parks are located are generally the most scenic in the area and if you are not pulling a trailer or camping, they provide small cabins or villas. The villas are similar to an apartment in accommodation, but priced around US $25 per night…impossible to beat the price. The newer ones are fabricated off site as a modular type small home, then brought in, and setup on a permanent site.

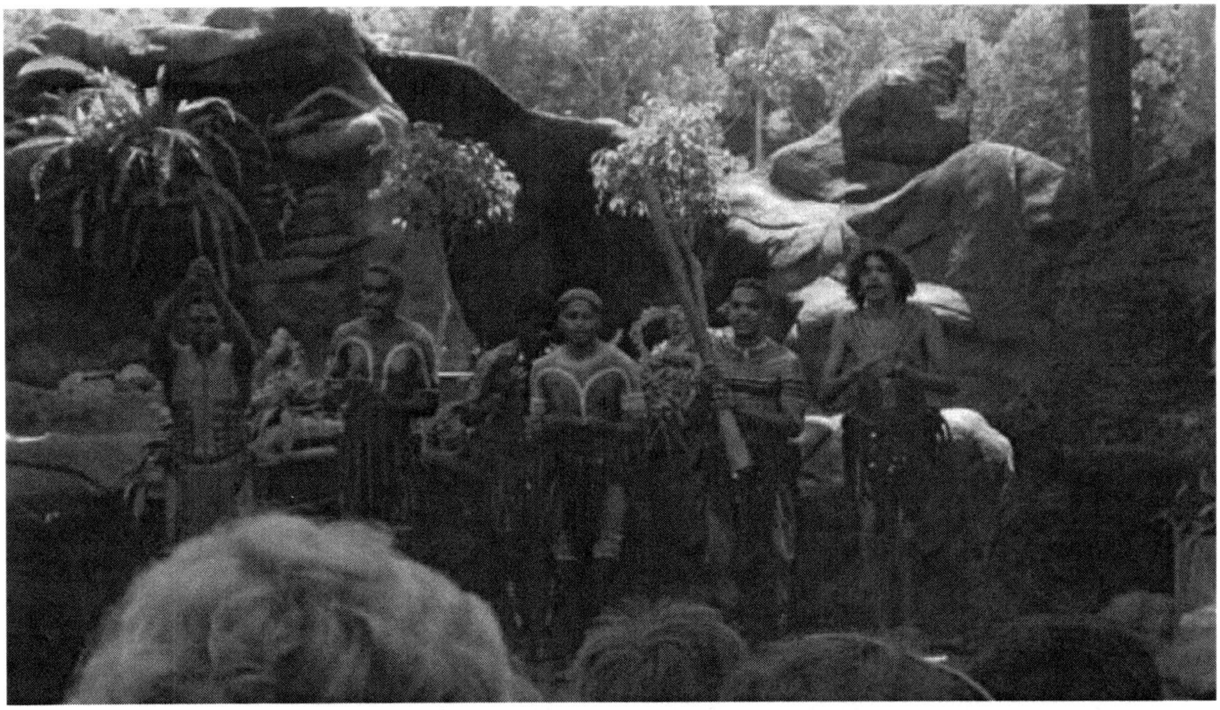

TIAPUKAI DANCERS, ABORIGINAL CENTER

Well, Oct. 6 was Australia's granddaddy of horse races, the Melbourne Cup. Every pub, club and restaurant around the country offers luncheon specials with sweepstake betting. Australian's are keen on horseracing and this was the 140th running of the cup with big prize money at stake. In Melbourne, the town is closed down so everyone can participate. Race day is the day women look forward to after months of designing and sewing fashionable race day clothes. A lively contest is held to pick the best-dressed woman. It rained before and during the race, but that did not deter the 92,500 race goers' spirits. The Mooloolaba Yacht Club hosted a luncheon buffet for the race, a wonderful treat for Pat and me. All you could eat ham, roast beef, beef Stroganoff, vegetables, salads and desserts for only $7.50 per person. Glasses of quality champagne were only $2.00. We bought $10.00 worth of sweepstake tickets and Pat won $36.00. The winning horse, "Ethereal," was from New Zealand and won AUS $2,400,000 for its owner. The trainer of "Ethereal," Sheila Lexon, 45, won some acclaim as the only woman trainer ever to win the Melbourne Cup. Even more impressive, in 1991 she went into a coma for eight days and almost died after a fall in an amateur horserace in Gisborne, New Zealand. She has fully recovered, but no longer races.

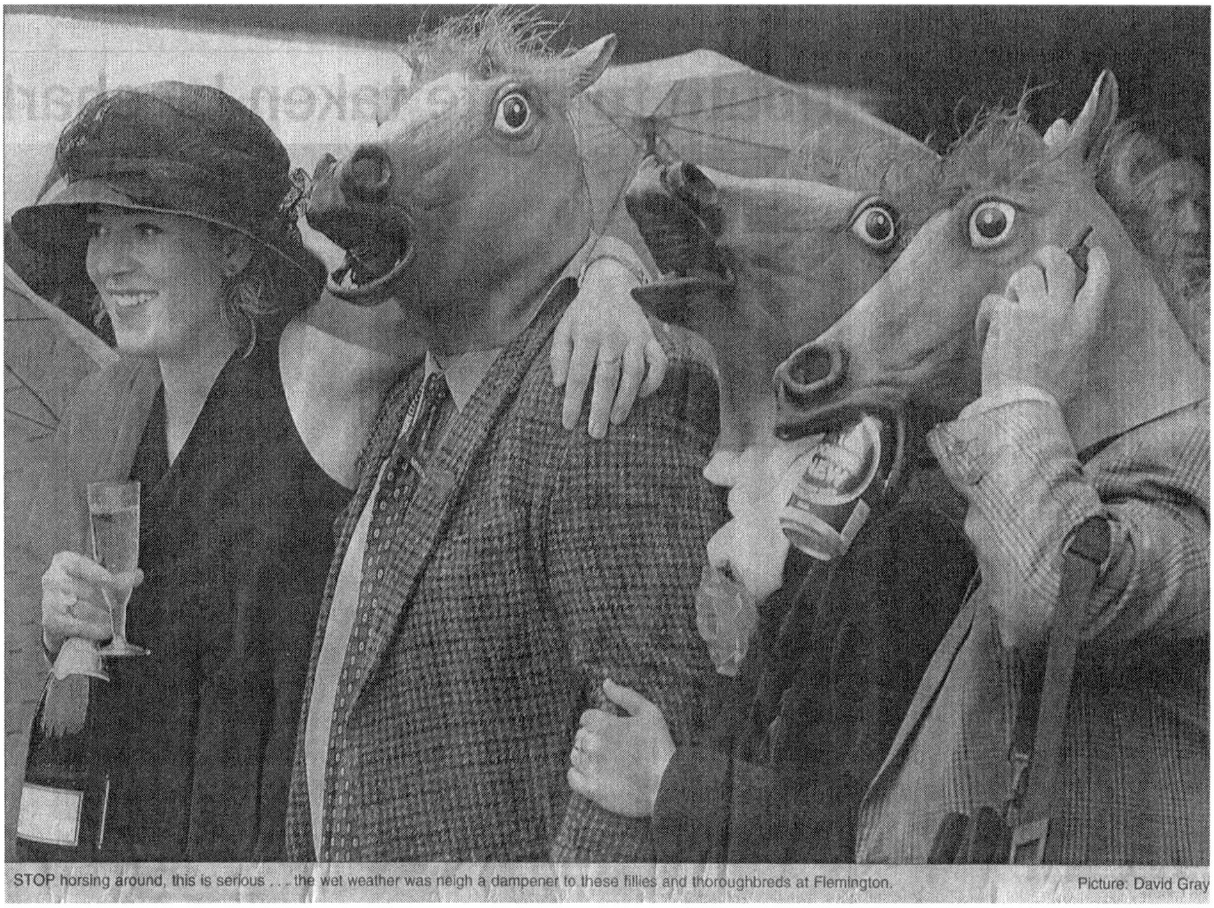

STOP horsing around, this is serious . . . the wet weather was neigh a dampener to these fillies and thoroughbreds at Flemington. Picture: David Gray

Photo courtesy of Reuter's news, photographer David Gray.

COURIER-MAIL NEWSPAPER PICTURE TAKEN AT THE MELBOURNE RACETRACK — HOW'S THAT FOR HUMOR?

Chapter 16

THE AUSTRALIAN OUTBACK

On Dec. 11, 2001, Pat and I flew from Brisbane to Ayers Rock (the Aboriginal name for this rock is Uluru) on Qantas Airlines via Sydney. This proposed trip initially held little interest for me. Traveling to see a red monolith in the middle of nowhere, even if it is the world's greatest monolith, seemed silly. This area is in the heart of the Australian outback located in the Northern Territory with the nearest significant cities about 1,000 miles away in any direction. It is a land rich in gas, oil and every conceivable mineral. I cannot find a good definition for the outback. It seems that the Australians consider anything rural the "bush" and if you travel, further you are in the "outback." If you continue for another 2,000 miles you will be in the bush again, and then a city and then the ocean.

We signed up with a good tour company to see this area, as the outback is seriously hard on ordinary cars. Daytime temperatures may reach 110 plus degrees, but we were lucky with daytime temperatures only around 80 degrees. Most of the local cars we saw were heavy duty manly types. I have seen bits and pieces of these vehicles in the states, but never the full complement. These bad boys are always four wheel drives, but their engines breathe through snorkels up near the roof line for high water foraging. Oversize all terrain tires are the norm, two spare tires on a roof rack, bull bars, big electric winches front and rear, extra fuel and water containers, heavy duty truck jacks, single side band radios and long handled shovels. There are no bridges over the streams and rivers, which are usually dry, but if it rains heavily, water flows hard over low spots in the road stranding ordinary cars for days. All the tour buses for this part of the trip are rugged, high quality 50 passenger buses. Occasionally they breakdown or are isolated by flooding, but they are equipped with single side band radios for reliable communications with their support base. Another significant problem could be just finding a gas station as in some areas they are one hundred to three hundred miles apart — more about the outback later.

We first arrived at the tiny town of Yulara, about twenty miles north of Uluru and our accommodation at the Outback Pioneer Hotel — a part of the Ayers Rock Resort complex. Our room was quite comfortable, air conditioned, but not luxurious. We just had time to unpack, have a cool drink and catch the 3 p.m. sunset and BBQ tour bus to the Olgas. The Olgas (the Aboriginal name for these rocks is Kata Tjuta) are 30 miles to the west of Ayers Rock. This massive cluster of red rocks is just as mysterious as Ayers Rock, but sit in an oasis-like Valley of the Winds. They are dramatic and vividly colored. The highest of the rocks, mount Olga, (named for a past Queen of Spain), raises some 1,650 feet from the valley floor. After a walking tour through the Valley of the Winds and a lecture at the "water hole," we settled back in a park near the Olgas. The Aboriginal people have many stories about creation time and refer to these stories as "Dream Time." I think of their stories as similar to the stories in Greek mythology, but they only share small portions of these stories with their white brethren. One of the stories took place besides a rock in the Olgas shaped like a giant serpent's head. The story is about a mother who kills the giant snake with a stick to protect her child.

Our three guides set-up tables, chairs, two gas barbeques and cooked beefsteaks and kangaroo steaks (there are about 7,000,000 kangaroos foraging in the outback that the government would like to exterminate to save scarce grazing resources). We relaxed in the shade of the bus with lots of Champaign to watch a beautiful sunset over the Olgas.

We arrived back at our room about 10 p.m., but we had to get up the next day at the uncivilized time of 4 a.m. to watch the sunrise at Ayers Rock — guess who worked out this schedule. The idea is to witness the varied color change occurring as the sun rises — I was not impressed with that idea. Driving to the rock my mood was rather pessimistic, but when I saw it I was instantly transfixed. There in the middle of this vast emptiness stands a thing of exceptional grandeur. It was much more arresting than I could ever have imagined. I have seen this rock all over Australia on calendars, photography books and posters, so I knew what to expect, yet this mighty monolith awed me. It is so arresting that I could not take my eyes off it. Driving closer it becomes more interesting as you see some of its irregularities, deep pot marks and deep impressions that look like waves. I am not that great with colors, but as the sun rose, I think I saw colors of red, mauve, blues, pinks and browns.

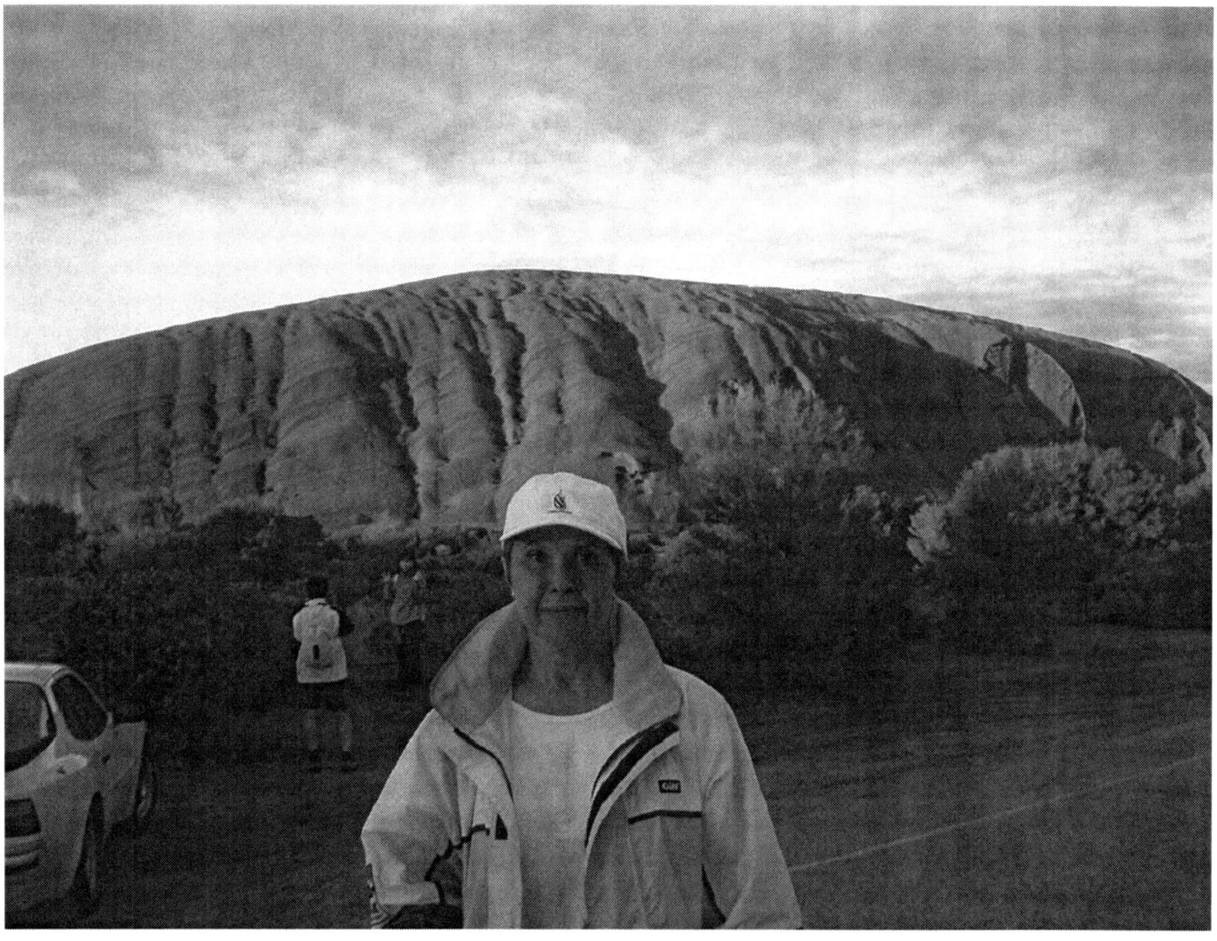

SUNRISE AT "AYERS ROCK" (Aboriginal name is "ULURU")

This rock rises majestically to about 1,100 feet above the red, sandy floodplain and the distance around the base is about eight miles. Geologists refer to this type of formation as a bornhardt, which is merely a weather resistant, rock that remains standing as everything around it erodes away. The floodplain consists of spinifex grass (clump-forming, perennial grass with pointed leaves), desert oak and many other plants (some 300 species) and flowers. The desert oak is one of the interesting trees in this region for its capability to find water. During its early years it will maintain a small structure with tiny limbs and stunted growth while its roots keep growing downward looking for water. If the roots find water, the desert oak will grow into a large tree. If water is not found, it will stay small. Some oaks have waited as long as fifteen years before their roots grew long enough to find water.

The outback as a desert is not the way we picture deserts. It is not a dry sandy place without vegetation. Instead there are small trees, grasses, flowers, plants, birds and animal life. Lizards for example are second only to Brazil in varieties of which there are sixty different species in the Northern Territory. One of the species, in the monitor family is called a perentie lizard and can grow to eight feet — thank goodness we did not run into that guy. The sandy soil is everywhere colored red from the iron oxide that exists in mostly sandstone. This year saw an exceptional amount of rainfall almost six times normal so the plants, birds, creepy things and flowers were happy. The guide said this heavy rainfall would provide food for the outback cattle if it did not rain again for 6 years. The cattle ranches or "cattle stations" in the outback, range in size from 75 square miles to 4,700 square miles. Cattle stations have to be enormous because of the scarcity of food. I heard several different estimates, but in general, it takes around one acre to provide food for six cattle. There are 240 cattle stations in the outback.

Both monolith sites are sacred places that go back to ancient times for the Aboriginals who live in the area. According to legends, two tribes lived here, the Loritja and Pitjanjatjara — how is that for a mouthful? They believe Uluru and Kata Tjuta monoliths date back to the time of creation. There are still cave paintings visible at the base of Uluru made thousands of years ago, but like the other cave paintings in Australia, there meaning is a mystery. The Anangu tribe now claims ownership of Uluru and they perform secret ceremonies for both men and women at different locations around the site. The ancestors of these people may have lived in the area for at least 30,000 years. The trail to the top of the mountain is sacred and a death in the tribe or religious ceremonies will close the trail to non-tribal members. The trail to the top of Uluru is steep at close to 42 degrees on smooth rock, no steps. There is a chain railing, waist high, fastened to steel posts along the more difficult spots otherwise it is open. The parks department usually closes the trail during rain or high winds.

Our guide suggested we not make the climb as he thought it was too windy. I was quite relieved, as I did not want to subject my out-of-shape body to such punishment, but might have tried. It was open however and people were climbing to the top. We chose to follow a trail part way around the base of Uluru to view some of the cave paintings. Leaving the area, our guide pointed out plaques that named people who had died climbing Uluru — not a good time to find out about that! The production of plaques has ceased, but so far, 38 people have died trying to climb Uluru. Some from heart attacks and others were from loss of balance — we made the right choice. When we looked at some tourists attempting that arduous climb, it was obvious to me that they were taking unnecessary risks. There were people using canes, overweight bodies, poor movement coordination and old age, all risking serious consequences.

About mid-afternoon on Wednesday, we boarded a coach for the 200 plus miles to the city of Alice Springs with a mid-way stop at Kings Canyon Frontier Lodge. Now, when you see the word "lodge," as in accommodation in Australia, you can never be sure of what to expect. But when we saw our lodge room with four sagging twin beds, no air-conditioning, no running water, steel lockers for a closet and the shared toilets 100 feet away, we were back in the office in a flash. We are not sure how our agent booked us in a lodge room, but for just $30 more, we could have a luxurious hotel room with a spa bath and a beautiful view of Kings Canyon — guess where we stayed? The hotel had a beautiful restaurant called Carmichaels that featured the best Australian wines, fantastic views and a great menu — what an unexpected pleasure in the middle of nowhere. The following morning we were supposed to tour Kings Canyon, but it was raining. The tour left, but we decided to skip the tour, enjoy a lazy breakfast at Carmichaels and luxuriated in our spa until our coach was ready to leave for Alice Springs.

About halfway to Alice Springs (a 4 hour trip) we stopped at a well maintained cattle station. Only this cattle station was into everything for weary travelers like us. There was a nice café with ice-cream, cold beer and a large variety of assorted pops — quite refreshing. There was a small U.S. made, Bell helicopter warming up for sightseeing and several Honda 4 wheel trail bikes for hire. This station was also interesting in that it raised camels for export as well as cattle for beef export on about 1,000,000 acres. The camels are single hump dromedary types imported originally for exploration, surveying and hauling. These camels can carry an amazing 1,000 pounds.

Australia hired Afghan immigrants to train and handle camels for exploration of the outback and the installation of the first north/south telegraph line. Other countries, now seek Australian camels, as they are healthy and disease free. It is quite remarkable that cattle and camels do coexist quite well together. For a long time, ranchers thought camels were destroying the cattle's food, but after much study, it was found that their food tastes are different. Another camel benefit is their soft padded feet do not harm the sensitive areas of the desert. We have heard that there are many large herds of wild camels roaming the desert as well as wild horses called brumbies. Just recently, there was a team of Americans there to teach the Australians our method of breaking in wild horses using kindness — some of our exports extol the better values of our wonderful country. About halfway to Alice Springs (a four-hour trip) we stopped at a very well maintained cattle station. Only this cattle station was into everything for weary travelers like us. There was a nice café with ice-cream, cold beer

Alice Springs, 300 miles from Uluru and 900 miles from any major city, was our next stop. Our agent booked us at a nice, in-the-heart-of-town hotel, the Mercure Diplomat. Our room had a nice balcony with cast iron railings in the theme of traditional Australian homes. The second floor room had a good view of the city's major street and of all things, a K Mart plaza. Even here, in the middle of nowhere, we have exported K Mart, McDonalds and Kentucky Fried Chicken. It seems like the U.S. has created a retail philosophy without aesthetics and visually regrettable in a city like Alice Springs. I could be wrong as they probably provide an alternate place to buy less expensive goods, but they distract from the outback's distinctiveness. I doubt if U.S. CEO's would understand this view and I suppose the locals will just delight in finding Martha Stewart towels for their homes.

We were not sure what to expect in Alice Springs as we heard varied opinions, but there is a lot to see so we programmed our stay for four days. The population is about 28,000 with Aborigines making up almost 25% of the population. From my observation, I'd say the majority of the Aborigines were friendly and behaved themselves, but there were some bad apples and troublemakers. The troublemaker types, mostly live alongside the Todd River, sleep on the grass, have no shelter and no means of support without government handouts. When they drink too much, which seems to be often, they cause trouble. The respectable Aborigines even dislike "those river people."

I'm not sure what they had been into, but every morning a group of five or six Aborigines, apparently from the river, would pass by our balcony. They had been to the hospital and had various bandages on their hands, arms, heads, etc. I assumed they had been fighting and they probably were. When local whites passed Aborigines, on the street, they would not look at them and the Aborigines would not look at the whites — two races, but no acknowledgement of each other. The Aborigines usually walked in small groups and talked silently among themselves. The police are quite visible in Alice Springs so personal safety was never a concern. Aborigines are probably Australia's greatest social failing as evidenced in published indicators of health and income. They usually fall somewhere between two and twenty times worse off than the countries general population.

Scientists think the Aboriginal people mastered open ocean travel, settled in Australia 45,000 to 60,000 years ago and never went to sea again. It is also interesting that they have no evident racial or linguistic relationship to any of Australia's neighbors. There are many documented and undocumented appalling stories of mistreatment of the Aborigines by whites that are hard to believe and a sad part of this country's history. One documented case, the most senior judge in Australia back in 1805 stated that they lacked the mental capacity for courtroom trials and gave settlers permission to track down offending natives and inflict punishment fitting the crime. This was an open invitation to kill Aborigines with no questions asked and they were hunted and killed. The last known slaughter took place near Alice Springs in 1928 where the police killed up to seventy Aborigines in reprisal for the murder of a dingo (native Australian dog) hunter. There is a visible police presence in Alice Springs and everyone told us it was a safe city as long as you did not walk near the river after dark.

As the Australians say, the town is "tidy." Alice Springs has lots of restaurants, shops, art galleries and a large casino (every major town in Australia seems to have a casino). The galleries feature a lot of original aboriginal art from local artists and some of it must have been quite good if high prices are any criteria. After looking all over Australia, I finally found an exceptional didgeridoo in one of the galleries. This one has some beautiful artistic work by a local artist, not truly authentic. Original versions used in native ceremonies are plain with no exterior paint or artwork. The interior of a didgeridoo is hollowed out naturally by the over abundant and hungry, native termites. Therefore, by merely tapping tree branches, natives can determine which branches are hollow. Then they are cut to a length where the diameter matches the musical note they would like to play. Keys, C and D major, seem to be most common — like magic, a musical instrument already tuned and ready to play with almost no effort.

We scheduled several tours into the MacDonnell mountain ranges and a tour of several historical sites in town. The tour company designed special off road vehicles for the mountain tours and they looked like high-tech vehicles straight from a Spielberg movie. They began life as a Mercedes, four-wheel drive fire truck chassis with enormous off-road tires. After the chassis arrived in Australia, a custom, 20 passengers, heavy-duty, off-road body was added. They are equipped with single side band transceivers, chassis jacks, bull bars, shovels, extra fuel and water and WWII airfield construction steel plates for tire traction in sand. The area abounds with sad stories of people traveling the outback's unpaved roads, getting stuck in sand and losing their life to the harsh elements. I now know why all the fuss over traveling in this driest, hottest, infertile and harshest of all of the inhabited continents. A heavy one-day rainfall had just stopped and the road to the 3,000 year old palm trees in Palm Valley was impassable because of waist-high swift water. Even in a star wars vehicle, the guide was afraid the swift running water might push against the side of the vehicle and carry us down stream.

Weather in this area has been unusual as they already had six times the normal amount of rainfall, which saturated the creek and riverbeds. The result is that a little rain results in instant flooding of low-lying roads. It was not a problem to cross most of the flooded roads so we toured most of the Eastern and Western MacDonnell ranges. Our guide was a perfect match for the six to eight people on his tour bus as he was obviously in love with the outback and knew it in great detail. He knew most of the plants, bugs, insects and animals the Aborigines ate and the most important, how it is prepared. Several of the plants are toxic and must be prepared properly, like soaking for several days, before they are fit to eat. He also knew many plants that had medicinal purpose and showed us one known to remove warts — I guess warts have been around a long time. You have to understand that this place is so inhospitable that tribes living here spent all their waking hours on food gathering and preparation. Finding food consumed so much time; no time remained for recreation or art and is probably the reason cave art is simple and sparse.

A couple of gum trees native to this area are the red river gum and the ghost gum. They only grow around riverbeds so if they are seen from a distance a knowledgeable person will know water is nearby. Even a seemingly dry riverbed will yield water if digging goes down deep enough. The ghost gum is extremely white because of a white powder, similar to talcum that covers the tree instead of bark. It will come off on your hands if you rub it — very cool. During periods of severe drought, this tree will cut off circulation to all its small branches to save energy. The selected branches die, turn black and fall to the ground. The red river gum is similar in appearance as it has no bark and is white with small amounts of red, but this tree cuts off circulation to all its large branches when required which then fall to the ground. I have heard campers being told not to sleep under these trees as a branch can fall off without warning. The branches will turn black after they have been chosen for sacrifice, but you cannot tell when they are ready to bonk someone.

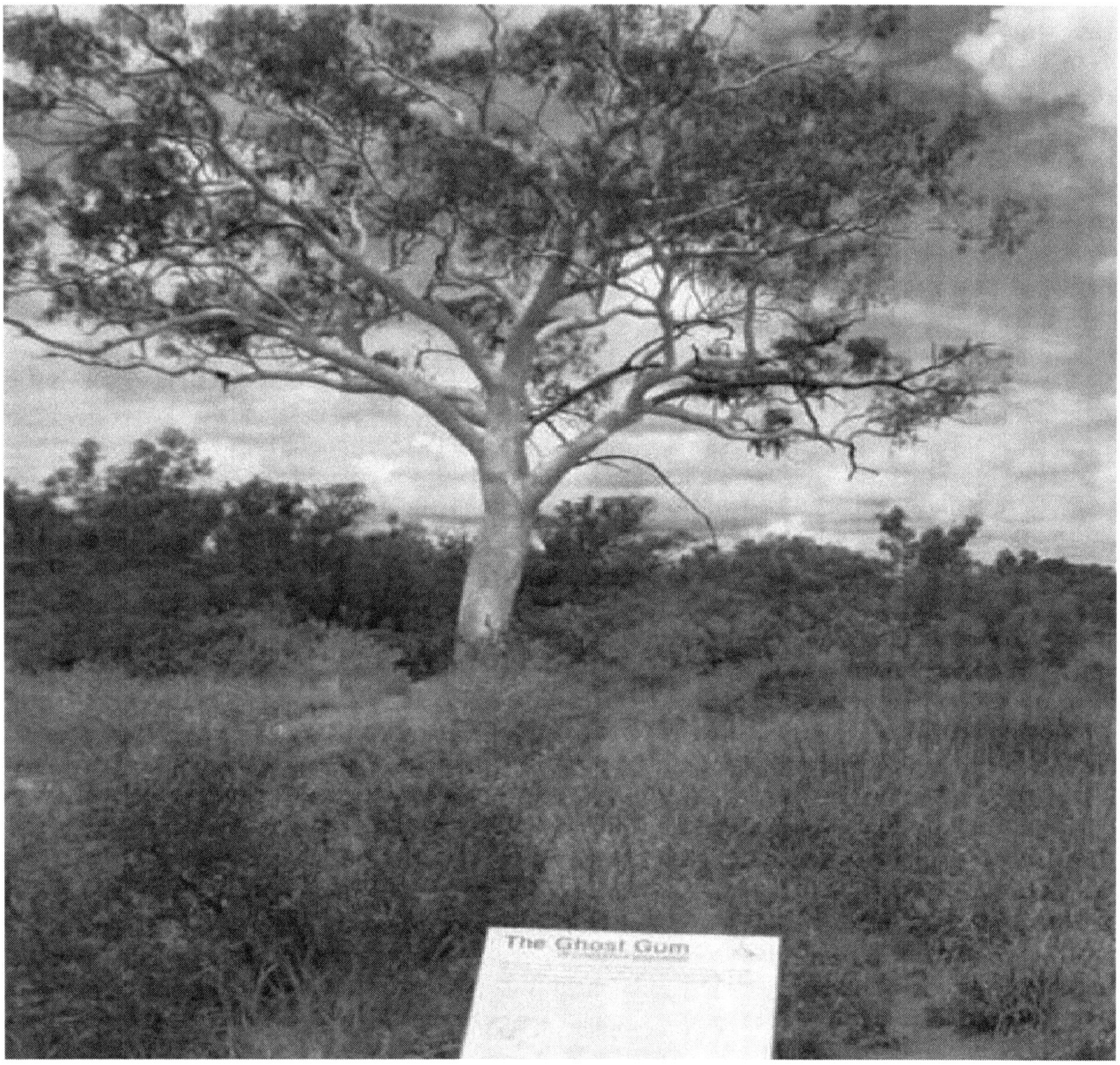

300 YEAR OLD GHOST GUM TREE, AUSTRALIAN OUTBACK

Australia is a place of great contrasts even its creatures evolved seemingly so different from the rest of the world:

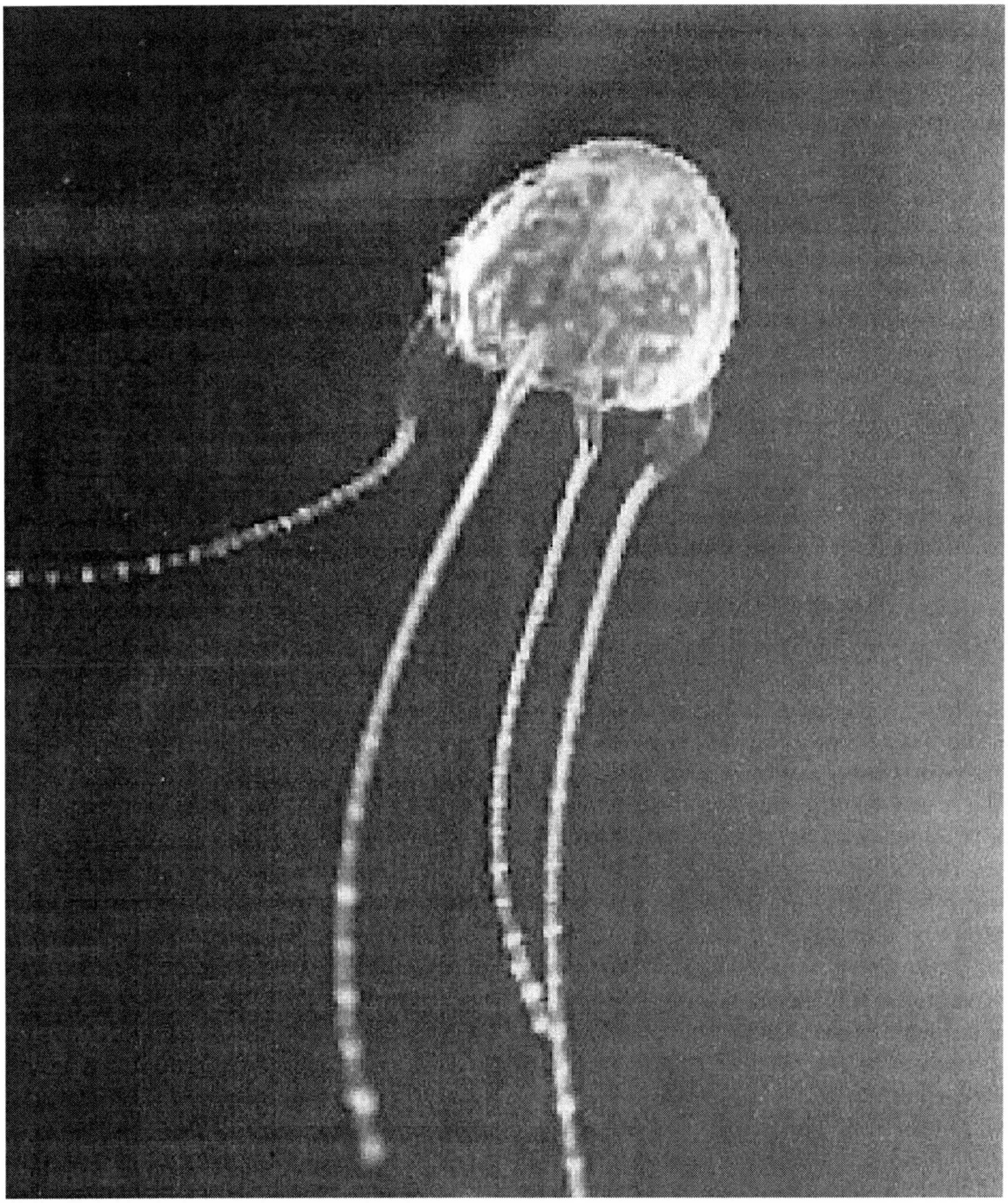

Photo Courtesy of Wikipedia Encyclopedia
DEADLY IRUKANDJI JELLYFISH, AUSTRALIA

- There is a fox that flies (in reality a large bat, but known as a flying fox).
- Giant seashells, big enough to hold a small person.
- Animals that bounce like balls across the land (kangaroos exist by the millions).
- A fish that once climbed trees.
- Something like 80% of the animals, plants, bugs and insects that live in the inhospitable areas are not found anywhere else on earth.
- The soil is practically inert yet creepy-crawly life exists in huge numbers so vast that 30% to 80% of the different species are thought to be unknown to scientists.
- The Great Barrier Reef is the largest living thing in the world.
- Australia is home to ten of the world's most poisonous snakes, several deadly spiders and many other lethal things like the box jellyfish, blue-ringed octopus, tick and stonefish.
- The mature box jellyfish carry the most lethal venom in the world, but the reason is unknown because their food source, krill, is easy to kill. When sea conditions are right for box jellyfish, a local fisherman told me, it is quite common to have small box jellyfish come up with tuna and land on your back. He believes the venom in small and immature jellyfish is not strong because it does not bother him.
- Australia is also quite old; something like 60 million years and many of the world's oldest rocks, riverbeds and fossils are found there.

There is another tiny jellyfish the size of a thumbnail, 2 cm in diameter, almost invisible, the irukandji. Its scientific name, carukia barnesi, after its discovery by Dr. Barnes who caught one after being stung back in 1964. There are four tentacles, one at each corner of the bell that can grow as long as 5 cm. It is responsible for the dramatic irukandji syndrome following its sting. This dreaded little guy is usually found in the northern parts of Queensland, Australia. Every summer about 60 people end up in the hospital fighting this potentially fatal syndrome. After being stung, nothing much happens for about 30 minutes. After that, the victim will suffer a severe backache, headache, muscle pains and pains in their abdomen and chest. Other signs might include nausea, anxiousness, restlessness and vomiting. While we were in Townsville, a tourist swimming at a resort in the Whitsunday Islands died after being stung by a jellyfish, probably an irukandji. He was on blood thinners and had a heart valve replaced so he might not have been in good health. However, the sting raised his blood pleasure by an estimated 300%, a level that didn't give him much of a chance. This potent little guy is tough on older people with high blood pressure and the real problem; it's almost invisible.

Victims of the irukandji frequently require hospitalization for analgesia and sometimes — intravenous antihypertensive therapy and alpha-blockers. Some doctors have resorted to supraventricular tachycardia and dilated cardiomyopathy to treat stings. At the time we left Australia, a treatment for the toxin was rigorously under investigation by their research unit. Many of Australia's beaches have jellyfish nets that work well for box jellyfish and larger species, but the net openings are not small enough to keep out the irukandji.

Shark nets have a significant presence in Australia at most ocean swimming beaches, but I think their effectiveness is doubtful. The nets, positioned in a straight line about a quarter mile from all swimming beaches, are open at both ends. The nets are not designed to enclose the swimming area. I think the theory is that a shark at sea looking for dinner will head directly for the sound of a swimmer and swim into the net. The holes are sized to trap medium and larger size sharks. I have heard people express feelings that the nets are more psychological than effective shark catchers are. The nets are placed in front the swimming boundary defined by the yellow and red flags placed along the beach by lifeguards. However, they do use spotter planes to look for sharks along the coasts and no one is allowed to swim where a shark is seen. The Australian lifeguards are probably among the finest in the world and save about 6,000 lives each year. I saw a report that claimed more people died from shark attacks in Florida than Australia, so maybe nets do lower attack risk.

Saltwater crocks inhabit the northern parts of Australia and have no regard for humans wandering in their territory. Walking anywhere close to the water's edge is a sure way to kiss yourself goodbye as they can fly out of the water for short distances at lightning speed. On land, they cannot employ their powerful tails to react against the water and are much slower. There are many stories here of the crocks' keen ability to get a death grip on farm animals, wild animals, dogs, cats and people walking too close to the water's edge. One interesting crock story is about a hefty, seventeen footer (they can grow to 23 feet) that did not go after people, but liked to chew on the outboard props of startled fisherman in their "tinnies" (Australian, for aluminum dinghy). No explanation was ever offered for her strange behavior, but she was moved to more isolated area.

We went on some significant tours within Alice Springs:

- Desert Park.
- School of the Air.
- Royal Flying Doctor Service of Australia.
- Road Transport Hall of Fame.
- Frontier Camel Farm.
- Alice Springs Telegraph Station.

In addition, The Boeing Company operates a large satellite tracking station just outside Alice Springs that employs about 1,000 local and 1,000 U.S. employees, but it is not open to the public. Our tour guide said that jobs with Boeing were vigorously sought after for their good salaries and benefits.

Our first stop was the **Telegraph Station**. This station was built as a repeater station and was one of twelve such stations built between Adelaide in southern Australia and Darwin in northern Australia. The system was interesting in that it used only one wire on the pole while the earth was used for the signal return. The distance between the north-south stations required the installation of an amazing 3,000 telegraph poles. Each repeater station manually decoded a received message and then the operator sent it on to the next station. These stations reduced the time it took, by several months, to hand carry messages by sea back and forth to Darwin, which was the terminus for a transatlantic cable to the UK.

The station location was chosen for its closeness to a permanent water hole in the Todd River. A spring near the water hole was named "Alice" after the wife of the then Superintendent of Telegraphs, Charles Todd. Hence, the area became known as "Alice Springs." The station sits on a nice piece of open land in a park like setting with all the original stone buildings nicely restored. After the first year of operation they found about 1,000 of the painstakingly installed poles were a fond source of food for termites and had to be replaced with steel poles. Imagine the conditions back in 1870 when all the materials had to be transported by horseback and camels — quite extraordinary! The repeater stations were used until 1932.

The **Royal Flying Doctor Service of Australia** provides the medical service to the outback. This service was initiated only to provide good medical care throughout the outback, which requires a close relationship between medicine, aviation and short wave radio. A Presbyterian minister, John Flynn, who first saw the need in 1928, started the service. By 1930, the federal government recognized the importance of providing medical care to the outback and it became a national service. It is now regarded as the greatest single contribution to the settlement of the outback. Alice Springs was one of the early bases, but now there are 20 bases providing aircraft, pilots, doctors and flight nurses on an annual budget of 50 million dollars. However, the dollars required to buy capital equipment, like airplanes, is raised through public donations.

They now have a total fleet of 40 planes that fly 40,000 flights a year and evacuate some 21,000 patients. They fly quite a variety of aircraft including de Havilland; Beechcraft: Barons, Travelairs, Queen Airs, Dukes and Kingairs; Cessna: 180s, 182s and 421Bs; and Piper: Cherokees, Chieftains and Navajos. Most of the cattle stations now have a small runway, but dirt roads and dry creek beds are used in emergencies. Night landings may use car lights focused on the landing field or oil burning pots. In the early days, there were no reliable maps and pilots had to know their territories by landmarks on the ground.

Communications is quite a story in itself. A young inventive genius named Alfred Traeger from Adelaide designed a lightweight and inexpensive two-way radio for Morse code. A self-contained generator, at first using a hand crank and later by a foot-operated pedal crank, powered the radio. These systems were distributed to cattle stations, small settlements, missions and police stations. The base station in Alice Springs is located in a modest building with a café, gift shop (of course) and the radio station with an operator and radio equipment behind a glass enclosure. Updated SSB, HF radio communications are in use, but the telephone is by far the most common communication system now. As you might imagine, the stories of heroism, help and assistance involving the service are incredible and several books have been written detailing these fascinating stories.

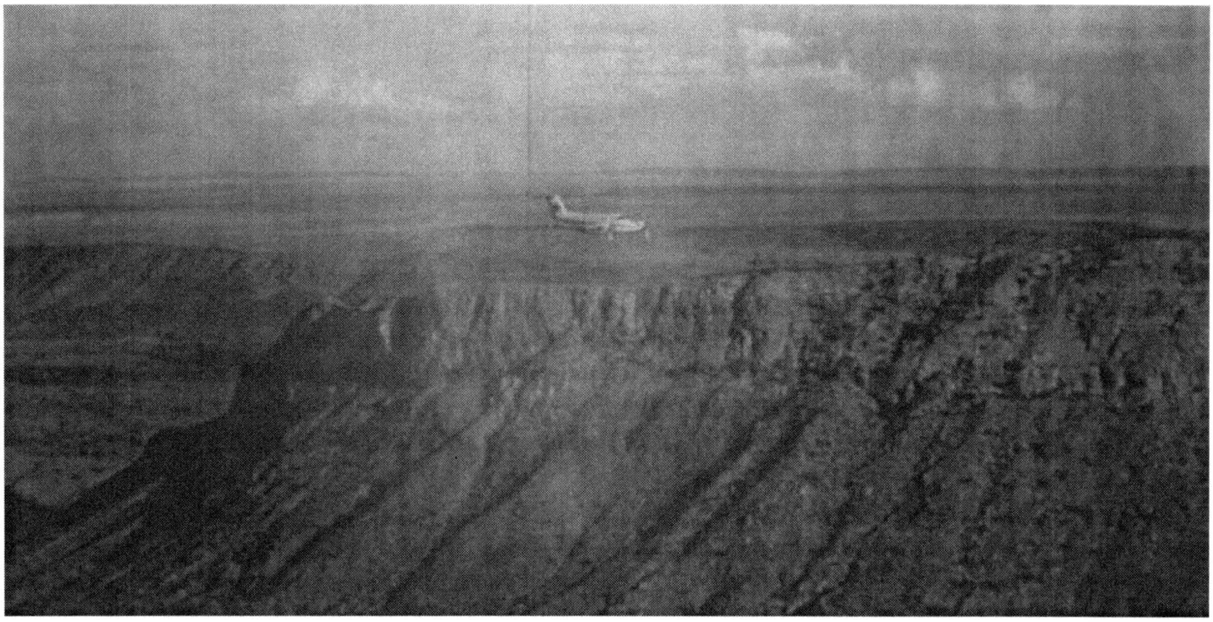

Photo courtesy of the Royal Flying Doctor Service
ROYAL FLYING DOCTOR SERVICE PLANE FLYING OVER THE OUTBACK, NORTHERN TERRITORY, AU

The next stop was the **Alice Springs School of the Air**. As you might have guessed, this school takes to the airwaves to bring schooling to the children of the outback. The school building is a one story, office like building, in a residential area. It has two broadcast studios, a large room at the entrance to display the children's schoolwork, a large conference room and a couple of small rooms used to organize the mail — an unpretentious minimal school facility. Visitors are treated to a short movie of how the school works and sound tracts of lively conversations between a teacher and her class. These teachers have a lot of patience to maintain a cheery attitude as they have to compete with the background hissing and crackling you would expect from short wave radio. It happened to be a school holiday during our visit so the broadcast studios were not operating. The idea is to bring a classroom experience to the 120 children, kindergarten through grade seven who live within the 800 mile radius of the station's outback region.

Schooling is mainly taught by mail correspondence courses with each teacher talking to their students briefly each day for about a half hour. Teachers take roll call, get the students to sing happy birthday if it's someone's birthday and may talk about a current interesting topic or schoolwork. Then each student spends about ten minutes once a week in a private session with his or her teacher, but the real schooling is by correspondence. It gets lonely for kids living in the outback with little or no possibility to mix with other children. Thus, the real thrust of the school's airtime is to help the school children with a quasi classroom setting where they can relate with other children living the same lifestyle. Each student is given a portable, single side band radio for the participation and some students are using computers if they are available at home and have a telephone line. Pat and I were quite impressed with this simple school concept bringing education under difficult circumstances to young children since 1951. We took the time to read some of the essays and look at the artwork on display. We were surprised to find excellent examples that demonstrate that this unique education system is inspiring young students in knowledge and comprehension skills.

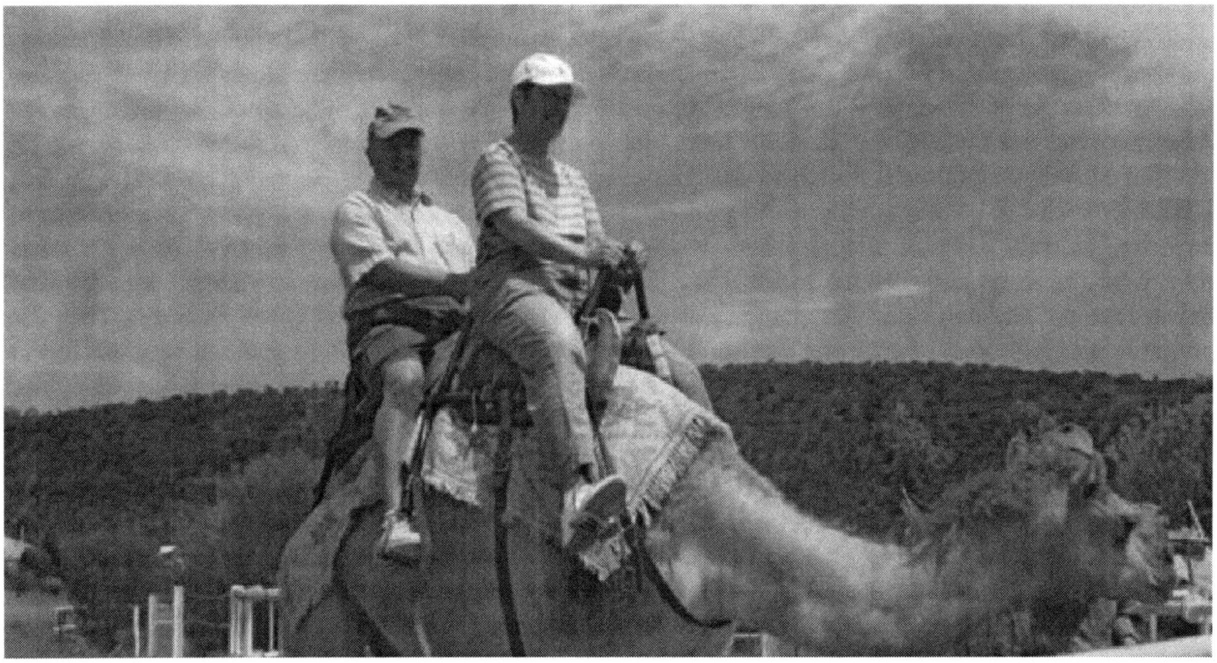

DICK AND PAT ON "TED," AUSTRALIAN DROMEDARY CAMEL, Dec. 14, 2001

Next was the **Frontier Camel Farm**. This is a place where you can go for a short ride or extended safaris into Rainbow Valley on a dromedary (one-hump) camel. Another option was the 45 minute, sunset camel ride to a restaurant for dinner. We opted for the short ride first with thoughts of the dinner ride. The motion on these big long necked beasts of burden is so uncomfortable we dropped the dinner thoughts quickly. The camel's odd gyrations rub against areas of your legs, thighs and butt that are previously unknown tender spots. On top of that, you find yourself using white-knuckle power to hang on because the hump is where one should be sitting. The awkward camel movements clearly tests ones balance skills — so much for the dromedary camel. Oh, they also have a racetrack here for the annual Camel Cup race. One camel story told to us was about a male camel during mating season. Apparently, the males can become quite mean. One of the early Afghan handlers got too close to a mean camel, and had his whole arm ripped out. Their neck muscles are super strong and used for pulling, so if he grabs you with his teeth, you're in for a whole lot of pain.

Two more stops: The **Transport Hall Of Fame** and **Alice Springs Desert Park**. The Transport Hall Of Fame has a fine collection of old vehicles used for transporting freight to outback cities like Alice Springs. One of the most interesting trucks was built from an English WWI truck chassis. Some Australian with a lot of inventiveness extended the chassis and added two more sets of four driven wheels on carriages for trailers that turned with the tractor. I think this truck was the beginning of the "Road Trains," so called because of the many trailers pulled by one tractor (the trains are currently limited to 150 feet in length). The monstrous radiator was right behind the driver and must have been unusual to drive with its airplane propeller size fan whirring behind him. The large radiator is a good indicator of just how debilitating the heat of the desert can be.

This truck was somewhat successful, for its time, on the unpaved desert roads. Its reliability and the limited horsepower of its huge, heavy, cast iron, Diesel engine needed improvement before decent freight loads could be hauled. At this point, the transportation story becomes quite interesting with the arrival of the U.S. Mack truck. The Mack truck arrived in Australia with its enormous horsepower, ruggedness and reliability to change the transportation industry overnight. This truck is credited with an important Australian milestone of carrying, reliably, heavy freight loads over the rough, unpaved roads of the outback. Who would have thought our American Mack truck would become such a successful contributor to the expansion of the Australian outback?

The **Alice Springs Desert Park** is a beautifully designed wild life park covering about 3,000 acres. At first, I didn't have a lot of interest in touring this park, but the park turned out to contain an unusual assortment of interesting animals. The walk-through aviaries with desert parrots like the princess parrot and about a hundred other beautiful desert birds was fun to see, They also have a large nocturnal house to view at least a hundred desert creatures that only come out at night and would not be seen if left to one's own resources. They also put on a show with birds of prey that featured an Australian wedge-tail eagle. This eagle swoops down from a high rocky hilltop to snatch up a dead piece of meat a trainer drags in front of the viewing stand — impressive! There were also some superb displays featuring the ecosystems of central Australia and their relationship to the Aboriginal people. We flew from Alice Springs on Dec. 17 and were back on ***Our Pleasure*** by 8:30 p.m.

I drove Pat to the Brisbane Airport where she then flew to Seattle and continued on to Buffalo to see her mother. Her mother was in failing health and recovery was not possible at this point. Pat and I met later in Seattle to travel the easy way, by Boeing's 747. We left Seattle in mid-April on our way back to Australia using round-the-world tickets. We stopped in Buffalo again for a week and flew from there to Florida, Munich, Rome, Singapore and Australia (more about that later). At that time, Mary's (Pat's mother) condition was pretty much the same as it had been for several years. Besides requiring oxygen full time, she takes fourteen different medications each day to combat pain, stomach problems, blood problems, breathing problems, memory problems and arthritis.

After we arrived back in Mooloolaba, Mary suffered a minor stroke, which added several serious care problems. Her medical care at a local hospital and nursing home restricted her treatment to the staff doctors. Even though the new doctors had a list of previous medication, they chose to follow their own inclinations and prescribed a different set of medicines. Their medication caused her stomach to rupture in two places with a subsequent loss of two pints of blood. The blood loss reduced the oxygen to her brain and caused her memory medication to be ineffective. Her family was extremely frustrated over their poor medical decisions, but finally got her to the right hospital and her personal doctors. Her doctor noticed black and blue marks on her stomach and surmised the nursing home abused her. She is back in her own home now and eating normally, but cannot walk without a walker and needs help for physical tasks. Her doctor told Pat's sister, Mona that he loved Mary like his own mother, but her body is worn out. He will keep the pain at a tolerable level for her, but he should no longer use any extraordinary means to prolong her life — aging with serious medical problems is a terrible way to live your last days.

Buffalo is not an easy flying destination from Australia as it takes 4 plane changes, and 20 hours of flying time. Therefore, the total travel time from doorstep to doorstep is an exhausting 31 hours. Pat's plan was to visit for 2 to 3 weeks then return to Australia so we can sail to our next destination the Louisiades Archipelago. The Louisiades are a group of isolated and primitive islands that are a part of Papa New Guinea about 1,000 miles north and east from Townsville, Australia. We plan to explore these islands for a couple of months and then return to Australia.

We left ***Our Pleasure*** in a boatyard for three months for maintenance work, but rainy weather held up completion of the bottom epoxy work and painting. The work, scheduled for completion before our return, required another two weeks. Refinishing the cabin floors inside resulted in a major dust problem that was just about under control. We rented a condominium nearby so we took advantage of the dishwasher, washing machine and dryer to help with part of the clean-up. Fine sanding dust is insidious though and manages to infiltrate everything in spite of dust covers. However, a lot of stuff still needs attention, like food buying, inspection of sails and rigging, etc. before we will be ready to sail again.

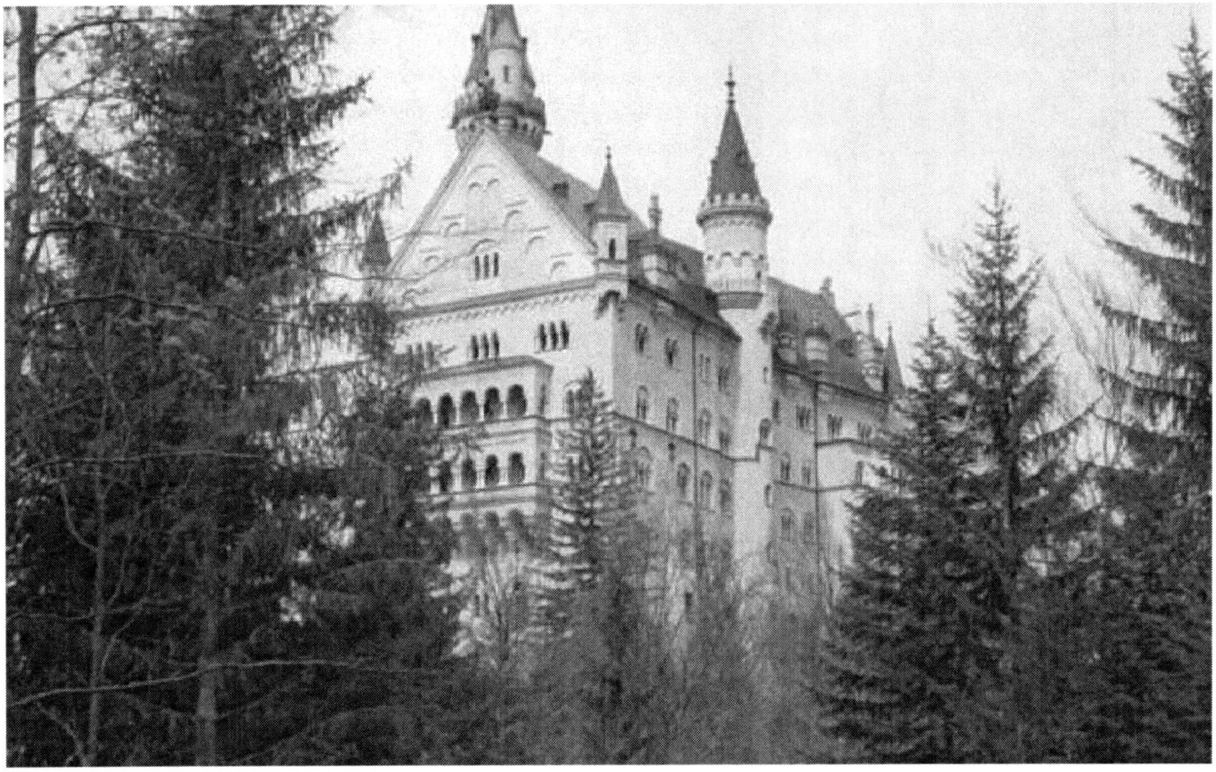

KING LUDWIG'S NEUSCHWANSTEIN CASTLE, GERMANY

When buying airline tickets in Australia to fly to Seattle, Buffalo and Tampa it was suggested that, a better alternative was to buy around-the-world tickets for the same price. The rules were simple: fly a circular route, do not back track, return to the starting point and limit the distance to 25,000 miles. We could have stayed at each destination as long as we wanted, but had to limit our time away so we could return to Australia for the start of the sailing season. We added Munich, Rome and a one-day stopover in Singapore before returning to Brisbane. It turned out to be too much traveling for such a limited time, but we did get to see a lot and enjoyed ourselves.

In Munich, we saw the Glockenspiel and St, Michael's Church built by the Jesuits in 1587. This church has about ten side alters with beautiful artwork and the tomb of King Ludwig II. We managed to navigate the German rail system (with one transfer) to see King Ludwig's Neuschwanstein Castle. While eating dinner in a Munich beer garden, two German software engineers sat down with us (tables are shared when chairs are available). Their beer is so outstanding I now understand why it is so revered. The two engineers spoke perfect English as they studied English in their school system for nine years. We had a great time discussing our different cultures and world problems while learning how to remove the skin from white sausages.

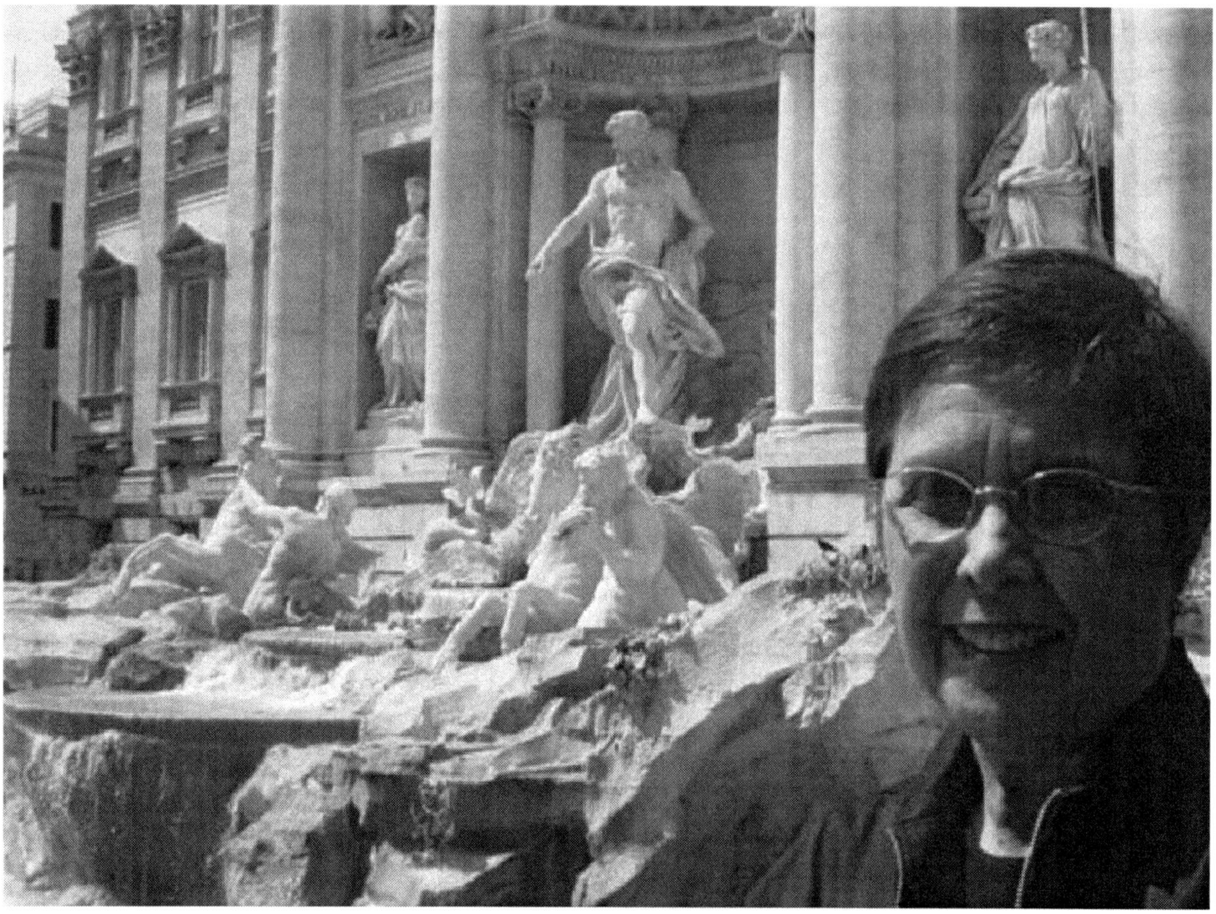

PAT IN FRONT OF THE TREVI FOUNTAIN, ROME

We spent five days in Rome and managed to see most of the major landmarks. Rome is so different from Munich. It is much dirtier, noisier and busier, a lot like New York without the tall buildings. Driving is a real problem as the motor scooters swarm around like a bunch of bees and the drivers are aggressive. There is absolutely no place to park and people will double park right across pedestrian walkways. A good thing, the majority of the people are about my size so I never felt short. At one church service, I towered over all the little old women. The Italians normally talk loudly and use many hand gestures walking along with friends. They create a rather pleasant, comfortable atmosphere that caused us to smile a lot. Our hotel was a short walk to the Trevi Fountain and the Spanish Steps. A good pair of walking shoes is an absolute must as almost every block has a beautiful basilica, a restaurant, café, pizzeria and coffee shop to explore. Someone told us that there are about 500 basilicas in Rome and you can always find a Mass celebration any hour of the day. I have no idea where they get all the priests, but some Masses had up to three priests celebrating Mass.

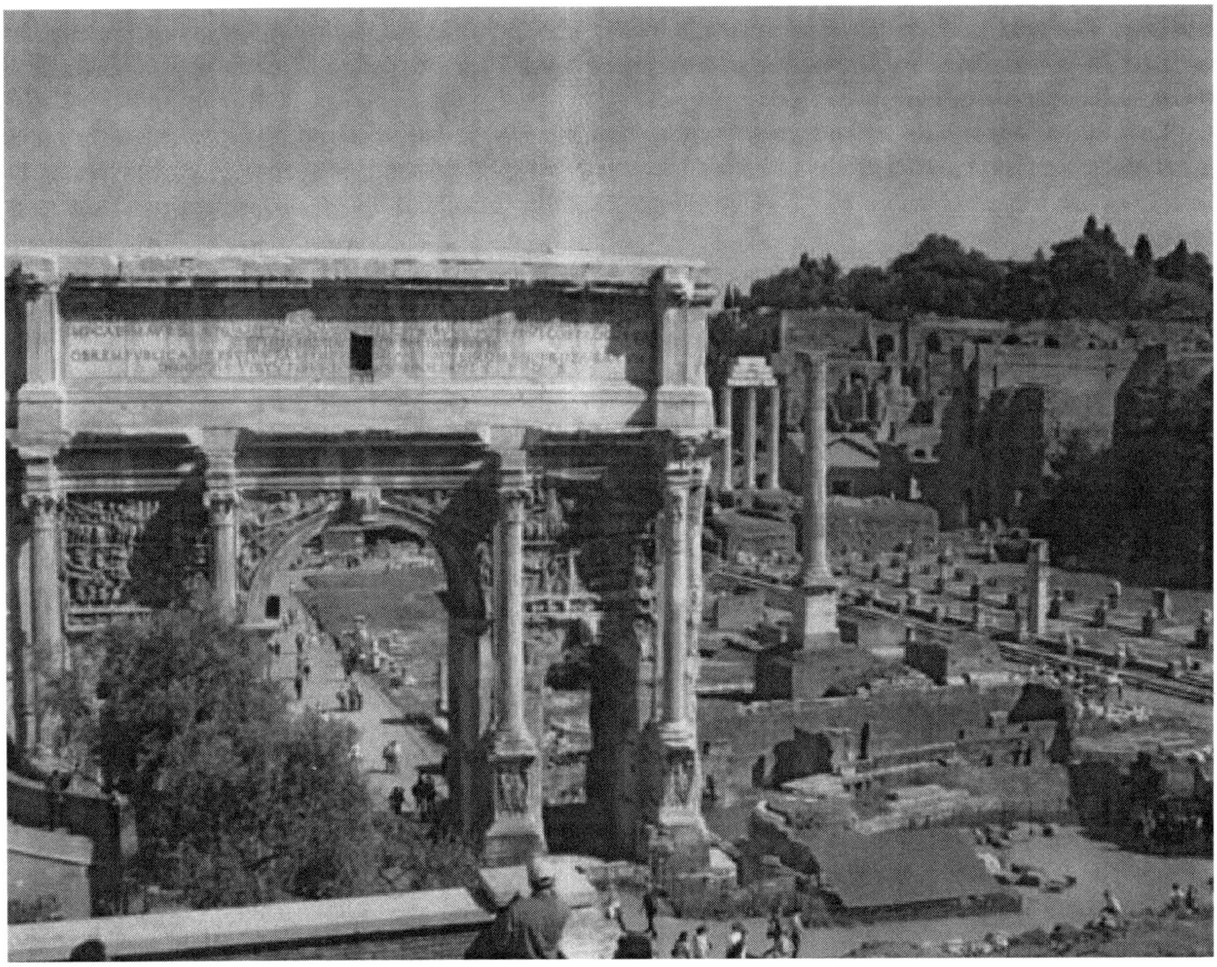

3,000 YEAR OLD RUINS OF THE ROMAN EMPIRE

The food was wonderful, as most of the restaurants are family owned and we never had a bad meal except on a bus tour that included lunch. Most of the waiters have a great sense of humor, which kept us laughing all the time. It is also apparent that they must keep all their best wines and export the mediocre stuff as every wine we tried was on the good or outstanding side. Another surprise was all the men's clothing shops; probably around 30% of all shops carry just men's clothing. One woman told us: "It was expensive to keep our men looking good, but worth it to see them look so smart and elegant." Some men that were dressed for business and seen eating dinner in some restaurants did dress well, but on average, I would say they dressed normally and not all that elegantly.

We managed to see a rock concert, the Coliseum, St. Peters, St. Maria Maggiore's, St Paul's (elegant when compared to St. Peters), the Sistine Chapel, the Vatican Museum, lots of piazzas, parks, statues, fountains, the Pantheon and the 3,000 year old ruins of Old Rome. Restoration work is going on everywhere, but I get the feeling they will never catch up. Many Roman marble and bronze construction pieces ended up in church buildings. The gold, artifacts, beautiful marble, artwork, mosaics, paintings and tapestries are everywhere. At first, the art overwhelmed my senses, but after seeing so much of it everywhere, it became common, a little brash, and maybe too opulent.

One fun experience was trying their subway system. It is easy to use once you figure out where to buy a ticket and which route and direction to follow. Like the New York subway during rush hour, you cannot be bashful or you will never get on or off as the people packing is close and uptight — pushing and shoving is mandatory.

The Singapore stop was only 14 hours, not enough time to do much except take bus tours of the city and their resort island. We expected to get a room at the airport hotel for some sleep, but it was full. Back in Australia, we got the boat ready for another adventure.

Chapter 17

LOUISIADE ARCHIPELAGO, TERRITORY OF PAPUA NEW GUINEA (PNG), JUNE 26 TO AUG. 26, 2002

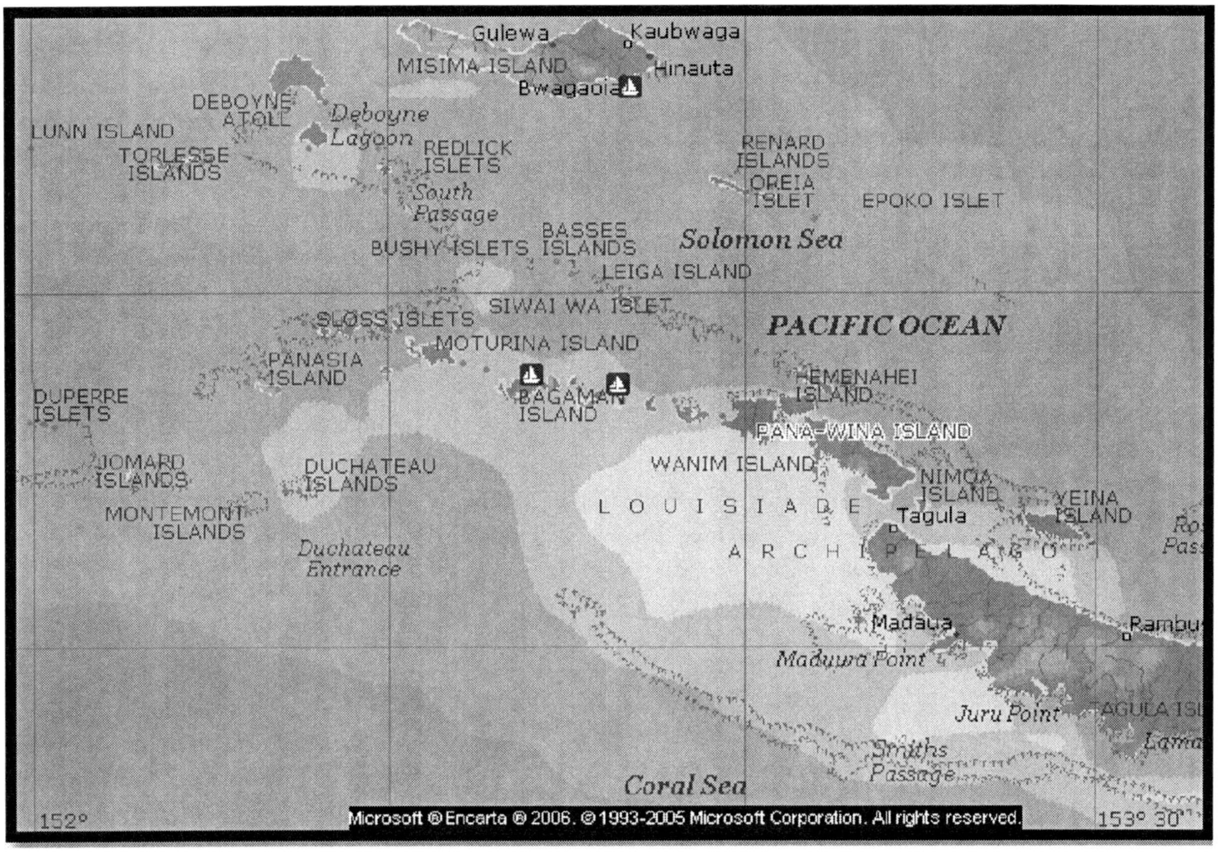

MISIMA, BAGAMAN & PANA NUMARA, LOUISIADE ARCHIPELAGO

Our Trip to the Louisiades turned out to be one of our finest cruising experiences in over 5 years of offshore sailing. It ranks up there with our visits to Palmerston and the Island of Niue. Getting to the Louisiades was difficult as we had to put up with and fix several problems soon after we left Mooloolaba, Australia, not fun, but part of the downside of this life style:

Our Pleasure with just Dick and Pat left the Mooloolaba fuel dock at 11:30 a.m., June 26, 2002 and headed out into the Pacific Ocean. The skies were clear with light winds from the NE. A high-pressure system of 1032 millibars was just moving off the southern coast of Australia. If the high-pressure system was lower, maybe around 1024 millibars, the wind conditions could have been near perfect. However, we had already obtained our clearance from Australian customs and our visas from the Papua New Guinea consulate in Brisbane so we were committed to leave. By 4 p.m., we were still motoring in light winds making 6.7 knots on a course of 20 degrees magnetic. Pat was napping and resting her left shoulder after receiving a shot from the local sports medicine doctor, Dr. Canavan. She had hurt her shoulder several months ago after tripping on the sidewalk at the marina. Her shoulder since that accident was constantly paining her and treatments in Australia and the states had not helped. This shot of cortisone however, injected after a thorough investigation including, probing, x-ray reviews and an MRI, had positive results.

The second day out was a disaster, it seemed like everything was failing. Two of the battery banks failed from what I think was an improper relay shutdown of the bow thruster. I saw the voltmeter momentarily drop to around 10 volts and two battery banks never recovered. One of the lead battery terminals had melted so completely the battery cable was no longer in contact with the battery — thank goodness the third bank (which was off) was unaffected. By this time the winds were blowing 20 knots, the seas were building and ***Our Pleasure*** was rolling as the larger waves passed under her.

Mysteriously we saw small amounts of water on the sole of the pilothouse, but after wiping the water up we saw more when we looked again. It was hard to find the water source at 1 a.m., but it turned out to be a failed, main engine, anti-siphon valve mounted in the wet locker. After some considerable fussing I managed to remove the old valve and install a make shift one with a manual shut-off valve. With the wind still building, I started the engine so we could head the boat into the wind and reef the mainsail. While reefing the mainsail, which rolls up into the boom, I managed to break the furling line.

This line is strength rated at 3,200 pounds, but boat rolling had wedged the main halyard into the jumper strut tangs. The halyard has to remain free to allow the mainsail to roll into the boom. This had never happened before so it didn't occur to me that the main halyard might be stuck. I could have prevented this failure by easing up on the electric winch when I heard it strain, but I thought it was wind pressure on the sail causing the strain. Line failure can be a problem with electric winches; they are powerful making it easy to break a stuck line. We were lucky that only about 10 to 15 feet of the mainsail was outside the boom when the furling line parted.

The next item to go south was the wind direction and anemometer masthead transducer. This guy had been acting up, but now was fully inoperative. This device is useful, but not a necessity. A high IQ is not required to determine the direction of a gale force wind. Where to go for repairs became the next worry. By this time, we were 200 miles off the east coast of Australia and a long way from a major port. I did not want to backtrack so we headed for Mackay 200 miles to our northwest. Mackay is near the southern end of the Great Barrier Reef.

Early Saturday morning, with the wind now blowing 30 knots, I looked to our stern to see the starboard davit had broken. This is one of the two davits that secure our inflatable dinghy. The dinghy and davit were now moving around wildly trying to break something. Tethered to my safety harness and hanging on to our wildly pitching rear deck I was able attach a line from the dinghy to the mizzen boom. I stabilized the boom with lines running port and starboard and crawled back to the safety of the cockpit.

The next day was Sunday, June 30 and two more systems acted up. First, the communication line from the GPS to the computer failed and the engine tachometer dropped to zero while the alternator voltage climbed to over 14 volts sending the inverter into an overload condition turning itself off. It took 30 minutes to find and solder the loose connection in the NEMA 0183 communication line to the computer. The alternator voltage corrected itself in about 5 minutes at 1:40 p.m. only three hours from Mackay. At this point, the wind decreased to 15 knots and the watercolor turned a beautiful light green. We talked to our friends on *Endurance*, with whom we should have been sailing with, reporting they were only 10 miles from the Louisiades — not cheerful information for us.

Mackay marina is only a few years old and probably one of the nicest marinas on the east coast of Australia. Gary, from the yacht *Shearwater*, heard us talking with the marina staff and met us at our assigned slip to grab our dock lines. By the fourth of July we had lined up all the local help we needed. There was Don Buckeridge welding our davits, Battery World rebuilt our alternator and found us a new voltage regulator. Greg Hamwood worked on the refrigeration system, Ian Masters repaired the mainsail furler and I ordered three new absorption glass mat (AGM) batteries from Brisbane.

Thank goodness, Gary was there to help carry the batteries down the steep ramp and the 200 yards further along the dock to our boat. The marina was able to loan us a small furniture type truck, but each battery weighed around 160 pounds and it became quite a chore to remove the old batteries and put in the new ones. Of course, the new batteries had a different footprint than the old ones so I had to move the original hold-down brackets. Mackay is a great stop over point for boats heading north to see the Great Barrier Reef or beyond to Darwin, Australia, There were several boats in the Marina, besides *Shearwater* that we knew like *Blue Banana* and *Strega* so we were not short on company.

We have two independent refrigeration systems on ***Our Pleasure***, but they are the most unreliable systems on the boat. Greg Hamwood put in a new pressure control system that was intended to start the, 120 volt ac compressor motor first under no-load. Then, with the motor running, change the pressure valve to add the compressor load. His changes worked good at the dock, but for some mysterious reason, the revision did not work at sea. They also have some other idiosyncrasies that seem to baffle the refrigeration experts. Before leaving Mooloolaba, we bought about three months worth or $200 worth of vacuum packed and deep frozen meats for the freezer and now we had to rely on only the engine driven system. This means running the main engine every 16 to 18 hours to keep the fridge and freezer at temperature. Whereas the generator is much quieter and uses a third of the fuel the main engine uses. Finding the problem, determining the solution that can be accomplished with available parts and resources can be a significant problem.

We left Mackay at 9:25 a.m., July 16, with a new clearance from Australian customs. We had intended to leave earlier in the morning, but Pat's brother Phil called at 2:30 a.m. from Buffalo, N.Y. unsure about the time change; we needed some extra sleep time. The best sailing route to the Louisiades from Mackay requires a passage through a channel in the Great Barrier Reef. The only one available for 120 miles was Hydrographer's Passage. The huge bulk-carriers carrying coal and sugar from Mackay mostly use this passage. We passed three freighters that were inbound toward Mackay and arrived at the pass entrance just before dark. The passage is fairly wide, but twists and turns through this part of the reef for 40 miles. We were lucky that no freighters were using the passage until we were almost through.

The first freighter we met in the passage was not happy with us. We were close to the channel's center to avoid any GPS or navigation problems. The freighter's captain got on the VHF radio and in an uncivil manner, said we should be on one side or the other. He was right of course, but sailing that zigzag course with strong currents in the dark is risky, so we opted for the most room possible. He was traveling at 12 knots so wind and currents were only a minor problem for him to stay in the channel. We were using our laptop computer next to the steering station for the passage through the reef. Connected to the GPS, a fairly accurate boat position is superimposed on an electronic chart of the area; otherwise, we would have to wait for daylight to make this passage. Just before leaving the passage on the east side of the reef, we met another inbound freighter, but this skipper was friendly. He wanted to know our names and our destination. This freighter's captain suggested passing portside to portside and wished us good luck on our journey — two similar freighters, but two personalities 180 degrees apart.

By Wednesday, we were sailing in 20 knots of wind and the seas were 3 to 10 feet high, Pat was feeling a bit seasick. We were now at the 200 mile limit of Australian waters, at a small reef group called Diamond Passage. The autopilot is steering the boat perfectly and making 7 knots with a 100% jib, shortened main and mizzen, the Louisiades are now a mere 353 miles away. On July 19 and 20, the weather turned lousy with a constant wind speed of around 30-knots and waves up to 12 feet. The waves slowed the boat speed down to three and four knots. The wind tore our staysail cover and the cover on the deck mounted dinghy. Pat's left shoulder is bothering her again and she is finding it difficult to find a comfortable position for sleeping

We entered Ducheateau Pass at 9:15 a.m., July 21, one of the main passes into the Calvados Chain of islands in the Louisiade Archipelago. This group of islands is rather unique as they are contained within a sunken reef that is about 120 miles long and 30 miles wide. The outer reefs are sometimes underwater, but the waves coming into this island area, are still diminished by the surrounding reef. The area is well charted with varying water depths, but good sailing depths can be found in waters around 30 to 60 feet deep. The area is quite tropical, as it lies about 650 miles south of the equator with thick lush growth and plenty of palm trees.

As we moved deeper into the chain of islands, the water turned a beautiful green and was clear down to probably 30 feet. White sandy beaches were evident on the islands we passed. We were headed for an island called Pana Numara about fifteen miles away. We had maintained radio contact since leaving Mooloolaba with our friends we knew were anchored there: *Endurance*, *Esprit* and *Tweed*. We dropped our big 120 pound Manson anchor in about 60 feet of water. It seemed like all our friends were welcoming us at the same time by radio: they and we were overjoyed that we finally arrived almost three weeks later than scheduled — time for a big Cuba Libra for me and chilled white wine for Pat (no drinking during passages).

Right after the anchor was down, some natives paddled out in their dugout canoes to trade vegetables for hammers and nails. The vegetables they raised in their gardens consisted of cherry tomatoes, limes, bananas, pawpaw (papaya), taro, sweet potatoes and squash. In this culture, the people are quite small in stature and trim. The only slightly overweight person we ever saw was a woman schoolteacher. They were polite; most were quite shy and spoke softly in varying grades of English. The clothes they wore were worn and soiled. They thoughtfully held their canoes away from our boat so as not to scratch it. Usually, one or more of their children were along to bail out water that always leaked into their canoes.

Their canoes are small, made from hollowed-out logs with one sponson and held together with lashings and tight fitting joinery. They float close to the water and small waves will easily enter over the top or through minor cracks in the wood. Most of the families have four or five children and some have a lot more. The mothers openly breast feed their children and may continue to do so for several years or until the next baby is born. They are dark skinned with brown eyes and short black hair. The men were lightly muscled with attractive athletic like features. The women all have short curly hair, physically trim, small busts and not as attractive as other Polynesian races we have seen in the Pacific. The children are a different story, as we thought they all looked beautiful and so happy with big beautiful smiles.

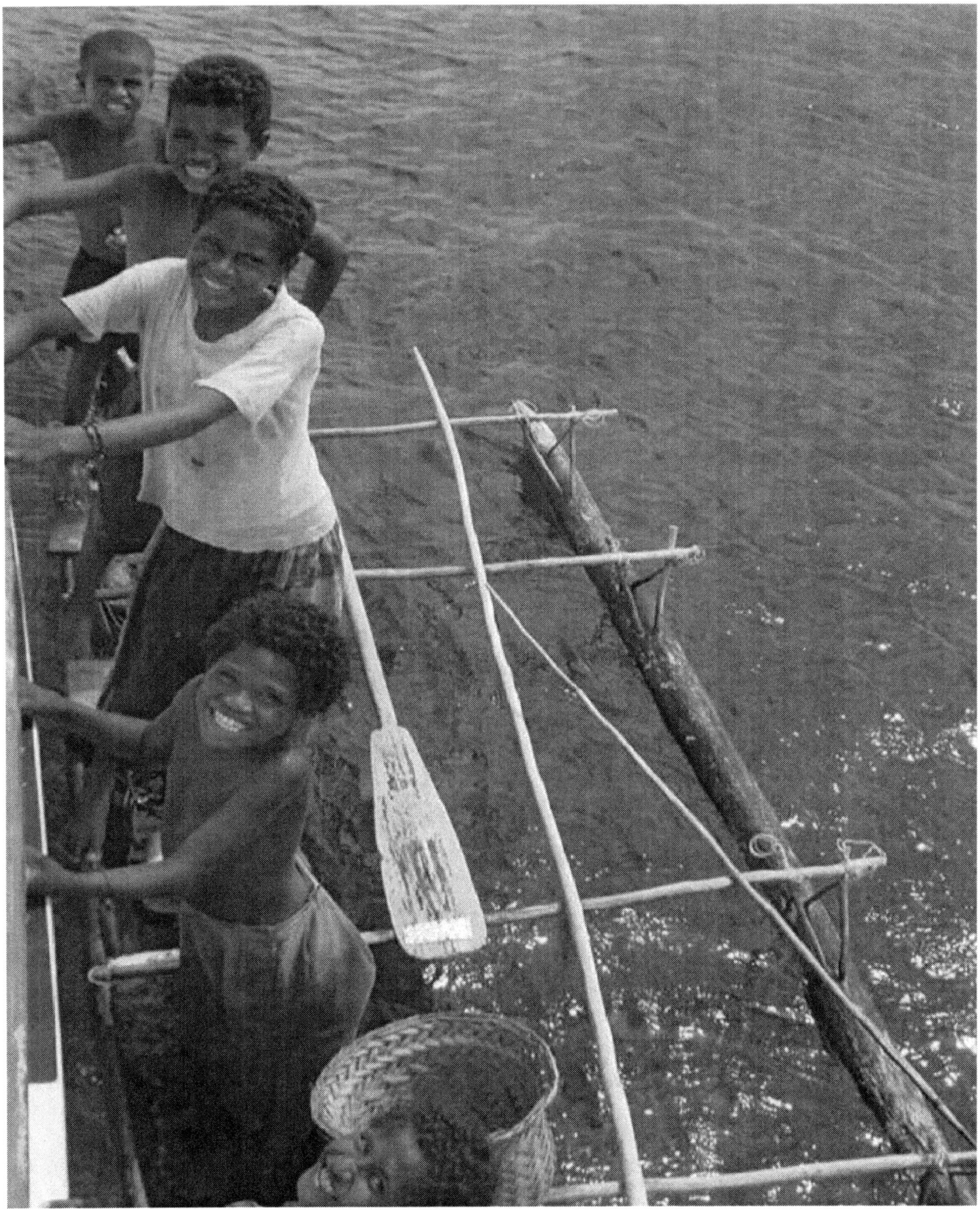

CHILDREN WELCOME US TO PANA NUMARA

Their clothes were mostly tattered with pins holding them together, no underwear, many holes, I wanted to cry and hug them at the same time. These Polynesian descendents are probably the poorest group of people we ever had the privilege to meet. It so happened we did not have an extra hammer or nails, but we always found something to trade with them. If they were willing to trade what little they had (often it was just one vegetable), and made the effort to paddle out to see us, we always made sure they received something in return. They keep one set of their best clothes reserved for church, as they are religious. I had some 30 odd shirts hanging in my locker so I was able to enhance a lot of men's church wardrobes.

For the next couple of days we just rested and worked on minor boat projects. Jalna on *Tweed*, had her sewing machine out and insisted on repairing our American flag and the torn dinghy cover. The first time I tried to run the water maker, since having it serviced, it would not run. By trial and error, I found that bypassing a new pressure sensitive switch the water maker company installed and fixing a leaky high-pressure fitting, we were in business. Without good drinking water out here, we would have to leave the islands after a couple of weeks. The islanders store rainwater, but the lack of rain was drawing down their reserves forcing them to conserve their good water. Their backup source of water is well water, but well water, like in Palmerston, requires boiling. The winds finally eased on July 25 so we pulled our anchor and headed for the island of Misima some 30 miles away for our formal check-in to Papua New Guinea (PNG) — all our friends had checked in before us.

Misima is not a town anyone would stay in voluntarily, we thought it quite depressing. Dusty dirt roads, no sidewalks, no streetlights, four minor grocery stores, one small bank in a trailer, a one-person post office, a bottle shop (liquor store), police station and a market. Oh, the public toilets are two out-houses built out over the water in the small bay where the children splash around – pretty disgusting. Directly across the bay lives a big old crocodile in the mangroves. He has not eaten any of the children yet, but wild pigs, stray dogs and some birds have disappeared. Many people sitting around doing nothing, but friendly. The market sounds good, but the most common items were betel nuts, lime powder and mustard leaves (to use with the betel nuts) and few vegetables.

The first time I heard of betel nuts was when my parents took me to see the musical South Pacific in New York. The songs were all about the lives of our WWII GI's with references to the natives as always chewing betel nuts. The nut itself is actually the seed kernel of the betel palm; it contains an alkaloid that acts as a stimulant and a tonic. It has a bitter taste so the natives chew them with pure lime powder also known as quicklime. The lime powder when mixed with the mouth's saliva will become quite warm. The nut and the lime powder are wrapped in a leaf from the betel vine or a mustard leaf. The combination stains their tongue and mouth bright red and will darken their teeth after prolonged use, not pretty.

It apparently provides an effect similar to kava juice used by the natives on islands where the kava root is found. Sort of a mellowing effect, unlike alcohol, people do not become aggressive or violent. Anyway, most natives that live on these islands cannot afford to buy it and we were told it would be good to bring some back for trading. Most men and some women love to chew betel nuts. The women bring their goods to the market in baskets balanced on their heads. Some baskets are so heavy it takes two people to lift the basket off and lower it to the ground.

Many natives living on Misima Island work at the gold mine where they receive a consistent income — unusual for PNG. However, the mine is closing, as the PNG government did not renew the mining contract with the Australian management firm. This is probably a blessing because the people have no idea what to do with the money. They never had money in the villages so the men spend it on loose women, drinking and having fun, not on homes, clothing, schooling, savings or property — just wasted indiscriminately.

We stopped in the bottle shop to bring a case of beer back for the folks on *Tweed.* The entire floor except for a tiny walking path to the counter and behind was piled waist high with cases of beer waiting for the mine payday. A case of PNG beer cost $45 in their money (kina), about $12 in ours, but a small bottle of imported rum costs kina $100. We were to find out later that the island Uniting Church pastors make about kina $25 ($6.25) every quarter and a schoolteacher makes about kina $25 a month for teaching primary grades.

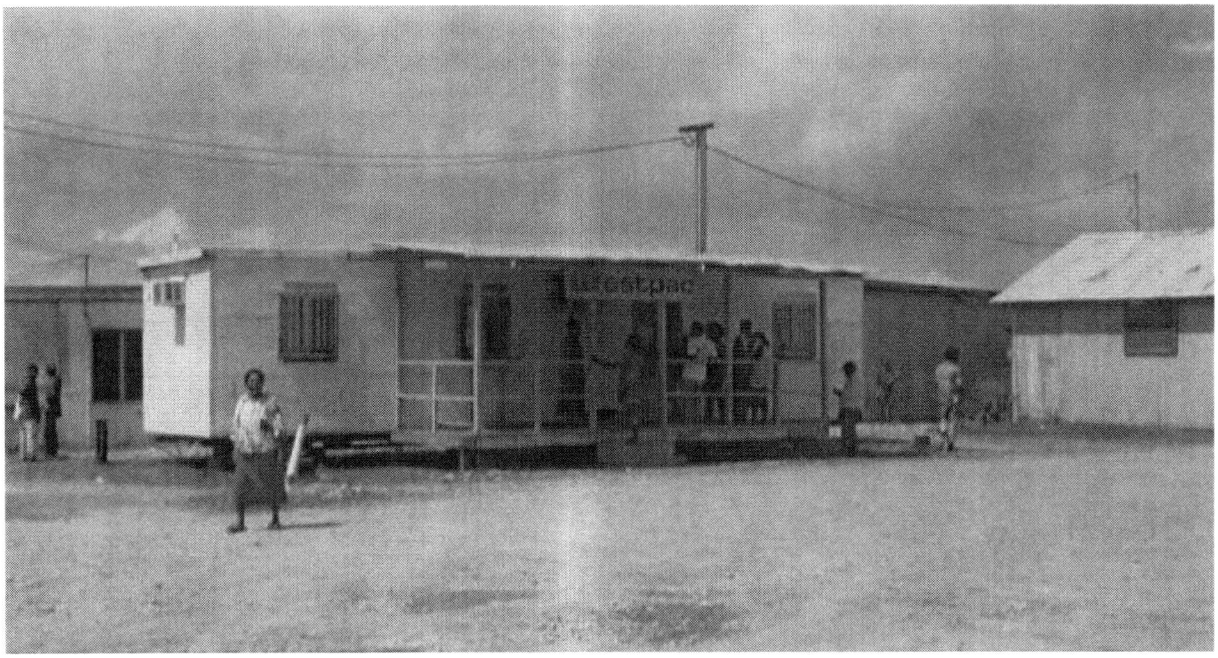

MAIN STREET OF MISIMA AND ITS ONLY BANK, WESTPAC

We have not tried this before, but we handed the customs agent two mostly empty bottles of rum for checking us in and out of PNG at the same time so we would not have to make this trip again. We merely said we were over the alcohol limit so would he take the extra? Pat and I were pretty much agreed we did not want to return to Misima and sail against the wind twice for thirty miles. The trip back is miserable and directly against the wind. We even waited at Misima Island in the harbor of Bwagaoia for two days for the wind to moderate.

We motor sailed to make Wuri-Wuri (worry-worry) Pass, unmarked and unlighted entrance through the Calvados reefs, before dark. With the wind and waves against us, we were managing a measly three to four knots. The current through the pass was also against us, which meant we would not get back to the anchorage at Pana Numara until dark. We radioed ahead and our friends said they would keep their lights on (like Motel 6) so we could judge where to drop our anchor in the dark. Their lights helped us judge distances properly, but the wind was blowing hard. By time the anchor reached the 60 feet to the bottom and dug in, we were blown back 300 feet from where we wanted to be. The next morning we re-anchored to move closer to the beach and for better shelter from the wind.

On Sunday we were invited to go to the Uniting Church[3] service on the island. Walking through two of the villages on the way to church was a pleasant surprise as the villages were clean and well cared for. Each home is built off the ground about four feet on strong pilings using a local wood that is rot resistant. The frame is made up of tree branches lashed together. The roof and walls are kept dry with tightly woven palm leaves. They open sections of the walls to let air and light in and provide a doorway. There is plenty of separation between the homes, palm trees, native island trees and some fencing for small gardens. Some of the owners keep their pigs, chickens and roosters under their homes. While other pigs are allowed to run wild, they return home each evening to be fed. No electricity or generators only kerosene lamps, if they have kerosene.

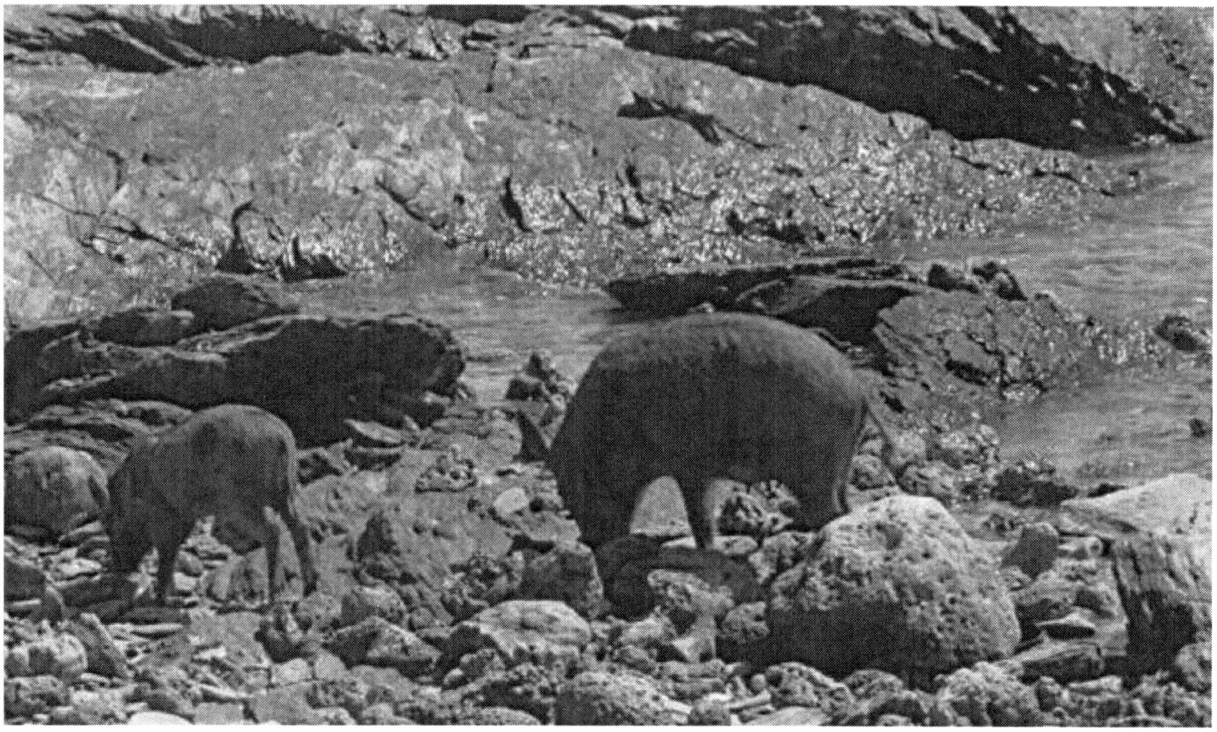

VILLAGE PIGS OF PANA NUMARA

3 The Uniting Church was formed in Australia in 1977, drawing membership from the Methodist Church of Australia, the Congregational Union of Australia, and the Presbyterian Church of Australia. Some Congregational and Presbyterian congregations decided not to join and to continue as before, but all Methodist churches were bound by the decision of their General Conference in favor of union. Microsoft® Encarta® 2006. © 1993-2005 Microsoft Corporation. All rights reserved.

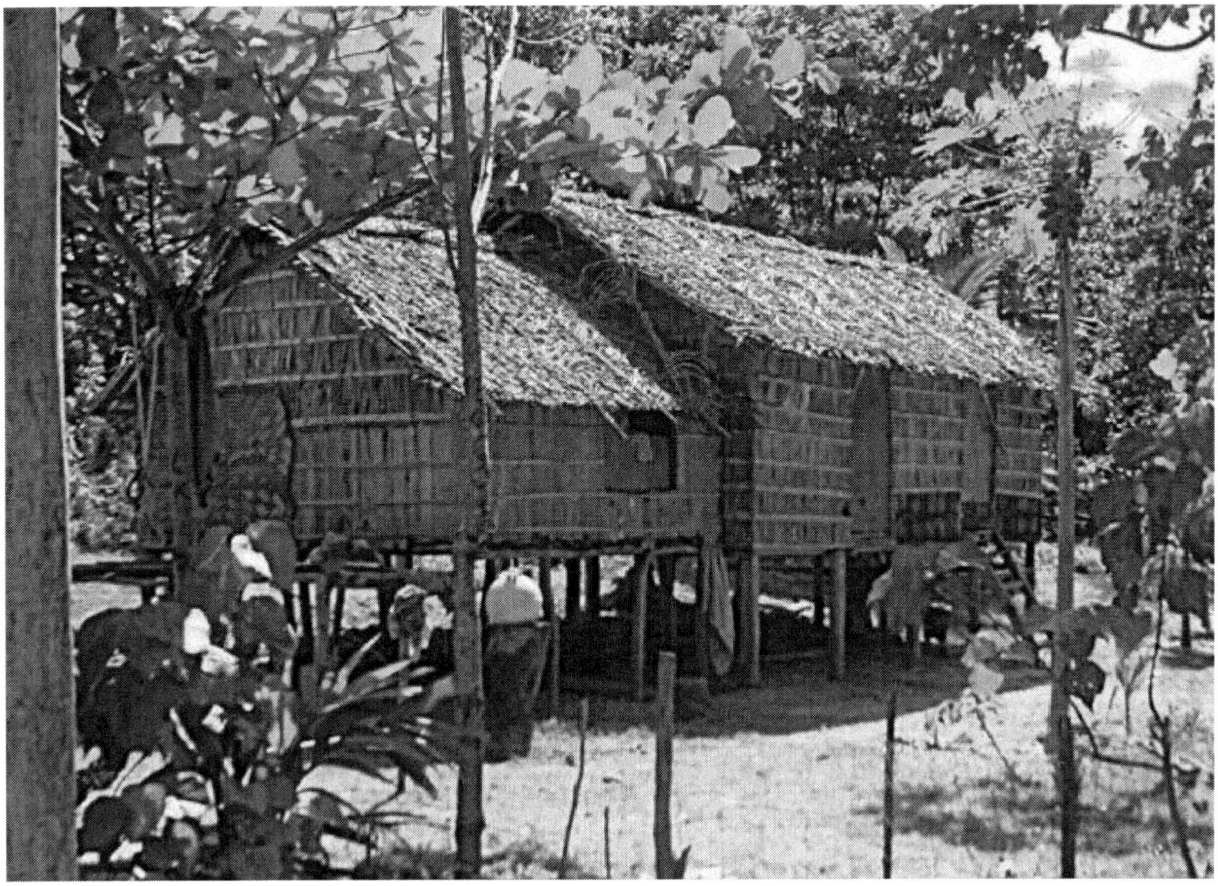

NATIVE HOME, PANA NUMARA ISLAND, LOUISIADES

The mining company in Misima provided the church building in Pana Numara. They also built several similar buildings on other islands (one good thing the mines contributed). The building was about 40 feet long by 20 feet wide with a small enclosure for a room at the far end. The construction was steel beams, steel roof, concrete floor and wooden sides about four feet up from the floor. The remaining space from the top of the wall to the ceiling is open with no way to close the opening. The islanders use this building for their church services, meetings and school up through grade three. We took our sandals off and dipped our feet in a bowl of water outside the door (the islanders do not have shoes or even simple flip-flops) and stepped onto a cold concrete floor.

The room was completely bare, no furniture of any kind, the men sat on the bare floor and most women brought woven mats of palm leaves to sit on. The women sat on the right side with the men on the left side, as is the norm for most of the Polynesian cultures. There were at least four women breast-feeding their children with lots of children sitting with one parent or the other. About 150 people live on this island including 50 children. We sat back and enjoyed the singing, which was in their native language. Two men played worn guitars and one played something like a miniature ukulele. The moving singing went on for about an hour. All church services begin with about an hour of singing followed by the formal service.

We quietly left at the end of the singing before the formal service started since it was in their native language. Imagine a church that does not take up a collection — not much point since the native's money exists in pigs and shell necklaces called "baggies." One of the village elders, Bernard, walked us out to the door and thanked us for coming. We all dug down to leave a donation for the church along with some writing books as the building doubles as a school.

As we got to know Bernard better, he turned out to be one unique individual. He was well-educated, former member of the PNG navy, humble, somewhat shy, and always delighted to see us. He was unique also because he never asked us for anything, but everyone wanted to give him what they could. He had once lived on the mainland, but his wife divorced him and managed to end up with their home and most assets. He chose to move to Pana Numara, as I believe he said his sister lives here. He remarried and now has five children. His oldest girl is thirteen and his wife is nursing a new baby girl. Bernard works every day from dawn to dusk clearing trees for a new vegetable garden. All gardens also require a substantial fence around them to keep the pigs out. Once the land is ready, his wife will do the planting and watering.

Monday was pig roast day! Bernard and several villagers got together to show their appreciation for our kindness by roasting a pig for us. We were quite surprised and delighted, but stipulated that we would pay for the pig. The villagers normally boil their pigs, but Bernard knew how to roast the pig western style. The process is an old-fashioned one and time consuming. The pigs are knocked unconscious with blows to the head. Then they are suffocated holding their mouths shut and sealing their nostrils with fingers — not a pretty sight. Most of the pig's internal organs were fed to the dogs and the natives also eat some organs.

Everything used for the process came from the land. The natives wove mats from palm leaves for sitting and to put the dishes and utensils on. The yachties provided the dishes and utensils. Two fires were started, one to boil water and the other to heat rocks gathered from the beach. The fires were started by rubbing wood together, no matches. Boiled water incrementally was poured over small areas of the pig to help loosen hair that was then shaved off with a sharp machete. The pig was roasted over the open fire spit and turned by hand. This pig was ready to eat around 3:30 in the afternoon from a process that started around 6:30 in the morning.

The best meat came from the legs whereas meat from the ribs contained a lot of fat. We brought applesauce, coleslaw and a cake for dessert. The other three couples also brought along other foods for the roast with enough to go around for the natives. We brought along balloons for the 10 or so native children watching the whole affair with great delight. Marv and Chieko gave the children sticks of gum. For ten dollars spent on the whole affair ($5 for the pig and $5 to the natives that helped), everyone had a marvelous day and what great value for a few dollars. We got back to our boats just before dark with great feelings of closeness to these kind and generous people.

We announced to the village that Tuesday would be children's day on Pana Numara. When our dinghies reached the shore, children with great big smiles, waited to great us. We had all made popcorn balls, which they had never seen or tasted before, *Esprit* also made chocolate candy, Marv passed out, gum, pencils, plastic water pistols and marbles. We had balloons and Jalna had tattoo transfers for the children that were a great hit. We were quite surprised that the children knew how to use the marbles and how to trade them. The children were so beautiful and happy, giggling all the time. Most of the children could say basic words in English like, "thank you," "good morning," "what is your name" and understood some of our questions.

There were about 30 children in the village and another 20 or so that were living on other islands for higher levels of schooling. When they go to other islands for schooling, they live with relatives. From talking to the natives, we learned that it is common for the families to have relatives on many islands in the Calvados chain and on the mainland. Pat and I agreed that the natives we met who were educated at the catholic mission school had the best command of English and were most likely to be leaders in their villages. When all the popcorn balls and candy were eaten and all the toys passed out, the children sang four songs for us accompanied by Bernard on the guitar. We clapped loudly and long and were delighted to see all those barefoot children in tattered clothes with proud beaming faces smiling back at us.

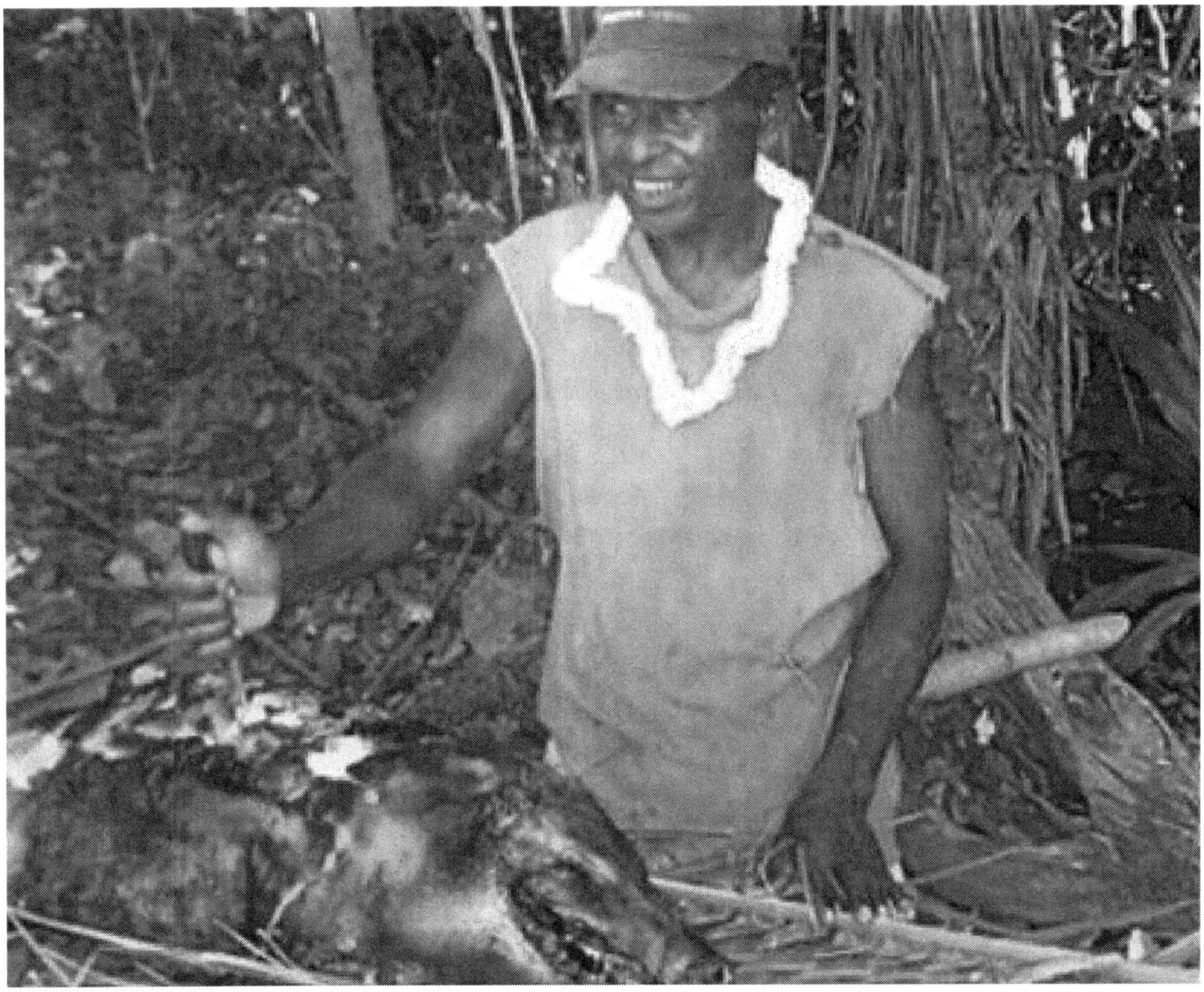

BERNARD, PIG ROAST, PANA NUMARA ISLAND

This day the village was also preparing a feast in memory of a chief who had died there. The chief had died some fifteen years ago and part of the ceremony was to dismantle the house he had lived in. We never did get an explanation of why no one could live there all this time or why it took fifteen years to honor him and remove his house. Walking back to our dinghies we could see the village was full of activity with the young men untying each pole from the house and neatly stacking the wood while others were cooking food in pots over several fires. In one of the larger pots, some men were making a strange looking soup that needed constant stirring with a large paddle. They had killed two pigs for this feast, but they were being boiled in the traditional way — probably a method left over from the old days when they boiled their enemies. We heard one nearby island had a pile of skulls left over from the days of cannibalism — not something we were anxious to see.

On Wednesday, the women from the four cruising yachts put together a women's day for the native women of the village. We could hear the village gong being rung for the women to gather at the church building. Every Wednesday the women normally gathered there for bible reading and fellowship, but today, decided they would see what the dim-dim (native term for white people) women had in store for them. Chieko was not feeling good that day so the dim-dim team was reduced to Pat, Jalna and Sheri. The idea was to help the native women with cosmetics and other feminine things that they could not afford or rarely came in contact with. So, the dim-dim women gathered up all their polishes and lipsticks and shared their secrets of applying toenail polish and lipstick. From the word I got back from Pat, the day was a complete success. The women were giggling and excited like children to be treated to a few hours of spoiling and attention. Afterwards the native women treated our dim-dims to several songs.

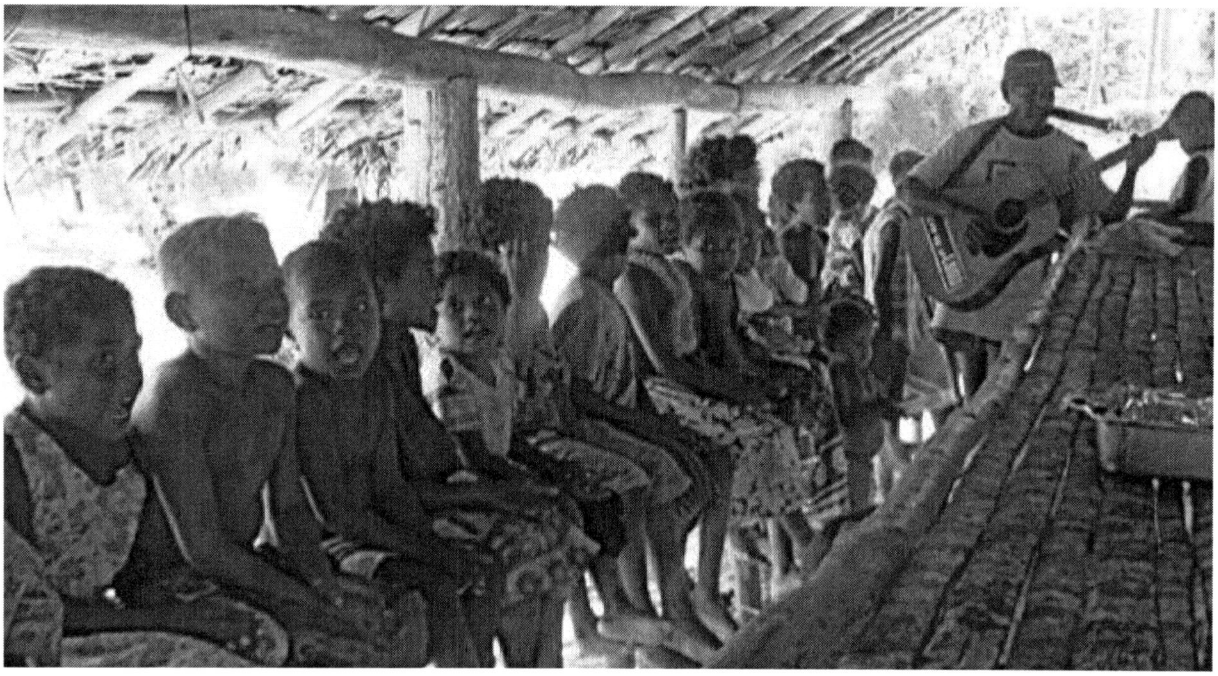

THE CHILDREN OF PANA NUMARA, LOUISIADES, PNG

The men, in the meantime, went crayfish hunting with three native men. We ferried them out to some nearby reefs to look for giant lobsters that grow here, but not much luck. These lobsters are vegetarians and inhabit caves and holes in reefs. Normally they feed at night and keep hidden during the day, but negotiating these reefs at night is even more dangerous. About five hours was spent in searching one reef, but the native divers found only one female whose body was about a foot long. The water temperature was over 80° F, but after five hours the native divers were shivering. Roger did some diving with the natives for a while, but swimming around the reefs with waves breaking against them requires a lot of skill and strong swimming ability. Much too tiring on bodies lacking exercise. On the other hand, the idea of putting one's hand into an unknown dark hole is not something I want to do, as there are a lot of creatures that bite in the tropics. I was surprised that the natives would use our snorkels and masks, but not fins or gloves.

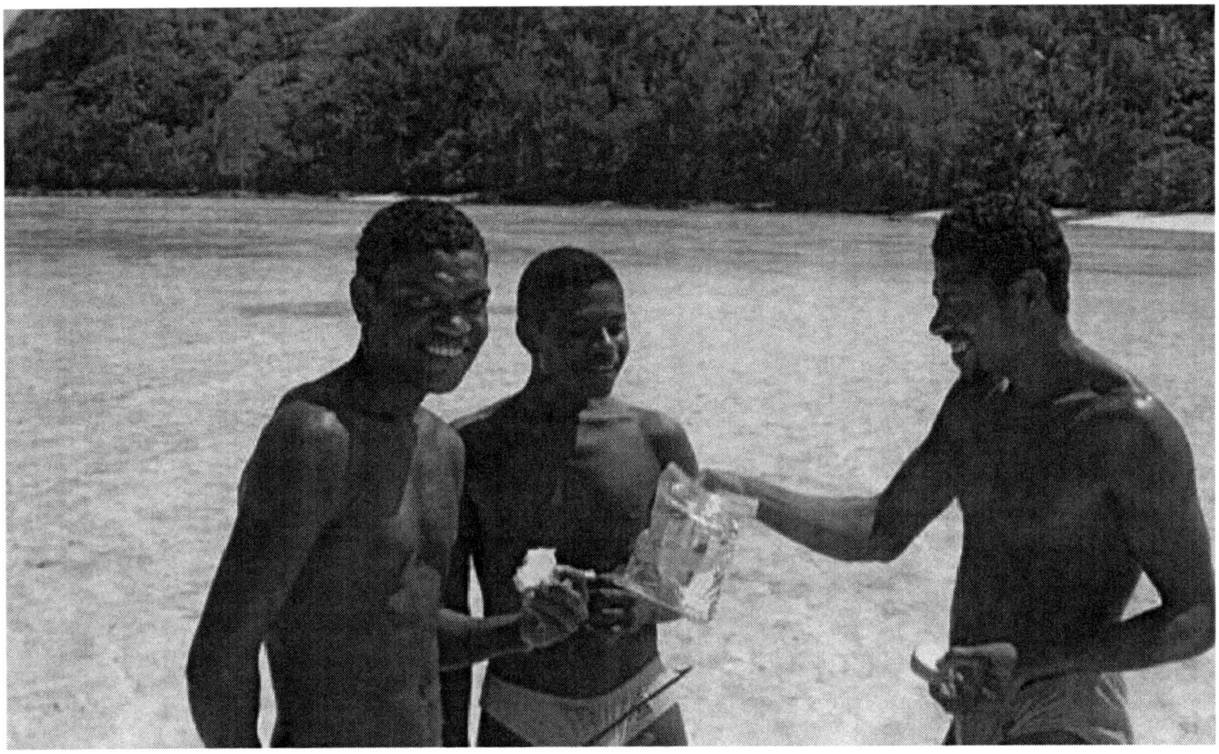

GETTING READY TO LOOK FOR LOBSTER, PANA NUMARA STYLE

On Sunday the 4 yachts pooled their food resources and had a beach barbeque. By this time the natives had found some lobsters for trading so surf and turf (turf from our freezers) was enjoyed by the dim-dims.

The next day, an old looking villager (they do not keep records, so most of the natives did not know their age) fell out of a tree while cutting off some branches. He was building himself a new home. He was thought to have broken some ribs as his breathing was labored and he was obviously in a lot pain. The pastor asked us if we could help organize the trip to the hospital at Misima. We gave him some strong painkillers and supplied the fuel for their outboard. Our boats were not fast enough to expedite his transportation to the hospital at Misima. As is normal in the villages, they did not have any gas. We also gave the pastor AUS $40 to buy gas for the return trip and a hospital bed if required. The care would be free, but they have to pay for the beds if an overnight is required. The other men would stay with relatives. The pastor returned the next day in their aluminum dinghy. The injured man would recover, but had to stay at the hospital and would be returned by his relatives. We never did get an accounting of how the money was spent, but I am sure it did not go entirely towards gas or the patient — it was probably like turning kids loose in a candy shop.

Tuesday, someone decided it would be Mexican night on board *Endurance*. Everyone brought Mexican hors d'oeuvres, a main dish and wore Mexican attire. Marv, from *Endurance*, still had one and a half gallons of Tequila left over from his cruising days in Mexico so he volunteered to supply the Margaritas.

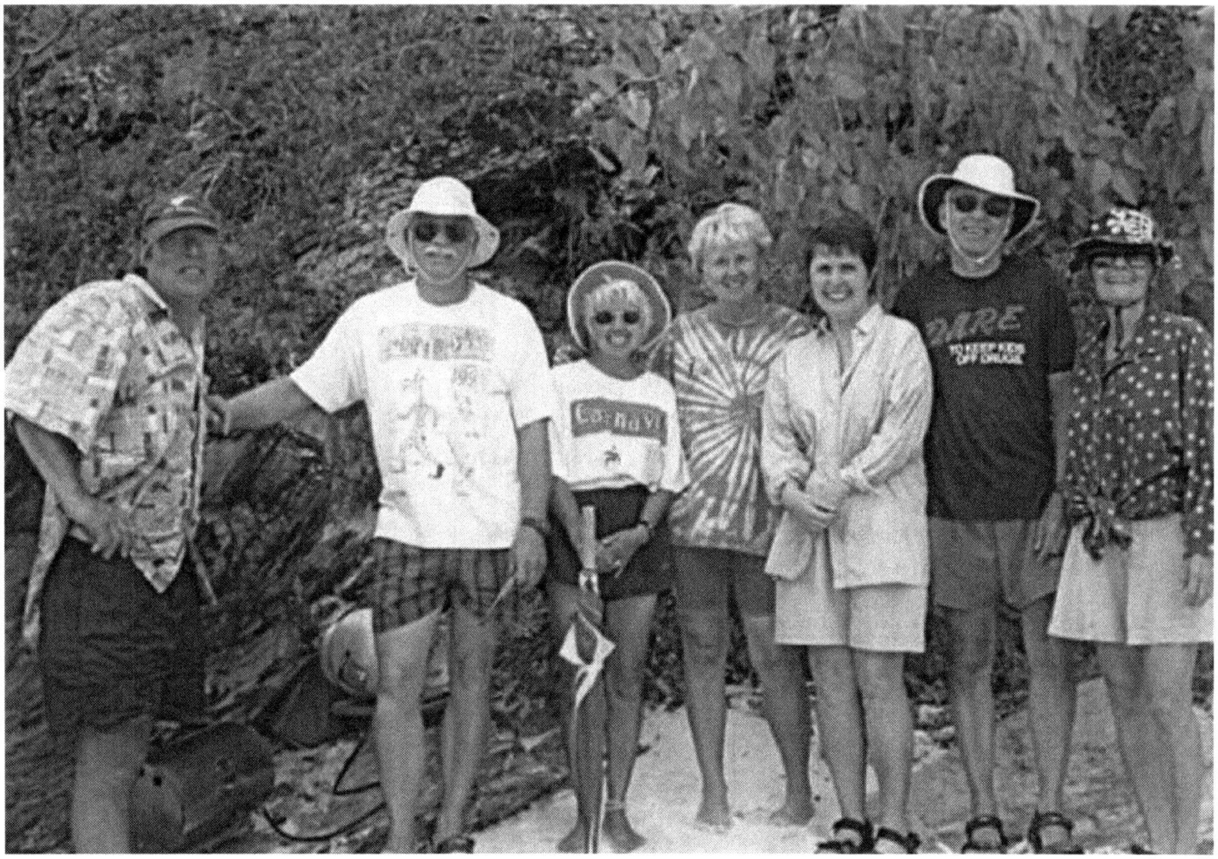

ROGER (*TWEED*), MARV AND CHIEKO (*ENDURANCE*), JALNA (*TWEED*), PAT (*OUR PLEASURE*), BILL AND SHERI (*ESPRIT*), PANA NUMARA ISLAND

We also invited Melanie and her 1 year-old son Jacob over, as her husband had to go to Misima to get some engine parts. Their boat was anchored near ours and she would have been alone with her son. She added a younger side to our conversations. She is an independent 20 year-old French Canadian who left home at sixteen. She worked while traveling a lot of the world until she met her Australian husband who was a charter boat skipper taking divers to the Great Barrier Reef. She had 2 visible tattoos and was not the least bit shy about nursing Jacob, but to her credit, did not drink any alcohol. The evening was warm and beautiful, with no light from the islands; the night sky was vivid with bright stars and planets.

On Thursday the islanders honored us again with another pig roast complete with island vegetables: yam, taro and sweet potatoes. However, we stipulated that we would donate the money for the pig to the village. The day was warm, sunny and pleasant with lots of children watching the whole feast with laughter and curiosity. This was quite an honor for us from people who are so poor, but enjoy the simple pleasures of life like sharing a meal. The occasion of the feast was to allow good friends to say goodbye, as it was time for us to move on.

The next afternoon we found Bernard working in his garden and presented him with a bright and shiny guitar. We asked Melanie's husband to bring back one of the inexpensive guitars made in China and available in Misima. Bernard never asked us for a guitar, but mentioned that his oldest daughter had some musical talent, but he would probably never be able to buy her a musical instrument. His joy was overwhelming; he tried to look away so we would not see the tears of a proud man. It brought tears to our eyes to witness his joy. Later he was seen with his head in his hands sobbing. The guitar cost about $135 in kina or $35, but if he ever saved that much money he would be obligated to share it with the villagers for kerosene or other necessities — it would probably never be within his reach.

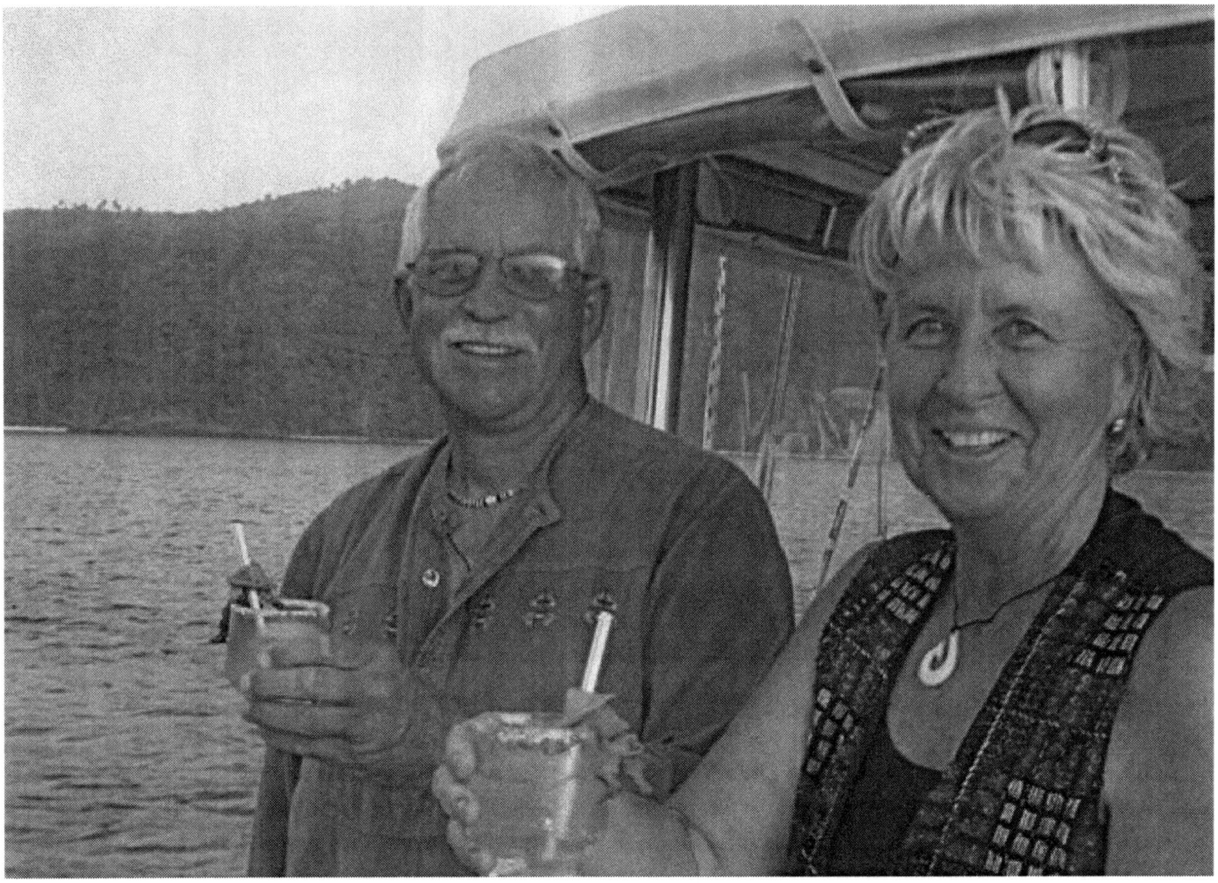

MARV AND JALNA, MEXICAN NIGHT, PANA NUMARA

We lifted our anchors at Pana Numara on Aug. 10, just after Bernard and another village elder, Tass, came out in their dugout canoes to say goodbye and give us some last minute gifts of handmade tablemats. We motored by the village, blew them a salute with our air horns, and then motored over to Bagaman Island about an hour away. Bagaman is an island similar to Pana Numara with swaying palm trees, native plants and trees, sandy beaches, a well-protected wide bay, but with a much larger land mass and a population of around 250 in five villages.

After we had set our anchors at Bagaman Island, a villager named, Gulu came out to welcome us. He brought paw-paws and bananas for trading. He claimed to be a chief and announced we were now free to visit the village. We were told later that he made it his goal to greet all arrivals first, he was not a chief, but a slightly eccentric old man believed to be 87 years old. If 87 was his true age he beat the averages as life span in his culture is reputed to be only fifty years. A week later he accidentally started a huge grass fire while cooking some fish. He is easily recognized by large holes in each ear lobe reminiscent from the old days when they put wooden disks in their ear lobes.

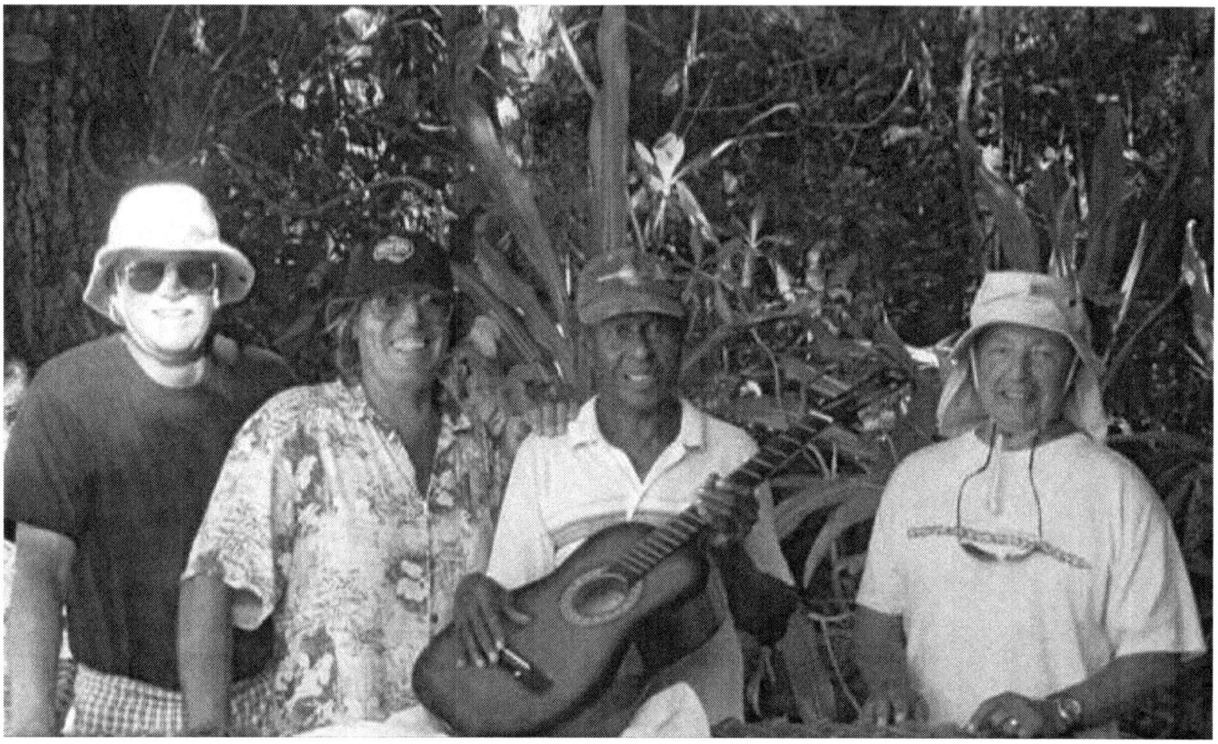

MARV, ROGER, BERNARD WITH NEW GUITAR AND DICK, PANA NUMARA

This day was also Marv and Chieko Millers (from the 65 foot schooner *Endurance*) 34th wedding anniversary and ***Our Pleasure*** hosted the anniversary party. Everyone dressed up; even some ties were seen on the men until the heat got to them. Roger played the role of steward and his wife Jalna was a hostess. We were able to find three bottles of Champaign (not French) to drink. Jalna at one time owned a restaurant in Victoria, BC. Much to Chieko's delight, Jalna made delicious sushi for hors d'oeuvres followed by Pat's main course of chicken divine. The wine was my favorite, gold medal winner Wyndham Estate's Bin 555 Shiraz wine from Australia. Dessert was white cake with a vanilla custard topping and Starbuck's coffee. The anniversary couple enjoyed all the attention and everyone enjoyed the occasion.

The next day Roger and I went over to help Marv find out why his new bow thruster stopped working. While anchoring at Bagaman, he used the bow thruster to keep the boat straight as he backed away from the anchor. Initially it worked, then he could hear the motor running, but the bow did not respond to turn commands. Eventually, after much poking and moving different parts, we found the motor was disconnected from the drive shaft to the thruster's 2 props. The electric motor puts out 15 horsepower and is a 100 pound monster. By positioning a table next to the motor and opening the access plates we were able to get a good hold on the motor for the short transition to the table.

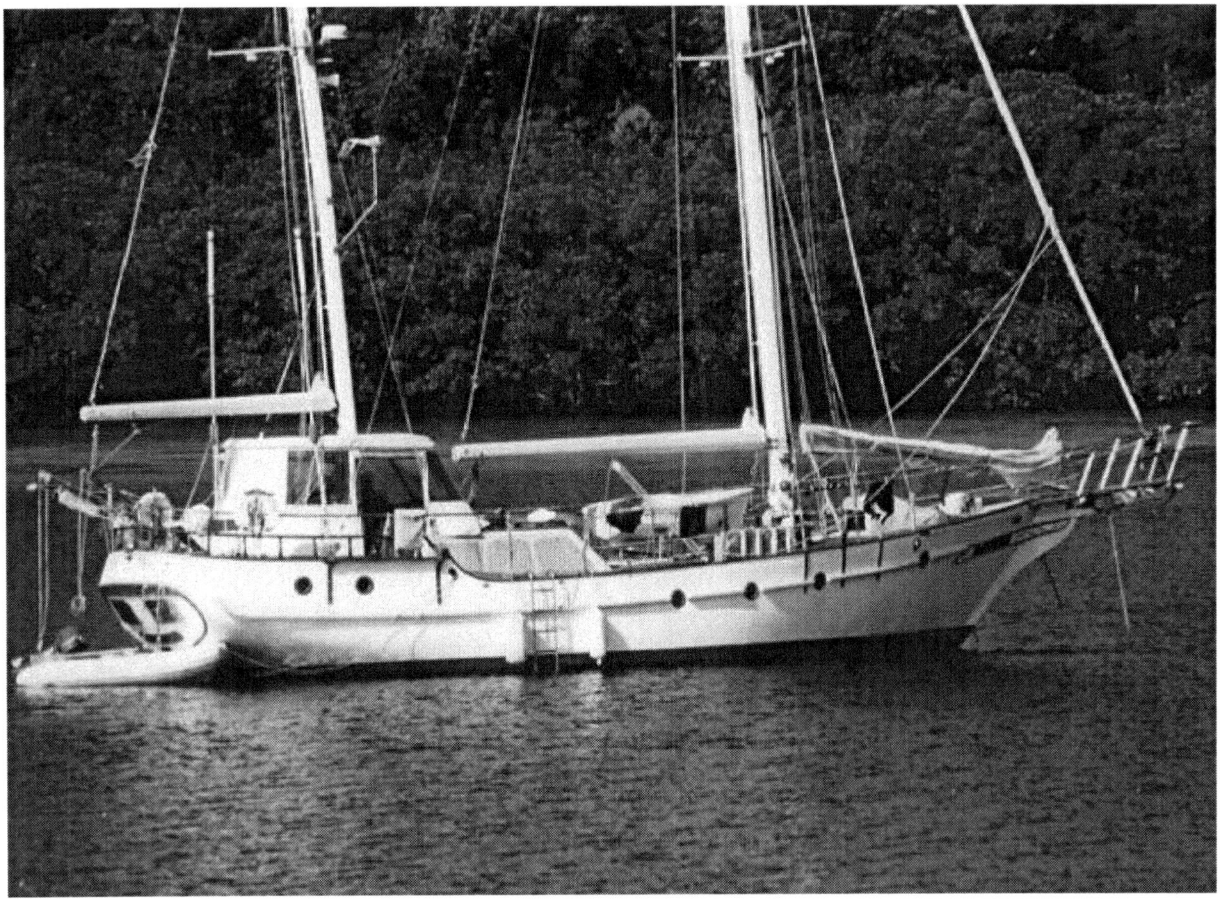

OUR PLEASURE ANCHORED AT BAGAMAN ISLAND

It looked like the fault occurred when the motor and drive shaft were connected together during the initial installation. The three bolts that were supposed to do the job worked their way out and fell inside the housing out of view. Marv was lucky there was no damage. We took plenty of care to clean out old grease, add new grease where needed and to Loctite® all set screws and bolts. The thruster was better than new and now worked perfectly. The power generated from his thruster can be compared to four strong men standing on a dock pulling a line attached to the bow, a huge asset when docking.

On Thursday the four skippers and their first mates were invited to the elementary school on Bagaman Island. There were 21 students at the school, which only teaches grades 1, 2 and 3. The children were all priceless, dressed in their traditional costumes. They managed to sing and dance their way through five dances much to everyone's delight. When we all clapped loudly their faces just glowed with pride. The girls were dressed in grass skirts; necklaces made from seashells, native flowers and make believe tattoos on their cheeks. The boys wore a string bikini made from palm fronds, feather headdresses and seashell necklaces.

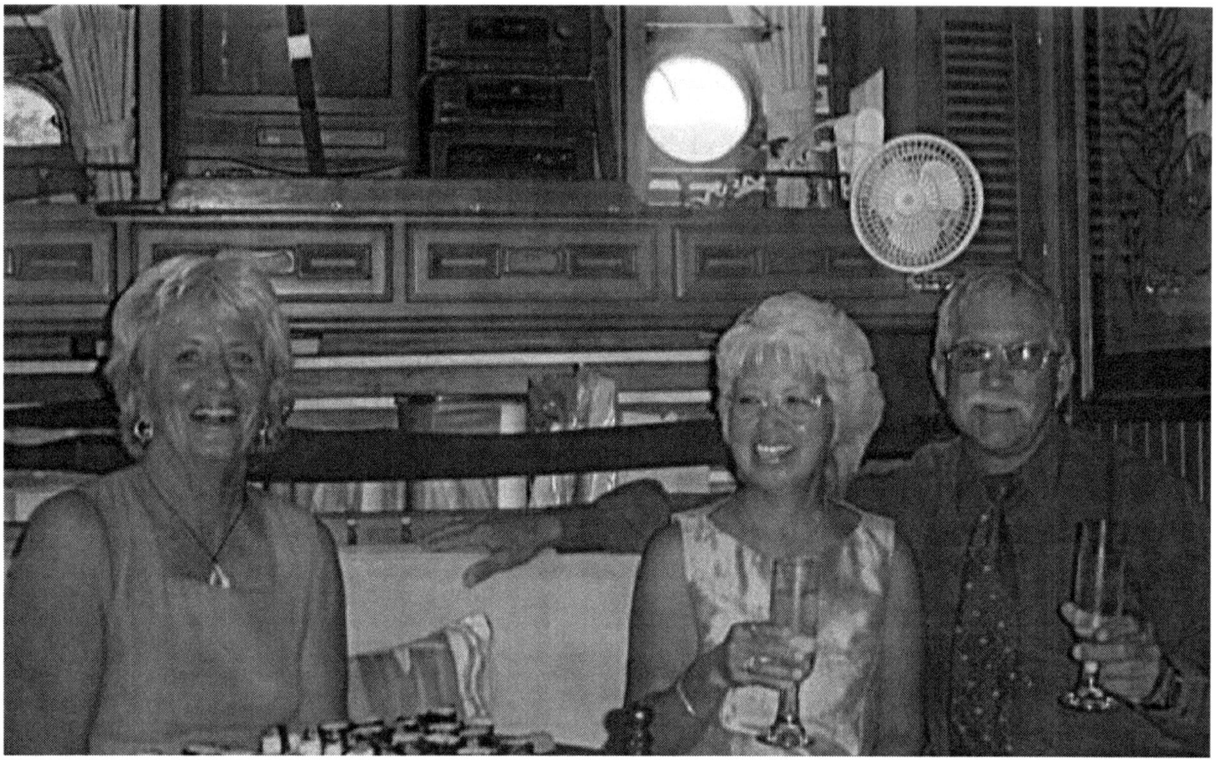

JALNA, ANNIVERSARY COUPLE CHIEKO AND MARV ON THEIR 34th

Pat and I gave the teacher about 50 exercise books for writing assignments, pens, pencils and chalk. She was almost out of chalk and the other school materials were about non-existent. Imagine, these small gifts made her cry openly and she hugged Pat hard with real emotion. Remember, she is paid an equivalent of about $6.25 a month with essentially no support from the PNG government. She has to teach school with little or no supplies and tries to inspire 21 children — tremendous dedication. She was probably one of the most educated of the islanders we met; I believe she said she finished 14 years of education. We had all made chocolate cupcakes especially for the children, but with enough for everyone. They weren't familiar with cupcakes, but one taste was all it took to see the big smiles all around.

Several days ago I gave Sam, probably in his twenties, 4 D-cell batteries so he could do some night diving for crayfish. Well, he never came back with the crayfish so we told the islanders if they could not keep their word we would no longer trade with them. Well, that really stirred things up. It turned out that Sam has a bad reputation as an aspiring conman and the villagers were not happy. Sam showed up today with 3 nice sized crayfish for us and was accompanied by his village elder. Sam looked a bit spent as it took him most of the night to find the crayfish. The village elder watched and listened to the whole exchange between us and asked if they could start trading again? With all accounts settled, everyone was happy. He also had made a present for us, a name board with our boat name carved into the wood — everyone was satisfied.

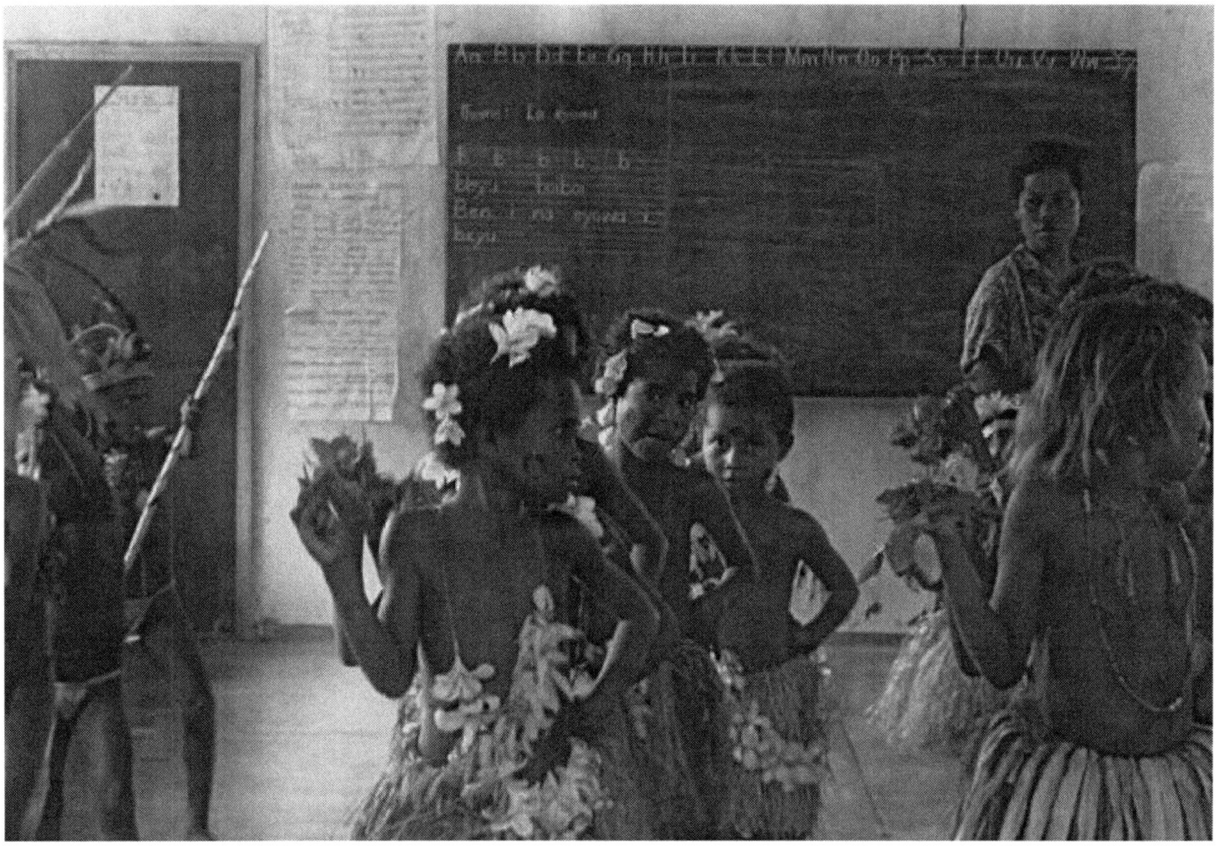

BAGAMAN ISLAND SCHOOL CHILDREN DANCING FOR THE DIM-DIM YACHTIES

When we finally left the Louisiades, besides the fruits and vegetables we traded for everyday, we ended up with the following items:

- Three hand carved name boards.
- One model outrigger canoe.
- Two model outrigger sailing canoes.
- Two hand carved dolphins.
- Nine hand woven and dyed purses.
- Two hand woven and dyed tablemats.
- One hand carved canoe paddle.
- Six shell necklaces.
- One clay pot.
- Two walking sticks.
- A strong basket used by women to carry heavy items on their heads.

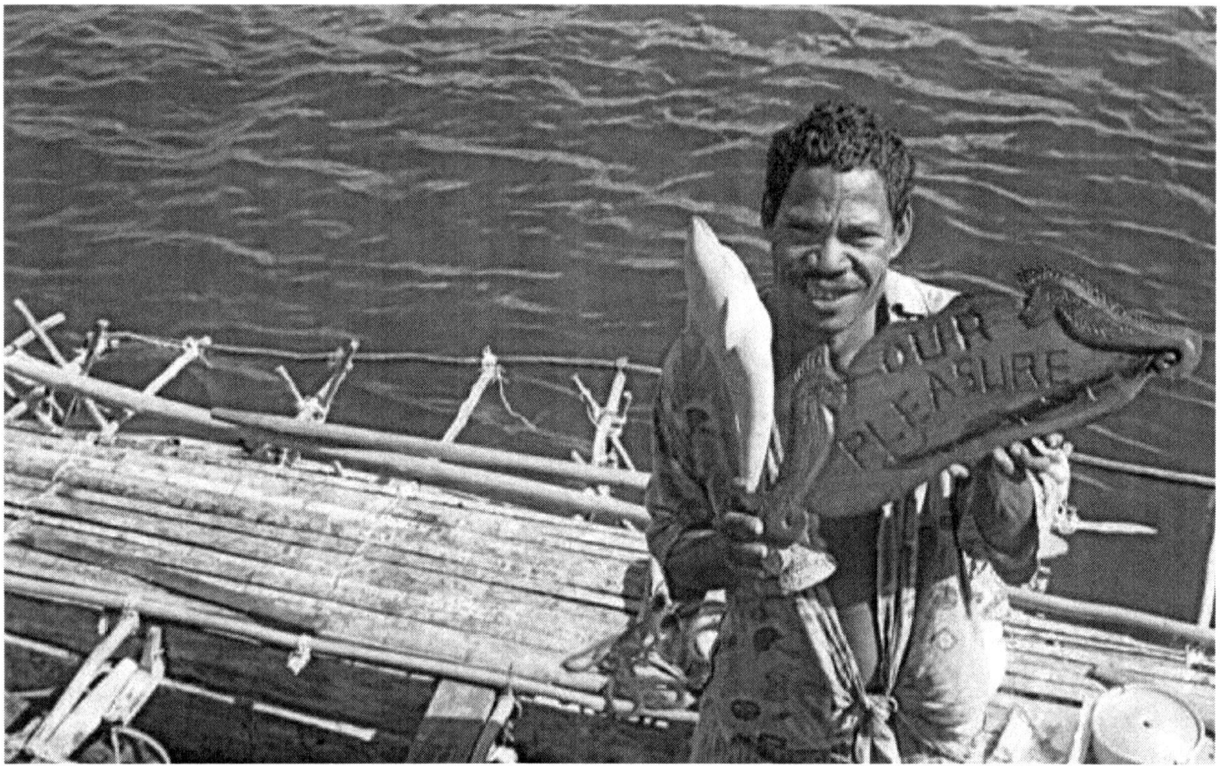

MORRIS, GIFTS OF A DOLPHIN AND NAME BOARD FOR *OUR PLEASURE*

We have no idea what we will do with all this stuff, but we felt that if the natives made the effort to bring us something we would reciprocate and always give them something in return. Our boat is now a lot lighter from the items given away. Besides all the school supplies, we traded tools, fishing gear, clothes, sewing stuff, material, mirrors, books and cooking pots. I gave away some hand tools like a hand plane and a hand drill that once belonged to my Dad. Pat gave one of the women she was especially fond of, Miriam, a new Timex wristwatch so she could receive training to become a mid-wife. The watch was required for timing contractions.

It is now Friday, Aug. 16. One of the men I am fond of, Morris from the village Oisi, paddled over to ask if I could help him fix his outboard. It ran well, but was not pumping cooling water. When I went over to the village he was happy to see me. He is one person who seemed to have it all together. His wife, Bilita, really stands out from most of the native women because she is personable, attractive and speaks good English. She was off at their new garden to do the planting and took the baby she is nursing with her. The older boy, Billie, was with Morris. Morris had just served three years as a councilman representing Bagaman Island and several nearby islands. He must have done a good job, as he seemed to enjoy a lot of respect from his fellow villagers. To do his council job the government gave him a used 25 horsepower Evenrude outboard motor and a used aluminum dinghy.

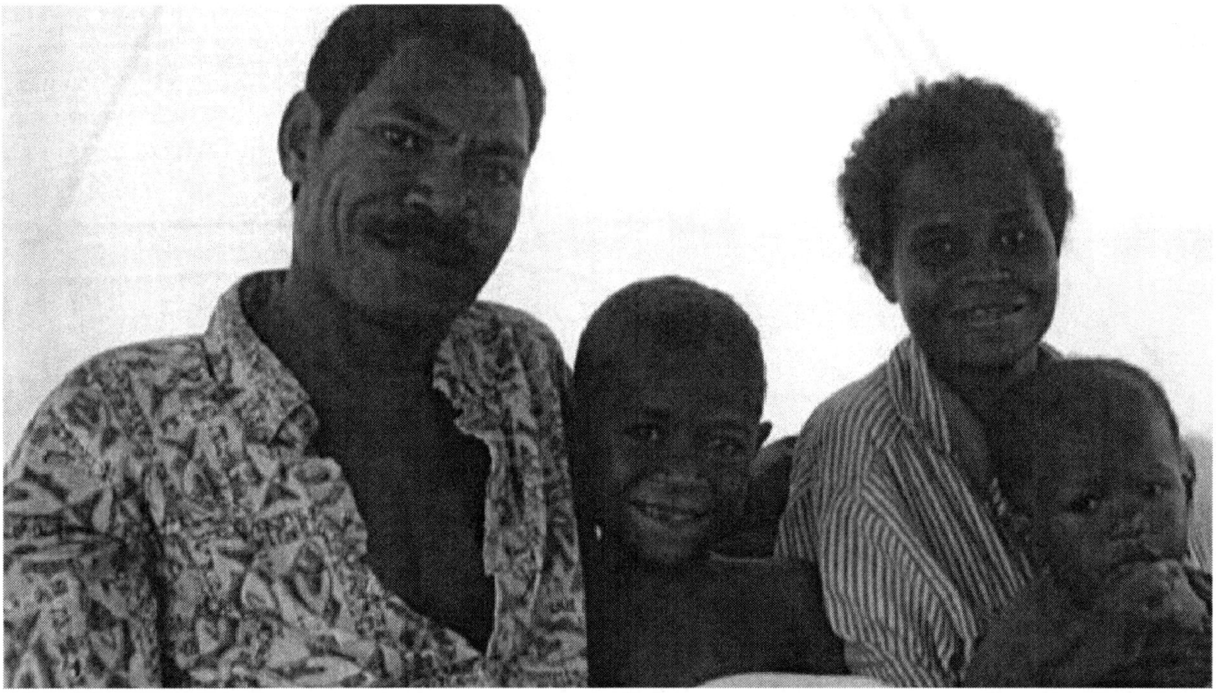

MORRIS, BILLY, BILITA AND BABY ON *OUR PLEASURE*

As we neared the beach, two men standing in waist high water waded out to greet me. I climbed out and they picked up my 200 pound dinghy with a minimum of strain and carried it up to the beach to avoid scratching the aluminum bottom on rocks. Bear in mind that the men and women of this culture are small in stature, about my height and shorter, but probably weigh in at around 120 pounds. Morris had managed to find a replacement impeller, but lacked the tools and maybe the knowledge to install it properly. This operation attracted the interest of the villagers including Gulu, but no women.

I took the two lower units of the outboard apart and then I cleaned out all the water passages with a chemical cleaner that Marv had given me. I had to make new gaskets and installed the new impeller. Morris had one-half of a plastic 50 gallon drum, which they used as a bath for the children; I wanted to use it to test the impeller. He had one man, watching the whole affair, carry it out and fill it with salt water. The village was out of outboard fuel and by this time I was almost out so we were not able to run the outboard. However, I was able to turn the drive shift by hand before bolting the upper lower unit in place and it appeared to pump properly. I gave Morris my small Sears® socket set for any future work as he only had a couple of rusty box wrenches. Skip Meredith, a Boeing engineering manager, gave me that set back in '95 as a Boeing retirement gift — it is now in a good place.

On Saturday, Simi and his wife Miriam invited all of us to their house for lunch in the village of Ho Hola. They are a typical family with four children. This village is a bit of a walk from our anchorage, but it is on a beautiful beach setting with lots of palm trees and beautiful green water. We all brought samples of American foods while they prepared their traditional dishes of taro, yams, sweet potatoes, boiled pig and tapioca cake. Their home was typical of island homes, built off the ground, close to the beach and simple with no furniture only woven mats to sit on and to place food on. There were 4 openings for light and air and 3 door-sized openings as well as shutters of palm fronds designed to close off all the openings. There were just 2 rooms, the smallest room contained cooking and eating wares on open shelves. The largest room was used for socializing and eating.

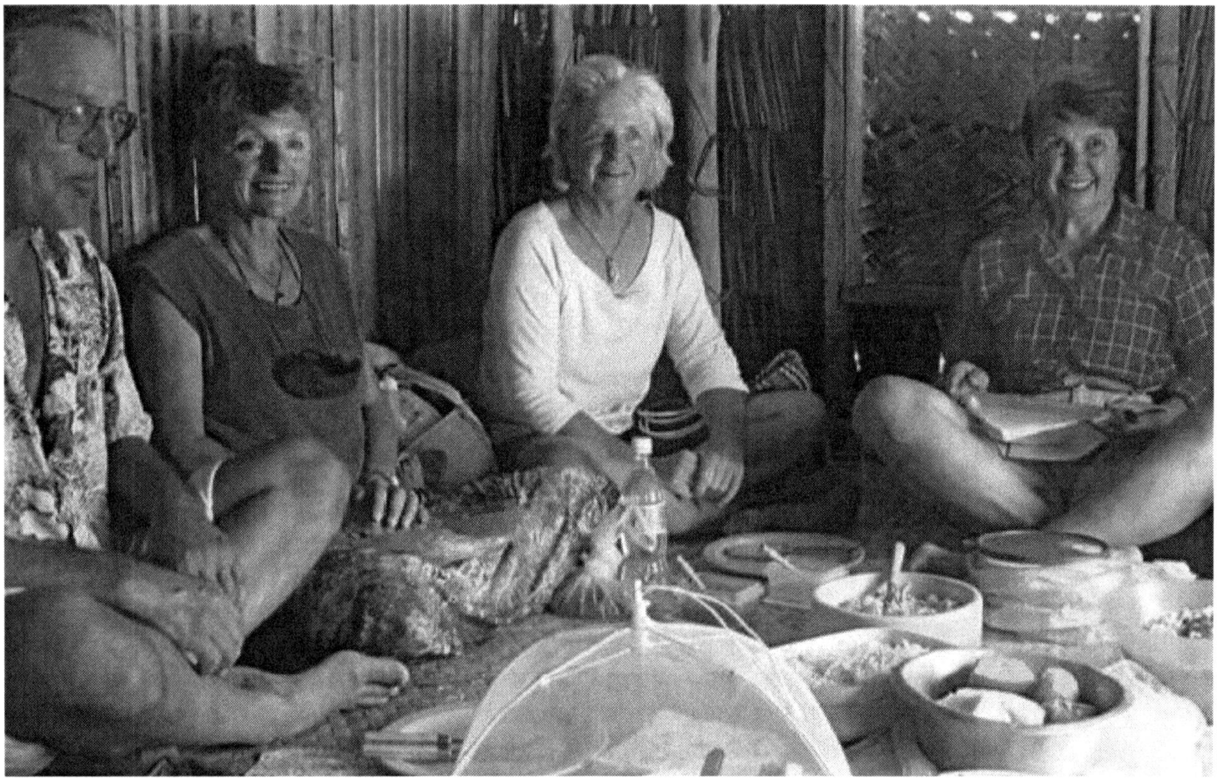

ROGER, SHERI, JALNA AND PAT ENJOYING LUNCH AT SIMI AND MARIAN'S

All cooking is done outside the house under an open sided thatched roof hut and an open fire area. They must have enjoyed our American food because there was nothing left over. Their food is all boiled with no added spices or sauces so it tastes bland. There was quite a gathering of people as it looked like all the villagers were also invited. The children and women all ate after us. Several women and the older children did the cooking and washed everything as soon as it was used.

After lunch everyone was invited to go sailing on Simi's ocean going sailing canoe, but only the men yachties were up to the challenge. These boats are exciting to sail, as they are fast and depend on the physical and athletic abilities of their crew. They are built from three solid wood planks on each side of the main hull. The planks are about thirty feet long, one inch thick and about a foot wide. They are fastened in clinker or lapstreak fashion so the edges over lap each other. The sponson or outrigger is a solid, 8 inch diameter log that is pointed at both ends and is the same length as the hull. The sponson was positioned about ten feet from the main hull by wooden poles and lashings. From the hull to the sponson there are lightweight planks to place cargo on. The hull planks form a point at both ends fastened into solid hardwood pieces that contain many elaborate carvings.

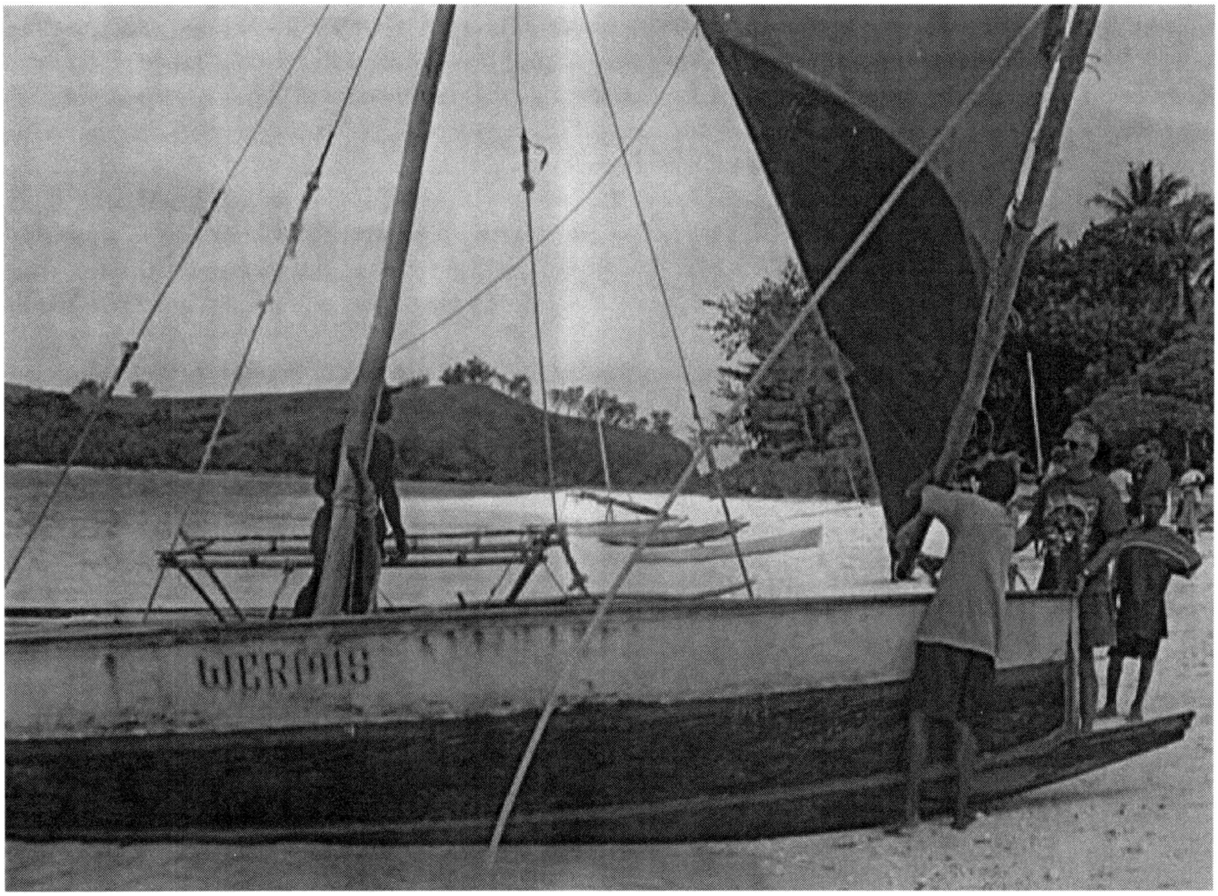

RIGGING SIMI'S OCEAN SAILING LATEEN RIGGED CANOE

The single, large sail is lateen rigged that allows these canoes to be sailed in either direction. They have one outrigger, no blocks or tackle and everything is lashed together. In light winds of probably 12 knots, we were doing about 10 knots on a beam reach, much faster than ***Our Pleasure***. Every lashing and every piece of wood on the boat was moving and there was a big bow wave driving water spray above the hull like a speedboat would. The native crew consisted of two men, one teenage boy and a young boy, the bailer. The task of bailing is a constant one as the faster the canoe goes the wetter it gets. The sail was made from pieces of plastic tarps stitched together. To change direction they lower the sail, move the low end of the boom to the opposite end, raise the sail, move the rudder (a simple paddle) to the other end and away they go. The person steering must be quite strong and the position is not for the weak-of-heart. The person steering stands on a flat board that forms the bottom of the hull and sticks out about two feet from both ends of the hull. He has to hold the paddle shaft between his foot and the protruding board. Moving the paddle to steer the canoe requires a lot of strength and is a position that requires crew rotation. The water rushing by his feet and legs is trying knock him continually off into the water. Holding the paddle shaft against the protruding board with a bare foot, while speeding along at ten knots is both wearying and demanding.

These sailors deserve a lot credit for their sailing skills as they often travel in the dark through reef areas without lights, charts, navigation equipment or life preservers. This type of sailing in the open ocean without knowledge of what storms maybe brewing is dangerous. We heard stories of men heading out to sea in these flimsy canoes disappearing never to return. Radio communication is mostly nonexistent. Their government is not going to send out a search plane for some lost natives. These sailors are on their own and know they must take responsibility for their actions because no one else will.

Talented village natives build some canoes, but if the talent or materials are not available, necklaces or pig trading is an option. One island has become the sailing canoe boat-building center and has a good reputation for building these canoes. Blocks or pulleys are not available so the lines wear and fray easily, which hastens their failure — a potential safety problem. Marv gave Simi a sheet block to raise the main sail and some new line to help with sea worthiness — a really nice gesture.

We had planned to go to their church service on Sunday, but there was a lot of confusion. We couldn't get a reliable word of where the service was being held and at what time. When we finally figured it out the service was over.

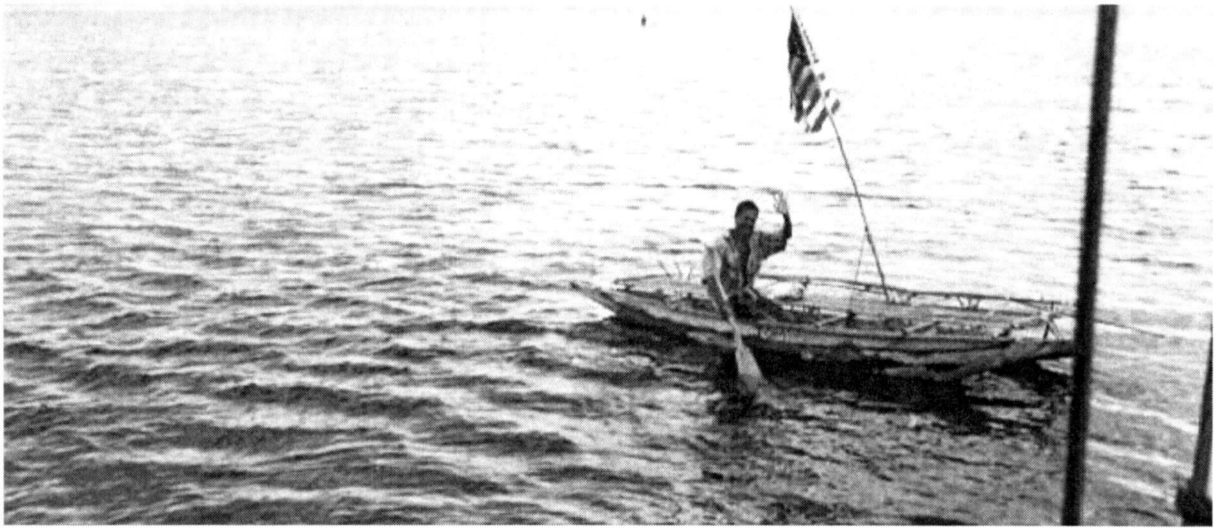

MORRIS, FLYING OUR FLAG, PADDLED OUT TO SAY "SO LONG"

Since it was now time to leave the Louisiades, we made one last trip to the beach to burn our garbage. Simon brought over a beautiful tablemat that his mother had made for Pat. Much to his delight, Pat had one more large cooking pot we had bought in Misima for his mother. Most of the day was spent getting the boat ready for the 700 miles of open water back to Australia. That evening, Simi and Miriam paddled over to say goodbye and had a beautiful shell necklace for Pat. While we were talking in the cockpit, their canoe became untied and drifted away. When they wanted to leave, it was nowhere to be seen and it was dark, real dark. We were lucky to find it with our search light about 100 yards away. It was caught in the mangroves, which was lucky as another 100 feet and it would have been in open water. Our dinghy had already been stowed for the crossing so Simi had to swim for it. He asked for a floatable cushion to swim with and I guided him with the searchlight. These people are strong swimmers so he was back in no time. The paddle had fallen out and was missing so he had to use his hands to paddle. He wasn't fazed by this problem and said he would just carve a new paddle tomorrow.

The next morning, as we pulled up our anchor, several natives, including Simi and Morris, paddled out to say goodbye. Morris was flying the large American flag we had given him on a long pole attached to his canoe — a nice parting tribute. The sail back to Australian waters was uneventful and took us five days, arriving Aug. 25. We had to anchor at Magnetic Island, just outside our arrival port, Townsville, to wait for high tide. Customs, Immigration and Quarantine were at the Townsville fuel dock waiting for us. Australia really has a great system for greeting the arrival of foreign yachts.

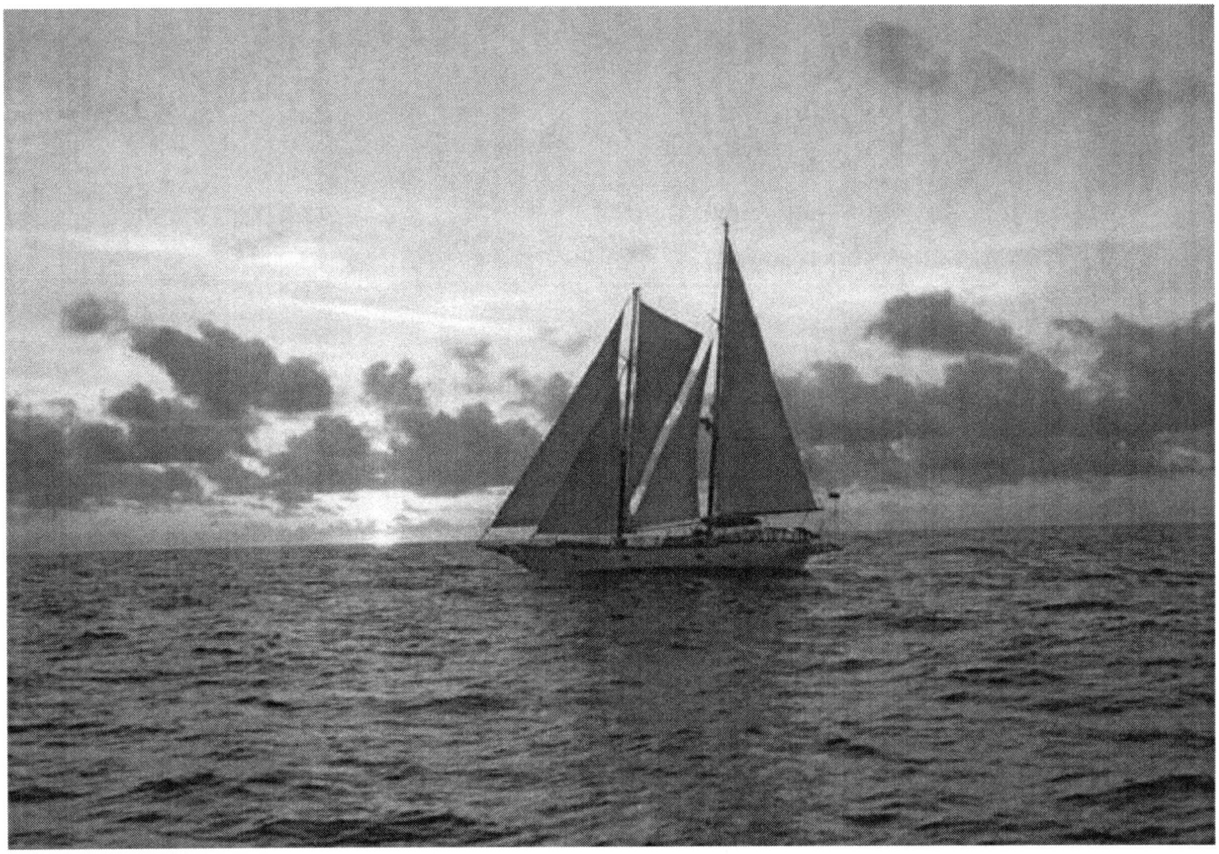

SCHOONER *ENDURANCE* SAILING BACK TO AUSTRALIA, Aug. 20, 2002

Chapter 18

TOWNSVILLE, AUSTRALIA THEN TO DARWIN

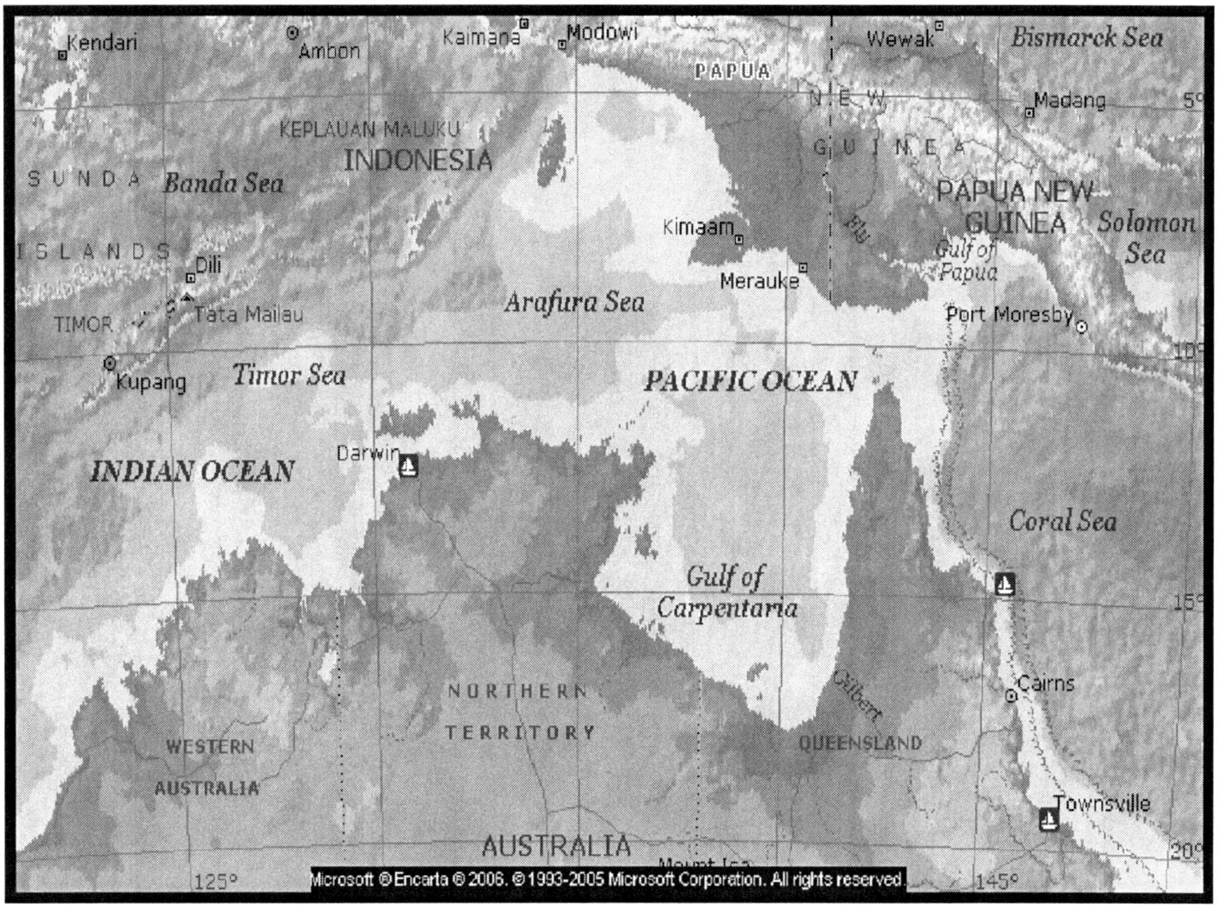

TOWNSVILLE, TO DARWIN, AUSTRALIA'S NORTHERN TERRITORY

After we cleared Australia's paper system and a slip became available, Pat and I tied-up to a long-term berth in Townsville from the Louisiades on Sept. 8, 2002. We decided to stay in Townsville rather than sail back to Mooloolaba, thus saving 1,600 miles off our planned sail to Darwin next season. Another good reason for staying put, the trip south to Mooloolaba would usually mean sailing against the wind. As it turned out, *Endurance* and *Esprit* were extraordinarily lucky to find good tail winds all the way to Brisbane. Of course during our radio contacts they chided us for missing the good sailing. We knew Townsville had a bad reputation for hot Australia summers, but saving 1,600 miles made good sense to us. Air-conditioning would become a necessity in Townsville and it helped to make our stay more pleasant.

Our first priority was to get our '93 Mitsubishi back with us from Mooloolaba. We left it with a storage company this time so we knew it was secure and would not be driven. Australian friends, Lynn and Barbara on the yacht *Strega* asked us to drive their car from Townsville to the Mooloolaba Yacht Club. They were traveling on their sailboat around the east coast of Australia and left their car near Townsville, but were heading to Mooloolaba on their sailboat. This gave us a chance to drive at a leisurely pace down the coast to Mooloolaba.

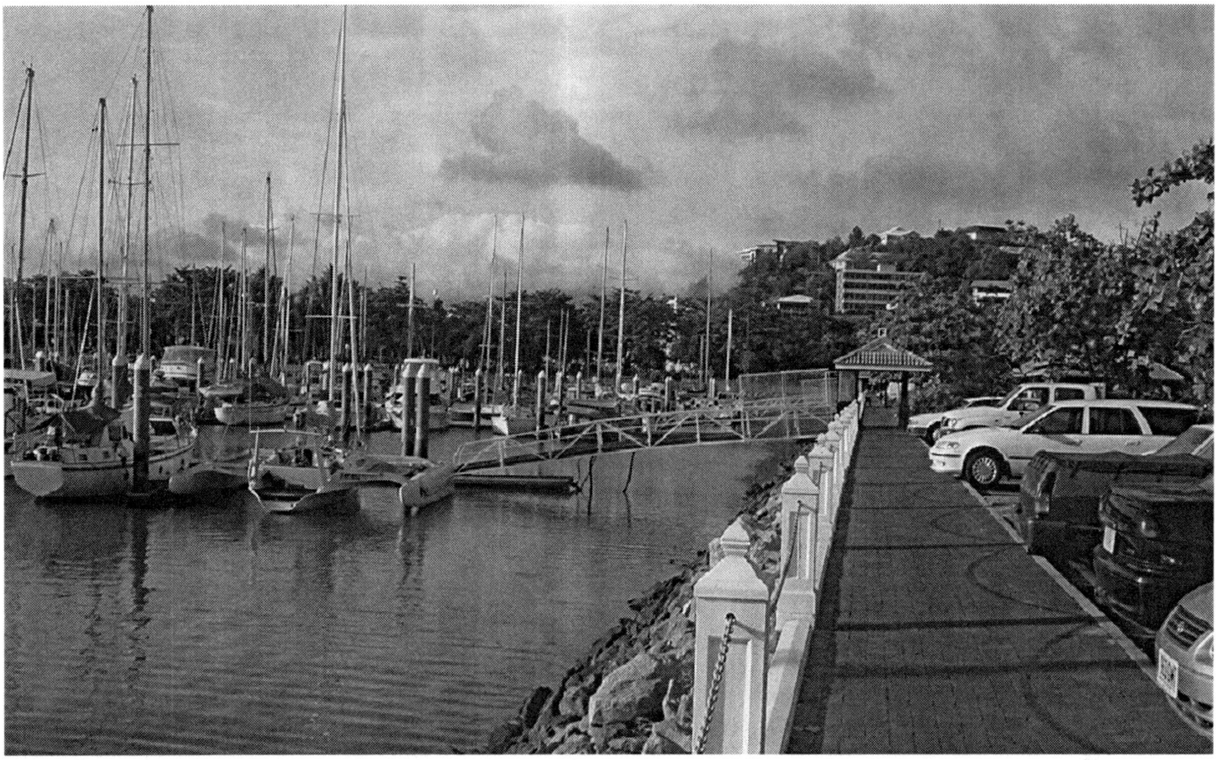

BREAKWATER MARINA, TOWNSVILLE, AUSTRALIA

We left Townsville on Sept. 23, stayed overnight at Rockhampton and rented an apartment at the Nautilus Resort in Mooloolaba for a few days. On the way back we found a new caravan park in the town of Bowen. The new modular villa we stayed at was right on the ocean, air-conditioned, spa tub, nice kitchen and a covered patio at the water's edge. We found the park so pleasant that we stayed two days and just watched the ocean waves roll-in.

Back in Townsville, we drove north to Cairns, Australia on Oct. 11 to pick-up our good friends Bill and Dianne from Seattle. They have a yacht similar to ***Our Pleasure***, but it was moored in Mexico and they were anxious to see Australia. The drive to Cairns is only a few hours from Townsville. Cairns is a well-established resort city with a resident population of about 70,000. The area attracts vacationers who want to see the Great Barrier Reef or ride the railroad to Kuranda. We took the railroad tour through the Macalister Mountain

Range and the cable car to the Tiapukai Aboriginal Dance Theater again with our friends. They were as equally impressed as we were. There are several other packaged tours to consider, but we decided to visit the Great Barrier Reef.

We rode out to the reef on the latest high tech catamaran design with so-called wave piercing hulls. Their ride is stable, fast and carries upwards of 200 passengers. The catamaran arrives at a large floating platform that has facilities for eating, snorkeling, scuba diving; helicopter rides and a boat ride with underwater viewing ports. We were a little disappointed in the reef, as it did not live up to the pictures seen in promotional brochures. Some coral was looking a bit sad and the sea life was lacking in quantity and variety. A trend that seems to be common lately associated with ocean warming and human indifference to protecting our oceans. They have scheduled times for fish feeding, which attracts many fish, but the quantity of fish before the feeding seemed low to us.

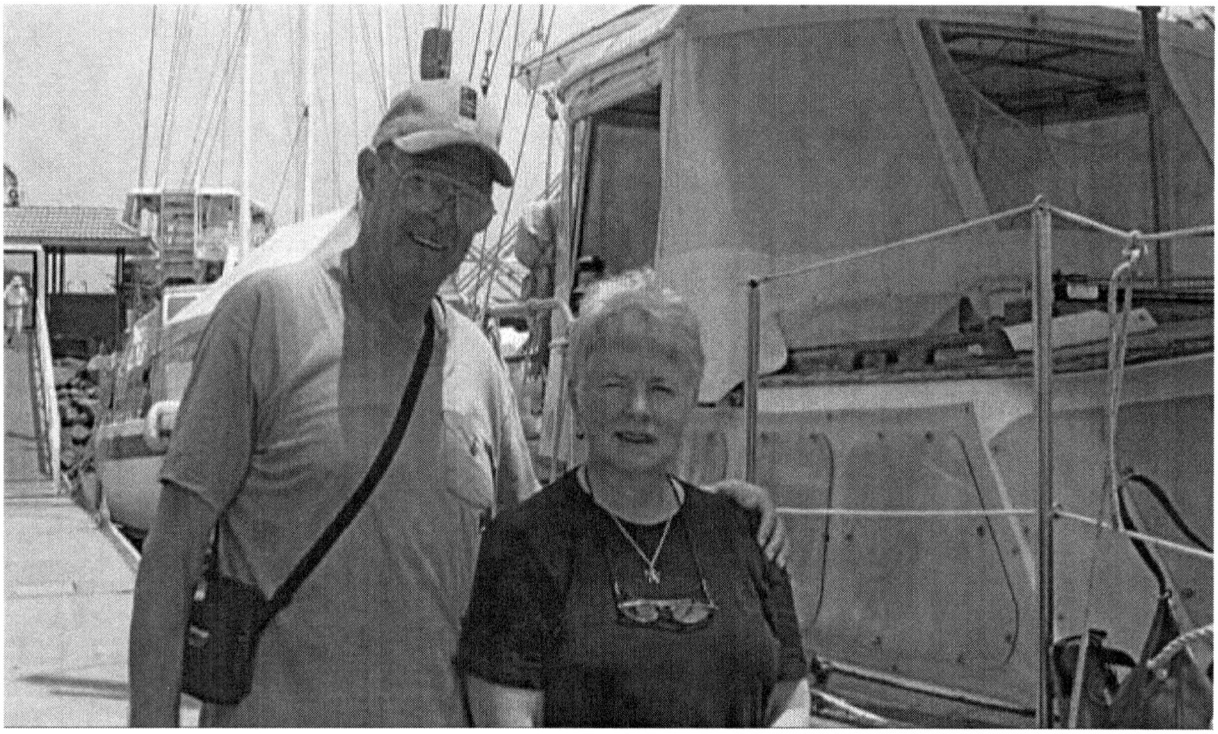

BILL AND DIANNE, YACHT *GOLDEN RING*, VISITING FROM MEXICO

Bill and Dianne spent several days with us back in Townsville using ***Our Pleasure*** as their base. Townsville is an interesting city as it is not a tourist destination, but is a family oriented city with a working class population of around 80,000. The main attraction for us was probably the water front park known as "The Strand."

This park is beautifully laid out for two miles along the part of the Pacific Ocean referred to as the Coral Sea. At the northern edge of the park is a large saltwater swimming pool known as the "rock pool" because of the barrier of large rocks that rings the pool to keep out the ocean. At the southern end there is an area called Anzac Memorial Park. The park is dedicated to WWI and WWII soldiers and to battles fought in the Coral

Sea during WWII. In between these two areas is a beautiful walk with lush green lawns, picnic areas with free stainless steel electric barbeques, a water park for the children, exercise areas, lots of bird life and two waterfront restaurants. However, Starbucks has not yet discovered Townsville.

There is an army base and an air force base in Townsville. Both of these bases have big orchestras and their concerts provide great family get-togethers in the park. There is a research center here for The Great Barrier Reef and the authority for the reef has offices here. There is a nice, modern museum and a maritime museum also. Reef HQ is a big tourist attraction here that displays living parts of the reef in air-conditioned comfort. The town has a Sunday market in the Flinders Street Mall. The Flinders Mall is getting a bit dumpy and sorely needs refurbishment, which is under consideration. The local Aboriginals tend to hang out there after they have been drinking. They talk loudly in their native language and shout out to their friends sometimes a block away. This has greatly dampened the mall's shopping environment. Shoppers and tourists just don't like drunken, loud and rude natives acting up in the mall. There have also been incidents in some shops between the natives and shop owners that also have discouraged locals from shopping there.

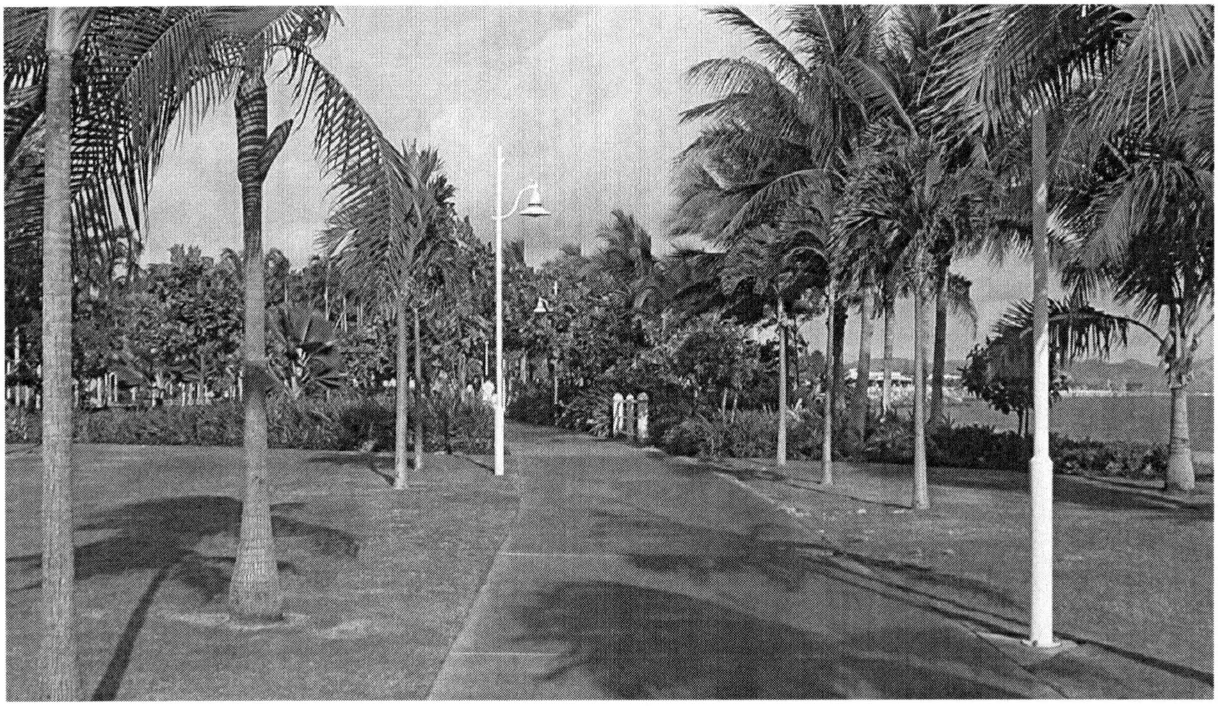

"THE STRAND," TOWNSVILLE'S WATERFRONT PARK, LOOKING NORTH

Right in the center of town is a recreation reserve known as Castle Hill. Castle Hill is about 600 feet high with a lookout area on top that provides great views of Townsville and the ocean. The road to the top is narrow with lots of turns as the hill is steep. Usually in the morning and in the evening when it is a little cooler, the road is congested with walkers, runners and bicycles. About half way up the hill is a theater for plays, but driving there is a slow process because of all the people using the road.

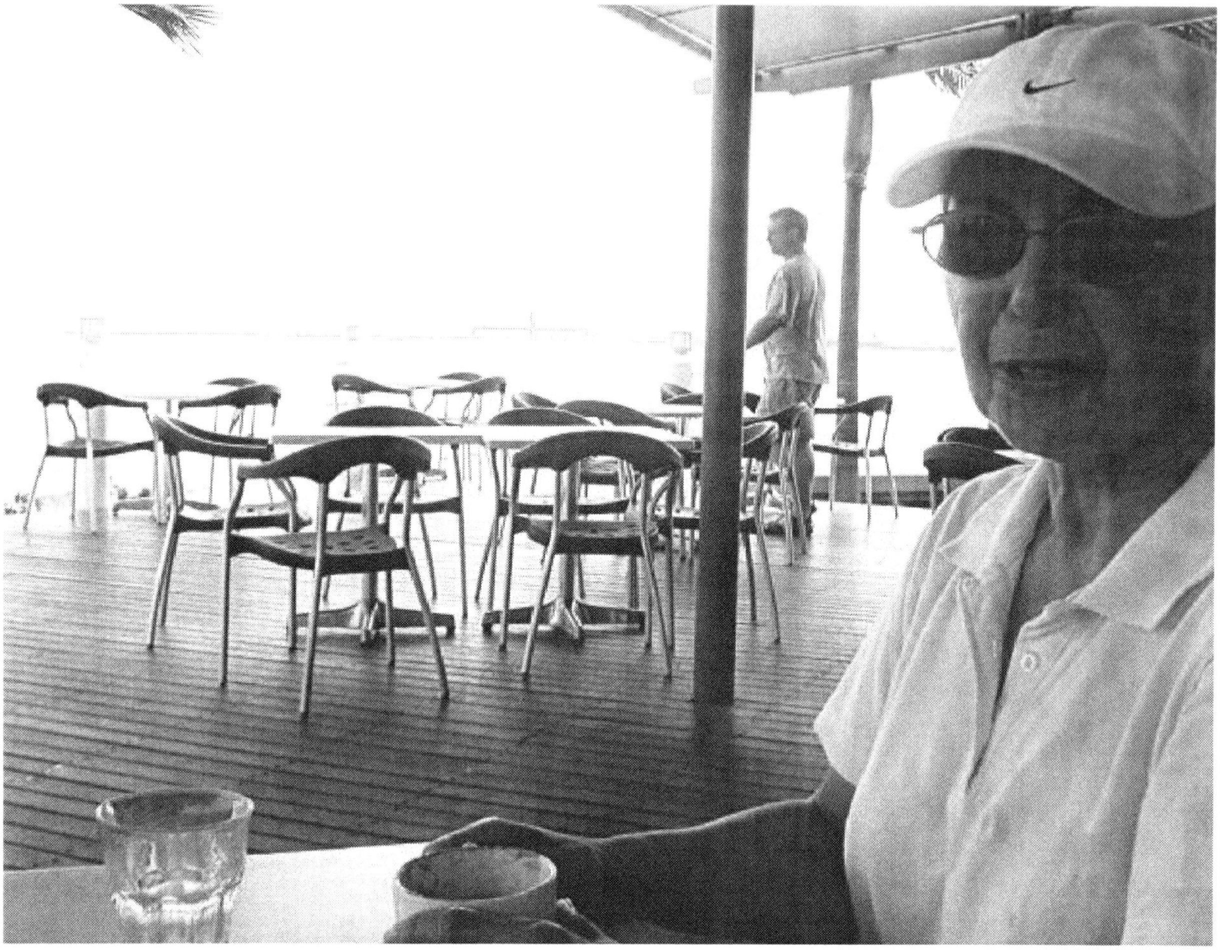

PAT W/CAPPUCCINO, "C BAR CAFÉ" ON THE STRAND

The Breakwater Marina, where we stayed, is well protected and within walking distance to almost everything. The Strand walkway crosses the road into the marina so we made it a habit to walk the Strand almost every day. The Olympic size swimming pool is right next to the marina and even the Catholic Church was only two blocks away. Several yachties we knew decided to stay in Townsville until the next cruising season. This is a bit unusual because most boaters head further south for milder weather. Our best friends here were Graham and Julie Sanders. They sailed across the Pacific the same time we did on their yacht *Phase III*. Graham is an Australian citizen and Julie is from Canada. They managed to get good jobs in Townsville, bought a home and sold their boat while we were there. They were instrumental in getting us acquainted with Townsville. We did a lot of fun things together while we were there including, plays, movies, dining out and coffee almost every Saturday morning at the marina chandlery/deli. Graham and Julie have a great backyard for barbequing and loved to have us over, which was always a special treat for us.

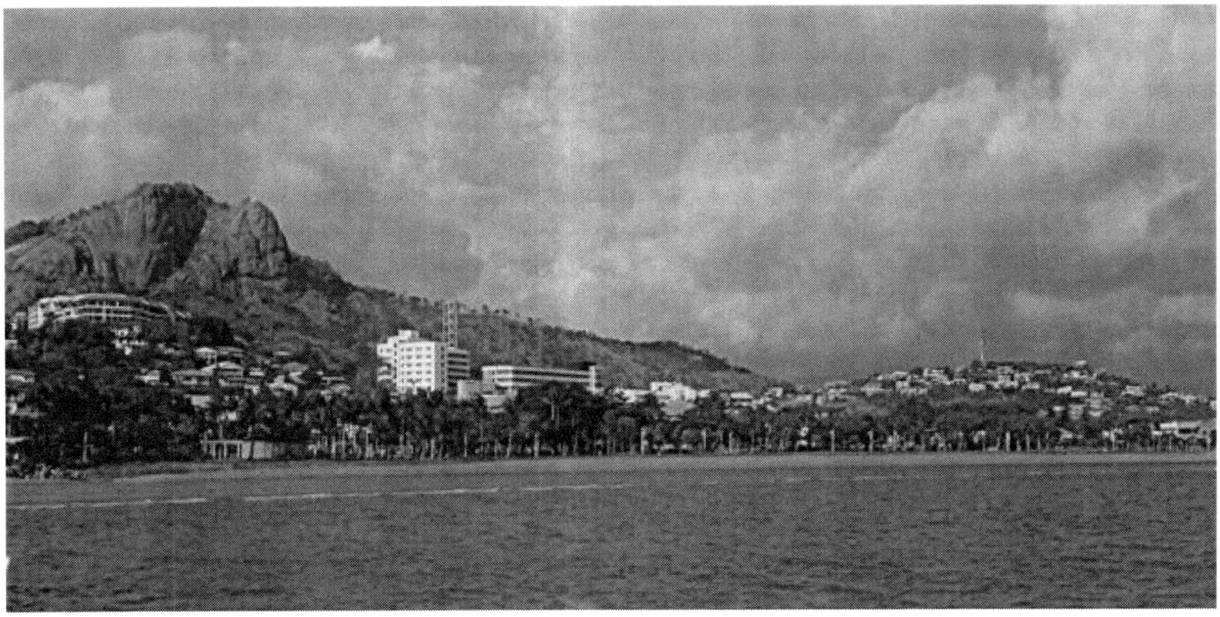

CASTLE HILL, TOWNSVILLE, AUSTRALIA AS SEEN FROM THE MARINA

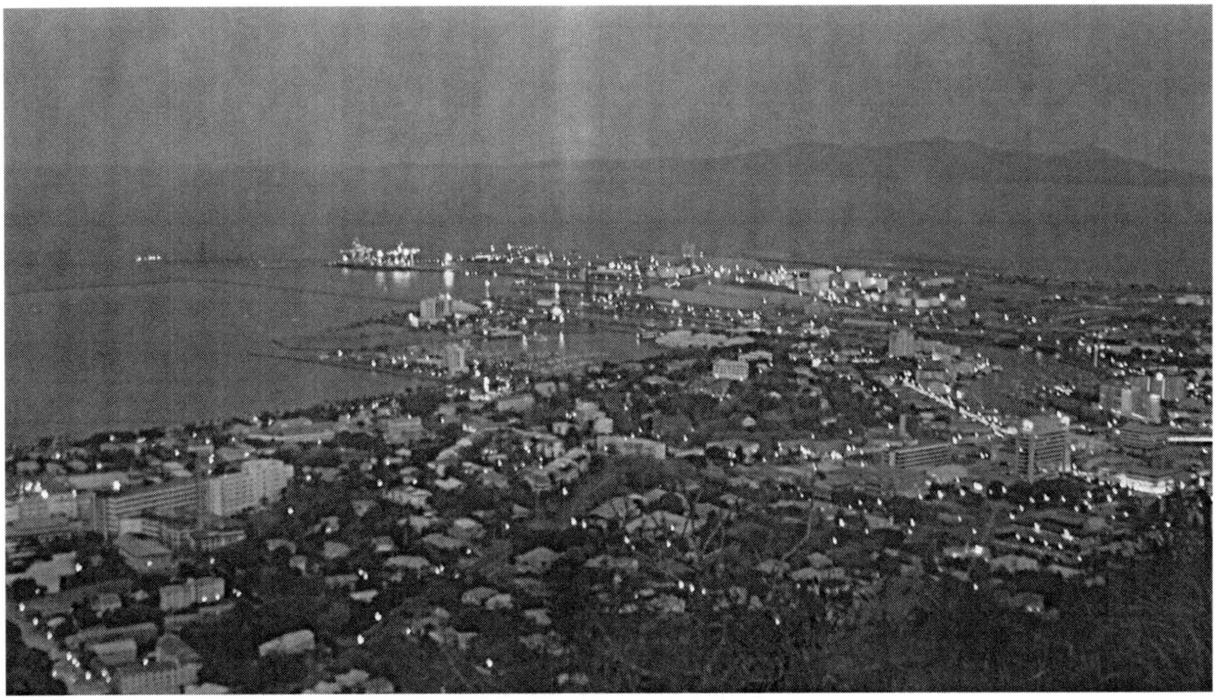

TOWNSVILLE AND COMMERCIAL PORTS FROM CASTLE HILL

Townsville has a pretty large commercial port for handling minerals, beef, wool, sugar and timber. However, when the wind blows from the south, dust from their commercial port operations lands on the boats in the marina. Normal dust would not be bad, but dust from the nickel ore operations is difficult to remove and tends to stain everything. The port uses large sprinkler systems to wet down minerals stored at the port, but some dust always gets in the air.

For the Melbourne Cup horse race this year we made reservations at a nice waterside restaurant, The Pier. It extends over the water near the marina and is built using a liberal amount of glass walls. We did not know it at the time, but The Pier, was hosting a private benefit luncheon for Townsville High School. All the teachers and school supporters were dressed in their finest for the luncheon. However, they made us welcome and even the school principal came over to introduce himself and invite us to visit the school. Some of the schools talented students put on a fashion show. We did not win any of the door prizes, but managed to get two bets on the horse race right. My strategy was to research all the newspaper articles on the race to see what the experts had to say about the horses, jockeys, track, weights and etc. In this case, the favorite horse, ridden by the favorite jockey won. The bets that experts recommended were mostly duds and I did not make enough to pay for our lunch — so much for experts.

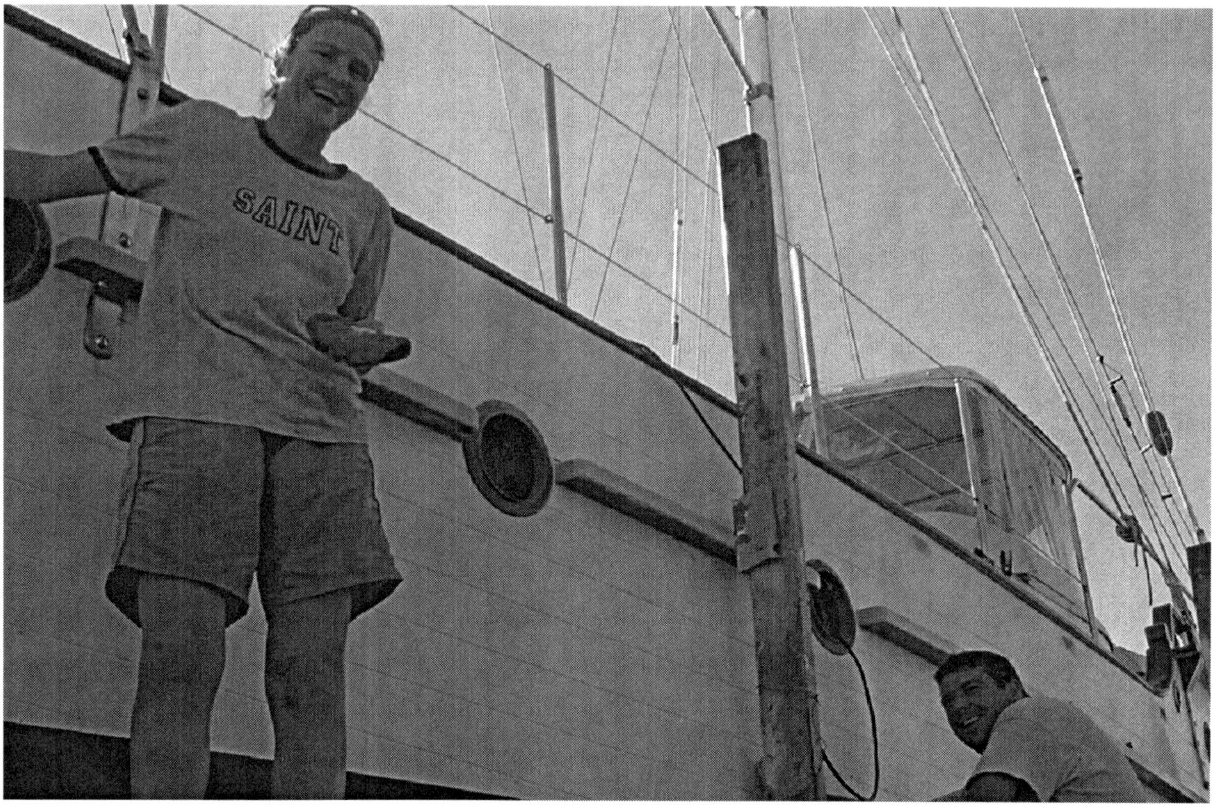

MARINI AND IAN POLISHING *OUR PLEASURE*

The rest of 2002 was spent working on boat projects and relaxing. For Christmas we drove down to Mooloolaba were we rented a two-bedroom apartment and invited Marv and Chieko to spend the holidays with us. Their yacht was moored at the marina in Scarborough, which is about a thirty-minute drive north of Brisbane and an hour from Mooloolaba. We made our normal trip back to Seattle near the end of Feb. 2003 to visit our family, friends and pay our federal taxes. Before leaving for Seattle we made arrangements with Ross Island Marine in Townsville to install all new rigging on ***Our Pleasure***. Brian Jones is a certified rigger in Australia, kept us up-dated by e-mail and did a fine job. The work was paid for by electronically transferring money from my Seattle bank to his Australian bank. While in Seattle, we made a side trip to Cortez, Florida to visit my sister and inspect our condominium, which was leased to long-term friends of my sister. We were back in Townsville near the end of April just in time to welcome our new crew Ian and Marini.

We hauled the boat at the marina on April 23 and Pat left for Seattle to be with our youngest daughter Leslie and her husband Bob. They were expecting their first child in mid-June and Leslie wanted her mother to be there. I also sold our car that day for AUS $5,800. Their dollar was stronger now, about 62 cents U.S. to one Australian dollar so it cost us about $1,400 plus maintenance to drive a good car from Dec. 2000 to May 2003 — not bad. With Ian and Marini working long days, we put three coats of bottom paint on ***Our Pleasure*** with an extra coat around the waterline.

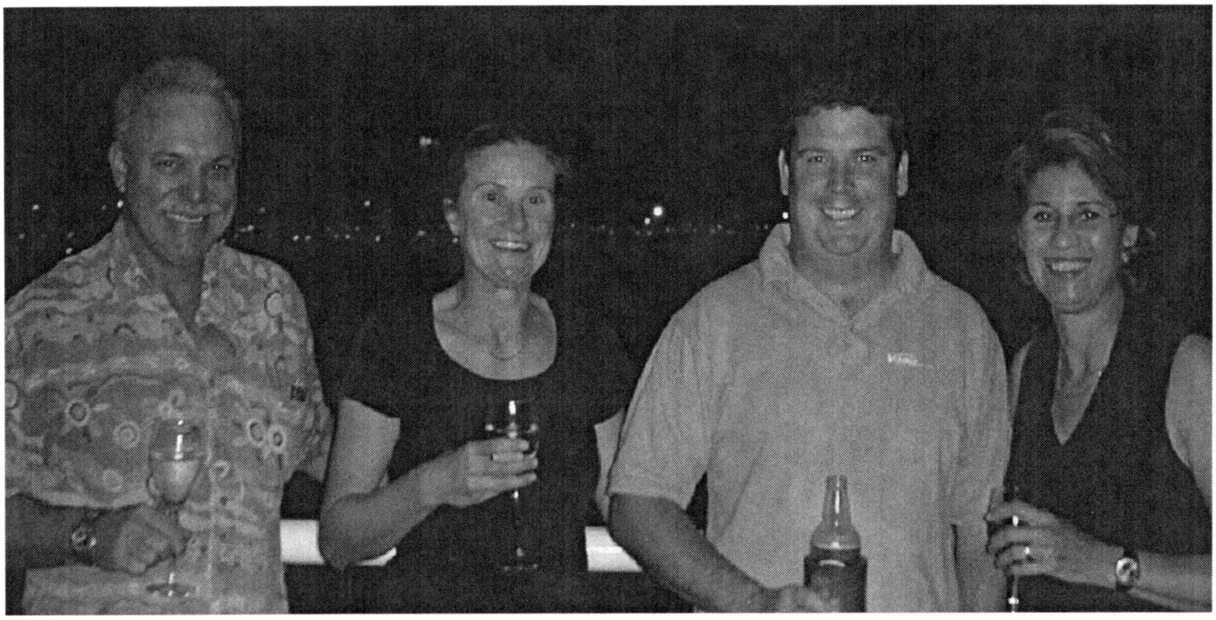

DINNER PARTY WITH ORISTIS, MARINI, IAN AND ZOLA, TOWNSVILLE

I purchased several Australian charts for the trip to Darwin and we were back in the water on May 28. Zola and Oristis invited us to dinner on Sunday. Their apartment overlooks The Strand and has beautiful views of Magnetic Island and the Coral Sea. He managed the nickel mining operations near Townsville and we had become friends through Pat's exercising class at the swimming pool. A boat yard in Fremantle was building a new 50 foot catamaran for him so we had a lot to talk about.

Malcolm checked out our refrigeration system one more time and we loaded it with vacuum-sealed, frozen meat from the excellent "Butcher on Bundock" butcher shop. One more barbeque at Graham and Julies and we untied our lines at the Breakwater Marina on June 3, 2003.

We made the 1,400 mile trip up the East Coast of Australia and along the top of Australia's Northern Territory to Darwin from Townsville with few incidents. We sailed between the Great Barrier Reef and the mainland for most of the trip. This helped make the trip more interesting with hundreds of islands, fishing boats and big freighters to watch. The many islands also reduced the swells by about three feet and that improves the comfort level immensely. Weather for the most part was close to perfect, but sleeping without a small fan blowing in your face would not be pleasant. This type of tropical sailing is only comfortable in bare feet, thin cotton clothing or bathing suits. The weather has some similarities to Florida, but much warmer and this is their winter!

The young couple crewing with me on ***Our Pleasure***, Ian (36) and Martini (34) did well. They took turns cooking and liked to experiment with new tastes, flavors and sauces, but they both ate a lot of groceries. Their past sailing experiences fit in well with my planned trip to Cape Town. Ian and I had a few differences, but they were always straightened out. Marini is an attractive Dutch woman, pleasant with many good qualities. They have been what the Australians refer to as mates for about two years. A "mate" can be a friend, a married couple, an unmarried couple, and the relationship could be straight or gay — they were not married.

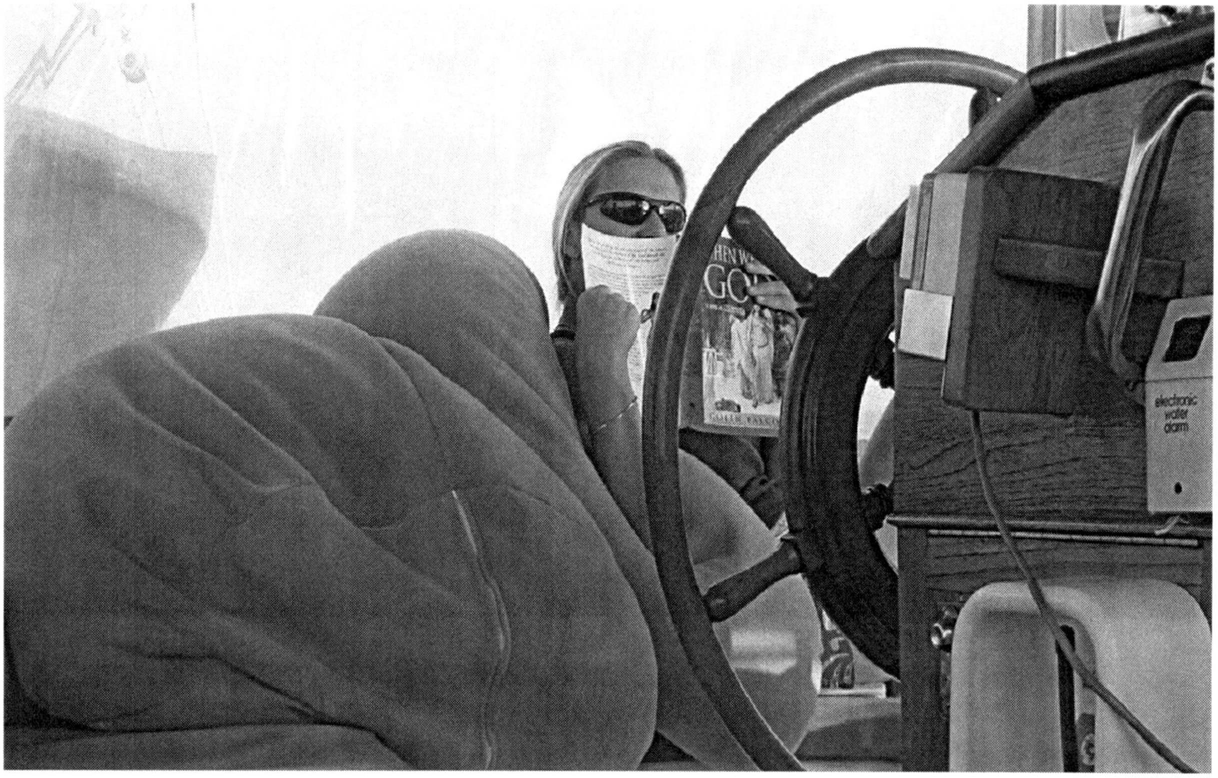

MARINI ON WATCH

Good news: Leslie and Bob just had their first child, Mitchell Jones Fischer, on Father's Day – what a great present for me. Pat tells me their dog, Max, is so curious he sniffs Mitchell all the time, Leslie thinks they will make great companions. While the baby was in the hospital he wore a cap that Leslie brought home to let Max sniff before Mitchell arrived. When Mitchell arrived home, the first thing Max did was sniff Mitchell's head —

too bad dogs can't talk to us. Pat has found a nice apartment overlooking Bitter Lake in Seattle, which is near Leslie so she can help out with all the trials and tribulations a new mother and baby face. She is hoping to catch up with me next year in South Africa if she can get rid of some of her bothersome aches and pains and then on through the Caribbean to Florida. We have some safari tours planned for Africa if it is still safe — should be exciting.

Approaching Darwin, past Cape Don, we experienced good SE winds and favorable current. Running south, we were able to sail at seven knots. However, once we were further into Van Diemen Gulf we ran into head winds of 25 knots with gusts to 40 knots. This forced us to motor sail to keep a safe distance off Abbott Shoal, but the strong head winds slowed us down to two knots. That in turn, prevented us from making the favorable current through Howard Channel. At Howard Channel, the tide turned against us flowing at 1.7 knots. It increased to a maximum of 3.8 knots keeping us in a negative current for four hours. By keeping the engine RPM at 1,700 we were able to make between 2.4 and 3.4 knots with help of a 10 knot breeze on our port quarter. The sea was calm in the channel, but the sun was sinking fast and the adverse current was going to make Darwin an evening approach. The steering station in the cockpit is set up to allow the laptop to sit next to the steering station. In the low light conditions, I was able to follow the electronic chart and my precharted route the last 30 miles into to Darwin without a problem.

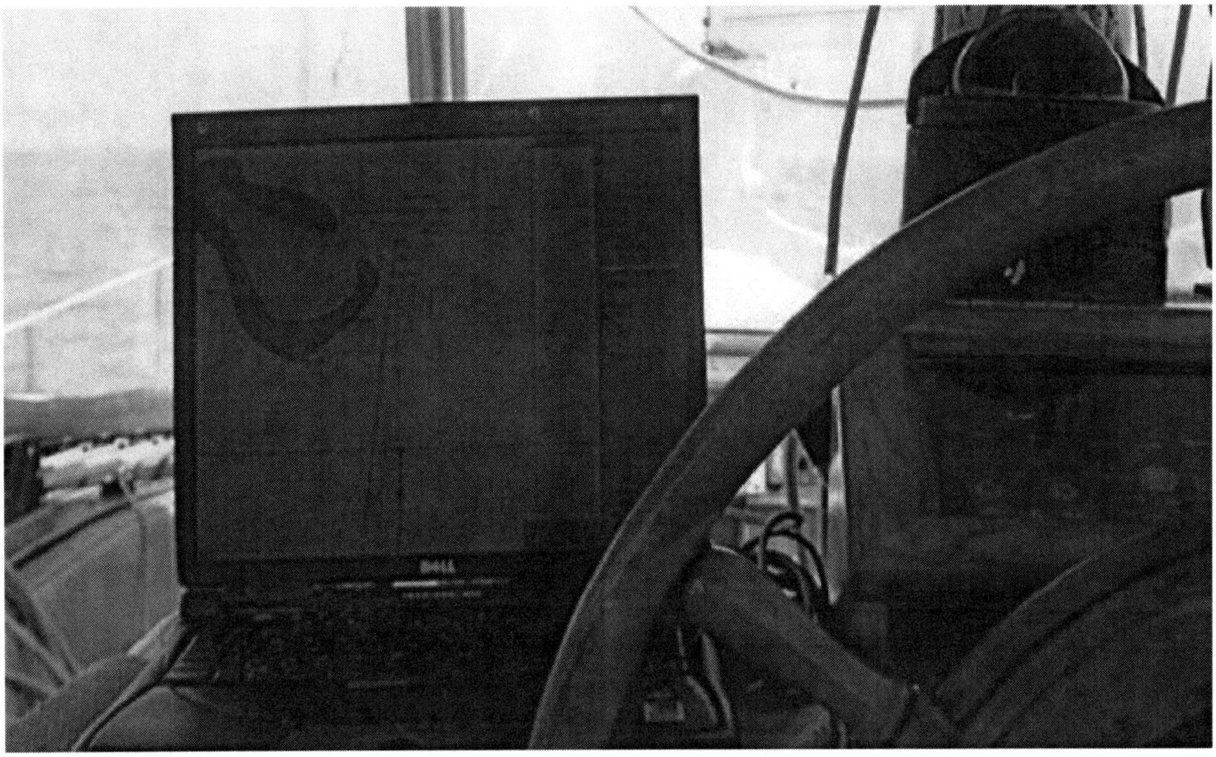

LAPTOP W/C-MAP ELECTRONIC CHARTS, OUTSIDE STEERING STATION

We arrived at Darwin's marina locks at 3 a.m. extremely tired. The fuel dock outside the locks was empty so, we tied up and conked out. A ferry arrived at the fuel dock at 7 a.m. followed by some loud speaking Asian tourists abruptly waking us from our deep sleep. Marini put together a nice breakfast around 8 a.m. and the lockmaster told us to be ready at 9 a.m. to go through the locks. Dennis and Martina, our friends from the yacht *Inti* caught our lines at our assigned slip, B13 at 9:30 a.m. on June 15, 2003. The marina has many similarities to marinas in Florida with its palm trees, canals, restaurants and expensive homes. After we washed the salt off ***Our Pleasure***, I treated Ian and Marini to a nice lunch at the Buzz Café overlooking Cullen Bay. Most of our time at Cullen Bay was spent changing oils, installing new filters, cleaning heat exchangers and replacing a leaky seal on the hydraulic pump. Lots of maintenance work for our next extended cruising. We usually managed to finish all work by four so we could be cleaned up for five o'clock happy hours with our friends.

I had not worked out all the navigation details of the trip at this point, but I knew it would be about 7,000 miles to Cape Town with stops at three minor islands that are still friendly to the US. The islands of Cocos Keeling and Chagos are rumored to be extraordinarily beautiful and should not be missed without a stopover of at least two weeks to a month. We stocked up with about $1,400 worth of food, which assumes there will not be much shopping along the way.

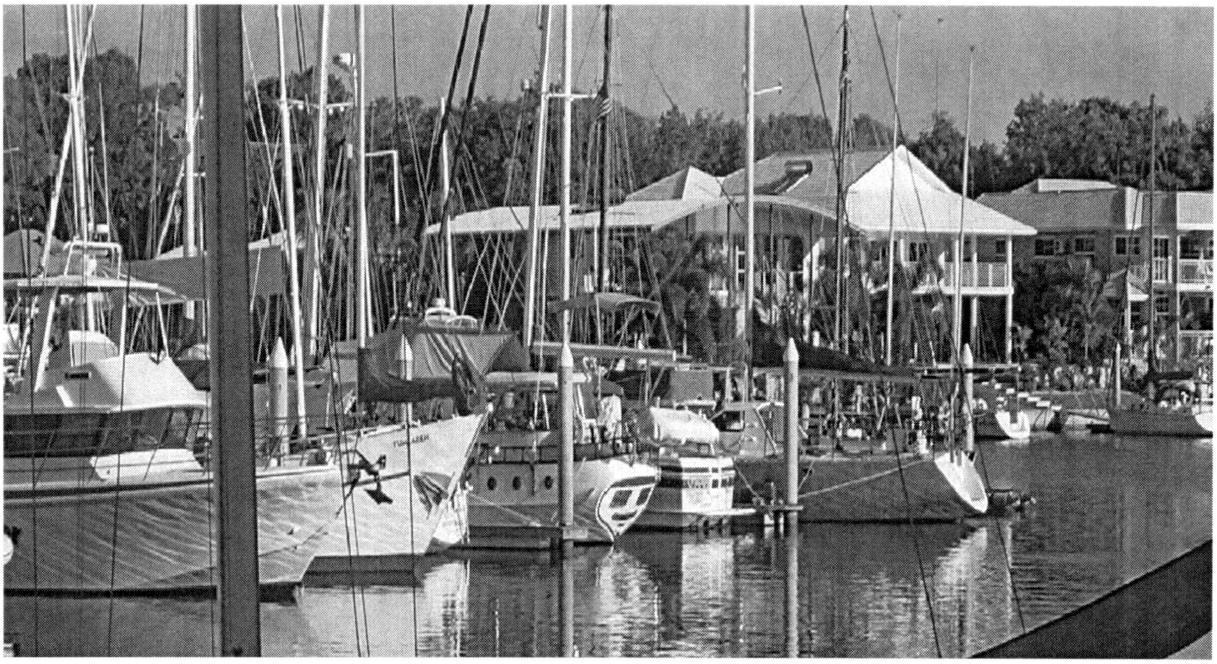

CULLEN BAY MARINA, DARWIN, AUSTRALIA

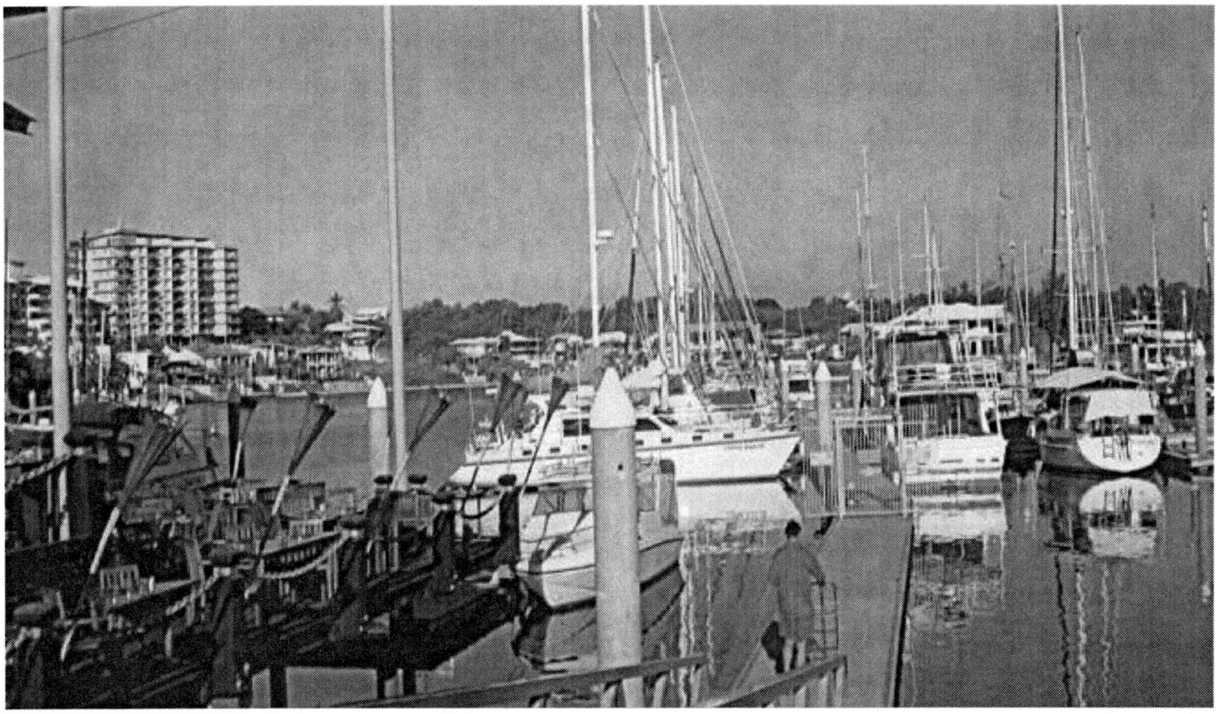

"BUZZ CAFÉ," BEST RESTAURANT IN CULLEN BAY, DARWIN

We took on 85 gallons of fuel, cleared customs, left the locks at 9:45 a.m. and headed out again on June 30, 2003. The winds were so light we decided to anchor in nearby Fannie Bay with *Endurance* and *Esprit* to wait for more wind. On July 3, with the wind starting to build, we had to check out once more with Australian Customs and left Fannie Bay the next morning.

Chapter 19

DARWIN TO COCOS KEELING (AUSTRALIA)

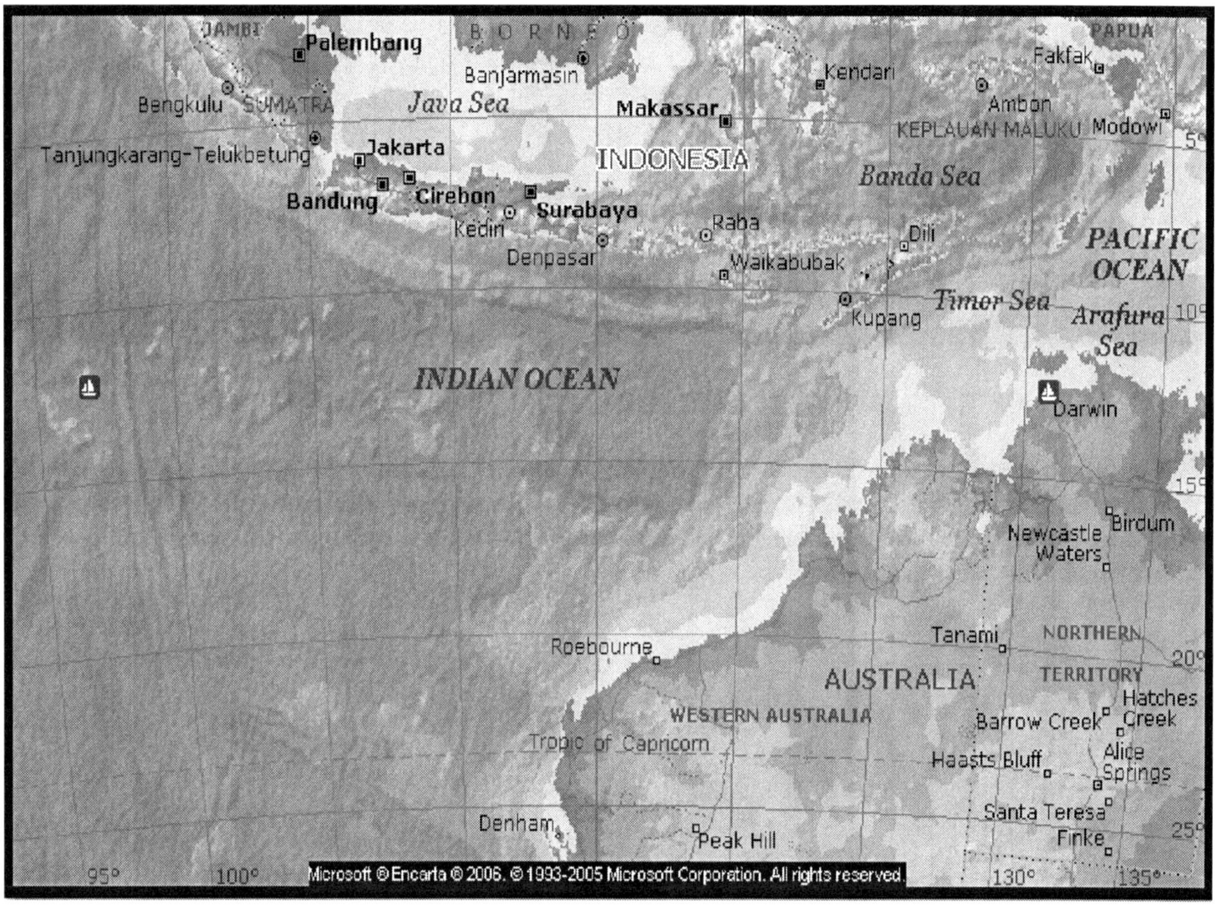

DARWIN, AUSTRALIA TO COCOS KEELING IN THE COCOS ISLANDS

Winds were still light for the next two days, but finally picked up on July 7. Ian caught a two foot fish that we thought was a Spanish mackerel; the name maybe wrong, but the firmness and taste were nice. We poled out our genny and started making good 24 hour average speeds. We passed by Ashmore Reef and Christmas Island. *Endurance* helped me work out my e-mail problems with Sailmail®. I had not been using the name "Sailmail" in the "Post Via" box in the recipient's address menu, making this correction cleared up the problem.

Most of the sailing was consistent with 20 knots on the aft quarter and the Indian Ocean lived up to its reputation of being bumpy, lumpy and rolly. Late one night and with a 40 knot gust of wind, Marini got a full dose of salt water through the main salon hatch right on her face — I didn't think anyone could scream that loudly. It was generally so hot at night that sleeping was difficult without some breeze blowing over you. That's why the hatch was open. The waves that night were probably below two feet, but we just happened to get hit with one of those odd balls. We always saw plenty of sea birds and flying fish with a few fish landing on our deck every night. If we had a cat on board he'd be in seventh heaven, but the fish were too small for us.

On July 16, we were about 200 miles ahead of *Esprit* and *Endurance*. *Endurance* was at a real disadvantage, without a spinnaker pole. He and *Esprit* had to tack back and forth across their rhumb line. By poling my genny out, I could follow the wind and did not have to tack. We managed to stay in radio contact using the single side band frequency of 4,030 KHz. Boat traffic was rather minor with a few Indonesian fishing boats and a couple of freighters on this 2,000 mile passage. Most of the boat hardware ran fine during this trip, but I did end up changing the water pump impellers on both the main engine and the generator.

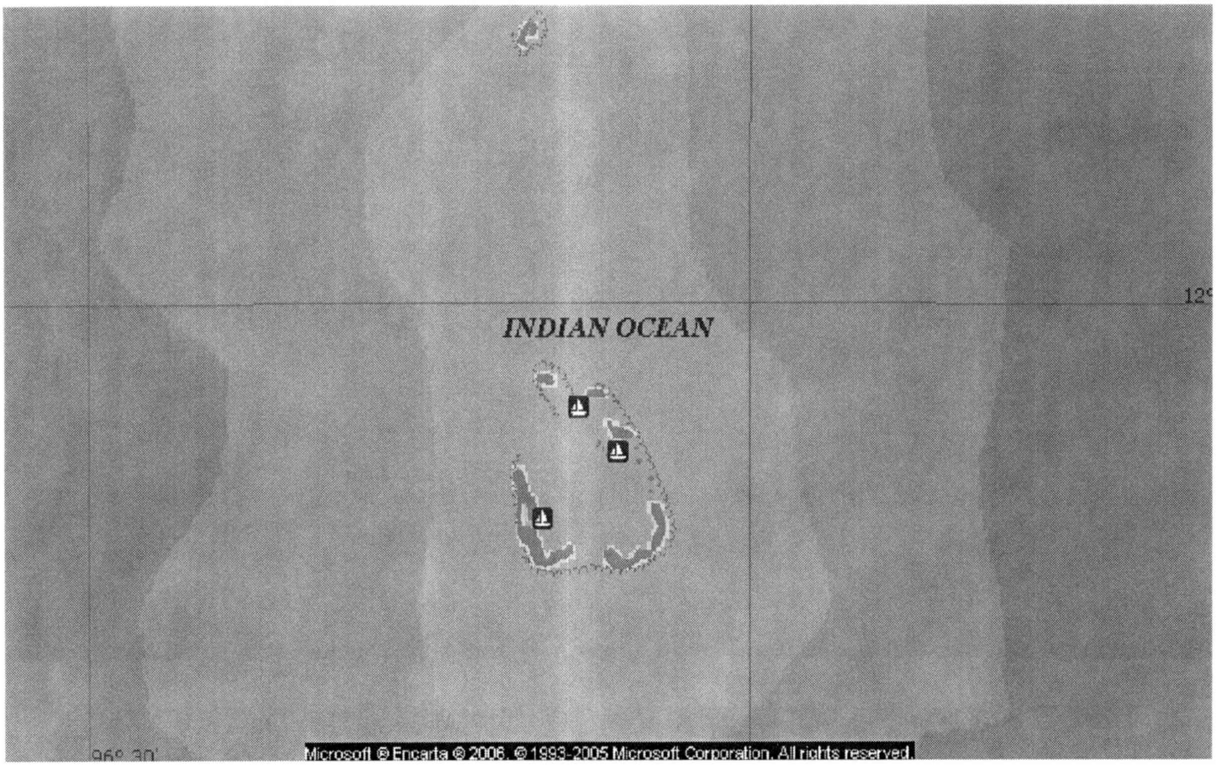

MAIN COCOS KEELING ISLANDS: DIRECTION, HOME AND WEST ISLANDS

This was my fault since I completely overlooked how many engine hours had passed since they had been changed. For the main engine about 1,000 hours had passed and about 600 hours for the generator. The main engine had only one impeller blade left out of eight, but it was still moving water and the generator had only lost two blades, but one was blocking the water passage. Both impellers had to be changed late at night of course in rolling seas. Bob and Leslie had given me an extremely bright LED lamp that fits on my head leaving my hands free to work. This headlamp turned out to be invaluable when working at night.

We arrived at the Australian islands of Cocos Keeling on the July 19 at 9 a.m. local time and a rising tide — perfect timing. The buoy system into Direction Island is not obvious, but luckily a passenger ferry that only comes in on Saturdays was just ahead of us and we followed him in. The customs boat was already at Direction Island and told us to anchor where we wanted instead of tying up to the quarantine buoy — another plus. The water inside the lagoon cannot be described adequately, but try to imagine bright, beautiful shades of blues and greens with clear water all the way down to the bottom. We finally set the anchor after two tries, which is a bit unusual for our 120 pound, plow anchor.

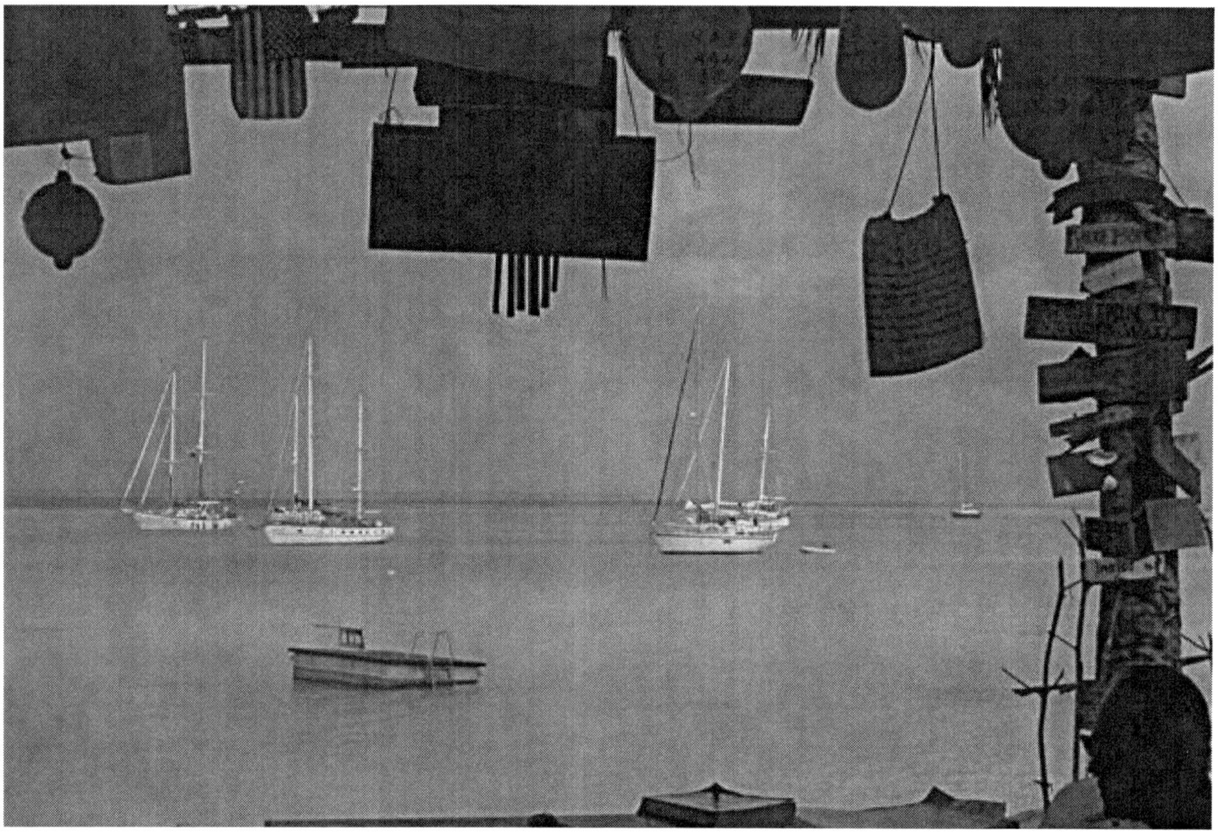

DIRECTION ISLAND, COCOS KEELING, NAME BOARDS FILL THE SHELTER

The bottom was sand that eventually provided good holding. Looking around we saw several bommies, which we knew would difficult to extract the anchor from if it were snarled in one of those guys. Anchors and chains damage these small coral formations, which in turn hurt the natural environment for small sea creatures. This is an anchorage where you can swim directly off your boat without fear of sharks, which is a rare treat. These islands consist of a group of 27 islands in the Eastern Indian Ocean. The islands are a dependency of Australia, which maintains a small military base and airport on the largest island, West Island.

The "Keeling" name comes from an East India Company captain (Captain Keeling) who made a short stop in 1609. The "Cocos" name from the abundance of coconuts once processed for their meat. Australia purchased Home Island from the Clunies-Ross family, the island's principal landholder from 1886 to 1978 and gave it to the Malay natives. Australia has controlled all the islands of Cocos Keeling since 1955 and considers them of strategic importance. Probably around 700 people live on the islands on a total area of around 12 square miles.

We launched the dinghy the next day so we could help *Endurance* and *Esprit* into the anchorage, but my new 15 HP Yamaha would not start. Ron and Beebe from the yacht *Hanna* rose to the occasion and helped them in. Later I found a clogged passage in the carburetor because after the last use I must not have run all the fuel out before storing the outboard.

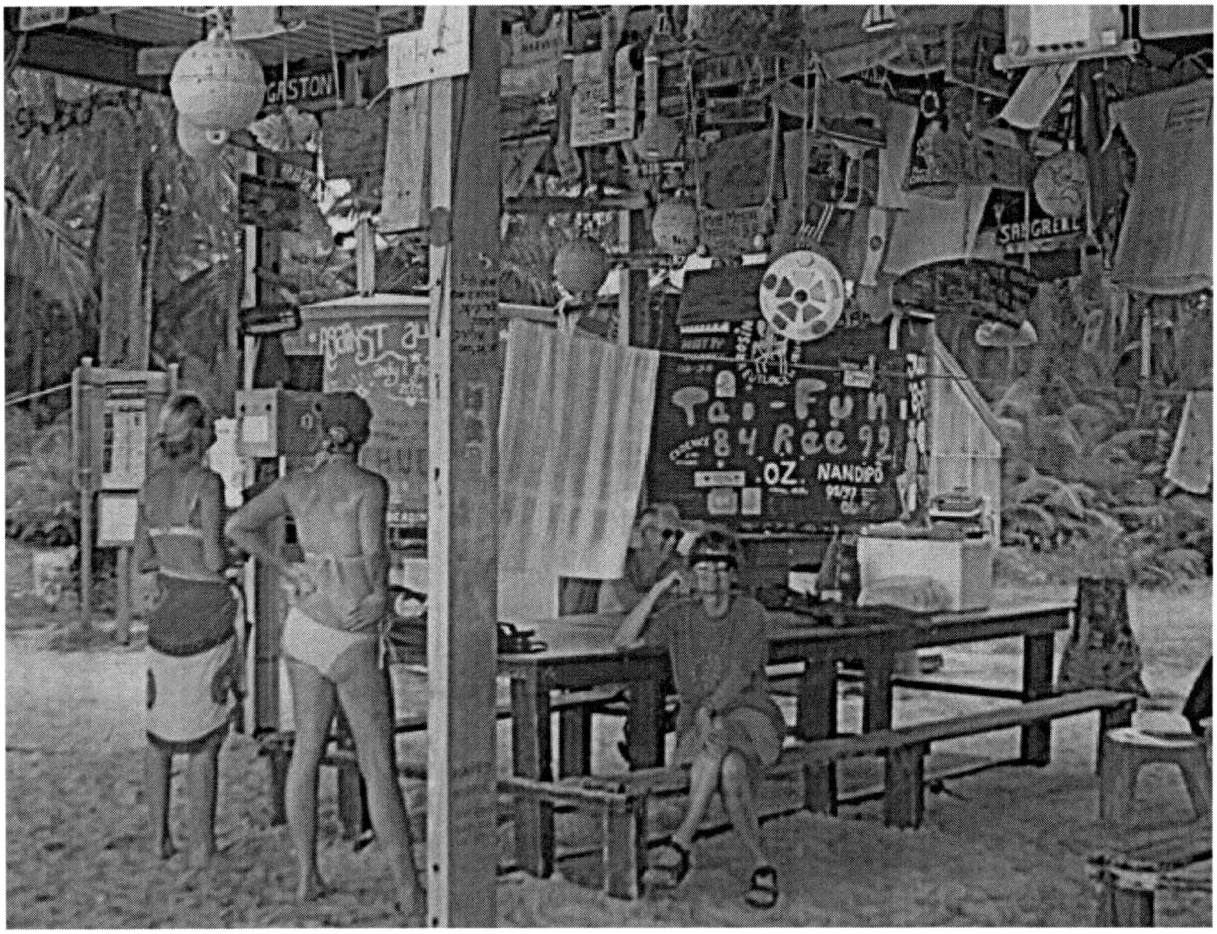

MARINI *Our Pleasure*; JULIA *Endurance*; BILL AND SHERI *Esprit*; DIRECTION ISLAND

I think I fell in love with Cocos Keeling. It is such a pleasant place to just sit and relax, read, swim or follow the hiking trails around the island. The shelter is filled with hundreds of yacht names hanging from the shelter roof that were left by previous yachties. The large roof of the shelter funnels rainwater into two huge water tanks that are probably around 500 gallons each — convenient for people wanting to wash clothes or in need of drinking water. Australia also maintains two compost type toilets there. The most amazing convenience of all though is a modern telephone that does not require money — quite extraordinary. In the shelter there is a makeshift phone booth with a free household type telephone and a Western Australian phone book. You can make free calls to the other two main islands in the group, Home and West. I was able to call home using my Australian phone card or I could call the available services on the other islands for assistance. In medical emergencies, the hospital on West Island or the clinic on Home Island was just a call away. It was just incredible to sit in the shelter with my feet in pure white sand, in my bathing suit and talk to Pat in Seattle.

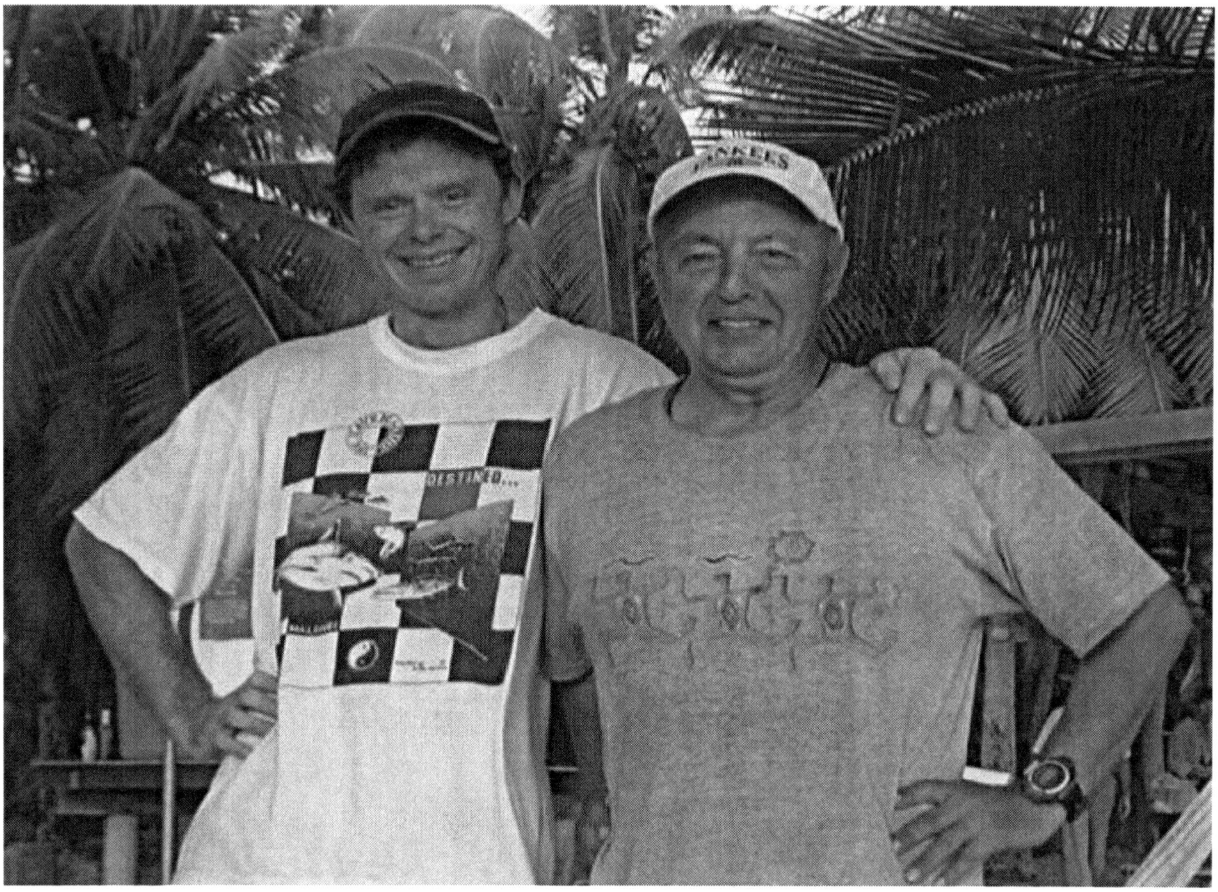

HARALD AND ME, DIRECTION ISLAND, COCOS KEELING

Ian and Marini had to make plane reservations from here as Ian's rental property in the UK lost its tenants. He was not able to rent it through an agency because it needed too many repairs and Ian didn't have the money to make mortgage payments for more than a few months. So they flew from Cocos to Christmas Island to Jakarta to Singapore to Amsterdam to England — long trip. Their problem left me with a bigger problem, no crew, essentially in the middle of nowhere. I offered to make Ian's mortgage payments until we arrived in South Africa, but he did not want to do that. Marv was going to lend me one of his crewmembers, Julia, until we arrived in Chagos. Julia changed her mind or Marv changed it when he decided to go straight through to Madagascar and not stop at Chagos. He was worried about wind angles and having enough time to see Madagascar.

I was in the process of sailing alone to Chagos when a wonderful Australian couple, Bea and Diane came to my rescue. They were living on their catamaran, *Sortilege* at Direction Island waiting for December's seasonal wind change to take them back to Australia. They knew a keen sailor, Harald (German spelling), who lived in Albany, Australia and thought he might be able to crew for me. Diane called him first and setup a time for me to call. I called, made the arrangements, he agreed, cancelled a home remodeling job and in four days, much to my delight, he was on ***Our Pleasure***.

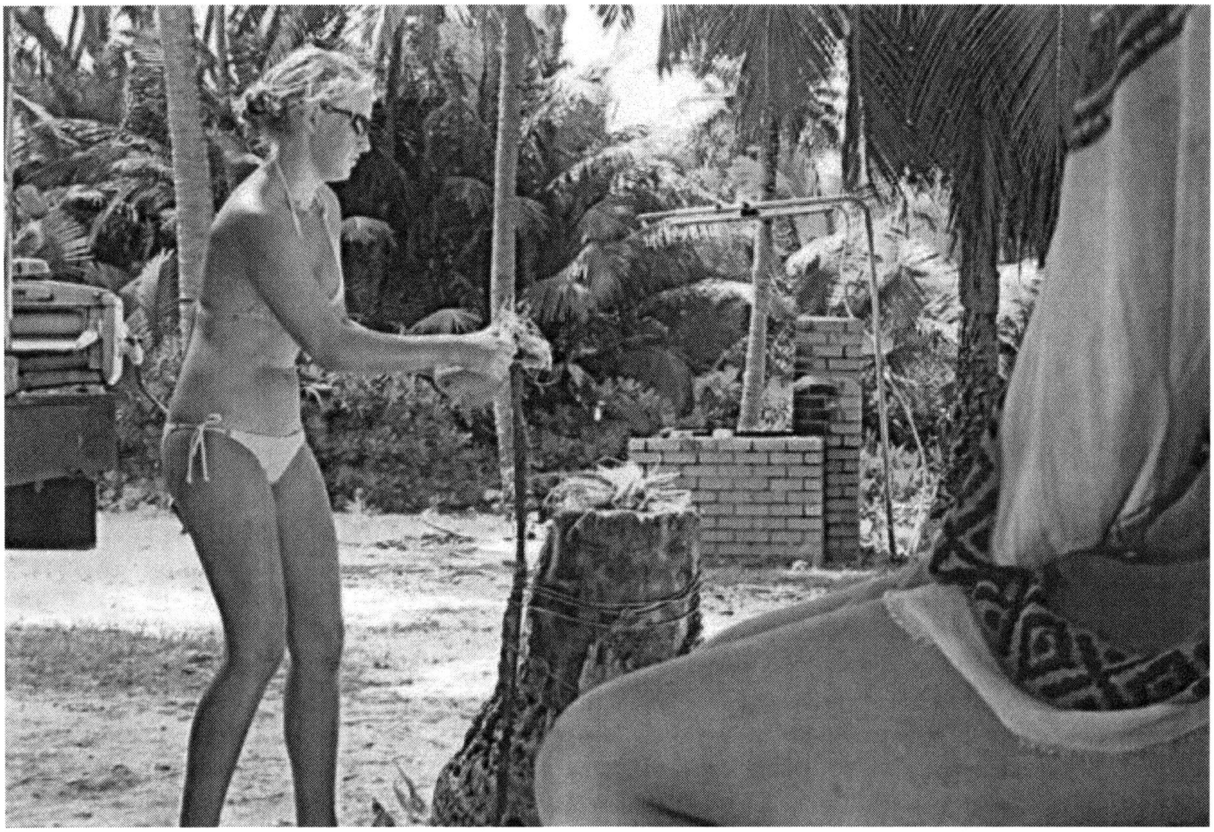

JULIA OPENS A COCONUT WITH MARINI WATCHING

My plan at that time was for Harald to sail with me to Chagos where I would add 2 new crew members, a French couple Serge and Pascale. This unfortunate couple had lost their sailboat *Marimba* and many of their possessions. Only a few weeks before, *Marimba* hit a reef entering an uncharted passage into Chagos. After our Chagos arrival, Serge and Pascale would go with me to South Africa as crew. I would then drop Harald off at the French island of Mayotte (the next island on my route) and he would catch a plane back home to Albany, Australia. This plan sounded good to me at the time and it would benefit all concerned parties. Serge and Pascale were contacted by single side band radio and made aware of the plan.

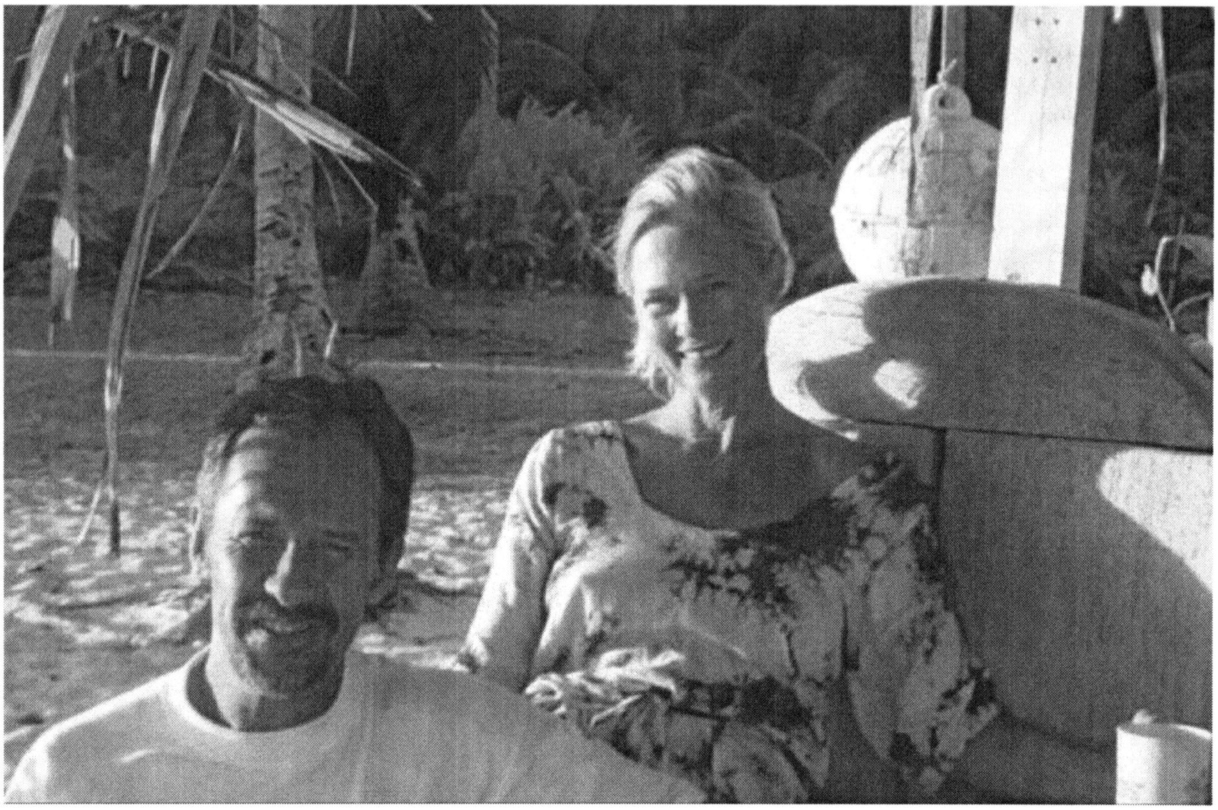

BEA AND DIANE; MARV AND CHIEKO'S 35th WEDDING ANNIVERSARY

I invited Bea and Diane over to ***Our Pleasure*** for happy hour and to thank them for all their concern and help. Diane baked a homemade pizza for the occasion, which tasted mighty fine. This was their second time to be at Cocos Keeling so they were a great source of knowledge. They moored their catamaran in an ideal spot quite near the beach with the stern facing a nice group of coconut trees. Diane had cleared a waterfront spot in the nearby palm trees to provide, as her sign said, "Massages in Paradise." They are headed back to Darwin, Australia, but are waiting for the prevailing winds to change direction, probably Nov. or Dec.

Diane was repairing one of Marv's sails when her Bernina® sewing machine got out of sync and the needle started hitting the bobbin. They brought it over to ***Our Pleasure*** to see if I could find the problem. Well, this is one of those machines that can do several hundred kinds of stitches, which makes it a mechanical nightmare. I did manage to change the timing so the needle did not hit the bobbin, but it would only sew straight stitches and would not zigzag. I felt bad and was disappointed that I could not get it back to its original sewing form because they use it to keep their sails in working order and help others.

Bea put together a useful island schedule for visiting yachties to detail operation times of all the island's various businesses. Without this schedule everyone would be totally lost, the schedule included:

- The supermarkets (a real misnomer) on Home and West Islands were open 8:30 a.m. to 3 p.m. Monday through Friday, closed on Sunday, but the Home Island market opened 8:30 a.m. to 12 noon on Saturday.

- The only bank, Common Wealth Bank, opened from 7:30 a.m. to 1 p.m. Tuesday and Thursday on Home Island. On West Island, it opened for the same hours on Wednesday and Thursday. Both banks are closed on Friday.
- The post office is open on Home Island on Tuesday from 1:30 p.m. to 3:30 p.m. On Wednesday and Friday it opens from 7:30 a.m. to 12 noon. On West Island, it was open Monday, Tuesday, and Thursday from 8:15 a.m. to 10:45 a.m.
- The only hardware store was on Home Island and it only opens from 9:30 a.m. to 10:30 a.m. or 11:30 a.m. every day except Tuesday, Saturday, and Sunday it is closed.
- Propane is available on Home Island from 10:30 a.m. to 11:30 a.m. on Monday and Thursday. A small tank costs around AUS $60.
- You can buy fuel on Home Island from 7:30 to 9:30 a.m., Monday, Wednesday, Thursday and Friday with an additional hour on Friday from 1:30 to 2:30 p.m.
- There is a small, fast, passenger ferry that runs between Home Island and West Island five times each week day for AUS $2 each way.
- The bus to the center of West Island is only AUS $.50 for the 15 minute ride.
- Going to Home Island (closest to our anchorage) requires a two mile dinghy ride, which is almost always a wet ride in choppy water.

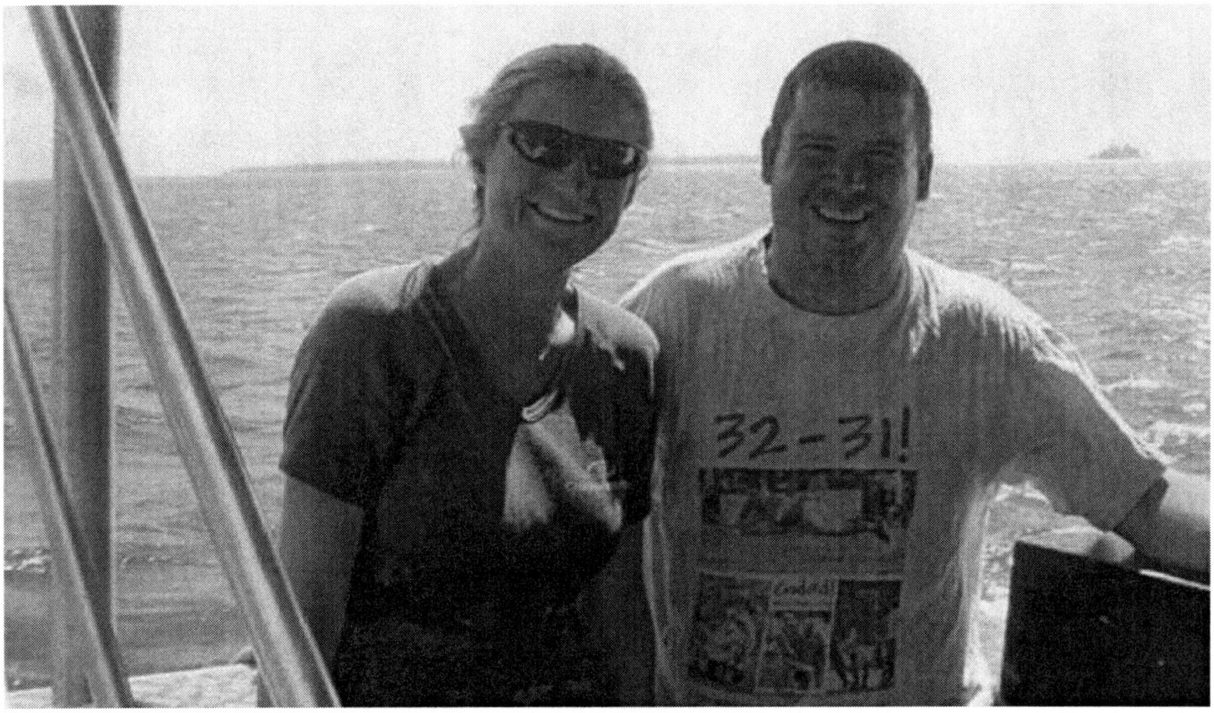

OUR PLEASURE'S **CREW ON THE FERRY TO WEST ISLAND**

There were many parties at the Direction Island shelter; the most memorable was Marv and Chieko's 35th wedding anniversary celebration. Harald, Bea and Diane spent the afternoon blowing up balloons and all the yachts were cooking up something special for potluck sharing. Originally, Bill and Sheri on *Esprit* asked Marv and Chieko to their boat to have a nice quiet dinner. I didn't like that plan, as this was the main event that we all were waiting for. I had to go over to Marv's boat to explain that for their anniversary I had already invited all their friends to a surprise beach party — so much for surprises. They liked the idea of the beach celebration and asked Bill and Sheri if they would mind moving their invitation to the following day? With everyone marching to the same drumbeat, we had the party late in the afternoon on Aug. 10, 2003. The food was wonderful. Harald made a potato salad that was gone almost immediately and we brought pork loins for the BBQ. There were fourteen invited people and two couples that invited themselves, which usually happens when people see a gathering on the beach.

Snorkeling in the lagoon is quite good and large fish like butterfly fish would always swarm around the boat if we threw in any scraps. While they fought for the scraps, small white and black tip reef sharks would swim over to see what the commotion was all about. The reef sharks were about three feet long and although they were common, they ignored people swimming near them. They might come over and have a look, but would then swim off disinterested. Everyone seemed quite comfortable to swim with them.

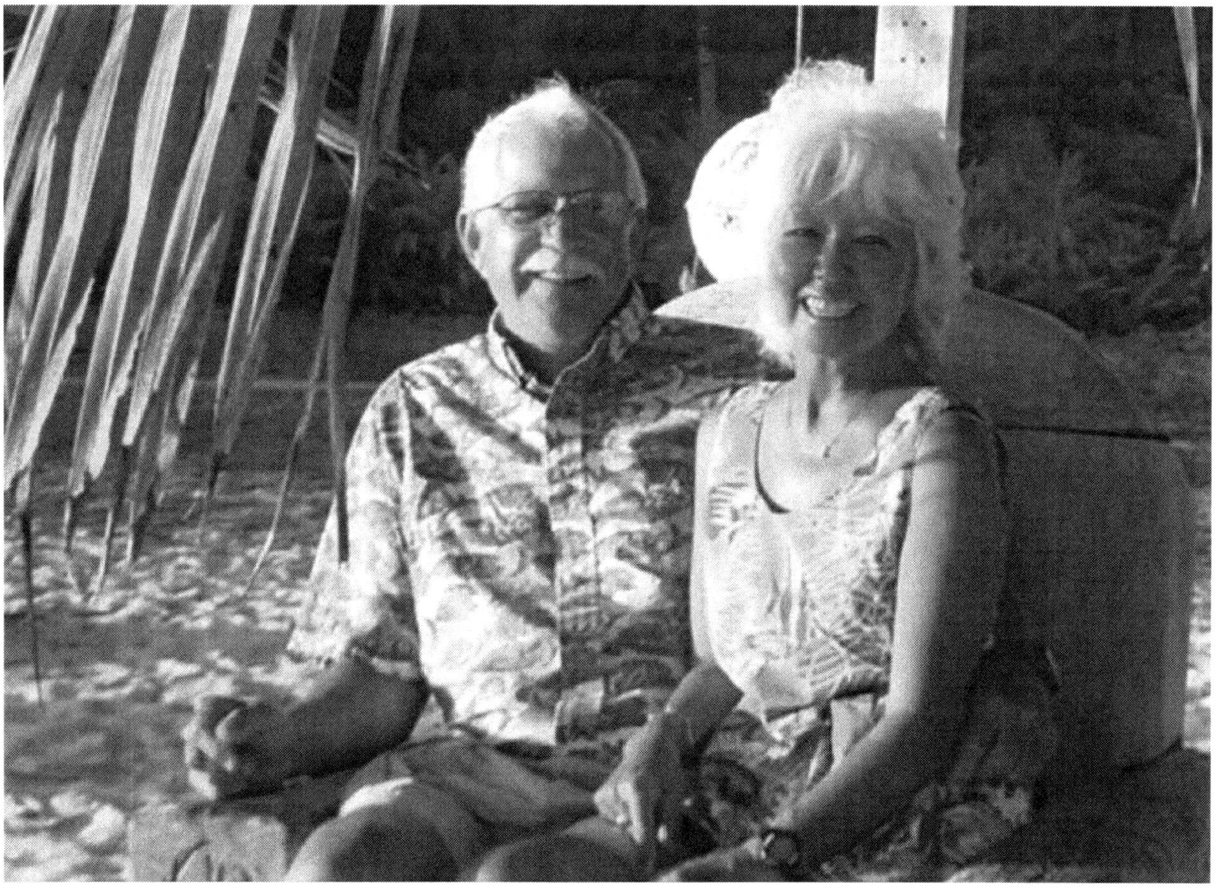

MARV AND CHIEKO, 35th ANNIVERSARY, DIRECTION ISLAND, 8.10.03

A ferry runs to and from Direction Island to West Island on Saturdays to bring the local Australians to the swimming beach. As the beach on Direction Island was the best beach in the islands for swimming. The ferry brought the swimmers in the morning and returned for them in the afternoon. The beach on Direction Island is the best and in the South East corner there is an area portioned off with lines and floats. This marks an area known as the "Rip." One can snorkel there while the continuous current carries you along to view coral and fish life. However, the current can be overly strong if one picks the wrong tidal range to snorkel. Rumor has it that someone was swept out into the lagoon and hence the ropes to grab onto.

Peter, an Australian single hander from Perth, on the yacht *Yvonne Elizabeth* was moored near me and was quite a character. This was his first long voyage and arrived at Cocos with engine problems. He had taken his engine apart and was waiting for replacement parts to arrive from Australia when we first met. However, because of a mix-up in wording, some parts were shipped by freighter instead of by airfreight. After a wait of six weeks, the parts did show up, but after putting his engine back together, it would not start. His sister Carrie came to visit him for a couple of weeks and took his mind off his engine. She was active and got him to take her fishing, snorkeling, over to Home Island and West Island and on diving expeditions.

I asked them over one night and really enjoyed their company. They laughed easily, had many interesting things to talk about and were quite relaxed like old friends. When I left Cocos, Peter had taken the engine apart one more time to dress the valves, but still no joy. He was going to send the valves and injection pump back with Carrie to have them reworked in Perth. It looked like Peter would be stuck in Cocos for quite a while, but hopefully we will catch up again in South Africa.

After talking to the Australian Met Service on West Island, it looked like tomorrow would be a good time to leave for Chagos. Diane took Harald over to Home Island to buy what fresh vegetables might be available and I called Pat to let her know we were leaving. Diane and Harald hit the jackpot at the grocery store as they found tomatoes, bananas, celery, frozen bread and some meat that had just been flown in. Of course, the prices were a bit extreme as two plastic grocery bags cost $50 Australian to fill. That night I had the *Esprit* and *Endurance* folks over for a last hurrah for a long time. The next meeting for the three boats would probably be at Richards Bay, South Africa, about 6,000 miles away. Harald and I prepared for our next stop at Chagos Archipelago some 1,600 nautical miles to the West.

Some facts about Cocos Keeling (Latitude 12°49'S, Longitude 96°53'E):

- There are two main island groups that make up Cocos Keeling, North Island and South Keeling.
- North Island is an atoll with a continuous reef that surrounds the lagoon. It is covered in coconut palms, a nature reserve and uninhabited.
- South keeling, where we moored, is an atoll where the main islands are connected by a reef with a large lagoon inside the reef. There are about ten islands in this group with the main islands being Direction, Home, and West.
- The islands were first reported by Captain William Keeling in 1609 and first settled by John Hare and John Clunies-Ross in 1826. The pair setup a copra plantation, but disagreements forced Hare to leave.
- Clunies-Ross imported labor from Malaya and built a large copra plantation.
- In 1857, the British declared the islands a British Dominion, but in 1886 Queen Victoria awarded the islands to the Clunies-Ross descendents.
- During WWI, the German cruiser *Emden* blew up a communication center on Direction Island. The *Emden* is now an historic wreck on North Keeling after a sea battle with the *HAMAS Sydney* in which it was badly damaged. The German captain decided to ground the damaged cruiser on the island.[4]

---

4 Microsoft® Encarta® 2006. © 1993-2005 Microsoft Corporation. All rights reserved

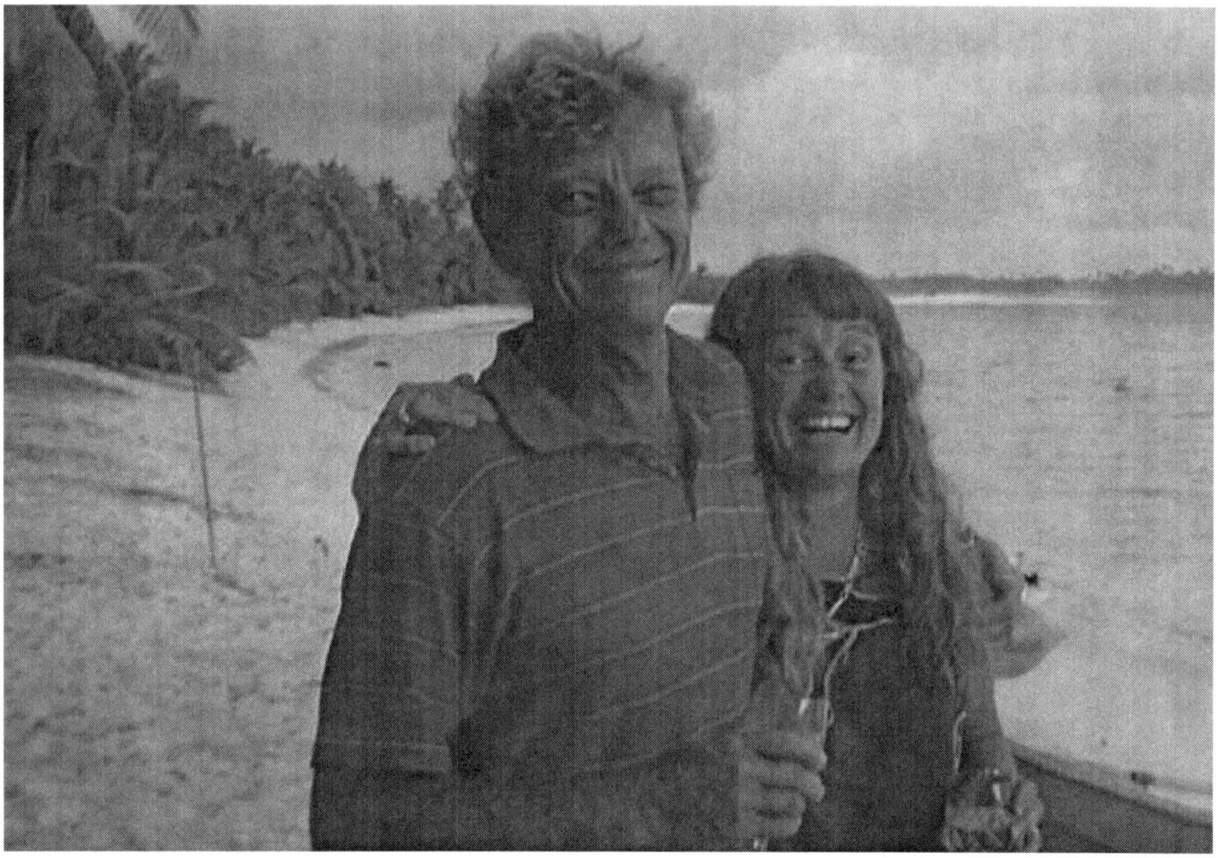

PETER, YACHT *YVONNE ELIZABETH* AND SISTER CARRIE

- During WWII, Direction Island was the base of a U.S. search and rescue service for downed airmen. They flew amphibious PBY's and some of the site is visible where the planes were hauled up to the beach for service and hiding.
- The Britt's made the islands an Australian dependency in 1955 and purchased the property from the Clunies-Ross descendents in 1978. Rumor has it that the purchase price for their mansion and property was $6,500,000. The family lost the money on a business venture in which they bought a freighter to keep Christmas and Cocos Keeling Islands supplied with goods. My understanding is the Australian government would not give them an exclusive supply contract and they went bankrupt. Their mansion still stands on Home Island with many artifacts intact and I think there are plans to restore it to its former glory.
- John Clunies-Ross also built boats on the island and the museum there has about four of his boats on display. An interesting feature of the boats is they contain ironwood and teak, both native island woods. Ironwood was once plentiful on the island, but was no longer evident and I think teak can still be found on one of the southern islands.
- Home Island is now the main settlement for the Malays that remained and is administered by Australia, but is locally self-governed.

The Malays live in nice air-conditioned homes; some have aluminum fishing dinghies with newer outboards. They all drive Honda type; all terrain vehicles with four big off road tires and a back seat or storage bin. Their religion is Muslim and the women wear clothing that covers everything, but their face. I believe there are about 600 in the native population and about 80 Australians living and working on mostly West Island. They have their own club on West Island that opens at 3:30 each afternoon. All alcohol can be purchased duty free at the supermarket and there is a duty free store with limited items to choose from. The banks will exchange American dollars for Australian dollars, but do not provide any credit card services like cash advances — this was a puzzle to us. Direction Island has no permanent inhabitant

Chapter 20

COCOS KEELING TO CHAGOS (UK)

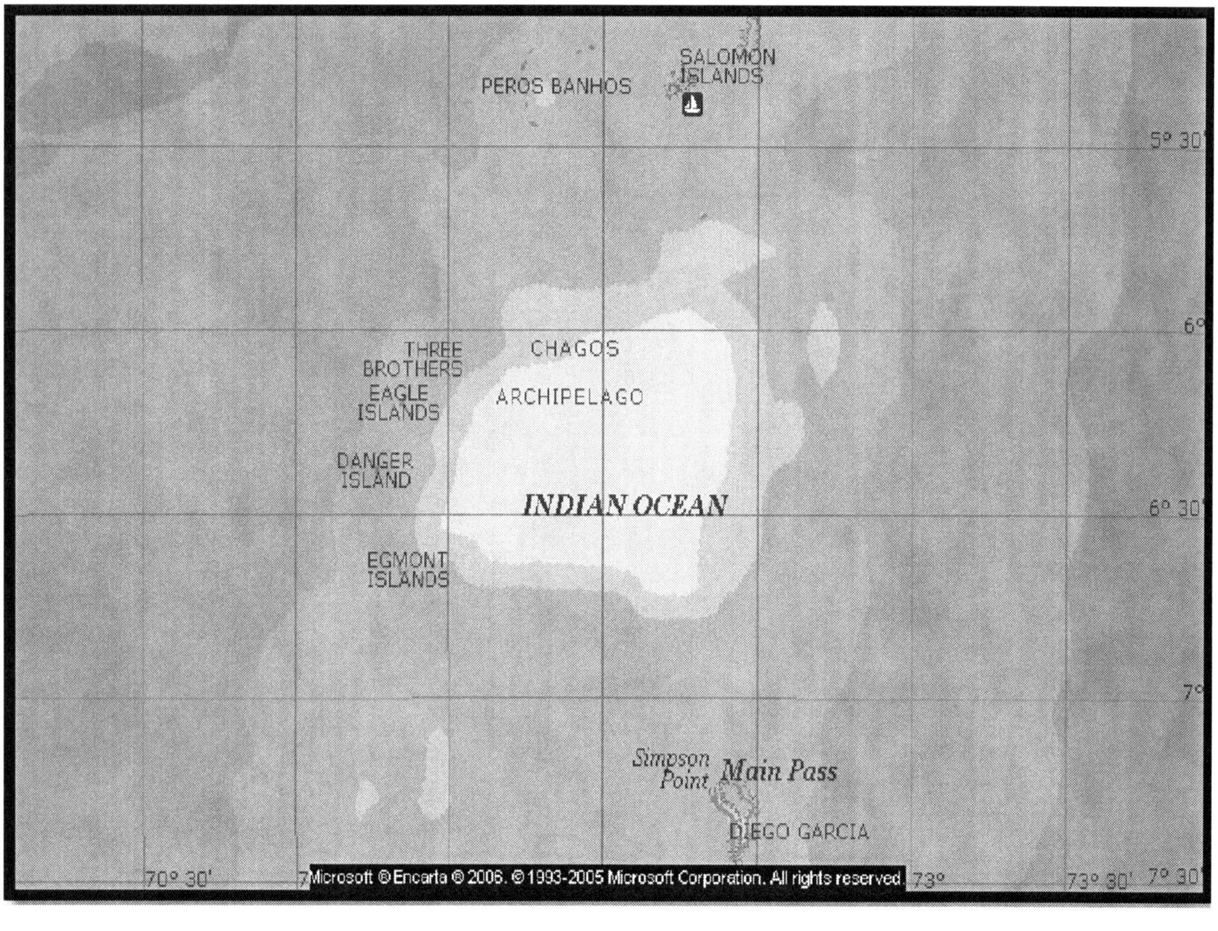

SALOMON ISLANDS IN THE CHAGOS ARCHIPELAGO 8. 27. 2003

On Thursday, Aug. 14, Harald and I started the process of picking up the anchor. By 9:30 a.m., the anchor was stowed. We blew our air horn several times and felt a warm sensation as boats in the anchorage responded with their horns. There was a lot of hand waving and feelings of sadness in me for I had developed a unique connection and fondness for Cocos Keeling, hard to express, but deep rooted like a spiritual relationship.

It seems like some of the yachties there like Peter on *Yvonne Elizabeth* and Bea and Diane on *Sortilege* were permanent residents. Like a small town setting, you soon know everyone, you're aware of the problems they were dealing with and somehow their lives become part of yours. Anyway, we were off, the sky was blue, only a few wispy clouds, the temperature was 82° F. The wind was perfect at 18 knots from the East South East and filled our sails from the aft, port quarter.

I keep track of the hours used by the main and genset engines and apply an estimate to the fuel consumption. The main engine uses around 0.6 gallons per hour on average while running between 1,250 to 1,500 RPM. The genset uses an average of 0.3 gallons per hour. Using these estimates I figured ***Our Pleasure*** consumed around 66 gallons since leaving Darwin. Since I usually run the genset twice a day for refrigeration, our totals looked good so far. If I could fill the tanks completely we would have about 280 gallons available. However, Diesel fuel contains air from the pumping process and tends to bubble back up from the tank's fill port if the fuel is pumped too fast or you try to overfill the tanks.

The next day we ran into rain showers and collected water for the starboard water tank, water jugs and the teakettle. The slowly dying winds reduced our sailing speed average to 122 NM for the next 24 hours. I talked to Diane on SSB and found out Bea had cut his finger badly just as we were leaving. I heard her call the medical clinic via VHF radio, but did not hear the whole conversation. Diane managed to patch up wound and thought it would heal properly. I suffered a minor rope burn on my index finger about the same time when I released the Spinlock® (line locking device) for the main sail furler. I thought the furling lock on the boom was engaged, but it still had a couple of inches to go before the drum automatically locked. I was lucky there were only a few inches before locking otherwise the burn would have been quite serious. Harald put together a big salad of fresh vegetables from Home Island to go with lamb chops.

I talked with *Endurance* on Saturday morning and they were just leaving Cocos with *Esprit* and a Finnish boat, *Ida. Ida* was going to Chagos, while they were going some 3,200 miles directly to Madagascar. The wind was steady now at 15 to 20 knots so our progress was good. We were trailing a fishing line with a lure that made good use of chicken feathers. A fisherman in Darwin assured me, that this lure would catch fish. Well it did, but the fish was so big it swam off with the lure and several feet of broken fishing line.

Our heading from Cocos to Chagos was northwest as we left 12° of south latitude and headed toward 5° south latitude. Chagos is actually some 420 NM closer to the equator than Cocos and only about 300 miles from the equator. The winds tend toward the light side; the water is warmer and the rain more frequent. Information from Chagos on a marine radio net let us know the boats there had already been through two weeks of steady rain. While the rain hampered some outdoor activities like volleyball, it allowed them to fill their water tanks with good water. We experienced some light wind days of ten knots, but that allowed us to polish some of the stainless steel and for Harald to bake bread.

We arrived at Chagos on Wednesday, Aug. 27 and anchored off the Ile Fouquet after 13 days and approximately 1,600 NM. Our average distance per day was quite low because of light winds while *Endurance* and *Esprit* were enjoying 160 mile day runs just 400 miles to the south of us. Chagos is an archipelago made up of atolls and reefs in the middle of the Indian Ocean. There are about 50 islands, several atolls, lots of reefs and submerged shoals. The great Chagos Bank is the largest atoll in the Indian Ocean. Ile Fouquet is in the most popular island group for yachts, the Salomon Islands.

After coming cautiously through the bommies at the Salomon entrance we first anchored off an island called Ile de la Passe. Harald had stopped here once before when he was a crewmember on the yacht *Sortilege*. Crewing was how he met Bea and Diane. However, the area had lots of bommies and was a bit rolly and no one else had picked this island as an anchorage. As we looked around for a better spot a dinghy came over with Larry and Lena from their yacht *Allons'y*. They were snorkeling in the area. We were all amazed when they told us they were from Friday Harbor near Seattle — small world. They suggested we move to Ile Fouquet, as it was more sheltered from the trade winds. That was a good suggestion as it was sheltered and we had a good view of the dense palm trees on shore and waves breaking over a reef nearby. We were invited to a beach party that night which Harald went to while I preferred to rest on ***Our Pleasure*** with a Cuba Libra and a barbequed steak — good move on my part because Harald did not get back until 11 p.m., without having a decent meal.

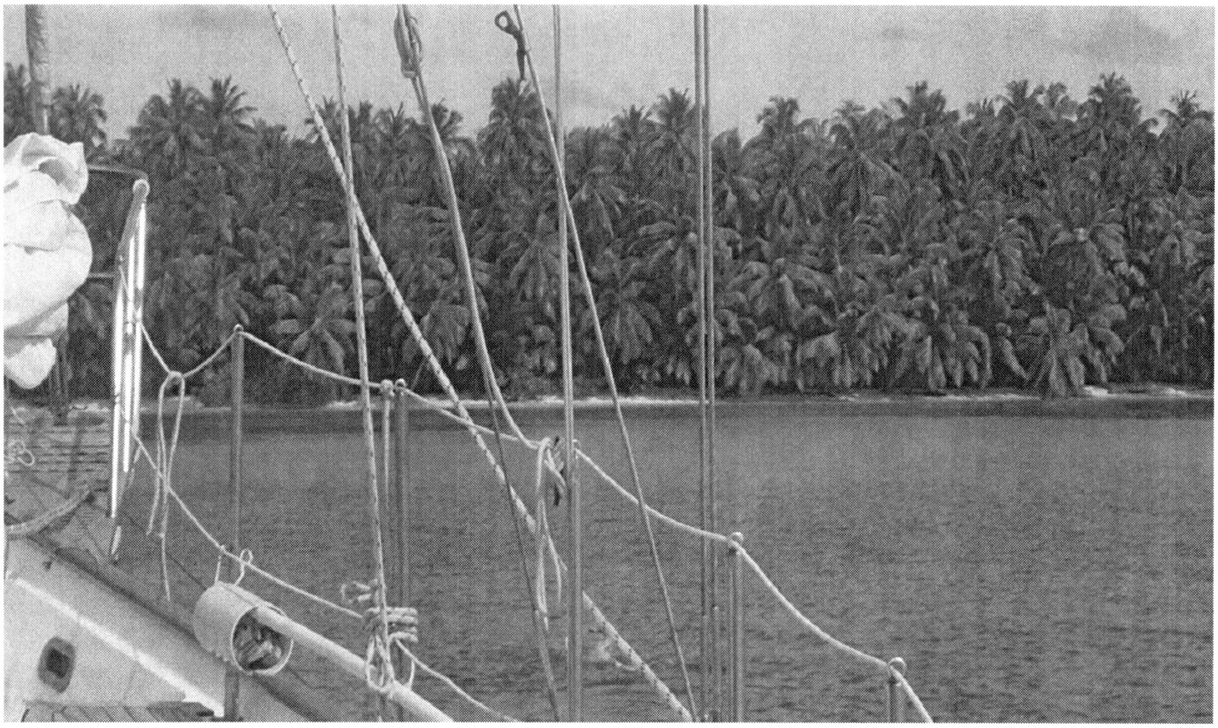

OUR PLEASURE, ILE FOUQUET, CHAGOS ARCHIPELAGO, AUG. 27, 2003

Adrian, from the catamaran *Ctar*, came over the next morning with Serge and Pascale, the French couple who lost their yacht *Marimba* a few weeks ago. We discussed our plans and how we could get them to South Africa on ***Our Pleasure***. Before we arrived in Chagos, the British officials who administer these islands would not allow the French couple to camp on shore. The islands are a natural preserve and no one can live on the island's land. Originally, they had moved their salvaged gear from *Marimba* to Ile de la Passe and were happily camped there. The Brits had other ideas though and proposed to fly them to Singapore where they would then be on their own.

A South African yacht at Chagos, *Scavargo*, offered them a berth and space for their salvaged gear until Mayotte. This satisfied the Brits so Serge, Pascale and Kami, their dog, moved aboard *Scavargo*. Walt and Judith's 50 foot *Scavargo* had room to carry their personal belongings and items they thought sellable in Mayotte, but it was a bit crowded. By the time I arrived, they were well situated on *Scavargo*. This actually was a blessing for me, as they had salvaged a lot of gear that would have burdened and crowded ***Our Pleasure***. The plan now was for Harald and me to sail on ***Our Pleasure*** to Mayotte where Serge, Pascale and Kami would move aboard for the trip to South Africa. Since Mayotte is a French possession, the thinking was to sell the salvaged gear there to fellow nationals and make a few Euros. Everyone was happy with the plan so we looked forward to enjoying Chagos.

Looking around our anchorage, we could see Chagos has many similarities to Cocos Keeling, except no one lives on these islands and facilities are limited. The British Navy now provides administration for the islands in the Archipelago of around 20 square miles and collects an $80 service fee from yachts anchored there. A service they do provide is collecting garbage from containers placed near the concrete jetty on Boddam Island and that's about it except for shooing campers off the islands. These islands are designated as a conservation area and all fauna and flora are protected. The Chagos atoll is much smaller than Cocos Keeling with the lagoon roughly two miles across. Rainwater is collected at Boddam Island in a rusty steel tank and the island also has a well. Washing clothes by hand is the norm for yachties using rain or well water. A shower hose and nozzle had been installed on the water tank by some yachties for showering. Boddam Island has a unique history going back over 45 years when people lived there. Workers were brought there to process coconuts for oil and copra.

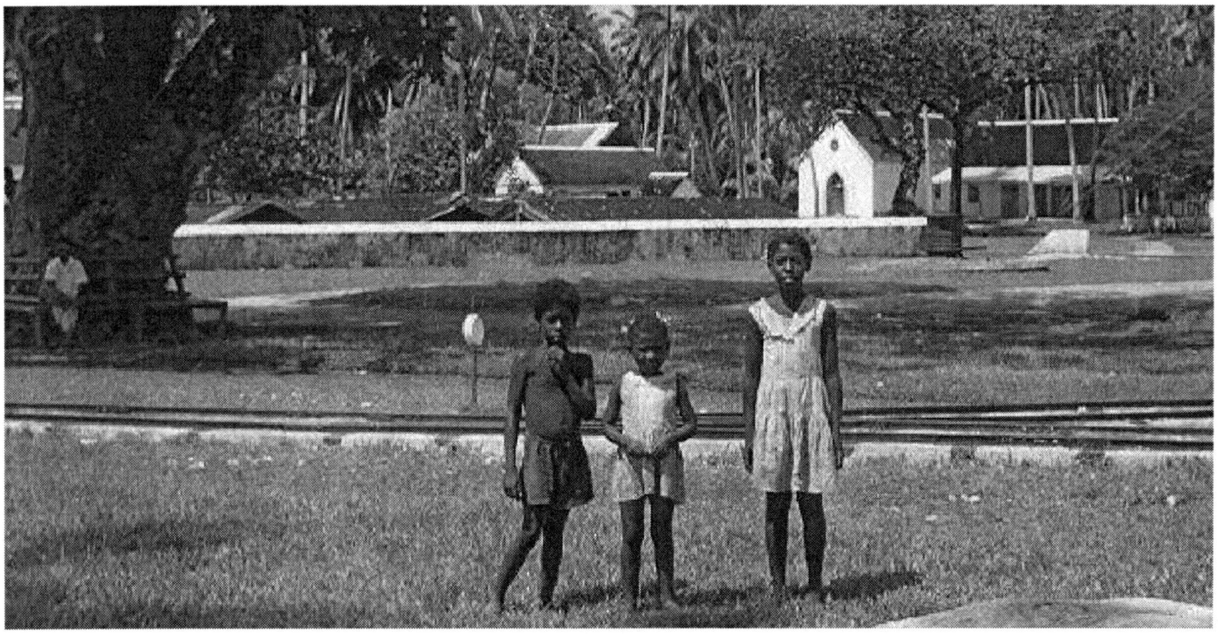

Photo courtesy of the Chagos Conservation Trust (CCT)

BODDAM ISLAND, CHAGOS — HOSPITAL & CHURCH IN BACKGROUND, 1963

The British moved all the people to other nearby British islands like Mauritius, around 1970. I am not certain why they were moved, but it probably had something to do with the military development of Diego Garcia that is now leased to the U.S. Navy. Diego Garcia has a communication center, big naval base and large runways for the largest of our transport planes. Diego Garcia is part of the Chagos archipelago, about 130 miles south from the Salomon Islands group. The building remnants at Chagos are still standing because they were heavily constructed of coral stone using a cement binding. Building walls are about two feet thick and big timber beams supported steel corrugated roofs. Window frames and roofs have mostly disintegrated as most woods used in the construction have rotted away, but the stonewalls have weathered the years well.

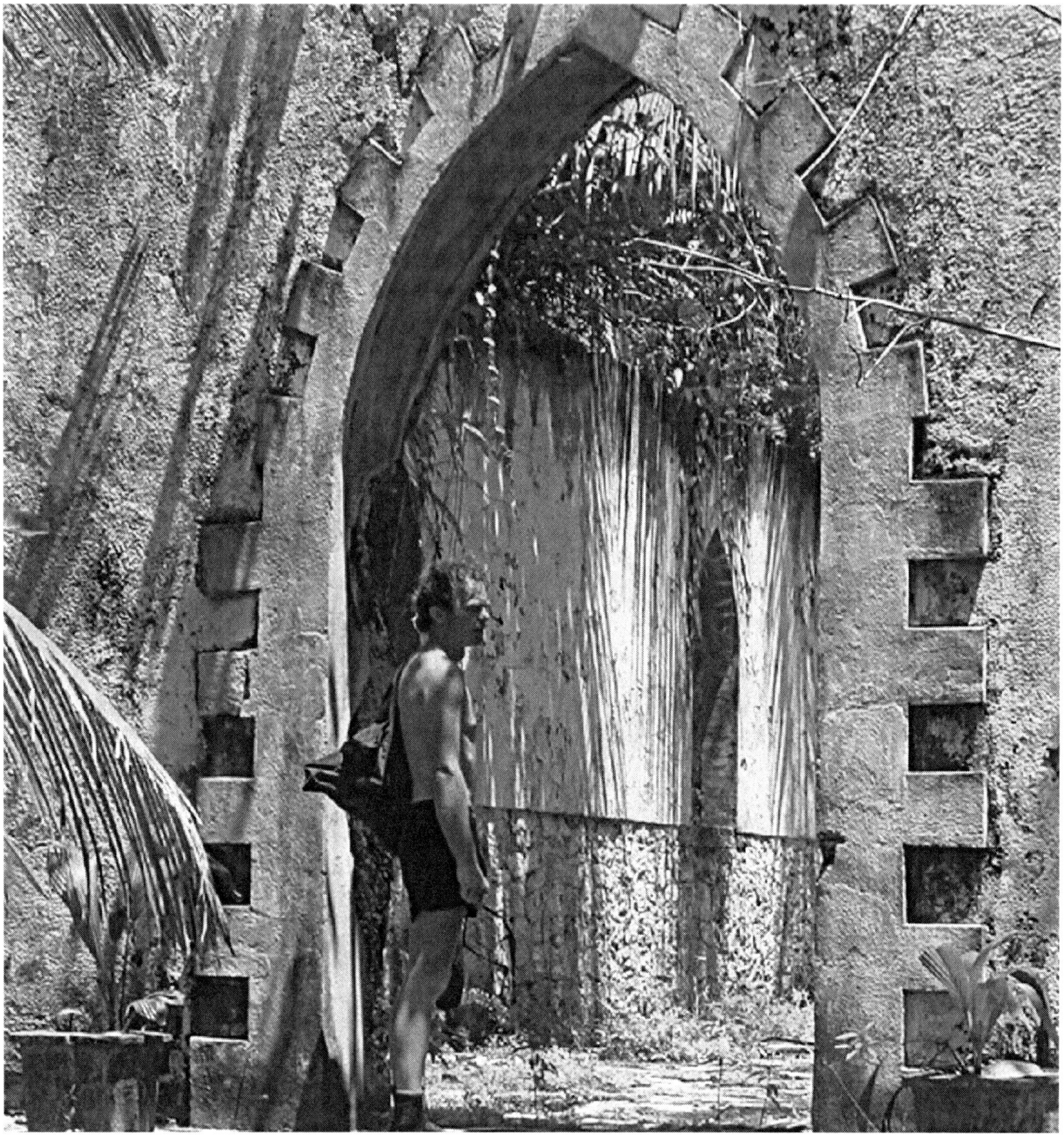

HARALD AND CHURCH RUINS, BODDAM ISLAND

There is a stone and concrete jetty and with an oversized concrete cross on the right side of the jetty. The function of some buildings is obvious like the jail with four small rooms, the church and the processing buildings with ovens and piping. The church architecture is good looking with a rounded wall behind the altar and extra detailing in the window framing. Two nicely detailed concrete flower boxes still exist at the entrance to the church. Early photographs of the settlement show nice lawns and open spaces between the jetty and buildings like the church, but this whole area is now densely overgrown. It was rumored that the natives or their ancestors now have permission to move back to the island. However, the lack of water and infrastructure would make it difficult. There are hiking trails on the island kept cleared by yachties. One couple we met was making a map of the island using a GPS. However, mosquitoes were making their presence known on nearby trails and I did not have repellent with me.

The yachties use the area near the jetty, under the shade of coconut palm trees to barbeque, chat, relax, meet or play volleyball on the makeshift court there. The view looking toward the lagoon and yachts anchored nearby is pleasant and picture-postcard-perfect. Some past yachties tried to make use of the best remaining building that still had an intact roof. They fashioned it into a shelter similar to the shelter at Cocos Keeling. The British authorities however, claimed that use of the building violated regulations and removed all yacht names and memorabilia. That ruling seemed rather shortsighted to us as no one would be living in the building — big government strikes again. Yachts that cruise the Indian Ocean on a regular basis, drop off chairs and tools to keep the islands more inviting and civilized.

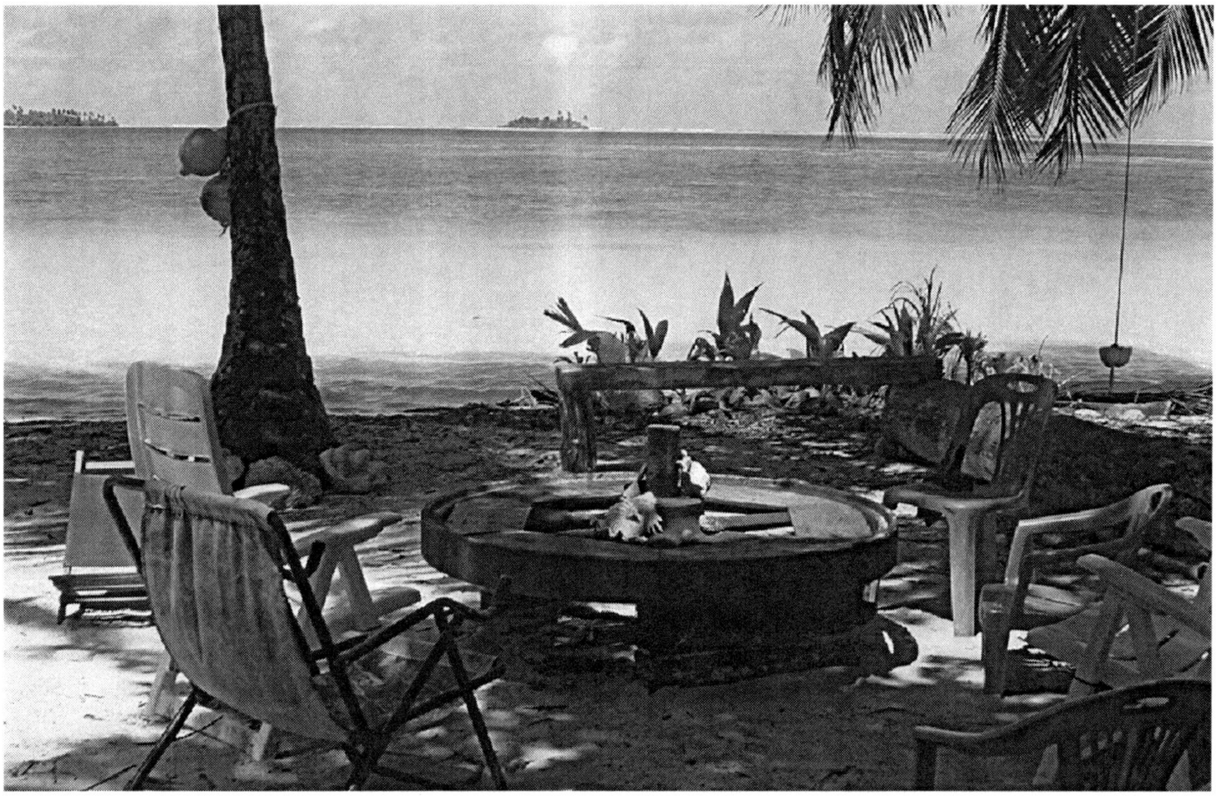

INVITING, PEACEFUL AND SERENE, BODDAM ISLAND

Harald took me for a tour of the island Ile de la Passe, his previous anchorage the last time he was on Chagos. We saw some large coconut crabs, hermit crabs, and the island water well (still useable) and some of the old island trails which are now overgrown and not passable. We went over to the reef between this island and Ile Mapou to see the remains of *Marimba*, Serge and Pascale's yacht. The yachties at the time of the grounding, only a few weeks ago, helped remove all food, personal belongings and hardware from the boat except the engine. Initially it was thought *Marimba* could be refloated, but pounding on the reef cracked the fiberglass hull. With the structure failing, everyone concentrated on moving *Marimba's* gear to the island. The mast, boom and rigging were all removed so the yacht is now completely empty except for the engine. Quite a few of the salvaged items were sold to the yachties on Chagos at the time, which helped raise money for Serge and Pascale.

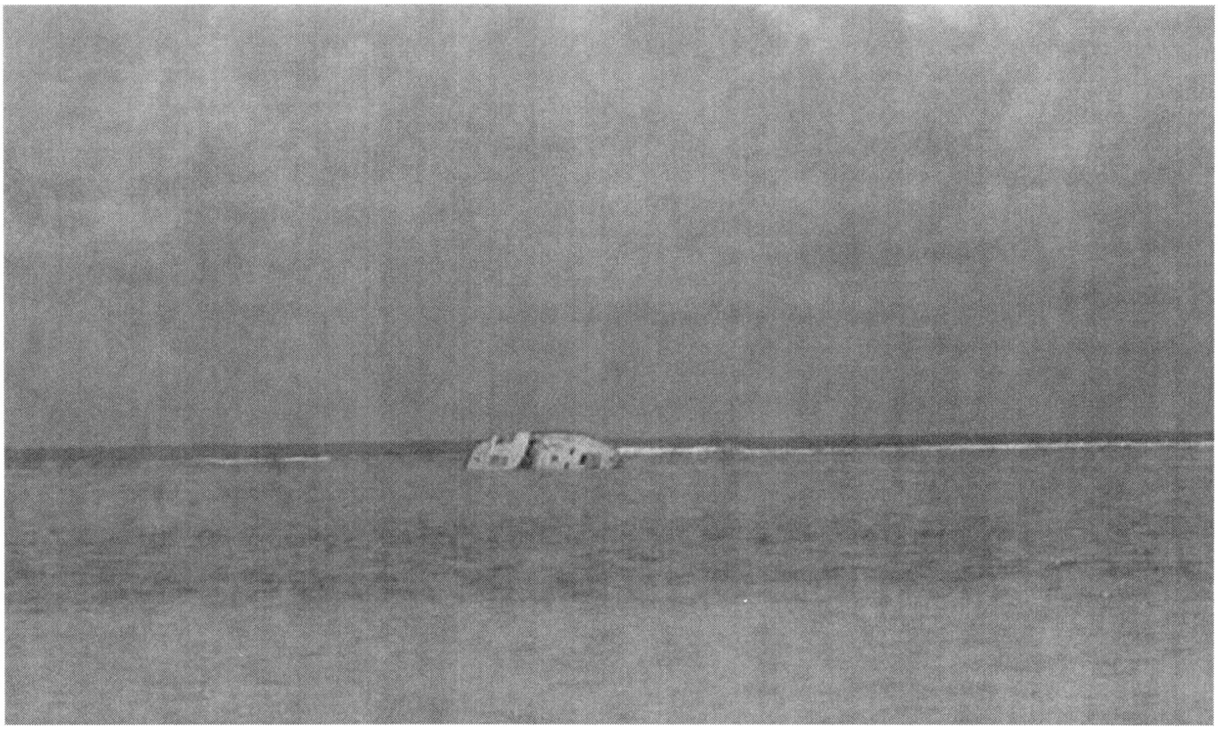

REMAINS OF *MARIMBA* GROUNDED FOREVER ON A REEF, CHAGOS

On the way back to ***Our Pleasure*** we stopped at Ile Takamaka to see why a fairly large sloop was careened on the beach. There we met an Australian national, Russell, who was repairing the hull of his sloop, *Spike*. His hull was composed of five layers of diagonal hardwood planking covered by fiberglass. It seems that marine boring worms had managed to get through the outside glass and weaken four of the inner wood layers. He noticed the problem when the hull started leaking in rough weather. He was quite a salty character with his shaven head, full beard, black thong and half of a tee shirt. He was an experienced shipwright and the builder of *Spike* so we were confident that he would repair her. However, it seemed to me that the spacing of the repaired planks should have been fitted closer together.

He had already been there for about a month working on the repair, but it was still a long way to completion. It had taken him five days just to move the boat through shallow water, on its side, to the beach. He had repaired most the starboard side, but still faced moving the boat out to deeper water, turning it around and moving it back to the beach for the port side repair. He had tied a hammock with mosquito netting to a couple of lines going to the shore for a place to sleep. He had a large pot with water boiling over an open fire to bend the planking, a generator and some power tools.

A few weeks before we met Russell, the British authorities questioned his occupation of the beach. Living ashore in Chagos is prohibited, so they arrested him and carted him off to Diego Garcia — not much compassion shown for his problems. As I remember the conversation, he said he was in jail for three days before the officials in England said he should be released. In a technicality of maritime law, a person is allowed to use the shore to affect repair to his vessel in an emergency. To make amends for his unjust imprisonment the Brits bought wood, fiberglass and epoxy from the Americans on Diego Garcia and provided him with other supplies. That was a good thing for him since he told us he did not have enough wood or epoxy to repair *Spike* without help.

One other positive outcome of the internment was the treatment for a serious infection. It seems a rat had bitten him and self-treatment had not been working. So the Brits treated the infection properly and he was healing nicely. However, they still did not want him to become entrenched there and asked him to complete his repair by the end of Sept. He thought the time allotment somewhat of a joke and said to us; "It would be finished when it was finished" — he may be there a long time. He works and lives alone, understandably, as no woman I know would put up with his attitude or life style.

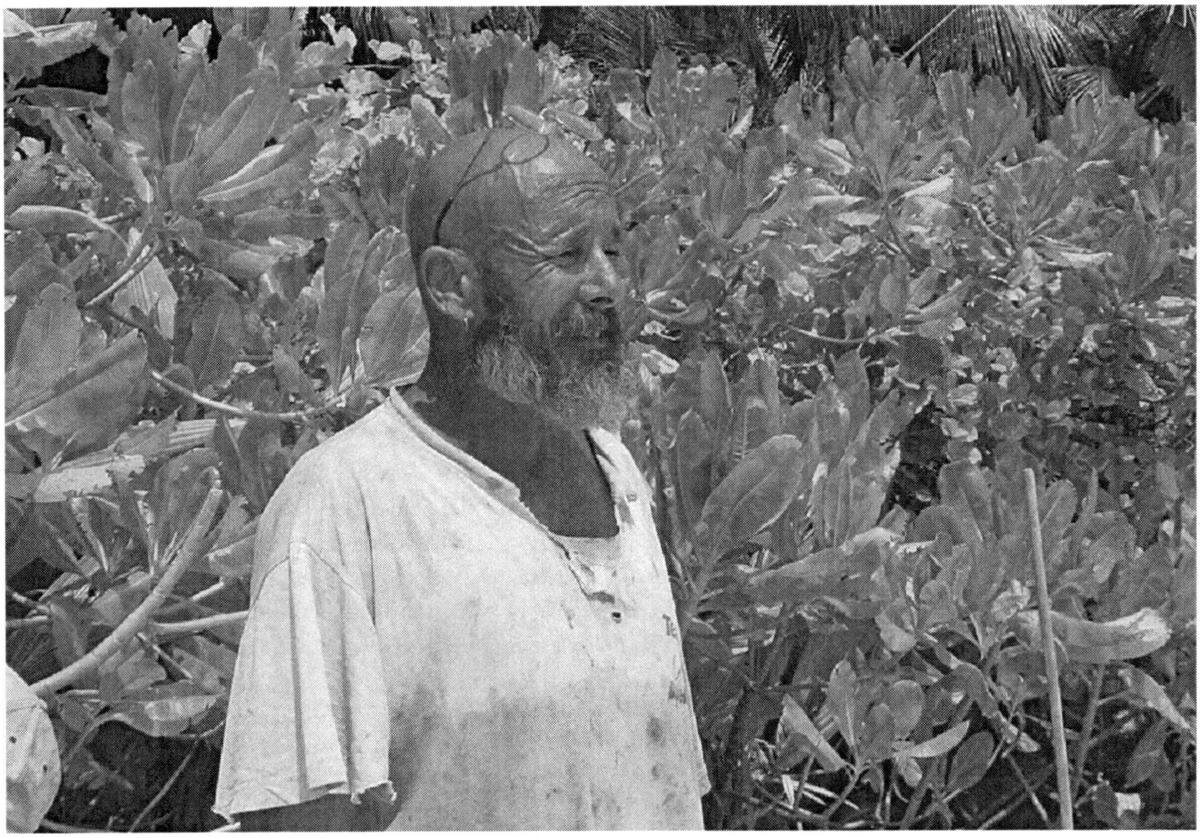

RUSSELL, LOOKING AT *SPIKE*, FROM THE BEACH AT ILE TAKAMAKA

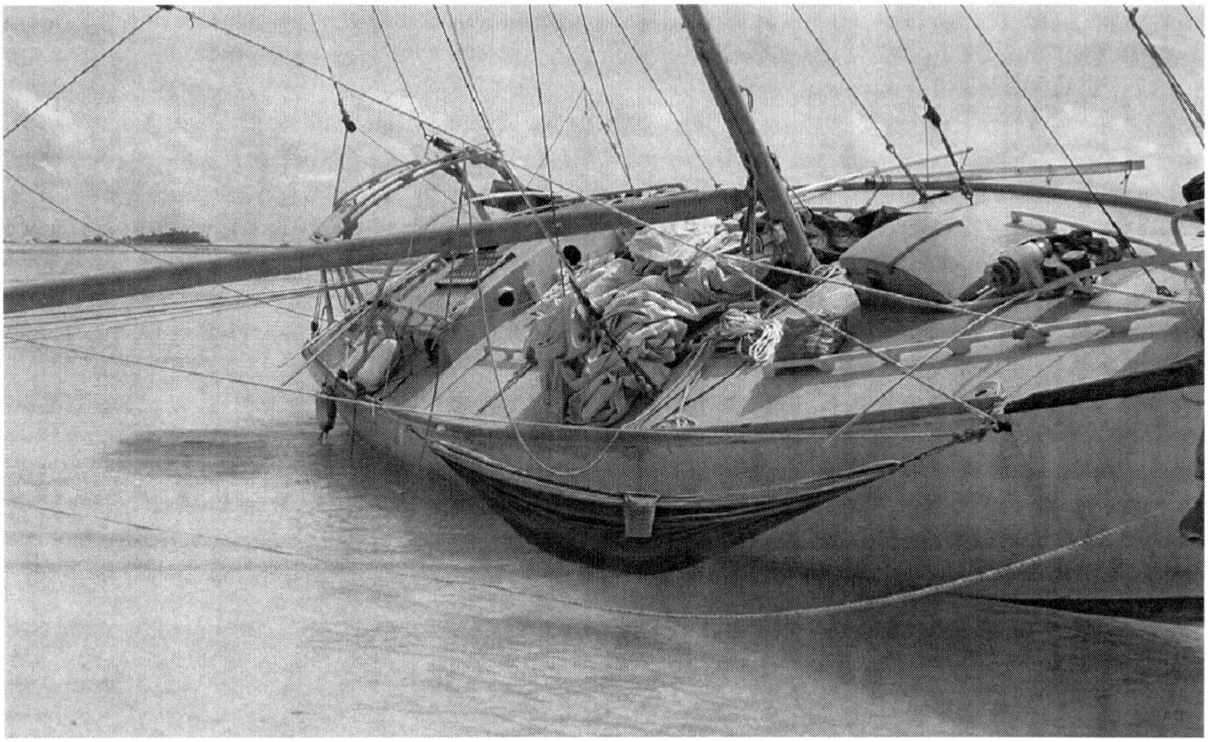

SPIKE, CAREENED ON THE BEACH, ILE TAKAMAKA, CHAGOS

One more stop to say hello to Herby, a single hander from Germany, who was visiting on the yacht *Ctar*. Herb's sloop *Beule* was without a working engine at this point in his adventure. *Beule* is a steel boat and the rough translation of the name in German would mean bumpy. The bumps occur on the steel plates between welds and the naming was indeed appropriate. Adrian, his wife Hiltrup and young son Eric on *Ctar* had become good friends with Herby as they helped him on several occasions. Last stop for Harald and me was a short snorkel at a ferro-cement sloop that had dragged its anchor in the lagoon at Ile Fouquet.

Apparently this drama happened in June 2002 when strong winds blew her towards shallow water were it hit a coral head and sank in about eight feet of water. The rumor mill suggested she did not drag her anchor, but anchored near the coral head without knowing it was within range of her anchored circle. There was not much left as almost everything had been removed. The hatches were open and the hull and deck were mostly in good order. The overly stout mast, boom and some rigging had been moved to the shore under the coconut palms and were still there. By time we got back to ***Our Pleasure*** I was ready for a nap. Herb came over to ***Our Pleasure*** that night for happy hour and we talked late into the evening.

My single side band radio had not been doing well since leaving Townsville. I knew the SGC automatic antenna tuner was no longer working, but according to Marv, I sounded like I was talking from the bottom of a water barrel. He was only about 1,400 miles away and said that both the voice quality and my signal strength were poor. I was having a hard time finding a solution for this problem as I had the transceiver realigned and tuned in Townsville. The Seattle manufacturer, SGC had also sent some new firmware to update the system. I tried dragging a 100 foot wire in the water to improve the ground plane, but no change was noticed. I did find that a three-pole filter I had installed right at the 12 volt input to the transceiver would oscillate at some frequencies, so I disconnected it.

Another factor that was puzzling was the ability to send/receive e-mail via the Sailmail SSB system. That system was working great and had no problems. Larry on *Allons'y* asked me if I disconnected the Sailmail, Pactor modem while using voice transmission. I told him yes because I turned off its power. I found out later that I actually had to pull the cable's plug to the modem during transmission and that turning the power off was not sufficient. I found out this little known fact while I was talking on a marine SSB net and one of the boats said his ICOM sounded the same way until he pulled its communication line. Not all, but quite a few of the problems encountered while cruising, can be corrected by minor fixes.

Harald and I were making plans to leave Chagos on Sept. 1, but Larry on *Allons'y,* thought we should wait a few more days. The atmospheric pressure was now reading high at 1035 millibars and the main part of this high pressure system was only 1,000 miles to our south. *Allons'y* told us he had been caught in a similar system just after leaving Cocos Keeling. Normal sailing winds, but high waves had knocked his new outboard off its storage mount on the stern and into the water it went. Even though the winds predicted were good for sailing, the sea heights predicted were as high as 20 feet. Low wind speeds generating high seas were abnormal and the usual thought is the predictions are wrong, but it's much better to play it safe. So we agreed the prudent thing would be to wait for a few more days. When everything is stowed for sailing and systems are checked out, it becomes almost painful to wait.

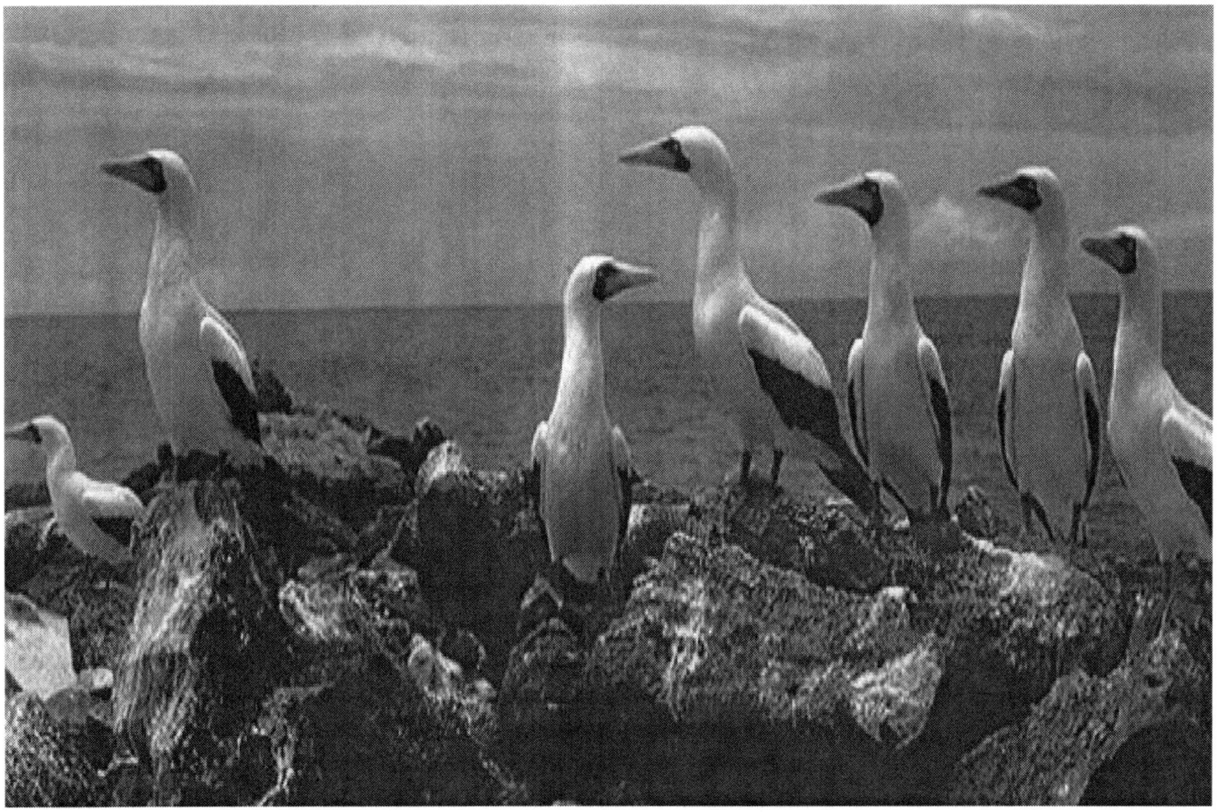

© Photo courtesy of Professor Charles Sheppard of CCT

GROUP OF MASKED BOOBIES

One of the highly regarded boating superstitions is never leave port on Friday. We normally try to comply with this superstition, as do most of the yachties, but it usually adds another day to departures. I took the dinghy to shore to have a closer look at Ile Fouquet. I walked the full length of the island on the lagoon side and also on the ocean side where there was good access. Quite a few sea birds have made this island home. I saw five species including a red-footed booby, a brown booby, a friendly dark gray bird with webfeet, probably a lesser noddy tern. A small white bird with a long narrow tail feather, probably a fairy tern and a frigate bird. The white birds with long tail feathers always flew in pairs in a tight formation, with wing tips almost touching. To me it looked like a flight training school something like the Top Gun school for Marine fighter pilots. They always flew fast and flew intricate maneuvers like might be required to catch flying fish.

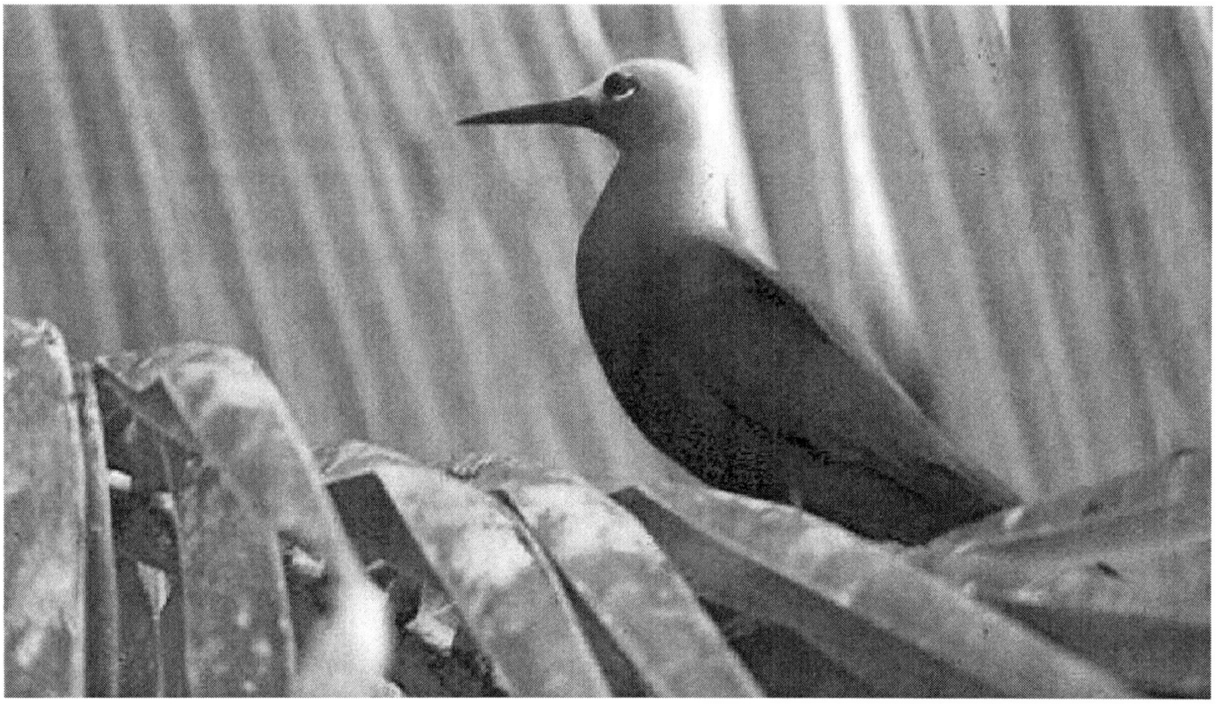

© Photo courtesy of Professor Charles Sheppard of CCT

LESSER NODDY TERN

A small manta ray swam slowly by me and close to the beach. Following right behind was a small, black tip reef shark. I was amazed to find a beautifully colored conk shell about the size of a baseball cap exposed in the sand. A large land crab had been digging a hole in the sand and exposed this shell about 4 inches below the surface. I was tempted to keep it, but it was so beautiful and still alive so I put it back where it belonged. I saw hundreds of hermit crabs, both white and red always retreating into their borrowed shells when they sensed my presence. The island also has coconut crabs, but I saw only a few of the smaller variety. I found two areas off the beach that had been cleared by previous yachties for get-togethers. One had a volleyball court with boundaries marked by a large diameter hemp rope. There was even a volleyball there ready for action. Some kind soul had left the ball hanging from a tree limb inside a small net. The volleyball net was a simple long, white board tied between two trees.

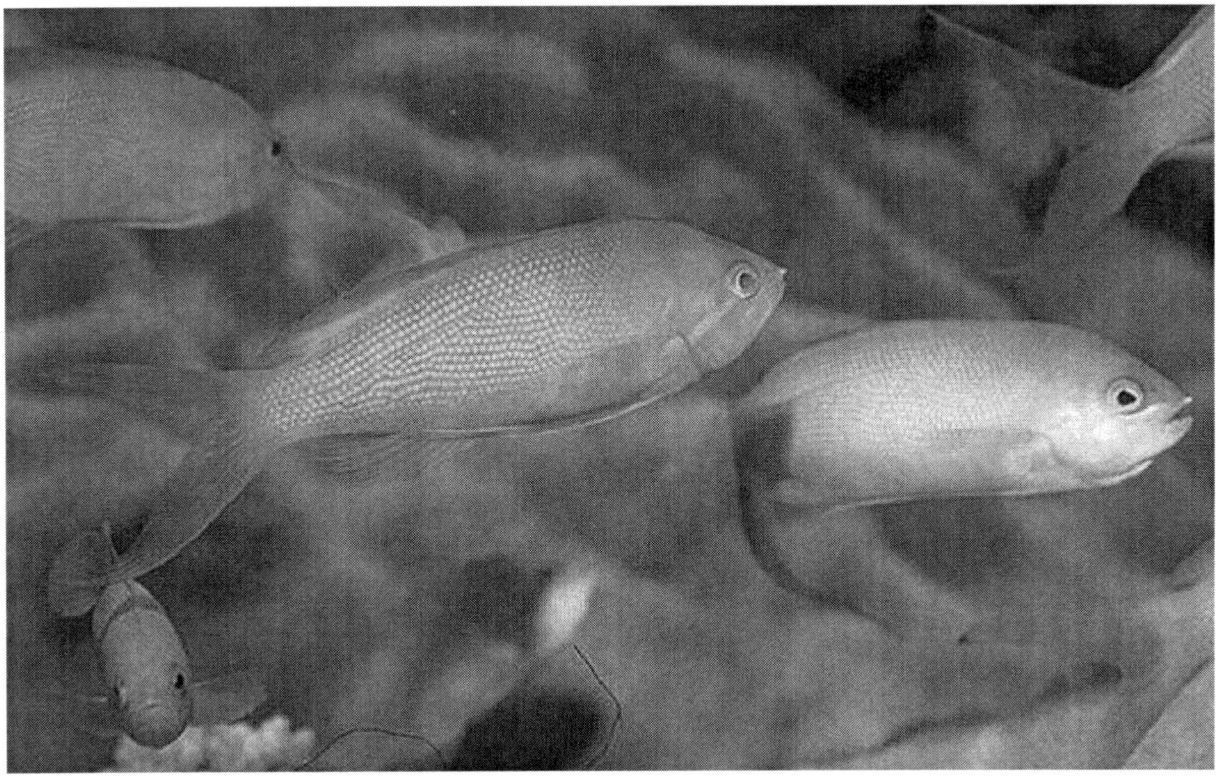

©Photo courtesy of Dr. Charles Anderson of the CCT

ANTHIAS FISH ARE RELATED TO THEIR LARGER GROUPER COUSINS

Along a path to the ocean side of the island, I found a shrine, probably to a loved family member. It consisted of a small wooden building similar to a pagoda about the size of a shoebox. Next to the building was the carved face of a man about the size of a softball. Colored paint was used to emphasize his features and outline the building. The woods were stained dark and polished as if they were rubbed in oil. The whole shrine was placed on a stone table, which rested on small rocks. The wood did not appear to be weathered so I don't think it had been there long. The significance of the shrine was not clear, but appeared to be a tribute to a young man who had passed away. Who placed it there was a real mystery as it appeared to be a native type shrine and these islands are supposed to be uninhabited. All that aside, whoever built the shrine was an excellent craftsman with talent.

These islands, in general, are unique because no one has openly lived on them for 45 years; the indigenous birds, coral, sea life and land creatures have flourished. At the end of the island I ran into Serge and Pascale making bread over an open fire for the trip to Mayotte.

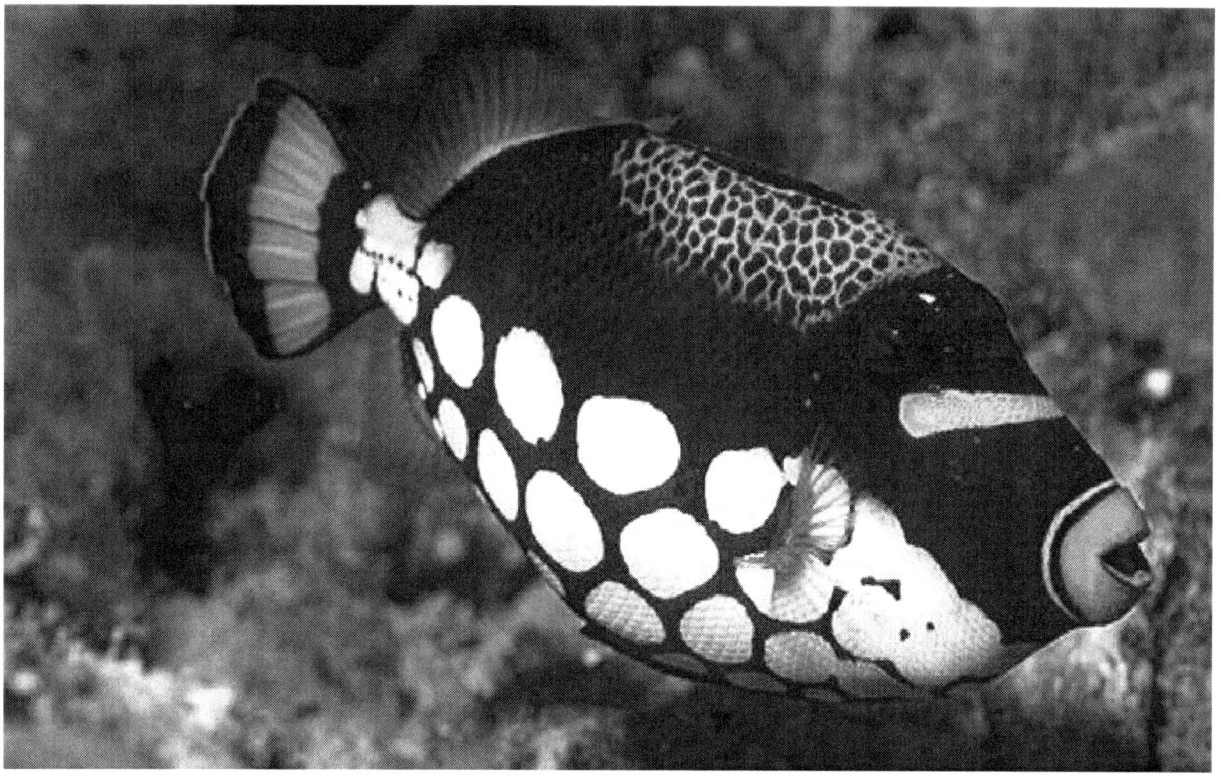

© Photo courtesy of Dr. Charles Anderson of the CCT
CLOWN TRIGGER FISH

Wind direction, wind speed and barometric pressure are predicted by NOAA for most of the world and are provided as part of the Sailmail e-mail service. On Sept. 6, the weather for the first five days to Mayotte was looking good. The anchor was up by 9:30 a.m., Harald stood on the bow to direct us past the bommies and we were in deep water by 10:15 a.m. I followed a straight rhumb line course to Mayotte that would pass by the northern tip of Madagascar by at least 50 miles.

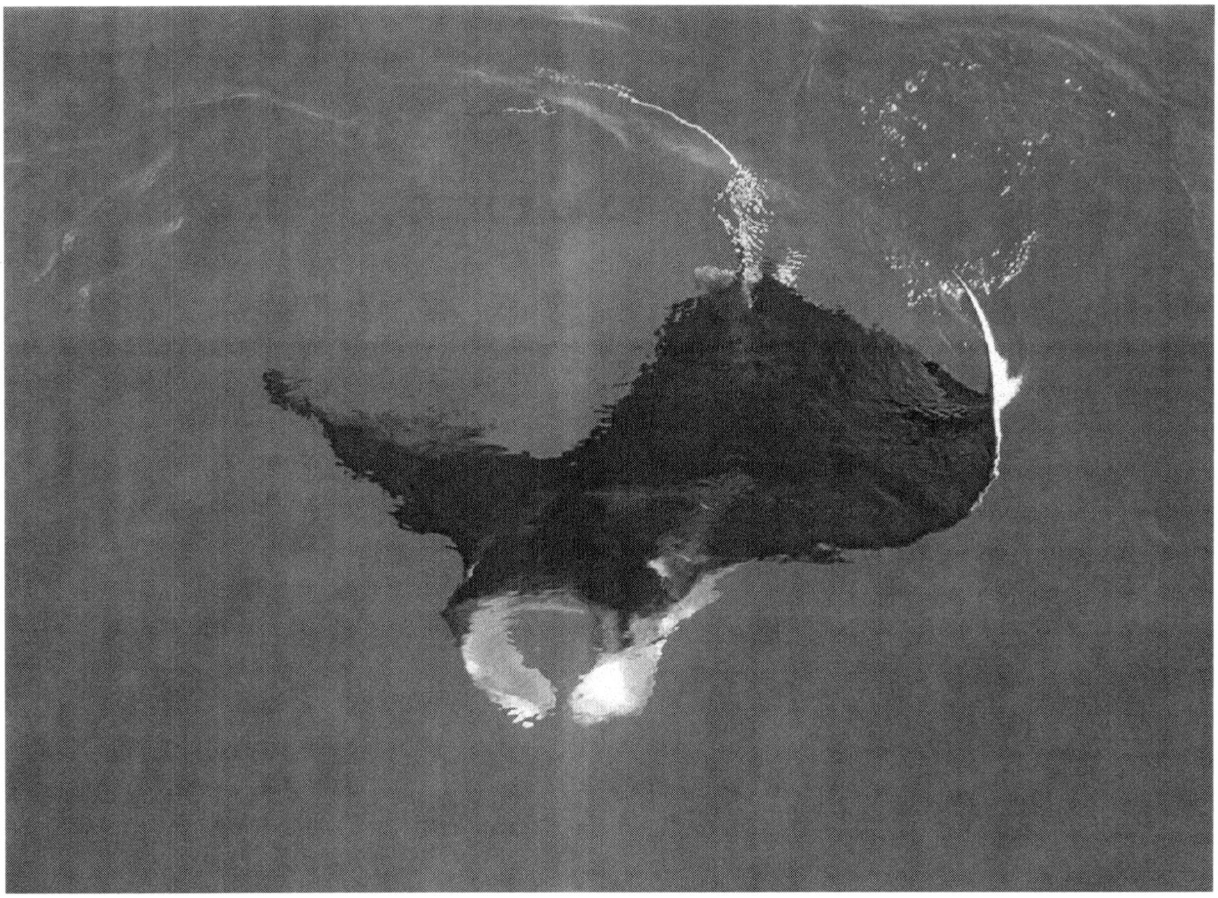

STRING RAY INVESTIGATING *OUR PLEASURE*, ILE FOUQUET, CHAGOS

Chapter 21

CHAGOS TO MAYOTTE

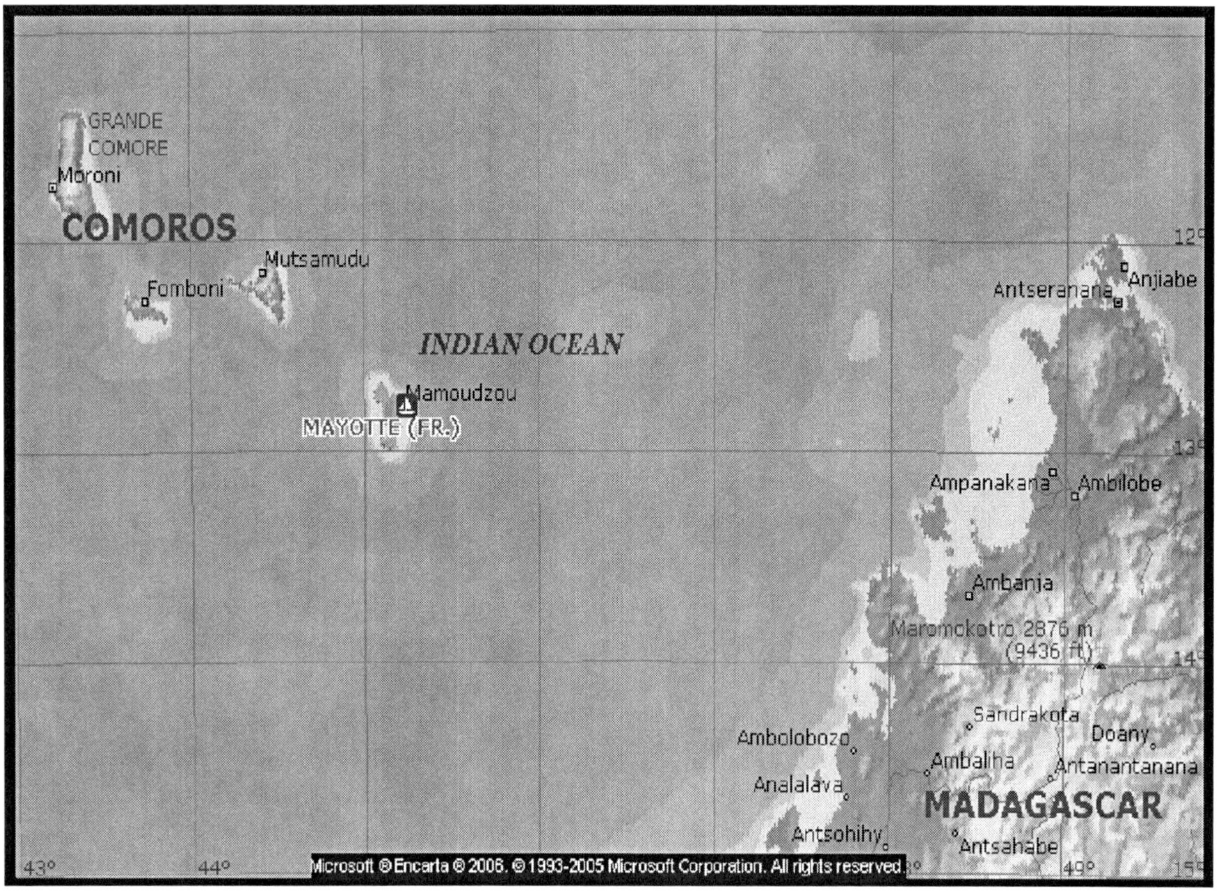

**COMOROS ISLANDS (Independent); MAYOTTE (French)
AND MADAGASCAR (Independent Republic) 9.19.2003**

The first four days we encountered light winds and only made a total of 416 NM. The Indian Ocean seas had been uncomfortable for us. The waves had two major components; one large swell always came from the southwest while the other was generated by the trade winds from the southeast. These two systems mix resulting in waves with no regular symmetry. The resulting waves can be larger or smaller than either of the two major wave systems. Sometimes they hit us head-on, sometimes on the beam and sometimes on the stern. Everyone describes them as lumpy because their pattern is so random. In light winds these waves cause the sails to dump their wind, while causing the main sail and genoa to snap hard enough to rattle the rigging. When the sails snap, the rigging will rattle loudly. The usual counter measure is to reduce the sail area to minimize stress on the system. Of course, reducing sail results in slowing the boat speed, so we go around in circles trying to minimize the effect of lumpy seas.

Sailing this route to Mayotte we encountered the most sea birds trying to hitch rides at night of any previous sailing route. It may have some relationship to the number of fish in these waters as we passed by some areas of large shallow sea-banks. Almost every night a number of boobies would try to land somewhere on the boat. If they landed on top of the mast they could not be dislodged by loud noises like the air horn, nor lights like spotlights or the masthead strobe light. Sometimes the mast would move through twenty-degree arcs, but no matter, they would stick like they were glued down. One morning I turned to look over the stern at the sunrise and to my amazement, there were three boobies sitting on top of my white dinghy cover. They were chattering away with each other, grooming themselves and looking contented. Of course, they had left their little calling cards all over my nice clean white dinghy cover. They looked so surprised at me when I shooed them off, like what did I do? Washing the vinyl cover immediately seemed to do the trick.

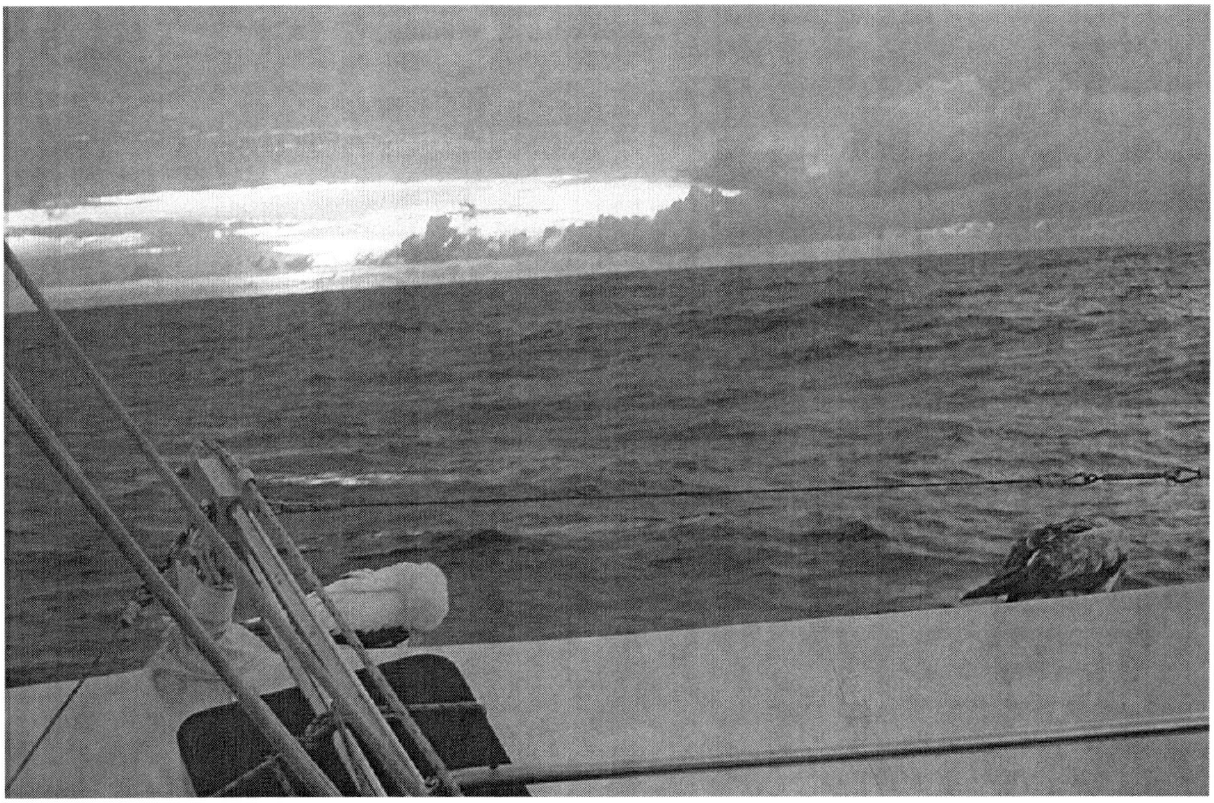

SEABIRDS HITCH AN ALL NIGHT RIDE TO MAYOTTE ON THE DINGHY

One night a booby hitched a ride on our stainless railing and a big black sea bird landed on our small diameter lifeline. The bird on the railing had a good chance of hanging on and he did, but the small diameter lifeline, no way. Well, to my amazement, this bird wrapped his webbed feet around the lifeline, tucked his head over his back between his wings and went to sleep. His tail feathers were continually moving up and down to maintain his balance when the boat heeled, so how he managed to sleep there all night is a real mystery. The boobies, however, do not look like they sleep as their eyes are open and they are always looking around. The birds provided a nice diversion as sometimes they would miss-judge landing on a mast spreader, hit the rigging wire and splash down in the ocean. Some of them will peck away at the instruments at the masthead like the wind vane or anemometer — not good. On this leg, one of the birds managed to destroy our wind direction device that provides a visual aid for wind direction — the nearest replacement, South Africa.

By Sept. 11, our fifth day from Chagos, the wind picked up and we were now making 143 mile days. The outside temperature remained consistent at close to 83° F and the humidity was similarly consistent at 80%. Harald managed to hook a beautiful yellow fin tuna probably around two and a half feet long. He was nice and round with a firm body, big eyes and beautiful coloring. While removing the bad parts we found out why flying fish were always leaping out of the water like something was chasing them. Well, they are chased by tuna because tuna eat them. This tuna had two recently caught flying fish in his stomach and three other partially digested fish. The next day the wind was blowing from the southeast at 20 knots and we were making 160 mile days.

On Sept. 14, Harald noticed the pin holding the mizzen boom to the mast was working its way out. We were doing 7.2 knots at the time so parting of the boom from the mast with the sail up would have spelled disaster. We furled the sail into the boom, maintained our sailing speed and rigged up a tackle system to the boom using the mizzen halyard. We had to put a piece of plywood between the dodger frame and the vinyl dodger so Harald could work without fear of falling through the dodger. The aluminum-furling boom is quite heavy so it took a lot of difficult maneuvering to align everything to reseat the pin. Apparently, the cotter pin that holds the pin in place had worked its way loose or had not been installed. Anyway, we managed to correct the fault in time, put the mizzen back up and we were back in our groove.

The wind was gradually increasing the next few days until Sept. 16 when the wind was consistently 30 knots with peak gusts to 46 knots. The waves were responding to the increase in wind velocity with big waves around 12 feet. ***Our Pleasure*** was doing 7 to 8 knots with all sails slightly reefed. The NOAA wind predictions for this area did not show any winds over 20 knots, but we are used to predictions on the low side. We were closing on the tip of Madagascar's Cape D'Ambre that we had planned to miss by 50 offshore miles. The evening of the Sept. 16, the wind was a consistent 40 to 45 knots with gusts to 55 knots, obviously affected by the land contours of Madagascar. The wind was a few degrees ahead of the beam and ***Our Pleasure*** was doing 9 knots. The sails had one reef in the mizzen, two and a half reefs in the main and about 30% of the jib out. Our twenty-four hour average, 181 nautical miles, a new high for this leg.

The wind completely disappeared by 4 p.m. on Sept. 17. We motored slowly the next two days to time our entrance for sunrise into Mayotte's north pass. Our anchor was down and set by 9:22 a.m., Sept. 19, 2003 close to *Gryphon* and *Allons'y*. Lena, from *Allons'y*, bless her heart, helped us to clear in with the French authorities. She speaks French (I wish I had paid more attention to French in high school) and knew where all their offices were located.

The next problem was getting Harald back to Australia, We thought we had lots of time, but the French bank, BFC on Mayotte, slowed us down to a snail's pace. Their computer was acting up and I could not get Euro dollars using my VISA credit card to pay for Harald's airfare. Harald cashed in a travelers check and that took an hour and a half to get $70 as their printer became intermittent. The teller was banging on the printer and the customer lines were getting longer and longer — some fun. By time we left the bank and taxied back to the docks we had spent two and a half hours, the day was shot and we were frustrated. We found the supermarket, but it was closed only to find out later that it opened again at 3:30 p.m. If we had waited about fifteen minutes it would have opened. The Air France agency would close tomorrow at noon (Saturday) so we had to make reservations to Australia and pay Harald for his flight to Cocos Keeling by noon the next day.

The manager at the Air France office spoke good English and worked out a good plan for Harald. The original thought was to fly to Mauritius and wait on standby for the flight to Perth, Australia. However, the flight from Mauritius to Perth flew only once a week and if he missed it he would be stuck in Mauritius for one week — not sounding good. The next choice was to fly to Reunion, Mauritius, Djibouti and Perth with an overnight stay in Djibouti. This looked like the best option since the seats could be confirmed. I paid the Euro $1,100 airfare and Harald was off to Australia on Sunday.

Monday, Serge, Pascale and their dog Kami started moving aboard ***Our Pleasure***. They had a lot more gear than I expected, diving gear, spear guns, books, charts, food in plastic jugs, cooking gear, bedding and clothes. This was after Serge talked the Mayotte, ACHM Yacht Club, into using their large shipping container for storing the gear he planned to sell. Those items included lines, rigging, the aluminum boom, mast fittings, sextant, compasses, anchor windless, fiberglass dinghy, 15 hp outboard, spare parts, tools etc. They had arranged with the yacht club to display and sell their gear at the clubs bar. The sale was set for the next weekend, Sept. 27 and 28.

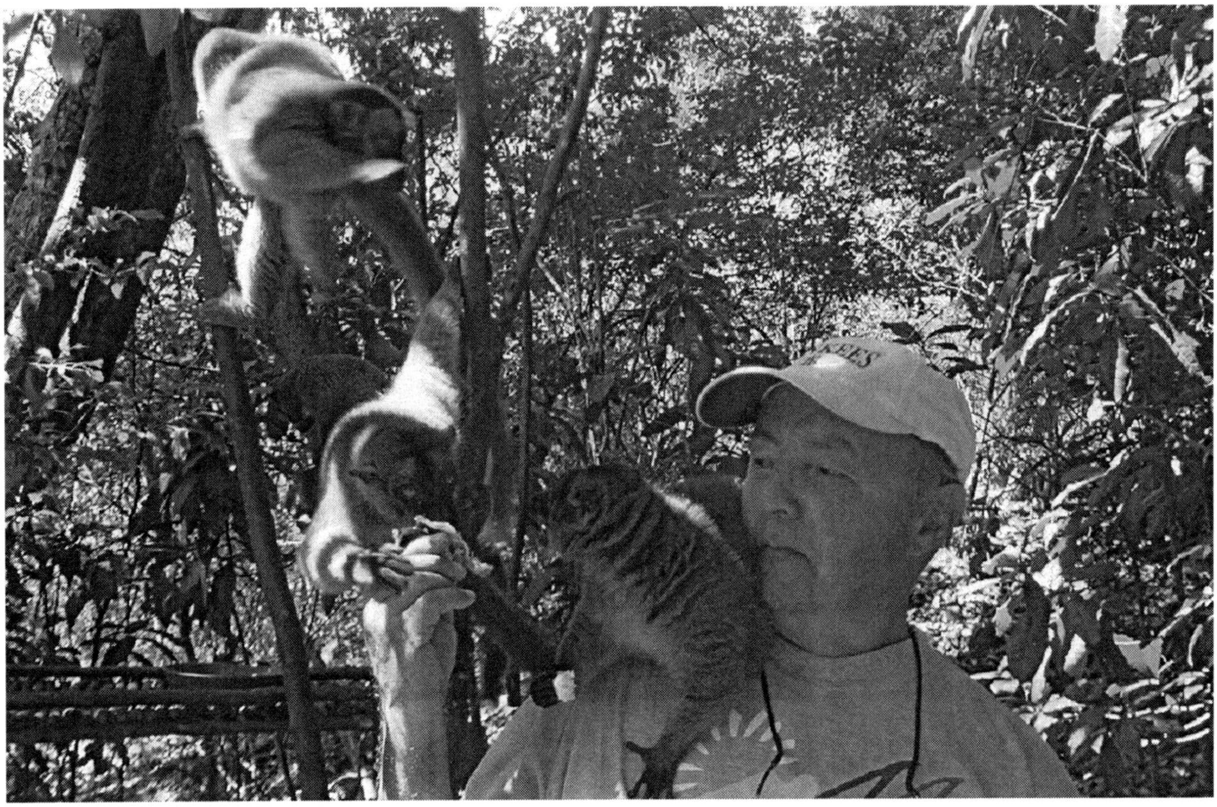

CAPTAIN DICK FEEDING LEMURS BANANAS

On Tuesday, Lena (from the yacht *Allons'y*), using her French, was able to arrange a tour of a nearby island, Ilot Bouzi. Not that it was hard to tour the island, but it was necessary to have a good knowledge of French to get information and make arrangements. The tour costs Euro $15 per person that includes a boat ride (open 20 ft dinghy with a 15 hp outboard) to the island and a conducted tour, which takes about three hours. The money goes to the association for protecting the island's fauna and safeguarding the lemur monkeys. Few people speak English on Mayotte so knowing some French was necessary. If a person knew a few hundred French words, one could do just fine. The island is home to a colony of 350 protected lemur monkeys. One dedicated French woman lives on the island, cares for them and conducts tours. She has lived there for 8 years and claims to have names for all 350 monkeys. We assumed that claim was a bit exaggerated. Walking through the colony she does call them by name to eat some banana, but seeing bananas is probably all the motivation needed to come a running. She did not speak English so the wealth of information she possesses about the monkeys would be wasted without a translator.

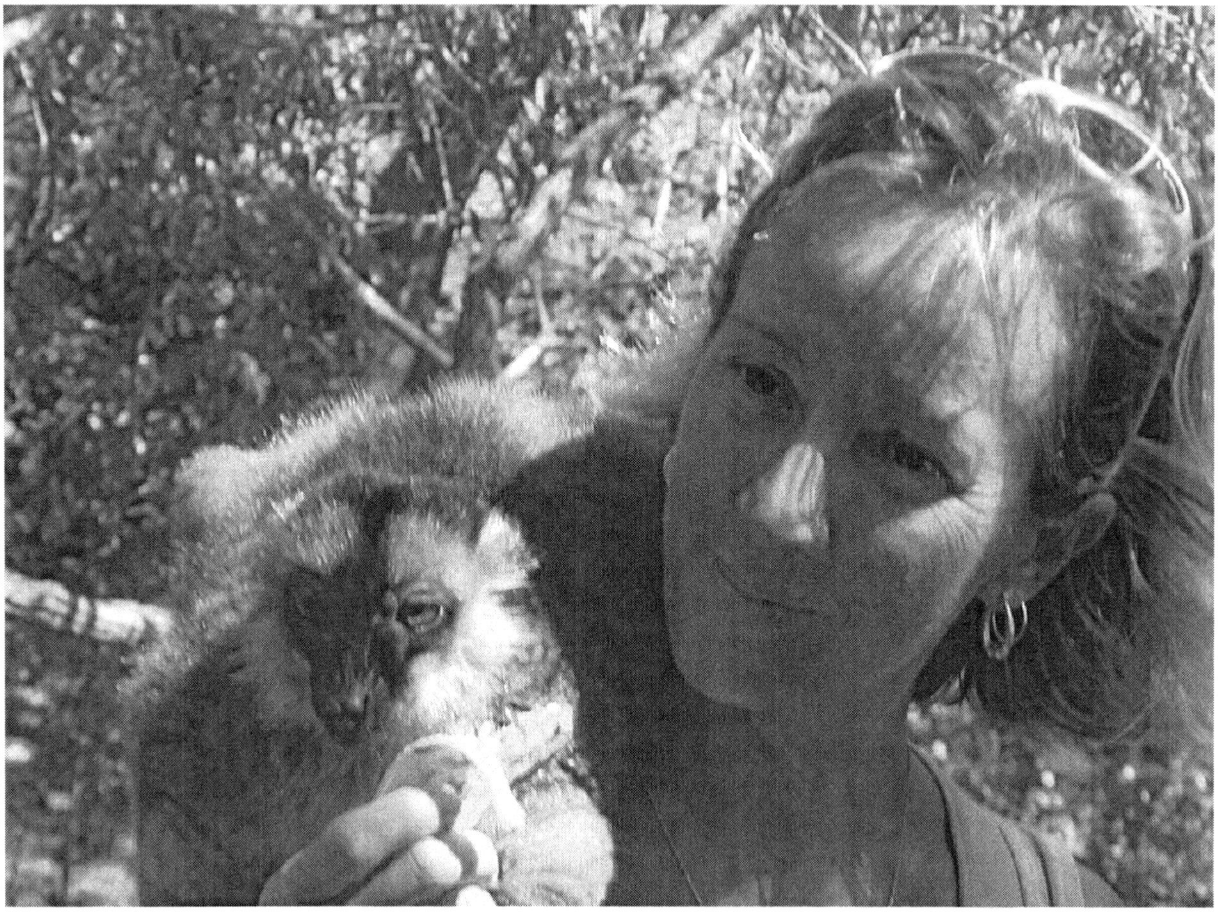

RAINE WILLIAMS, *GRYPHON*, BOSTON, MA, LEMUR AND BANANA

There are several species of the lemur monkeys living on the island, which provides them with unique variations in facial features and coloring. They were trusting, gentle and tame. They stand about 2 feet high and weigh between 6 and 7 pounds. Their faces are cute and their fur is soft like cashmere. They must have a strong grip to swing through the trees like they do, but they gently rested on our shoulders to eat hand-held bananas. They live not in family groups, but in groups that have similar dispositions — I thought that fact rather unusual. At one time, they lived all over Mayotte to the extent of around 50,000 of them. Originally, the monkeys were often seen around cemeteries and the natives thought they were safeguarding their relatives and protected the monkeys. However, as situations changed, the natives started eating them and their numbers dwindled. They do not have any predators on the island now except for large birds that may go after a baby separated from its mother. The babies were seen wrapped around their mother's stomach and holding on with great tenacity as the mother swings through the trees.

Wednesday, Serge and Pascale announced that there plan to buy and restore an old trawler in South Africa was ill conceived. With only $20,000 to spend on purchasing, repair and outfitting for the trip across the Atlantic to French Guiana, they realized their plan was destined for failure. I was disappointed at first and felt dismayed at the turnover of crew on this cruise. However, I always had doubts about their plan and knew it made good sense for them to find work and start over with sufficient funds in hand. A good job with steady income for a couple of years was really what they needed. Pascale did have a job waiting for her in French Guiana teaching high school sports; she just had to get there. At one time, she had been a woman's handball champion in France so this job was right up her alley. A kind French soul provided them with an interim boat so they could move off ***Our Pleasure***. Actually, it was considerate of them to give back my privacy so I could look for crew. I am sure I was suffering a little mental stress over the thought of a dog living aboard ***Our Pleasure*** on long passages.

Their dog Kami seemed to be quite smart and well behaved, but he was shedding hair in huge quantities all over the place. Other unwanted attributes, Kami had flees and worms. I saw further problems at sea because he would be doing his business on my nice clean teak deck — yuck. Serge did not allow him inside the boat, but with the companionway open, his hair managed to blow inside. They vacuumed every morning and washed the deck off, but of course some hair managed to avoid all efforts of removal. Also, both Serge and Pascale smoked frequently, which was annoying.

Anyway, they did move off on Thursday and I had the boat to myself once more. Their final sale of salvaged goods at the yacht club was a success in that it paid their airfare to Paris where Pascale's parents lived. Following a short visit in Paris, they would fly on to French Guiana. They took their now hairless dog, flees, worms, tobacco and left Mayotte on Tuesday of the following week — actually, I was relieved to know there was a God, now if He would just help me find a good crew.

The French phone system is something else. They do not want competition because I could not find a phone card that would discount international calls. Their phone cards that cost Euro $6.20 would last about 3 minutes when I called Pat in Seattle. You get enough time to say, "Hello, how are you?" and the phone connection dies. There is no warning or no chance to insert another card, just silence. Raine suggested I call Pat using the phone card and quickly have her call me back in the phone booth. Well, there is only one booth in town with its phone number stenciled on the inside of the booth. That booth is in better repair because it is just outside the entrance to the French Foreign Legion gate, offering some protection in the evening.

If you make any calls at night you have to bring a flashlight as the booth lights are missing, probably stolen along with the door and one window. It took Pat and me several phone calls to figure out that incoming calls do not ring in the booth. Instead, if you can read French, the tiny display announces in French that someone is calling that number. One more problem, the international code for Mayotte is 269, but that number is also used in the nearby Comoros Islands. We were told that some calls may go to the Comoros by mistake, but we were lucky and I am not aware that this occurred during our calls. After working out these little details, Pat and I were actually able to carry on a decent conversation.

I found a message waiting for me on the bulletin board at the end of the dock on Friday. A French woman, Francoise, in response to my notice "Looking for Crew," left it on the board. I had written one note card in English and Pascale had written another translated into French. Serge and Pascale had generously posted the notices in strategic locations around the city during their travels. I called the phone number Francoise listed and we had a conversation in fairly good English. We set up a meeting for Tuesday morning, 11 a.m. at the yacht club. When I got to the club, Serge, Pascale with their dog Kami were standing outside waiting for their ride to the airport so I got to say a last goodbye. After Francoise arrived, we took my dinghy out to ***Our Pleasure*** so she could see the boat, tell me about her plans and sailing background. She explained that she had two problems that required solving before she could leave Mayotte:

1. Her passport was expiring and the replacement had not arrived.
2. Her VISA card was expiring at the end of Oct. and her French bank wanted her to pick up the new card in Paris — the French are very logical.

Well, both problems were in work so I agreed we could wait a few more days hoping French mail would deliver these items in time. I am not sure, but she was probably in her late forties — not polite to ask. She is a scuba instructor so she is athletic and looked fit. The French always do things differently, so the eight dive shops in Mayotte all fed her the same stupid logic: because she was certified in the U.S. and not in France, she could not teach diving in Mayotte. This is rather absurd since France and the rest of the world use the U.S. developed PADI® system for diving instruction, procedures, regulations and safety — leave it to the French.

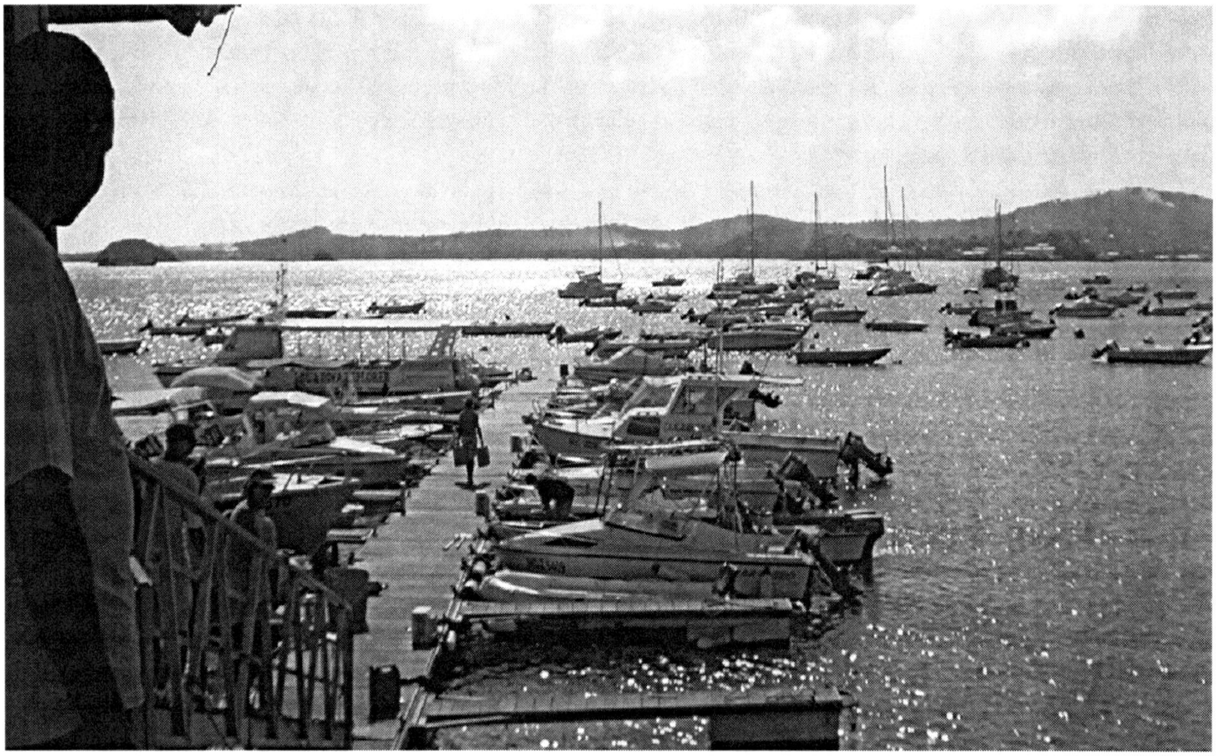

DZAOUDZI (PETITE TERRE), MAYOTTE SMALL BOAT MOORAGE

I took Father O'Duill and his new replacement, Father Andre, out to dinner after the 5:30 p.m. Mass on Saturday. He said he was anxious to speak in English for a change. I do not think he is invited out often because he said, "Bless you," when I invited him out for dinner. We went to a local restaurant and had a nice dinner with wine, desert and cappuccinos for Euro $50. It was an enjoyable evening and he had many questions about my sailing adventures. Father Andre was able to speak a little English and could follow most of our conversation. Father O'Duill is Irish and had been a priest in Mayotte for 8 years and 30 years had been spent in Africa before that. He was 66 years old at the time and said it was now time to go back to Ireland. He is so much like our Irish, family priest back in Seattle, Father Ibar. Just like Father Ibar, he greets everyone at the door of the church and hugs all the children. Because of the French culture he also gets to kiss all the women on both cheeks — something not seen in Seattle. He just finished building a new church on the main island of Mayotte in the city of Mamoudzou, which I understand is quite nice.

I attended Father O'Duill's church service on Petite Terre, conducted in the church that was one of the islands original buildings. I thought it was a rather pleasant structure with its thick, white, stucco walls and unique arch design for the windows and doorway. There was no glass in the church, which is not unusual in the tropics, instead, the windows were wood shutters and made to swing out for light and ventilation. The older of his two churches, actually belongs to the French government. Using his persuasive ways, he managed to get the government to commit funds for restoration, which the old church sorely needs. He also got the government to send 12 Catholics to Rome last year. It seems the French have been sending Muslims from Mayotte to Mecca every year so he evened the score a little. About fifty people attend Mass every Saturday at the small church with a mixture of native Catholics and French Catholics. Some of the native parishioners have moved to Mayotte from other French possessions so it is difficult to tell if they are from the native Mayotte population.

Monday, Marv, Bill and I made four trips to the fuel dock at Dzaoudzi to fill our fuel tanks. Sharing the 5 and 6-gallon jugs from the three boats we had 20 jugs. I ended up with 117 gallons at a duty free price of 43 cents per liter or Euro $191. My port tank was still about 25 gallons low, but there is enough fuel to motor to Richard's Bay, South Africa, if we do not have any wind. This is only the second time we have fueled by jugs, but it makes a good case for an electric transfer pump as moving jugs around by hand is both messy and tiring. The fuel always finds its way into the dinghy and onto our deck.

Some yachts do tie up alongside the stonewalled fuel dock and a long fuel hose is available to reach their tanks. That method will work at high tide with lots of fenders assuming your boat does not stick out into the nearby ferry landing. There cannot be a swell running at the time and someone familiar with the operation must throw you docking lines from the two bollards available along the wall. The attendant only speaks French, hands the hose down to the boat and does not do any line tying. We were lucky that Julia on *Endurance* spoke French well enough to organize the language parts needing interpretation. We were now in good shape for leaving except for the last minute veggies and crew.

On Thursday Marv, Chieko and I decided to try the new Cora Mall at the capital city of Grand Terre Mamoudzou. It required a ferry ride to the main island and a taxi to the mall through some poor sections of the town. The Cora supermarket is similar to K-Mart as it carries a large variety of food, clothes, outdoor furniture and hardware. The selection of French cheeses, meats, wines, and etc., was impressive. However, almost everything is imported except for eggs, potatoes, onions and some veggies. I have not seen any fresh milk, only long life types. There is a nice coffee shop and patisserie in the mall along with several stores selling good quality clothes.

Chieko showed me a nice jewelry store and I found Pat a gold charm to add to her charm bracelet. It is a map outline of the island of Mayotte with some gold filigree that highlights the edging. Her bracelet is rather heavy now with charms from all the countries we have stopped at that have jewelry stores. We stopped at the patisserie and had the best cappuccinos and pastry in all of Mayotte. The patisserie even has an electronic flycatcher, proving that some people are doing something about the flies. The taxi back to the ferry terminal takes about twenty minutes. The route has many commercial buildings mostly in disrepair, but the hovels some people live in are so dirty, very sad. Most islands we visited, where the population was poor, the people were neat and their homes were clean and cared for. Here, there is garbage strewn in front of the shacks like they opened a window and threw it out. The homes are thrown together with bits of rusty sheet metal and old lumber pieces — no pride.

The general, "I do not care attitude," of the natives about their garbage and homes makes large areas of this city ugly and full of flies. I have been told this is the slack season for flies; it gets worse during the rainy season. Mayotte is the dirtiest of any of the French cities I have ever seen. Every other French city we have stopped at has been neat and clean. It must be the local native Muslim population that takes the cities of Mayotte to such poor extremes. I also get the impression the natives do not like foreigners or the French, as the few that have been friendly, can be counted on one hand. In Fiji for example, you could not pass by a native without a friendly greeting, here they look the other way.

The three major islands of the Comoros and Mayotte belonged to France all the way back to 1912 when they were looking for a naval base. Some of the islanders wanted to be independent of France and the islanders cast their votes in 1974. Mayotte stayed with France — I bet the French have regretted that decision. The other Comoros Islands: Grand Comore, Mohéli and Anjouan voted to be independent — huge mistake. The economy of those islands is in shambles and most of their natives try to immigrate to Mayotte to find work. The mostly Muslim population of Mayotte is close to 200,000 and they live on 150 square miles.

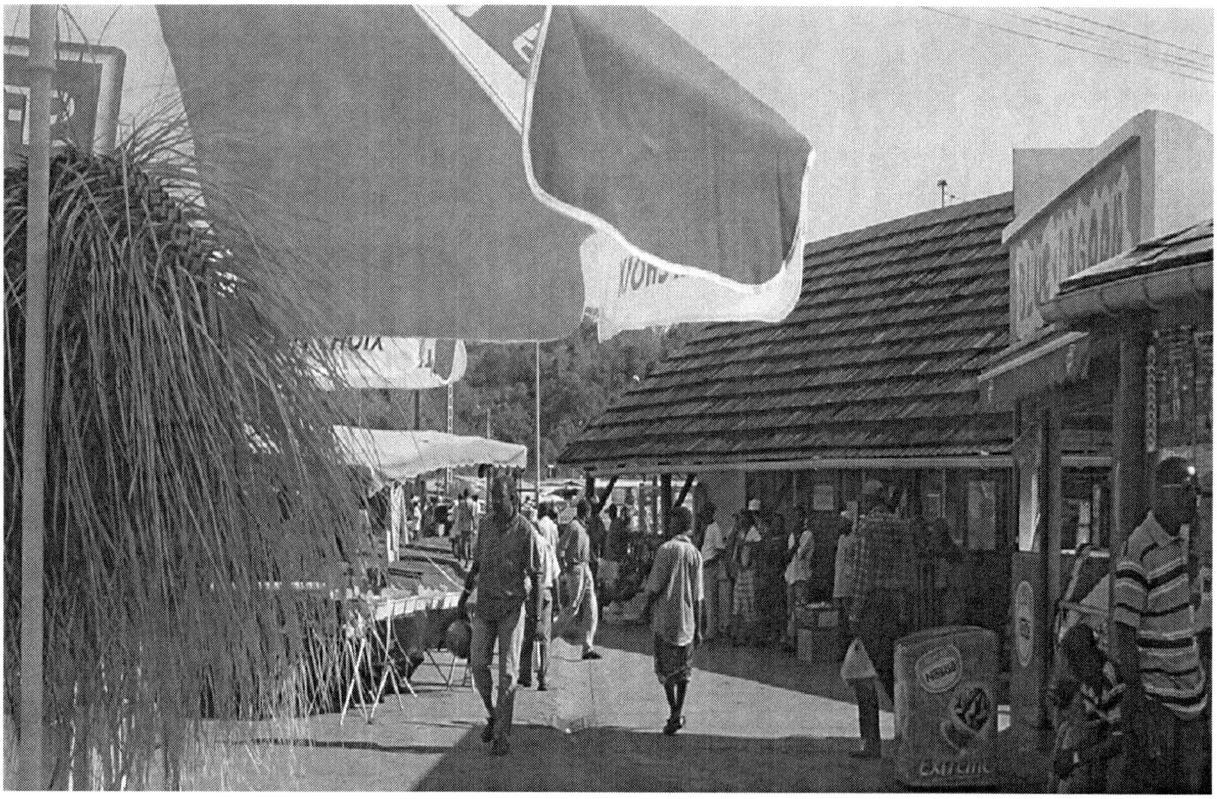

CAPITAL CITY OF MAMOUDZOU, GRAND TERRE, MAYOTTE

The natives are called Mahorais and speak a language called Shimahore mixed with some words barrowed from immigrants that came from the nearby island of Madagascar. Only about two percent of the population is Roman Catholic, mostly people from the French occupation. The people depend on subsistence farming, fishing and France, which is obviously subsidizing the economy. The *Gryphon* folks stopped at Anjouan, Comoros before Mayotte and ran into many problems with corrupt officialdom. The officials were hostile and tried to plunder $100 from them just to anchor in the bay. They said they wouldn't pay such exorbitant fees and were threatened with reprisal. *Gryphon* left, but they were afraid of being followed by the Comoros navy or customs, which never happened.

The usual temperature in the afternoon here is always around 86° F and the summer season has not started yet. The skies are sunny all day long, no rain and the breeze non-existent. At night, the temperature dips as low as 78° F. The usual clothing worn on the boats is bathing suits or thin cotton clothing. Inside a boat you can forget about underwear, shoes or hats. In this heat with its accompanying high humidity, even watchbands and belts are uncomfortable.

I was invited to *Endurance* in the afternoon for happy hour. Marv wanted me to try some of the cinnamon aged rum he bought in Madagascar. I think he said he paid about $1.50 for a liter and you bring your own bottle to the rum factory. This is potent stuff at 105 proof so a little goes a long way. I thought it tasted good and so did everyone else who tasted it. He also had some different French cheeses that we tasted. After happy hour, we took a dinghy ride into the dock where we bought some pizza from a truck that bakes pizzas in the ferry parking lot. This pizza took the prize for thin crusts. It was so thin that three minutes took care of the baking — electricity must be expensive. They did not go overboard with the toppings either, but the overall taste was good. The cost of a large pizza was only 8 Euros — I couldn't complain too much. We carried them back to ***Our Pleasure*** and had a nice leisurely pizza party in the cockpit.

On Oct. 10, the yacht club hosted a blues concert featuring two German yachties that are long time cruisers. Stan played the electronic keyboard and wife Cora, played a vibrant tenor sax. There was extra support from an electric guitarist and an occasional harmonica player. Everyone was tapping their feet, clapping their hands and really getting into this couples fine renditions of blues music. The enthusiasm of the 75 people or so really sparked the musicians to give it their all. Stan and Cora support their cruising by playing jazz, usually at restaurants along the way. I heard they have been at it for 23 years. They started playing at the yacht club around 7 p.m., which is late enough for all the flies to go to sleep.

Mayotte flies seem to be especially drawn to the yacht club during the day and will fly into any beer bottle or beer can that goes unprotected — yum, yum. Eating a sandwich at the club with one hand and keeping the flies at bay with the other is a real challenge. I met one of my new crewmembers that night, Francois. He is a young chemical engineer of 28 looking for a sail back to his home country, South Africa. He had been crewing with Stan and Cora while they were in Madagascar and wanted to go to Richard's Bay, South Africa. It seems Francois was thinking about changing his profession and work his way into chartering or professional crew aboard mega yachts. He had paid a lot of money to go through a sailing school at a South African academy that teaches all aspects of sailing. The academy provides its graduates with certificates and licenses for different levels of boating up to "Master of Large Yachts." He had finished their coastal navigation course and was obtaining sea miles to meet the academy's requirements for the next level of courses. Marv had met Francois while cruising in Madagascar and had told him about me needing crew to South Africa so it became a done deal. Francois moved aboard two days later to get familiar with ***Our Pleasure***.

The next day Francoise called me on the VHF radio to say she expected her passport in Thursday's mail and the French bank was sending her VISA card to the bank in Mayotte. So it sounded like everything was coming together on schedule. We all made one last trip to the fuel dock to top off the fuel used between the last fillings and to fill all fuel jugs. It seemed to me we were going a bit over the top on fuel supplies, but there is a real concern for running into strong head winds in the Mozambique Channel. Headwinds with big accompanying waves are quite a reality on this leg as well as having no wind for the 1,500 miles.

On Wednesday, Oct. 15, the wind was perfect for going south and was predicted to stay that way for at least four days. *Endurance* and *Esprit* left the Mayotte anchorage about 9 a.m., headed out the south pass and pointed their boats directly towards Richard's Bay, South Africa. Needless to say I was disappointed that I was not leaving with them, but thought Françoise's paper work would be ready by Friday. When I talked to Francoise on Friday, she was sadly disappointed that none of her paperwork had made it to Mayotte. I told her that it looked as though good winds would last for probably two more days. We agreed I should not wait any longer since there was no real way to tell when her paperwork would actually show up.

Disappointed about not having a third crewmember, Francois and I left Mayotte without Francoise on Saturday, Oct. 18. As we were leaving the harbor, Francoise managed to get to a VHF radio to wish us luck on our journey and apologize for holding us up. At first, I did not realize she was calling me, as she didn't use the normal VHF protocol of calling the ship's name, in this case, ***Our Pleasure***. Instead, she called me by my first name in her cute English with a French accent. Her pronunciation of Dick became Deeek, which she said several times before I finally woke up. We said our friendly "farewells and good lucks." Several of my friends also heard her calling me and have kidded me ever since. I think I now have a new nickname. We cleared the harbor around 10:30 a.m.

Chapter 22

MAYOTTE TO RICHARD'S BAY, SOUTH AFRICA

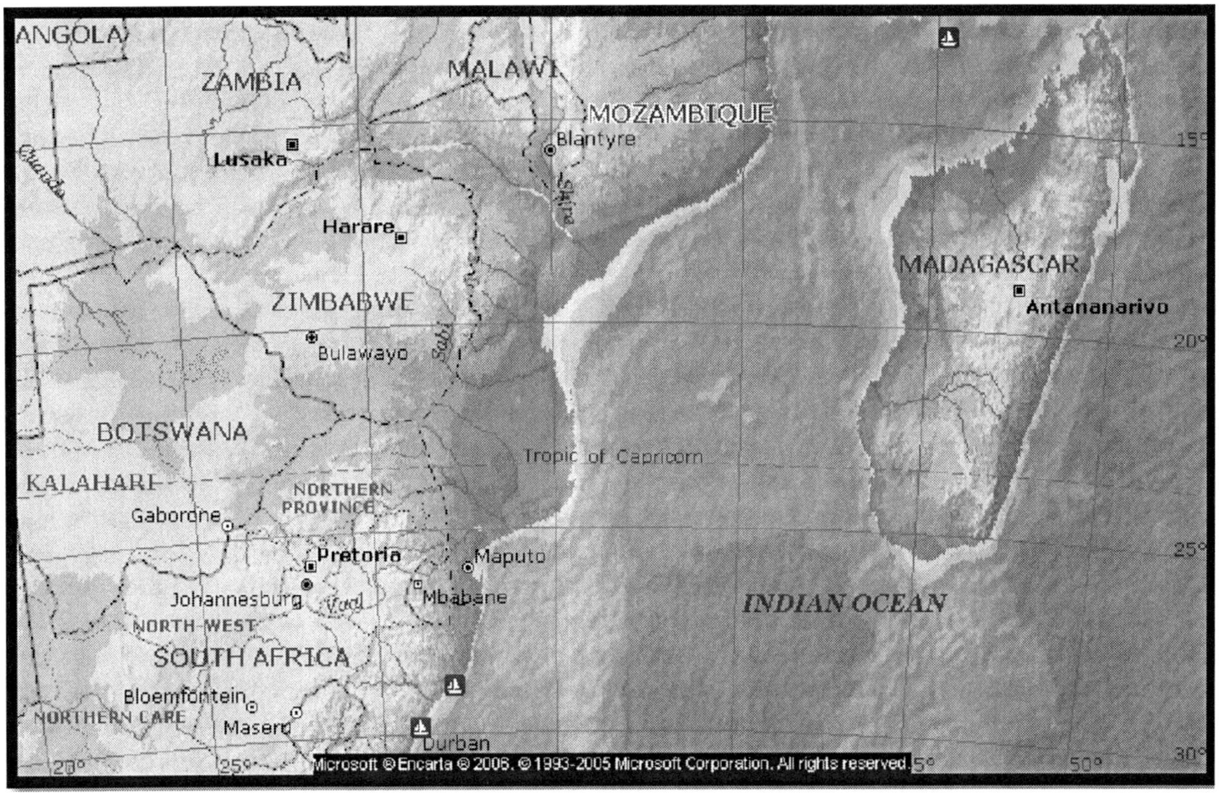

RICHARD'S BAY ON SOUTH AFRICA'S EAST COAST JUST NORTH OF DURBAN

Sailing during our first day since leaving Mayotte, Oct. 18, 2003, we experienced good weather with calm seas and about 15 knots of wind on our port quarter. However, late in the afternoon of Oct. 19, the wind dropped to 5 knots, but with favorable current, we were able to make 4 knots. We could see a pattern of light winds developing and they did. The wind on Oct. 20 blew from a good direction, but was still only 6 knots, not enough to move a heavy boat like ***Our Pleasure***. We found there was a counter current running at one knot against us now and we had to motor to make headway towards Richard's Bay. The barometer was holding steady 1019 millibars and the sun was heating up our interior to 87° F while the outside temperature was 82° F.

We started seeing large ships now plying up and down the sea-lanes between Mozambique and Madagascar, in the Mozambique Channel. These big guys were tankers, freighters and container ships. They usually gave us a few miles of sea room when passing. For the most part, they were considerate and changed their course allowing us to maintain our sailing course. They always have the right of way, but I think the more experienced of the captains realize that a short-handed sailboat crew might not have detected them. Also, anyone who has sailed before knows that changing course while under sail in heavy winds can be difficult. In light winds sailboats have a lot more flexibility for jibing or reefing sails quickly. If the genny is poled out with a preventer on the boom and there is only one crewmember on watch, sail changes in strong winds are challenging and time consuming.

On average, cruising sailboats are manned by two persons, usually a husband and wife team. Sometimes at night, big ships could be seen altering course if they were coming up from behind or coming towards us. That usually happened at around 8 miles where the angle between the high, white bow light and port or starboard navigation lights can be seen changing. Every now and then, a ship would pass quite close causing us some concern until we were sure his course was not coincident with ours. If my course is close to theirs I use my horn signals to indicate which side I intend to pass on. My air horn uses compressed carbon dioxide and sounds like the Queen Mary. However, I have yet to hear a ship answer my horn signals. I am not sure why they go unanswered as the international rules state that they respond in agreement or disagree with a different passing signal. One ship did respond by VHF radio, that he intended to pass on a side different from my horn signal. Another ship abruptly changed course as if I had woken the helmsman from a nap.

Our radar has a system that will sound a loud alarm if an intruding ship slips into an electronic boundary, which we program into the radar. This alarm can be time activated at predetermined intervals or can be run continuously. We always use the alarm system with the intrusion distance set for 8 miles and automatic scanning every 10 minutes. Big steel ships will always show up on our radar screen at that distance and trigger the alarm. It has been my experience that small ships radars do not have the power to detect boats constructed of wood or fiberglass until they are between 2 to 4 miles away even if the boats have a radar reflector. If the sea state is wild with big waves and my boat is rolling, the system will usually not reliably indicate the presence of another boat at long distances. Big waves can trigger the alarm or an approaching squall will also trigger the alarm. In general, the radar system works well, but the bottom line always rests with the person on watch to make the right call.

The next several days were pretty much the same with light winds and low 24 hour distances of around 100 miles. We relied heavily on the engine to keep us going in the right direction. On Oct. 21, we established a new record for ship sightings at 6. It was unusual to see that many big ships in one 24 hour period. Clear skies and lots of sun was making the days pleasant even though we had to listen to the dull, throaty sounds of the Diesel engine. The current in the Mozambique Channel is unusual in that one-day we may have 2 knots with us, but the next day, 1 knot against us. Besides the helping and hindering currents, there is a major current component always pushing us west towards Africa. To overcome this strong current we normally had to steer 30° away from our rhumb line course.

Most days the sea state could be labeled as moderate, but we ran into some unusual swells on Oct. 21. We had been motoring with 2 knots of positive current helping us to make 6 knots with little or no wind. For no apparent reason we ran into huge waves on our port side ranging from 9 to 12 feet in height. They started out unnoticed, but gradually built up during the day. They rolled the boat as they passed underneath us making the ride uncomfortable as all get out. These uncomfortable conditions lasted for close to 18 hours. What actually drove these big waves was a mystery to me since there was no wind to drive them, they must have received their energy from adverse currents or a distant storm.

For the next few days we did a lot of motoring in light winds. At 5 a.m. on the 27th — just 120 miles from Maputo, Mozambique — the wind from the southeast started howling. The 40 knot plus winds were driving big

9 to 12 foot seas just a few degrees ahead of our port beam. Boat motion was so uncomfortable that working in the galley or eating for that matter, was avoided. However, with the boat speed averaging around 7.5 knots, the sea miles were ticking right along. Late that afternoon the wind moderated between 30 and 35 knots. Francois managed to hang on with one hand while cooking some bacon and eggs with the other hand. This condition was caused by a low-pressure system moving up the east coast of South Africa, a common occurrence in this part of the world. The next 2 days the wind moderated, but with help from the east coast positive current, we managed to keep our average speed at 7 knots.

Just 30 miles from Richard's Bay on Oct. 29, the winds started blowing 35 to 40 knots again with ***Our Pleasure*** responding with increased boat speed. We managed to squeeze by the sterns of two big freighters moving south along the east coast. With our speed at 7.5 knots and theirs about 12 knots it was hard to judge just how close we would pass. Our courses were perpendicular to each other at that point. I talked to both captains to make sure they thought we would pass with good clearance. They were both very polite, said they appreciated the call and said they had started to change course slightly to give us more room to pass. I changed our course to point into the wind as high as I could, which slowed us down slightly and provided a better visual sense of our course past their sterns. We were thankful that they helped us out, which they were not obligated to do since they had the right-of-way.

Those sea conditions and winds made it difficult to make big course changes. The best alternative would have been to turn south and run with the wind until they were past, but then we would have been faced with beating to windward to get back those lost miles. In the wind and sea conditions at the time, beating to windward would have meant running the engine hard and driving the bow into big waves. Instead of making 7.5 knots toward our course we would be reduced to 2.5 knots with the bow crashing into each wave — not much fun.

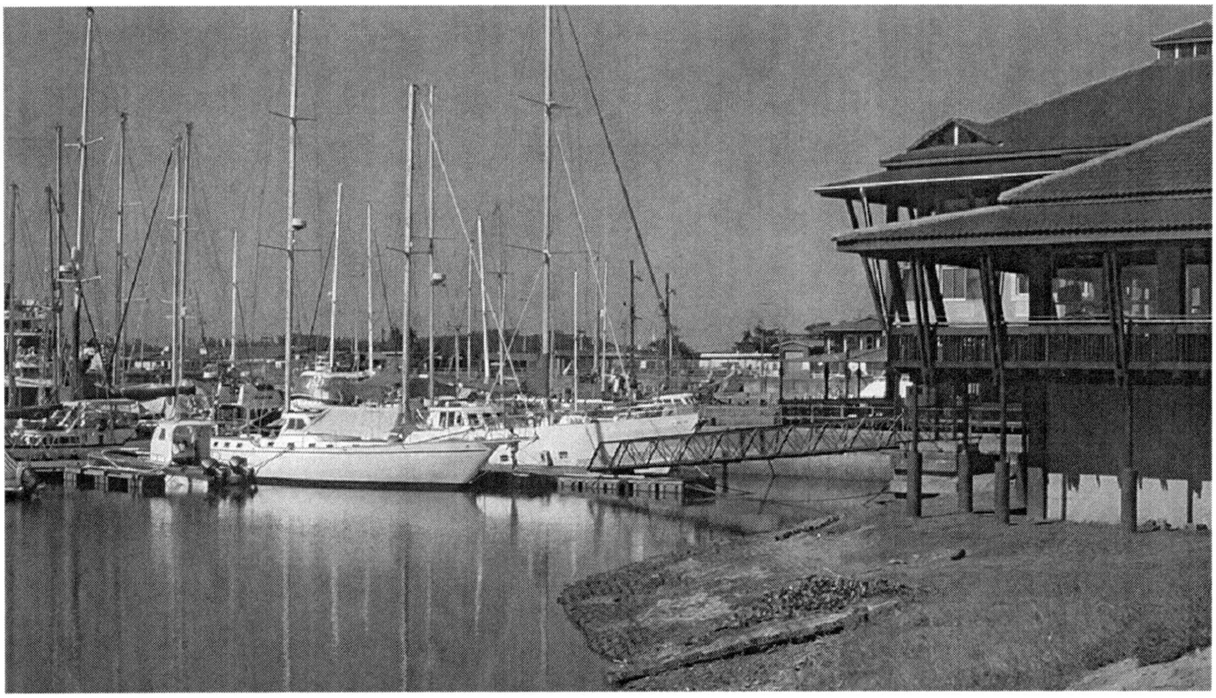

TUZI GAZI MARINA, RICHARD'S BAY, SOUTH AFRICA

We arrived at Richard's Bay entrance at 11 a.m. and were securely tied to our dock by 3 p.m. We were in radio contact with Marv on *Endurance* every day and by VHF radio when we were 10 miles off. Therefore, on arrival at the Tuzi Gazi Marina several cruising friends were waiting to catch our dock lines. Cruising with friends is always helpful when coming into a new area and especially here, where space is tight. The marina had not been designed to maneuver a sailboat our size. Francois stayed on the boat for 6 days to help get her cleaned up before he went off to visit his family near Durban, South Africa.

Pat flew into Richard's Bay on Nov. 9 from Seattle and instead of going directly to ***Our Pleasure*** I took her to the Ridge Hotel. The Ridge Hotel is high on a hill and overlooks the ocean and all the shipping activity on Richard's Bay. The hotel was once the family home for the Richard's family, the original settlers in this territory. Our room was perfect for Pat to rest after her long flight from Seattle (flight time about 20 hours, in two days) and for us to catch up after almost 6 months of separation.

Richard's Bay is one of the world's largest coal shipping ports so there is a constant movement of big freighters to watch. The down side is the small coal dust particles that land on the deck when the wind direction is from the southwest. The food and service at the hotel were truly outstanding and we both agreed the hotel was a fitting start to our time together in beautiful South Africa. After staying 3 nights at the hotel, we moved back aboard ***Our Pleasure***. Next, we rented a car and traveled about 80 miles to Mkuze Falls a private game reserve and the highlight of our time together in South Africa. Mkuze Falls is a 50,000 acre, five stars, private game reserve situated between Durban and the Kruger National Park.

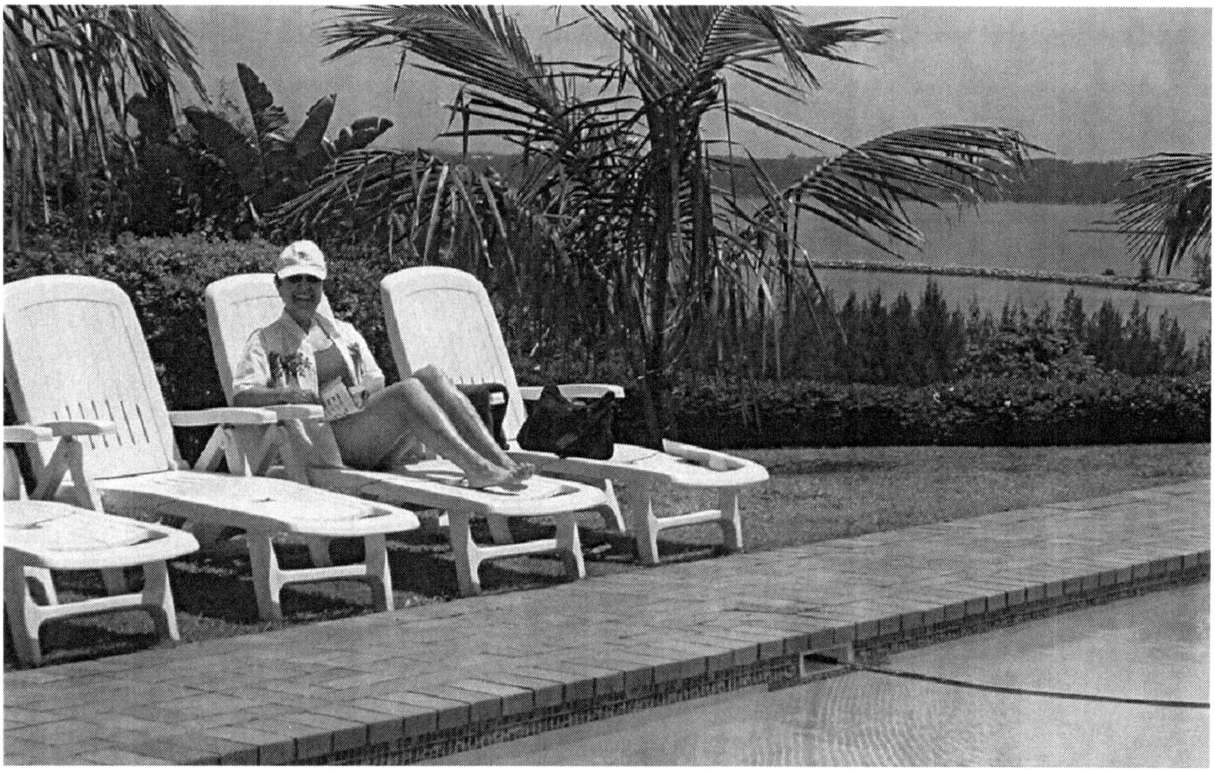

PAT RELAXING BY THE RIDGE HOTEL POOL, RICHARD'S BAY, SOUTH AFRICA

In between Richard's Bay and Mkuze Falls is a Zulu craft village called "Ilala Weavers." The village is really a Zulu cultural museum, restaurant and gallery. Their claim-to-fame is the largest collection of traditional Zulu baskets in the world. The gallery also features collector items of antique Zulu beadwork, woodcarvings, hand printed fabrics and woven rugs. The Zulu artwork and craftsmen's ship turned out to be an unexpected source of delight. Initially we thought Ilala Weavers would be a tourist trap of typical knick-knacks that no one would ever spend good money on. Boy were we wrong, we were truly amazed to see so many high quality items of Zulu culture on display. Looking at so many baskets and artifacts takes a long time, so much so, we worried about missing the welcoming high tea at Mkuze Lodge. I am sure I have never seen Pat shop that fast. Realizing we had little time remaining to arrive at the lodge on time, she managed to look at almost everything in under two hours. Of course, the remaining space in our little rental car became filled with baskets, artwork and other purchases. The high level of artwork among the Zulu people is quite extraordinary. One of the baskets, now in our home, is called a "beer basket" because the weave is so tight it will hold beer — I'm inclined to believe the claim without attempting to disprove it. The stone and woodcarvings of people's faces and all of Africa's animals are of superior quality. In our travels, we have seen many good examples of carvings and woven baskets, but the African examples are the best we have seen anywhere.

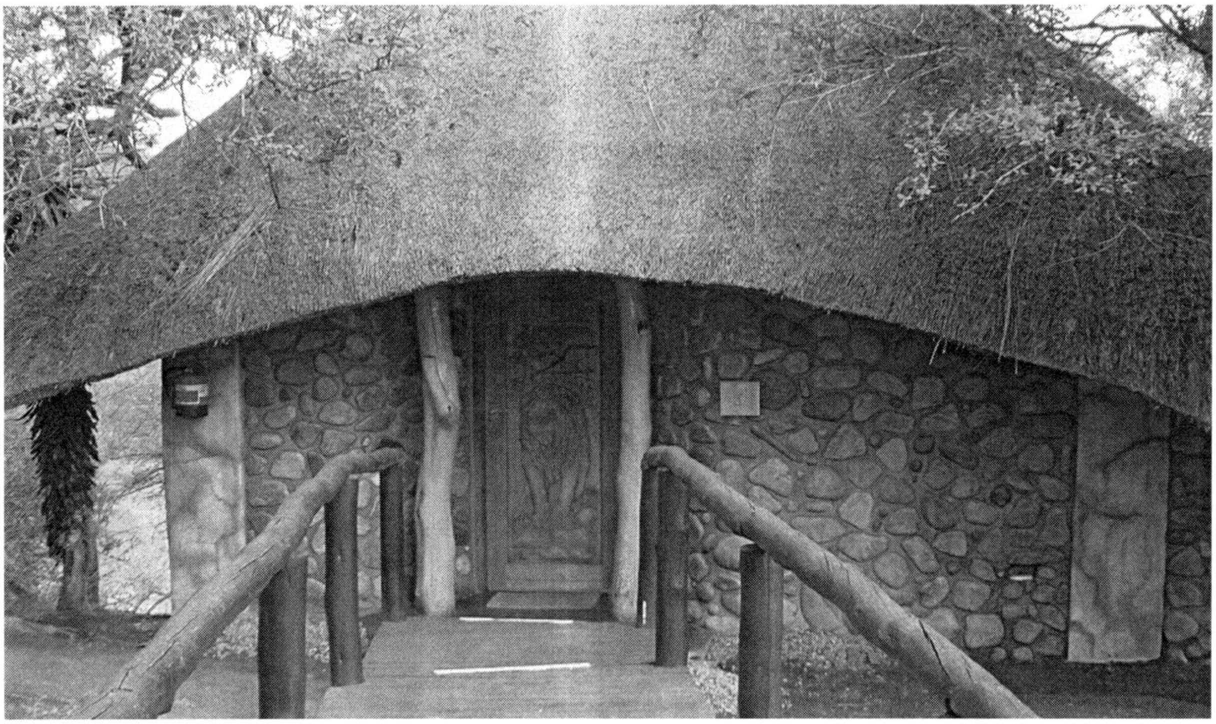

ENTRANCE TO OUR CHALET, MKUZE FALLS GAME RESERVE, SOUTH AFRICA

At the lodge, we were treated like royalty as our accommodations were in a luxurious chalet with spectacular views of the Mkuze River and the Mkuze Falls. The chalet was so nice and comfortable we thought about forgoing the tours just to enjoy the sights from our private terrace. Each of the lodge's chalets is secluded for privacy with beautiful African decor and furnishings. The roofs are thatched Zulu style to about eight inches thick. Each of the eight spacious chalets feature a large king-sized bed and a headboard outlined with simulated elephant's tusks.

Each night on returning from dinner, we found the bath drawn, a sheer lace curtain drawn around the bed and rose petals decorated our bed. White chocolates in fancy decorated boxes were on each of our nightstands.

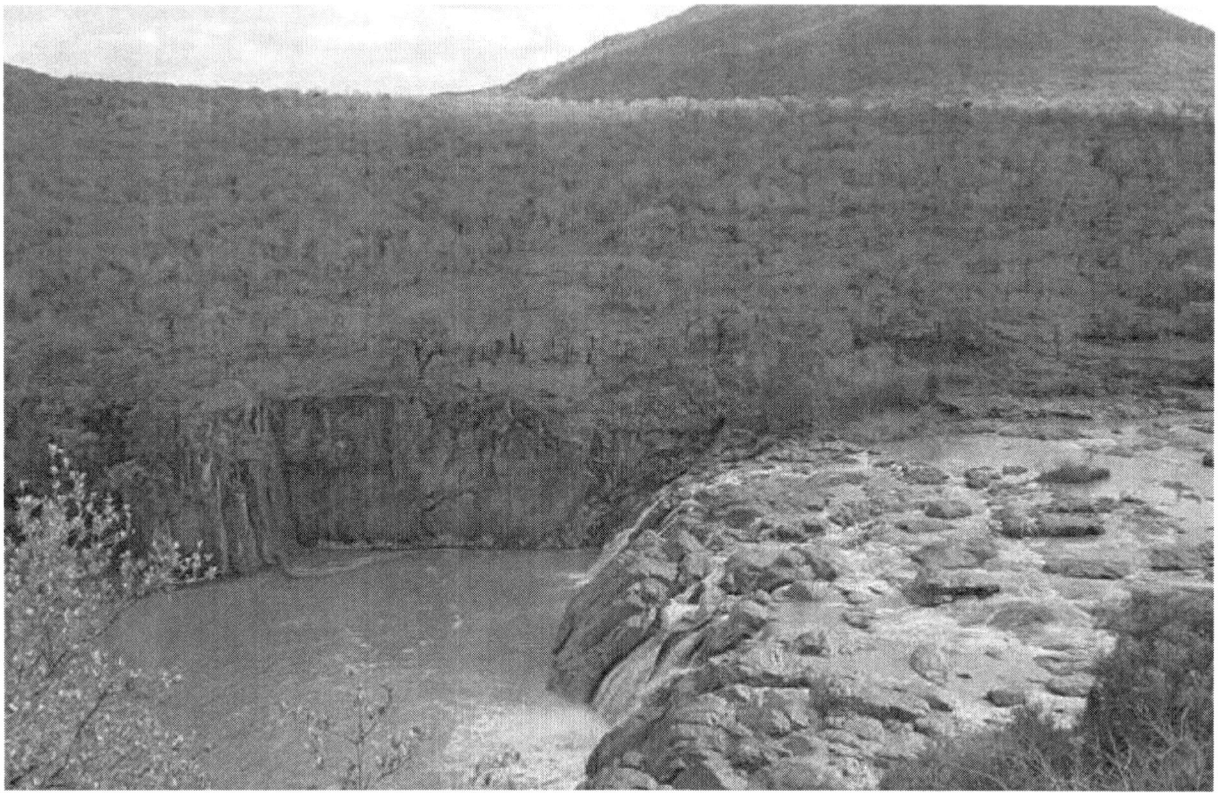

MKUZE RIVER AND FALLS FROM OUR CHALET TERRACE

The chalet's air-conditioner was big and quiet, the bed's bottom cover can be heated, there is a stocked wet bar and the bathroom was huge. The finishing touch was an outdoor shower and spa with views of the river and falls. The food was beautifully prepared and overeating seemed to be the norm at each meal. On top of that, our sightseeing Land Rover was equipped with a small picnic table, wines, liquors, pops, juices and snacks — quite unbelievable, but truly marvelous!

However, our big treat came when we witnessed the rare sight of 2 young male loins (brothers) devouring a nyala (a small South African antelope) in an open field. Our ranger guide said we probably missed seeing the actual kill by less than an hour. Pat got the ranger really laughing when she asked if they fed the wild animals in the reserve — nope, all natural. On the next tour day, we saw six elephants pulling up small trees to eat their roots all within 50 feet of our open Land Rover. Pat kept a list of all the animals and birds that we saw at the game reserve. The sightings included rhinos, giraffes, wildebeests, hippos, zebras, warthogs, nyalas, antelope, monkeys, lizards, and impalas. We did not get to see any cheetahs or leopards. We saw probably about 15 of the 400 species of birds in the area. Our ranger was especially knowledgeable about the bird life, which added a lot of informative knowledge to our tour. Seeing these incredible animals up closely while they move freely around the mountains, hills and plains of this vast country is an emotional experience that I cannot adequately describe. There are few places in the world that can rival the diversity of our experiences and adventure in Zululand, Africa.

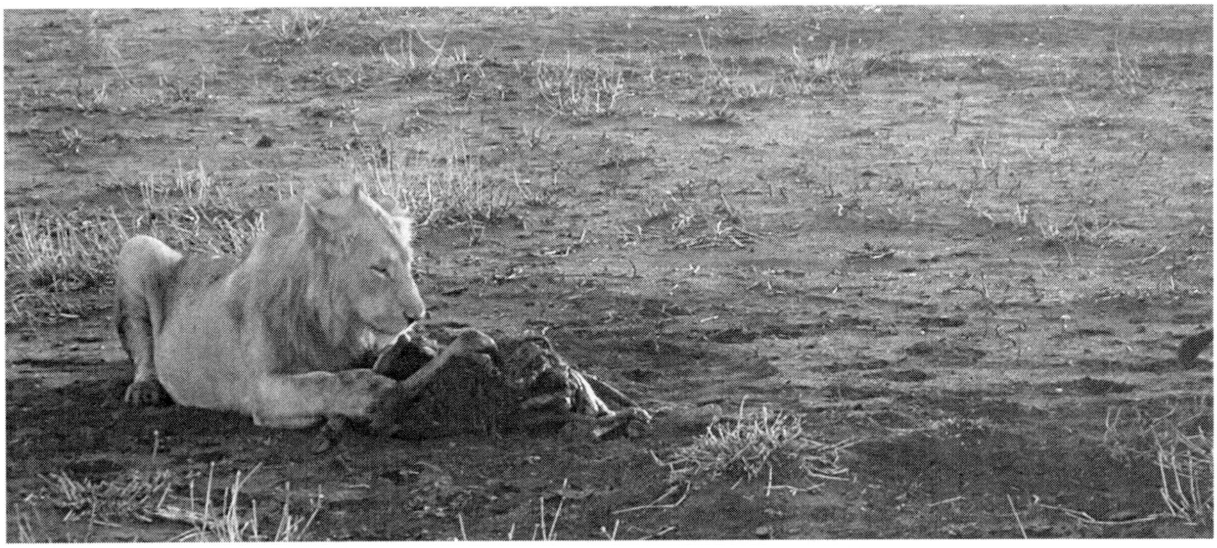

TWO-YEAR-OLD MALE LOIN FEASTING ON A NYALA

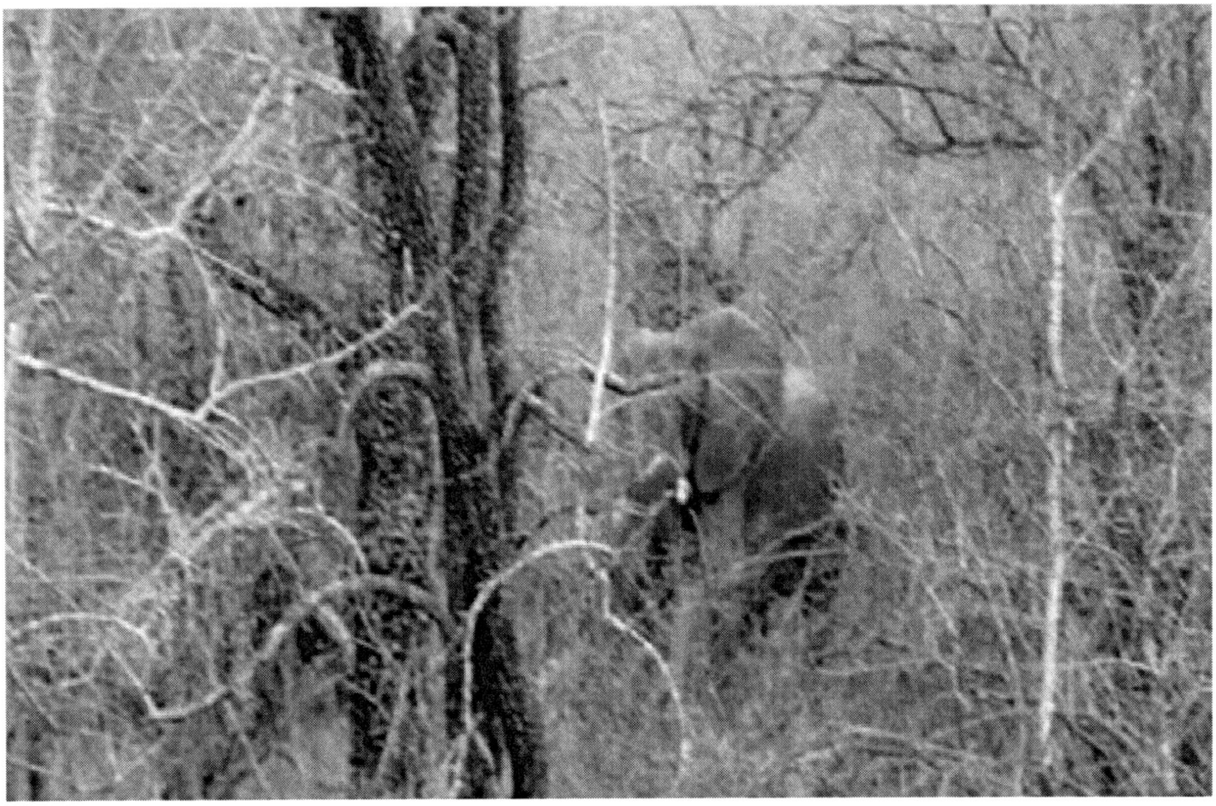

ELEPHANT HERD LEADER CHOMPING THROUGH THE THICKET

One of the more difficult parts of our experience was the ranger's wake-up call at 4:30 each morning. To hear the phone ring while luxuriating in a big comfortable bed, dead to the world, is just uncivilized. However, he nicely explained that early morning was the time to see the big cats. They like to roam the plains before the sun comes up. When the sun comes up, they head for the cover and shade of the bush. They do not really need protection of the bush since they are rather high up on the food chain. They use it more for spying for their next meal and shade rather than for protection.

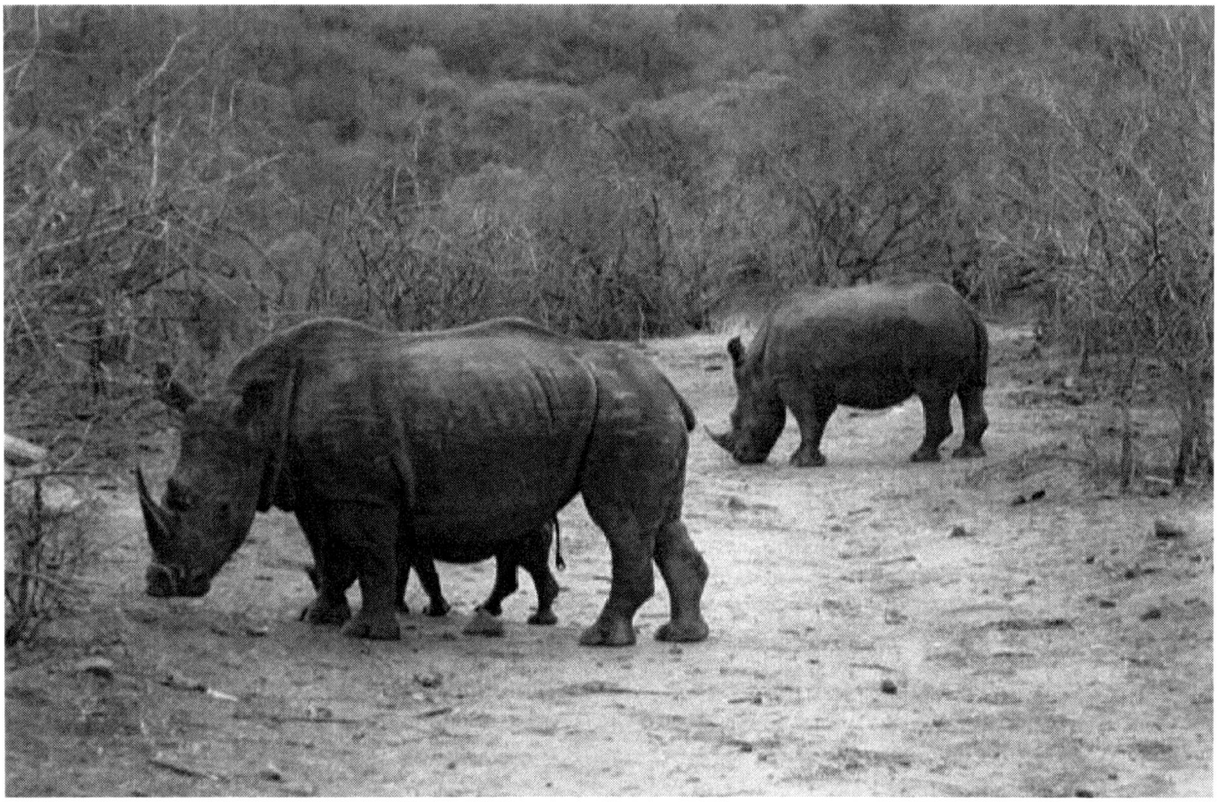

MAMA WATCHING APPREHENSIVELY, HER CALF ON THE FAR SIDE

While we were in the reserve, everything was extremely dry as there had been little rain all winter. Most of the trees had only a few leaves and green grass was hard to find. Our ranger said it was the driest winter in 50 years. Since the animals in the reserve are not fed, they have to find their own food. Luckily, it rained after we left, which changes the physical appearance of the African bush. With a little rain, everything grows amazingly fast especially the grass. We were told the grass is normally so high it will hide most animals, so the dry season makes it easier to catch a glimpse of the animals. The trees miraculously get their leaves back, which make the animals happy. Quite a few of the animals depend on vegetation for their diet so they experienced some difficult times before the rains came. All my photographs look black and white instead of colored because of the extreme dryness.

We had to leave the lodge Saturday morning at 6:30 a.m. so Pat could make the plane leaving Richard's Bay for Seattle. Leaving this early, we were going to miss the early morning bush drive and the morning breakfast. However, when the staff heard we had to leave early they took our orders the night before and we had a fully cooked breakfast waiting for us at 6 a.m. in the dining room. The cook and our assigned waiter and waitress, had to arrive early at the dining room to serve our breakfast — now that is service with a capital "S." In the manner of cruise ship custom, we left generous tips in envelopes for the ranger, the tracker, and the staff.

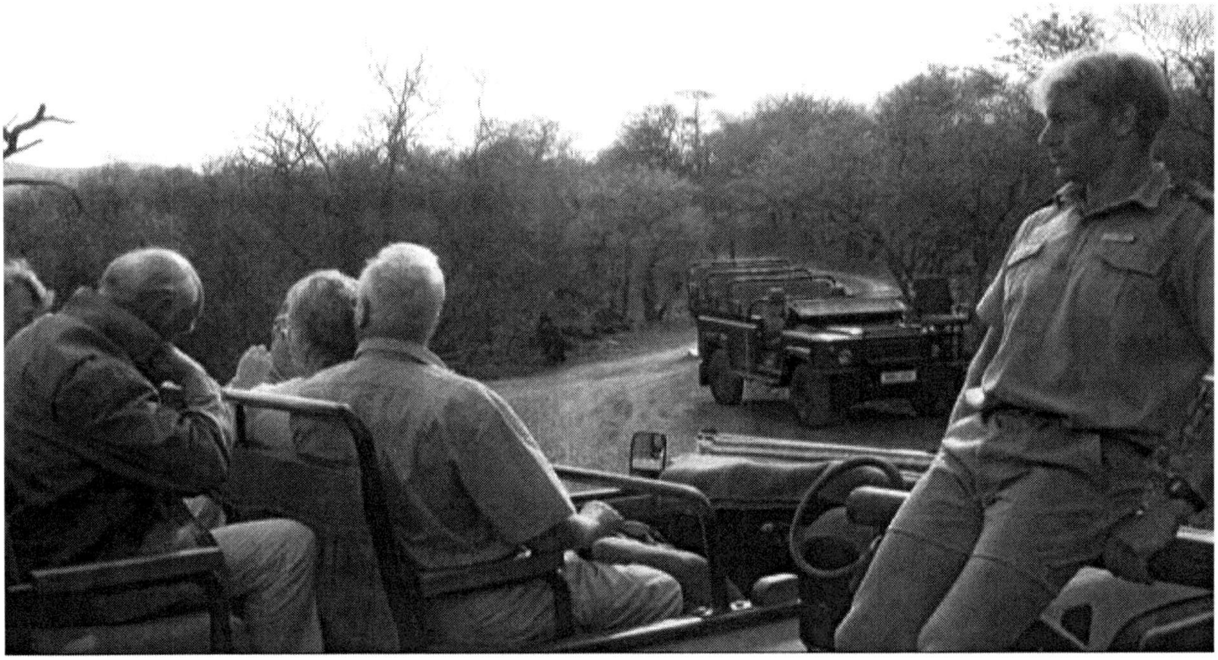

RANGER AND TOURISTS WAITING FOR THE HERD OF ELEPHANTS

That is about all the exciting stuff that happened at Richard's Bay. There is not a lot to do at the bay and the town is a fair distance away. There are several nice restaurants, a travel agency, a deli, a liquor store, beauty salon, gift shop, police station and condominiums so the bay is well self-contained. Most free time is as an eight-hour workday spent on boat projects and planning the trip to Cape Town. There is also a nice yacht club in the Bay, but the moorage there does not accommodate large yachts. The town has a central business district and a large mall where one can find food, theaters, banking, nice shops, a post office and other mall type stuff. Without a car, a shopping trip requires hiring a taxi. The taxi fare runs about $5.50 each way for the fifteen-minute ride. The inconvenience of taking taxis results in putting off shopping until one finds someone else to share a taxi. There is bus service from the bay, but the locals said it is not safe to take a bus or walk outside the bay's gates, especially at night, and Richard's Bay is one of the safer cities in Africa.

With unemployment around 40%, the incidence of crime is high. Any person that looks like a tourist or might have some money is a likely victim. The marina has fulltime security guards at its entrance and they also walk the docks. The toilets and showers require a key and were strategically built in view of the guardhouse. The marina office is enclosed by a heavy steel bar door that can only be opened from the inside. If you take a rental car or personal car to the mall, you have to pay a guard and rely on him to watch your car in the parking lot. The parking lots do have security guards to watch cars for a small fee. They record your plate number, they wear uniforms and look official, but they are not armed. A person posing as an attendant tried to get me to pay him, but he was an obvious imposter. We were warned that unscrupulous characters in the mall may try to see your pin number at the cash machine. If the thief can get your pin number, he will try to steal your card and will not be kind. This actually happened to two yachties we knew from the marina. To avoid cash machine problems you need a friend to make sure no one is trying to see your pin number.

Carjacking and robberies (often violent) are high on the crime list. Violent carjacking in South Africa is so prevalent that a special court in Johannesburg has been set up to deal exclusively with those cases. Going into a bank is quite an experience. Outside the bank, a guard with a metal detector will give you the once over and looks into bags or parcels in your possession. If you pass that check, you enter a one-person glass chamber and the doors into and out-of the chamber lock automatically. The chamber contains another detector, if you pass that test, a green light comes on and you can open the door into the bank. On leaving the bank, one must repeat the process through another set of doors. One of our friends, coming into Johannesburg by plane, was told by a well-dressed person that he was her assigned shuttle driver. Luckily, she was alerted by sharp airport personnel and averted who knows what? Africa is trying to get crime under control, but it certainly is not there yet.

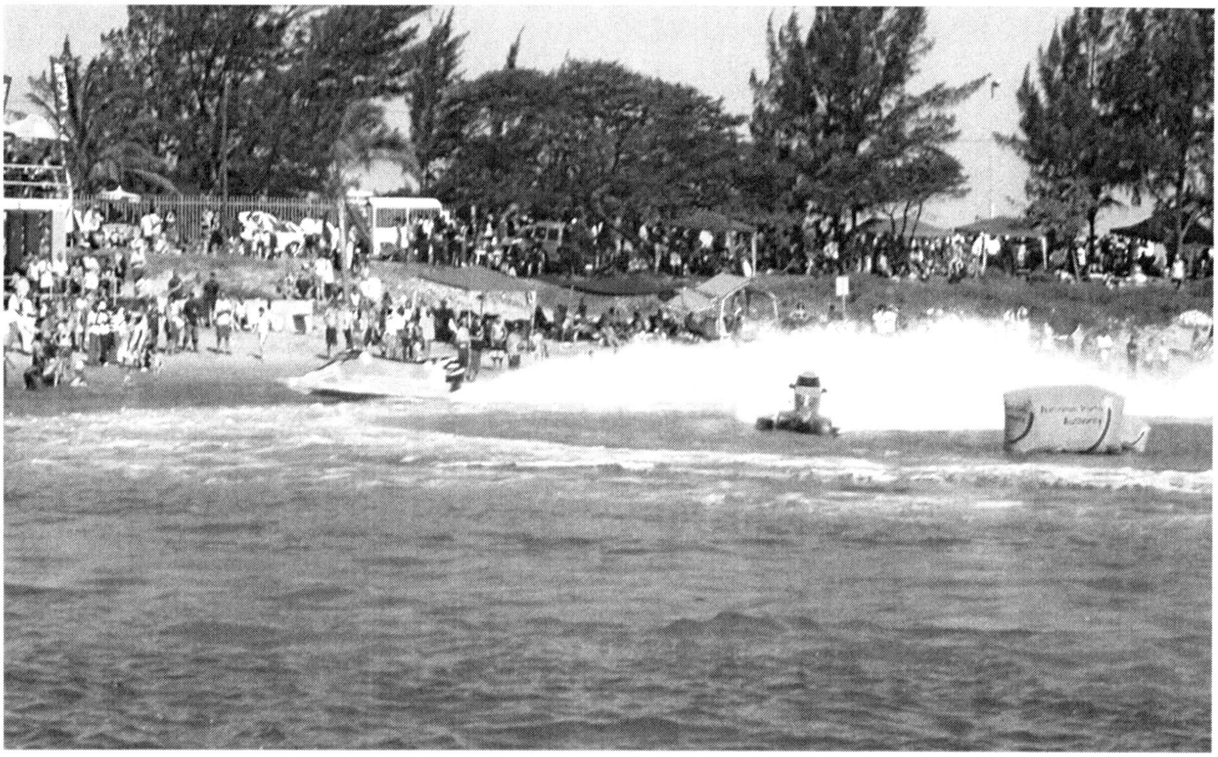

HYDROPLANE RACING, RICHARD'S BAY

On Nov. 27, Mimi on *Silver Cloud* from Houston, Texas arranged our Thanksgiving dinner at a nice restaurant at the bay. She planned the dinner menu and the restaurant hosted a private party for the yachties with turkey and dressing as the main entrée. For a small fee, 60 yachties enjoyed the afternoon together with good food and good South African wine. Each yachtie brought along a favorite dish to help overindulge this group and they tasted everything. Since Pat was in Seattle by this time, I was left floundering to whip something up. Pat told me that we had a nice Cadbury chocolate cake mix on ***Our Pleasure***, which saved the day. I managed to follow the recipe and ended up with a good desert even if it was out of a box. This was actually my first experience at baking a cake of any kind — luckily, it was good and I was quite proud of myself.

A few more noteworthy events happened at Richard's Bay. My crew to Cape Town, André, arrived Dec. 4. He is a big, six foot four inch, South African teenager with quite a lot of sailing experience. Another event was Marv's birthday, which we celebrated at the Portuguese restaurant on Dec. 5. On Dec. 16, South Africa enjoys a national holiday called Day of Reconciliation. We thought we would be gone by then, but the weather was not cooperating. The day was spent watching boat racing on the bay. One leg of the course came right by the stern of *Esprit*, which included a tight 180° turn around a buoy. Big 350 horsepower outboard engines powered the hydroplanes and they were fast. We watched Zulu dance competitions, checked out some of the food stands and enjoyed their Day of Reconciliation.

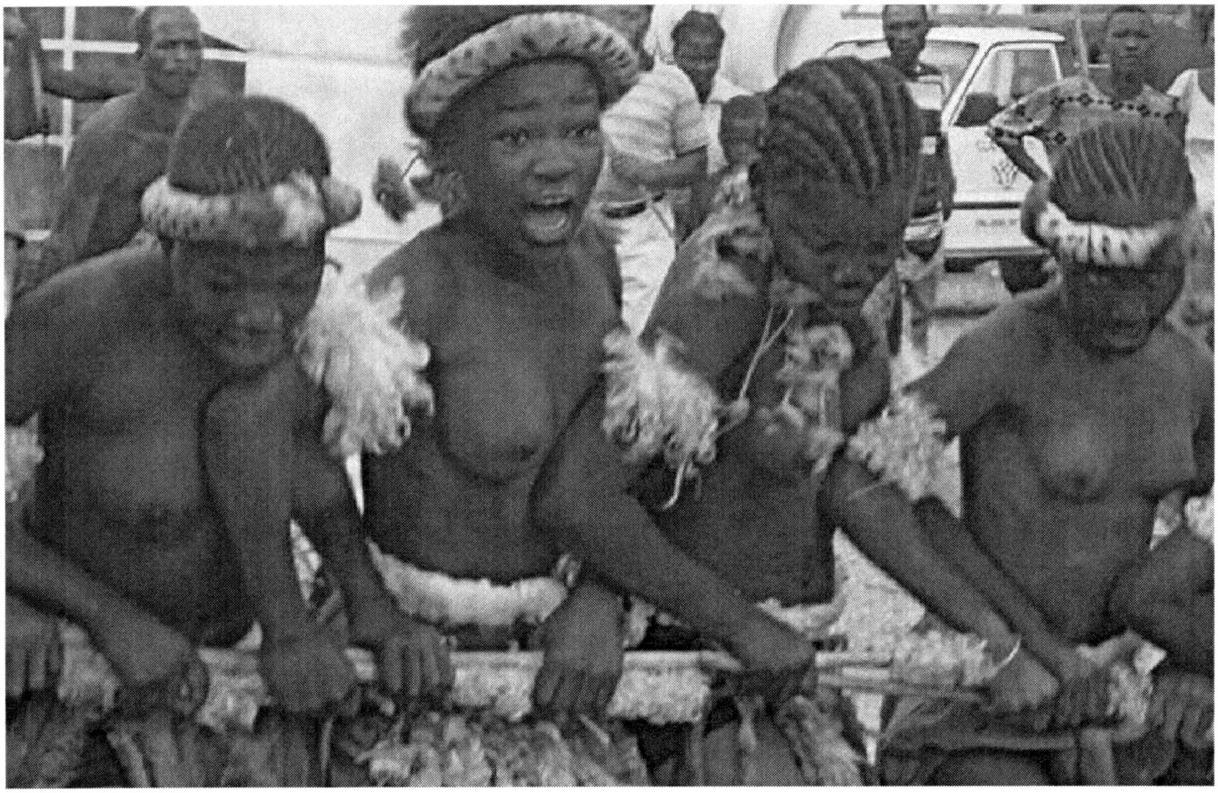

YOUNG WOMEN, ZULU DANCE COMPETITION, RICHARD'S BAY, SA

I spent a lot of time looking at paper and electronic charts for the right course to Cape Town. I finely managed to decide on 18 good waypoints down the east coast. I included major stops at Durban, East London, Port Elizabeth, Mossel Bay and Cape Town. Weather down the African coast is really tricky. One can expect only a few days of wind in the direction you intend to sail and the rest of the time, you had better not be out there. The southwest winds, "**Southwest Buster,**" come through with a ferocious intensity every few days. These winds are counter to the direction of the cape winds and can cause waves up to 60 feet if they run into the strong, south setting, Agulhas current. This current is strongest between Durban and East London, which is why this 250 mile stretch is known as the "**Wild Coast.**" Actually, the name does not adequately describe the furry that wind and wave can lash out.

Just sitting at the dock in Richard's Bay when a Southwest Buster comes through is enough to question one's sanity to sail here. The docks bend, their shapes distort as the strong winds try to pull their welds and fasteners apart. Boats heel, mooring lines fray and all this takes place in a well-protected harbor. On the water, these conditions can cause serious harm to life, limb and vessel in minutes. When the air-pressure drops quickly, you pray that your timing was right and you are in a safe harbor. We waited at Richard's Bay for almost two months to make sure we had the best weather for the 80 mile run to Durban.

There are two dedicated ham operators in Durban, Fred, ZS5FM and Alistair, ZS5MU, who watch over this area and the South Atlantic. They take to the airwaves twice a day to help sort-out the weather for those silly enough to be sailing in it or those waiting to make their move. They receive all the weather resources available in this part of the world, review it according to boat locations and tell sailors what to expect for the next several days. They have been providing this weather service and their vast knowledge of the coast for years without fan fare or remuneration except for the thanks we sailors accord them. I often wonder how many small boat sailors may owe these hams their lives and do not even realize it.

We finely got a good break in the weather on Dec. 19 and passed the harbor breakwater at 3:15 p.m. Six boats left Richard's Bay at the same time and experienced good sailing weather. We arrived at the Durban breakwater at 10:15 a.m. and tied at the visitor's float until there was room at their international jetty. Tying to the float was quite an experience as it is too low in the water for our freeboard. André stepped on the float so he could run a line through its mooring ring. While he was on the float, strong winds were blowing ***Our Pleasure*** further away. For a few minutes, I thought he would have to swim back, but our bow thruster managed to get the bow back to the float.

After moving to the international jetty, we filled in their paper work and were through by 1p.m. The marina office stayed open past their 12 noon lunch time to help us check in, but we could not move to a slip without immigration check-in. Immigration would not be available until Monday as they had five commercial ships to clear-in. Why all the paper work is required is a mystery since we had already cleared into South Africa at Richard's Bay.

Chapter 23

DURBAN TO CAPE TOWN, SOUTH AFRICA

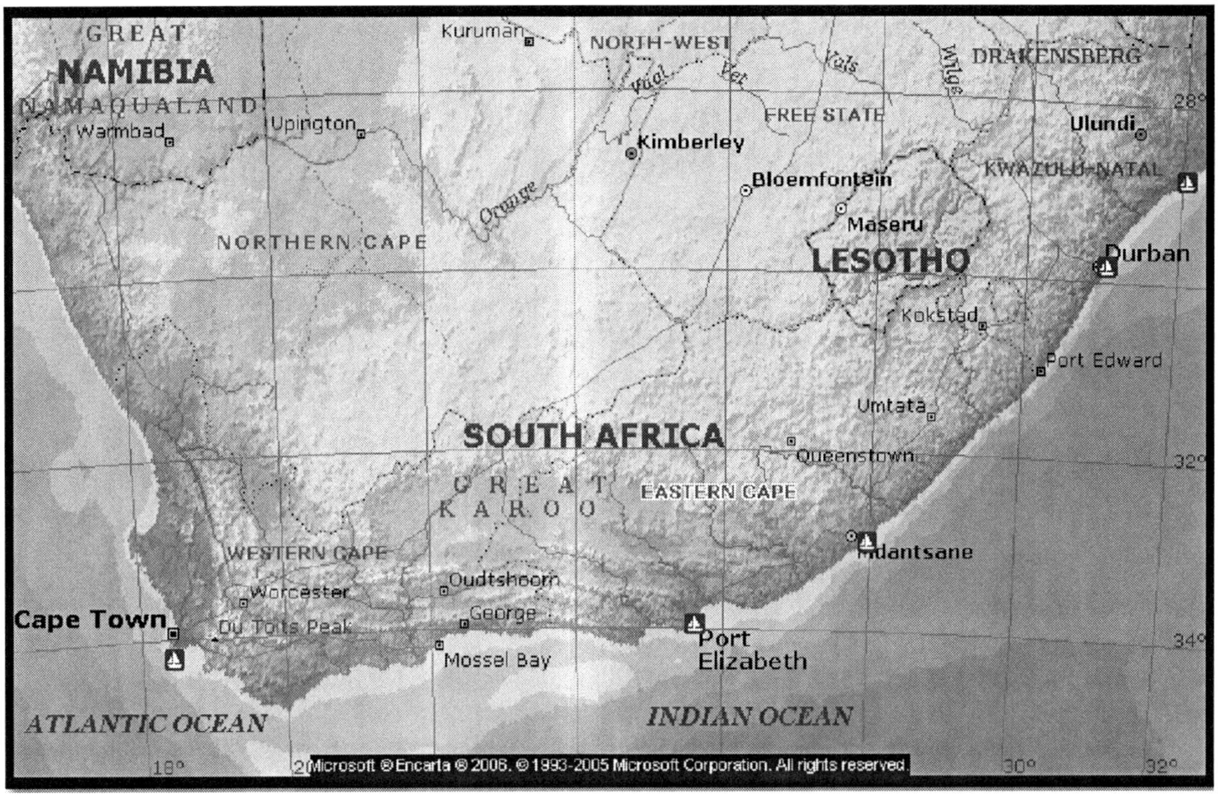

DURBAN TO CAPE TOWN, SOUTH AFRICA, DEC. 20 TO FEB. 18, 2003

Near the end of the fifteenth century, Portuguese explorer, Vasco Da Gama sailed into what is now Durban. He called it "Rio de Natal" or Christmas River because of the forests surrounding the river at that time. The word Natal still is in use today and refers to the local province. Around 1820 a Zulu chief and military genius named Shaka organized the clans of the region into an almost irrepressible army. It took the British Empire about 60 years before they could subdue the Zulus. Today Durban is a large city of three million people all in a hurry.

The city is the third largest in South Africa and their port is the largest in South Africa. The buildings are tall and impressive. Our assigned slip must be on the longest dock in the world, if not, it is the longest that I have ever been on. It takes a good five minutes just to walk to the gate, showers and toilets. If you feel the urge to use the toilet facility, you have to get a-move-on because you cannot dilly-dally. A few of the privately owned slips have power, but by far, the majority does not. This struck me as a little odd for a large, big city marina, to have water for all the slips, but not power. No dock power means running the generator every twelve hours to keep the batteries charged and the refrigerator/freezer cold.

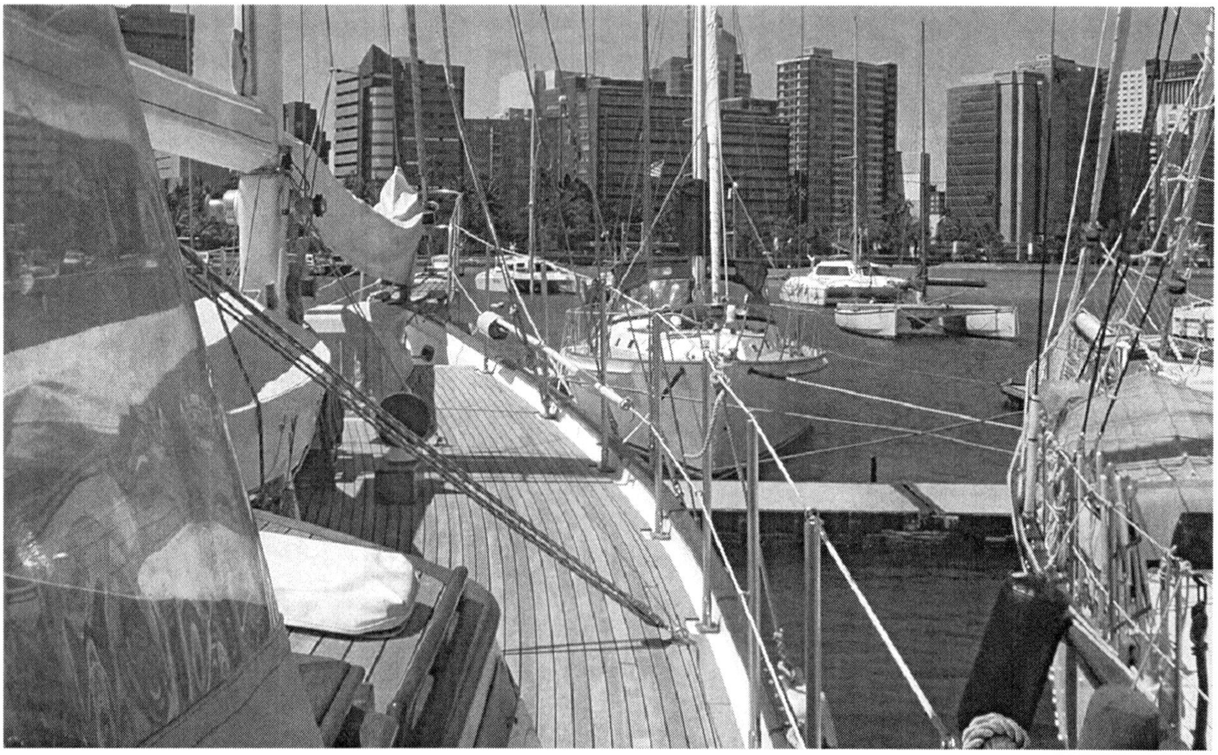

OUR PLEASURE, AT THE TRANSIENT YACHT PIER, DURBAN, SOUTH AFRICA

The South African people are friendly, but there are safety concerns. Like Richard's Bay, we were warned not to walk alone after dark. This does not include the marina area that has security personnel for the docks and yacht club. Walking in the city seems quite safe, but being white certainly puts you in the minority. Almost everyone is a black African or Hindu. The Hindu population is supposed to be the largest in the world outside of Asia. 152,000 laborers were brought in to work the sugar plantations between 1860 and 1911. They were offered free passage back after five years, but over half decided to stay in South Africa. Today their population is estimated at over one million.

It is nice being in a big city again with all its markets, services, restaurants and coffee shops. Boating related services are quite good compared to Richard's Bay. Right after we arrived in Durban it looked like a good weather window was forming to sail further south. We checked out of Durban, with Fred's help, he runs Peri-Peri Radio for cruising yachts. He drove us to all the scattered government offices on Dec. 24, 2003. Our plan was to leave on Sunday Dec. 28, but the safety window became too small to sail the 250 miles south to the next city, East London. Therefore, we had to look for another potential window and go through the checkout procedure again. Somehow, the bureaucracy managed to spread all the agencies as far apart as possible. Starting the checkout procedure at 8 a.m., we finely finished visiting the four agencies and completed their paper work by 11 a.m.

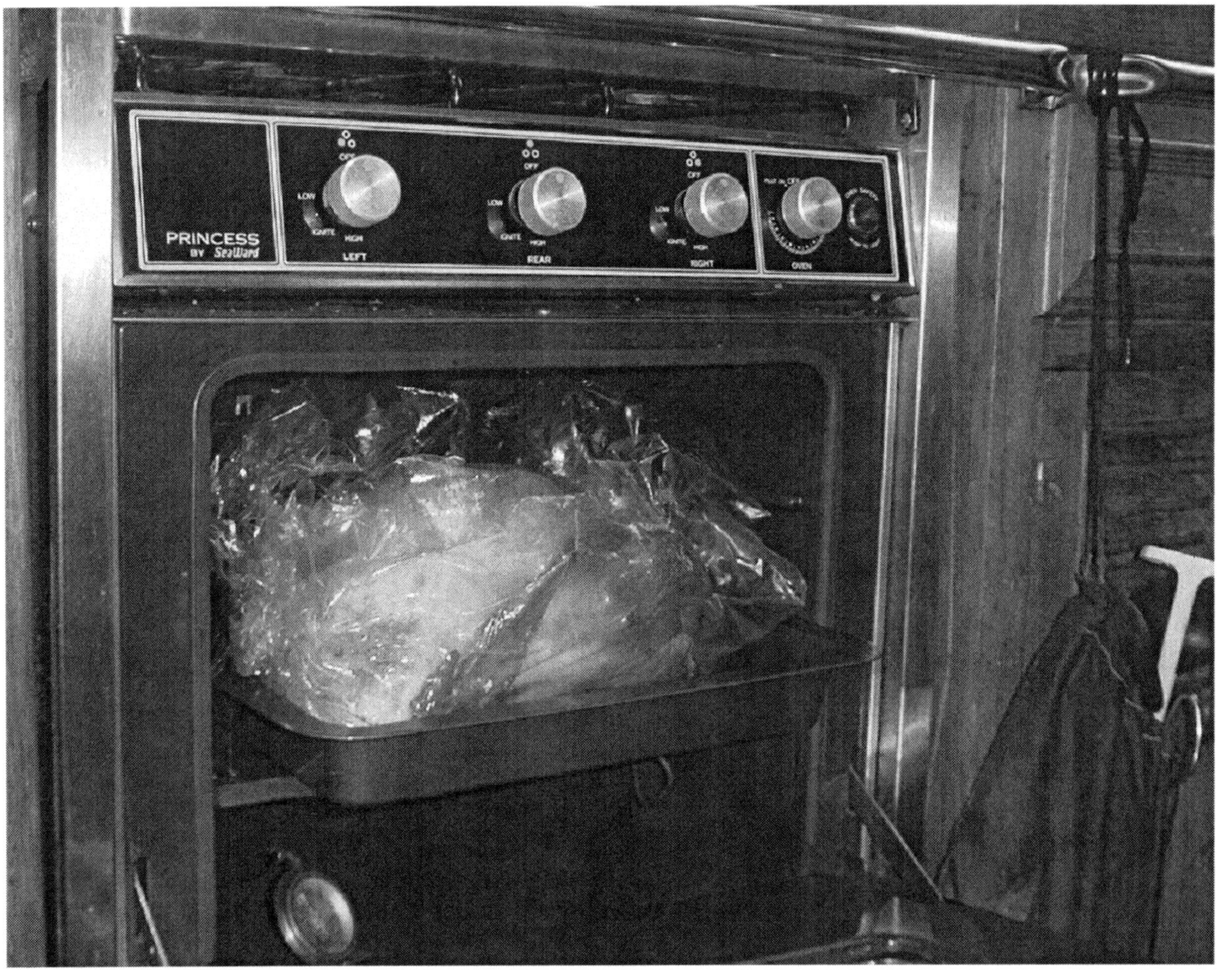

CHECKING THE CHRISTMAS TURKEY, *OUR PLEASURE*, DEC. 25, 2003

Everything in Durban closed for the Christmas holidays, which includes Boxing Day. So the big holiday treat was to dine on *Endurance*. I was tasked with cooking one turkey on ***Our Pleasure***. So I got off fairly easy as Sheri did the stuffing for it and Marv had a baking bag for our nice 13 pound tom. Surveying all the food spread out on the dining table, I was impressed.

Raywin baked a fruitcake and a pecan pie for dessert. She claimed the pecan pie was baked just for me and managed to save two pieces for me to have later. Eating all that food was tiring and after a couple of hours passed, everyone needed a nap.

On Dec. 27, 2003, we got six couples together and went to see an African five star musical named *UMOJA*, or "*The Spirit of Togetherness*." We went to the Saturday matinee so tickets were only $7.30 for the best seats in

The Playhouse Theater. All the musicians, dancers and singers were native Africans. The music and dancing was designed to celebrate the history of African music from early Africa to the present. The musical had toured about twenty countries around the world; the rave reviews told us we would like it. The singing was sensational; the dancing was energetic beyond imagination. The thirty performers had the whole theater waving their arms and singing along with native songs. Women depicting Zulu dancing and singing from early periods wore topless costumes with brightly colored beads. The men wore animal skin coverings, beads, and animal hair and carried animal skin shields. The dancing was extremely physical with kicking high above their heads to the tempo of the drums.

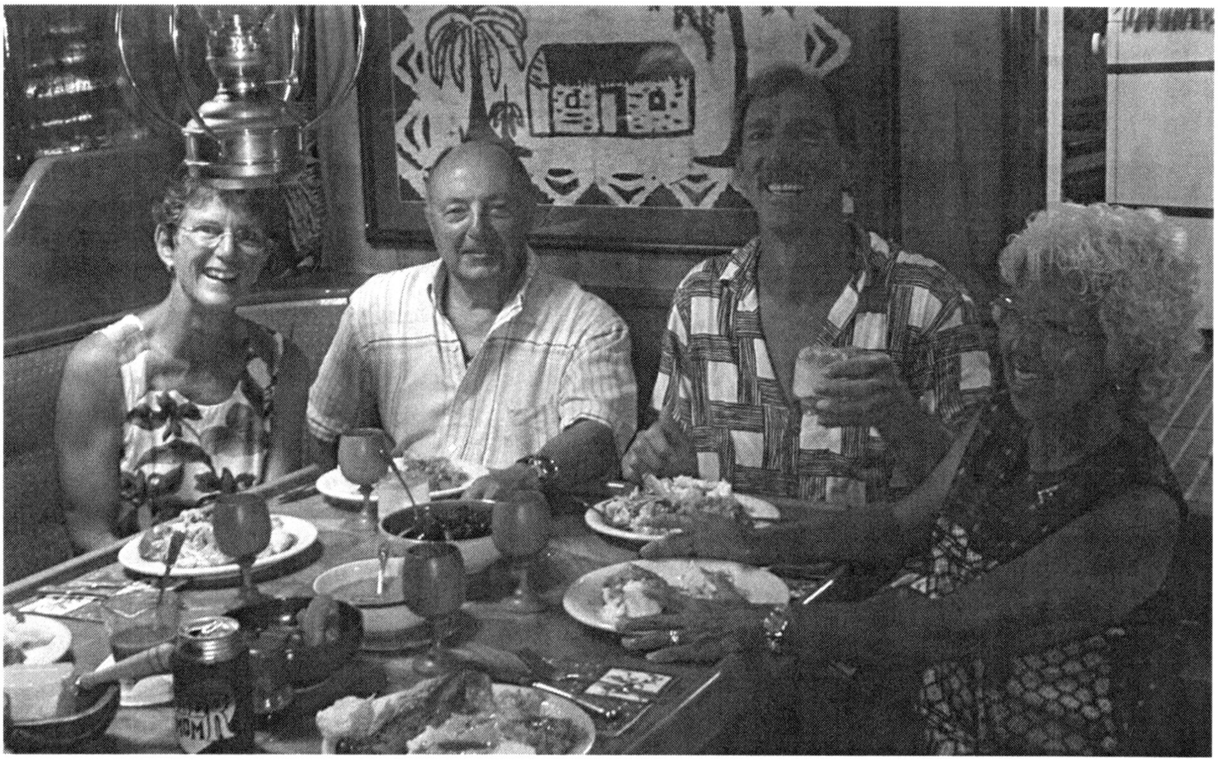

RAYWIN, *SAVEKE*; CAPTAIN DICK; MYRON AND CHIEKO, *ENDURANCE;* CHRISTMAS, 2003

Besides the jazz band style orchestra there were four muscular men providing the main rhythm through large animal-skinned drums. As the history continued, we saw their version of the jitterbug right up to the present rap period. The energy never wavered or slowed for three and a half hours, truly amazing. The costumes, lighting and sound were excellent. The scenery was basic, but was designed to fit with the costumes and time periods without much variation. One thing that you do not see in U.S. theaters, people bring their snacks and drinks to have in their seats during intermission. Most of the audience was dressed casually, while only a few men and woman were well dressed. Of course, it was a pretty hot day outside the air conditioned theater, about 84° F. that probably accounts for some people in shorts. Our group must have been feeling the need for some American food as we went to a nearby Pizza Hut after the show.

On New Year's Eve, I was invited to the yacht *Gryphon* (Jeff and Raine, Boston, MA) as were Larry and Lena from *Allons'y* (Friday Harbor, WA) along with Tom and Lou from the English yacht *Token*. Raine went out of her way to make wonderful hors d'oeuvres that just kept coming out of the oven all night long. Lena also brought along some wonderful treats, which made my little tray of snacks a bit embarrassing. The fireworks were mostly out of sight from the harbor, but their pops and booms made their presence known. African rules for foreign yachts are restrictive for leaving harbors. Paper work must be completed for a departure or a South African skipper must be onboard — we stayed in the harbor.

On Jan. 2, Eva, Fred's wife, drove us around Durban so we could complete our departure paper work. It takes close to half a day to visit customs, immigration, the port captain and marina manager. Clearance papers include several forms and official rubber stamps; the good part is no money is involved. Fred is a ham operator who provides weather info to yachts in the Mozambique Channel and keeps track of their daily positions. His service is a volunteer effort performed every day year after year. His SSB station in Durban is known as "Peri-Peri Radio." The next day Marv and I bought Eva and Fred lunch at the Point Yacht Club and I did some last minute grocery shopping and e-mailing. On Sunday, André and I motored past the break wall at 8 a.m. and headed south down the coast toward East London, SA.

After motoring all night we saw the wind pickup to 18 knots early Monday morning. It kept on building and by late afternoon, it was blowing between 35 and 45 knots. With several knots of current in our favor we were making 12 knots — ***Our Pleasure*** loved it and so did we. We had started with a full set of sails out, but in the strong winds, we eventually had to roll in all the sails except the staysail. The staysail is the workhorse of our sail inventory as it is strong and easily managed. It is on a boom that keeps it from flogging around and can be tied to a preventer line when going down wind.

We made good time and entered the East London harbor at 7 p.m. *Endurance* and *Saveke* were there to help take our mooring lines to a concrete pier designed for large commercial ships. Their marina for yachts was designed for yachts around 40 feet and not large enough for *Endurance* and ***Our Pleasure***. They were also limited on the number of yachts they could accommodate, therefore, the concrete pier. We were invited over to *Endurance* for Cuba Libras that were refreshing after our journey through wind and waves. We finally settled in around midnight. The next day we had to move from our spot on the wall to make room for a large commercial boat. The wind in the harbor was light so we were able to add our boat to the three-boat raft that *Endurance* started. Mooring to concrete piers is always hard on boat gear, as tide changes tend to scratch up fenders and our wooden rub rails.

East London is the second largest city along South Africa's East Cape region and the countries only river port. This area is famous for its many shipwrecks, which probably had a lot to do with the nickname "Wild Coast." This area is claimed to be mostly underdeveloped and an area where rural communities still follow old traditions. The natives here and south to Cape Town speak a language called Xhosa and own most of the land. We did not go into town here so I cannot comment on it, but Larry and Lena from *Allons'y* did and were stopped by a police officer. He told them it was not safe to walk to town. He asked them where they wanted to go and took them to a shopping center he considered safe. He asked them to be ready in an hour and a half and he would meet them and drive them back to their boat. Again, pointing out the real problem of crime in South Africa. There is lot of effort being expended to reduce crime all over South Africa and the latest statistics show good progress is being made.

We left East London at noon on Jan. 7 and 24 hours later entered Port Elizabeth some 120 miles south. Our wind died about four in the morning and our helpful current also petered out. Our moorage turned out again to be next to a concrete pier. The yacht club at Port Elizabeth was told previously by phone to expect the arrival of 15 boats. The message however did not get to the right people so moorage was limited at the yacht club. Marv said he called at least three times to alert them of the big influx of yachts, but the secretary never passed it on. I think they only had slips for about three boats and Marv helped the club manager find various pier ties and raft arrangements. The Algoa Yacht Club turned out to be super friendly and the best of all the clubs we have stayed at. The first drink at their bar was free and they had a barbeque party for us the first night. The second night they arranged live entertainment for us in the bar. I had a great cordon bleu dinner there including a glass of wine for less than $5.

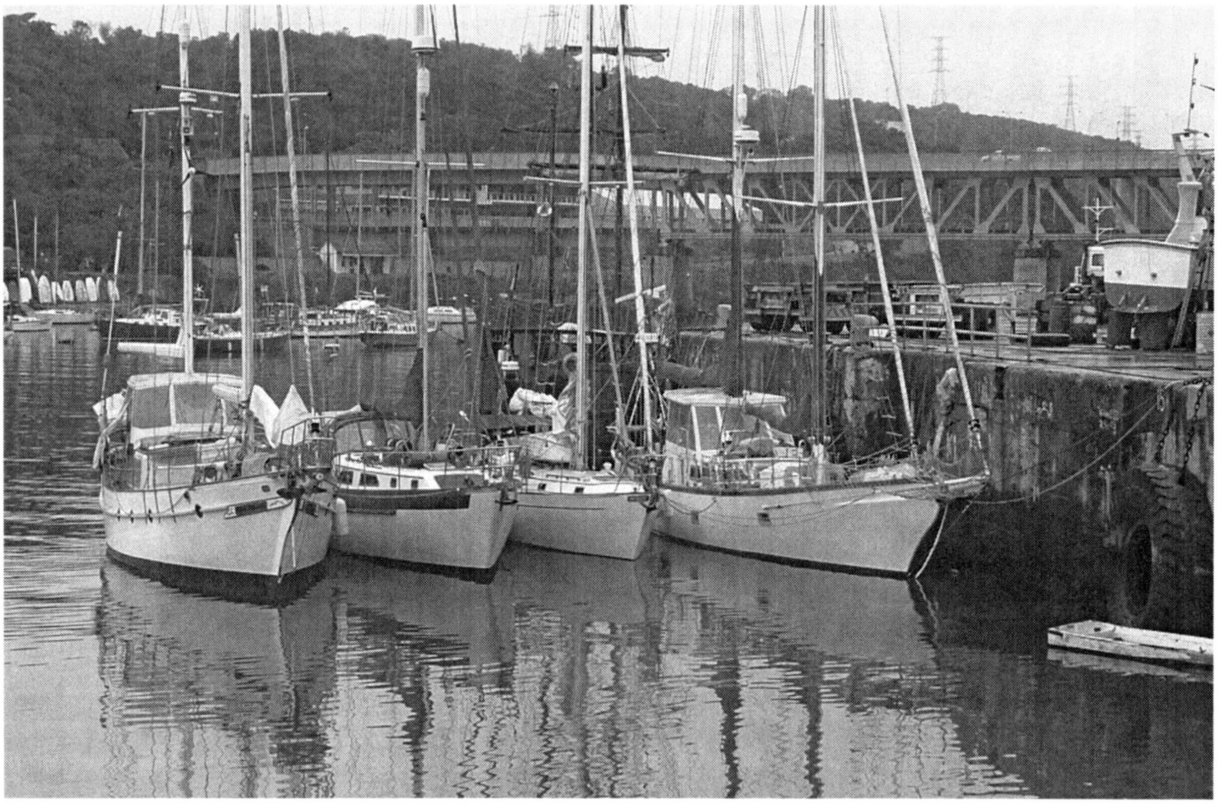

OUR PLEASURE, ALLONS'Y, SAVEKE **AND** ***ENDURANCE*** **EAST LONDON, SA**

Our pier tie was a much better moorage than East London. However, dock power was not available and water required a 150 foot hose to reach the club's nearest water. The pier was actually a working dock and unloading facility for commercial fishing boats. This activity went on all day long and mostly blacks handled the off loading. For some reason they talk loudly to each other, which made the pier a noisy place during the day.

Port Elizabeth is Africa's third largest port and fifth largest city with about 1.3 million people. We saw attractive beaches on our sailing approach that ran for about 40 miles along the Indian Ocean. The people we talked to there were quite friendly. According to the guidebook, their Homewood Golf Course is the best in South Africa. An unusual attraction in town is the 1905 life-sized bronze figures of a horse about to drink from a bucket held by a kneeling solder. The horse memorial is dedicated to the estimated 347,000 horses that died during the Second-Boer War (1899-1902). The British brought most of the horses into Africa through Port Elizabeth, but other countries like Australia and the United states also contributed many horses.

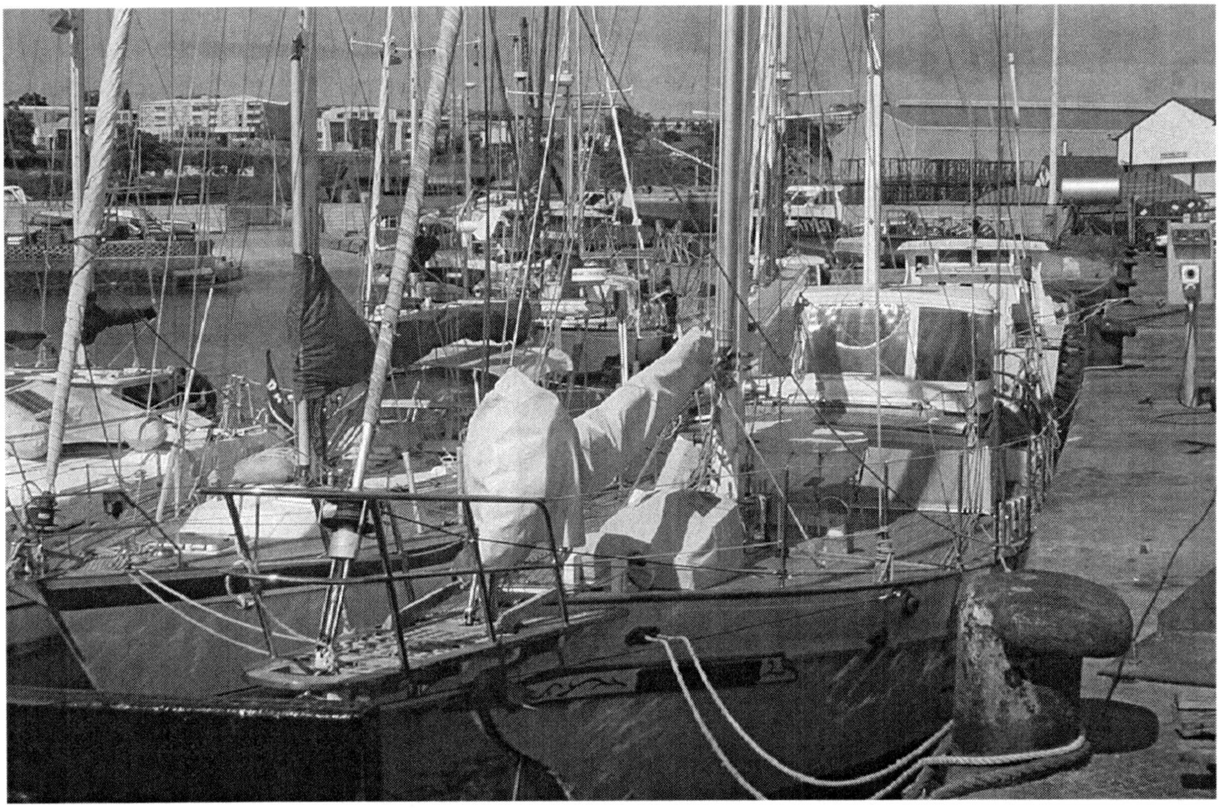

OUR PLEASURE AT PORT ELIZABETH

We had to wait at Port Elizabeth until Jan. 10 for the wind to switch away from the South West, a perilous sailing direction. When the South East winds started to blow, we hurried to leave the harbor at 2 in the afternoon. I had wanted to call Pat before leaving Port Elizabeth so she would know my plans, but our time differences were a conflicting problem. Pat was 10,000 miles away in Tempe, Arizona after attending her Mother's funeral in Buffalo, New York.

We steered a southerly course to pass Mossel Bay, SA by only a few offshore miles. If the weather turned foul we would duck into their bay. The next day the wind had built up to 30 knots with gusts to 50. The wind was from a good sailing direction, but trimming the sails to find the best balance was not always easy. We decided a reduced main and a boomed out staysail was the best combination. This combo worked well until the heavy stainless steel pivot pin on the bow's staysail boom disintegrated. The boom started banging around like some crazy guy. The noise was intolerable and we knew we had to constrain it fast. After subduing the boom and untying it from the staysail, we managed to re-rig it as a loose-footed sail. We tied the boom to the stanchions until we could repair the pin that broke. The next major problem was an accidental jibe, which broke one of the main boom traveler pulleys. The starboard traveler had to be fastened down with a strong line until the broken hardware could be replaced.

We listened to Alistair on the ham radio predicting one of those nasty sou'westers tomorrow. Talking with *Endurance* and *Esprit* by radio, we decided the most prudent course would be to head for Mossel Bay. By that time, however, ***Our Pleasure*** was 35 miles offshore and well past Mossel Bay. Trying to sail to Mossel Bay put the wind at 5° off the bow, a direction no yacht can sail without motoring. We ran the engine for two hours forcing the boat into the wind and waves, but made no real forward progress. Marv radioed that his autopilot was not steering properly and they had to hand steer. On top of that, he took some water down the dorade that was directly over his computer, which stopped his computer from working — really bad. The decisive factor was the loose deck hatch over their bunk; it allowed water to leak onto their bedding. *Endurance* and *Esprit* decided to heave-to until dawn while they were only 20 miles offshore. In daylight, they would go into Mossel Bay and sort out their problems.

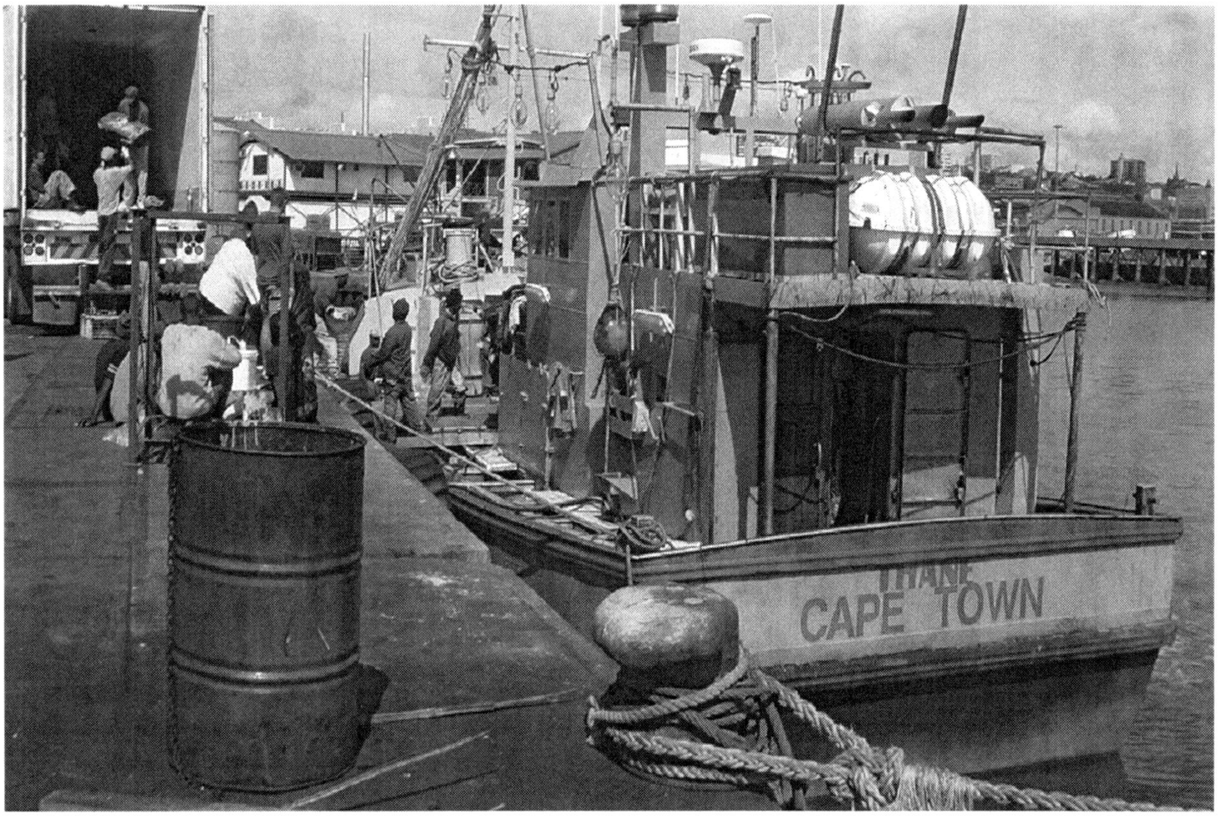

OFFLOADING FISH THE OLD FASHION WAY, BY HAND, PORT ELIZABETH

Our effort to make Mossel Bay was becoming foolhardy. Reviewing the coastal charts, I decided to run with the wind and seek shelter in a bay further south. The boat was now sailing better as I headed toward St. Sebastian Bay some 84 miles away. The predicted big blow never materialized and the next morning we were motoring toward St. Sebastian Bay in light winds. After listening to a weather report that morning predicting light winds, we changed our course and headed for Cape Agulhas. Cape Agulhas is actually the most southern point of Africa while the Cape of Good Hope is several miles north of Cape Agulhas. By 6 p.m. we had rounded Cape Agulhas and were headed toward the Cape of Good Hope in 14 knots of wind from the SE. Cape Town was only 120 miles away and we should make that by morning. However, by 7:30 a.m., a dense fog that came in out of nowhere surrounded ***Our Pleasure***. The wind direction had moved to the north against the direction we wanted to sail. The wind then increased to 35 knots blowing directly into our bow rapidly building the height of the waves.

I kept hearing an odd squeaking sound coming from the stern of the boat, but when I walked aft, it stopped. When I walked forward, it started again. Then I heard the same sounds coming from a location near the mast. We finally solved the noise problem when André found the first of two large crickets. How the two of them found us so far offshore will forever remain a mystery, but we had other problems. By 10 a.m., the wind was blowing upwards of 45 knots directly against us and the fog still enveloped our boat. We could not make any forward progress and decided to heave-to.

The dense fog was nerve racking as we were in the center of the shipping lanes with the biggest of ocean going freighters going north and south near our fixed position. We had our automatic foghorn going and they were blasting theirs. We watched them on radar maneuvering to avoid each other and us when only about two miles separated our positions. The fog was so thick we could hear them pass by, but never saw them. We were continually ready to start the engine if one came too close, but the angels were watching over us this time. The apprehension of not knowing if they will make the right choice in time is frightful. Heaving-to makes us rather vulnerable because we need time to change the sail attitude, start the engine and pick a non-collision course. I really credit the skippers and their high level of seamanship that kept everything orderly in a difficult situation.

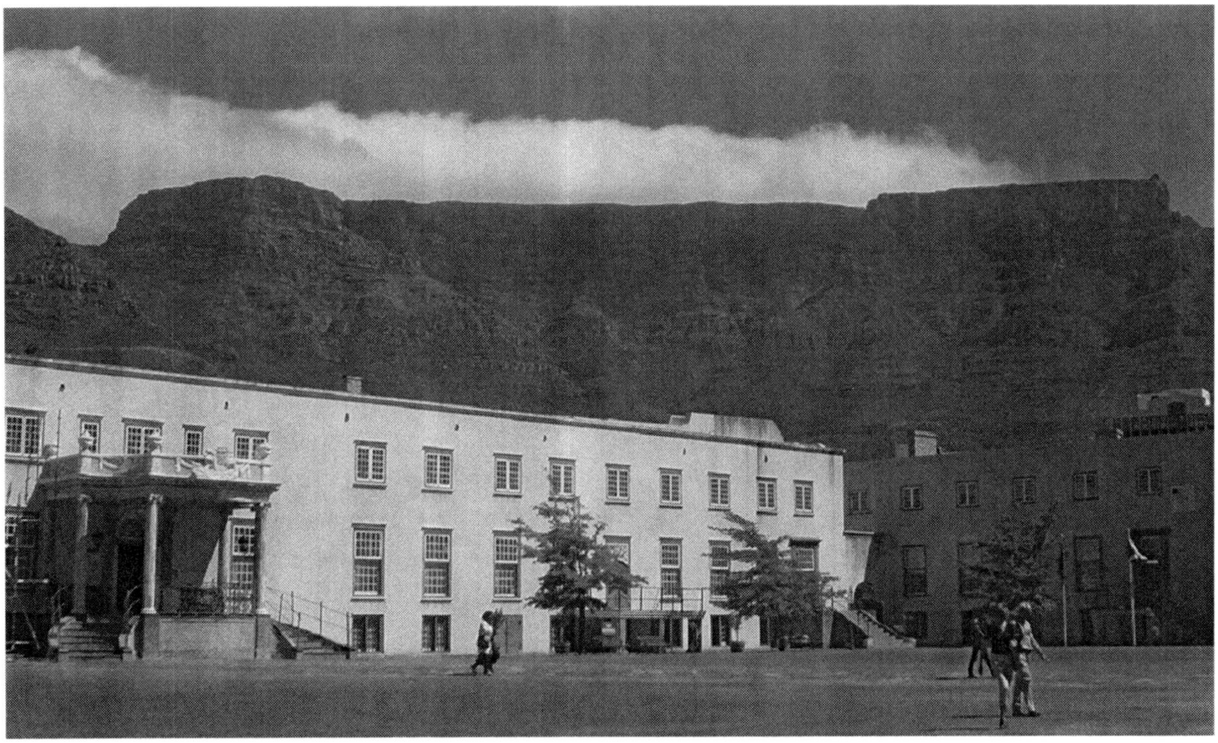

TABLE MOUNTAIN FROM THE PARADE GROUNDS OF THE CASTLE, GOOD HOPE, CAPE TOWN

At 6:30 p.m., the wind switched to the NE at 25 knots moving the fog and allowing us to power through the sea at a better wind angle. The wind speed continued to be persistent, but varying in direction. Sail changes required to coincide with wind direction changes tested our resolve and strength. We made it to Cape Town on

Jan. 14 and tied up at the Victoria and Alfred (V&A) Marina at an early 2 a.m. It was quiet at the port except for a few freighters moving to their berths. Cape Town Radio, Port Control, and Cape Town Bridge Control are always on duty and directed us through the port to the marina. The bridge control people operate two small walking-bridges that cross over the boat channel into the V&A Marina. One bridge swings to open and the other is a drawbridge called the Bascule Bridge. The bridges provide people access to and from the city to the huge V&A shopping mall, theaters, restaurants, I-Max Theater, native arts and crafts, hotels and aquarium. When I saw the lights of the city with Table Mountain lit up behind the city, I knew I was going to like Cape Town.

Our moorage at the upscale Victoria and Alford Marina was a perfect resting place after the 8,000 miles we had sailed since leaving Townsville, Australia. The marina was wisely constructed using steel and concrete with wide docks, wide berths and plenty of maneuvering room for large yachts. The marina was only four years old and well maintained. All possible voltage requirements were available at each dock. However, South Africa uses a standard frequency of 50 Hertz instead of our standard of 60 Hertz. This made our motors and clocks run about 16.7% slower — tolerable for heavy-duty motors. The toilet facilities were the best and cleanest that we have had in any marina with copious amounts hot water.

We were moored in the midst of several super yachts from around the world. One sloop, *Philanderer*, was about 130 feet long and our mast was only about one-third the height of hers.

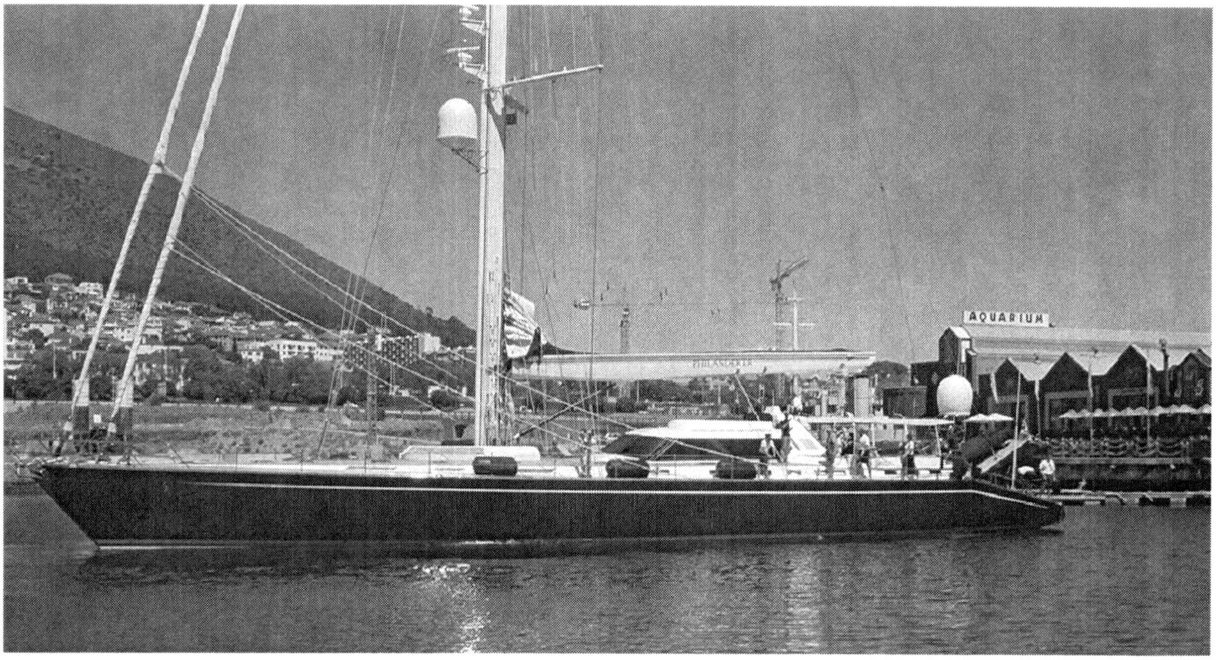

130 FOOT SUPER YACHT, *PHILANDERER*, V&A MARINA, CAPE TOWN

At 10:30 a.m., four days later, *Endurance* and *Esprit* arrived at the V&A Marina and I showed them to their slips and handled their dock lines. Four Champaign bottles were opened and we toasted each other on our successful trip around one of the world's great capes. André went off to visit his parents near Johannesburg and I worked on boat cleaning and projects. I met Pat at the Cape Town airport on Jan. 23 and we had another great Champaign party on *Endurance.*

Cape Town ranks right up there as one of the most beautiful cities we have had the pleasure to visit. The city is a beehive of activity with new building construction and planned developments in work. The history of the area, the places of interest and abundance of scenery are almost endless. There are so many tours that a month of just touring might limit what could be seen. Pat could not believe her eyes when I took her through the local mall only five minutes from our moorage. Until she spent a few days there and learned her way around it was easy to get lost. The V&A district is a vast complex of shops, eating establishments and businesses all developed along the harbor waterfront. The areas used for mooring fishing boats and dry docks were left in their working states. In walking through the area, you can expect to see large boats being repaired and painted. All the commercial activity adds interest and an unusual flavor to the whole area. Security is visible everywhere in the complex and they have made that a number one priority.

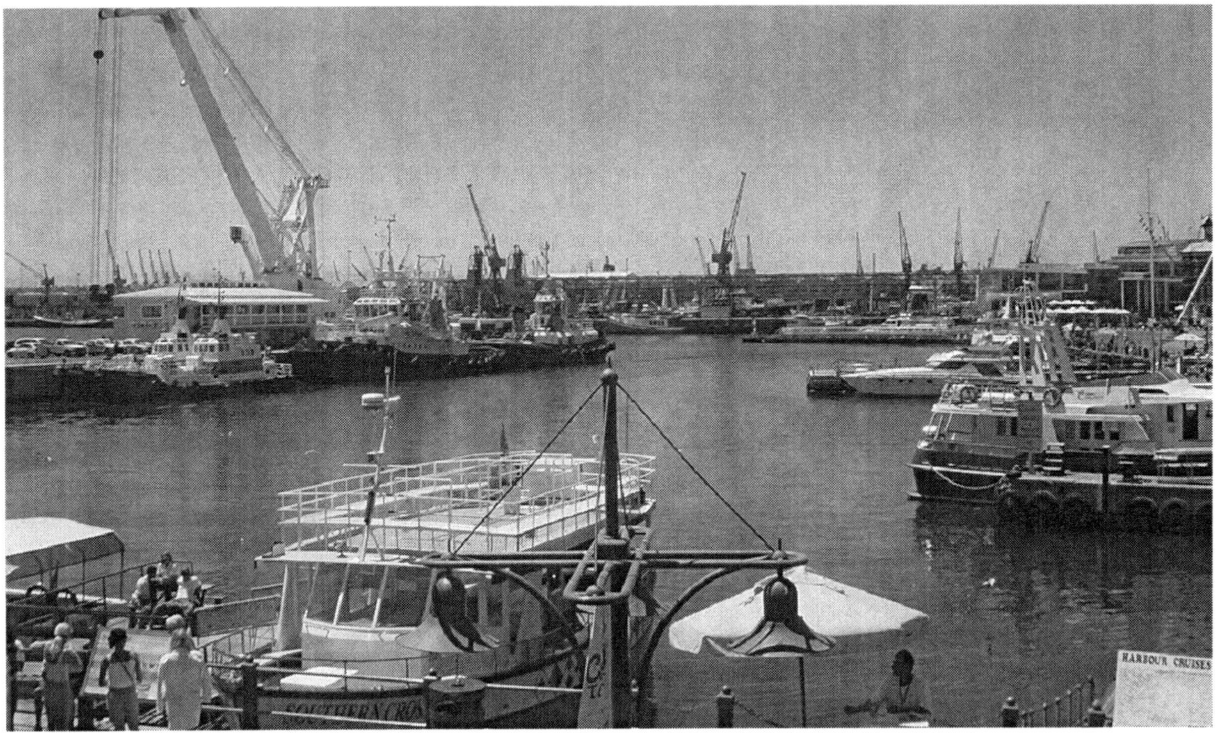

VICTORIA AND ALFRED MALL HARBOR, CAPE TOWN, SOUTH AFRICA

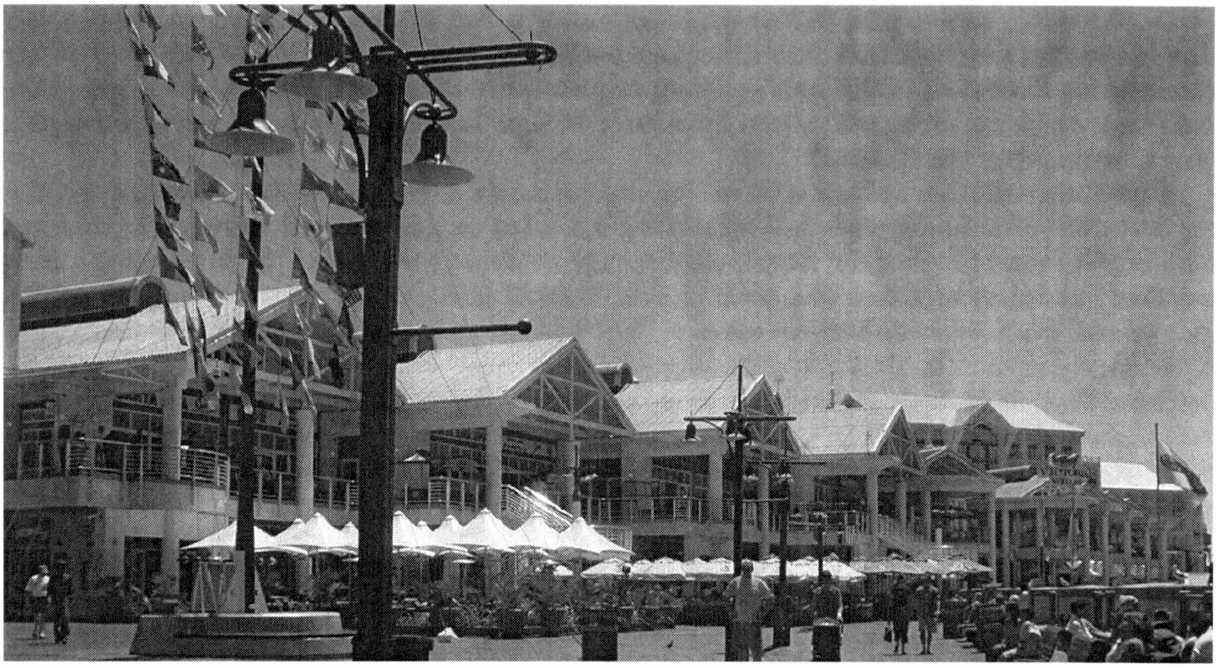

SHOPPING MALL, VICTORIA AND ALFRED WATERFRONT, CAPE TOWN

The V&A Marina happens to be right in front of the elegant Cape Grace Hotel. This is the hotel that President Clinton and his staff took over in its entirety when he visited South Africa during his presidency — our tax dollars at work. I talked with the hotel staff about the visit and they were quite impressed with the then president Clinton. They were particularly impressed with his friendliness and talkativeness with the staff. He went right into the kitchen and talked to the head chef and his staff. Another thing that intrigued them was the private room that was reserved for President Clinton's dog, Buddy — of course, it's a real necessity to reserve a private room for your spoiled dog.

This five stars hotel is a beautiful five-story building of good-looking architecture. The dining room, its food and service were all first class. Breakfast was a super treat with endless options. There was a help-yourself buffet in addition to table service from a fine menu. With the U.S. dollar about seven times the value of the rand, we ate like kings for around $5. Another big feature is their Bascule Whisky Bar. It features the largest liquor selection in the southern hemisphere. The wine cellar also appears to be well stocked. Friday, after work, is the time to howl at the bar for young working class Cape Towner's. There is live entertainment and the place is people-to-people packed. The crowd is so large that they cannot be contained in the lounge area of the bar and they spill out onto the large, concrete wharf of the marina. Walking through the noisy, tightly packed crowd to get to our boat was a test of one's resolve. It is apparent, the Bascule Whisky Bar is the place to take business guests and the "it" place to be seen on Friday nights in Cape Town.

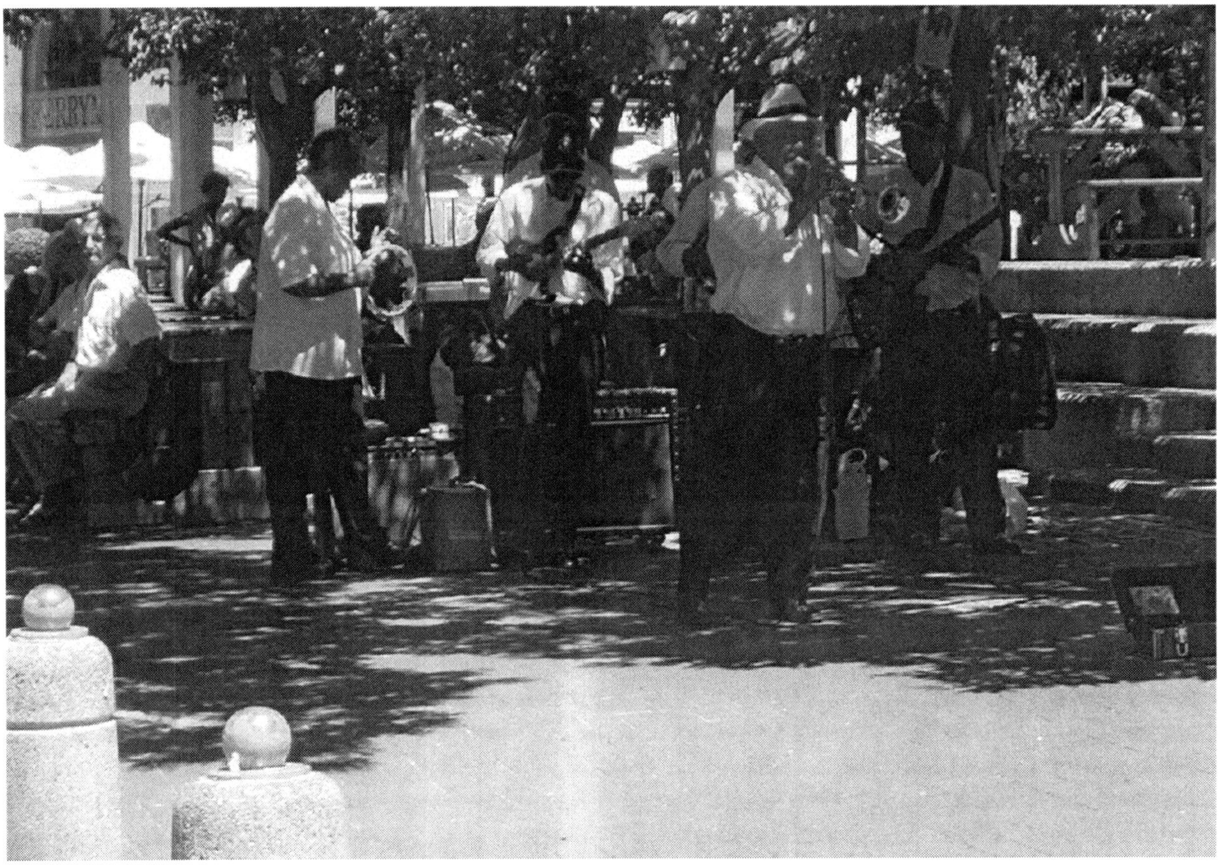

JAZZ GROUP ENTERTAINING SHOPPERS, VICTORIA AND ALFRED MALL

The first tour Pat and I took was the Cape Peninsula. The tour includes Cape Point the tip of peninsula's mountain chain, the Cape of Good Hope, the lighthouse there and fabulous views. The drive along Chapman's Peak Road, a narrow high mountain road to Hout Bay was impressive. Next were the Twelve Apostles an impressive outcrop of twelve towering rock formations. A drive through upscale neighborhoods of Cape Town that lie along the Atlantic Ocean, like Camps Bay, Clifton Head and Sea Point.

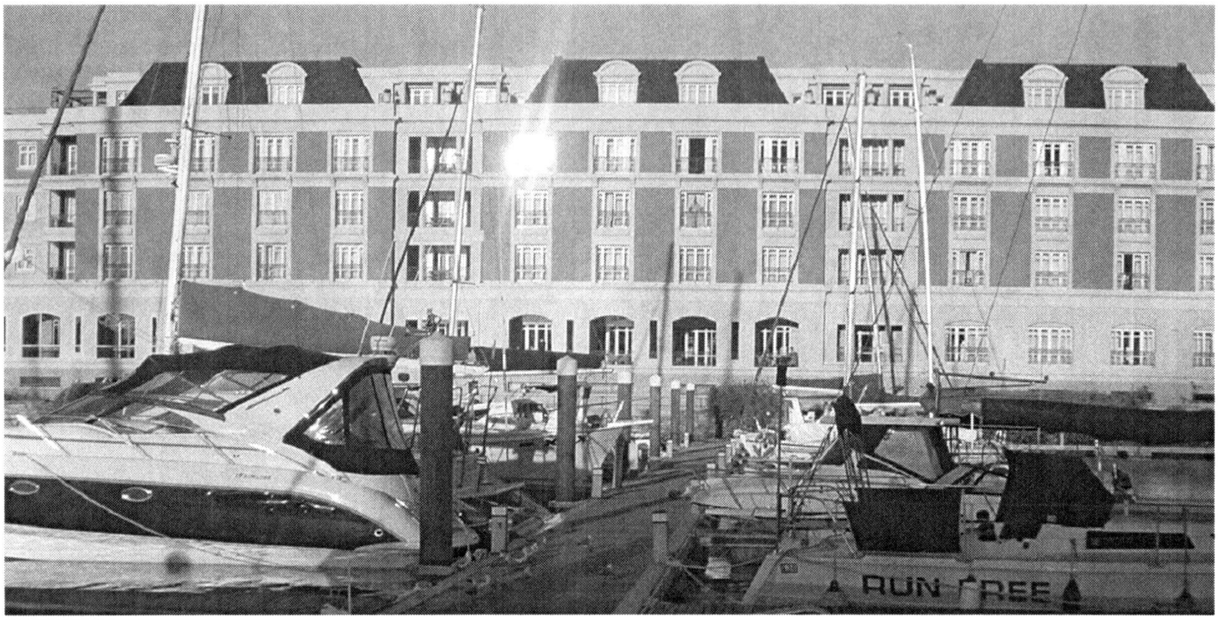

CAPE GRACE HOTEL, VICTORIA AND ALFRED MARINA, CAPE TOWN

One of the final points of interest was Castle Good Hope. Built between 1666 and 1679 it is the oldest structure in South Africa. The castle exhibits included period furniture, glass, metalwork and paintings by old masters, featuring Thomas Baines. There is also an impressive military museum of weapons and uniforms from the Dutch East India Company and periods of British occupation. One unique feature of this huge castle is a large private pool built for Lady Anne Barnard around 1790. The pool is built around a bronze dolphin sculpture and hence is known as the "Dolphin Pool." Lady Anne was married to the then colonial secretary Andrew Barnard. The beautiful courtyard and pool were quite extraordinary for their time. The pool and its surroundings must have been a place of tranquility and the site of lavish entertaining for Cape Town's dignitaries.

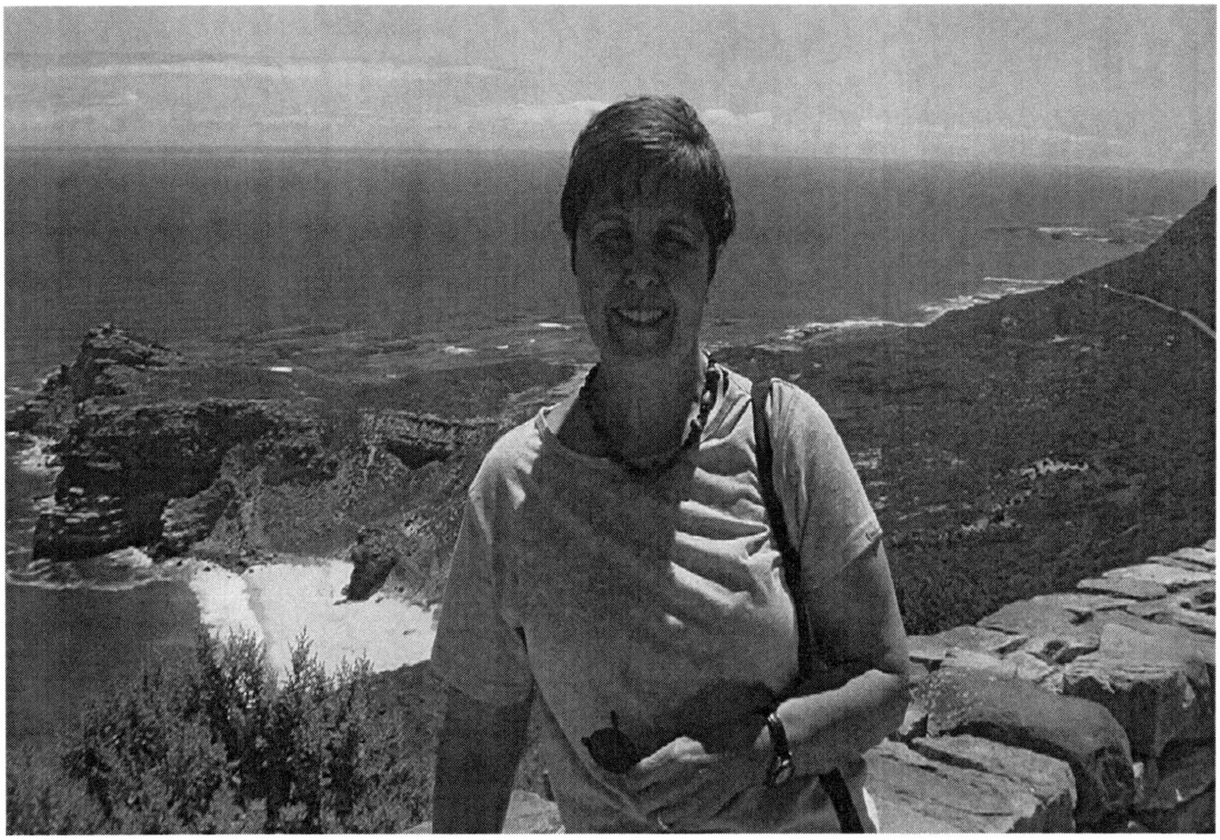

PAT AT "CAPE POINT," SOUTH OF THE CAPE OF GOOD HOPE NEAR THE MOST SOUTHERLY POINT IN SOUTH AFRICA, "CAPE AGULHAS"

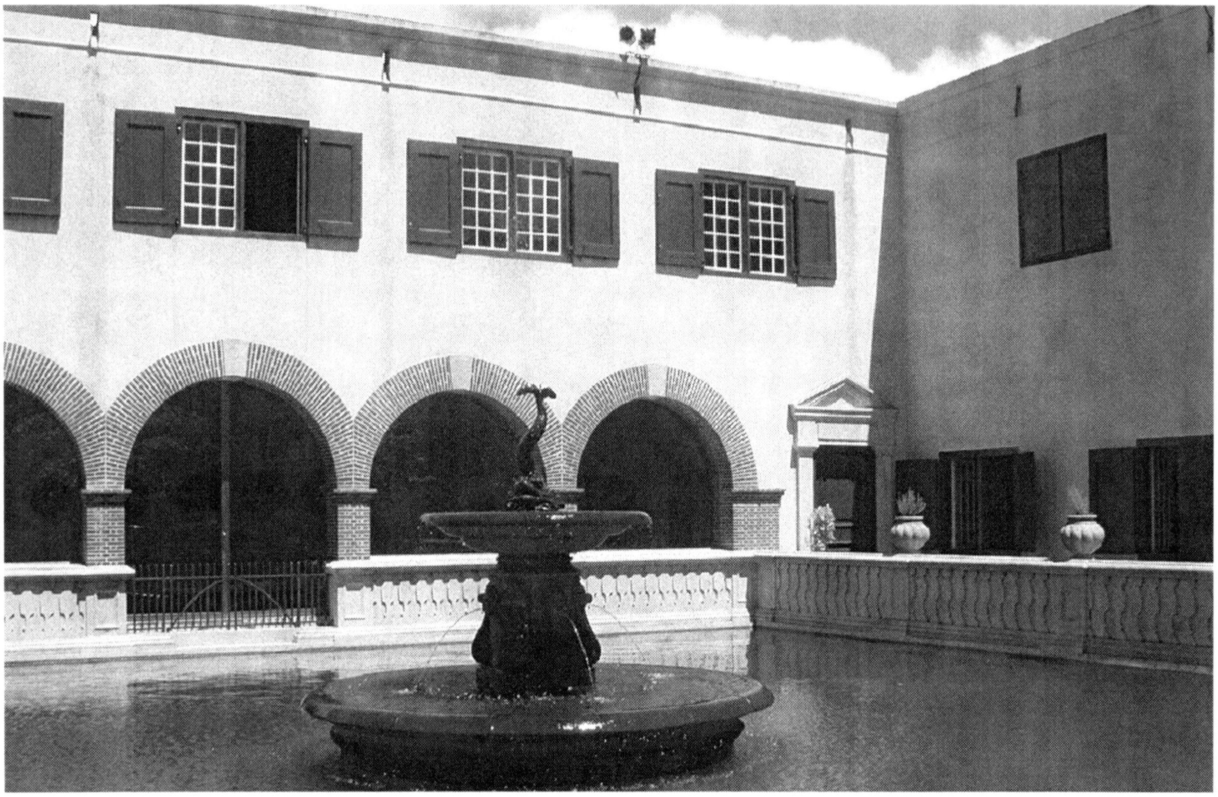

CASTLE GOOD HOPE'S "DOLPHIN POOL" FOR LADY ANNE BARNARD, CIRCA 1790

The Robben Island prison tour was probably the most significant of the tours for Pat and me. It is all about the Apartheid years and Nelson Mandela's fight against oppression. It was only back in 1948 that the white Afrikaner-based National Party came to power and imposed harsh laws on black Africans. They managed to control the composition of parliament to strip black Africans of their human rights. They established racial classification laws to dictate where people could live, work, be buried, what schools children could go to and what they were taught. People were classified according to their skin color. Sex between different skin colors was punishable with imprisonment and possible confiscation of land. If a husband and wife were classified as having different skin colors, they could not live together and were separated. All blacks had to carry passbooks, which were permits to work in white areas. They contained detailed descriptions of the carrier and had to be presented to police on demand.

The final blow was the law requiring black schools to teach using the Afrikaans language. A language developed from seventeenth century Dutch. This law resulted in bloody revolts during which some 575 people died. White solders used real bullets and fired on protesters. A famous news photograph published in newspapers around the world during the riots, showed a lifeless boy carried by his brother and mother. The revolts did eventually lead to negotiations between the blacks and the white government. On April 27, 1994, South Africa became a democracy. This was truly one of most significant events in modern times. Two adverse cultures both claiming ownership to the same land put their differences aside and reached a compromise that they both could live with — there may still be hope for Israel and Palestine.

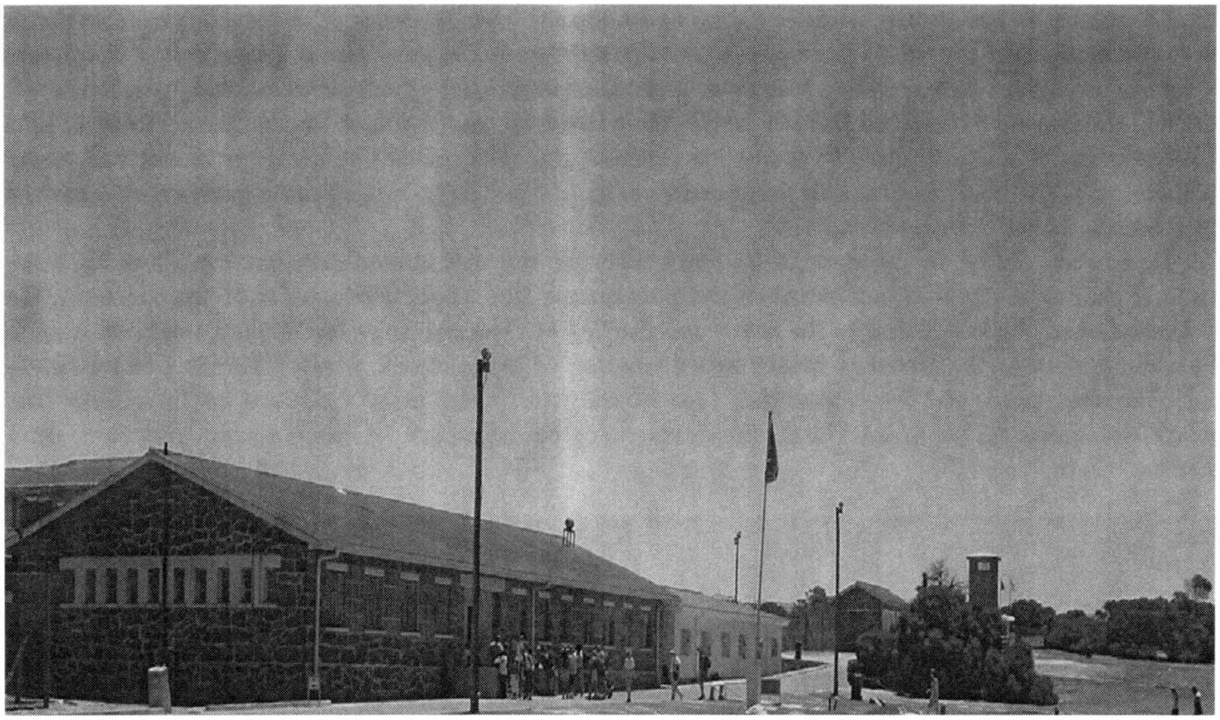

MANDELA'S PRISON HOME FOR 18 YEARS ON ROBBEN ISLAND

Mandela spent almost 28 years in prisons, from 1962 to 1990, for his leadership roles in the African National Congress (ANC). He spent 18 years at the Robben Island prison, an offshore island seven miles north of Cape Town — not a nice place. His leadership along with Desmond Tutu forced State President Frederick Willem de Klerk to move toward reconciliation. On April 27, 1994, 63% of the population voted for democracy and Mandela was elected the new State President. The prison tours are conducted by former prison inmates and the gruesome details of their treatment is pretty sordid. The sleeping space was so limited prisoners had to decide what side of their body was going to be on the floor mat. Once in place there was no room to change positions. Beds were finally brought in near the close of the prison. The jail cell where Mandela spent most of his time has been spruced up by bright paint for the tours. The small cell is tiny about 8 by 6 feet.

Ten years of democracy has seen many changes, but Mandela's government inherited a monumental mess back in 1994. The population was fragmented, the government was bankrupt, the economy was failing and the white civil service workers were not cooperative. International trade and investment was hampered by Africa's burden of foreign debt.

Another rugged mountain next to Table Mountain is called Loin's Head; it rises 2,198 feet in clear view of the city. About halfway up this mountain a wonderful tradition in Cape Town takes place precisely at noon each day. A huge vintage cannon is fired from Signal Hill, just a stone's throw from ***Our Pleasure's*** moorage. The British placed a battery of cannons there in 1890 to defend the harbor. They load the cannon with three pounds of gunpowder and the resulting blast is so loud it can be heard all over Cape Town. The smoke from the cannon can also be seen from most of the town, but it's the thunderous blast that gets everyone's attention.

Of course, we had to take the cable car up to the top of Table Mountain. The mountain itself is always in the background of the city — just a glance over one's shoulder. The cable cars employ a unique design that is circular to support their revolving floors. As the floor revolves, about thirty riders can enjoy good views of the city, the Atlantic Ocean and Robben Island. Only two cable cars are used for the Table Mountain ride. Their movement is synchronized so as one car descends the other ascends to lessen travel time and power requirements. The total trip takes only four minutes to travel 3,600 feet. Once on the summit we were amazed by the beautiful 360 degrees views.

Because the top of the mountain is flat, like a table, you can walk around the entire top. There are many viewing platforms, places to buy souvenirs and a restaurant. The height allows views of the entire city, the Atlantic Ocean, Robben Island to the north and the Indian Ocean to the east. When a southeast wind is blowing, the top of the mountain usually gets a covering of wispy clouds, which resemble a tablecloth — rather unusual, pretty and always changing. One of our crew, Jason, actually climbed up Table Mountain, which took a grueling five hours. The climb was certainly a challenge, but the inspiration probably came from a lack of funds.

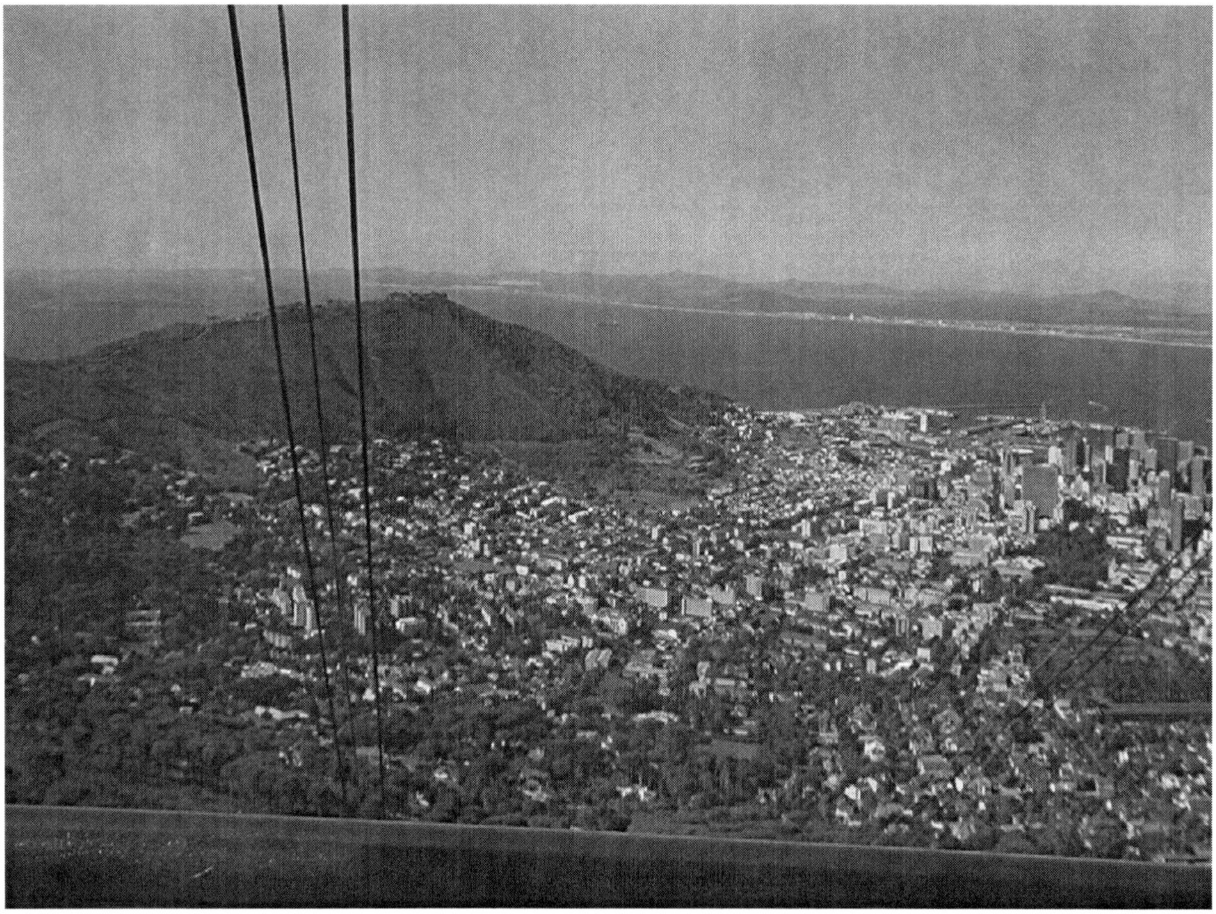

TABLE MOUNTAIN SUMMIT LOOKING NORTH, CAPE TOWN, SOUTH AFRICA

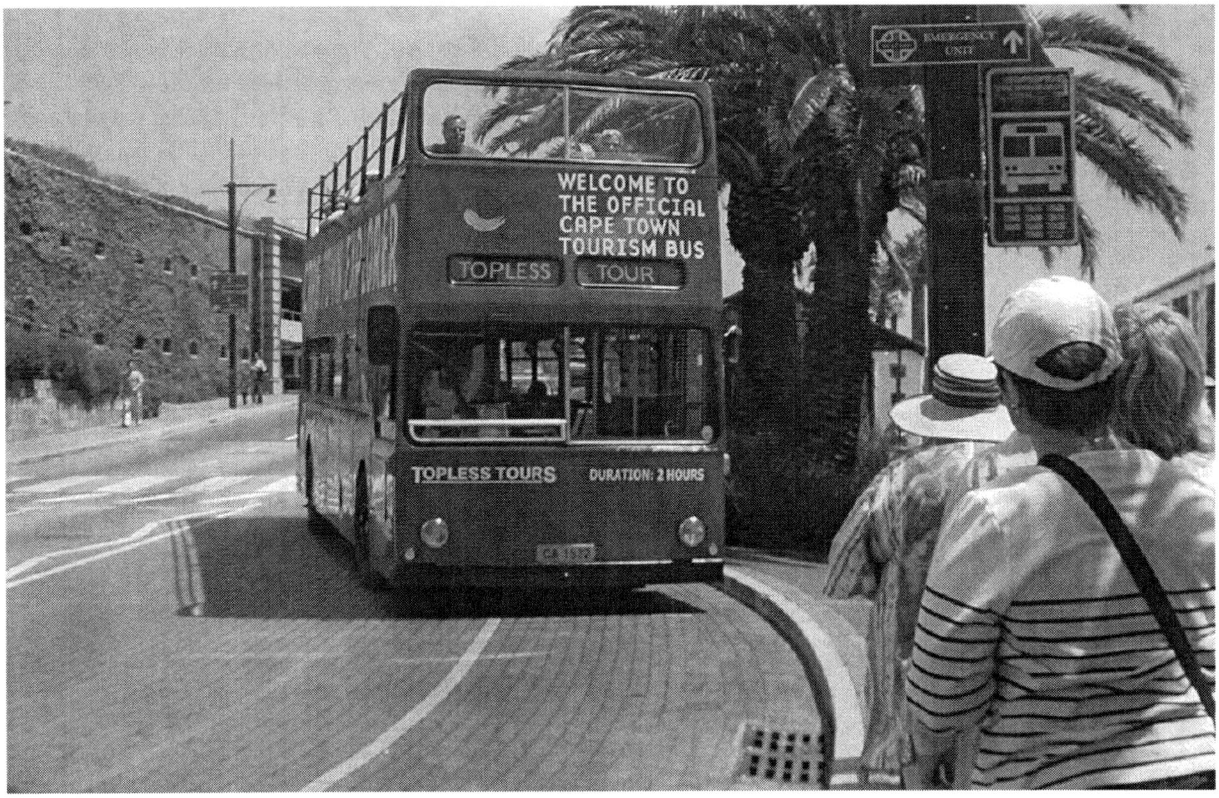

PAT WAITING FOR TOPLESS TOURS BUS, CITY OF CAPE TOWN

Endurance and *Esprit* left Cape Town on Feb. 1 and headed for St. Helena. Pat and I still had a lot of exploring to do and the next day we saw the African musical "Foot Prints." The following night we went to a hotel that had just been restored and according to a newspaper article, boasted an excellent chef. The Metrapole Hotel is nicely furnished with soft colors and lighting. We arrived early enough to be seated at a window table with views of a busy city street. However, as the night went on we noticed that the diners were mostly couples of the same gender — maybe a coincidence? The food was good, nicely presented and Pat enjoyed the whole experience.

Another tour on our list was the city bus tour called "Topless Tours." This two hour tour was conducted from an old English double decker narrated by a retired doctor. He made the tour interesting in that he was a long time resident of Cape Town and witnessed many of its major changes.

However, the most interesting changes that took place in Cape Town were highlighted on the Cultural Tour. This tour started out at "District Six," which once was the heart of Cape Town's black population. The District Six Museum located on the edge of this former Cape Town precinct has a vast collection of photographs. The photos depict life in this area before and at the start of the apartheid years. This mostly Muslim community was eventually completely leveled starting in 1966 to comply with the Group Areas Act. This drive toward Afrikaner Nationalism removed the blacks (Xhosa — natives of the Cape area) out of the city and resettled them in several areas miles from the city.

Mandela's father was once a Xhosa chief. The government policy in effect claimed that only whites could live in the cities. This put an extra burden on the blacks that had jobs in the city as now they had to pay for public transportation to get to work. Of course, the areas that they were moved to were sordid shantytowns. To this day millions of blacks live in shacks of scrap wood and sheet metal. One sink and a toilet are placed in a 4x4 concrete block building to be shared among the families living in four of the shanties. The families must go outside to use this facility. The government at this point has moved about a million families into government built homes. They have a long way to go before a dent can be made in relocating these poor blacks into decent homes.

Pat and I walked through one of these black ghettoes and were deeply moved by the poor conditions these people lived in. When Pat pulled out some suckers, commonly known as lollies in the southern hemisphere, the children came running. Some of the children probably have never had a lollie before as they put them directly in their mouth without taking the rapper off.

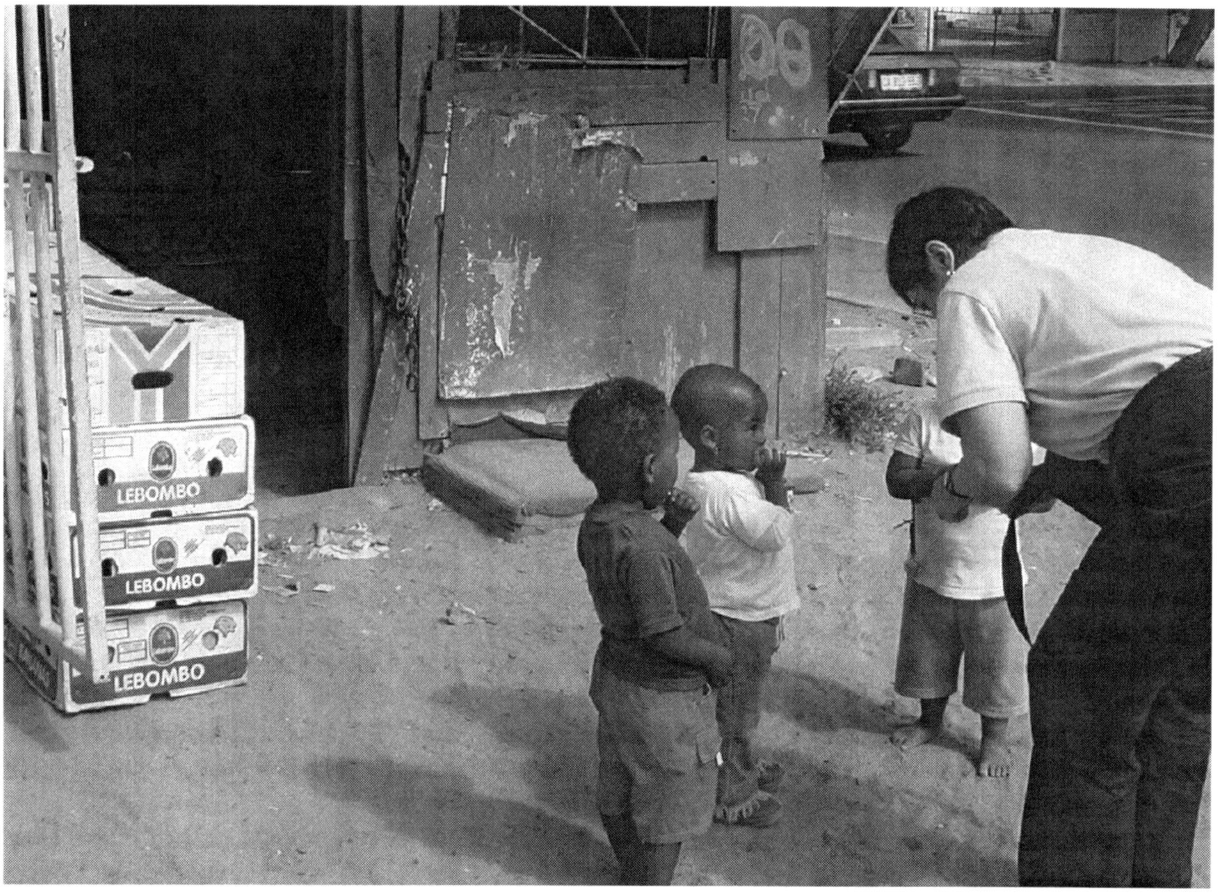

PAT DISTRIBUTING "LOLLIES," AT A CAPE TOWN SHANTY TOWN

The local healers, known as sangoma, (an African shaman) are practitioners of herbal medicine, divination and counseling in traditional Zulu and Xhosa societies of South Africa. These medicine men still practice their craft in the shantytowns. We went to visit one of these healers who practiced in a dark smelly building with all sorts of unknown skins, roots and herbs. He put on his headdress when we walked in with our cameras and was happy to pose for us. The hundreds of bottles with weird looking stuff were all over the room, the bottles were mostly unlabeled. During the conversation he had with Pat, he made some startling remarks. He said becoming a medicine man was not something he wanted to do. He claimed some mysterious force directed him toward that calling and did not allow him to sleep until he started helping people. We found out later that their philosophy is based on a belief of ancestral spirits. Both men and women can be called by their ancestors and if they don't respond, they may feel physical or mental anguish. He had no formal training, but said he was guided by a spiritual force that provided the right medicine to the people asking for help — who are we to question that? Of course, most of the people who call on him are poor and probably could not afford to seek out a medical doctor. Our guide saw our skepticism and was quick to explain the importance of these healers in their society. Anyway, we were left with the thought that this healer might be more genuine than we gave him credit.

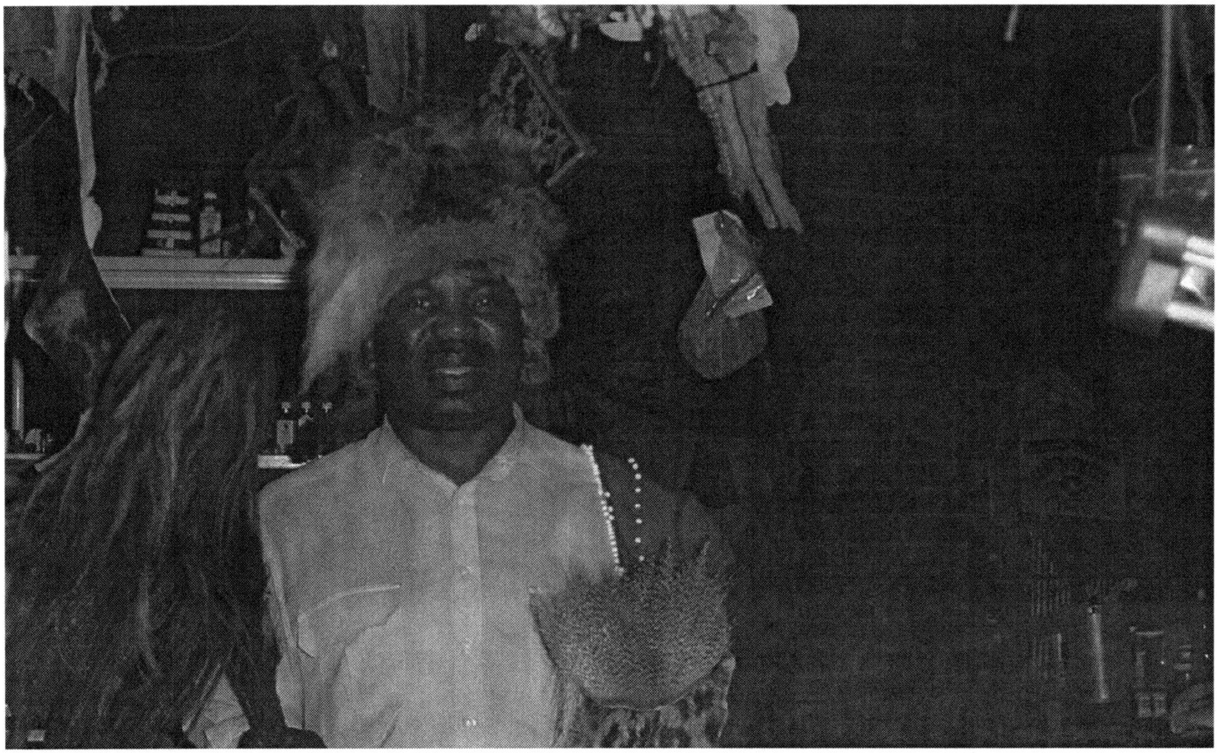

SANGOMA, MEDICINE MAN, WITH MYSTERIOUS COLLECTIONS OF DEAD ANIMALS, PLANTS, TREE ROOTS AND OTHER UNKNOWNS

We then visited a shebeen, an illegal drinking establishment. This shebeen did not advertise, as there were no signs or lights, you just had to know it was there, but I don't think authorities pay much attention. Two women were busy in back of the single room, dirt floored shanty, making the lightly alcoholic beer. The women's cloths and aprons were soiled from their work — cleanliness did not seem very important. About 10 men, no women, were sitting around in a big circle on make shift chairs socializing with each other and drinking this homemade brew called umqombothi, a beer distilled from malt and cornmeal.

The beer is concocted in big drums with very little time to ferment. The beer is scooped out into 5 liter buckets, which are passed around for drinking. The cost is 75 cents a day and that entitles you to drink as much as you want for a whole day. Pat and I bravely tried a mouthful of the beer and were not impressed. The taste was similar to a watery wheat cereal, rather light and the alcohol content was weak. They served the beer to us in a clean and polished can; quite different to the cans the natives use to drank their illegal alcohol. Their cans were well used, discolored, dented and probably never saw any soap, after all, alcohol kills germs.

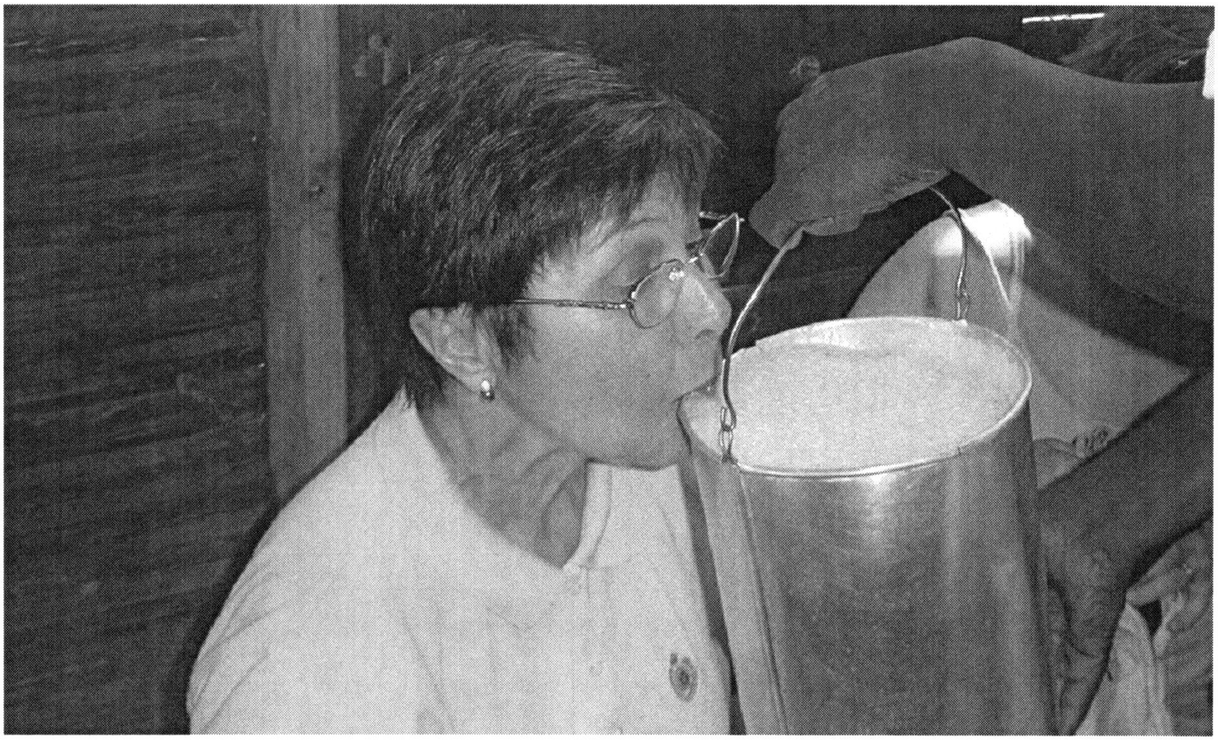

PAT TRIES SOME OF AFRICA'S ILLEGAL MAIZE BEER AT A SHEBEEN

Later in the tour, we were surprised to find a bed and breakfast in this vast town of shanties. This B&B was called "Vicky's" after the owner who started it. Vicky is famous in Cape Town for her big heart in helping her fellow Africans. One of the ways she helps is to provide a display space in her living room for arts and crafts of her people to sell to better healed tourists. However, most of her income goes to help the poor in her community. Her wall is full of newspaper articles and awards attesting to her generosity. Once, Queen Elizabeth recognized her for her generosity and aid to the poor. The Queen actually invited Vicky to England for the Queen's coronation. Her B&B is extremely modest with two small bedrooms and an outside toilet. The beds are doubles with well-worn mattresses that sway in the middle. The rooms have a slightly damp smell, but they were clean and tidy.

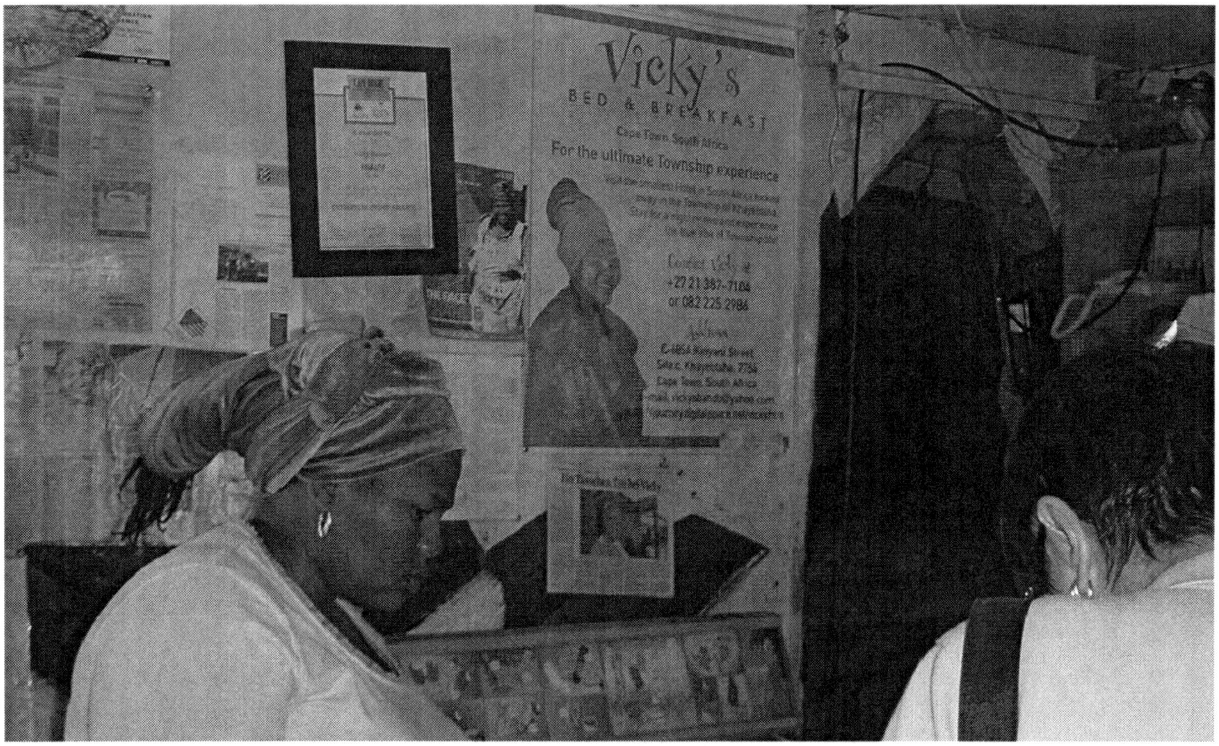

VICKY, SITTING WITH PAT IN THE LIVING ROOM OF HER FOUR ROOM B&B

Exposed wiring, non-conformity to wiring codes, illegal wiring and frequent power outages among the shanty communities has made daily living worse for the poor in Africa. Authorities rarely inspect shantytown wiring and potential dangers go uncorrected. A fire in one shack, if not controlled immediately, will spread rapidly. Just before leaving Cape Town, a fire destroyed several hundred of these homes before it was controlled.

The following Saturday the marina manager, Robin and his fiancée Melanie, took us on a grand tour of the famous Stellenbosch wine country. Stellenbosch is only one of the several wine regions within driving distance from Cape Town. Deciding which of the 101 wineries to visit in the Stellenbosch region was no simple task. The drive to and from Cape Town left us only enough time to visit three wine estates. We knew the Simonsig Winery had good reputation for fine wines and it became our first stop. We were overjoyed to find a year 2,000 Syrah Merindol that won two gold medals. Generally, wines in SA are an amazing value in American dollars, but high-end wines like these will cost around $20.

We stopped at the well-known Spier Wine Estate for lunch as the grounds and restaurants looked inviting. Their wines however, did not match our tastes. In addition, we found out that they don't put their wines into competition — not a good sign and after tasting a few I understood why — no wine purchased there. The last winery was Nederburg. There we purchased a case of their wonderful Cabernet/Sauvignon/Shiraz blend bottled in 2001 for about $5 per bottle. This blend of grapes had a nice smooth taste and besides, the Shiraz grape is my all time favorite. This winery has a well-known yearly auction presided over by British Wine Auctioneer, Patrick Grubb. His name did not mean much to me, but apparently, he is well known in real wine circles.

The most interesting thing happened in the winery garden. While waiting for the tasting samples to be delivered to our table, we had time to take pictures of our surroundings and ourselves. Hearing a strange voice behind me, I turned to find a friendly American offering to take a group photo. His name was Victor Rossi an Italian American who has lived in South Africa for thirty years. He was there buying wine with his charming wife Bonnie and two guests from U.S. college days, Jim and Deborah Pasquale. He was interested in our adventures and we became close friends for the rest of our Cape Town stay.

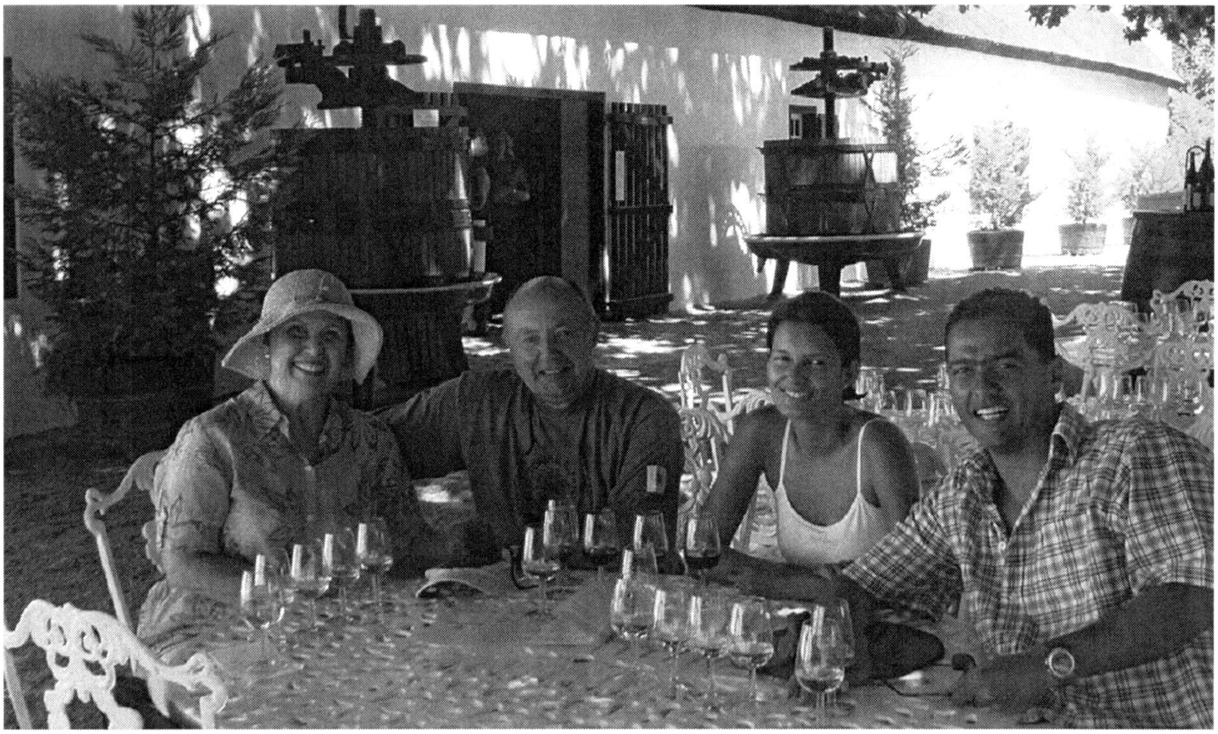

WINE TASTING AT NEDERBURG WINERY, STELLENBOSCH, SA; PAT, DICK, MELANIE AND ROBIN

The next night we invited the Rossi's, the Pasquale's and Victors close friends, Fonie and Sanet to our boat for Champaign. Later we were invited to tour the V&A waterfront and view Atlantic Ocean beach homes from Fonie's boat. His boat turned out to be a 40 foot Bayliner; a boat built in my hometown, Seattle and moored at the V&A marina. The Rossi's, Fonie and Sanet own homes in exclusive Cape Town neighborhoods facing the Atlantic Ocean. The view of Cape Town from the ocean at sunset is a marvelous sight. Afterwards Victor took everyone to his favorite restaurant, La Pearla, for dessert. Victor knew the whole staff there including the owner. He claims to have been their first customer when it opened 30 years ago.

Two days later, we were invited to the Rossi's home for a wonderful five course Italian dinner. We were treated to a rocket leaf salad using olive oil; shaved pecorino cheese and prosciutto; homemade cannelloni; homemade tortellini; fresh fruits; two red African wines and tiramisu for desert with coffee. It just so happened that an international mining convention was taking place in Cape Town and Victor invited Daniel, a customer and CEO of gold mine in Ghana. Fonie and Sanet were also invited, which made for a lively dinner conversation.

Victor asked everyone to talk about one of their most memorable experiences in life — for us it was easy as Pat and I have had many; interesting personal experiences continued late into the evening.

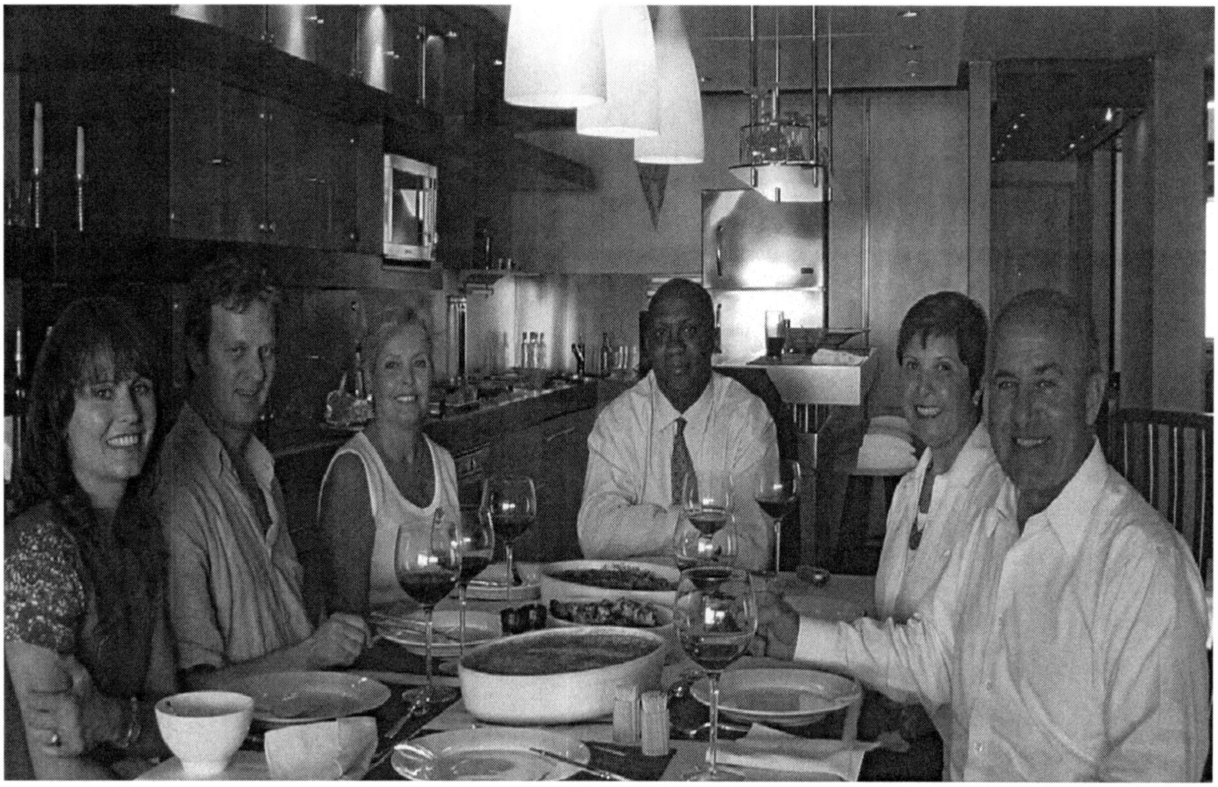

FIVE COURSE ITALIAN DINNER AT VICTOR AND BONNIE'S CONDO OVERLOOKING THE ATLANTIC OCEAN, SANET, FONIE, BONNIE, DANIEL, PAT AND VICTOR

Right across from our moorage workers brought in two large barges and started erecting grandstands. The barges became the seating and stage for a water opera. Along the back of the stage, artisans built a wonderful mermaid using wire mesh to form her outline. She had such a pretty face, somewhat serious, with long eyelashes, long flowing hair and a silver tail. She was about 80 feet long and formed a beautiful backdrop for the opera.

The interior of the mermaid was large enough to house all the dressing rooms. The barge that was lower in height, became the floor for the grand stand and the opera's large symphony orchestra. The opera was a mixture of several musicals that contained water themes such as *South Pacific*. They did a commendable job of tying the musicals with water themes together to establish a classy night at the opera. All the music was well known to the general public and it was obvious they enjoyed every song. Pat and I managed to get good seats close to the stage and were impressed with the voices, the music, the lighting and the overall superior performance of the whole cast.

Pat left Cape Town on Feb. 13, 2003, for Seattle and the crew, Jason and André, spent the next few days preparing ***Our Pleasure*** for the 6,000 mile trip to Trinidad.

Chapter 24

CAPE TOWN TO ST. HELENA

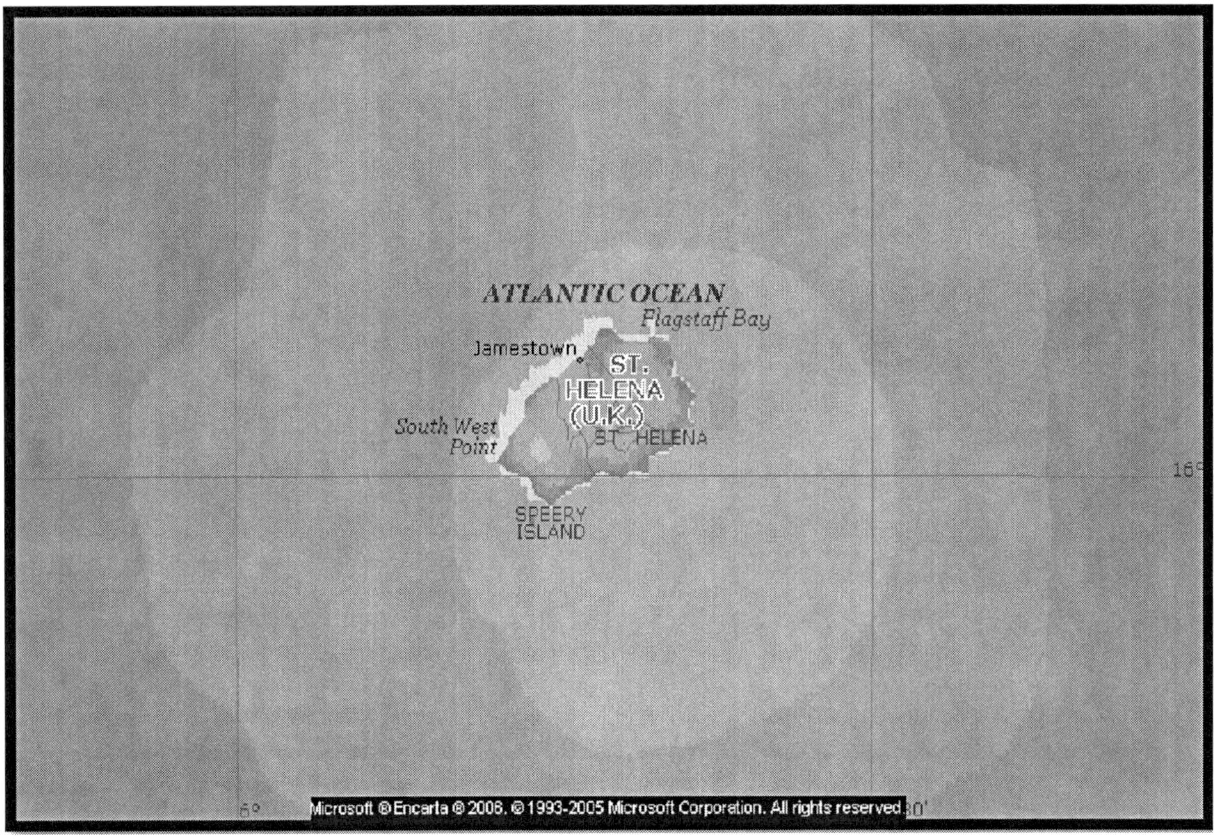

ST. HELENA, BRITISH DEPENDENCY, ATLANTIC OCEAN

Our Pleasure, along with Jason and André, left Cape Town under clear skies and calm seas with almost no wind. Jason and André would be sharing the cooking duties and I would help with galley clean up, navigating, sails, etc. Watches were arranged so each crewmember would be on watch for three hours and could sleep for six. It was so pleasant to look back at the big city buildings and the wispy clouds over Table Mountain. Starting out on a long voyage in good weather is always a boost for morale as we had 6,000 miles of sailing to Trinidad ahead of us. We steered a course to the north, keeping Robben Island to our starboard side.

The next day, Feb. 19, 2003, we had managed to sail 147 nautical miles from Cape Town by noon. The wind had picked-up quite a bit since yesterday and was now blowing 35 knots out of the southeast. We were making 7 knots with the wind blowing from a good position over our starboard aft quarter. The sea was rough now and the ride, the crew agreed, was not comfortable. We were told this type of weather would be the norm for the next four days or so until we reached the trade winds. In the trades, the wind speed should be steadier and not so boisterous, which will be reflected in calmer seas.

On watch in the cockpit, I noticed a group of whales about a quarter mile away to our north. They were to the starboard of us swimming in the same direction we were headed. At first, I noticed some water spraying in the air and wondered what was going on. Then I saw a tail and several other waterspouts. I counted about seven of them swimming in a rather spread out formation. At that point, I decided to start the engine to make our presence known. I had not been looking at the port side of the boat as all the action was to starboard — big mistake. The bow rose up a bit and a loud thump was heard coming from the forward part of our keel. Just then, a big whale's head appeared close to our starboard side and a mighty big eye was staring at me. His expression looked happy though as opposed to painful, if a whale's face can show emotions. When I saw his face, his tail was still near the surface on the other side of the boat. That probably made the whale about 30 feet long, I think it looked like a humpback whale, but I am not sure.

I turned my head to watch his whole body move away from our starboard side. We were moving rapidly north at that point and he faded in the distance to the south. I could not tell if he was injured, but he appeared to be swimming away in good fashion. I looked for any sign of blood on the surface, but did not see any. It was quite a jolt as the crew, who were sleeping at the time, all heard the large thump against the hull. I am quite aware that whales sometime sleep on the surface, so I try to keep a sharp lookout for them. In the past, noise from the engine running kept them from coming too close to the boat; I guess this whale did not get the message. This one caught me by surprise and I hoped he was not hurt. In the back of my mind was the thought that the hard structure of the keel might have injured him. From accounts, I have read in the past, injured whales have been known to ram the boat that injured them. Therefore, there were some anxious moments until we knew we were well away from the area.

Three days later the wind had moderated to 15 knots and the boat motion was once again pleasant. We were now 1,067 miles from St. Helena Island, our next planned landfall. We have been averaging over 153 nautical miles per day, but knew our mileage would drop as we entered the southeast trades. The inside temperature was averaging about 76° F at this point, but the humidity had been steady around the 74% mark. For dinner last night, André put together some hot dogs with diced potatoes and refried beans.

On Feb. 24 and 25, we encountered light winds and had to rely on our engine. The wind did not come back until Feb. 26. What a relief, it is so annoying to have the engine running night and day. I usually do not worry about the amount of fuel we use as we could probably motor to St. Helena by keeping the speed around four knots. We are now at 22° 37' south latitude and the inside temperature has risen to 80° F. The humidity however, is going down and is now averaging around 63%. The crew is doing a fabulous job of making dinner and keeping everything tidy. We use a lot of chicken in dishes like chicken and rice. Pasta is also a big favorite with ground beef and a red sauce. Our big freezer has plenty room for these long trips. As we approach the equator from the south, we see fewer sea birds, but more flying fish.

Marv overheard me talking to the South Pacific ham operator, Alistair, (call sign ZS5MU) who was broadcasting the weather from the east coast at Durban, South Africa. Marv was nearing the coast of Brazil to the west and knew I was having trouble connecting with any of the SSB Sailmail® stations, our commercial, offshore e-mail provider. He was able to send a short message to Pat saying I was okay and our location was about halfway to St. Helena. Earlier, I had asked Alistair if he would send an e-mail message to Pat using his

South African landline provider. He did send my message, but my e-mail provider, AOL, said my address was protected and he was not allowed entry. Anyway, sitting in the southern Atlantic Ocean, there wasn't much we could do about it.

By Feb. 28, we were 389 nautical miles from St. Helena, sailing wing and wing at about six knots in 12 knots of wind from the SE. We saw a freighter this morning, the first since leaving the South African coast. Flying fish are becoming more evident now as we usually find several on deck each morning. The barometer was steady on this trip usually between 1018 and 1020 millibars. The outside temperature was always around 80° F. while the inside temperature was generally around 83° F.

On the first day of March, we experienced a momentary power drop of voltage on the auxiliary and house battery banks. The voltage dropped below the minimum threshold of the autopilot and the GPS so they automatically turned themselves off. However, the batteries quickly recovered to 12.4 volts. When the voltage dropped, I heard the VHF radio protesting with a loud hum so I knew something was wrong. A similar problem happened before with this battery bank on the way to the Louisiades. I think it was a relay problem in the bow thruster electronics, but since it recovered quickly, I had no way of finding the fault. The VHS radio recovered without any problems, but I had to reprogram the GPS waypoints and reset the autopilot. It's a good thing I took the time to make a paper copy of the way points.

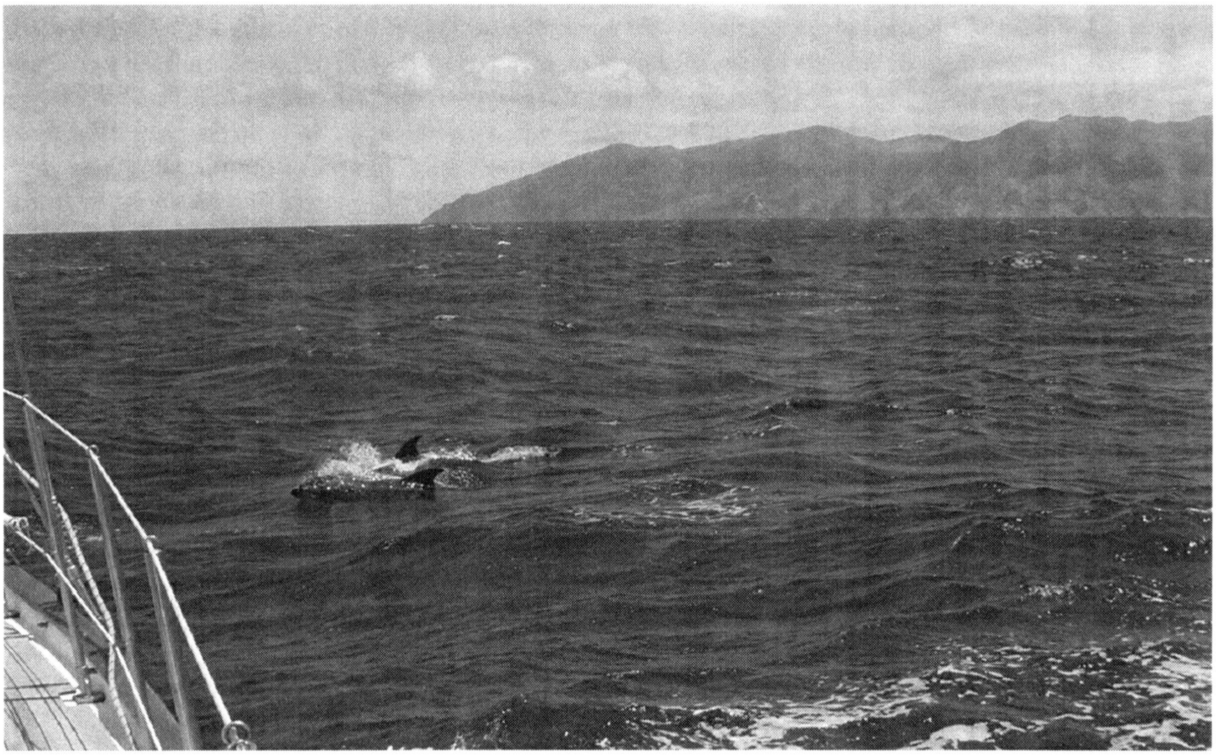

DOLPHINS PLAYING IN OUR WAKE WHILE APPROACHING ST. HELENA

We first sighted St. Helena on Mar. 2 from about 40 miles away. The highest point on St. Helena is Diana's Peak, 2,685 feet. As we got closer, we were selected by a large school of curious dolphins. They came over to our boat and swam across our bow for about 10 minutes. They put on a great show, sometimes with two or three of them crossing at the same time or crossing from different directions. I am always amazed at their great swimming skill, grace and speed.

Dolphins the world over love to swim in the bow wave of fast moving boats. They seem to take great pleasure in swimming across the bow of boats as if it is some kind of sporting event. They seem to lose interest though if the boat is not going more than five knots. Our boat has a stainless steel tube low on the bow that connects to the bow pulpit structure called a "dolphin striker." The name is appropriate as the lower end of this is tube at the waterline and moves up and down with the bow's motion. As the striker moves in and out of the water, it can hit a slowly maneuvering dolphin trying to swim across the bow. I saw it strike a dolphin in the Pacific once so I know it can happen. When that dolphin was hit, several other dolphins swam over to him as if they wanted to help. I believe he was momentarily dazed and was eventually able to swim away under his own steam.

As we got closer to St. Helena, we could see its rocky terrain rising dramatically from the South Atlantic. This island is mountainous, barren cliffs and shear rocky faces, drop straight down to the sea. The whole island appeared on the horizon as a black, foreboding, bleak and mysterious monolith in the middle of nowhere. Of course, St Helena is associated with the internationally renowned figure, Napoleon Bonaparte. The British exiled him there in 1815 following the defeat of his army in the battle of Waterloo. I tried to imagine what Napoleon must have thought when he saw the island for the first time — they could not have been happy thoughts. He would have seen it the same way we did, except his approach was from the north.

The British found him an exile location this time that was inescapable, in the middle of nowhere and looking extremely inhospitable from seaward. Actually, two deep valleys are the only places on the entire island where there is access to the sea. The first is at Jamestown, the capital city and only town, the other is at the opposite end of the island, Sandy Bay. There are no sandy beaches on St. Helena now, but there might have been in the 1800's. Sandy Bay is now accessible by a rough mountainous road, but would have been a murderous trek to reach during Napoleon's exile.

The following distances illustrate just how isolated this island is. Ascension Island, the nearest island, is 800 miles to the northwest. Tristan da Cunha is 1,200 miles southwest. Brazil is about 1,800 miles west and the nearest distance east, the west coast of Africa, is 1,200 miles. The island itself is not large, only 10.5 miles long and 6.5 miles wide at its widest point. The coastline is rugged and uneven making the total area only about 47 square miles. There are no airports on St. Helena so the only way to get there is by ship. Their newest ship, the HMS *St. Helena*, started serving the island in 1990. This ship was specially designed for St. Helena to provide passenger and freight service between St. Helena and Cape Town. She was alternately going to England, but that route is destined to be cancelled to save costs. When we left St. Helena, two companies were negotiating proposals to build an airport on St. Helena. One proposal would build an airport for small jet service and the other proposal would build a large hotel and an airport to support larger jets. Both proposals were meeting a lot of opposition from locals wanting St. Helena to remain quiet and isolated.

We arrived at James Bay at 4 p.m. local time. Our approach was watched by their Harbor Control and they advised us by radio where to anchor. By time the anchor set, the wind and current moved ***Our Pleasure*** past the intended 30 foot depth into 50 feet of water. Luckily we had plenty of chain so 50 feet was not a worry and the holding turned out to be excellent. The bay is on the upper northwest side of the island and opens to wind and waves from the northeast to the northwest. There was a consistent swell running from the southeast trade winds. This swell manages to find its way around to the northern tip of the island and varies with trade wind speed. The swell was tolerable though and only a minor irritant while we were at anchor. Harbor Control then advised us that the island's small passenger ferry would pick us up the next morning to complete their paper work.

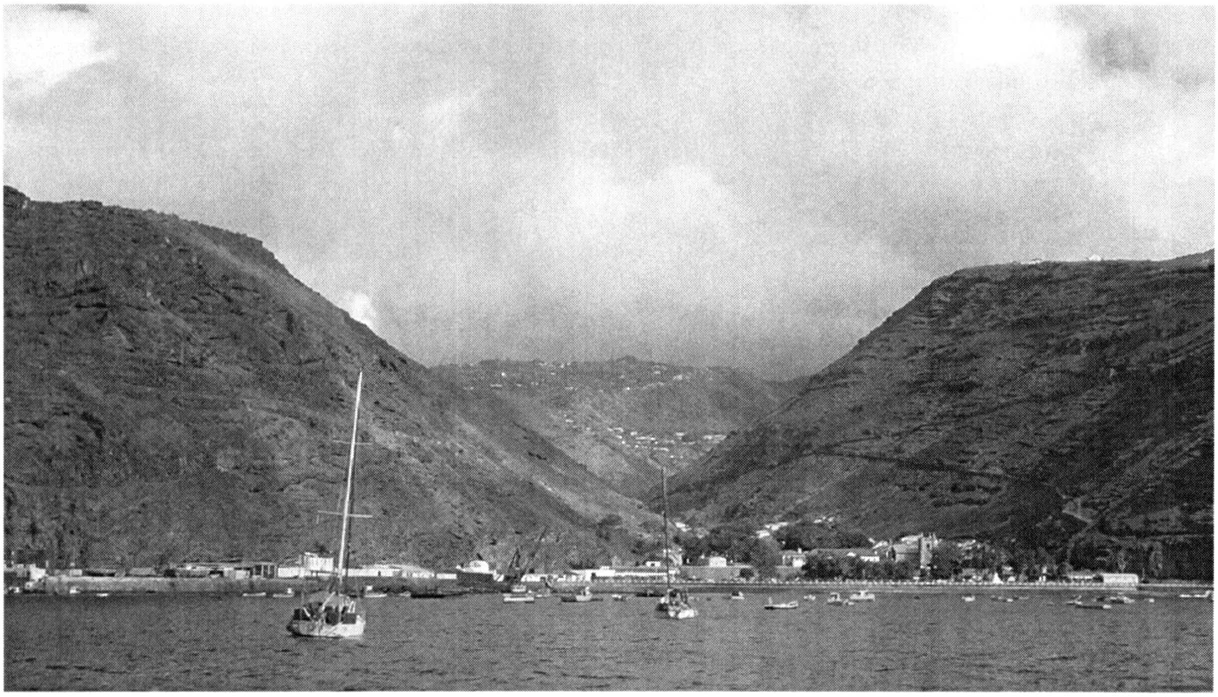

ST. HELENA'S MAIN HARBOR AND ITS CAPITAL, JAMESTOWN

The next day the ferry picked us up early in the morning, right on schedule. The friendly British port captain was waiting at the ferry landing to greet us. He welcomed us to St. Helena and led the way to the immigration office. The road was full of boulders from the construction project above us where crews were busy trying to stabilize loose rocks on the steep cliffs. All of St. Helena's entrance paperwork was straightforward, not complex or lengthy. We had to pay a harbor fee of £20.50, a customs fee of £11 for each person and £1.30 per person per day for health insurance. In addition the charge for the ferry was £1 per person per day between our boat and their pier. The passenger ferry was not elaborate, just a 20 foot runabout with a small enclosure to protect the pilot. All fees could only be paid using St. Helena pounds, which have the same value as the British pound, but with a unique St. Helena identity — of course everyone has St. Helena pounds.

Although there are no banks in St. Helena, some businesses do accept Visa and Master cards. One local business sold St. Helena pounds for American dollars and accepted Traveler's Checks. Cash advances on credit cards could also be obtained. The fees seemed a little steep to me, but we have no recourse to fees countries levy on cruisers. At least in this case, they did provide services like water, showers and toilets. Usually fuel could be purchased for yachts, but their Diesel supplies were at a crucial low point and were not for sale until the supply ship arrived. The lack of fuel was not a worry for us, but another American yacht, *Tree of Life*, needed about 600 gallons badly. They had motored most of the way from Cape Town and were pressed for time to make the Antigua Classic Yacht Races. The last time I talked to the skipper, they planned to motor to Ascension Island for fuel. We saw them briefly again at the Portuguese Island of Fernando de Noronha where they were ferrying jugs of fuel between the wharf and their boat.

Our initial thoughts, while walking around the town of Jamestown, were quite fixed on the people, the buildings and terrain. This place is both unique and quite different from any other city I have ever been in. For one thing, the people have a unique racial mix with varied skin colors and facial looks. The buildings looked as though they were out of an old time movie set; set close together with varied bright colors, second story balconies, with shuttered windows, ornate ironwork and elaborate doorways. As we learned more about this place, we came to realize how its history shaped the architecture and its people. The Portuguese explorer, João da Nova, discovered the island over 500 years ago in 1502. He named the island for the mother of Emperor Constantine the Great. The present population are descendents of British settlers, East India Company employees, some of the 10,000 slaves brought here from South Asia, East Indies and Madagascar. Chinese indentured laborers were also brought to the island and many stayed.

Everyone on the island was friendly and the varied cultures seemed to have integrated well with no outward signs of race problems. There is a small police station and one police car. We saw about three officers, but never witnessed any blaring sirens or blinking lights. The total population of St. Helena is about 5,000 with 900 living in Jamestown. The town is built at the bottom of a mountainous valley with sheer walls on both sides. The main street through town rises along a long sloping incline from the water's edge to the top of a ridge, which is about 600 feet high. The roads are paved, but narrow and single lane. On the steep hills, roads are single lane with small recesses where cars coming downhill can wait for cars going up.

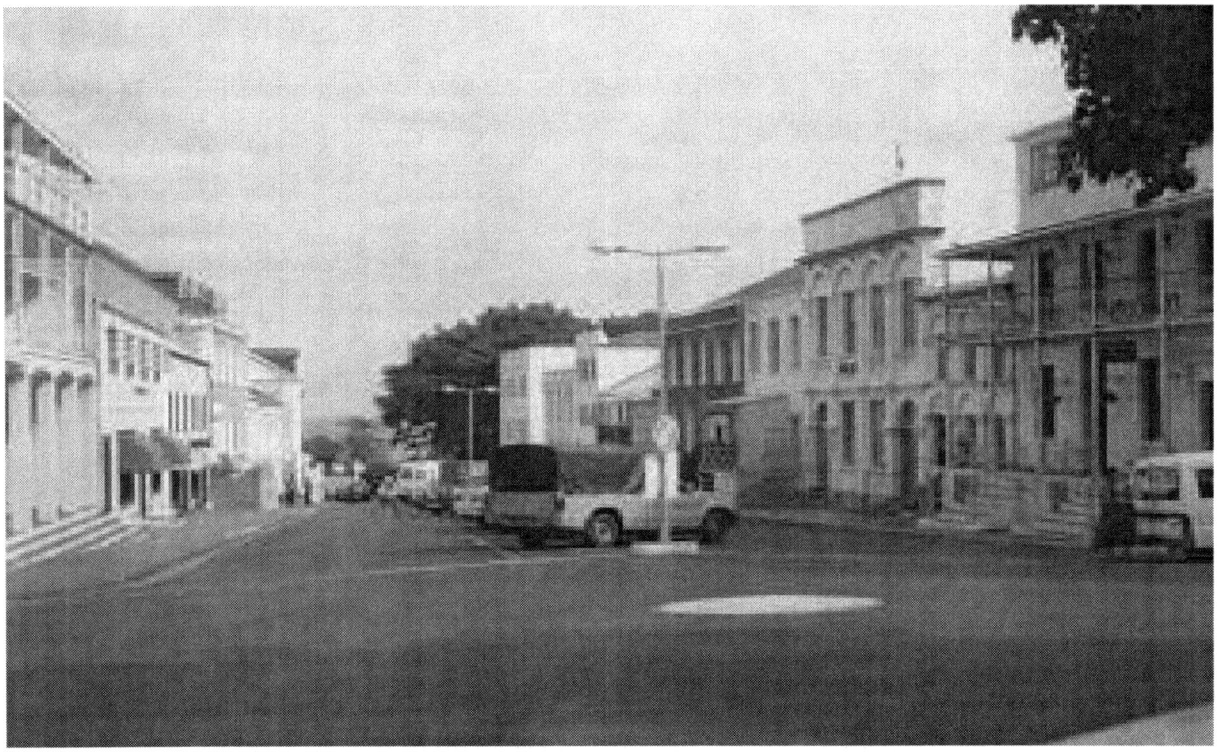

MAIN STREET OF JAMESTOWN, ST. HELENA

All the buildings in town have that old world look and most were probably built in the 1800's. The yacht club, for instance, was built in 1810, but has almost been destroyed by rocks falling from the cliffs above it. The original castle of St. John, at the entrance to Jamestown, was built in 1659. The castle has been well maintained and is now the seat of the St. Helena government. The building for the public library was built in 1813 and is the oldest library in the southern hemisphere. Tourists were welcome at the castle and library. Fighting between the Dutch, English, and Portuguese on the island destroyed the real early structures like a chapel that was active in 1601. Even though the majority of the buildings are quite old, they are painted nicely and maintained nicely.

I made dinner reservations for us at an eighteenth century building that is now "Harris's Guest House." This building was previously an alehouse known by sailors as the "First and Last" because of its position close to the water. Irene, the owner, would serve a home cooked meal based on our preferences if given a day to put it all together. Since Jason, our Australian crewmember, had not been back to his home for several years, we asked Irene to do a lamb dish. Of course, lamb is probably the most popular meat in all of New Zealand and Australia. Irene put together oven-roasted lamb, three vegetables, fruit salad, homemade ice cream and homemade cheesecake. The dinner was fabulous especially when compared to our boat meals.

We sat at a big comfortable dining room table and drank South African wine without rolling all over the place as sometimes happens on ***Our Pleasure***. We had the dining room to ourselves as one guest staying at the house scheduled his dinner late evening. The house was decorated in what I imagined was old English furniture, heavy dark pieces, delicate china, crystal glassware and lots of red color in the décor for draperies and overstuffed chairs. The total cost was unbelievable at only $8. We had to pre-bribe the ferry pilot to wait for us, as I knew the dinner would run past his last taxi run.

The women in the tourist office were super friendly and accommodating. An unexpected surprise was several nice brochures outlining the many places of interest on the island. The list of places to see was surprisingly long for a small island and included: Archives (island records from 1673) and Deadwood Plain (Boer War prisoner camp). The Boer war, 1899 to 1902, was a South African conflict between Britain and the Dutch descendents, known as Afrikaners or Boers (Boer means farmer in Dutch) that had immigrated to South Africa starting around 1652. They were Germanic ethnic groups descendents of Dutch, Flemish, French and German settlers. Their language, Afrikaans, was primarily derived from 17th century Dutch, and a variety of other languages.[5]

We thought the best places to visit would be:

- High Knoll Fort (completed in 1874).
- Jacob's Ladder (700 steps embedded into a steep cliff, built in 1829).
- Knollcombes (cemetery for Boer War prisoners).
- Museum.
- Napoleon's House and Tomb.
- Philatelic Bureau (stamps of St. Helena, Ascension and Tristan da Cunha).
- Plantation House (governor's residence and home of a giant, 172 year old turtle).
- Prosperous Bay House (old look-out station).
- Radio St. Helena (St. Helena's only radio station).
- St. James's Church (oldest Anglican Church in the southern hemisphere).
- St. Paul's Cathedral and Cemetery (built in 1850).
- Briar's Pavilion (first exile residence of Napoleon on the island).

5 Courtesy of Wikipedia®

There is no public transportation on St. Helena, but the tourist office will arrange taxis and cars for hire. They set up a tour for us with Thomas and his vintage Land Rover. This Land Rover was modified as a pickup truck with a sun canopy and hardwood bench seats on each side of the truck bed. The tour started in front of the tourist office at 8 a.m. Because of time constraints, we had to limit our tour to one day. The sites we agreed to included: The governor's mansion, Jacob's Ladder, High Knoll Fort, Napoleon's house and tomb and Briar's Pavilion.

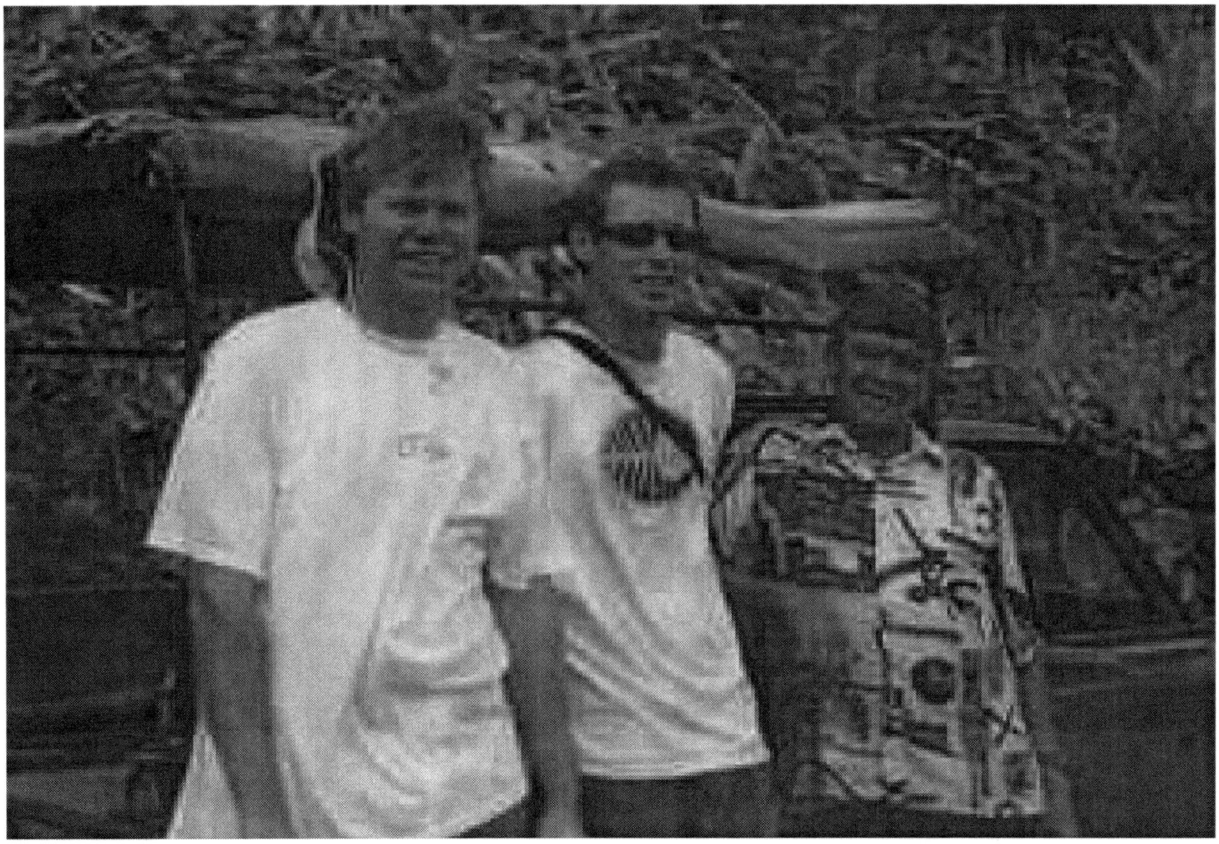

CREW: ANDRÉ & JASON WITH TOUR GUIDE THOMAS

The first tour stop was at the remarkable work of manual labor known to the local's as "Jacob's Ladder." This stairway was built back in 1829 and rises so high it can be seen from every part of the city of Jamestown. The base of the stairs starts near the waterfront of the city and rises at a steep angle to the cities protective fort. Just looking at 700 steps that were originally carved into the hard rock face is impressive, but the thought of the back braking labor it must have taken is mind-boggling. The steps end in the clouds at a place called Ladder Hill. We drove up the steep, single lane road in Thomas's laboring Land Rover to the top of Ladder Hill some 600 feet high. There is an old fort there with barracks and gun emplacements pointing out at James Bay. The ladder was an incline plane in its previous life that incorporated a platform to lift supplies to the top of the hill by ropes and pulleys. Jason and André actually thought they were up to the challenge and walked up to the top and down the stairs the day before our tour. The toll on their legs and other parts of their bodies was quite evident for several days.

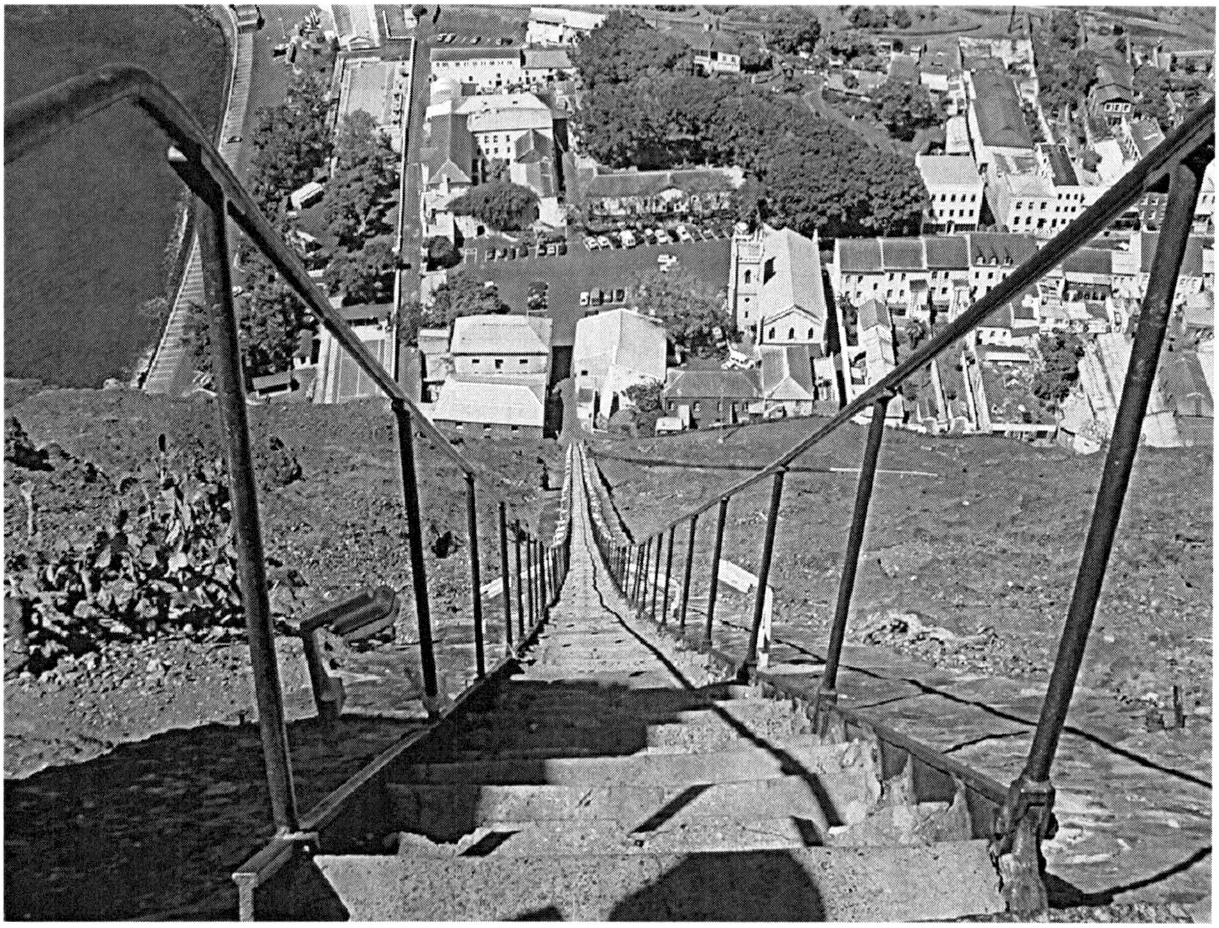

LOOKING DOWN THE 700 STEPS OF JACOB'S LADDER INTO JAMESTOWN

The governor's mansion is known as the "Plantation House." The original house was built in 1792 by the East India Company to house the island's resident governors, which were sent by England to oversee the functioning of the island. The house is now an impressive looking, two-story mansion, with Georgian façade that has been remodeled and expanded through the years. A large sweeping green lawn surrounds the house, which is more like a paddock or a large enclosed pasture. There are flower and vegetable gardens, walking trails and a forest of 110 acres. The plantation's forest contains trees of many varieties that were planted experimentally to see how they would do in the local climate. The trees seemed to have thrived, but the program must have stalled.

I understand the present governor's wife is not excited about her life on St. Helena and does not entertain much. Whereas former governors had lavish parties at the house and on the lawn, When British naval ships used to visit the governor, they flew in on their helicopters and landed on the lawn.

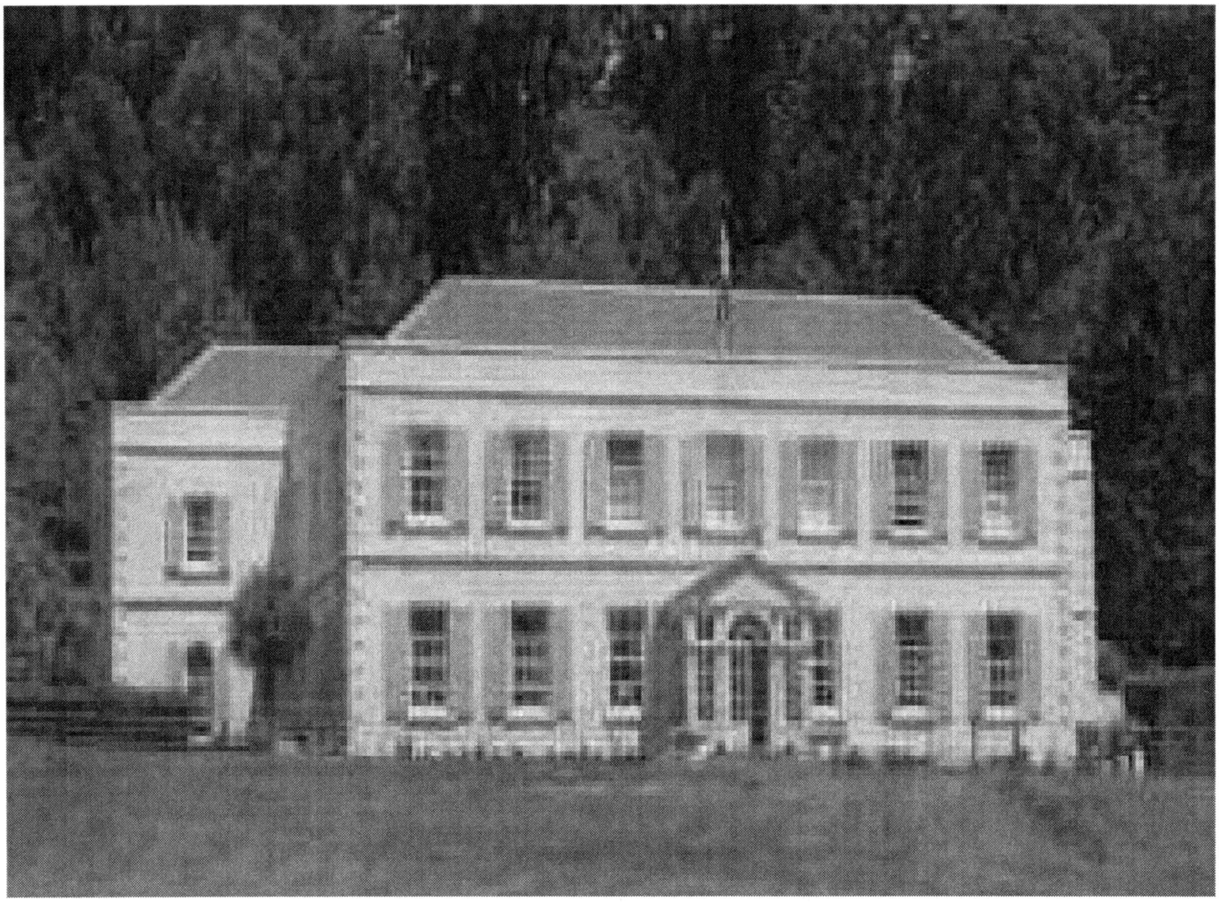

PLANTATION HOUSE (GOVERNOR'S MANSION)

A green iron railing encloses the grounds. Within the iron railing and on the vast lawn, there are five giant tortoises. Jonathan the oldest, is thought to be 172 years old. This old guy weighs about 400 pounds and was a gift from the governor of the Seychelles. He seemed friendly so we talked respectfully to him and petted his shell and head with no hostile signs from the huge old turtle. He actually did not pay any attention to us and kept walking toward his private waterhole.

Looking through history books about Napoleon, *The Age of Napoleon* by J. Christopher Herold, *Napoleon: the Immortal Emperor* by Gérard Gengembre, brochures from St. Helena and tour information, I pieced together information about his fascinating life. Napoleon remains a large figure in the Western imagination as an historical personality for his military and political genius. The aura that still surrounds him makes him a subject of great interest and fascination. Born Aug. 15, 1769, he rose from obscurity to become a charismatic and dominant leader like Alexander the Great. He seems to have had visions of an integrated Europe with a democratic form of government, inspired by the French Revolution. His "Grand Army" rolled across Europe in an invincible form until stranded in Moscow during the Russian winter of 1812. From there it was downhill for the French Empire as England, Austria, Russia and Prussia combined their forces to work against him. Thousands of soldiers were killed fighting Napoleon's wars. For example, in the Battle of Austerlitz, France lost 9,000 men, the Austrian and Russian armies lost about 25,000 soldiers — sad state of affairs.[6]

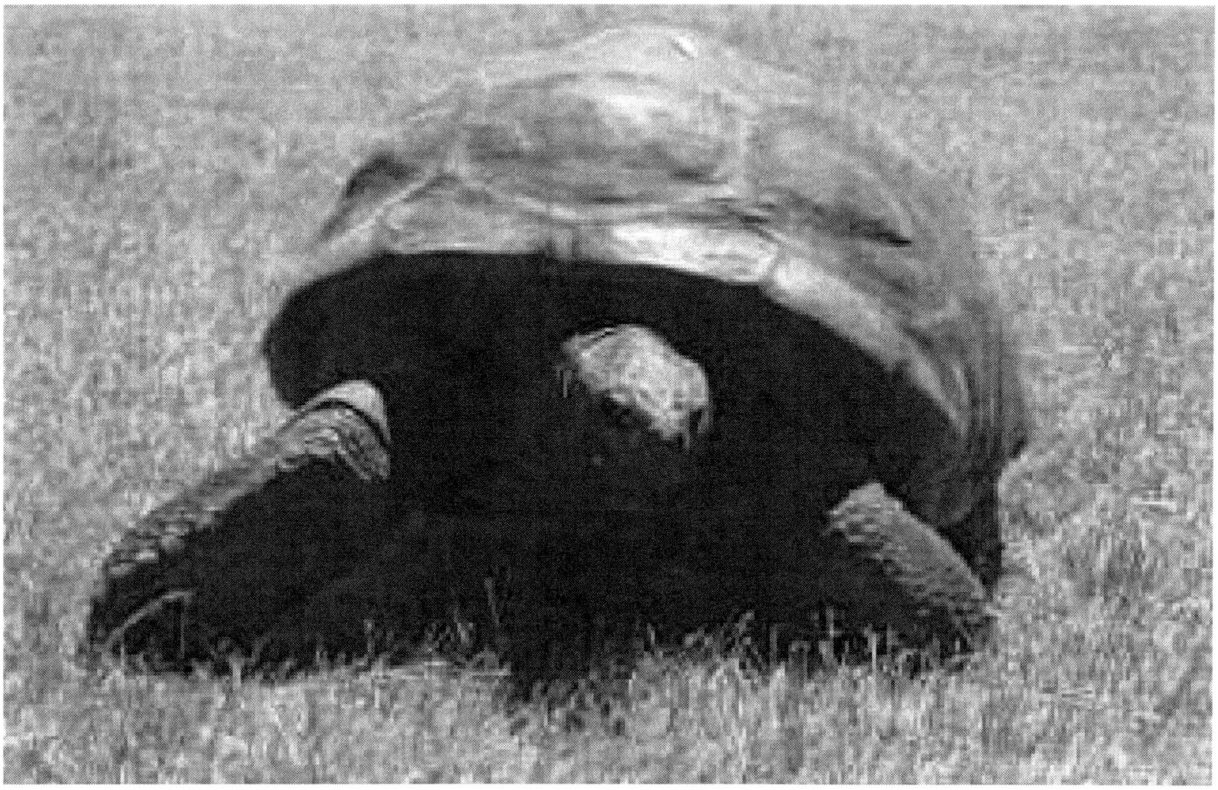

JOHNATHAN, 172 YEAR OLD TURTLE

Napoleon's generals deplored him to abdicate his throne to keep from plunging France into civil war. In the settlement, the Treaty of Fontainebleau, Napoleon was to become the emperor of Elba, an island off the west coast of Italy and receive annual revenue of two million francs a year. The empress received the same compensation and three duchies. The rest of his family was also to be well compensated. On April 20, 1814, Napoleon said goodbye to his loyal soldiers at the Chateau of Fontainebleau and headed for Elba. At Elba, Napoleon watched the disappointment and discontent of the people in France, Spain, Austria, Italy and Germany. There was lots of petty haggling and reneging on all promises by his victors.

6 Courtesy of Wikipedia®

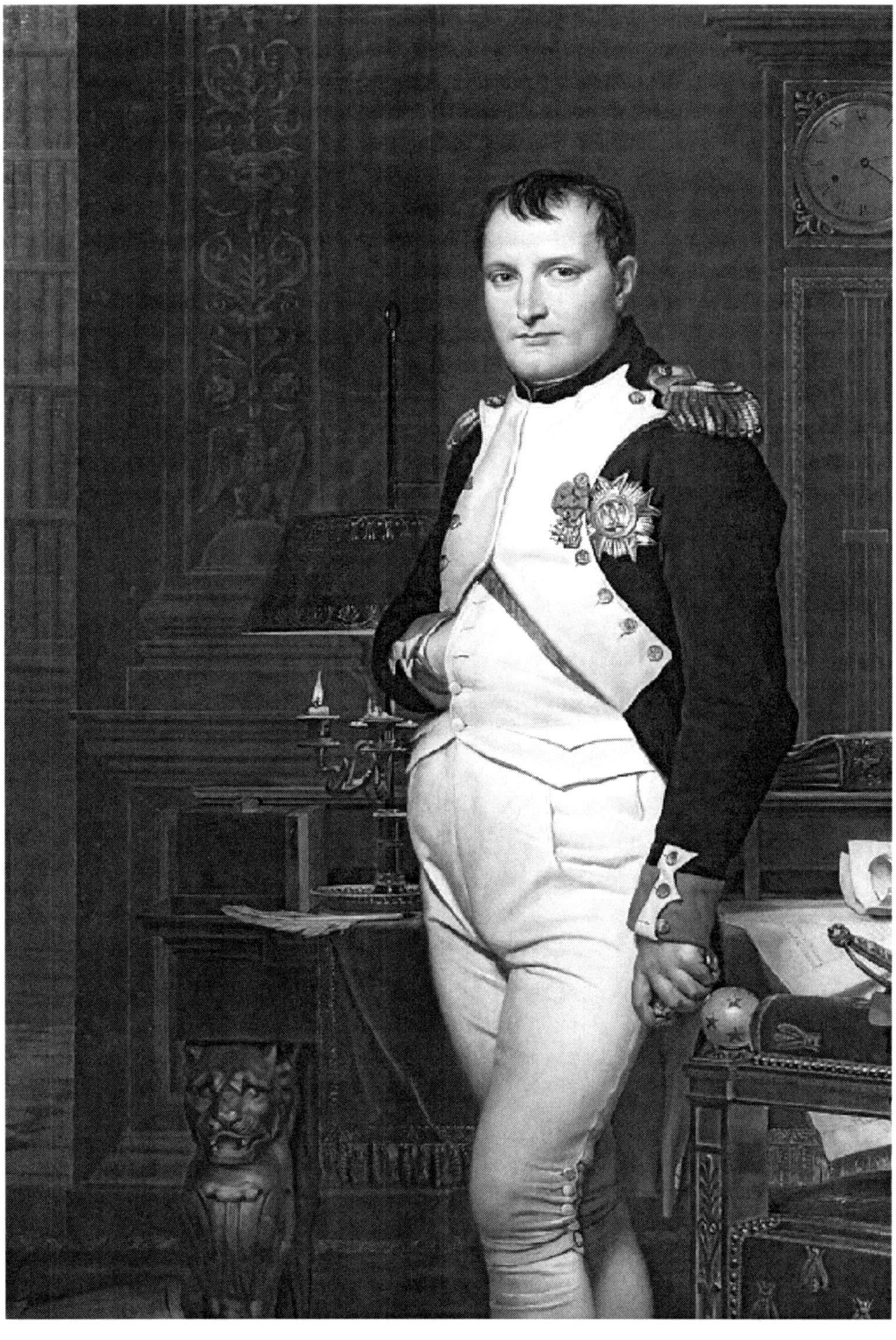

JACQUES-LOUIS DAVID, *NAPOLEON in HIS STUDY at the TUILERIES,* 1812

By March 1815, Napoleon managed to evade the British cruisers keeping watch on Elba and slipped back to France to reunite his former army as their leader. In Paris, the court of Louis XVIII folded and the king fled. All European powers, including the returned from exile, king of France, Louis XVIII, signed a formal alliance to declare war on Napoleon. Napoleon's army did well in several battles against the European armies and for a time, it looked like he might outsmart them. Weather, timing, and the steadfastness of the British army led to his armies defeat in Belgium at the battle of Waterloo, June 18, 1815. Napoleon escaped that battle and retreated to France. In France he made plans to leave for the United States (the Louisiana Territory), but was thwarted by a British blockade at Rochefort. If he had reached Rochefort a few days earlier he might have escaped, but bad timing and non-cooperating winds foiled his departure.

Napoleon threw himself at the mercy of England for the right of asylum. The British Government exiled him to the island of St. Helena via the HMS *Northumberland*, July 15, 1815. He died in exile there of stomach cancer May 5, 1821. He was buried at a site he chose for himself in the Sane Valley, St. Helena. After several years of negotiation, the British government, finally allowed Napoleon's body to be exhumed and returned to France. His coffin was lowered onto the HMS *Belle-Poule* whose rear deck was fitted out like a mortuary chapel that was on Oct. 15, 1840. In France, Dec. 11, 1840, his remains were treated to a grand funeral procession, passing through the Arch of Triumph, down the Seine to the open crypt at the church known as the "St. Denis of the Bonaparte's."

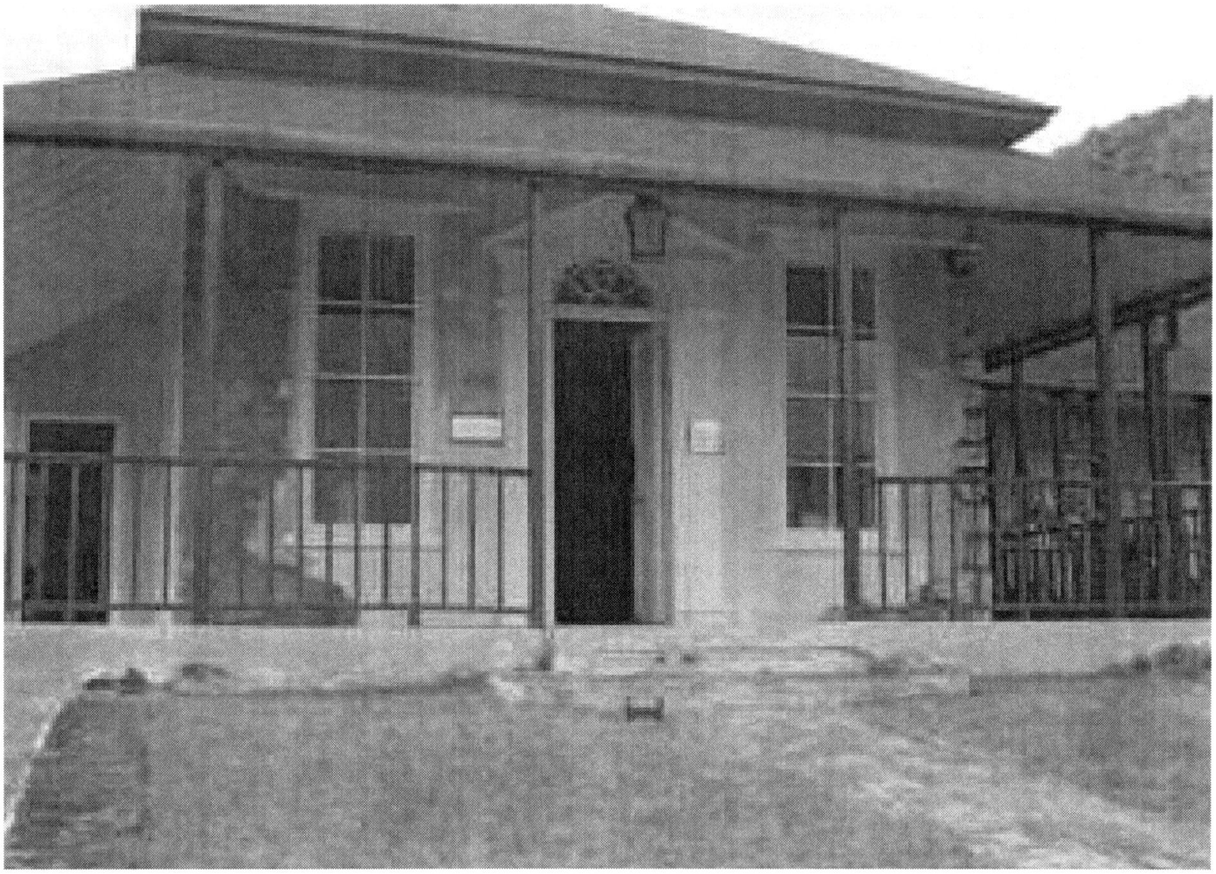

BRIAR'S PAVILION (BALCOMBE FAMILY HOME)

The French government maintains the three Napoleon sites on St. Helena: Briars Pavilion, Longwood House and the tomb at Sane Valley. We went to Briars Pavilion first. When Napoleon first arrived, this site was the Balcombe family home. It is situated on a high hill, far from town overlooking Jamestown, James Bay and the Atlantic Ocean to the north. The view is now obscured somewhat by tree growth, but when Napoleon stayed there, the views were probably awesome. The Balcombe family invited Napoleon to stay with them for three months until his house was ready at Longwood. The Balcombe house at that time was not much larger than a cottage. Now there is an effort to restore the cottage and locate the period furniture that belonged in the house, which is now a museum.

Next on the tour was Longwood House, the high point of our visit to St. Helena. Longwood House was originally a barn and converted into a house in 1752 for Lieutenant Governor Adamson. For Napoleon, the house was extended and repaired and is now maintained by a resident honorary French Consul. The tour guide at Longwood was knowledgeable about that period and Napoleon's life. One of the amazing historical facts relating to Napoleon is his mother, Letizia. She must have been an extremely outstanding inspiration for her family. Of her 12 children, 4 died in infancy, Napoleon became emperor of France, 3 of the boys became kings, one girl was a queen and another girl became a duchess. Napoleon had quite a career in his short life, as he was only 46 when exiled to St. Helena in 1815.

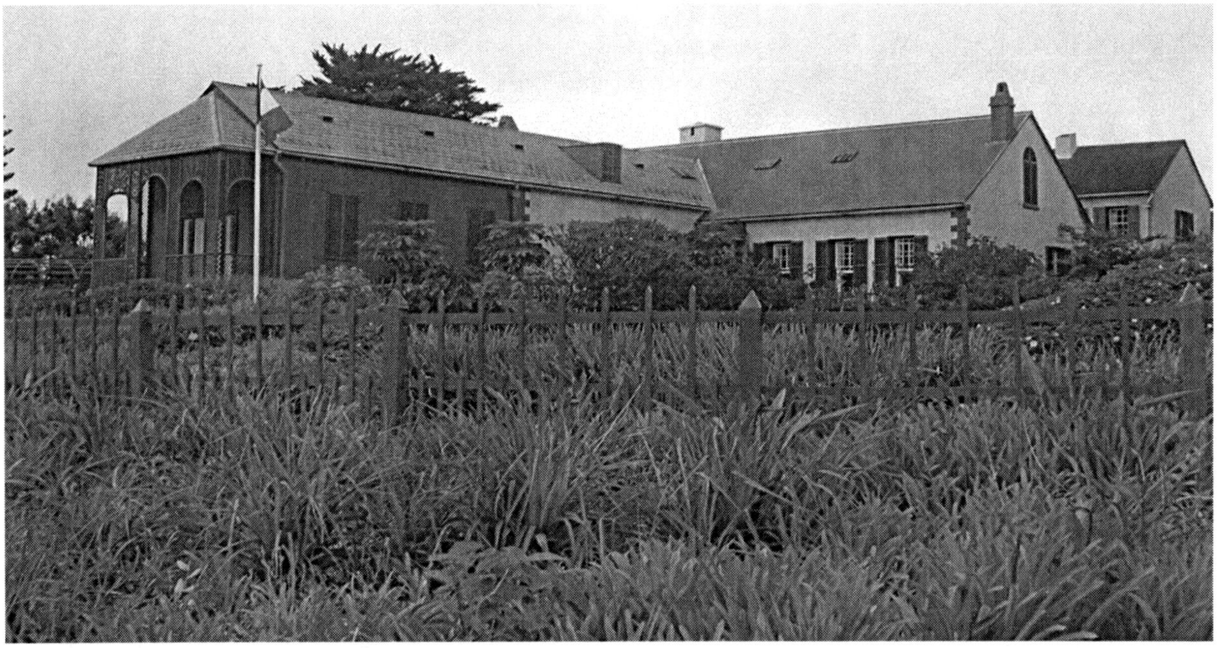

LONGWOOD HOUSE, NAPOLEON'S EXILE HOME ON ST. HELENA, 1815 TO 1821

The single storied Longwood House sits on high grassy plain near the middle of St. Helena with magnificent views. The grounds are spacious and well manicured with lots of flowers. The house is laid out in the shape of a "T" with the entry leading into the main social room. There were several out buildings to the rear and two large barns off to the left of the house at a respectable distance for a barn. There is a flagpole near the front entrance to the house flying a large French flag. The windows all have shutters with louvers that when closed, allow for the entry of some light, but privacy from prying eyes. Apparently, Napoleon liked to shut the shutters at night for privacy from the British guards that surrounded the house. However, the British guards liked to look in so they carved notches in selected louvers to spy on Napoleon.

The house is filled with copies of original paintings including the French Revolution, Napoleon at different times in his life, Empress Josephine and his second wife, archduchess Marie-Louise of Austria. He divorced Josephine (Dec. 1809) because she did not provide him a male heir for France. He married Marie-Louise after he had conquered Austria. He thought their marriage would provide France with a strong ally in Europe in addition to a son. Marie-Louise was only nineteen when they married in France, April 1810. One outstanding picture that screams for attention is the photocopy of the beautiful oil painting *Coronation* by Jacques-Louis David. The painting depicts an extravagant coronation ceremony with emperor Napoleon crowning Josephine with Pope Pius VII looking on. The ceremony was held Dec. 2, 1804, at the Notre Dame Cathedral, Paris.

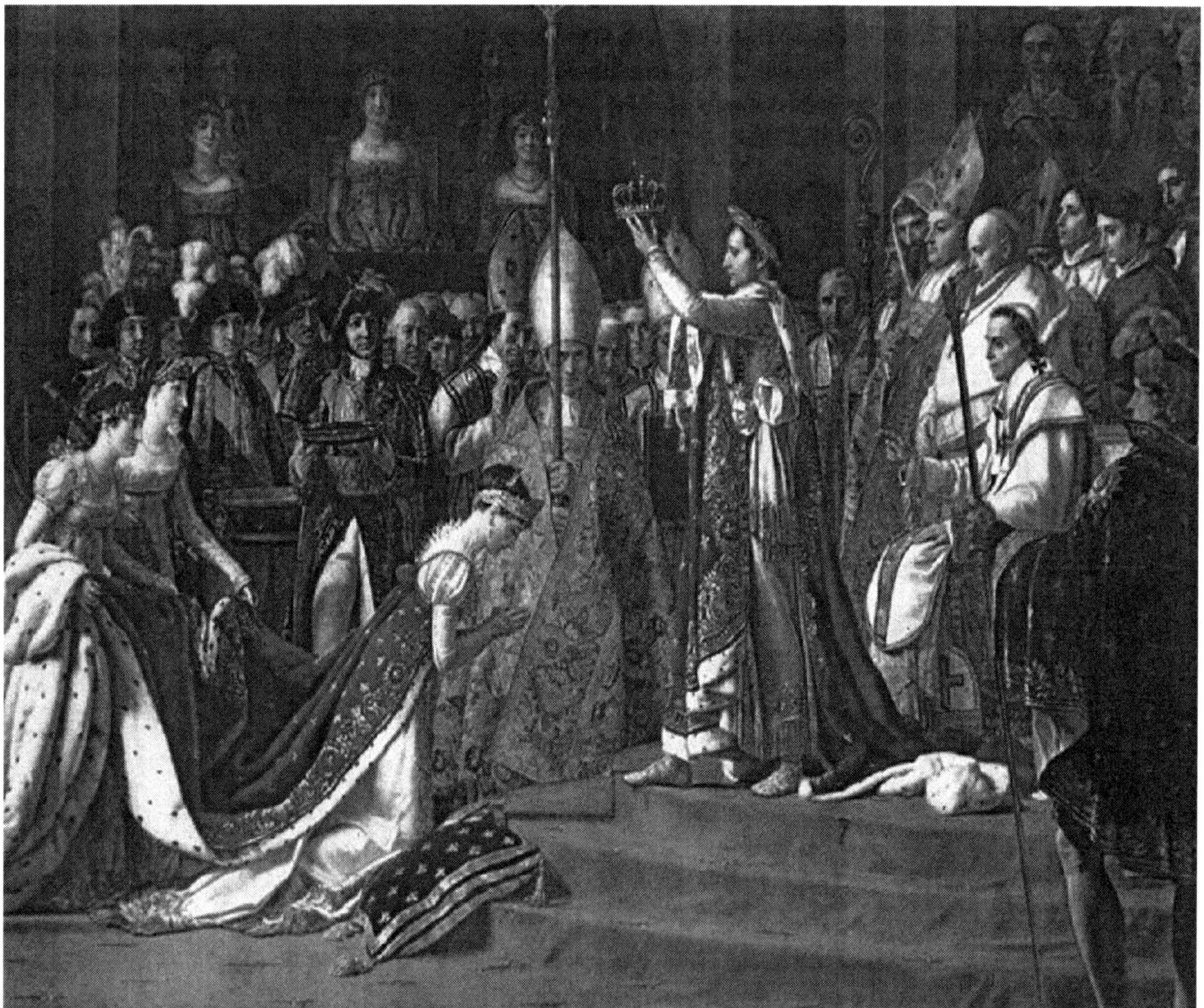

CORONATION by **JACQUES-LOUIS DAVID, JOSEPHINE IS CROWNED EMPRESS of FRANCE BY NAPOLEON I**

The original of this life size painting now hangs in the Louvre (Musèe National du Louvre), Paris. This museum was started when Napoleon was emperor of France and the original name was Musèe Napoleon. The museum was part of his dream to adorn France with the greatest art treasures of Europe. Napoleon's European conquest made it possible for him to assemble what was the greatest art collection ever gathered under one roof. He also had plans to make France the center of all Europe with Paris its capital city — he came close to realizing this dream.

Some of the original furniture still exists in the house along with copies of furniture from that period. A copy of his bed appears quite small, but people at that time did not sleep with their bodies stretched out. Using pillows at the head, they slept in a sitting position. There is also a copy of Napoleon's death mask in the house, which shows his true facial features. The tour guide told us that poor air circulation, damp days, smoke from the home's fireplaces and rats all contributed to an unhealthy environment in the home. The floors and even the wallpaper are part of the authentic restoration. The wallpaper is interesting in that it uses a floral design that was just introduced at that time. Before that period, wallpaper was blank. However, the initial process that added designs to wallpaper required the use of arsenic.

Arsenic was also used in early hair products. When samples of Napoleon's hair were examined years after his death, it was found to contain high levels of arsenic, which probably didn't do much for his health. Lots of theories and superstitions surround his death only five and a half years after his arrival at St Helena, including poisoning. According to the French tour guide, the accepted theory is that he died of stomach cancer, like his father. The date of his death was May 5, 1821. He died in great agony in the presence of 16 persons. His last words were not heard clearly, but those present agreed that he said "at the head of the army." No explanation was offered as to what he may have been trying to say.

His personal doctors diagnosed his illness as inflammation of the liver. They kept thorough daily records of his illness and how they treated this "inflammation." Actually, from studies of his illness records and autopsy, it was determined he suffered from stomach ulcers. Doctors studying his case proposed that the treatment he received for the supposed liver ailment actually made the ulcers malignant. It was later shown that his stomach was full of cancerous growths.

Napoleon's entourage at St. Helena consisted of a staff of domestic servants; a valet and secretary, Marchand; General Bertrand (an engineer) his wife and children; military officer and aide-de-camp, Montholon, his wife and son; General Gourgaud, chief orderly; and lastly, military officer, aide-de-camp, Las Cases and his son. Napoleon's only regular company was a British naval surgeon, Dr. Barry O'Meara and later, Dr. Francesco Antommarichi, his personal physicians.

Napoleon ran Longwood as if he was still the emperor of France, holding formal court in his palace. He insisted on being addressed as "Your Majesty." From tour information, he thought Longwood was inadequate for his needs. The British eventually agreed with him and started to build a new residence, but he died before it was finished. This was just one of the ongoing feuds between Napoleon and St. Helena's British appointed governor, Sir Hudson Lowe. These little feuds and disagreements must have kept life at Longwood interesting for everyone. The tour guide said that Lowe lacked the tact and intelligence necessary to handle a prisoner of Napoleon's stature. He insisted on calling Napoleon, "General Bonaparte," refuting (as Napoleon claimed) the status bestowed on him by the Pope and the sovereigns of Europe. After only a few months following Sir Hudson's appointment at St. Helena, Napoleon refused to receive Sir Hudson again. That was in Aug. of 1816.

It seems none of his entourage were important names in Napoleon's circle back in France except for General Gourgaud. Accounts I read suggested that most of the staff did not accompany him out of loyalty. For example, it was generally believed that General Bertrand would probably have faced court marshal if he had stayed in France. Most of his group was not happy at St. Helena and only Montholon and Bertrand stayed until the end. Albine de Montholon, Montholon's wife, left for England before Napoleon died. One persistent tale that pops up in books about Napoleon is his imperial habit of commanding women into his bed. While at St. Helena, Albine gave birth to a girl whom she named Napolèone. It seems Albine had been divorced twice for adultery before she married Montholon so the rumor that she was Napoleon's lover may have merit.

Another widespread rumor happened during the passage to St. Helena. The rumor is understandable in-that Madame Bertrand tried to throw herself out her cabin window when told that St. Helena was their destination. Compared to France, St. Helena must have seemed like the end of the world — England's version of Devil's Island. General Bertrand kept a daily diary of his days at St. Helena and noted that after Albine left for France, Napoleon made some unsuccessful attempts to make Madame Bertrand his mistress. He even tried to get Dr. Antommarichi to act as a go-between, but the doctor refused.

Las Cases, Dr. O'Meara, Montholon, and Dr. Antommarichi contributed to the published memoirs of Napoleon's life at St. Helena. The memoirs were written mostly from Napoleon's dictations. Even casual memoir readers saw that he cleverly embellished his actions, thoughts and ideas to enhance the way history would view his life. The memoirs provide strong contrasts on Napoleon's views when compared to the diaries of Gourgaud's, published in 1899 and Bertrand's, not published until 1950. Those two diaries were written for their author's personal interest, not the country at large. The guide concluded that those diaries provide the most accurate view of the real Napoleon, especially his character.

I found it interesting that some historians considered Napoleon the father of propaganda for the way his writings embellished his battles, his life, and his ideas. In the diaries, Napoleon is presented as an oppressive egotist believing all people are motivated by selfishness. The memoirs instead, depict Napoleon as a liberal humanitarian, always courteous to his comrades, with deep religious convictions and dreaming of noble projects. Las Cases, has a reputation as a skilled writer for the way he wrote and recorded Napoleon's conversations, quotations and dictations. Some of Napoleon's more emotionally moving remarks concerned his love for Josephine, his affection for his second wife Marie-Louise and his devotion to his son, Napoleon II.

Emperor Napoleon anointed his son, Napoleon II (1811-1832), King of Rome after his birth. However, when Napoleon was exiled to St. Helena, her father, Emperor Francis of Austria, ordered Marie-Louise back to Austria. He would not let her go to St. Helena and then Napoleon II's title was changed to the duke of Reichstadt in 1818. The duke never did reign as the allies refused to accept him. His mother may have abandoned him, as he never gained favor in Austria. His followers knew him as Napoleon II and his nickname the "Eaglet," a reference to the eagle coat-of-arms used by his father. Napoleon II was virtually confined to Austria and died there of tuberculosis 1832 at the age of 21.

Some historians have suggested that Josephine's death may have contributed to Napoleon's lack of decisiveness at the battle of Waterloo. Since, in some of his writings, Napoleon implied that Josephine's love brought him success in battle. During the battle, he was noticed to be withdrawn and his tactics were not up to his usual standards. The conditions at the scene were known to be rotten, heavy rains and muddy grounds. He then made what was certainly a problematic indecision when he delayed moving his cannons into their battle positions. Finally, he gave the command to move them into position in the afternoon, which may have cost him the battle of Waterloo. This was uncharacteristic of Napoleon, as appalling conditions in the past, had never deterred him from pushing his men to their limits.

According to Gourgaud's diary, the little St. Helena exile group, each day, consumed 17 bottles of wine, 88 pounds of meat, and 9 chickens. Liqueurs and champagne were also consumed all paid for by the British government. A huge amount of groceries to be sure, but more bickering occurred as Napoleon accused Sir Hudson of trying to poison them with spoiled meat. Actually, this period was a time of great prosperity for St. Helena. The large British garrison sent there to guard Napoleon contributed a great deal of money to the St. Helena economy.

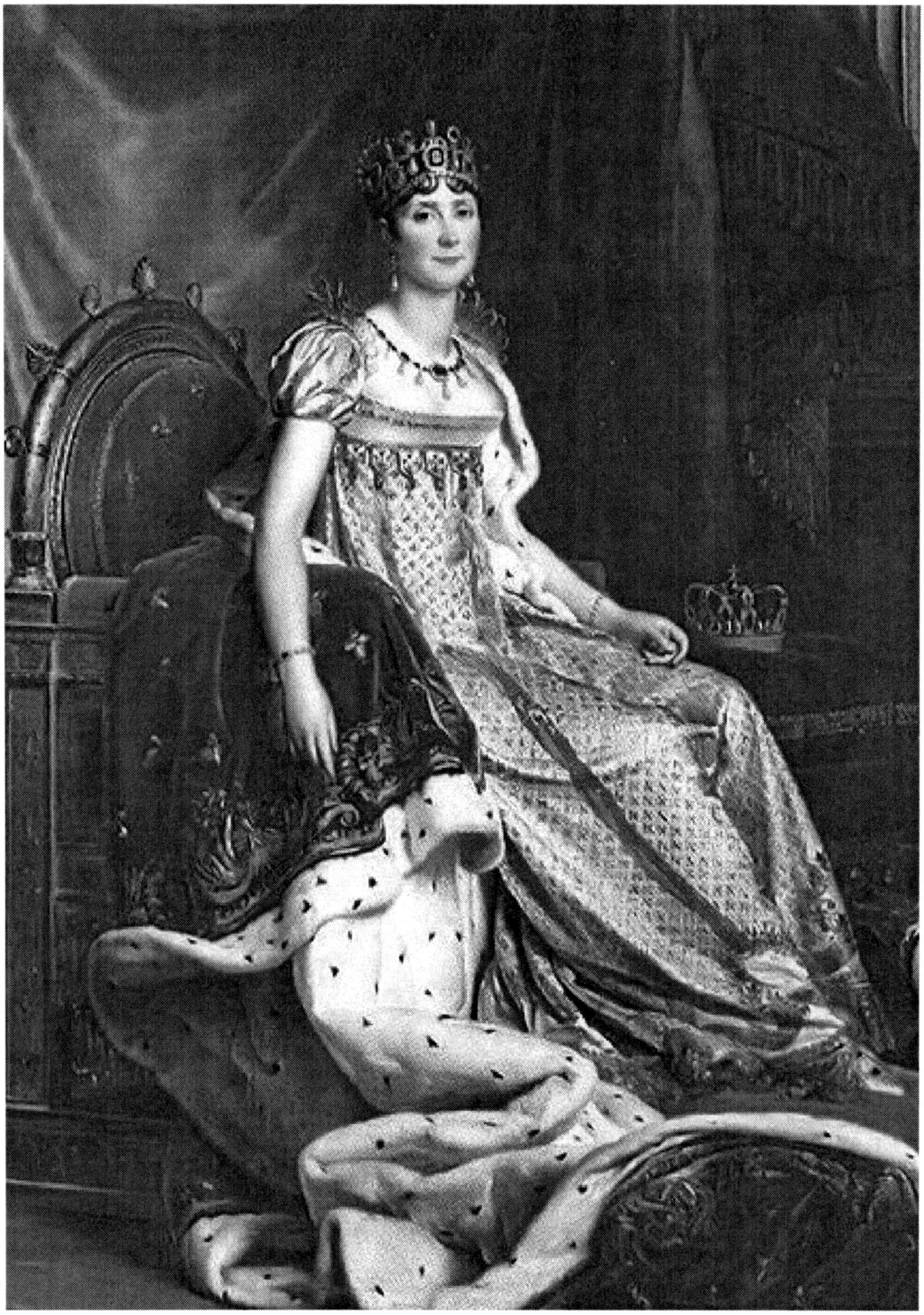

EMPRESS JOSEPHINE (1763-1814)
by FRANÇOIS PASCAL SIMON GÊRARD ca.1808

Napoleon used his exile to compare himself with Christ as wearing a crown of thorns instead of an imperial crown. These ideas probably started the legend of his poor treatment at St. Helena. Even Pope Pius VII tried coming to his aid asking the allied sovereigns to lighten Napoleon's sufferings in his hard exile. In a letter written in 1817 the Pope claimed the island of St. Helena is injurious to health and that Napoleon is dying. Actually, Napoleon's health was good at that time. However, the Pope's intervention is difficult for me to imagine. When Napoleon's armies marched through Italy, he confiscated most of the church's art treasures and cash. He then leaned on the Pope to crown him emperor of France. If that were not enough, Napoleon had the Pope imprisoned for excommunicating him when he divorced Josephine — Pius the VII must have been an extraordinary human being and a real example of how to live by Christian dogma.

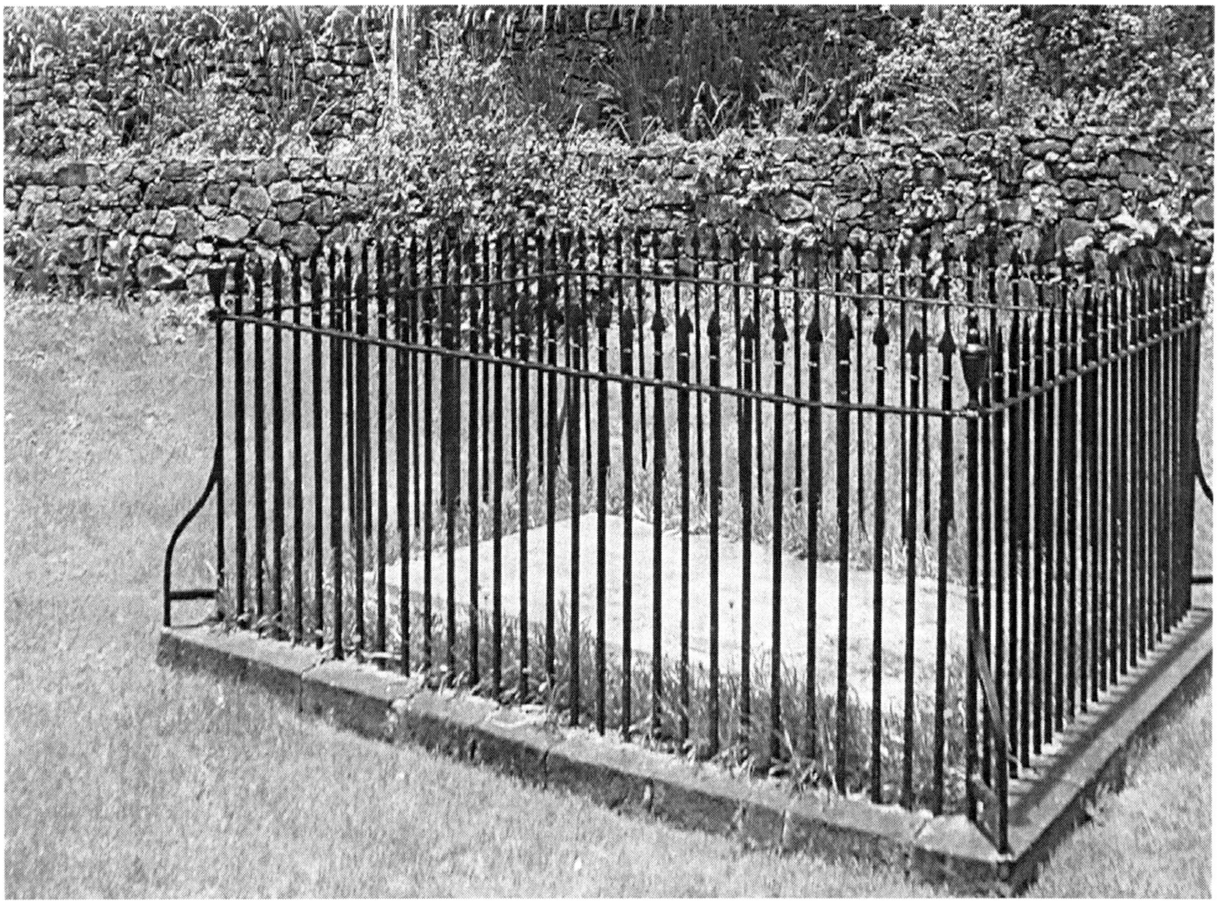

NAPOLEON'S GRAVE SITE IN THE SANE VALLEY, ST. HELENA

France's financial and military contribution to the United States helped to secure our independence from Great Britain. Napoleon realized he did not want to drive the United States into an alliance with England over territory held by France, namely, the Louisiana's. In 1803, President Thomas Jefferson sent James Monroe to Paris to obtain freedom for navigation on the Mississippi and free port privileges at New Orleans. Monroe was to work with our minister to France, Livingston, to buy New Orleans and West Florida from France. He was authorized to spend $10,000,000. They were both astonished when the U.S. was offered the whole Louisiana Territory for about $15,000,000. That territory included Arkansas, Florida, Iowa, Kansas, Louisiana, Minnesota, Missouri, Nebraska, North Dakota, Oklahoma, South Dakota and parts of Montana, Wyoming and Colorado. In all, it doubled the size of the United States. It was not clear what Napoleon had in mind for Louisiana, but he was delighted with the sale. He exclaimed, "The power of the U.S. will be consolidated forever and I have just given England a seafaring rival which sooner or later, will humble their pride." It is hard to imagine, but the U.S. senate was not impressed and referred to the sale as "Jefferson's Folly."

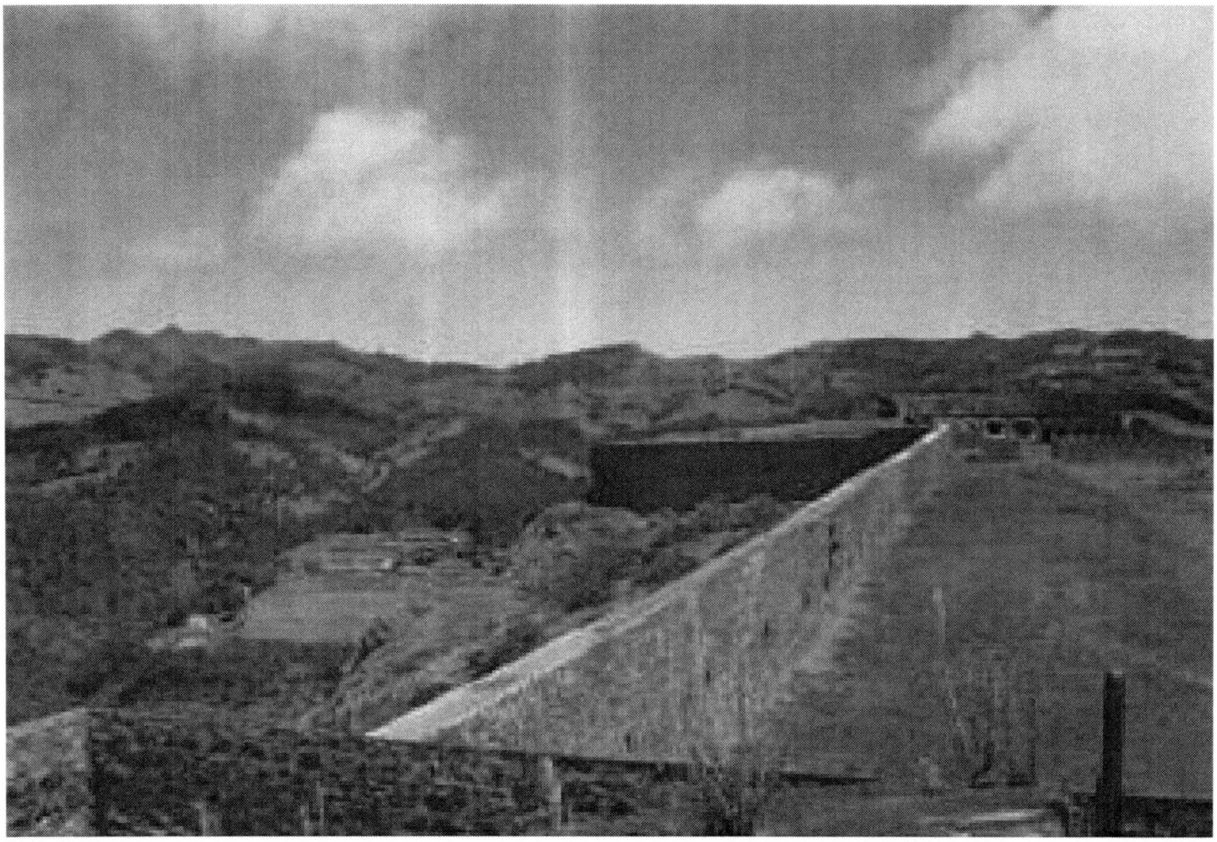

HIGH KNOLL FORT

When Napoleon died in 1821, he was buried in the Sane Valley on St. Helena. He probably chose this site for its peacefulness and beauty. The site is high on the island with expansive views, manicured lawns, and beautiful flowers. There was a gardener working on the garden while we were there, keeping the area in pristine condition. A small wooden guardhouse marking the site's entrance was probably once manned, but now it just adds a level of prestige to the site. His coffin originally was buried beneath the large concrete slab that rests flat on the ground. The slab is about four feet by eight feet, but with no markings to indicate that Napoleon was once buried there. That apparently was to conform to British requirements about the site. The tour guide emphasized how well Napoleon was incased in the tomb. Heavy steel plates and lots of concrete surrounded his coffin well below the large concrete slab. The British did not want the French to move him back to France or anyone else to break into the grave. When the British finely allowed his body to be shipped back to France in 1840, they found a well preserved body.

High Knoll Fort dates back to 1894 and sits on top of the highest point of the island. There is not much to see at the fort except the heavy and thick stone walls that would make penetration by an enemy difficult. The views, however, are quite extraordinary as is the wind that blows strongly across the top of the island. The fort was built to give St. Helena's population protection in case of an invasion, which never happened.

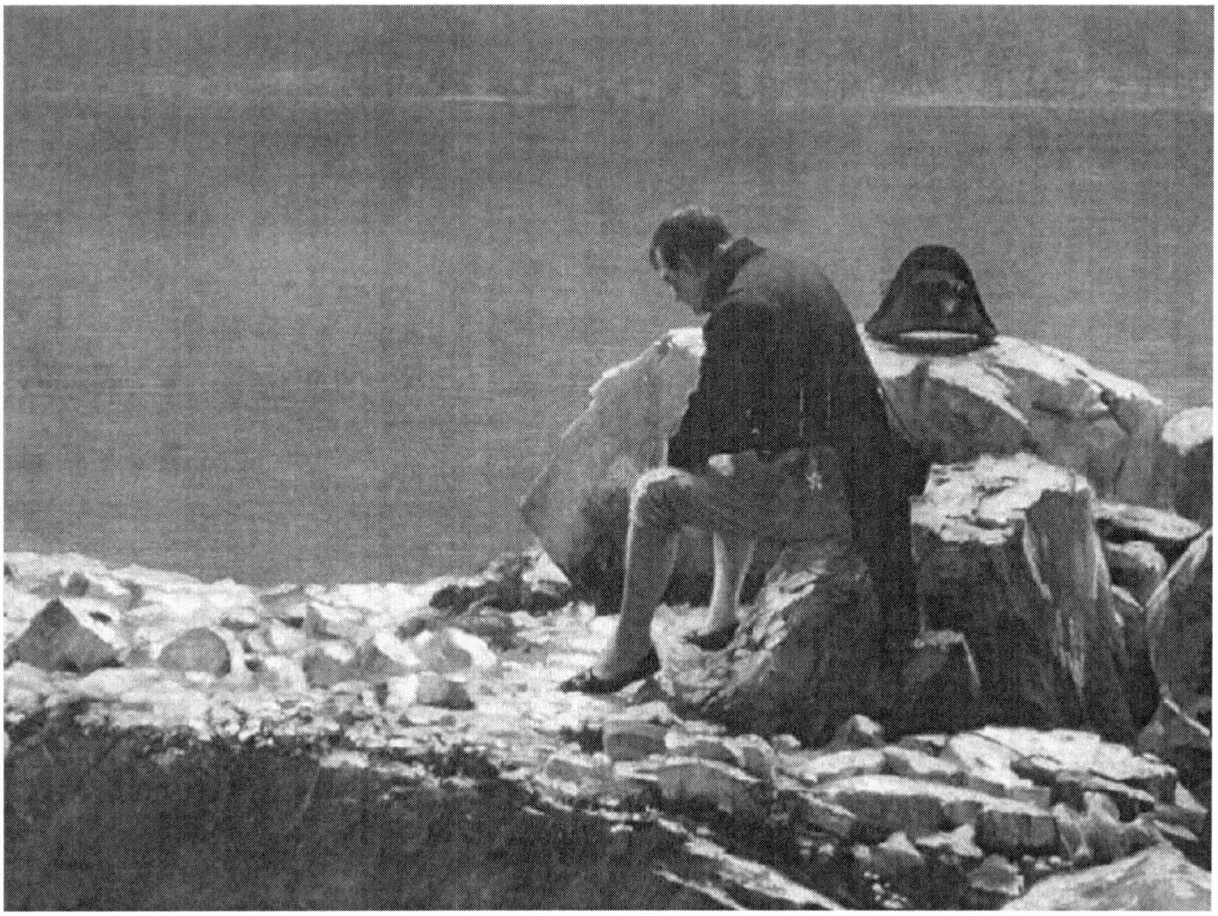

NAPOLEON ON ST. HELENA by OSCAR REX 1857: *IT IS FINISHED*

Chapter 25

ST. HELENA TO IHLA DE FERNANDO DE NORONHA

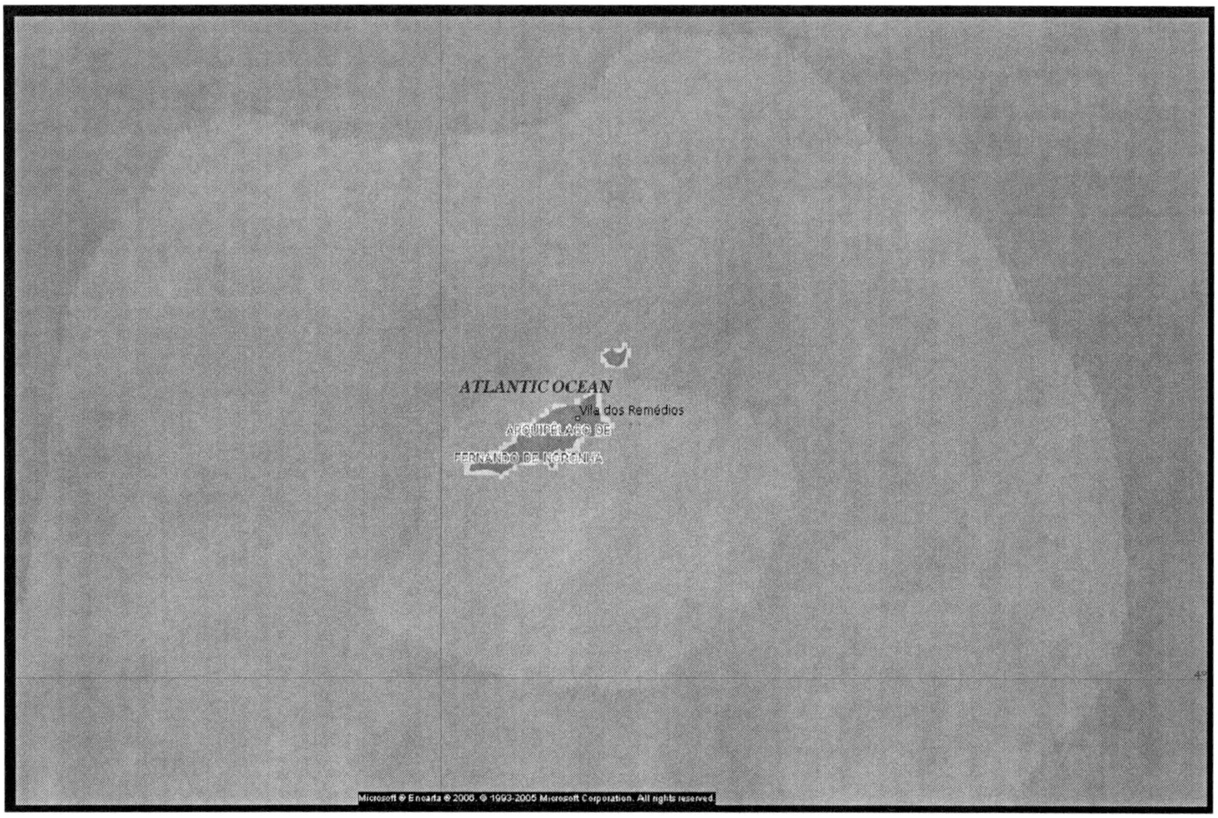

FERNANDO de NORONHA

Well, that is about it for St. Helena, we rounded up our chain and anchor on Saturday, Mar. 6, 2004, at 2 p.m. and headed northwest. About 20 miles out, we picked up the trade winds again. Poling out our jib, we moved right into our groove, sailing a steady 6 knots in 12 knots of wind from the southeast. We were sailing almost a rhumb line course to the Portuguese island of Ihla de Fernando de Noronha 2,000 miles away. This island is 220 miles from the east coast of Brazil and about 2,000 miles south of Trinidad. Credit for its discovery belongs to a Portuguese expedition led by Fernão de Noronha in 1501-1502. The main island appears to get its name from an entry in the logbook of explorer Martim Afonso de Souza, 1530 as the Ilha de Fernando de Noronha.

By Tuesday, the wind had picked up blowing 15 to 20 knots and we were still poled out doing 6.5 to 7 knots. We had sailed 231 nautical miles from St. Helena. The seas were now about 6 feet, the temperature was 83° F, the pressure was 1018 millibars and our course was NW at 318° magnetic. We were sailing close to another yacht, *Talisman* and exchanged positions and small talk with each other on single side band (SSB) channel six alpha each day around 12:00 UTC.

The sailing and wind pretty much remained the same for the next several days and everything was pretty quiet. However, a little excitement occurred during the evening of Mar. 13 as André spotted a white flare off to our starboard side. It was far off, as it did not appear to be high or bright. I made a general call on the radio several times, but no one responded. After some deliberation, we changed course and headed in the direction of the flare. We ended the search short of two hours with no further contacts from the radio or flares. The next day we reviewed the flare sighting with *Talisman* via SSB and decided it was probably a commercial ship indicating his presence with a white flare. This is legal under the Coast Guard "Rules of the Road," but I had not seen a ship signal this way. The night was clear and the water was calm so the conditions were good. I called in the approximate location of the flare to the South African ham net and it was relayed so other boats in that area could look for possible problems.

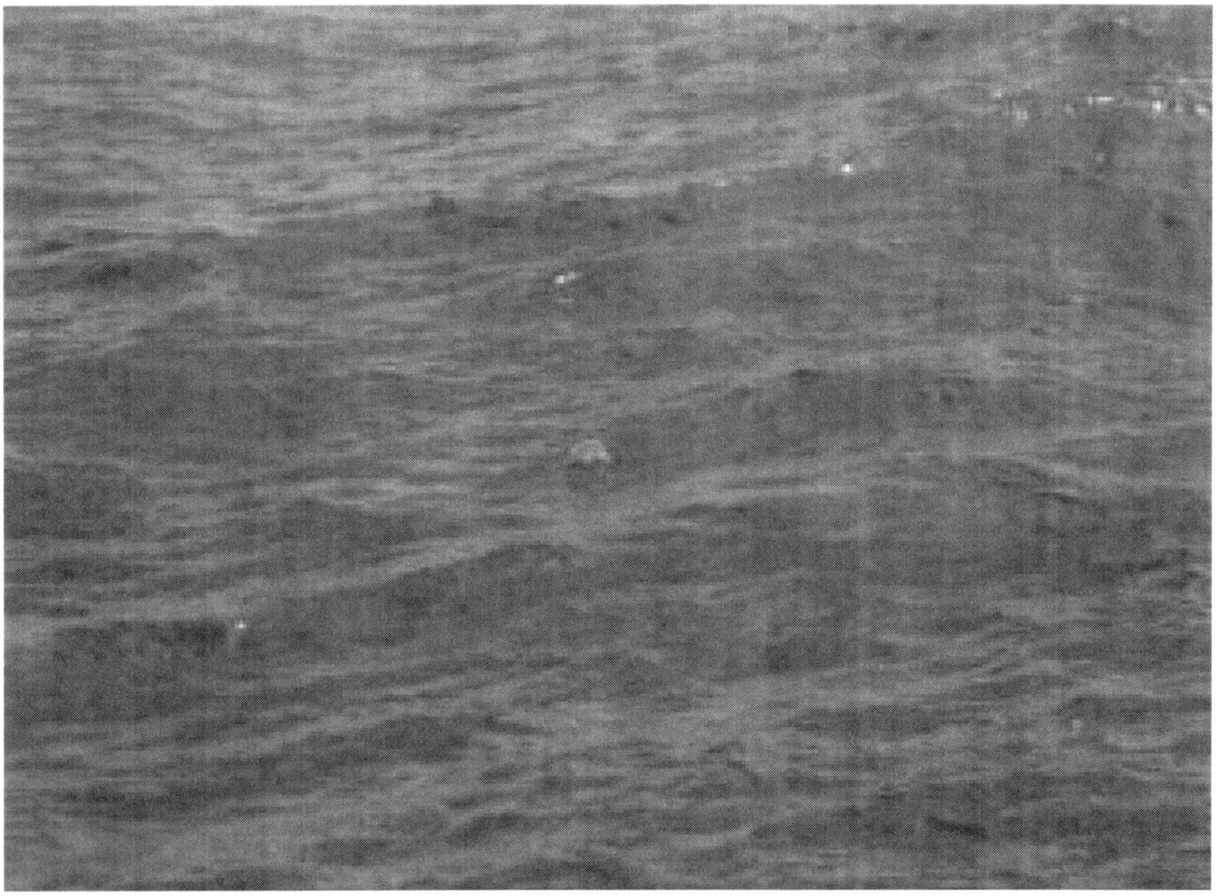

PORTUGUESE MAN-OF-WAR, SAILING SOUTH

For several days since leaving St. Helena, we noticed strange jellyfish sailing along on the surface of the ocean. I saw many jellyfish in Australia, but these were so unusual. They had a white translucent bladder like body that came in a variety of diameters varying from about 3 inches to 8 inches and slightly domed shaped. Their tentacles hung down about two feet on the largest ones. The unusual features were that their body colors appeared to be the spectrum of the rainbow and vivid in brightness and color. The other most unusual feature was that they were sailing upwind toward St. Helena. To sail, they had the ability to fold one-half of their body up in the air and control the shape of that half in the form of a wing foil. I am not sure of the angle to the wind they were sailing, but I think it was about 40 degrees. Sometimes a wave would break on them and it would flatten them or change their sailing direction, but they easily recovered and went back to sailing.

There was no apparent formation between them and it seemed they were sailing in a random pattern, but in the same direction. At first, I thought the larger jellyfish were leading the migration, but then I noticed plenty of the smaller variety intermingled. I do not know how far apart their east/west path was, but one passed by our boat about every two minutes or so, definitely not within sight of each other if they can see. Their numbers must have totaled in the thousands as we saw them almost all the way to Trinidad. I believe their coloring was probably due to the refraction of light through their translucent bodies, but I cannot be sure. Although, I do not think I saw any coloring in the half that remained in the water. Some people I later talked with thought they might have been Portuguese Man-of-Wars. Further research confirmed that they were indeed man-of-wars. Man-of-Wars do float on top of the water with brightly colored inflated bladders that turn into sails to catch wind. However, they belong to the class Hydrozoa, which is a type of animal not a jellyfish. Their lethal tentacles can grow to 100 feet — ouch!

I had noticed an engine problem in St. Helena that seemed related to bad fuel. Looking at the main fuel filters, I found the fuel was low in the filters and concluded the fuel pump needed replacing. However, it was no easy task, as I had to remove the engines main heat exchanger for access to the fuel pump. Then I found out one of the fuel pump bolts was not accessible without a special offset open-end wrench. I was lucky to have a bench grinder on board to modify an old half inch open-end wrench to fit. I found the fuel pump worked, but the pump's hand primer did not work and the fuel inlet hose on the bottom was not tight. I decided to replace the pump. When I finally put everything back together the engine started and ran smoothly. I figured, that problem was solved, but no, a few days later the engine RPM would slow and go back to normal over a long period of time.

Looking at the fuel filter again, it did not look too bad, but I replaced it anyway. The engine started right up. I have never had dirty fuel during the entire 30,000 miles up to this point. I reasoned the fuel we took on in South Africa must have been contaminated. Looking at my spare filter supply, I knew I was in trouble. The filters would only last for about 30 hours before clogging again. Talking to *Talisman* about cleaning the dirty filters I received some discouraging news that the filters probably could not be cleaned. They had a guest on board that was a Caterpillar Diesel mechanic and should know. He said the fuel entered the center of the filter through a small hole, which made the interior cleaning a bleak task — rather disheartening.

I decided to cut open a dirty filter to get a better look into to interior. I only had two more clean filters so I was under a strong compulsion to find a way to clean and reuse these filters. I found I could heat the plastic handle of a toothbrush and bend it to a shape that would fit into the hole. From there I was able to brush the interior of the filter with turpentine. Then I plugged the bottom hole of the filter and connected the hose from the dinghy air pump to the upper filter hole. By forcing air into the interior of the filter, I was able to blow the dirty particles out of the filter membrane. This cleaning procedure worked almost like installing a clean filter. I was lucky to have found a cleaning solution, as I now was able to use a dirty filter repeatedly. I knew I would find many windless areas requiring the help of the engine once we entered the region of the equator — my guardian angel was still looking over my shoulder!

We were about 650 miles from Ilha de Fernando de Noronha when the spinnaker-lifting guy broke. The outboard end of the pole came down and hit the rub rail putting a dent in the aluminum 4 inch diameter tubing. This pole is a telescoping version of the Forespar,® spinnaker poles and now the last 2 feet of the extension would not fit into the pole's main tube. To put the pole back in use I had to crimp a new stainless wire cable around the end of the main tube. The pole could be extended out; I just could not shorten the total length enough to fit into its holding fixture clamp on the mast. This was a repair task that could wait until we were in port.

On Mar. 16, we heard that a typhoon hit Madagascar several thousand miles east of our position. Our position was not affected, but the typhoon left about 100,000 people homeless. Most of the people that live there and their country are so poor already that the storm must have been devastating.

Our weather had been constant in wind direction and speed after leaving St. Helena. The barometer has not varied more than a couple of millibars. The skies have been clear with no rain, but the temperature has been slowly creeping up to where the days are now around 86° F. We are getting closer to the equator now and about 300 miles from Ilha de Fernando de Noronha. We have been averaging about 140 miles every 24 hours.

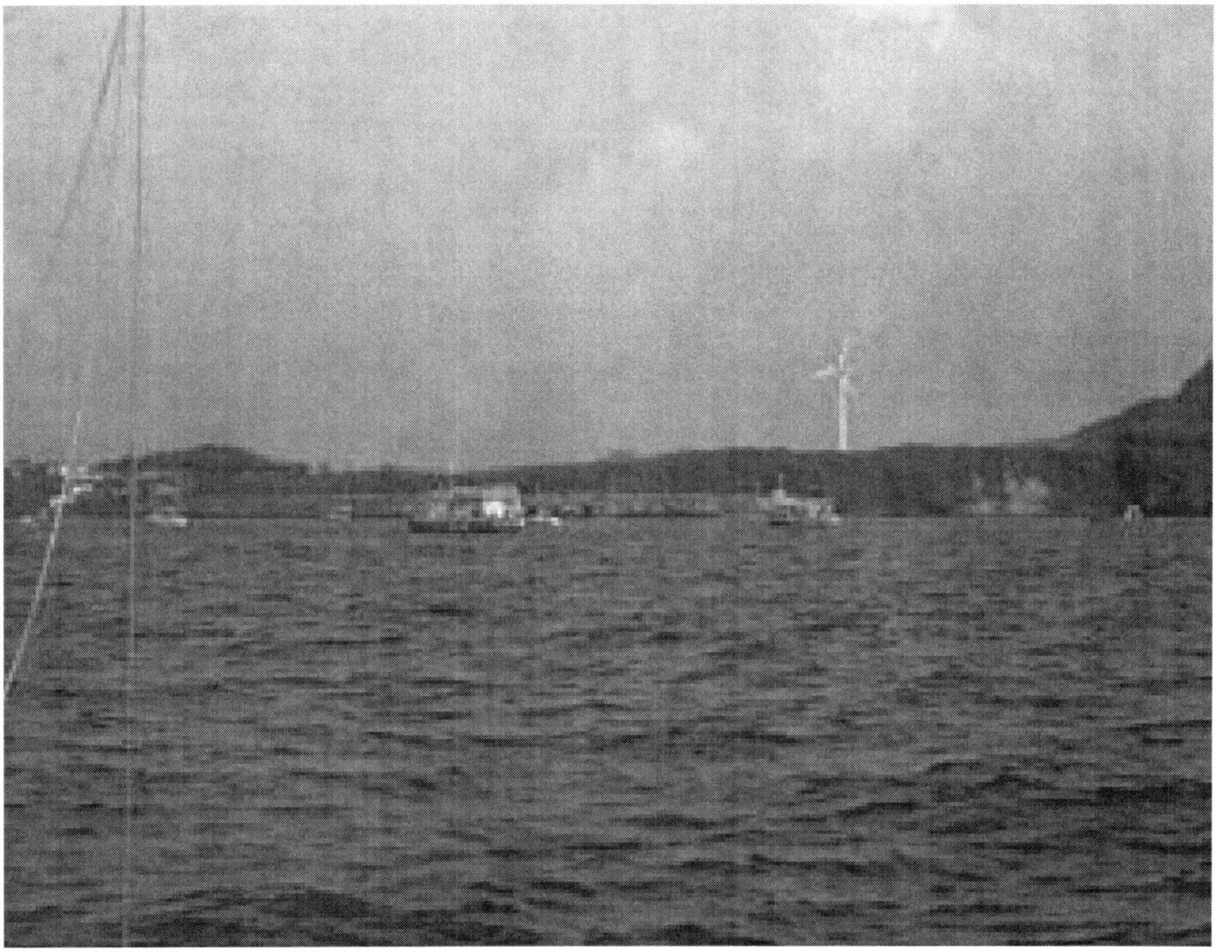

ILHA de FERNANDO de NORONHA

We arrived at the Portuguese island of Ilha de Fernando de Noronha on Mar. 19 at 2 p.m. and anchored on the north side of the island in the shadow of a large wind generator. The bay was full of local boats and fishing boats painted in bright colors. There were three dive boats and a couple of tour boats. Looking at the island from our anchorage and during our approach we could only see a few buildings and in general the island looked sparsely settled, but with beautiful lush green vegetation. There is a new small boat harbor, but the depth is limited and it is small. It consisted of a large "L" shaped rock breakwater with a nice looking wooden dock attached along the harbor side of the break wall.

The breakwater arms face north and west to keep out the trade wind swell. There is a beautiful white sandy beach protected by the break wall with quite a few young women lying on the sand in bikinis. If I had anchored inside the breakwater, there would not be room for local boats to maneuver and the water depth was not friendly to sailboats. One thing that got my attention right away was the largest colony of frigate birds I have ever seen. There were hundreds of them just flying around as if they were on vacation or looking for a mate.

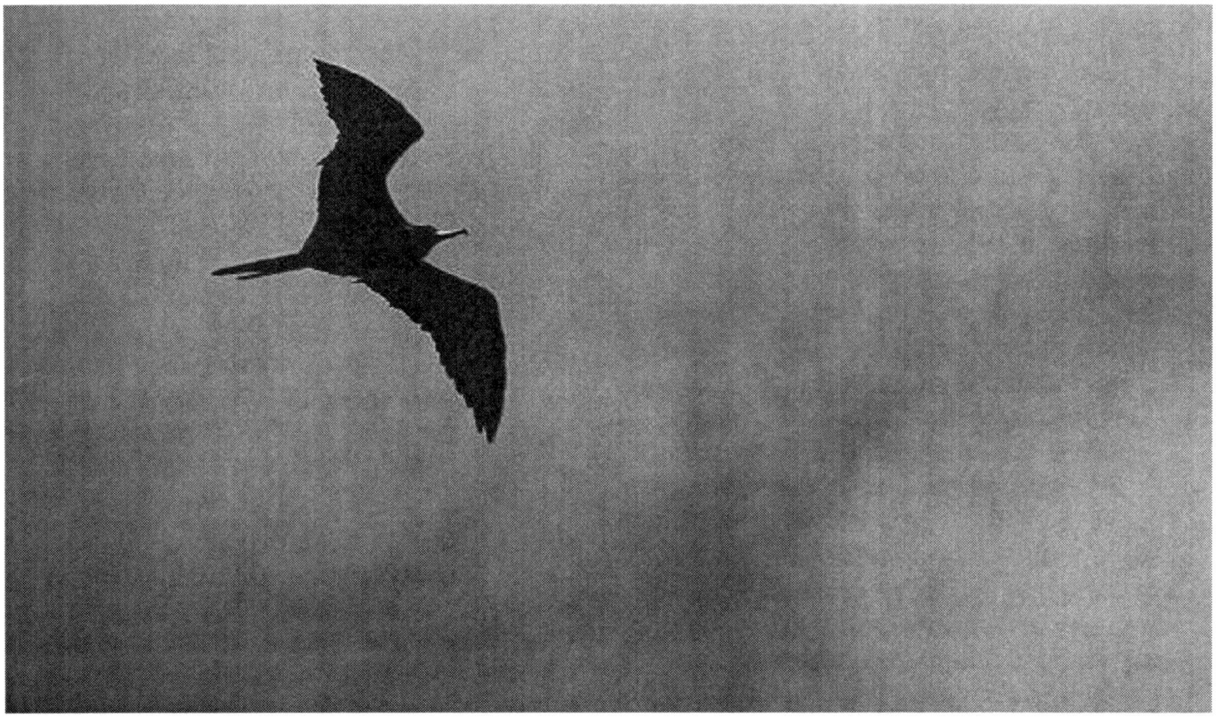

FRIGATE BIRD, ILHA de FERNANDO de NORONHA

With plenty of daylight left we launched the dinghy and went in to find immigration and customs. One person handles the whole operation, Harbor Master, Antonio. His office was just a short walk from the harbor in the center of town. However, the town consisted of only 10 buildings. They accept U.S. dollars, but fees are a little steep. The total for the five day visit amounted to $240, which included harbor fees and visas for our two-crew members. Water, showers, and toilets were available near the beach for an additional charge. We could have bought our visas in South Africa, but that would have required bus rides and long walks. Actually, it worked out fine to purchase them on the island for the same price. The ship's captain is excluded from buying a visa for some reason unless I misread what the port captain was saying. There is only one cash machine on the island and it is at the airport, at the other end of the island. Antonio understood almost no English except for some major words used by travelers. This island belongs to Brazil so everyone speaks Portuguese. They can mostly understand Spanish, but their spoken language did not have any words of Spanish origin I recognized.

Antonio drove us to the airport in his Japanese compact import, but almost all the other cars and taxis on the island were dune buggy type vehicles on a Volkswagen chassis — resort like place. We managed to arrive at a bad time, as a plane full of passengers was just unloading. It became readily apparent that this island is a favored vacation destination. Also surprising was that three airlines provided jet service to this tiny island of 7.1 square miles. Most of the passengers were fit young men with surfboards and fishing gear. We also saw many good-looking young women anxious to hit the beaches. We later found out the island boasts some fine resorts, beautiful white sandy beaches and good surfing. It is not as sparsely populated as we thought, but is rather small. We saw several hotels, resorts and homes converted to bed and breakfasts along the main road to the airport. Officialdom here is no different from any other place in the world. By the time the officials finished our paperwork and exchanged our money for Portuguese "reals," the day was shot. Of course, Antonio caught up on socializing with all his friends in customs and immigration before driving us back to the harbor.

André and Jason looked all over town, but could find only one vacationing engineer from Brazil who spoke English. He was helpful and answered our questions about buying phone cards and groceries, etc. Only one store sold phone cards and that required a taxi ride back near the airport. I never could figure out the procedure that would allow Pat to call me back and pay for the call, but I was able to leave messages on her answering machine. The grocery store was also a taxi ride, but the exchange rate was good. One of our dollars was equivalent to 3 of their "real" dollars so riding a taxi to the airport was about $4.50.

Grocery store shopping was disappointing. All their fresh food must have gone to resorts and restaurants because nothing was left for us. There were no vegetables, just empty bins where the vegetables should be, no fresh milk, no cheese, but lots of potato chips, beer, wine, soft drinks, canned goods, bread, soaps and baby food. We walked our mostly junk food back over a hot highway to the harbor. We managed to get all the stuff into the dinghy and back to the boat without getting too wet. The water outside the break wall was generally rough and ***Our Pleasure*** rolled slowly in the swell.

On the Mar. 23, we decided we had better get some extra fuel on board just in case the winds around the equator were light. However, the nearest Diesel fuel was at a gas station just outside of town. Carrying five gallon jugs of fuel back and forth from the boat to the station in the hot sun was not pleasant and it was tedious. The road from the beach to the gas station was up hill and about a quarter mile away. The 10 minute dinghy ride out to the boat was wet and we had to make 4 trips. Jason had hurt his foot while climbing down a rocky hillside to a beach full of pretty young women in bikinis. The view might have been worth it for him, but he couldn't help carry the fuel jugs — not good for us. We were not in shape for so much physical work and ended up being darn tired.

While we were going back and forth between the beach and the boat, *Talisman* came in and dropped their anchor about 4 in the afternoon. They had to repair their genoa the old-fashioned way, by hand. They laid the sail out on the deck, but boats rocking motion made the stitching repair difficult. After I told them about the procedures and cost to check-in they decided not to go ashore.

I took my crew out to dinner that night at a restaurant overlooking the harbor. I was able to figure out the name of the restaurant, which I thought was pretty good for my poor language skills. The Portuguese name translated to, "Restaurant with a Port View." We had planned to go to a different restaurant, but after hiking there, we found it had closed early that night. There was only one other couple having dinner at our restaurant so we had plenty of one-on-one conversations with the owners and the cook trying to decide what the menu said. The cook did know some limited English so we managed quite well. The young couple that owned the restaurant was blest with good looks and treated us graciously. I had shrimp cannelloni and two glasses of excellent Portuguese wine. The crew had two bottles of beer and I forget what they ordered for dinner, but everything was truly outstanding for a total evening expense of about $30, what a bargain.

Chapter 26

FERNANDO TO TRINIDAD

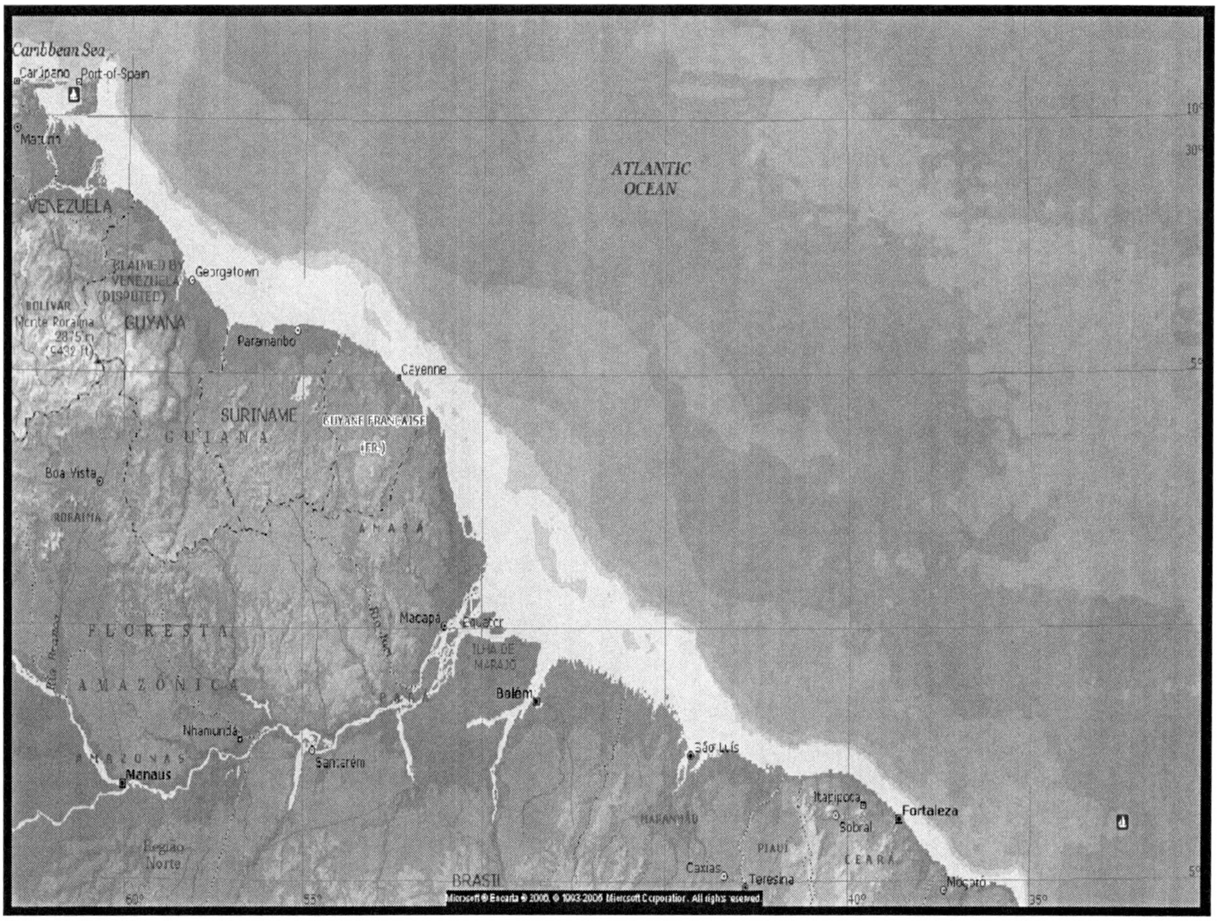

FERNANDO de NARONHA TO CHAGUARAMAS, TRINIDAD

We managed to leave Fernando about 9:30 a.m. the next day, Mar. 24 and headed toward Trinidad. We were about 200 miles south of the equator and the 88° temperature required running the refrigeration system for longer periods. Today is sunny with only a few broken clouds. Humidity is always around 75% or more, making us feel clammy. One happy surprise, we are sailing with one knot of positive current.

Conditions remained constant for several days. On our forth day from Fernando, we crossed the equator and the winds dropped off to zero. This happened while I was sleeping, of course, at 1:30 a.m., so the sails were lowered and the engine started. It started raining later and the rainwater tested to a wonderfully pure number of 40 parts per million of salt. We raised the main sail about 25 feet so we could collect water on the sail. The rainwater runs down the main boom interior to a spigot and into the starboard water tank via a plastic hose.

The wind started to rise on our starboard beam about 2:45 a.m. and I let out the full genny. Our speed picked up to 8 knots and the water tank was now overflowing. It is always a treat to fill up with pure rainwater and not have to use fuel to run the generator for the water maker. The water maker works well in calm water, but develops air bubbles in the water inlet when the boat is sailing fast. The pump in the water maker does not like air bubbles and will try to shut down unless it receives plenty of water.

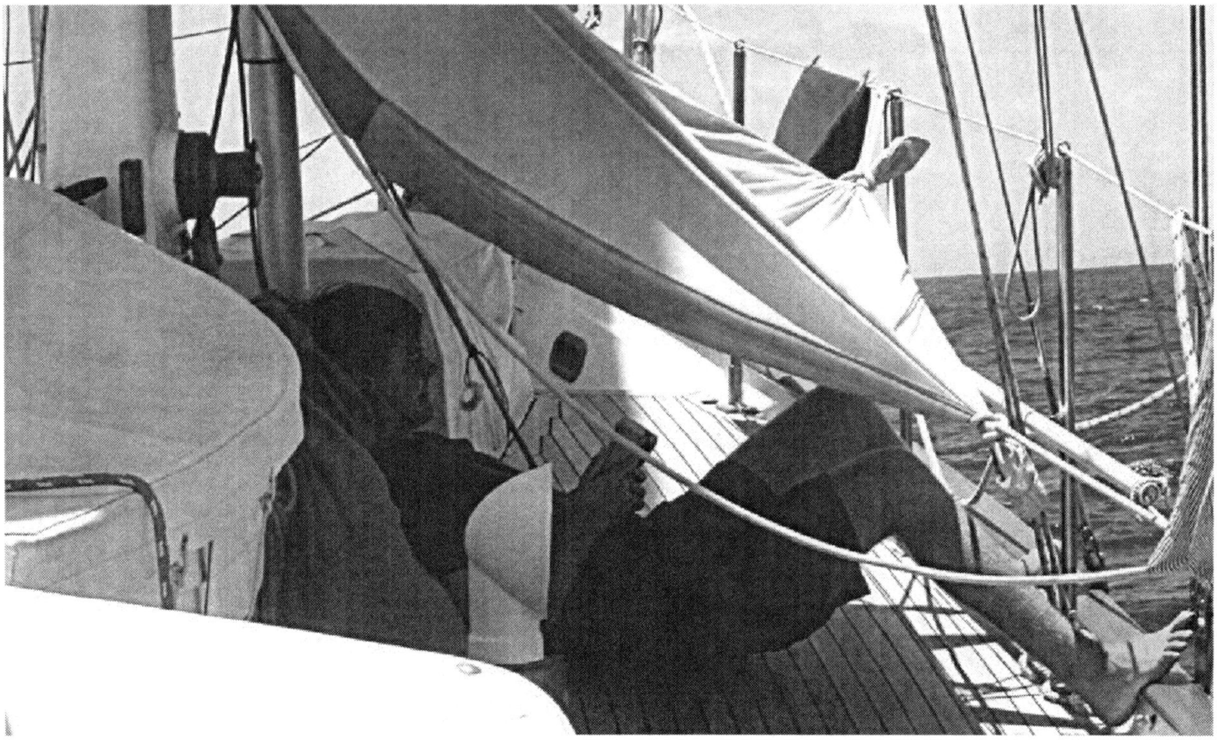

JASON MAKING SHADE ON THE FOREDECK

The wind speed around the equator is notoriously slow and we found it is still slow. In fact, if we made over 100 miles a day we were ecstatic. Some days we find currents that oppose our direction and slow our speed and some days the current helps. On the north side of the equator, the wind blows mostly from the NNE, which is not our good point of sail. We are still seeing some of those sailing jellyfish. *Talisman* has managed to find some better sailing winds gaining about 60 miles on us. They have sailed close to the Brazilian coast to find currents that are more favorable.

We arrived at the harbor at Chaguaramas, Trinidad just after midnight with no wind. The glassy water reflected all the lights from harbor's marinas and work facilities. We were surprised to see hundreds of masts in the harbor and on the land in dry storage. We had made reservations beforehand at Crew's Inn, a marina, and resort hotel, but thought we had better wait until daylight. We found a commercial buoy to tie to and easily slept the rest of the night away. The next morning we had to go through all the formal check-in requirements.

Trinidad customs insisted on completion of their paperwork before we could move into our slip. The customs agent, we had the misfortune of drawing, had a strict interpretation of the rules and in addition was a bit of a curmudgeon. He wanted my crew to leave Trinidad as soon as they signed off the boat as crewmembers. I filled in all the blanks, went back to ***Our Pleasure*** and motored over to our slip at Crew's Inn. John Ebel, a super friend and an outstanding lawyer from Seattle, was there in his dingy to help tie our bowlines to pilings as we backed into our assigned slip. Jason decided he would go back to a job he had waiting in Australia and stayed for about a week. André managed to work his way to Antigua for some race week sailing and found a boat delivery job. I stayed for several weeks at Crew's Inn and then moved the boat to Peak's Boat Yard for the hurricane season so I could go back to Seattle.

Chapter 27

SUMMER IN SEATTLE, MAY TO NOV. 2004

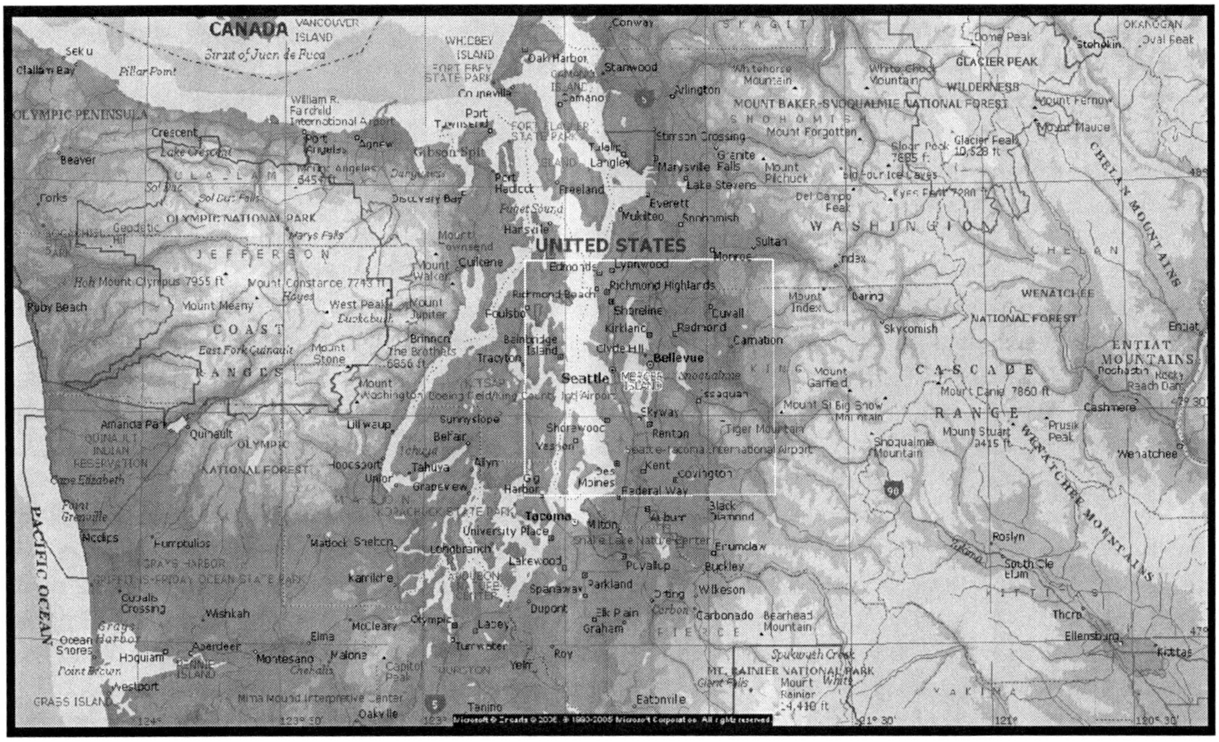

SEATTLE, WASHINGTON IN THE PACIFIC NORTH WEST, USA

I left ***Our Pleasure*** in Trinidad on May 3, 2004 for the hurricane season and flew back to Seattle for the summer. I had about three weeks to sort out the paper work, get Jason and André off the crew list, and get the boat secured on dry land storage at Peake's Boat Yard before I left. Meanwhile in Seattle, Pat had been living in a small, but comfortable apartment overlooking a small city lake, Bitter Lake. The view of Bitter Lake from our third floor apartment was not quite the same as the ocean view I'm use to, but it was a soothing view. On clear days, the impressive snowcapped mountains of the Cascades, about 30 miles away, come into view.

I had not seen my new grandson Mitchell yet and being acquainted with him was a wonderful new experience. He was almost a year old and the son of my daughter, Leslie and her husband Bob Fischer. The same crew we started out with from Seattle on the first 18 months of our voyage. They made it all the way to New Zealand before flying back to Seattle to start a so-called "normal life." Pat had to leave ***Our Pleasure*** at the Breakwater Marina, Townsville, Australia on May 23, 2003, so she could be in Seattle for Mitchell's arrival into the world. She had wanted to stay with the boat to at least Darwin, Australia which would have her in Seattle just after the predicted due date. However, Leslie was insistent that she wanted her mother home for Mitchell's birth. For me, Seattle weather was a drastic change from the ninety degrees of Trinidad. Now I had to wear shoes, no more shorts, I could still wear tee shirts, but under a sweatshirt.

Seattle was a whole new lifestyle compared to cruising and now my daily routines became scheduled with appointments, lunches, birthdays, baby sitting, changing diaper and a whole new world of activities. Schedules and cruising do not go well together as weather will always be the deciding factor no matter what your objectives might be. It was good to get an up-to-date physical and PSA test for prostrate health. Long time friend, Dr. Steve Albright, made sure my teeth were in good shape. It seemed like every day there was someone to visit or event I had to attend. When I arrived, I learned that a long time friend, Francis Peterman, was in the hospice care unit at Seattle's Veterans Hospital. He had lived most of his life on Seattle's Queen Anne Hill. He had been in failing health for some time, but now he was dying of stomach cancer. He never married and had only a couple of relatives. So Pat and I joined several of our St. Anne's church friends making sure there was someone at his bedside 24 hours a day.

Terry and Judy Casey, from St. Anne's took on the task of organizing and scheduling people to make sure he did not pass-on without someone at his bedside. Pat and I always went together to stay with him for about four hours once or twice a week. We both felt a bit uncomfortable at first, like what do you say to a friend who has only a brief period in his life left? I think Frances's easy manner helped us to feel more at ease with the circumstance. It did not take long before we knew a lot about Francis, his interesting life, his likes and dislikes. His life was full of interesting stories. He had done a lot of traveling and had philosophical comments about almost everything. He was fond of poetry and music and liked hearing his favorite poems read to him. The experience turned out much different from Pat and I ever imagined.

We learned a lot from Francis and he was so appreciative of the time he was able to spend with all his friends. He told Terry one day that the visits and time spent with his friends was one of the happiest of his life. The prognosis when we started visiting was three weeks, but he enjoyed the socializing so much we think it extended his life for another three months. His funeral at St. Anne's Church was a big event and filled the church with his friends. Several people spoke about Francis from their hearts. He will be missed as will his friendship. He was always ready to help his friends fix, repair and paint whenever the need arose.

Probably the most important reason to be in Seattle was to help Pat recover from shoulder surgery. She had been experiencing a lot of pain in her right shoulder that kept her from participating in boat functions like docking and sheet handling. Thanks to Frank Furtado, a good friend and quasi-retired Seattle Sonics Basketball team trainer, we made an appointment to see shoulder surgeon, Dr. Kirby. A funny incident happened at the hospital when we met the anesthesiologist. Pat had a small grocery bag with overnight stuff just in case she had to stay over. The bag was from "Pick and Pay," a chain of South African grocery stores. The anesthesiologist recognized the store name immediately as he was from South Africa. He was interested in hearing details of our sailing adventure and curious to know what we thought of South Africa. We became so caught up in conversation we ended up delaying the surgery.

Dr. Kirby performed the rotator cuff surgery to reattach Pat's shoulder muscle ligaments. The operation was successful and performed as day surgery. He and his surgical nurse used the utmost of care to minimize incision size and scarring. However, the most difficult part for us was the recovery. Without the use of her right arm, she needed help in doing almost everything from dressing to cooking. The most difficult time was probably the first three weeks. Doing minor exercises, she gradually regained full use of her right arm in about three months. She was careful to not to lift anything and to follow Dr. Kirby's instructions without rushing the recovery period.

We had many grandchildren events on our calendar like kindergarten parent's night for Melina our six year old. She is the daughter of our son David and his first wife, Jennifer. Melina is such a ham, not at all shy and loves to sing and dance for the crowd. Our grandson, Mitchell, was just turning one so, Bob and Leslie had a big first birthday party for him. There were many children there along with their young parents. It seemed so long ago that Pat and I were young parents. We had moved to Seattle from Buffalo, NY with the promise of an engineering career at Boeing. When our first son was born we were alone, separated from parents and friends 3,000 miles away. Our children and grandchildren do not realize how wonderful it is and will be for them to have their parents, grandparents, and friends around when they grow up. Grandmothers especially, thrive on that close association with their grandchildren.

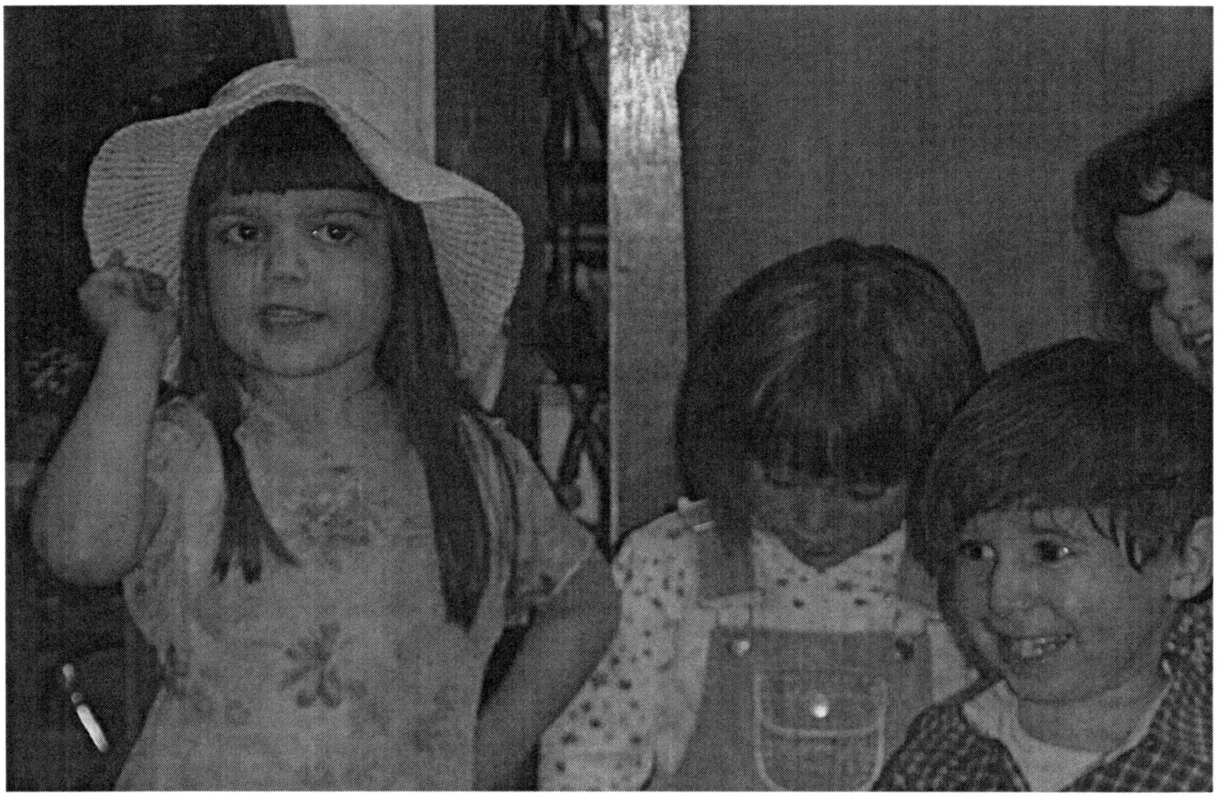

MELINA AT HER KINDERGARTEN'S PARENT'S NIGHT

A fun trip we were able to fit in after Pat's recovery from shoulder surgery was a car trip to Vancouver, BC. The city has grown by leaps and bounds since our last trip there — so cosmopolitan. There is so much to see there. We took the tour around Stanley Park, a city tour, and the Grouse Mountain cable car. On the mountain, they had substituted skiing with lumberjacks throwing hatchets, climbing poles, logrolling, sawing logs and all those forest things with a lot of humor thrown in. Just walking around the city is an interesting experience, many nice shops and all the hurried people, never a dull moment.

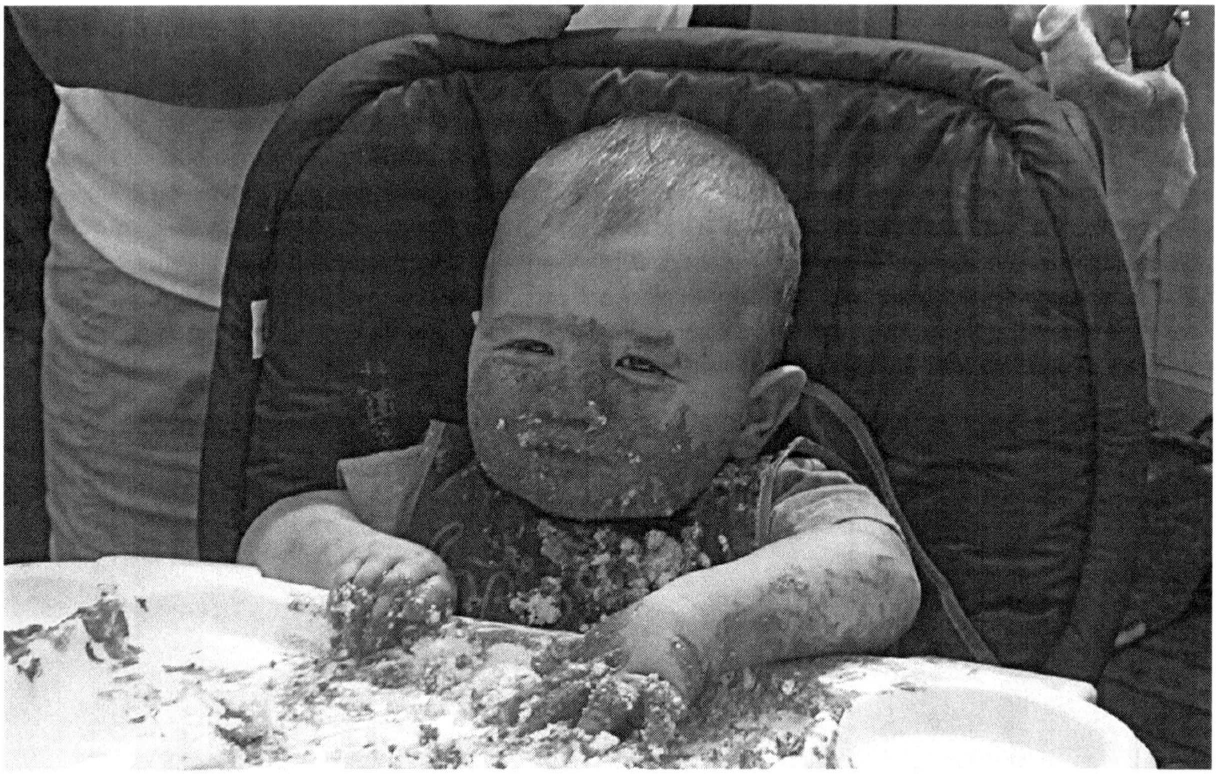

MITCHELL DEVOURING HIS FIRST BIRTHDAY CAKE — SOO GOOD!!!

We found some nice restaurants to eat at and had a special dinner at our hotel. The restaurant in our hotel was at the top of 36 floors and revolved slowly. We made our reservations so we could settle in before sunset to see the city in sunlight and in the evening. Vancouver is a busy shipping port and there was plenty of commercial boat traffic to draw our interest. It was a clear night so visibility was outstanding. Sunset was brilliant and by the time, we were enjoying dessert, we were able to witness the sparkling lights of this important Canadian city.

St. Anne's church sponsors a tour of Queen Anne Hill homes one weekend every summer as a fundraiser for their grammar school. Murray and Betty Ferguson always volunteer to chair this popular event. Queen Anne has some magnificent old homes around the hill that overlook the city to the south and people are curious to see them and look inside. Since Queen Anne Hill is about 500 feet above the city, views are endless. On a clear day you can easily see the 54 miles to snow capped, 14,400 foot high, Mount Rainier, and it is breath taking. Pat and I volunteered to show one of the grand homes that had just been remodeled to its former elegance. The views of downtown Seattle, Elliot Bay, Harbor Island, Bainbridge Island, the Ferries crossing Puget Sound and Mount Rainier helped make this weekend enjoyable. On clear days this view is probably one of this most remarkable I have ever seen. Then as a treat to all the volunteers, the Ferguson's hosted a "thank you" party on Sunday night to end the home tours in style.

Every Friday, small groups of retired Boeing Aerospace engineers meet for a long, three hour lunch. It's a lot of fun to rehash old programs and some of the staggering problems we helped solve on the Minuteman

Intercontinental Ballistic Missile System. Boeing was the prime contractor for Minuteman and most of this talented group of engineers worked in the highly regarded, Project Design Engineering Group. The number of lunch bunch members can vary from 6 to 16. We meet at the gambling casino, "Grand Central," in the nearby city of Tukwila. It is an unlikely place since no one gambles, but the food is always good, the service is good and the decor is comfortable. We also like the waitress who reserves the same table for us every week. She knows each of us well now and brings our favorite beverage when we sit down. Chuck Goggio always picks up Ralph Winnie and picks me up as he passes our Seattle apartment. Ralph Winnie, a long time lead engineer on the Minuteman Program is now confined to a wheel chair. For me, one of life's difficult problems is to see once vibrant people aging and losing their mobility and health.

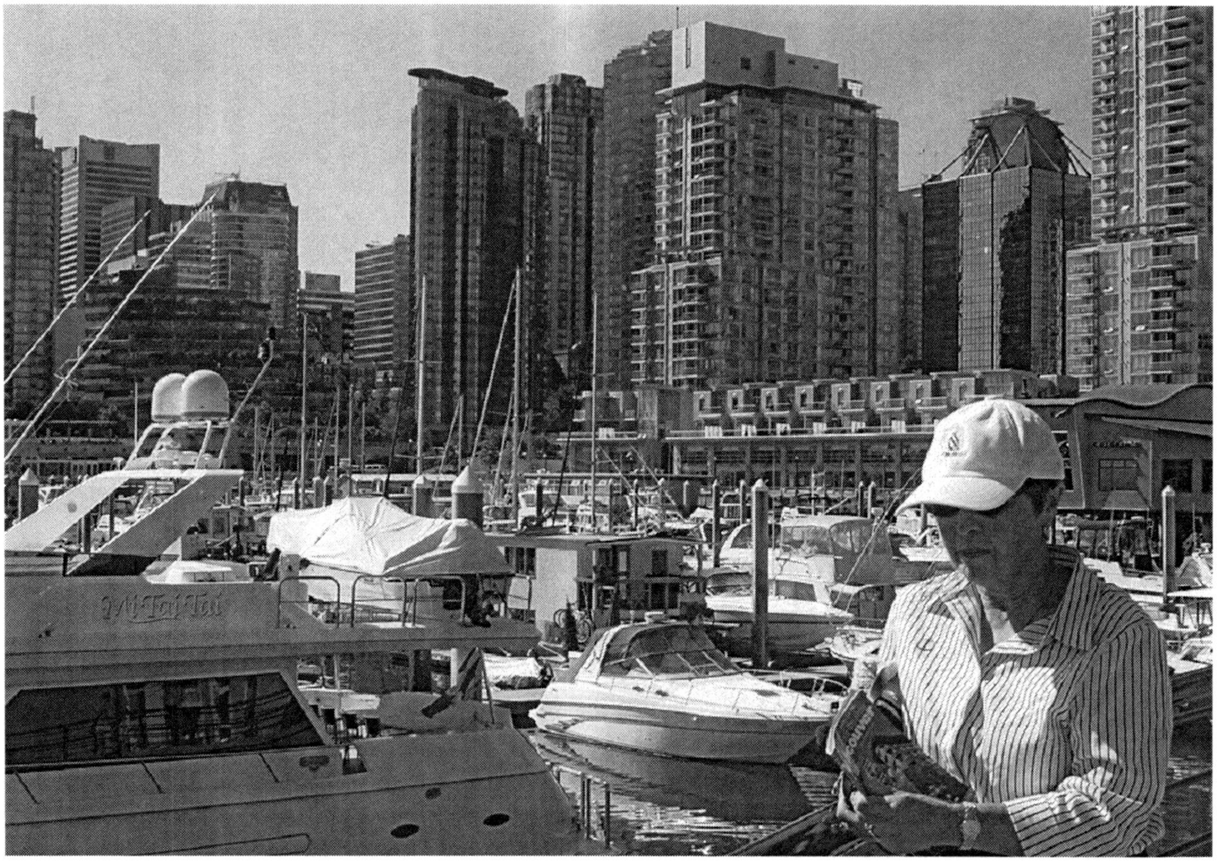

PAT, DOWNTOWN MARINA, BAYSHORE HOTEL, VANCOUVER, BC

On Sundays, I try to sing the bass parts with the St. Anne's choir even though I had no formal training (not hard to figure out if you listen closely), I enjoy singing. An Irish pastor in a church we attended while working a job for Boeing at the Harris Corp. in Melbourne, Florida, once said, "Even if you don't have a good voice, or can't carry a tune, sing all the louder to get back at God."

In Sept., we took a trip to Cortez, Florida to visit my sister Barbara and her husband Dr. Jack McCormick. Cortez is just 15 miles north of Sarasota and their condo is on the intercoastal waterway facing the barrier island of Bradenton Beach. I'm not sure why this city is called Cortez since Hernando Cortez never visited this part of Florida. Hernando Cortez or Hernán Cortéz (1485-1547) was the Spanish explorer who conquered the Aztec Empire and was not a nice person. He spent most of his time in Central America, Cuba and Mexico, but not Florida.

Our condo is on a canal that connects with the intercoastal waterway and the Gulf of Mexico. We always enjoy our trips to Florida. My sister and brother-in-law always make us feel so welcome and include us in all their activities at their golf club and with friends. You would think they would get tired of seeing us after all these years of visits, but no, she always wants to know when we are coming. She is the ultimate in fundamental beliefs of strong family ties and togetherness just like Pat.

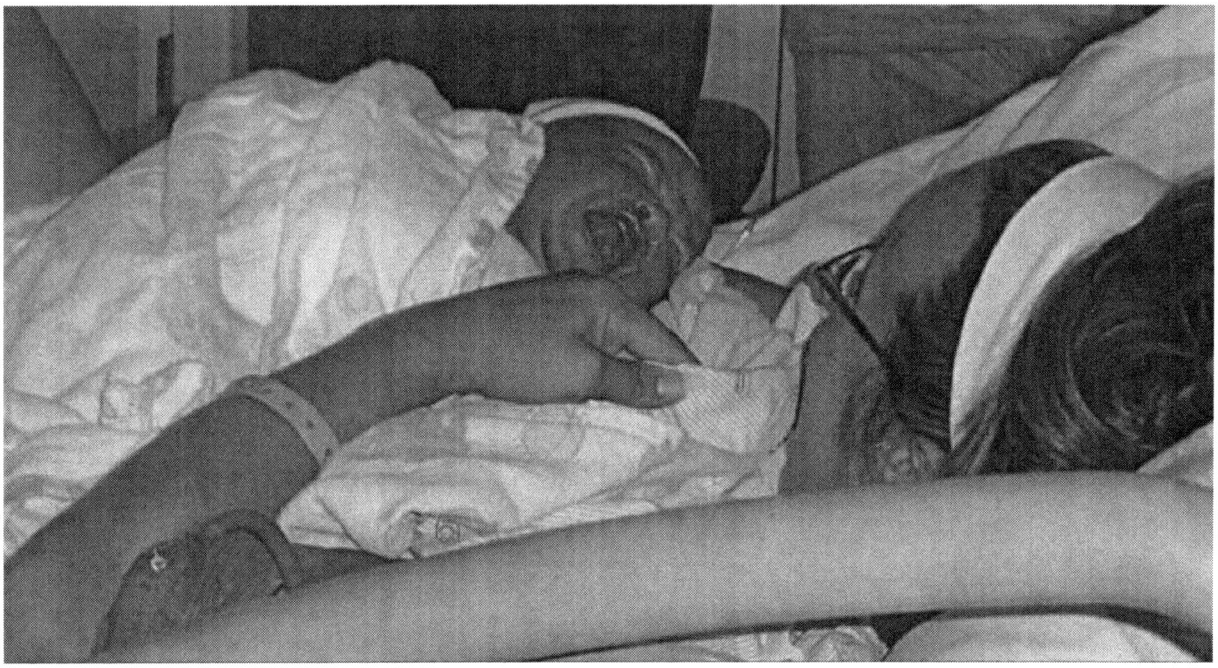

ARRIVAL OF MIA FISCHER TO EXCITED PARENTS BOB AND LESLIE

The most exciting part of our time in Seattle was the arrival of a new granddaughter on Pat's 67th birthday. Just after we got back from Florida, our daughter Leslie invited us to witness the birth of her new baby girl, Mia on Sept. 24, 2004. It was quite an occasion for our family. Swedish Hospital has individual birthing rooms equipped with the latest in high tech equipment. The room is large with a built-in incubator for the baby, warming ovens for blankets and flat panel displays for monitoring any conceivable function. There is even a built-in bed for husbands or family members to stay overnight.

The nurses could not have been friendlier or more helpful. When I told them, I had a bottle of champagne waiting in the car I was told to bring it in. The nurse found cups and ice and everyone toasted our newest family member. What a major change since our three children were born. Pat's obstetrician would not allow me to be in the birthing room for any of our three children. He felt so involved in the birthing process that he reasoned he could not deal with me if I should faint — what a difference 30 years can make. The doctor and nurses seemed so relaxed and at ease now, that they are happy to have people present.

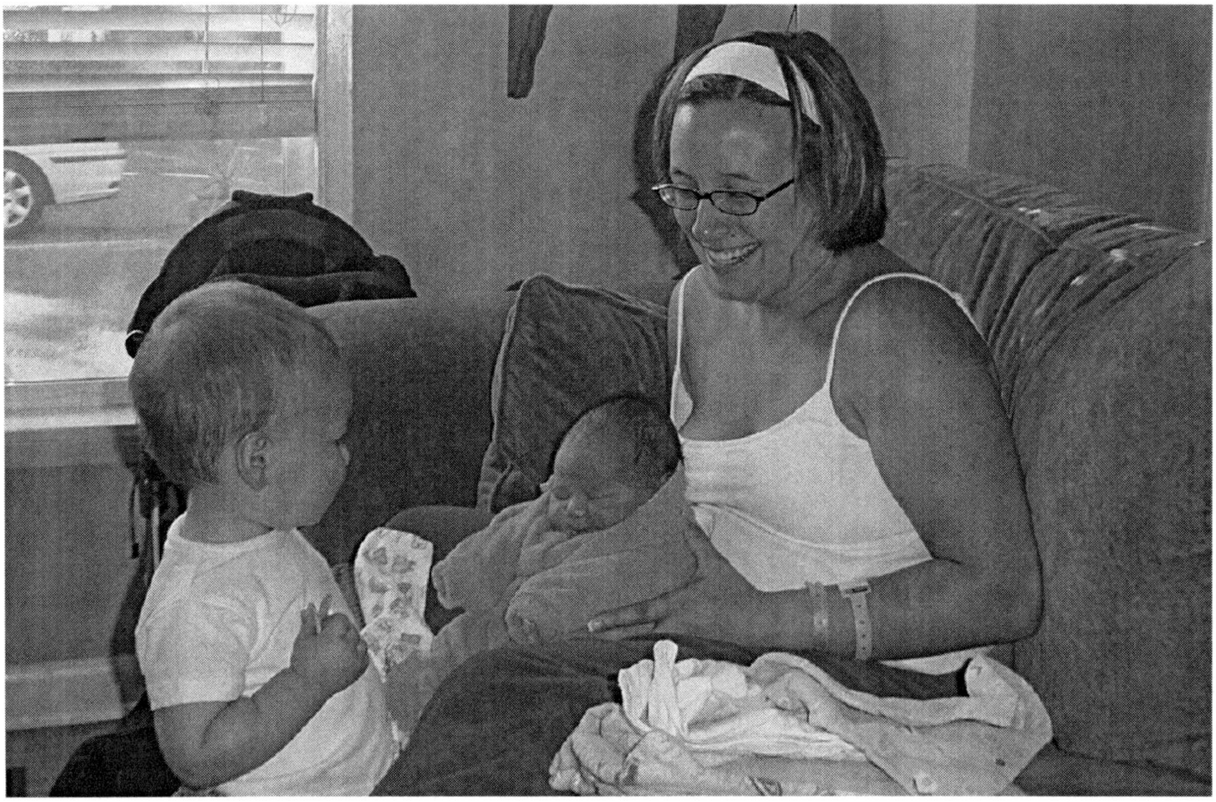

MITCHELL MEETS HIS NEW SISTER MIA FOR THE FIRST TIME

We were at Leslie's house when she first introduced Mitchell to his new sister. He knew right away were she came from as he rubbed his tummy when Leslie said, "baby." Max their dog and cats, Coal and Trixie showed only a momentary curiosity. Although Max did spend time smelling Mia's head. Leslie had brought home Mia's cap from the hospital and let Max smell it several times before Mia arrived home. He undoubtedly knew who wore this cap. I hope someday we will have a better understanding of all animals and the roles we play in each other's lives.

Chapter 28

TRINIDAD

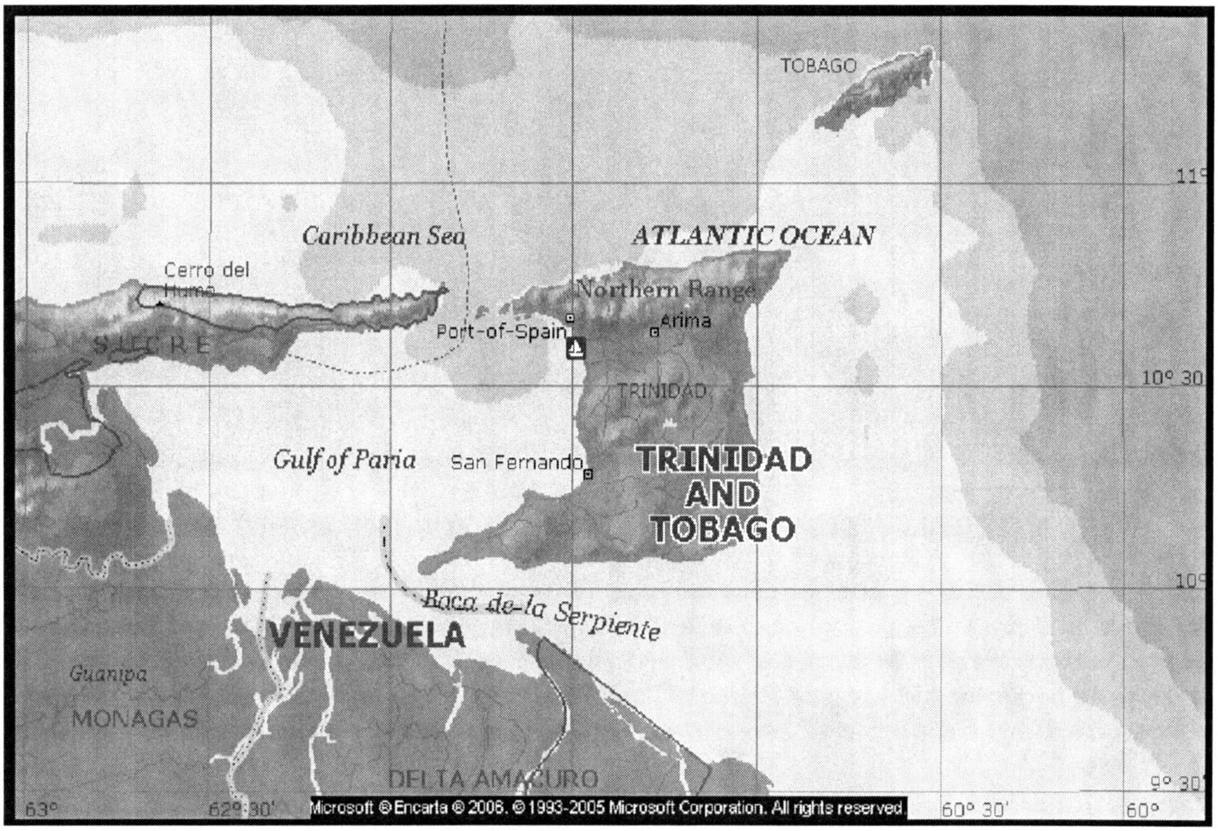

WEST INDIES NATIONS OF TRINIDAD AND TOBAGO (T and T)

I arrived back in Trinidad on Nov. 2, 2004; Pat was to follow after I cleaned up the boatyard dirt. ***Our Pleasure*** spent the last seven months in dry storage at Peake's Boatyard in Chaguaramas, Trinidad, not a clean place. The new hull paint and stripping done by KNJ, a company in Chaguaramas, was beautiful. The rest of the boat was dirty from yard dust, nearby boat work and high humidity. All the sheets that had been exposed to the Atlantic's salt water were coated in green mold, not unlike what happens in Seattle. I made the mistake of not having plastic shrink-wrap placed around the boat to protect the topsides.

For about $500, a company called Dynamite Marine will install a plastic pipe structure around the boat and cover it with a white, UV protective, plastic shrink-wrap. Next year I will be more prepared with shrink-wrap and my dehumidifier connected to an outside drain. Usually boaters are full of unsolicited advice, but no one warned me about potential mold problems. When I left Trinidad my dehumidifier was running, but with no one checking the boat, I found the power cord unplugged on my return. Actually, the interior was in good shape from vents that allow some air circulation. The two temperature-recording monitors were both maxed out at inside/outside temperatures of 120° Fahrenheit, a good indication of how hot it gets here in the summer time.

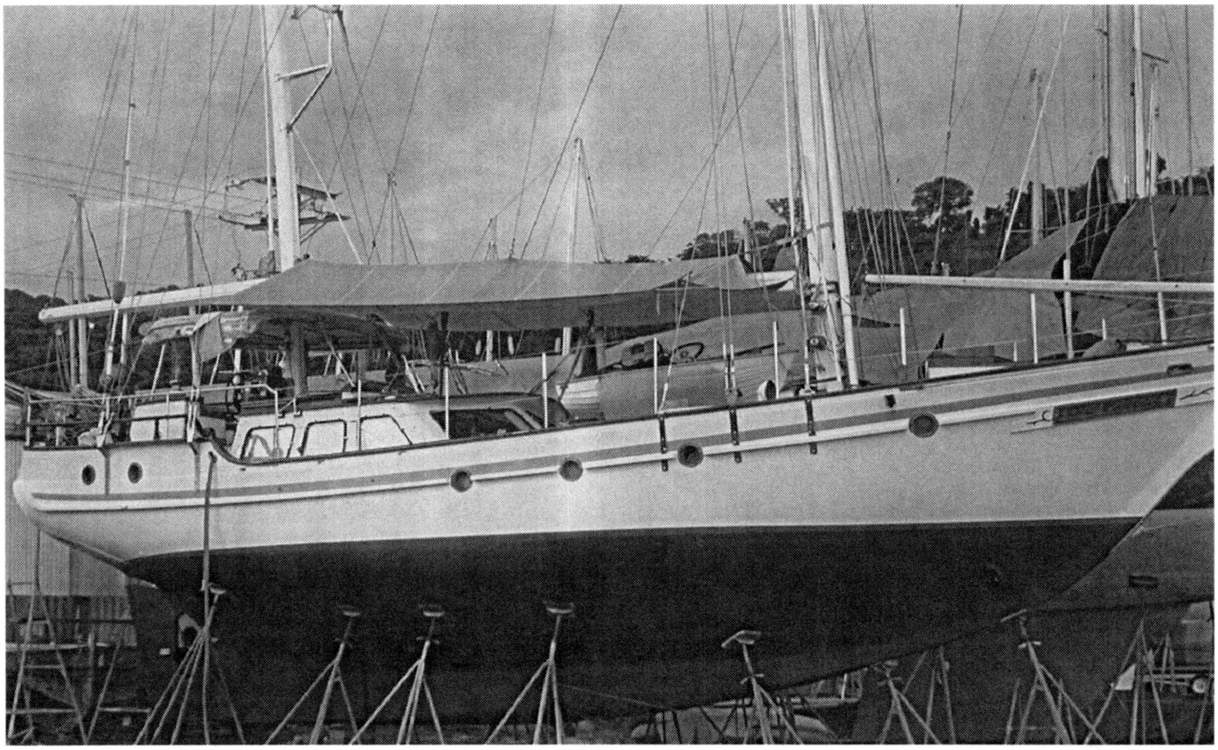

OUR PLEASURE, GLEAMING IN NEW PAINT, PEAKE'S BOATYARD, TRINIDAD

Peake's yard is well run and equipped with first class boat handling equipment. Their 150 ton travel lift handled my 26 tons easily and there was no need to remove any of the standing rigging first (always a must do job with smaller travel lifts). They also have a unique lowboy hydraulic tractor to move boats back and forth to the travel lift. It is equipped with six hydraulic arms to support the hull, which the driver can set remotely. This arrangement allows boats to travel around the storage yard quickly instead of using the slow moving travel lift.

This boat trailer also contains several steel box beams that can be moved in or out of the frame to accommodate any width catamaran or trimaran. This yard is run on a professional level, but all costs are based on U.S. dollars and prices — no cost bargains in this third world country. Pat arrived on Nov. 30 and stayed at the Crews Inn Hotel until we could get our slip back. Our slip reservations were for Dec. 4. The bigger slips were fully booked which eliminated an earlier launch date. We were assigned a slip on Dec. 3, and launched as the last boat that day. One of the surprising things about Trinidad is the hundreds of boats that are stored there each hurricane season. Official estimates I saw range from 800 to 1,200 boats depending on the season. Looking over the boat yards, all you see is a sea of masts.

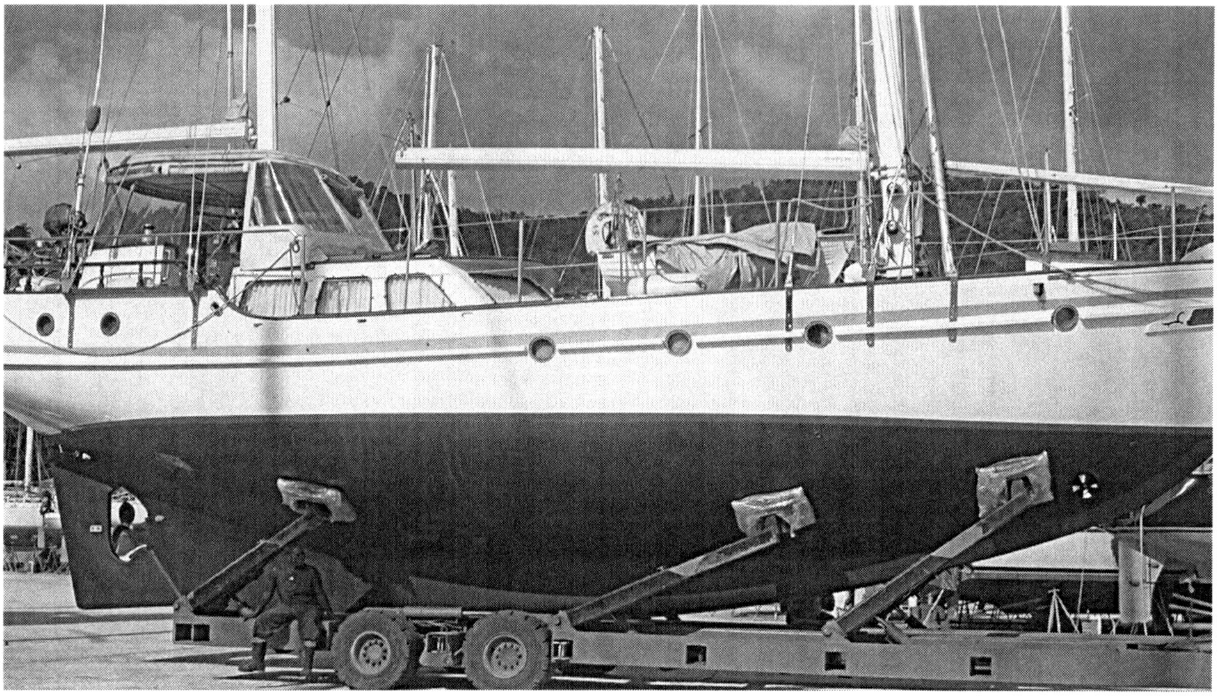

CUSTOM LOWBOY MOVING *OUR PLEASURE* TO THE TRAVEL LIFT

The government is working on plans to expand the marina and storage space since the boating industry has such a positive impact on their economy. This area is considered to be out of the hurricane belt, which makes it popular for east coast U.S. and European boats. The path of hurricane Ivan in 2004 came close to Trinidad's north shore and worried most boaters watching its path at home on their TV's. Ivan only reached 35 knots in Chaguaramas, Trinidad. However, Grenada only 90 miles north was directly in its path and was almost destroyed by Ivan. Grenada had been considered a safe haven for hurricanes until 2004. Insurance companies no longer consider Grenada safe during the hurricane season; a result of many damage claims filed by boat owners with boats damaged in that storm.

Trinidad was swamped with boat repair work as a result of Ivan and the repair work filled Trinidad's yards when I arrived in Nov. The few marine support type companies that have earned good reputations in Trinidad were swamped with work. I asked a rigging company to replace my wind vane, which was previously destroyed by a big bird in the Indian Ocean. The poor guy looked frazzled when he looked at it and said he did not want to take on any more jobs. This job looked simple to me, maybe an hour at most, but he could not deal with the pressure of all the extra work.

Most boats traveling the islands of the Caribbean stop in Trinidad for the excellent yacht services. Since ***Our Pleasure*** was docked at one of the largest docks at Crews Inn, we saw some beautiful mega-yachts. In the background of the next picture is the gorgeous mega-yacht sloop, *Georgia*. Pat and I first saw her after her New Zealand launching, just in time for the start of the year 2000 America's Cup racing. If I remember correctly, she is about 180 feet long and at the time, had the highest mast in the world for a sloop. ***Our Pleasure*** is centered in the picture with *Endurance* to the right.

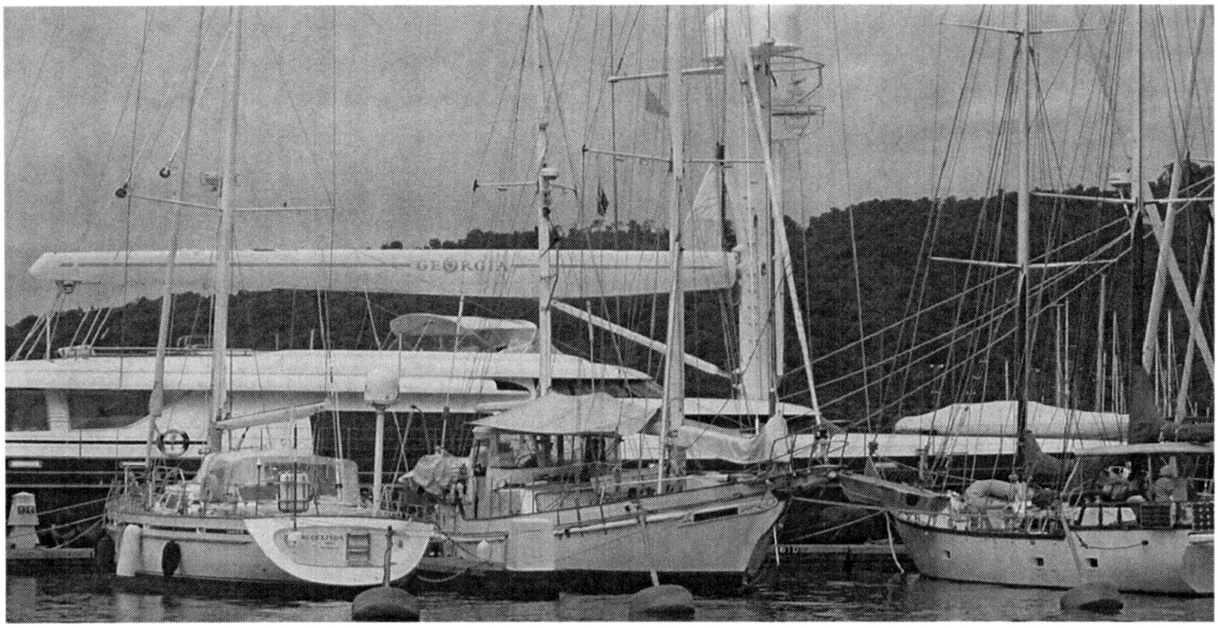

MEGA-YACHT *GEORGIA* PAYS A SHORT VISIT TO CREWS INN

An unusual commercial ship that docked behind us was the *Seaway Kestrel.* She is specialized for ocean pipe lying in support of the offshore oil industry in this region. The pipes are unwound from a large reel that must be around 50 feet in diameter. It looks like she has a big array of satellite, navigation, and communication equipment. There is a large landing pad for helicopters built over the bow. She must have several thrusters because she can move sideways without the help of tugs. She also carries a number of different sized cranes and emergency lifeboats. She has a sister ship that is built for the same purpose, but is not as frequent a visitor as *Seaway Kestrel.* When she is docked for loading supplies or maintenance, some of her crew will stay at the Crews Inn Hotel. The bar at the hotel's pool does a big business when one of these ships is in port.

A fascinating natural phenomenon exists in Trinidad called Pitch Lake. Sir Walter Raleigh discovered this lake in 1595 and it is the largest natural asphalt lake in the world. This 100 acre site of tar appears to be a large parking lot of oil, clay and bubbling sulfurous water. A form of petroleum, natural pitch, which seeps into the region, supplies the lake. You can actually walk on the lake, but you cannot stand in one place too long as you will sink in. In some areas of the lake, fluid tar is easily extracted. According to local folklore, an entire village submerged into the asphalt as a punishment for eating the sacred hummingbird. The great spirit of the Amerindians issued this punishment decree to the king of the local tribe.

One of the nice marina amenities at Crews Inn is their beautiful swimming pool. This is a popular spot in the afternoon when boat projects are ended for the day. The water temperature is always warm from the sun's ever presence. The air temperature on most days is close to 90° F so the pool is always refreshing at 84° F. Many boats do not have air conditioners and when the inside temperatures soar they hit the pool. Some women have organized pool exercise classes so between exercising, swimming and cooling off, the pool is very popular.

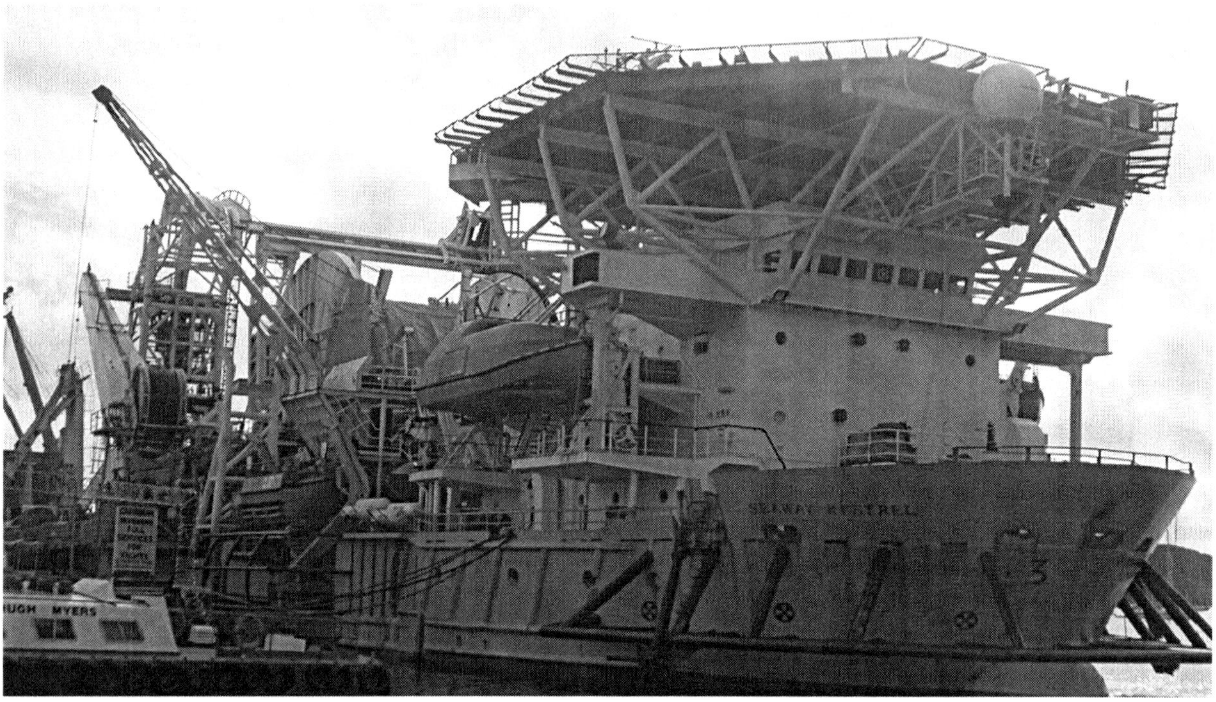

OCEAN PIPE LAYING SHIP, *SEAWAY KESTREL* WITH HELIPORT

Our boat has a built-in air conditioner that allows us to gratefully keep our inside temperature around 78° F. Working inside without air conditioning is close to impossible after 11 a.m. When the conditioner fails we become grumpy and miserable so not much is accomplished. Short-term failures are frequent; as dirty water in the area will clog water filters in about a week if not cleaned. The harbor water is barnacle prolific in that the water inlet screen will fill with barnacles if one is not vigilant. In addition, our aging conditioner now requires almost constant attention. I think I have replaced almost every one of its parts. It is a good thing Jeff Stone and his wife Dawn from Nau-T-Kol Refrigeration decided to open their business here. Jeff is always looking for parts for me like the contactor, capacitors, etc.

He installed a new rotary compressor I brought from Seattle and installed a high-pressure cut-off switch on it, which is worth its weight in gold. Besides the barnacle problem, the harbor water is full of debris, which frequently clogs the water pump filter reducing water flow to the air conditioner. If debris does clog the water inlet, the compressor operating pressure will rise, but the new switch will sense the problem and turn off the air-conditioner before serious damage.

An additional bonus in Trinidad is the daily marine radio net that starts at 8 a.m. and lasts for about 20 minutes. We can order roasted chickens to pick up at the local "Hi Lo" grocery store or arrange for a taxi to the Tuesday night movies in Port of Spain. All local activities are announced on the net and range from domino playing to ordering a custom-made dress or bathing suit. There is a section for people needing help to locate parts or services or to trade hardware. There are several yachties that have been coming here every year for many years and know the best doctors/dentists/hospitals or where to find technical services — it is a wonderful volunteer system that provides a needed service for new arrivals and old hands.

The year's end is a good time to be in Chaguaramas because of all the activities. Nov. 25 was the Thanksgiving dinner for yachties at the Trinidad/Tobago Hospitality and Tourism Institute. This school prepares students to work in all phases of the hotel industry. As a result, we were treated to an American style Thanksgiving dinner including pumpkin soup, turkey, stuffing, ham, mashed potatoes, candied sweet potatoes, vegetables, and apple pie. Pat had not arrived in Trinidad yet so I sat at a table with yachties from the yachts *Four Winds* and *Sea Wolf*, who had also sailed around the Cape of Good Hope. Joyce, from the yacht *Mood Indigo,* sang a beautiful version of "Our Father," and Carol, a Christian pastor from the yacht *Trinity*, led everyone in a Thanksgiving prayer. There were several other round-the-world yachties there from the yachts, *Aldebaran*, *Allons'y*, and *Holding Pattern.*

On Dec. 4, YSATT, a local marine organization, held their annual Christmas party they named, "Lime by the Sea." In Trinidad, to "lime" is to socialize, relax, and talk with friends. Boat yard and marine suppliers, using their own favorite recipes, prepared the food. There was a bar; a steel band and a disc jockey that played music so loud no one could carry on a conversation. Shouting worked some of the time, but I think if the DJ saw anyone talking, he cranked up the music a few notches. The food was good and everyone enjoyed himself or herself. The money collected went to the Grenada Hurricane Relief Fund, a good cause.

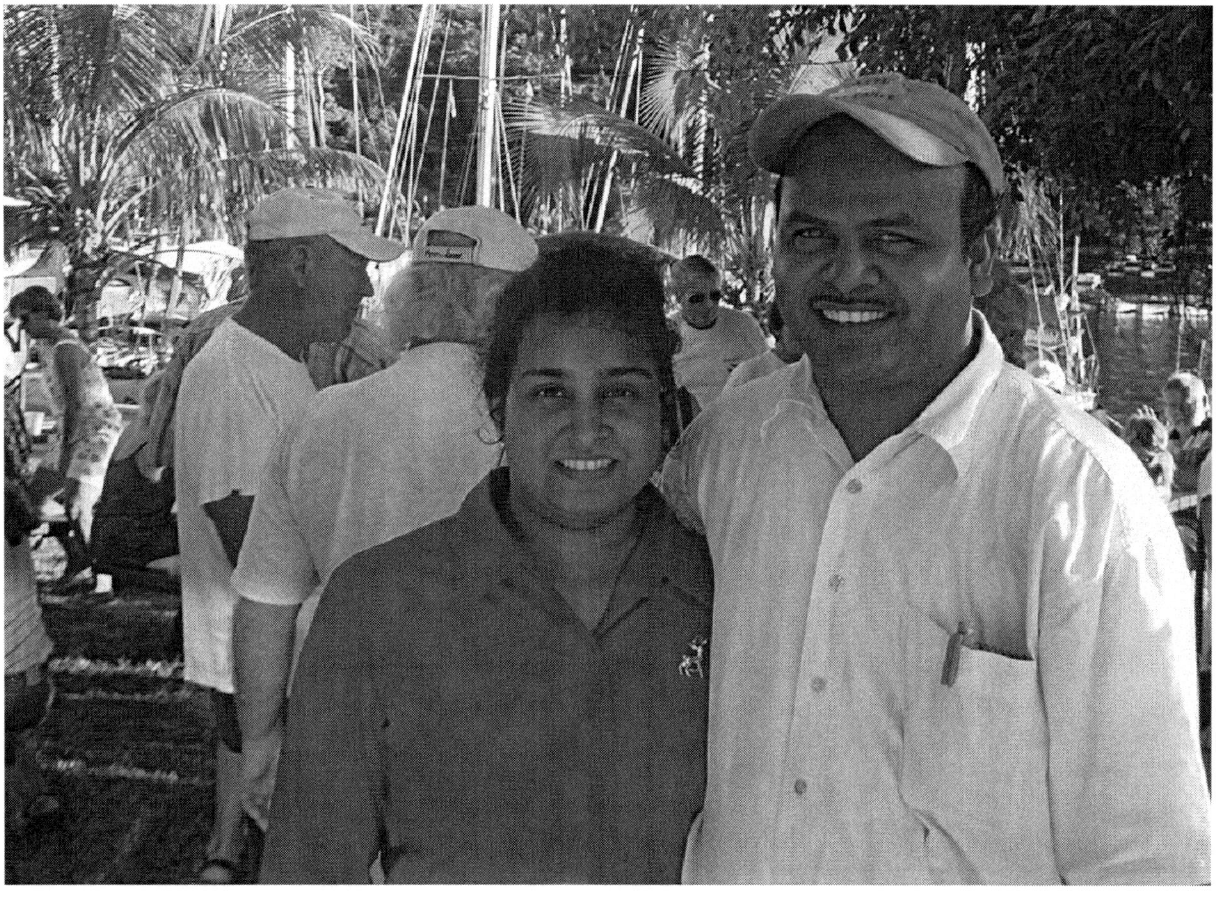

CHRISTMAS PARTY, JESSE AND WIFE SHARON ROSE, JAME'S TAXI SERVICE

On Dec. 6, Crews Inn hosted a Christmas dinner in the area of the hotel grounds called the Village Square. Everyone was greeted at the entrance with a glass of rum punch. The hotel staff hosted an open bar with a wide range of free drinks. Chefs at the hotel's Lighthouse Restaurant prepared the food, which included ham, turkey, scalloped potatoes, vegetables, rice, prawns, chocolate mousse, and ginger squares. A steel pan band provided good music and the group "Stiks," sang Venezuelan Christmas songs in Spanish. Each boat crew received a gift of fruitcake rapped as a Christmas present. The next day we went to see the Christmas movie Polar Express with Marv and Chieko from the yacht *Endurance*. On Dec. 16, we went to a Christmas party hosted by Jesse James, his wife Sharon Rose and Irena Travel. There was lots of sorrel rum punch and roties. Sorrel is a native plant that is naturally sour, but when spiced with sugar and spices has a nice taste. Roti is a local dish made with East Indian flat bread wrapped over a vegetable or chicken curry.

On Dec. 19, we went to a musical Christmas show at the Queen's Theater, a modern theater with comfortable seating well suited for musicals. The polished wood interior reminded me of the Sidney Opera House, but on a much smaller scale. The group is called the Lydians and it was their 25th anniversary. Lydian is a musical term referring to the natural tones of a major or minor scale. The group was around 100 strong with 75 of its members in the choir. The orchestra was a steel pan band with two pianos, conventional drums, African drums and several guitars. The group had four soloists with beautiful strong voices. You might have heard this group as they travel extensively around the world giving concerts.

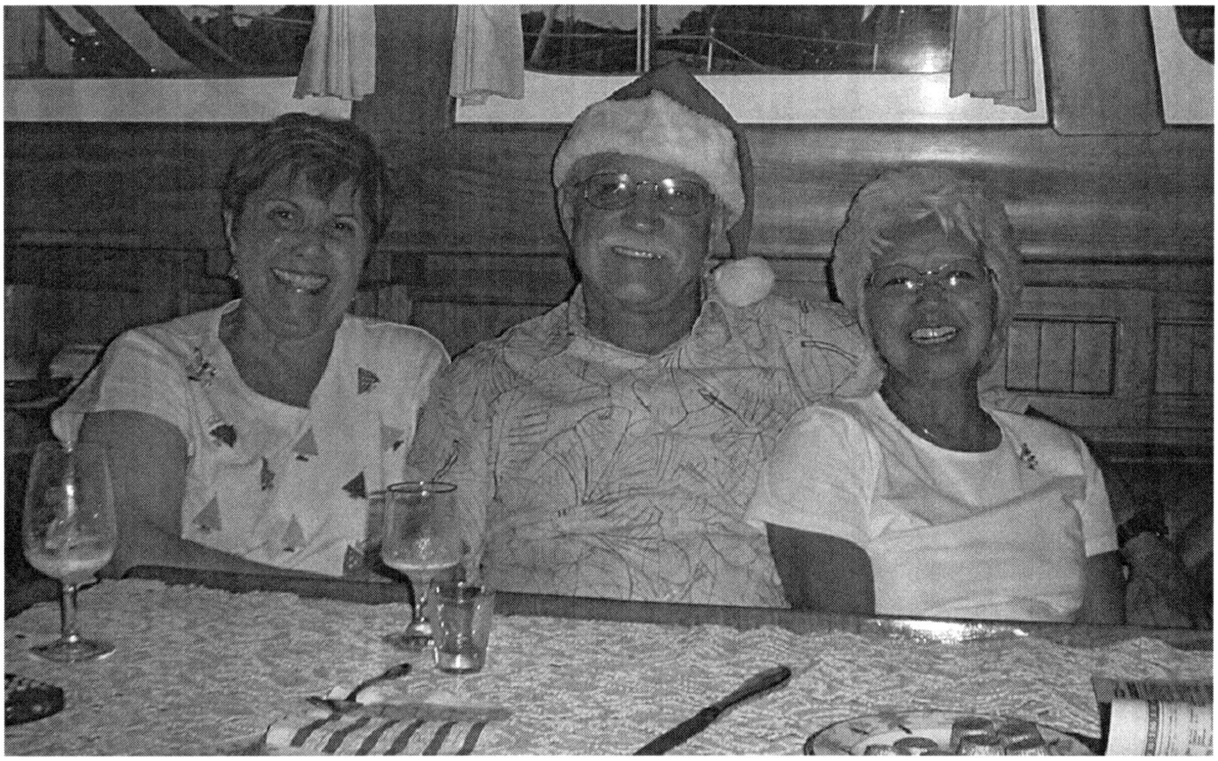

CHRISTMAS DAY, ON *OUR PLEASURE*, 2004, PAT, MARV AND CHIEKO

The Christmas music was varied with 31 different songs; ranging from *Comfort Ye* (George Handel's *Messiah*) to Handel's complex and difficult *Hallelujah Chorus*. Their music arrangement and presentation of the *Hallelujah Chorus* was probably the best I have ever heard. We have included this song in our Christmas music several times at St. Anne's church in Seattle. As always, the singers with training can follow along well, but there are those who get lost temporarily until they can get back in harmony. After several years, I think I have finally caught on.

On Christmas day, we had Marv and Chieko over for a Turkey dinner on ***Our Pleasure***. The day was hot and sunny with temperatures hovering around the ninety-degree mark.

New Years Eve was spent on *Endurance* with Bill and Sheri from *Esprit*. We watched the activity in Times Square on TV. There is a one-hour difference between NY and Trinidad time so we managed to stay quasi awake until past 1 a.m.

Local members of the Seven Seas Cruising Association (a worldwide organization for boaters) put a nice party together on New Year's Day. This was a potluck BOB party and everyone brought a dish for ten people, about 93 members and guests attended. The food and guest speakers were great.

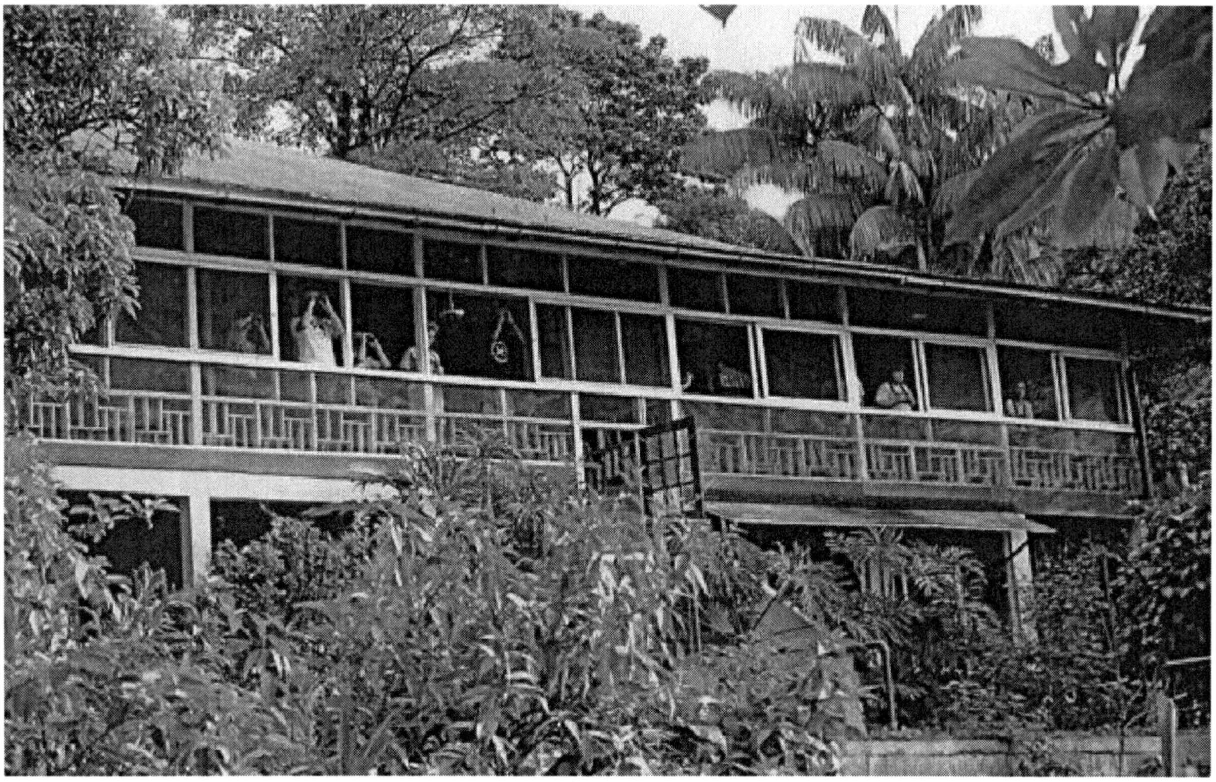

ASA WRIGHT NATURE CENTER VIEWING PORCH

On Jan. 3, we all had the garlic shrimp dinner with June and Andy at the Inn Place. Dinner, drinks, and desert were a bargain at around $15. However, the occasion was a sad gathering as Andy had just been to see a Trinidad urologist. Andy is a doctor and was sure he had a bladder problem. Tests confirmed he had bladder cancer — not good. In three days, they put their trimaran, *Gold Eagle,* in storage and flew to the states to consult with specialists. We heard his surgery was successful. During our travels, we have known people who found themselves with sudden medical problems. In most cases the problems have forced abrupt changes in their life styles and cancelled future plans. It seems that problems with cancer are especially life threatening. It just proves that one should not put off dreams, but instead be encouraged to pursue them while in good health.

One of the must see tours in Trinidad is the ASA Wright Nature Center, high up in the north hills of Trinidad. We went there with June and Andy (*Gold Eagle*) as well as Allen and Adel (*Celerity*) on Jan. 4, 2005, several days before Dr. Andy's surgery. On the mountainous road before the center, we saw farmers growing a popular Trinidad vegetable called christophene. This vegetable is like a bland squash that grows on a horizontal vine kept shoulder high off the ground by nets and poles. These vegetables cover large areas of the mountainside and must be a difficult challenge to farm, as the terrain is steep. Pat decided, after some experimentation in cooking with it, that one must acquire a taste for it.

This nature center is situated on a 200 acre conservation estate at an elevation of 1,200 feet. Within its rain forest a colony of Oilbird's may be seen, as well as, Manakin leks, Toucans, Bellbirds, Trogons, Motmots, Hummingbirds, Tanagers, Honeycreepers, Woodpeckers, Antshrikes and many others. There are reported to be approximately 430 bird species in Trinidad and Tobago and 2,300 flowering plants. Many of the plants and trees are identified along the center's nature trails. The center has a nice restaurant overlooking the valley and rooms for 24 overnight guests. The estate was once a cocoa and coffee plantation and the restaurant continues to feature those coffee beans, which they roast on site. The coffee is surprisingly good, probably the best of Trinidad's coffee's.

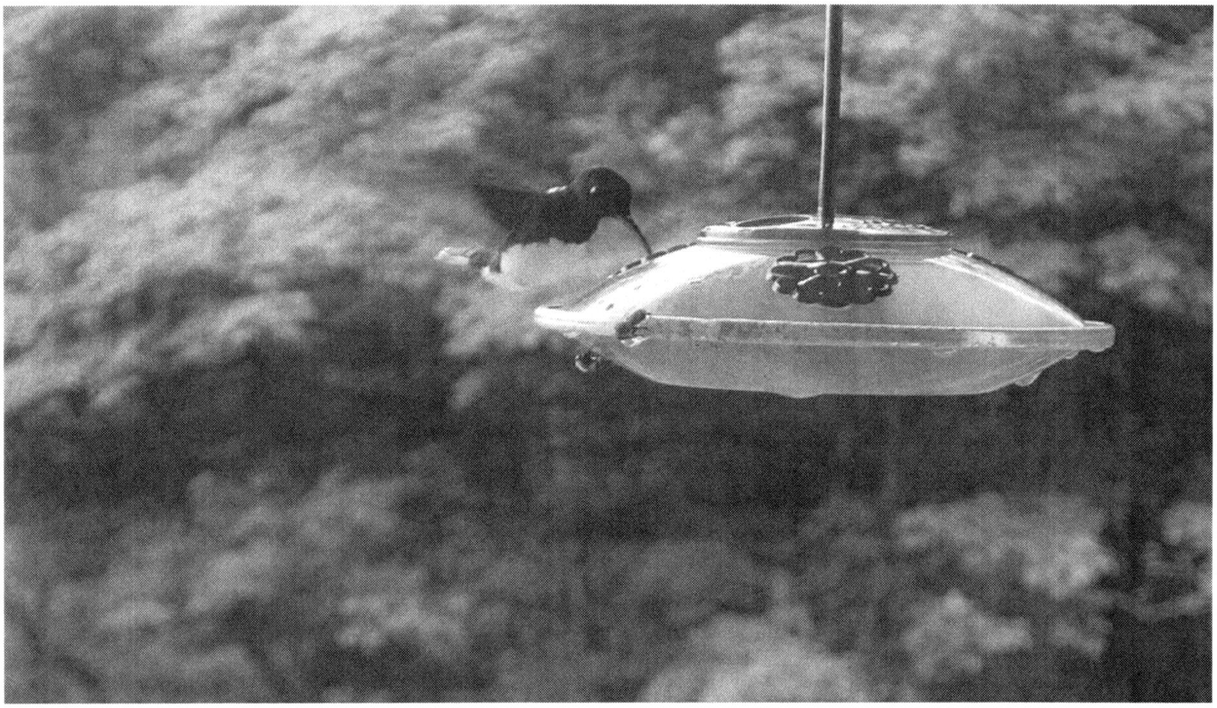

HUMMINGBIRD FEEDING AT THE ASA WRIGHT BIRD SANCTUARY

The original mansion has a huge veranda across the front overlooking a beautiful valley where hundreds of birds nest. There are 17 species of hummingbirds in Trinidad and 14 of them have been recorded at the ASA Wright center. The hummingbird feeders are at eye level right in front of the veranda. There were several other raised bird feeders just off the ground attracting birds that can also be seen from the veranda. There are several guides to help sort out different species and answer questions. We observed a family of agouti (large tailless rodents, with gray flecked hair) just below the raised feeders, eating the food that fell from the feeders — I actually thought they were as interesting as the birds.

The center features several well-marked hiking trails and the guided tours are interesting. The center does not receive government support and depends on donations and income from tourists. I found it surprising to see so many people interested in bird watching. Many people stay for days and bring bird identification books, binoculars and sophisticated camera equipment. I got the impression from overheard conversations that foreign tourists are the most ardent bird watchers.

After a nature walk and lunch with some of their good coffee, Jesse met us at the center at 2:30 p.m. to take us on a tour of the Coroni Swamp. This mangrove-lined swamp, in central Trinidad, has extensive streams, tributaries and lagoons. The swamp is the only home to the Scarlet Ibis in Trinidad. The Ibis in South America will nest in flocks of up to 10,000 birds. I am not sure how many we saw, but it must have been several hundred along with an equal number of White Egrets. However, this was not a good day to be bird watching in the swamp. The heavy rain was non-relenting, the mosquitoes were feasting on us like crazy and we were traveling in a slow, leaky, open, flat-bottomed boat with no protection from the rain. By time we saw the birds flying to their island-nesting tree, we wondered why we were subjecting ourselves to this ordeal. Allen remarked that if he never went on another bird tour it would be too soon.

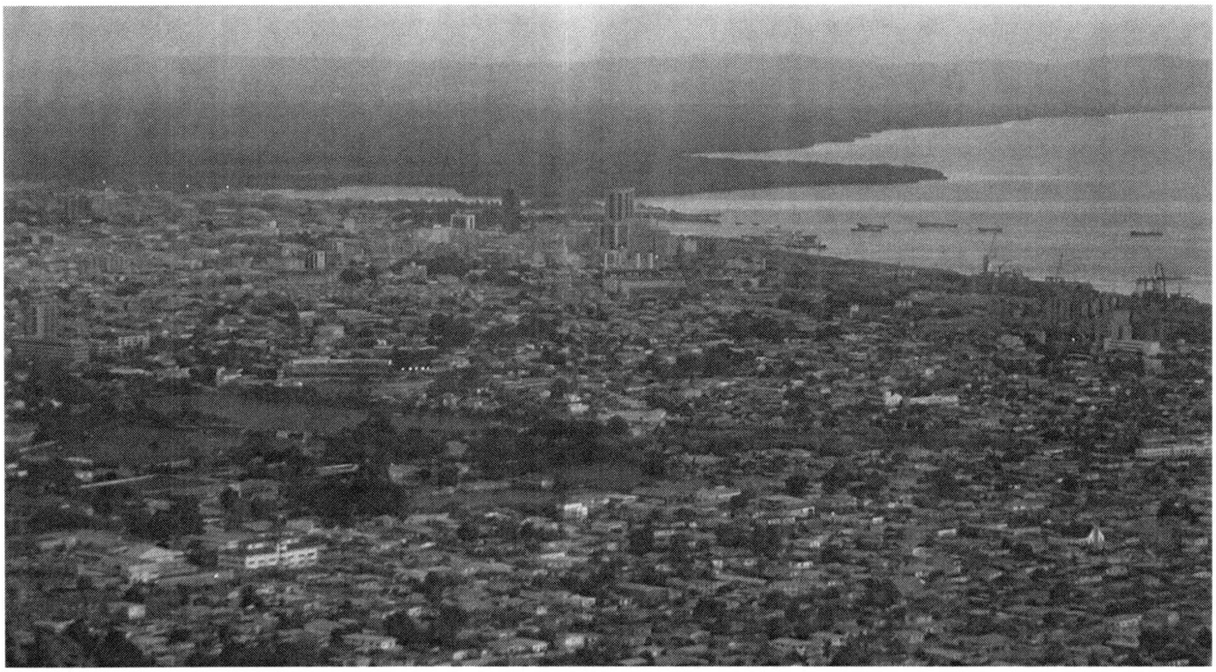

PORT OF SPAIN AS SEEN FROM FORT GEORGE

On Jan. 26, we went on an evening dinner tour of Fort George. This was a sunset tour high on the mountains overlooking the capital of Trinidad, Port of Spain. The evening was beautiful with semi-clear skies and breathtaking views all the way to Venezuela.

The next big event, where everyone goes crazy, is the pre-Lenten activities on the islands of Trinidad and Tobago, Carnival! Carnival or from the Latin translation, "farewell-to-flesh," is nothing like I expected. It is one huge outpouring of energy and creativity from Trinidad's multi-cultural roots. Carnival has evolved from its early roots into a spectacle of the streets where each cultural group of immigrants has added their own touch. There are weeks of events leading up to the final two days of parades e.g., King and Queen Competition, Calypso Competition, Steel Pan Competition, Kiddy Carnival, Extempo, J'Ouvert, Panorama, Dimanche Gras and Old Time Carnival.

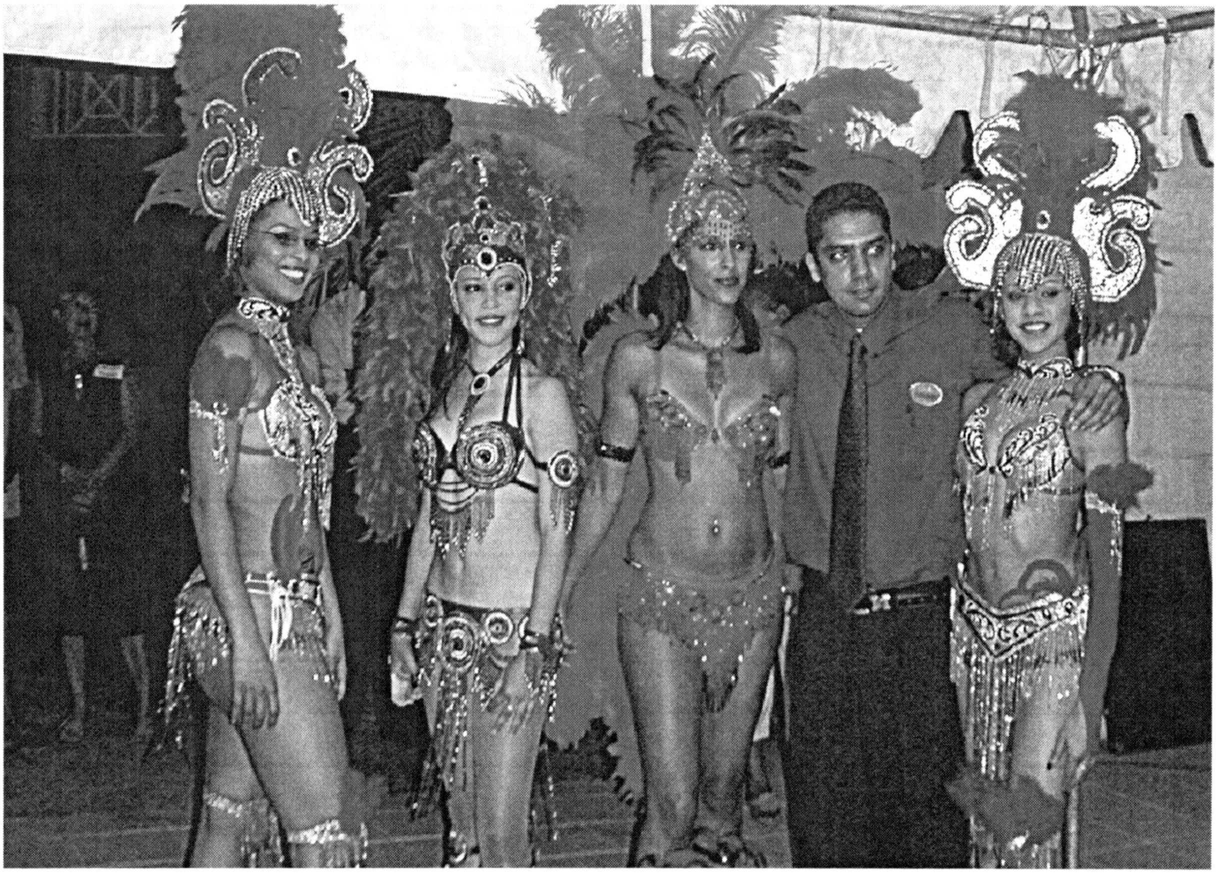

FOUR CARNIVAL COSTUME DESIGNS AT CREWS INN

Crews Inn hosted a cocktail party for their guests just before the start of Carnival. The models wore costumes related to the different festivities of Carnival. The above picture shows examples of some of the costume choices for revelers who will dance alongside their chosen bands in the parade. Also shown in the picture, is a small sample of the many attractive women in this country, the result of the many variations in races and cultures. Each band organization may have designed up to 20 different costume choices for revelers who want to associate with a particular band. Costume costs vary from $200 to $400, very expensive for Trini's. A good wage in the city for skilled labor, like lifeguards or firefighter, is around TT $200 to TT $250 a day or equivalent to $33 to $44. The enthusiasm and pleasure they receive from the festivities must far outweigh the cost. I understand it is common to take out loans to be part of the festivities. Each female costume design has a male counterpart, usually based on wearing shorts, armbands, leg bands and a headpiece.

Jesse James taxi service organized tours to see all these events and visits to several factories making costumes. He can provide several "Maxi Taxis" (12 passenger vans) that are safe and reliable transportation just for yachties in the Chaguaramas (main area of marinas) area of Trinidad. There are hundreds of **steel pan bands** in three categories, small, medium, and large, from 30 to 150 members as well as junior bands and school bands. Many of the steel band drummers play more than one drum and as many as six drums. An estimated 7,000 pannists are involved in the preliminary Steel Band Panorama competition. The prize money for first place in the large steel pan bands categories is TT $400,000, making competition formidable. Another carnival category is the **bands** that march in the Parade of Bands also known as "Pretty Mas."

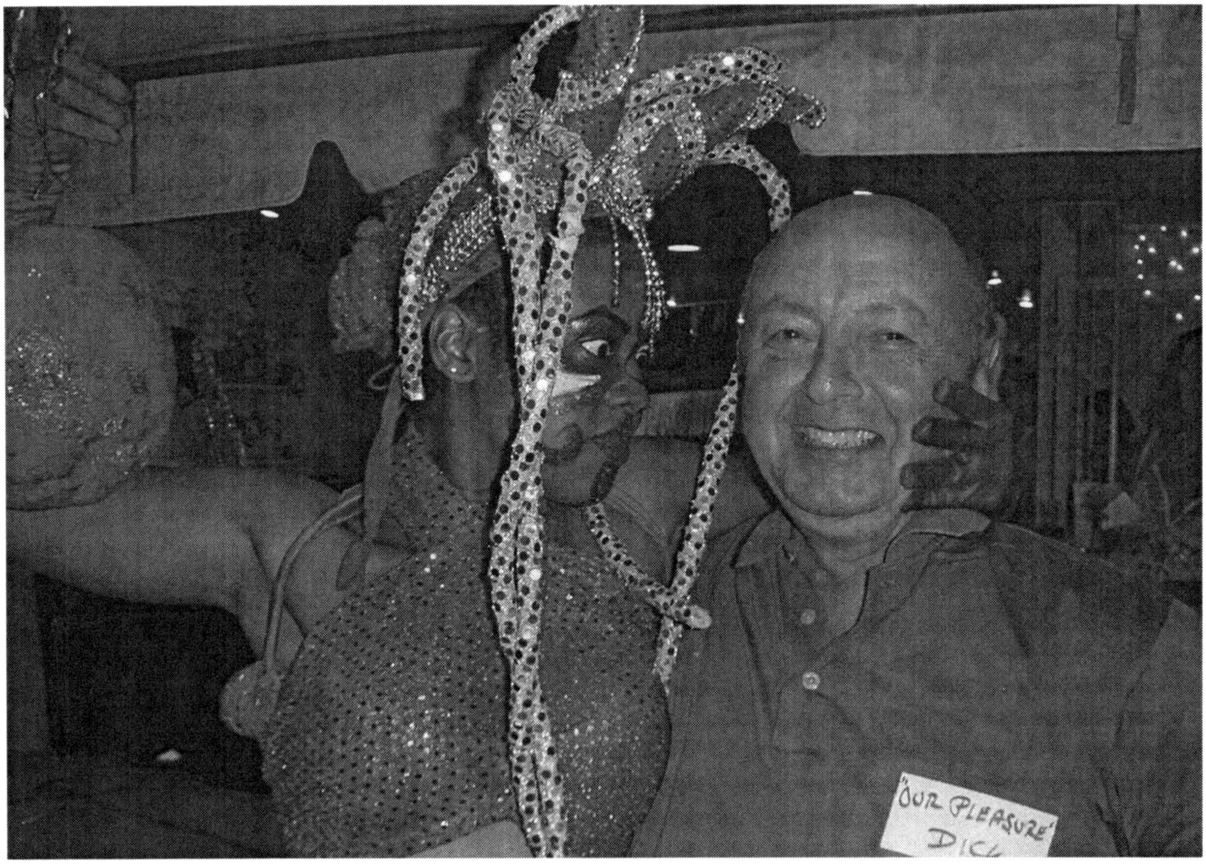

A J'OUVERT DEVIL TRYING TO FEED THE CAPTAIN "THEE" BAD APPLE

The Queens English is rather brutalized in Trinidad with island speak. One example is the word "Mas" which is short for masquerade. "De" or "d" are often used as a substitute for "the." So members parading with a

band are made up of costumed masqueraders dancing (chipping) behind their tractor-trailer, mega-watt sound systems. The chipping is an animated movement of the whole body to the beat of the music — something akin to an African war dance. The music they chip to is called soca music. Soca is an acronym for soul-calypso and provides an intense beat from steel pans and drums. The music is perfect for chipping. Not counting the rural villages of Trinidad and Tobago, which also have parades, the costumed revelers parading with 71 registered bands in the Port of Spain, were estimated at 50,000.

When we talk about sound systems, we are talking about **monster** sound systems. These systems are constructed with up to 50 speaker enclosures on each trailer. The speaker enclosures are mostly ducted port types with base speakers in the 12 to 15 inch diameter range. I saw a few speakers that were probably 30 inches in diameter. Each trailer contains a commercial size Diesel generator system in the 50,000 watt range. These babies supply ear-shattering, chair rattling, chipping music from big power amplifiers. The base frequencies are so intense my body felt them from 40 feet away. The low frequencies felt like they could change my heart rate. Soca, chipping music, is played at the threshold of pain, probably around 120 decibels.

The Trini's seem to love these sound levels, the louder the better! Those of us worried about keeping our hearing for a few more years wore good earplugs. Each sound truck or **band** carries a DJ to run the sound system. In addition, many of the trucks carried their own singers and a live band to blast away on top of recorded sound tracks. I do not know about the Trini's, but visitors have no chance of understanding the lyrics. Even when you think you get a few words there is always some doubt. Most lyrics repeat over and over in an endless, monotonous manner. However, the sound levels are so high words are distorted beyond recognition.

The biggest **bands** are enormous in size. One such **band**, "Legacy," had approximately 7,000 masqueraders in 17 different costumed sections (and this was not the biggest **band**). Each section wore a different costume, but with a central theme. During the Parade of Bands, they did a choreographed dance routine in front of the judges that took over an hour to complete. To organize that many dancers in a routine that intertwined all of their sections was quite a feat and an amazing spectacle to watch.

Another big competitive event involving **bands** requires elaborate costume designs for the King and Queen Title. Around 50 band organizations design these beautifully extravagant costumes. They are all competing for the title, King or Queen of the **Bands**. In many cases, their costumes are so elaborate and of such a large scale that their weight must be distributed on a metal framework. Up to three wheels, generally casters are used to support the costumes. The largest of these costumes are like 20 feet high by 30 feet wide. The wearers use muscle power to move the costume while they dance to the rhythm of the music along the parade route. These costume wearers must be fit, strong and spend months in weight training to participate in this demanding competition.

The most popular themes for the King costumes seem to relate to war, dragons or the spirit world. Whereas, Queen costumes relate to butterflies, sails, creativity, the bountiful earth and the brighter sides of life. The King picture below was taken from the Kings Semi-finals amongst 18 competitors. The person moving this costume is hardly visible in the picture. The back is finished with all the detail afforded the front with some added features like a tail. To understand the scale of this costume, the wearer's head is about eight feet below the mask. The tail at the bottom of the picture can be moved up and down by remote control. A number of the costumes had several technical features like belching smoke, emitting sparks, motorized control of costume parts and lighting small pots of fire. All the costumes displayed a lot of movement through the use of spring steel and/or fiberglass rods in the long panels. In the costume above, each colored panel is designed to be separate from the others, to allow independent panel movement as the wearer dances along in the parade.

The majority of women's costumes are designed around bikini style wear, but decorated ornately. The variations in color and decoration are imaginative. The parade **band**, "Trevor Wallace," based his costume designs on the theme "City Lights." In this case, he designed about 8 different costumes where each costume represented a major international city like New York, Tokyo, Las Vegas, etc. His costumes were a mix of bikini, single piece swimsuits, and body wraps that were discrete. Other designers took approaches using many yards of colorful material that completely covered the masqueraders. One such group was Brian MacFarlane's **band**, "The Washing by Fire by Water." They won in the medium band category wearing costumes that were ornately decorated, loose white dresses.

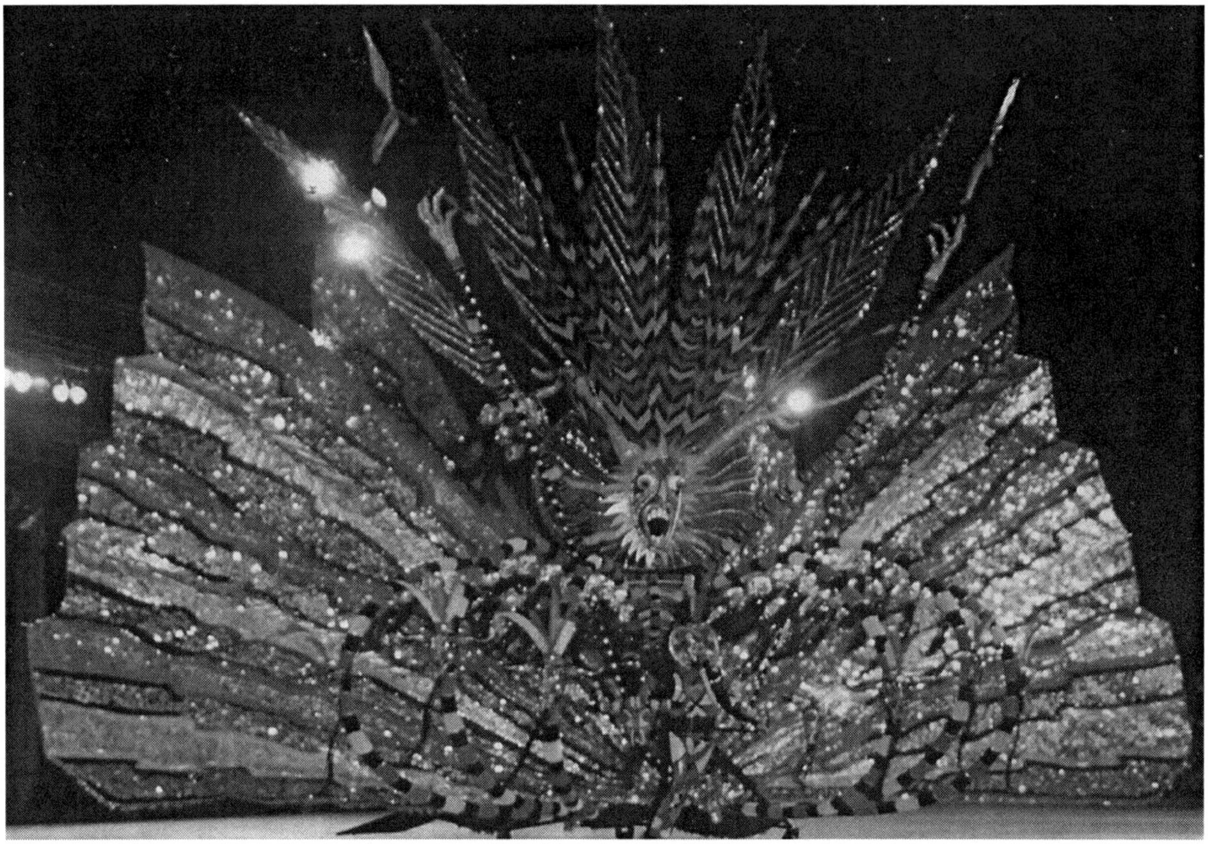

KING OF CARNIVAL WINNER, "WAR CHANT, D RISE OF TATANKA"

Some music concerts around town featured calypso and soca singer competition lasting until the wee hours of the morning with lots of rum drinking. The concerts can draw upwards of 25,000 devotees that watch the competition for the monarch title worth TT $100,000. The resulting traffic jams on the small, narrow roads can be frustrating. For example, on Sunday, Jan. 30, 2005, the usual 10 minute taxi ride to the 7 a.m. Mass at St. Peters Catholic Church took an hour because hundreds of revelers were just leaving a nearby concert from the night before.

The first calypso singer we heard in Trinidad was David Rudder. Calypso music is a popular form of West Indian music that had its origin in Trinidad. Originally, it was songs sung in the slave fields with a rebellious call response. Today the lyrics are a stream of political commentary laced with sexual innuendo. The rhythm is lively, set to a form of musical debate. David sang at a non-competitive concert at the up-scale Normandy

Hotel to several thousand of his devoted fans. His performance was energetic and most important his word pronunciation was good. A small group of good musicians accompanied him, His music is well known in Trinidad where he has won past competitions and recorded several CD's. He now lives in Canada, but returns to his native Trinidad every carnival season.

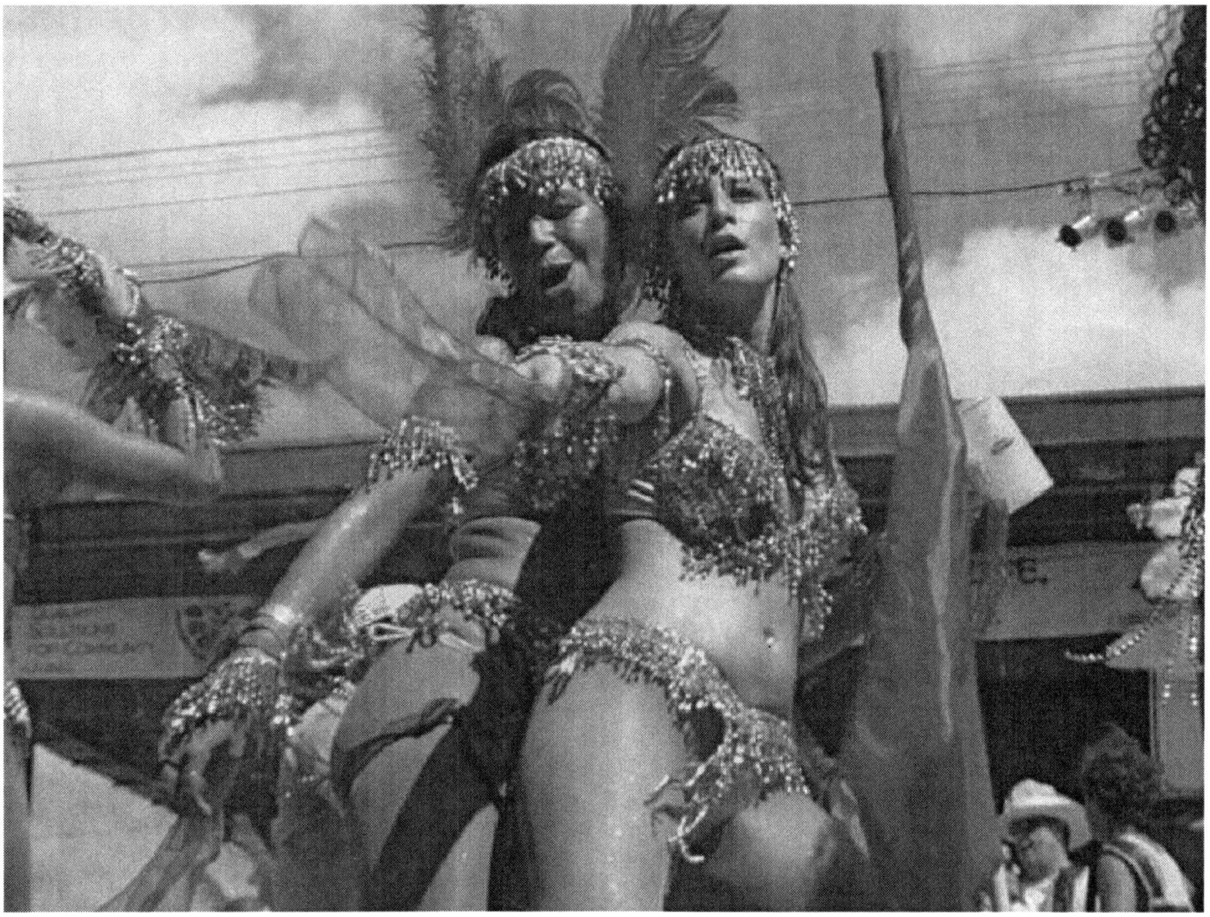

TWO YOUNG WOMEN "CHIPPING" ALONG

Calypso music is unique in that the singer usually writes his own lyrics about local events or problems. Popular subjects include crime and government ineptness. The monarch title this year went to veteran calypsonian "Chalkdust." This was his seventh title and he sang two songs in competition, "I In Town Too Long" and "Ah Doh Rhyme." The first song was about the pop culture of Trinidad and Tobago from the forties to the seventies comparing them against the political rat race of today. His second song featured comments on what he considered foolish behavior of politicians. For his effort he received the TT $100,000 and the monarch title.

The only female calypso singer in the senior category was the colorful "Singing Sandra." Her songs were titled, "Judge Me Not" and "Clean Heart." She came in third behind two of the art's most formidable performers, Chalkdust and Cro-Cro. She is not new to the calypso stage as this was her 21st year of competition. She is the only woman to have won the national calypso Monarch Crown twice. The Monarch Crown is the most prestigious of all the carnival competitions. Calypso is an art form that may be dying as some of the older singers expressed that thought referring to new calypso singers. Chalkdust said many calypso singers do not have the expression of art required by calypso music.

Bunji Garlin regained the soca monarch title. His performance was quite spectacular singing his winning song, "Blaze It Up." Initially he descended onto the stage in a cage belching sparks and fire. Later in his performance he was completely engulfed in flames protected by a pyrosuit. We did not see his performance, but saw the pictures in the local newspaper. It appears that he could have easily burned up himself and the stage. I doubt if an act like this could be sanctioned in the U.S. Naturally, there was some criticism about the way he won, as it was not on song merit alone.

In my mind, I do not see a big distinction between calypso and soca music. They both can use any subject, but usually pick on the government. Soca music is sung much louder than calypso and usually the main lyrics are repeated over and over again. Listening to both types, I guess I have not been here long enough to tell the difference.

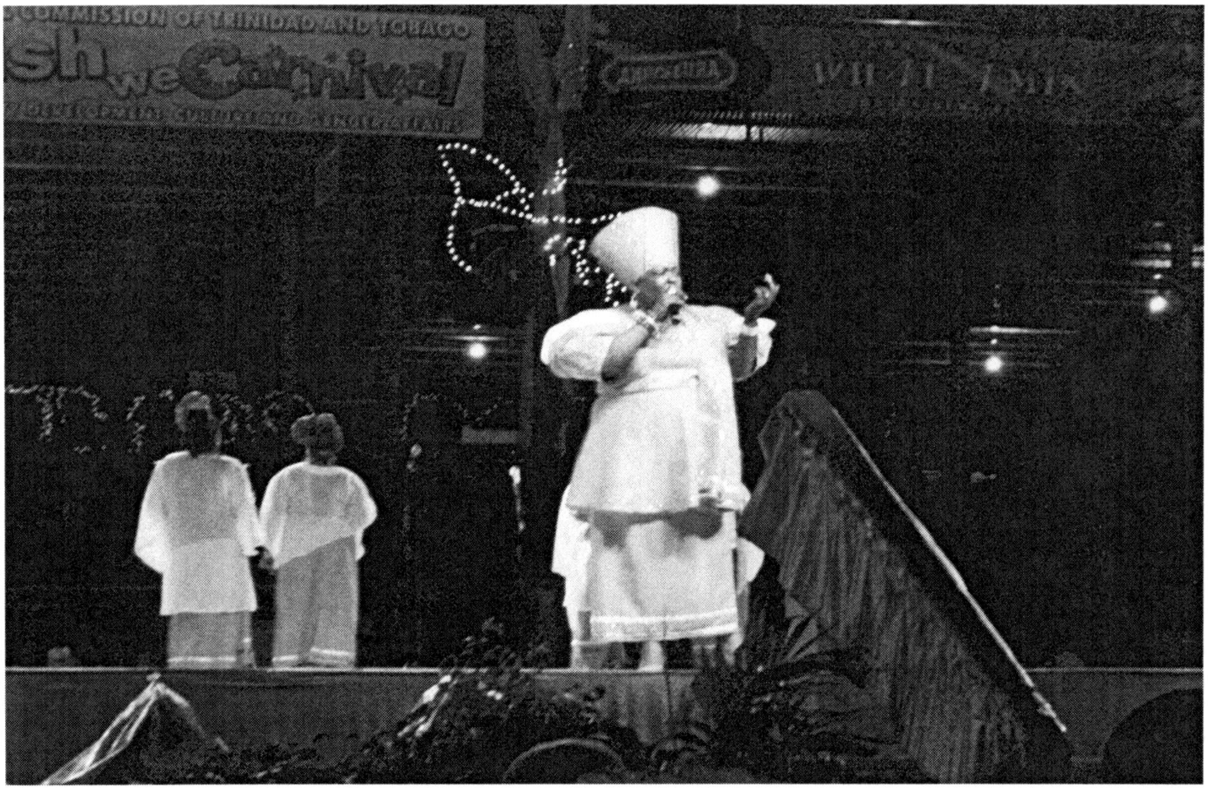

THIRD PLACE WINNER, "SINGING SANDRA," SINGING, "JUDGE ME NOT"

A couple of hundred yachties decided to participate in the parade called J'Ouvert. J'Ouvert is short for jour ouvert [joo vay] meaning "the day having been opened or day break." In the Caribbean, it is always the Monday that is the eve of Mardi Gras when the festivities begin. It becomes a time for creatures of the night like bats and devils. Our band parade costume consisted of a T-shirt, a straw hat and a hula skirt for the theme "hula-hula." The **band** organizer, Trevor Wallace, has been organizing groups for a long time and was chosen by Jesse to be our parade group. To make the Monday, 4 a.m. start, we were picked up at 2 a.m. — no sleep that night. At the assembly point, we were painted in bright colored water paints. There was coffee (instant — most Trini's have no idea of what a good coffee house is all about) and a so-called breakfast, one slice of ham and cheese inside a hotdog bun.

Trevor, a coastguardsman, had hired a large group of coastguard personnel to provide security for his **band** of about 2,000 people crazy enough to do this. If there was a problem, I'm not sure they would have been able to react fast enough. However, security is an extremely important component if you want to be in a **band**, as we were to find out. Heavy drinking, craziness and probably lack of sleep, seems to bring out the worst in people. On Wednesday, the local paper reported that over 40 people were "stabbed, chopped, slashed, and beaten" between Monday and Tuesday in carnival related violence. There were three murders and several shootings. Most of the larger cities and towns have their own J'Ouvert celebration so the mayhem is spread all over Trinidad. Thank goodness there were no incidents in our **band** group. The cities and towns of Trinidad are dangerous and there seems to be little confidence in the police or justice system. As of Mar. 3, there have been 53 murders since the beginning of the year in this small country of 1.3 million people.

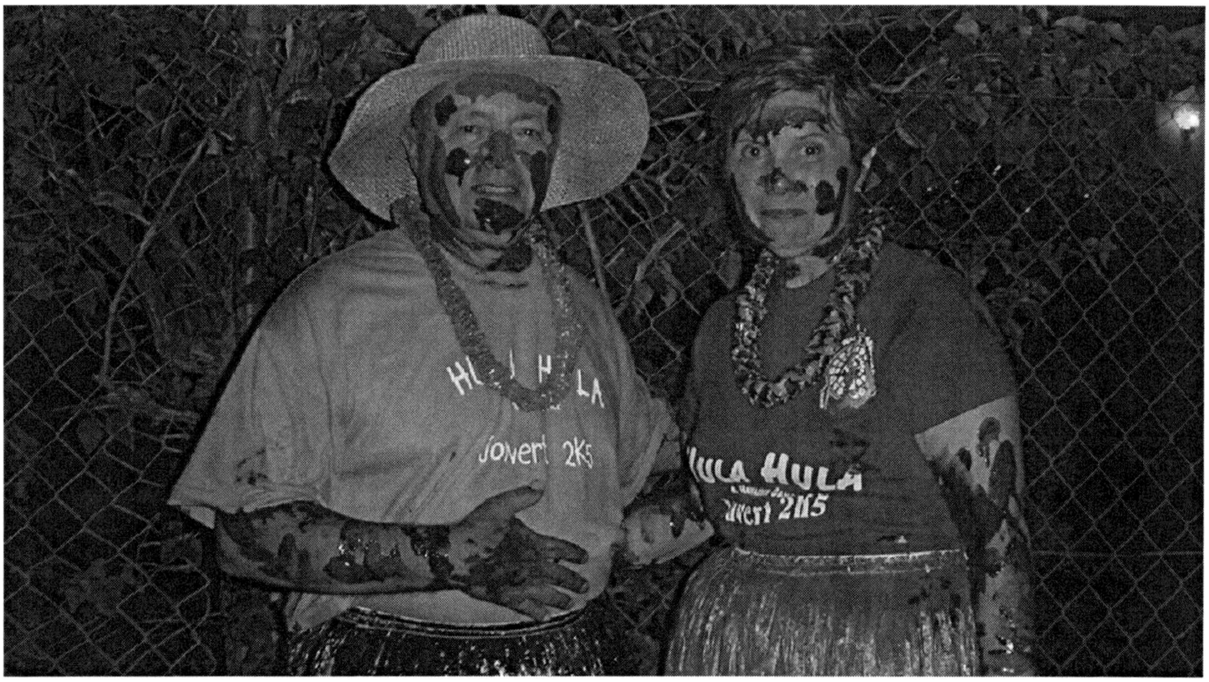

DICK AND PAT ALL PAINTED UP FOR THE START OF J'OUVERT

The **band** started its march about 4:30 a.m. with all the participants looking fairly clean except for the paint. As the sky began to lighten most of the crazy people in the parade were full of mud. Some of the band members went out of their way to cover themselves in mud from head to toe. After 4 hours of bouncing and dancing to the soca music, we were exhausted. We crawled back to the starting point at about 9 a.m. completely exhausted. We had to cover ourselves with plastic garbage bags to ride in the taxi back to our boats. Back at the boat, we had our hose ready to wash off the paint and mud on the dock. As you can imagine, the marina did not want anyone to use the showers to wash off the mud. Once in bed we slept to about 3 p.m. Well, that's about it for Carnival. If we ever did Carnival again we would skip J'Ouvert and find comfortable seats in the grandstand to watch only the major competitions.

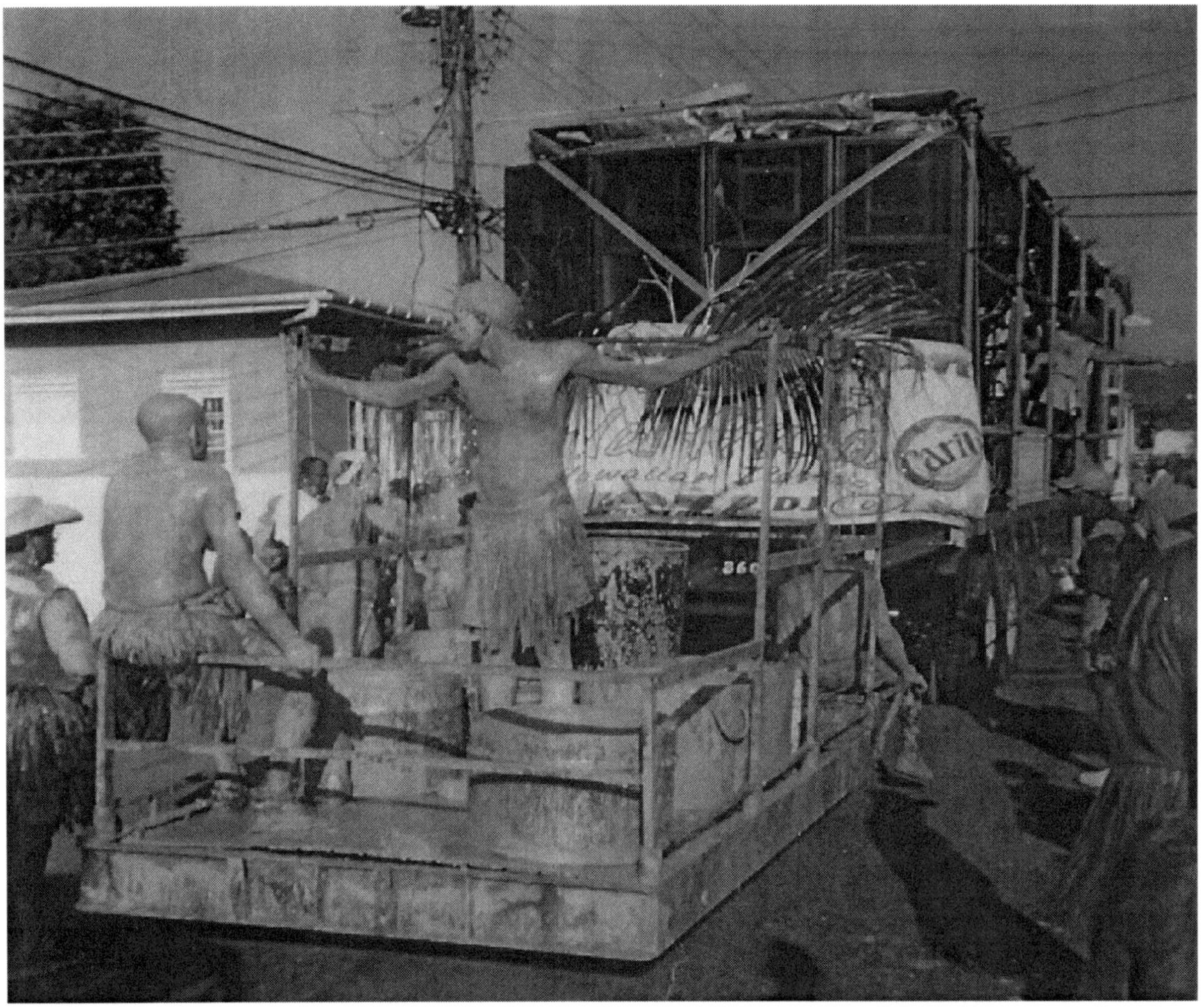

MUD TRUCK TOWED BY THE SOUND TRUCK

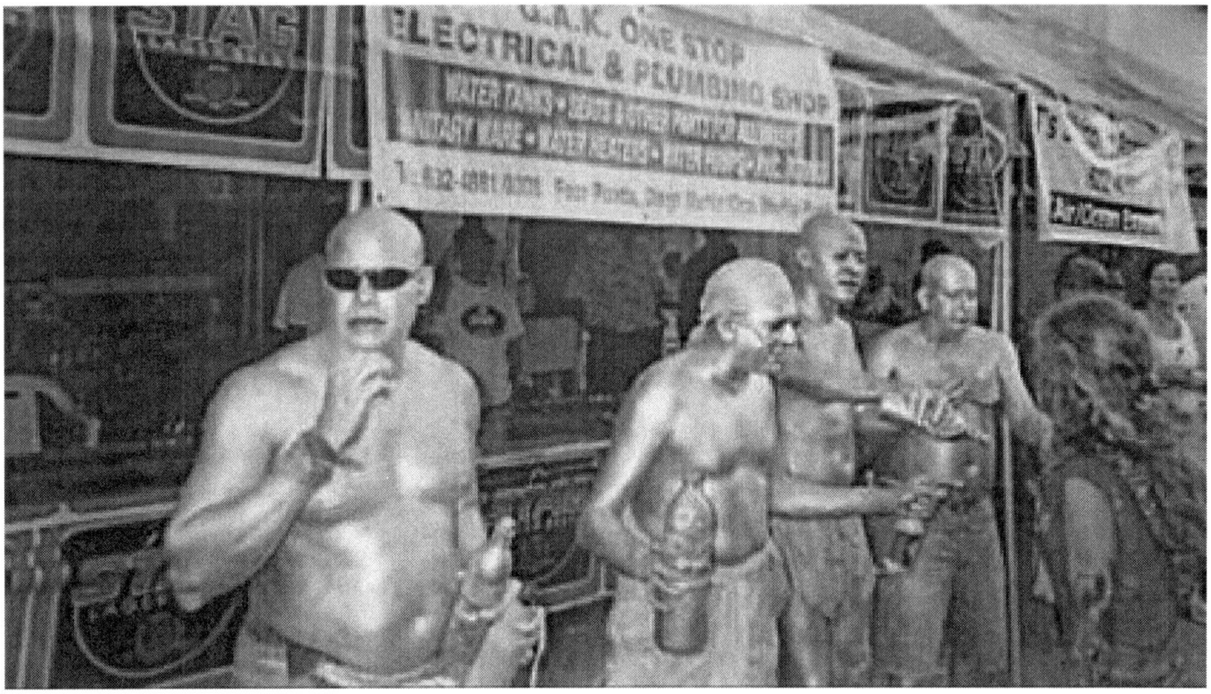

SOME BAND MEMBERS WERE A LITTLE OVER ZEALOUS WITH PAINT

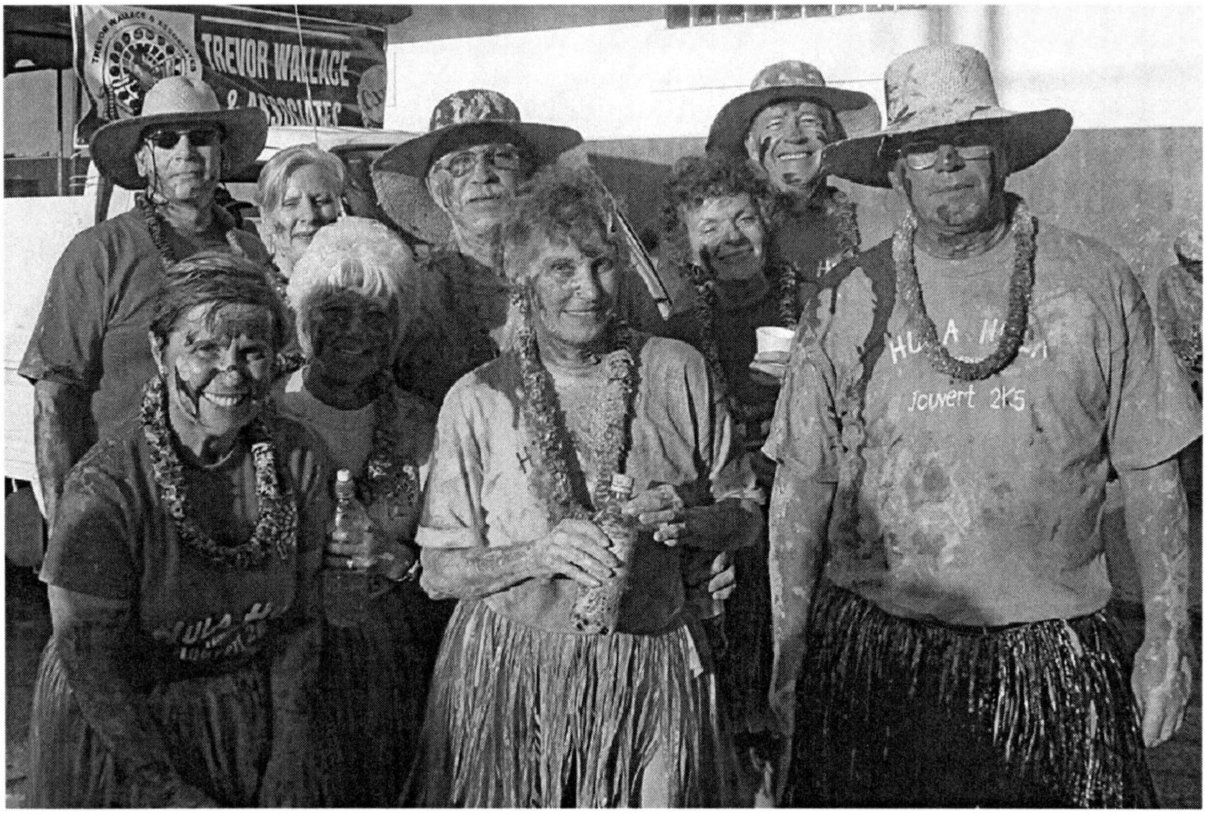

PAT AND FRIENDS NEAR THE END OF J'OUVERT

Chapter 29

MÉRIDA, VENEZUELA

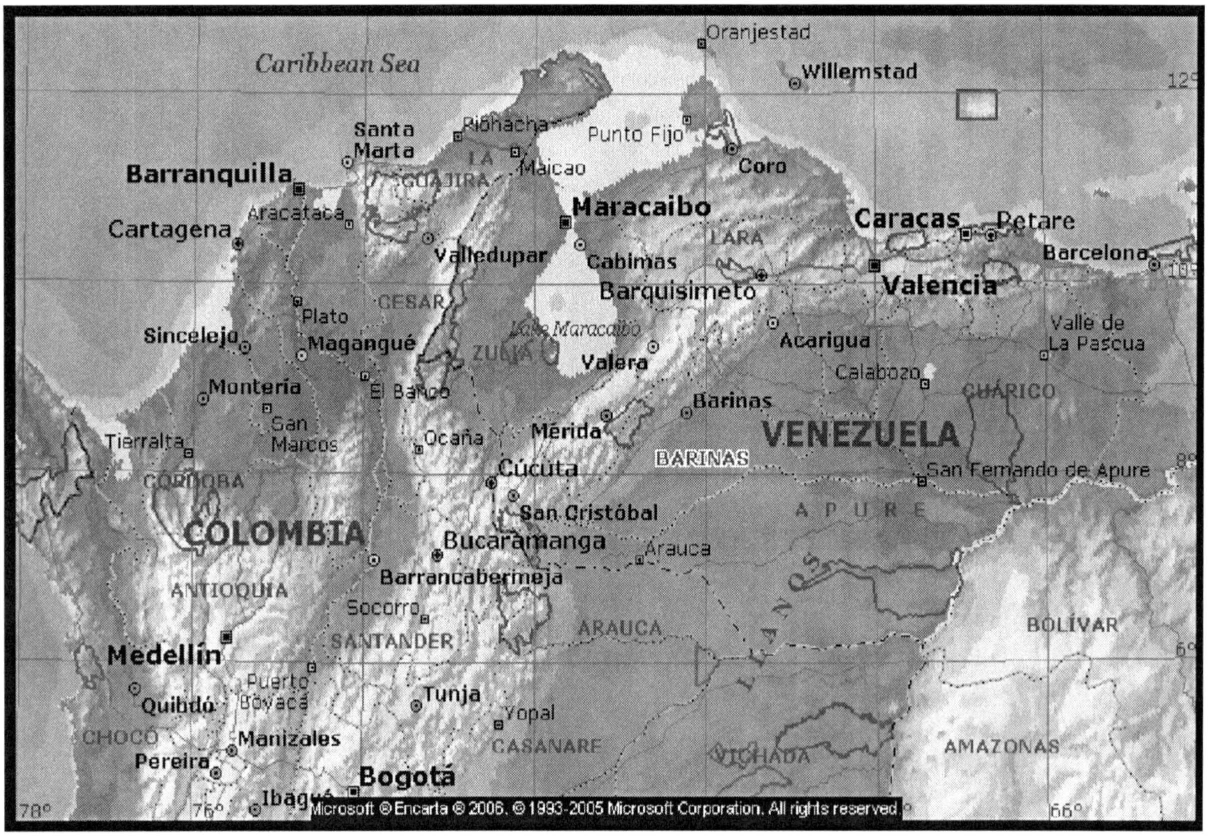

THE CITY OF MÉRIDA AND THE STATE OF MÉRIDA, VENEZUELA

Pat and I along with Susan and John Ebel (long time friends from Seattle), off the yacht *Alessandro*, flew to Venezuela from Trinidad for a little sightseeing. It was a short trip leaving on Feb. 19 and returning on Feb. 26, 2005. Susan planned our trip to Mérida where we would stay with a Venezuelan family. Our host's name was Gioia (Italian for joy), a lively and gracious young woman of Italian descent. She lived with her mother and daughter in a large house her father had designed and built in the heart of Mérida. Mérida is not your average Venezuela city. It is the capital of the State of Mérida and sits on a high plateau, which is in a long Andes

Mountain valley. This places the majority of the town's elevation at 5,177 feet above sea level. The daytime temperatures are very comfortable with low humidity and cool nights. We flew low and fast over the city to see a sea of brightly colored red tiled roofs.

Looking down on the airport, I was startled to see a runway that looked too short. The twin-engine, ATR-42 propjet, banked hard left, lined up with the north-south runway and as the wheels touched, I could feel the power of the engines at full reverse thrust. The landing was slightly up hill into the wind, which helped to slow us a bit. Everything went smoothly so I am sure the same pilot had made that landing many times. The plane used only about 60 percent of the runway and was able to turn off at the terminal without using the whole runway. We arrived in Mérida three hours early, as the flight from Caracas we were supposed to take was fully booked. The domestic airline, Santa Barbara, added our earlier flight to absorb over booking. Luckily, our flight from Trinidad arrived in Caracas in time to catch the added flight.

Flying domestic airlines inside Venezuela is a bit tricky; as we did not get confirmed reservations from our bookings outside the country — we just thought we did. We were given a tentative reservation and told, "There should be plenty of seats, on the Santa Barbara plane, but confirm our reservations in Caracas" — nothing like adding a little stress to life in a foreign country. The earlier flight was also a full flight, but had four vacant seats so we were quite lucky to get a seat. The luggage handling was also a surprise as mine was the only suitcase to arrive on our flight. To our relief the three remaining suitcases arrived on the flight of our original reservations. Gioia expected us on the later flight anyway so rather than call her we waited at the airport for three hours and the rest of our luggage.

We had an inexpensive large lunch at the airport while waiting for our luggage. The food and service was excellent. For one of our U.S. dollars we had 2,300 Bolivar dollars to spend. When we exchanged 700 U.S. dollars, we received 1,610,000 Bolivar dollars — a bushel basket full. They do not deal with small denominations in Venezuela and the common paper bills are ten and twenty thousand Bolivar's. The smallest coin we used was 100 Bolivar dollars. The Bolivar exchange from U.S. dollars took place on the sidewalk between the international and domestic airline terminals. This was strictly a black market type transaction, but the exchange rate was about 20% better than bank rates. We relied on information from other visiting yachties before us on how to get the best rate for our U.S. dollars. John Ebel nicknamed the money exchanger the "one eyed bandit" because one of his eyes was obviously glass and couldn't be focused.

The exchange procedure is simplicity in itself; just tell your porter you are interested in exchanging money. He is the guy who walks you and your luggage from the Caracas international terminal to the domestic terminal (about a 100 yard walk). He arranges to meet with a money exchanger to negotiate the rate and make the exchange. This group of local dealers understands U.S. dollars and they speak good English. When we told Gioia how we obtained our Bolivar's, she was not happy that we made this transaction in the open in broad daylight. She said the showing of that much money in public could be extremely dangerous. We knew that Caracas has a bad reputation for crime and not a safe city to walk the streets without an AK-47, but all visitors we met exchanged money the same way. The "one eyed bandit," had a roll of American dollars about the size of a softball. A group of American workers we talked to was able to negotiate a Bolivar $2,500 per U.S. dollar exchange rate because they were exchanging more money. Well, it all worked out, our missing luggage arrived on the later flight, we had a pocket full of Bolivar's and Gioia met us on schedule.

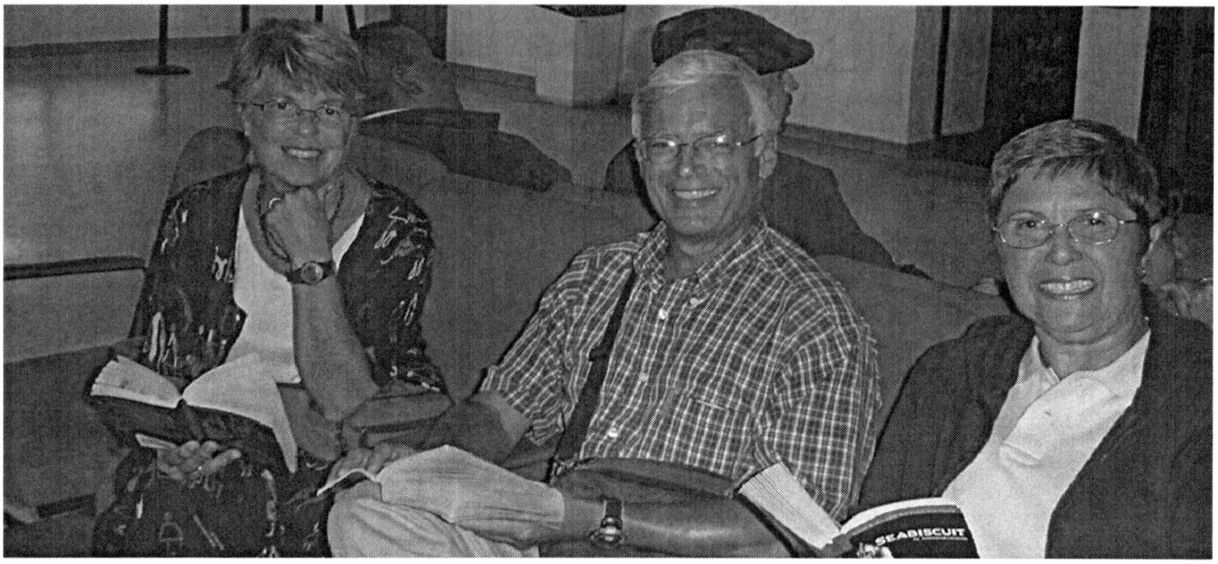

SUSAN, JOHN AND PAT WAITING FOR LUGGAGE AT THE MÉRIDA AIRPORT

Gioia is charming, attractive, fun to be with, a good conversationalist and always perky. She had lived in the U.S. for several years and spoke excellent English. Her mother speaks Italian and Spanish and usually makes yearly visits to Italy. Her family comes from the island of Elba, Italy, the short-lived first island Napoleon was sent to live in exile. We lived with Gioia's family for four nights and enjoyed our stay immensely. Our arrangement did not include meals so we ate all our meals out, but usually spent our free time at Gioia's house. However, their home was lively. The two housedogs, Lucky and Vicky, barked every time the doorbell rang or a new person came to visit.

An elderly aunt lived on the lower level and sometimes there were loud conversations between everyone in different rooms and different floors. Workers were remodeling the kitchen and when they rang the doorbell at 7 a.m., the dogs began barking and loud conversations started — never a dull moment. Gioia's family lost a little privacy and we lost some sleep time, but it all worked out. Gioia's mother, who spoke to us only in Italian and Spanish, one day, asked John in good English if we wanted to watch television. We were completely dumbfounded. Gioia is definitely a people person and was quite happy to answer all our questions and help us with our limited knowledge of their language and culture.

Their house was originally designed to be three stories high, but to preserve the natural light that came through a central open courtyard; they limited the height to two stories. They made what was intended to be the third story into a roof a garden — perfect for the dogs to leave their calling cards without going out to the street to find grass. Buildings within the city are built together to conserve space so there are no windows on the sides of the buildings. Sonry, Gioia's 79-year-old mother, loved plants and even traded plants with a neighbor, resulting in plants everywhere. Our bedroom had its own private bathroom, but John and Susan shared a bathroom with Gioia's family. The basic house was large since Gioia has three brothers and three sisters who grew up there. Gioia's late father was an engineer and everyone else in the family is some type of engineer, except Gioia who is a commercial illustrator. Her daughter, Sabrina, had just graduated from law school at the University of Los Andes and Gioia was beaming with pride.

Mérida is a university town of 35,000 students and the university enjoys a good reputation for its faculty and facilities. The university is one of the largest and oldest in Venezuela, founded in 1810. It had its beginnings as a seminary in 1785. The undergraduate schools are essentially free to Venezuelan citizens. To their credit, the government has managed to keep basic costs like taxes, fuel and food low. The city population is close to 250,000 mostly middle class workers. The city was clean and maintained in good repair, compared to Trinidad; it was a giant leap nicer. Gioia said only one section of the city could be a safety issue, but in general it would be smart to be off the streets after 10 p.m.

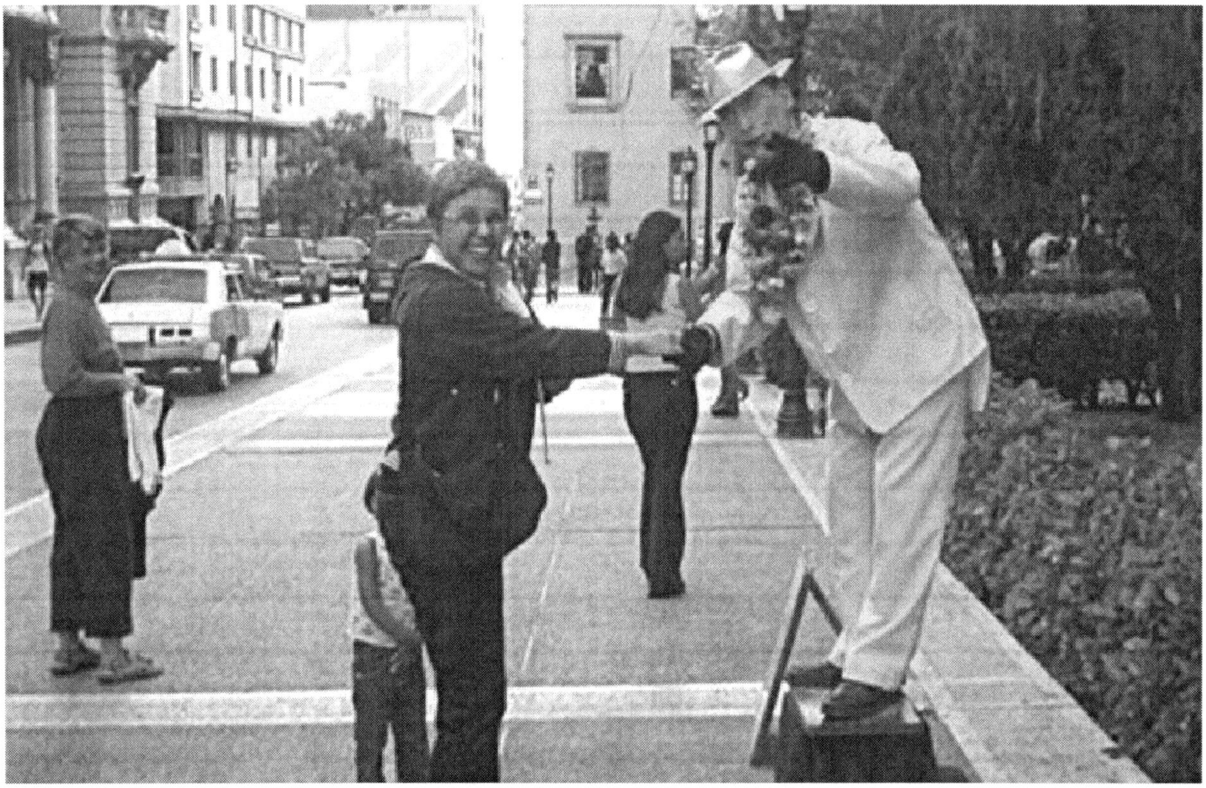

SUSAN, A LITTLE GIRL, PAT AND MIME HOLDING TIGHT, TOWN SQUARE

Gioia was our tour guide for the next four days and a good one; she impressed us with her knowledge of Venezuela. It was not just the simple stuff; she always knew what altitude we were at, had a good knowledge of trees, flowers and plants and geological facts like the location of earthquake faults.

Our first tour on Sunday was the Mérida cable car known as the El Teleférico de Mérida. The French built this cable car system in three years, the completion was in 1960. It is the highest cable car in the world and the longest. There are three independent stations along the way with the fourth station, Pico Espejo, 15,633 feet above sea level. The length of the system spans 7.7 miles over the rugged terrain of the high Andes Mountains in their national park, "Sierra Nevada," or serrated snow. The serration comes from the appearance of the mountains whose sides look heavily serrated. At this time of the year, there was no visible snow except for a small glacier, "La Concha," even though the tops these mountains are well above the clouds.

If one were to go straight to the top, transferring to the next station at each level, travel time would be around one hour. The average time between stations is about 12 minutes, but everyone stops at each station to walk around and take in the breathtaking views. We could only go to the third station at 13,272 feet as workers were replacing the cables to station four. From station three, we could see the Andes highest peak, "Pico Bolivar," which raises 16,427 feet above sea level. From travel brochures, this peak is supposed to be snow capped, but snow was not visible from the third level. I was surprised at the lack of snow since Mount Rainier in Washington State is close to the same height at 14,027 feet, but snow is always visible. The difference of 36 degrees of increased northerly latitude must be quite significant for Mount Rainer's colder environment. At level four there is a statue called the "Virgin of the Snows," she is the patron saint of skiers.

From level three we could see below us the old mule path leading to the high altitude village of Los Nevados. Being a city person myself, I do not understand living in such remote isolation at 8,000 feet. Any work at that altitude would make breathing difficult for normal humans. Just a small walk at our 13,000 foot level was all we could manage. The village is only accessible by foot, mule, or four-wheel drive vehicle. The drive to the village is so difficult only experienced village drivers are allowed to negotiate the rugged terrain. However, anyone curious enough to visit this village can pay a guide and ride to the village by mule or four-wheel drive vehicle. The trip requires an overnight stay and takes around five hours by mule. At one time, we had considered making the mule trip, but thank goodness, we came to our senses after seeing the rugged terrain. Pat, however, announced early on that she did not intend to make that trip by anything.

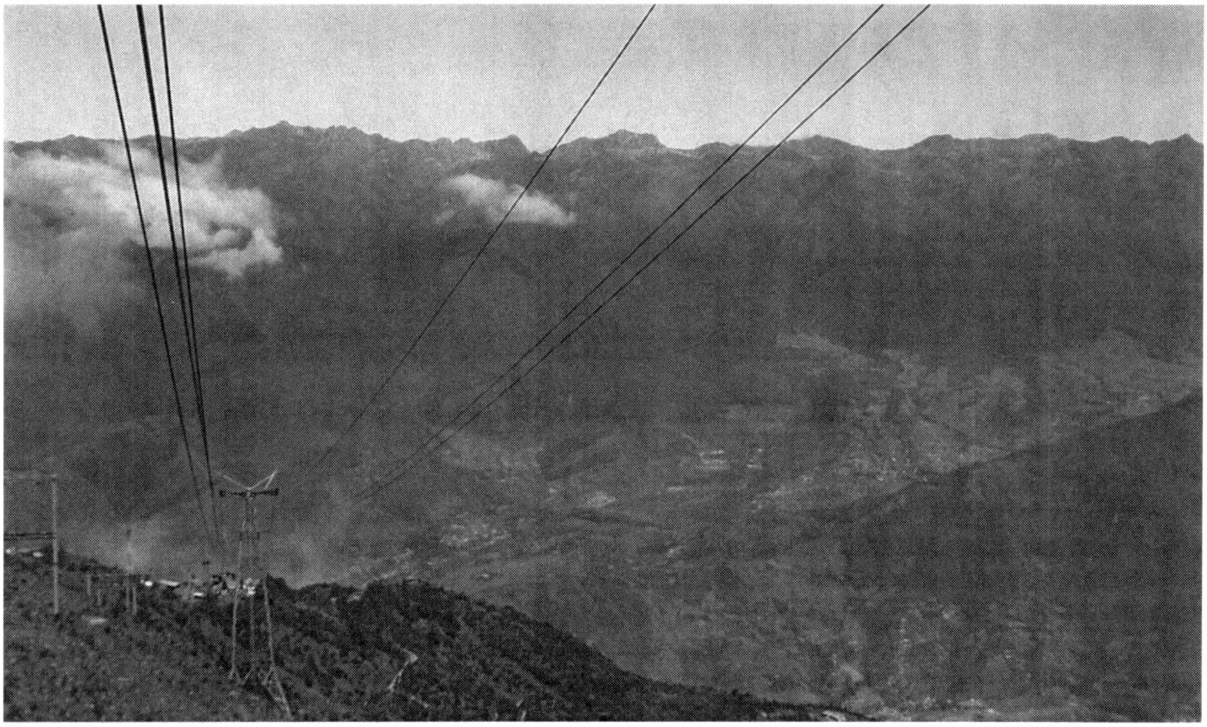

LOOKING DOWN FROM 13,272 FEET AT THE THIRD STATION OF THE TELÉFERICO

The cable car ride cost 35,000 Bolivar's or $15.50 in U.S. money for two seniors. The cashier looked at our passports to determine if we were over 60 to be eligible for the senior discount. We were eligible, but the Spanish language uses the word "ancianos," which John said meant ancient ones, we laughed.

Later that day we went to six o'clock mass at the cathedral, Basilica of the Immaculate Conception. The basilica faces one side of the town's square "Plaza Bolivar." Every town in Venezuela has a town square and a Roman Catholic Church facing the square. We should have gone to mass a little earlier as it was standing room only for the 6 p.m. Mass (94% of the population is Catholic). Of course, most of the Spanish homily passed right over our heads, but it must have been quite serious as no one smiled. The recently refurbished church was ornate and beautiful. The front doors were heavy works of art covered in metal with ornate figures. The massive doors were probably 12 feet high.

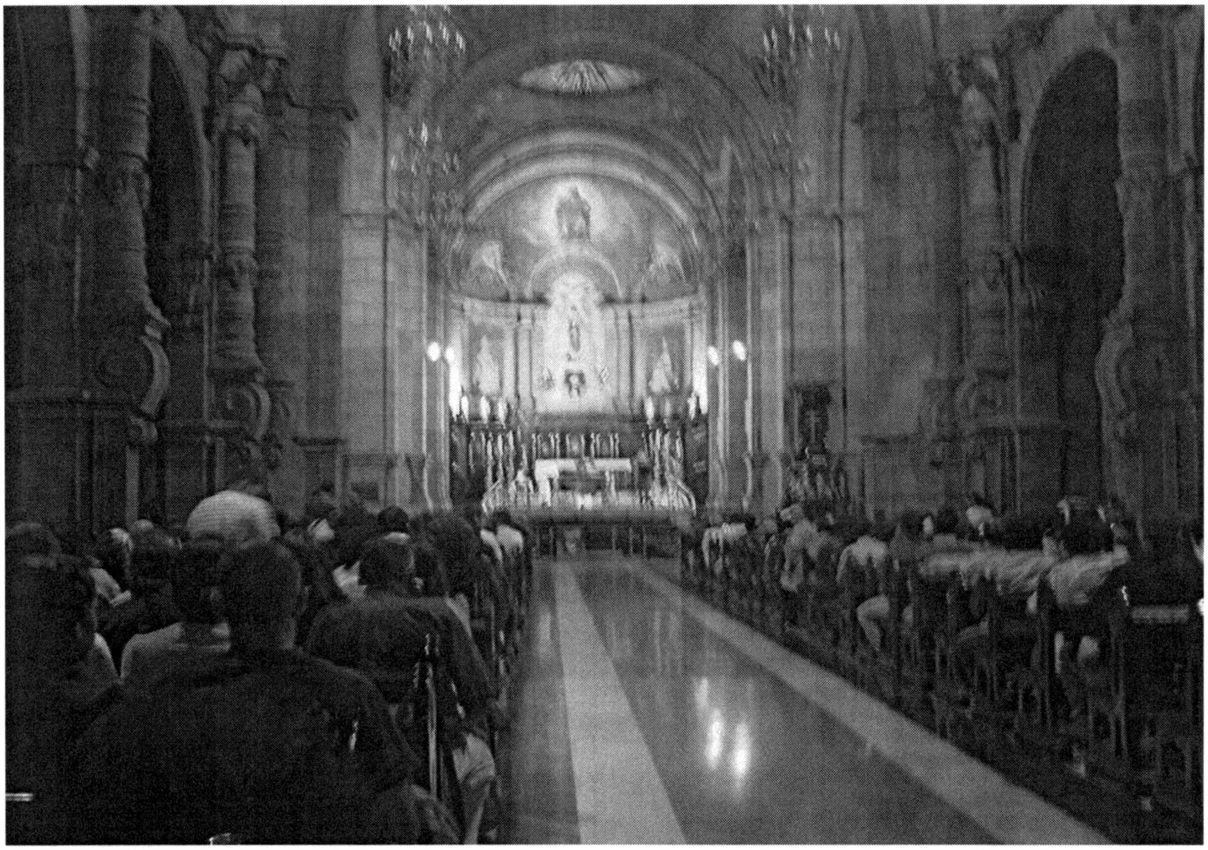

STANDING ROOM ONLY, BASILICA, IMMACULATE CONCEPTION, MÉRIDA

On Monday Gioia took us northeast on the Trans-Andean Highway to see some sights in the State of Mérida. Compared to Trinidad roads, the roads in Venezuela are in great shape. Drivers stayed on their side of the road and obeyed the posted speed limits. We noticed in the city, drivers tend to use their horns more than necessary and pedestrians need to exercise caution when crossing the street. If you step off the curb, all bets are off as to whether drivers will stop and we didn't want to find out. This highway took us through higher elevations in the valley that Mérida sits in. We passed through many towns of typical Spanish architecture and farmlands where the seasons do not see significant changes.

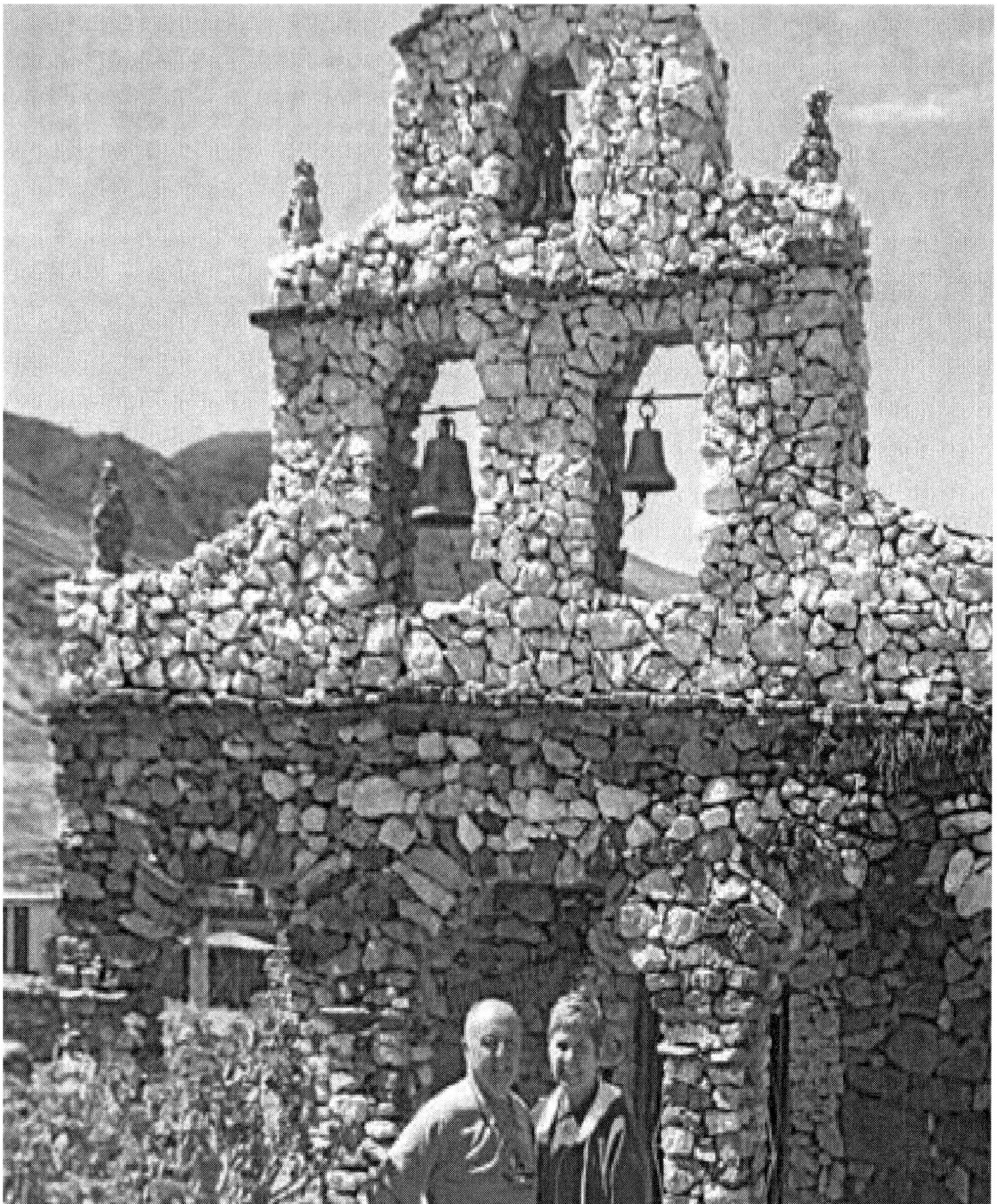

DICK AND PAT, CHAPEL AT SAN RAFAEL BY ARTIST JUAN FÉLIX SÁNCHEZ

The farming along our tour route was accomplished on steep, terraced slopes that are difficult to work. Modern farm machinery in this area is not as popular as mules and oxen — probably due to the difficult terrain. The farmers appeared to be poor. We passed through the town of Mucuchíes noted for a breed of dog originating there in the early 18th century. Spanish monks imported Pyrenean mountain dogs to guard their flocks, but cross breading with local dogs lead to a St. Bernard looking dog, the Mucuchíes. These dogs are prized for their loyalty, strength, obedience, and ferocity. Down the road, there was an interesting roadside chapel at San Rafael built by artist, Juan Félix Sánchez. In Venezuela, he is a well known artist and a revered mystic.

Sánchez finished the chapel in 1984 at the age of 84. At age 90, he was honored with the National Prize for Art. The chapel structure used thousands of stones taken from the local area and placed by hand in intricate patterns. The burial coffins of Juan and his wife are inside the chapel. The coffins are visible at the front entry to the chapel, but the interior is not accessible.

Next, we decided to visit Black Lake. This lake is 10,960 feet above sea level in the high Andes Mountains near the town of Apartaderos. The water is actually clear, but appears black from a distance because of the rocky bottom and surrounding terrain. The problem with visiting Black Lake is accessibility. The only way to get there is by a 45 minute horseback ride over a mountainous pathway strewn with rocks, stones and boulders. Pat had never ridden a horse and at first said "no way," but in the end, peer pressure won out. In addition, Gioia was able to tell the guides that Pat should have a small gentle horse, which the guide was to lead. It was at times like this, where having Gioia along to work out the small details in Spanish, was a real plus.

English is taught in high school, but with no chance to use it, few people spoke English. We did find that shop and restaurant people spoke some limited English. In addition, there is an inherent shyness in the population so I suspect they would be leery to try. We found the horses are on the small side, but Pat's horse was quite small, not much bigger than a pony. The guide was cautious while leading Pat's horse and Pat soon was confident that the ride would be okay. At first, she wanted to turn back as learning to balance and stay in the saddle on the steep terrain was not easy. The guide was showing her when to lean forward or backward to balance herself. It took all of us a little time to get the rhythm right. The bouncing, slipping and turning horses tried hard to get us into a lighter position — the ground.

We stopped at Black Lake for about 30 minutes to look around a bit and to rest the horses. The scenery was pretty, rather desolate like a desert, but with mountains all around. The high altitude makes the air temperature comfortable on the cool side. The lake was small and looking around the trees, I could see all of its shores. The day was sunny and with almost no breeze, it was quiet. The area is isolated with no homes or visible people or for that matter; I did not see any animals.

After the Black Lake trip we drove further north to the hotel Los Frailes for lunch. The hotel is halfway between the towns of Santo Domingo and Apartaderos. This hotel was originally built in the seventeenth century as a monastery and is probably the most popular resort in Mérida. With its cobblestone courtyard, fountain, white stucco walls, bell towers and red tiled roofs, it was the essence of Spanish design with lots of character. There are 48 tastefully decorated rooms, a cozy bar, a lounge with a fireplace and cable TV. The dining room atmosphere was masculine with big wooden beams, nice heavy wooden tables and upholstered chairs — comfortable.

When we arrived at the hotel it was already two o'clock in the afternoon and no one was in sight. A well-dressed man appeared in the dining room and said we could be accommodated for lunch. Menus were passed out and we were all surprised at the international and Andean cuisine available. I wondered how they could put these meals together on such short notice. The parking lot was empty except for one other car so I think we were their only customers. We ordered refreshing drinks and in no time, our lunch was served. The vegetables and salads were fresh and the meats tender. It seemed to me that the food in Venezuela was always good and so was the coffee.

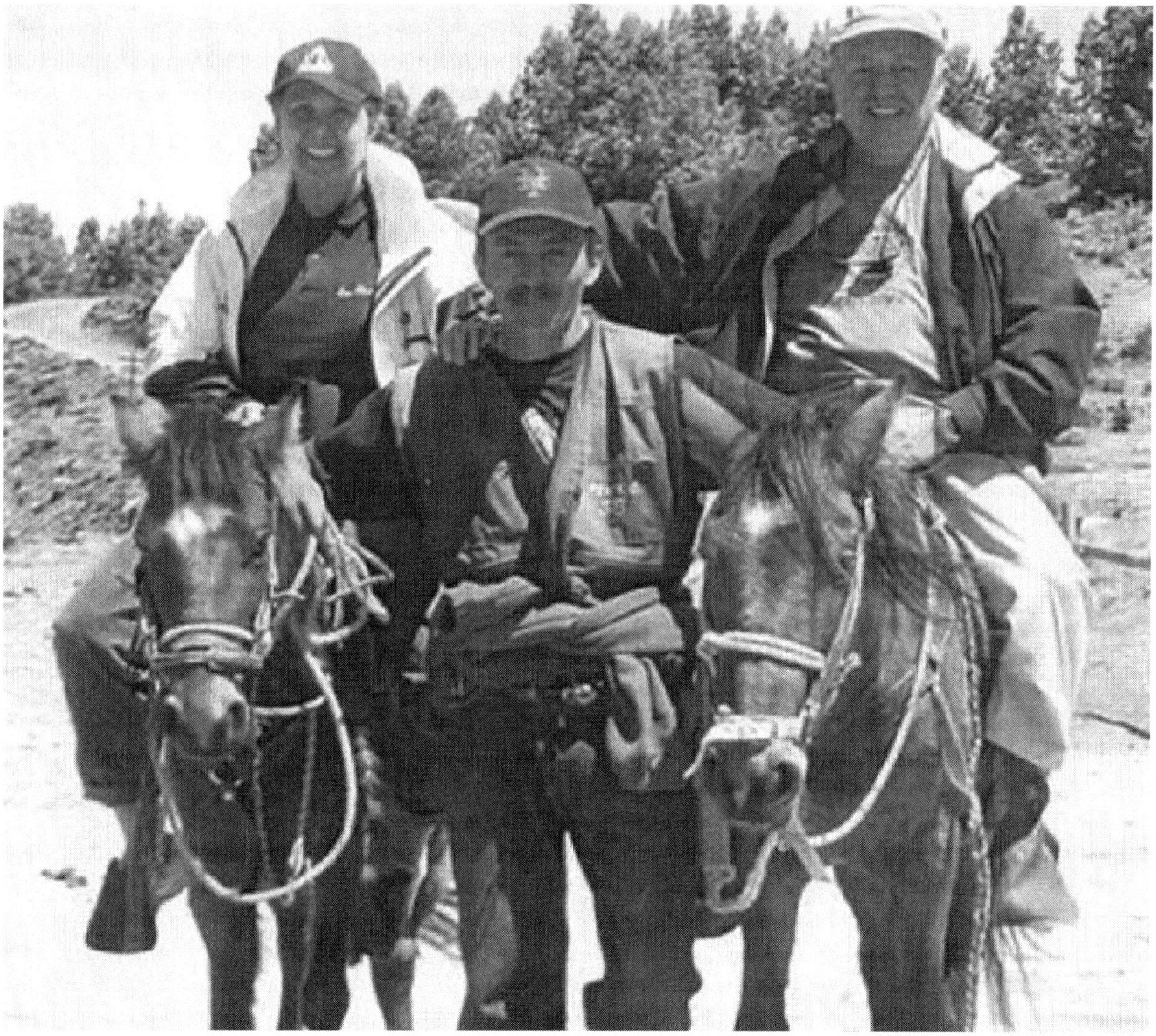

PAT, GUIDE AND DICK, BLACK LAKE, HIGH ANDES MOUNTAINS

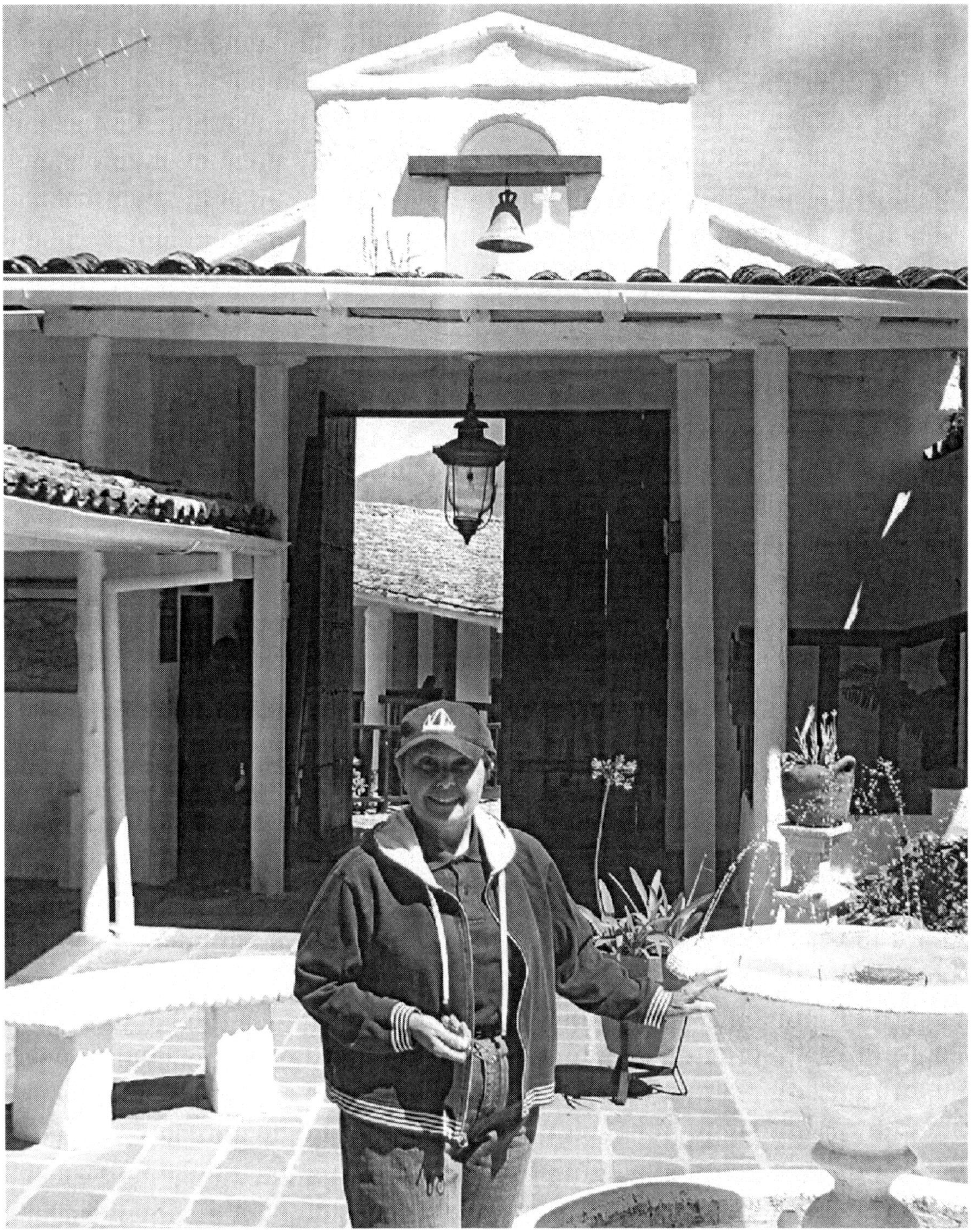

PAT IN THE COURTYARD OF THE HOTEL LOS FRAILES

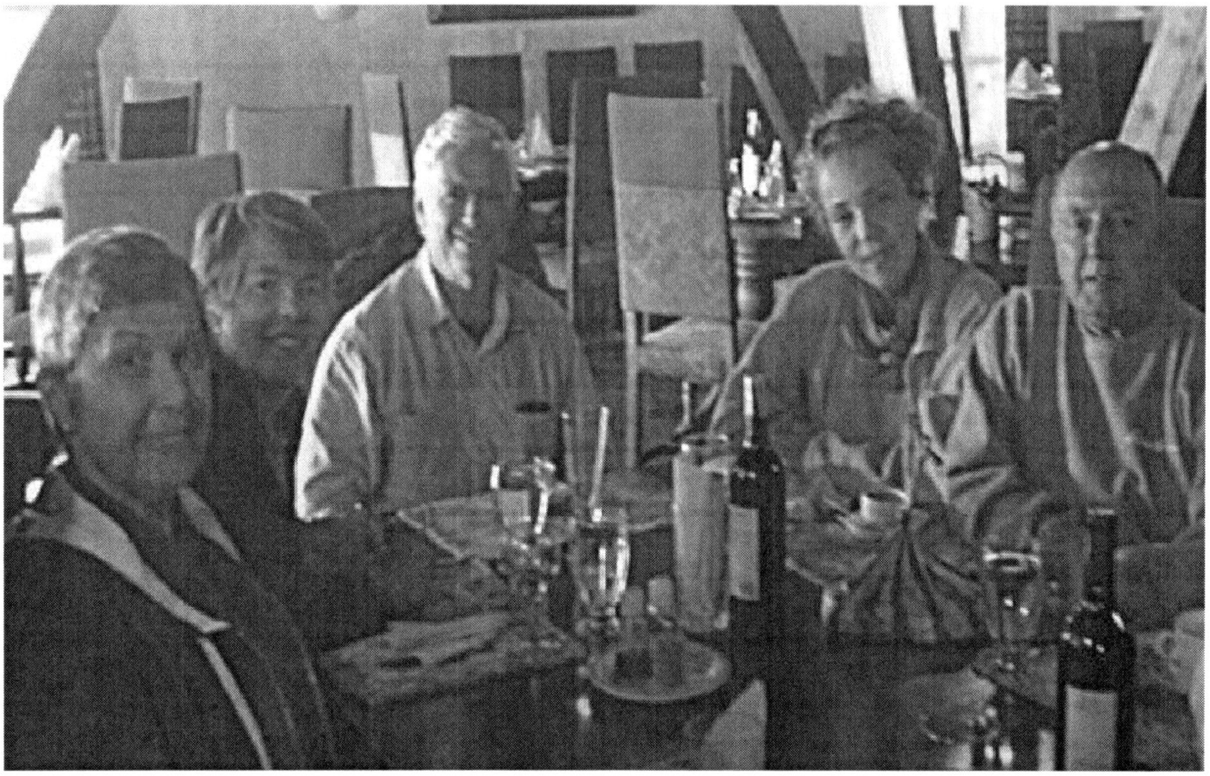

PAT, SUSAN, JOHN, GIOIA AND DICK, DINING ROOM, HOTEL LOS FRAILES

Coffee was so inexpensive about 40 cents, but the portions were smaller than we are used to. Every deli and restaurant had an espresso machine and made lattés. Some restaurants made cappuccinos, but quite different from those in the states. Deep rich coffee comes first, then a large topping of thick whipped crème, more like a coffee dessert. By time I managed to get past the crème, the coffee was cold. Everyone enjoyed their lunch. The hotel was as far north as we went. The only way back to the city was over the same highway.

On Tuesday, Gioia took us 24 miles northwest to the restored colonial village of Jaji. The drive offers splendid views along a winding mountain road that is often washed by streams and waterfalls.

We had hoped to drive south of Mérida to pick up the Pan American Highway, but that highway was heavily damaged a few weeks earlier by rains and landslides. In many places, the roads were completely washed out and impassible. Many people were still missing and unaccounted for, so the normal vacation sites to the south were closed. The village is clustered around its plaza with a typical Catholic Church and souvenir shops. The homes all have traditional wooden grilles over their windows. A little way from Jaji we stopped at a picturesque hacienda called El Carmen. The setting overlooked lush and fertile farmlands in a mountain valley. We had cool refreshing drinks there and then headed back to Mérida for a wonderful grilled lunch.

On Wednesday morning, we went to the local Mérida market, Mercado Principal, to look at local artwork, crafts, and goods. Stands were packed with regional produce, arts and crafts. The third floor contained some impressive art done by local artists. We all bought T-shirts and a few other souvenirs, but were not overly impressed. It seems most the goods for sale were imported and not made in Venezuela. From the market, we drove to the resort La Sevillana where we would stay for 2 nights before flying back to Trinidad. La Sevillana is about 30 minutes out of town perched on hill 6,600 feet above sea level. There are lots of hiking trails to explore. The buildings are all Spanish colonial-style with accommodations for 12 couples in nicely decorated rooms. The resort was originally a family home until 9 years ago when the resort additions were constructed.

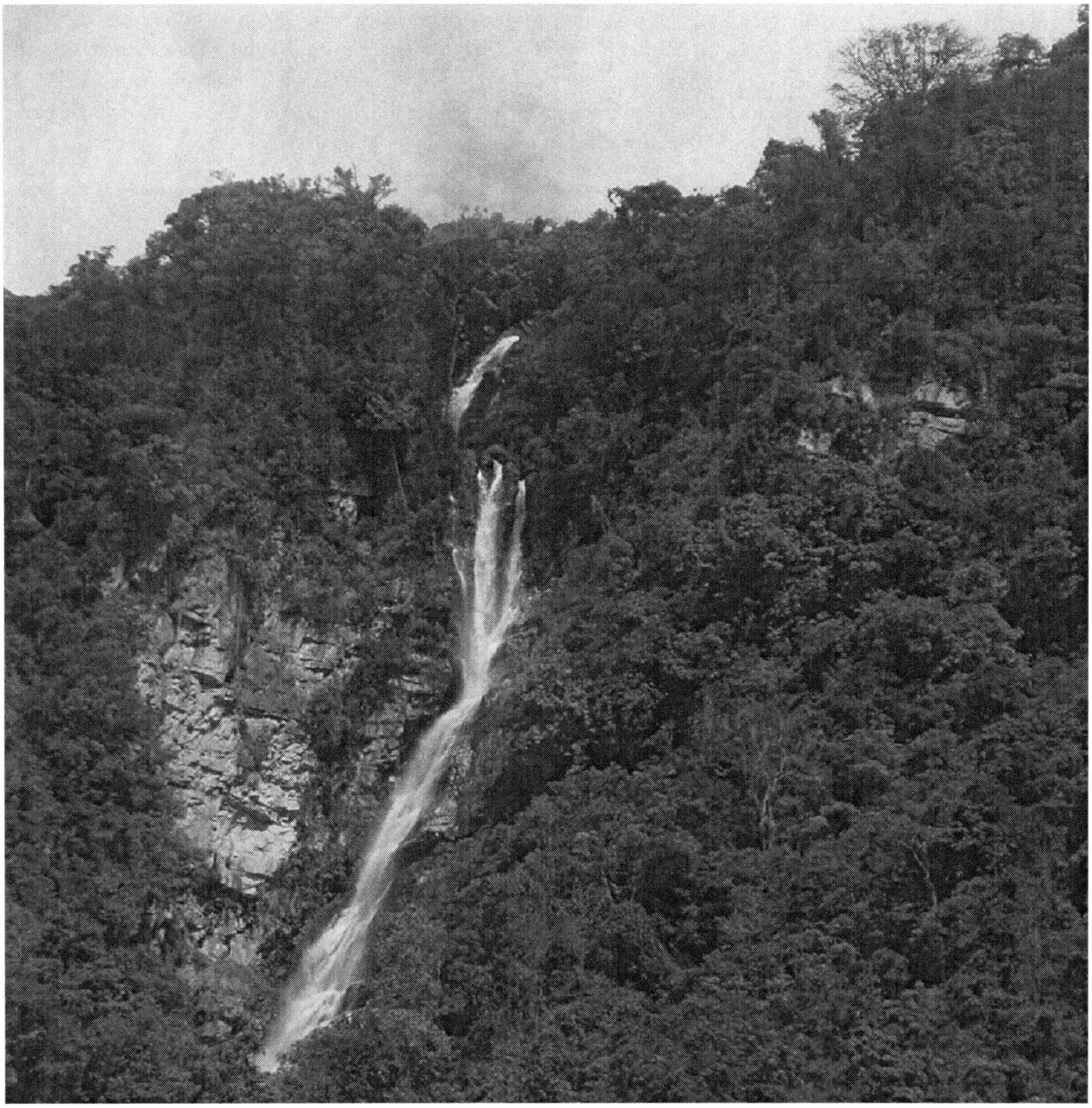

WONDERFUL WATERFALLS ALONG THE ROAD TO JAJI

The resort is a tranquil place meant for relaxation away from everyday noise and commotion. Pat and I took advantage of their spa services like massages and the Jacuzzi. The Jacuzzi was constructed as an elevated affair with glass windows and a 360 degree view of the hills and forests — just the perfect combination for relaxation. The resort food was of wonderful quality and their chef cooked all our food to order — how special is that? The family dog, Beni, was a big, lovable, English sheep dog overloaded with fluffy, grayish hair. If he spotted anyone heading towards the walking trails, he bound over with hair flying to take his favored place as the resort trail guide. If we could manage the walk to the highest point (the trail goes to a lookout point about 3,800 feet higher than the resort), we were visualizing what outstanding views might be seen. The trail is well marked with steps carved out where needed, but the climb is steep with lots of switchbacks. We only managed to climb probably 1,700 feet above the resort before heading back. Climbing at that altitude is difficult when you are not used to it and our well out-of-shape body issues did not help.

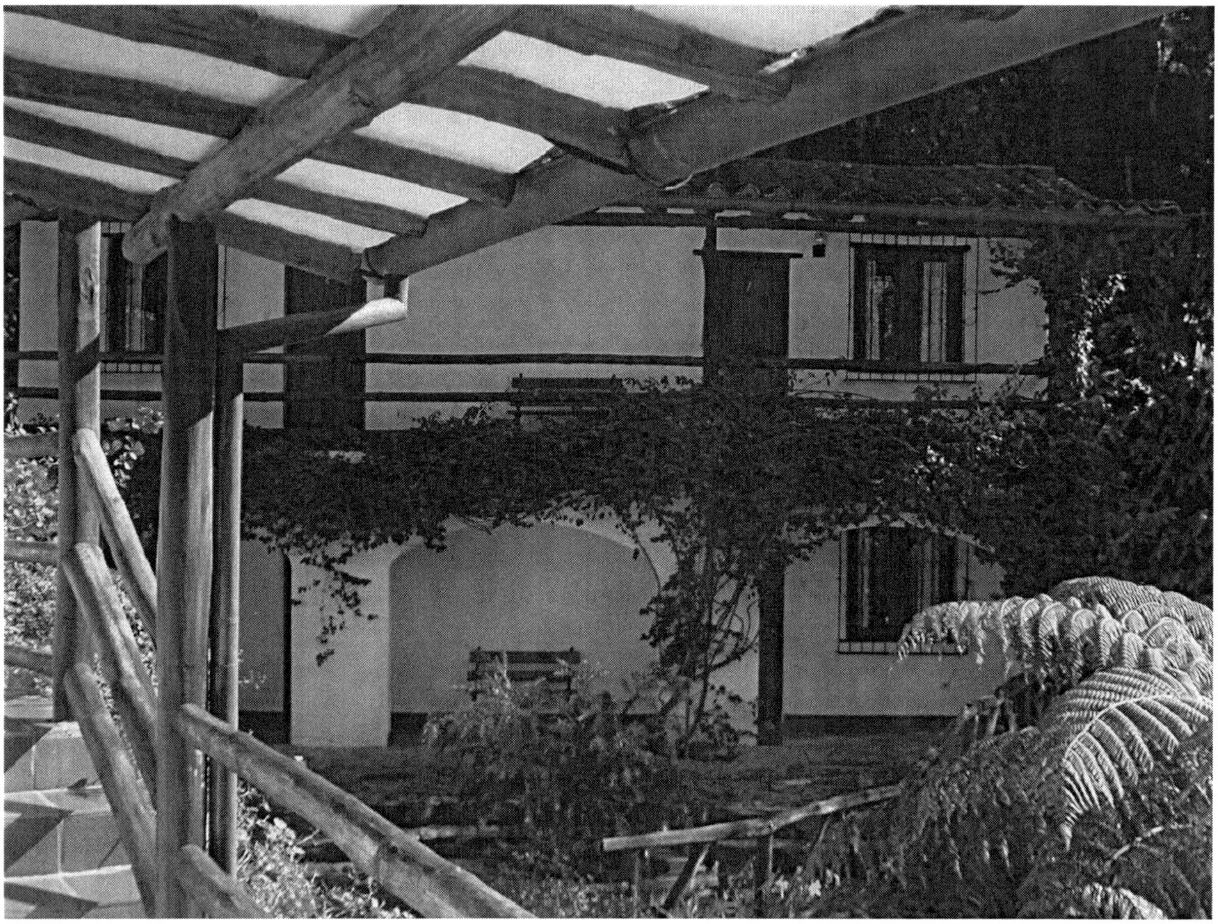

COURTYARD AND ACCOMMODATIONS AT THE RESORT LA SEVILLANA

Leaving Venezuela for Trinidad turned out to be a simple procedure. The resort arranged a taxi to the airport and we were off. Our plane was an hour late arriving at the Mérida Airport, which seems to be a common occurrence. The 3 or 4 hours of extra time for connections evaporates fast. At Caracas, the baggage check-in lines were long. The amount of money needed for the airport tax and departure tax was a bit excessive at about $42 each person. Filling out forms took-up the remaining time so by the time we reached the gate it was time to board

Chapter 30

BACK TO TRINIDAD

When we arrived at Port of Spain, Trinidad, Jesse's Taxi was waiting and we were back onboard ***Our Pleasure*** by 12:30 a.m., Feb. 26, 2005.

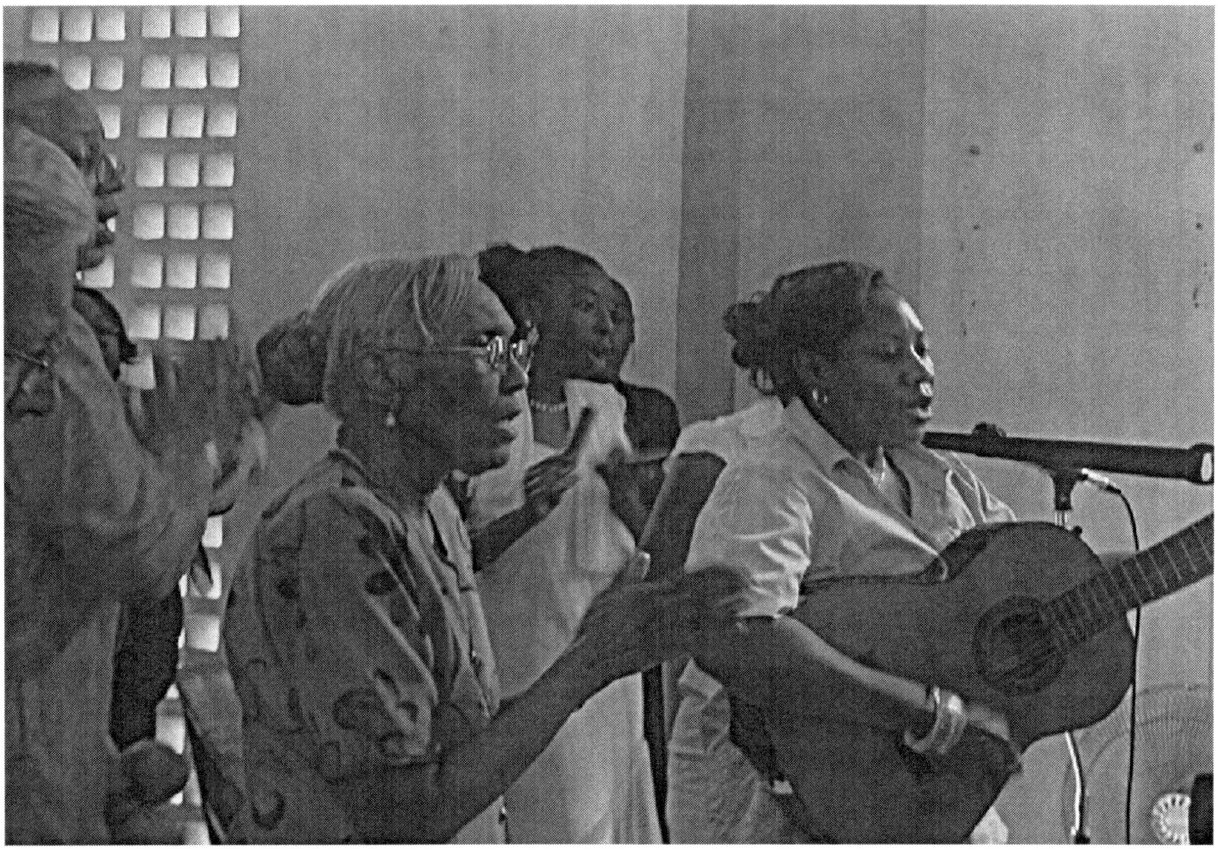

MUSIC GROUP, NOTICE THE CLAPPING TO THE MUSIC

Easter Sunday that year was Mar. 27. Pat and I along with Sue and John from the yacht *Stardust* took a maxi-taxi to St Peter's, Roman Catholic Church in the nearby town of Carnage. This small church is not in an affluent neighborhood, but it was packed with people all dressed in their Sunday best. The young girls all wore brightly decorated hats for this special day. It was also baptism day for over 20 new-born babies. The small music group featured a guitar, steel pan and African drums all played with great enthusiasm. Even the pastor, Fr. Guisippi, joined the congregation in responding to the rhythm of the music by dancing in place behind the altar. The Mass lasted over two hours, but the music atmosphere made the time go by so quickly.

Trinidad is referred to as the "Rainbow Nation" because of its diverse mix of cultures. When Columbus stopped in 1498 only Arawak and Carib Indians inhabited the island. Through the years it saw settlers from Britton, France and Spain. African slaves were also imported to work the sugar plantations until emancipated. Then, East Indians were offered five year contracts to work the plantations and most stayed. The diversity is noticeable today in skin color variations, styles of dress, celebrations, and music.

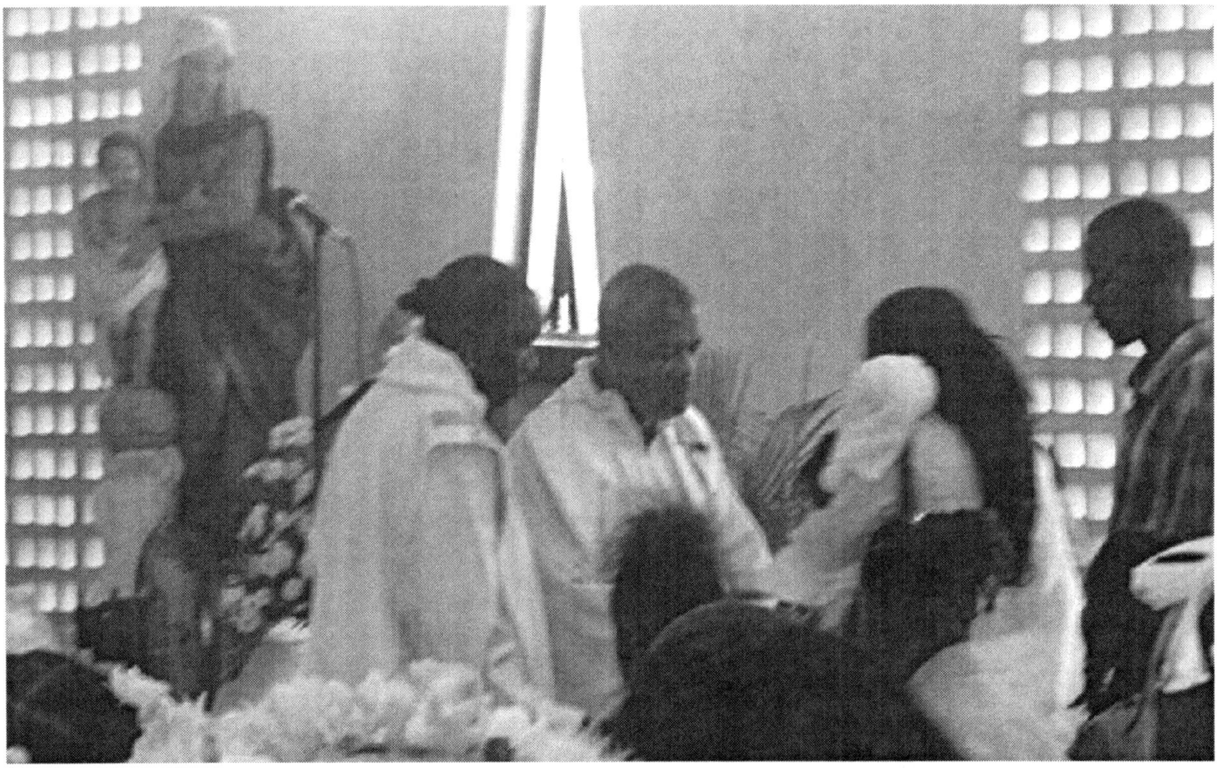

FR. GUISIPPI BAPTIZING BABIES, ST. PETERS, EASTER SUNDAY

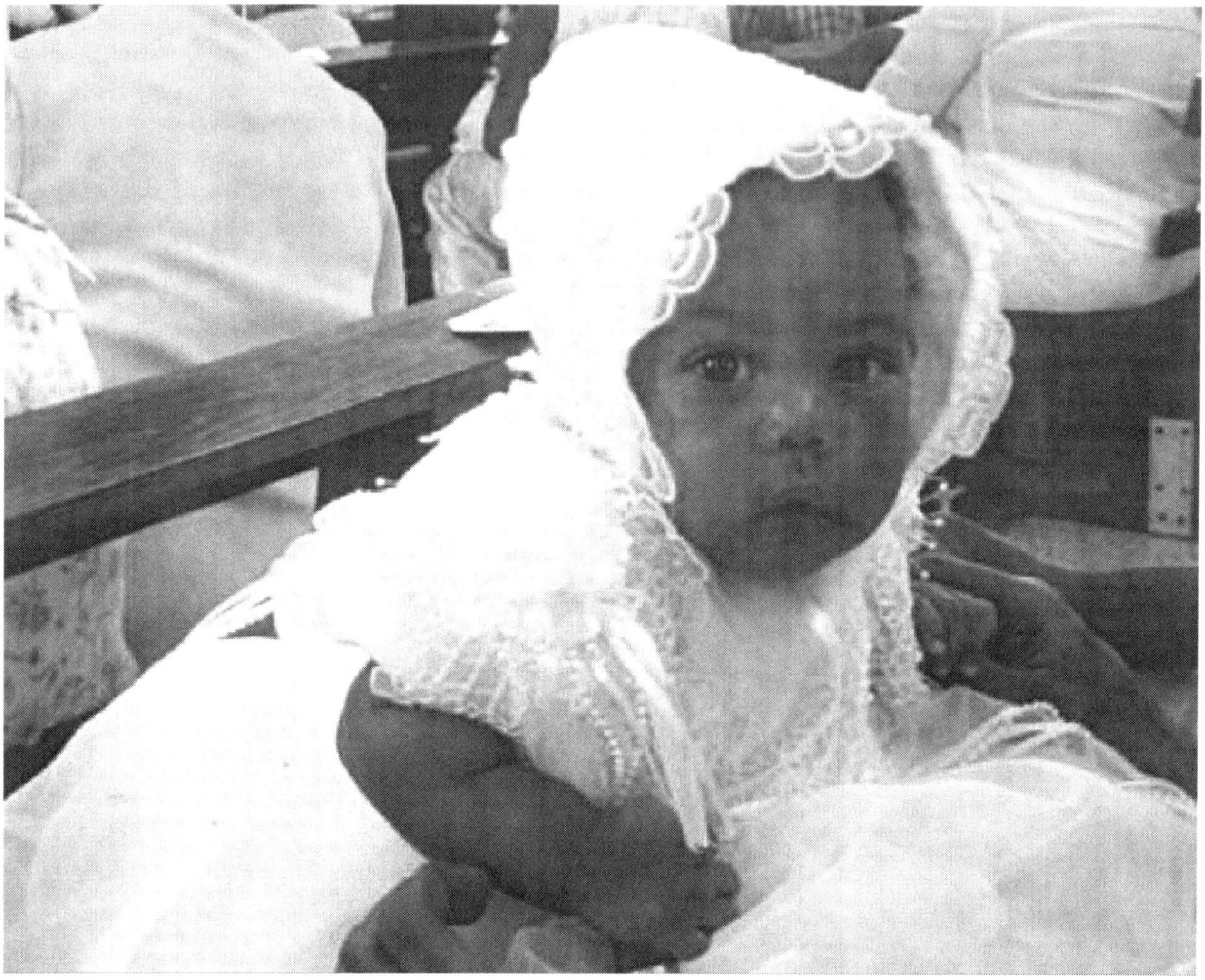

BEAUTIFUL TRINI IN HER BAPTISMAL GOWN, EASTER SUNDAY

Around the beginning of April, several sections of gigantic steel platforms with complicated piping and mysterious looking hardware, sitting on a long barge, docked at the commercial dock near our marina. We later found out this platform was named *Cannonball* and was built in Trinidad to extract newly found natural gas — a new industry in T and T. The platform is expected to extract and process about 700 million cubic feet of natural gas daily from a gas deposit that is 40 miles off the coast of Trinidad. The platform will sit on large diameter steel tubes to reach the gas deposit 235 feet below the Atlantic's surface. The project is interesting in that British Petroleum and the Trinidad and Tobago government built this platform in Trinidad as a joint project. The idea was to create a local fabrication industry, build a local engineering and fabrication capability, and reduce all future platform costs by using skilled local labor.

Somewhere around $10 million was spent to train 55 welders, 25 engineers and 150 other workers. When *Cannonball* was completed, T and T nationals performed 65% of the management, engineering, and fabrication work, 40% of the design work and supplied 70% of the project man-hours. I believe they expect to build at least two more platforms in Trinidad. The T and T government has invested $31 million so far to develop this capability so I hope it becomes successful. Good paying manufacturing jobs are important to any country. T and T's goal is to leave their third world status well behind by the year 2020. From my vantage point and other comments in the press, I think that will be a tough go.

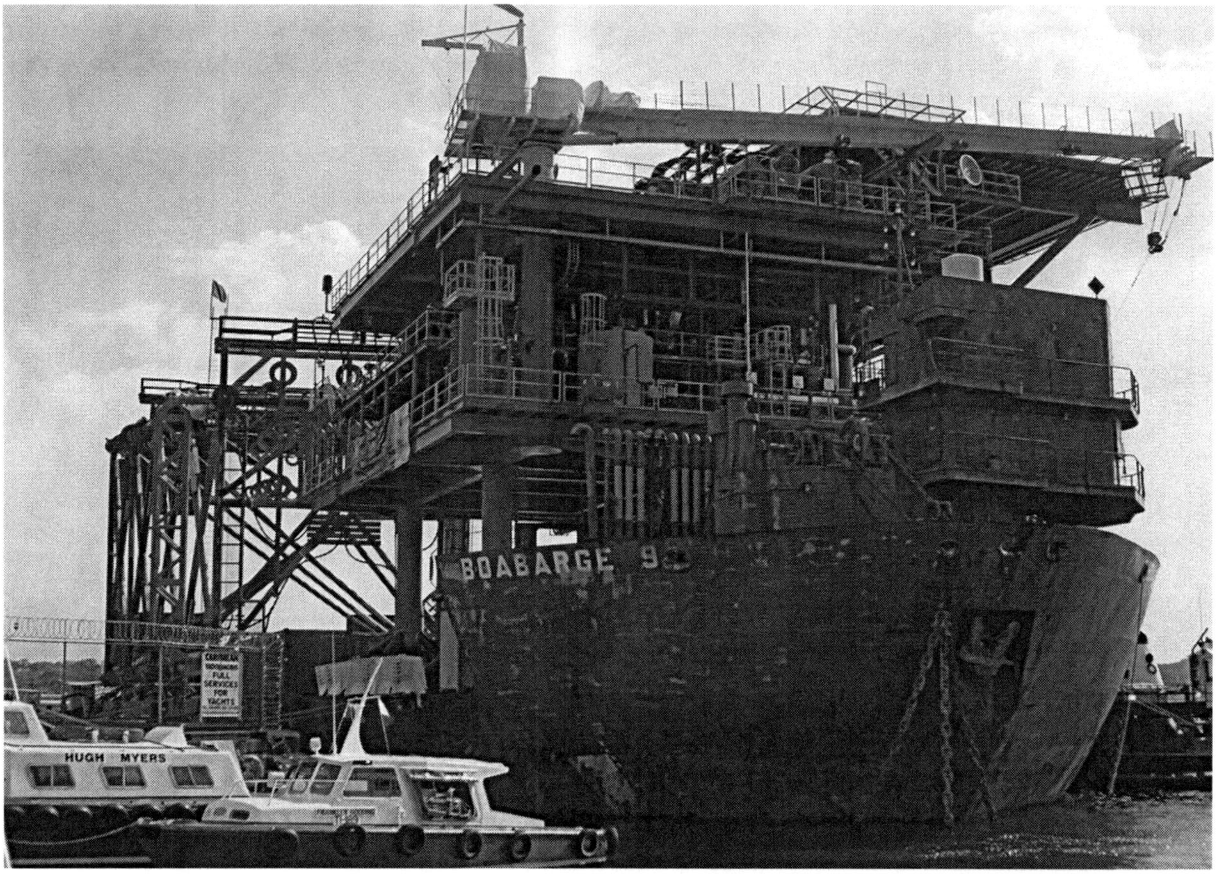

CANNONBALL — NATURAL GAS PLATFORM ON BOABARGE WAITING FOR TUGS

On April 5, Marv and Chieko sold their much-loved schooner, *Endurance* in Trinidad. Marv put together his own web site with detailed pictures of her construction, interior cabins and deck layout. He included pages of her equipment and vast spares. He and Chieko completed building the 65 foot *Endurance* over 20 years ago in their backyard. Marv's father, a cabinetmaker, applied his skills to finish the beautiful interior. At that time, they sailed her around the Pacific, then in '97, sailed about the same route we did across the Pacific Ocean, Indian Ocean, around South Africa and into the Atlantic to Trinidad. He arranged all the writing material and pictures and had the final web site put together by professional web designers in Trinidad. He managed to sell *Endurance* in 10 days to Doug, a fisherman from Alaska, who was pleased that he was the successful buyer. Marv had received several firm offers, but Doug was first. After a month, over 4,000 people visited Marv's web site — a good way to sell boats. Marv and Chieko decided to do the rest of their travels in a motor home. We will miss them as sailing companions as they have been extraordinary friends.

One of the outstanding inherent features found in the T and T culture is the pleasure derived from music. We went to another concert at Queen's Hall last night to hear the twentieth anniversary presentation of the Signal Hill Alumni Choir. This choir of about 36 members plus a small five member jazz group is from Tobago. Their musical director, John Arnold, is a well-known cultural icon in this region. Signal Hill is a secondary school in Tobago where John directs their school choir and another chorale group called "Signalite." Under his direction, his groups have dominated musical festivity victories in the folk category for 20 years. I believe the competition here in all categories of music is the driver that inspires everyone to excel. It seems that every type of music endeavor has its own competition within the Caribbean countries.

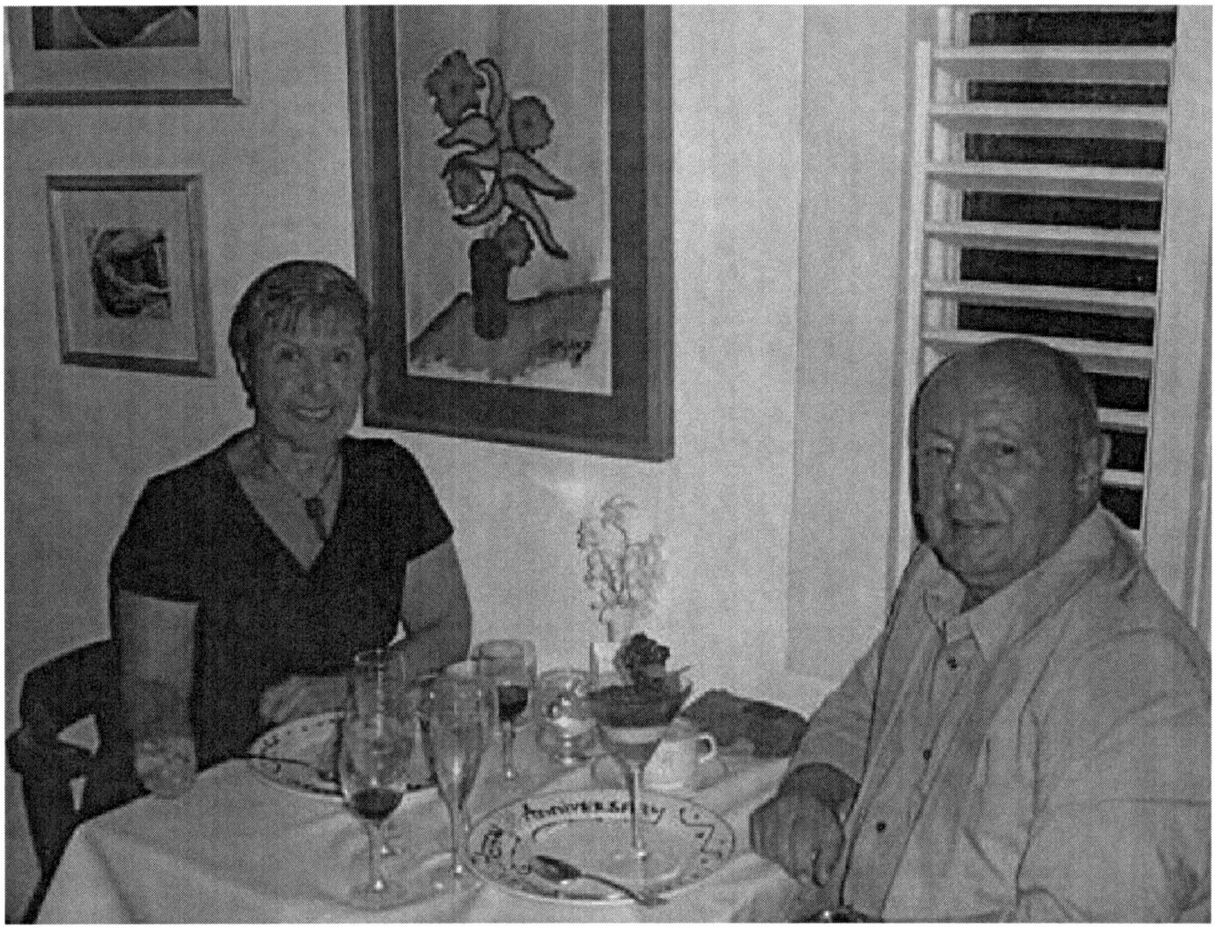

46th ANNIVERSARY DINNER, á la BASTILLE RESTAURANT, TRINIDAD

This choir pleased everyone in the audience with their wide range of music categories and their unique and skilled presentations. They sang 31 songs in the varied categories of gospel music, folk, African, jazz, contemporary, calypso, and soca. They even took on the difficult Handel's *Hallelujah Chorus* in a wonderful arrangement. A unique thing about this group is their syncopation between sound and movement that tells the story. Another fun thing about these concerts is how the Trini's get completely involved in the rhythm of the music. They can be seen throughout the concert hall bouncing, swaying, and moving in their seats to the music — you just can't sit still in Trinidad and listen to music! One big Trini woman next to me tried to demonstrate the proper way to move one's body to the rhythm of the music, but she didn't know who she was dealing with. We ended up having a great laugh at my inadequate attempts to move my body parts in sync with the music.

A secondary special treat at this concert was the appearance of two other outstanding chorale groups, the Marionettes Chorale and the Lydian Singers. We have been to previous concerts to hear these two choirs and were once again impressed by their wonderful music. These choirs are accomplished groups that also feature professionally trained soloists; they are so successful they travel all over the world to deliver high quality concerts. Both choirs sang several songs in tribute to Signal Hill's 20th anniversary. What a great night of entertainment value for $16 per person.

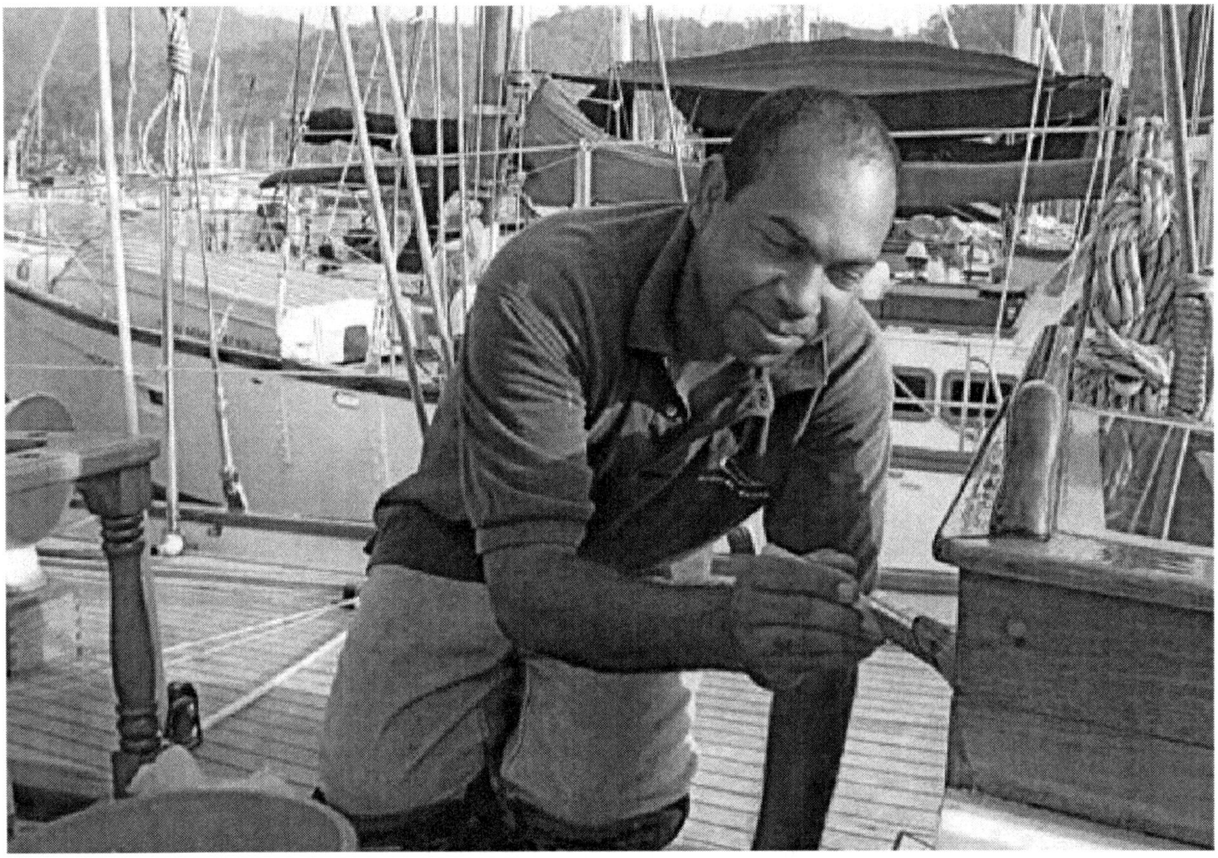

ROLLINS APPLYING VARNISH TO THE FORWARD HATCH

On April 11, Pat and I celebrated our 46th wedding anniversary. We went into Port of Spain to eat at the á la Bastille French restaurant. We heard other yachties offer comments about their outstanding menu and we were not disappointed. We had a fine Australian bottle of "bin 555" Shiraz wine from Wyndham Estates and pear Champaign from France. We had French onion soup and rack-of-lamb for the main course. The lamb came from New Zealand of course, and cooked to perfection. Rack-of-lamb was our favorite menu choice when we were in New Zealand, but the costs were significantly higher in Trinidad, more akin to U.S. prices. For dessert, I had a white and dark chocolate mousse, Pat had a trio of homemade sorbets. "Happy Anniversary," written in dark chocolate arrived on the large white dessert plates along with two glasses of Champagne. Cappuccinos finished off the evening. Our leisurely dinner took over two hours, our taxi, arranged by Jesse James, was waiting to take us back to the marina. The total cost for this evening was just under $200 dollars, an extravagant expenditure for sure, but 46th anniversaries come along only once and we enjoyed the evening immensely.

It was time once again to spruce up ***Our Pleasure's*** varnish. We were lucky that the best varnisher in all of Trinidad, Rollins, was available. People with mega type yachts, will actually fly Rollins to various destinations to varnish their yachts, that's how good he is. Anyway, he added three more coats of high gloss Flagship™ varnish to the outside and revarnished the interior of the main cabin. The varnishing was our last boat work before moving ***Our Pleasure*** into the Peake's secure storage yard for the summer. The secure part of their storage features a high fence enclosure, security cameras, night lighting, and a pit bull named Chompers. Boat work of any kind is verboten, no work dust, no debris and no contractors. Last year we made the mistake of storing our boat in the general yard at Peake's with appalling results. On our return, we found our boat covered in dust and grime as well as mold growing on all our outside lines (ropes). This was the year when hurricane Ivan whirled by close to Trinidad and stirred up a lot of the countryside. The lines most affected had been soaked by seawater during the sail from South Africa. The sun last summer was particularly hard on the teak plugs that cover the teak decking fastening screws. I replaced about 30 plugs this year and still couldn't complete the job because the local chandleries ran out of 3/8th inch plugs.

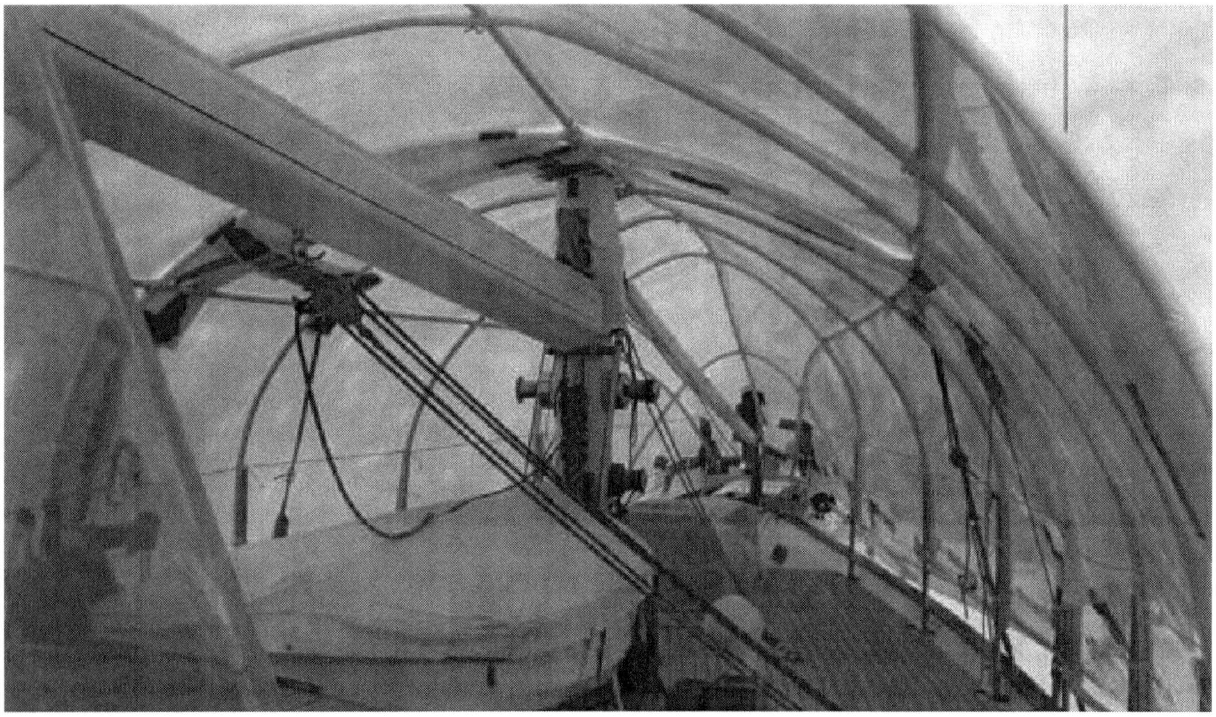

***OUR PLEASURE* SHRINK WRAPPED, AWAITING THE HOT SUMMER**

As time in Trinidad was running short, Pat and I celebrated my 70th birthday with Canadian's John and Barbara Thurston. They worked directly with contractors during the build of their Ted Brewer designed yacht *Emerald.* Naturally, their favorite color is emerald green. The restaurant we invaded was in the heart of downtown Port of Spain, La Trattoria Guiliano's, strictly Italian menu. After Guiliano decided we looked okay, he unlocked the heavy steel entry gate and let us in. Later during our meal, Guiliano himself came around to see if we were enjoying his food. The food was excellent with a big varied menu of Italian specialties and for Trinidad, reasonably priced. John and Barbara had a rented car and bravely volunteered to drive from the marina to the restaurant and back. Trinidad driving is not only difficult, but it risks one's life and limb. All their roads are poorly paved with large potholes, narrow-narrow streets, speeding drivers and the locals speed along with no notion of safety or courtesy.

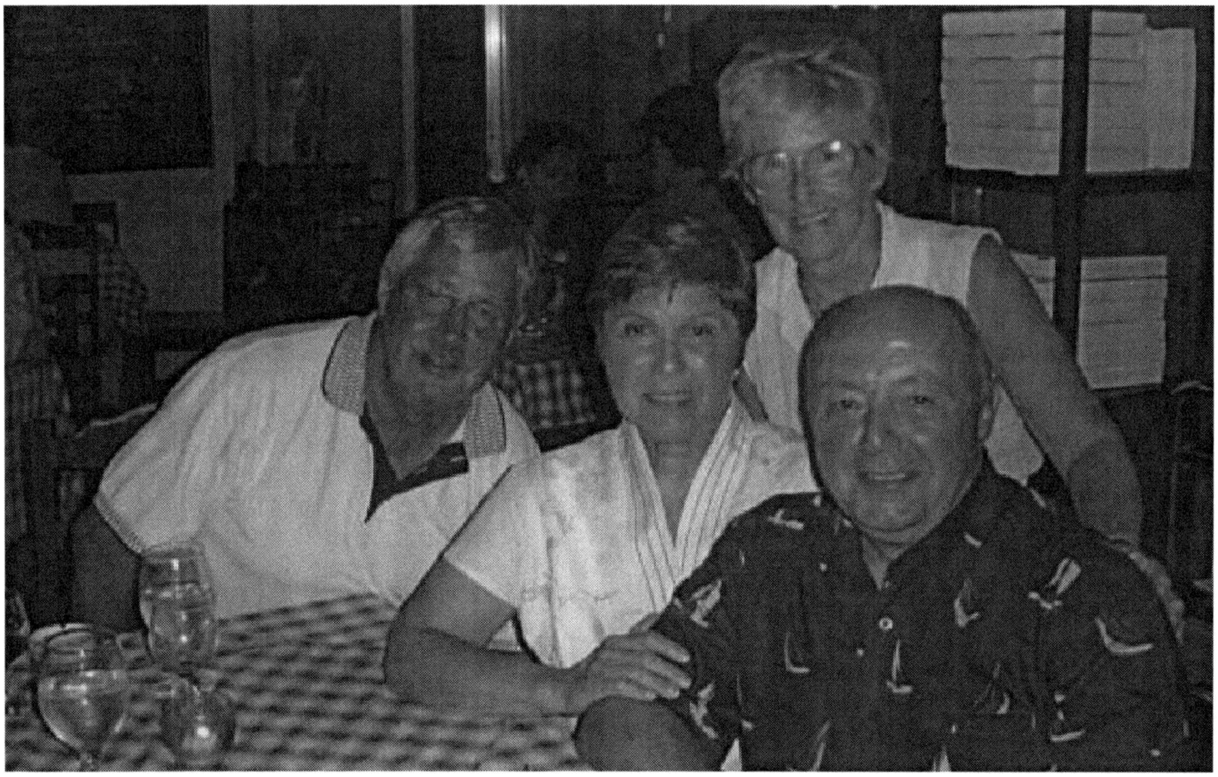

CAPTAIN DICK'S 70th BIRTHDAY PARTY; JOHN, PAT, BARBARA AND DICK

After my birthday party, I did a little more work on the boat and flew back to Seattle on May 3, 2005. Jesse picked me up at the Crews Inn Hotel at 4:15 a.m. for my 9 a.m. flight to Miami. By 7:15, my luggage had been checked aboard British West Indies Airline (BWIA) flight 484. I had gone through screening and enjoyed a cappuccino while I waited to board. The BWIA plane was a new Boeing 737-800 with all leather seating. The breakfast was a lot better than our U.S. airlines and the flight was smooth and uneventful. However, in Miami, before I could board the American Airlines flight to Chicago, there was an intense lightning storm. All planes were grounded and ground crews were not allowed to work on the tarmac. The planes that had landed had to sit on the tarmac until the storm moved through the area. Well, by time our plane off loaded passengers, handled baggage, cleaned the interior and loaded the new passengers, we were three hours late. I missed the plane in Chicago bound for Seattle by one hour. Luckily, another flight to Seattle had room and I arrived at 11:30 p.m. instead of 9 p.m. My son David and his wife Kelly were there to meet me.

The next evening I drove back to the Seattle/Tacoma airport, in one of David's cars, to meet Pat's plane. Her plane landed at 7:30 p.m. without any flight complications. Pat had left Trinidad before me to catch-up in Arizona with several of her longtime Seattle women friends. These gals have followed a get-together tradition over many years to celebrate their birthdays and always have a great time together.

Chapter 31

TRINIDAD TO BRADENTON, FLORIDA

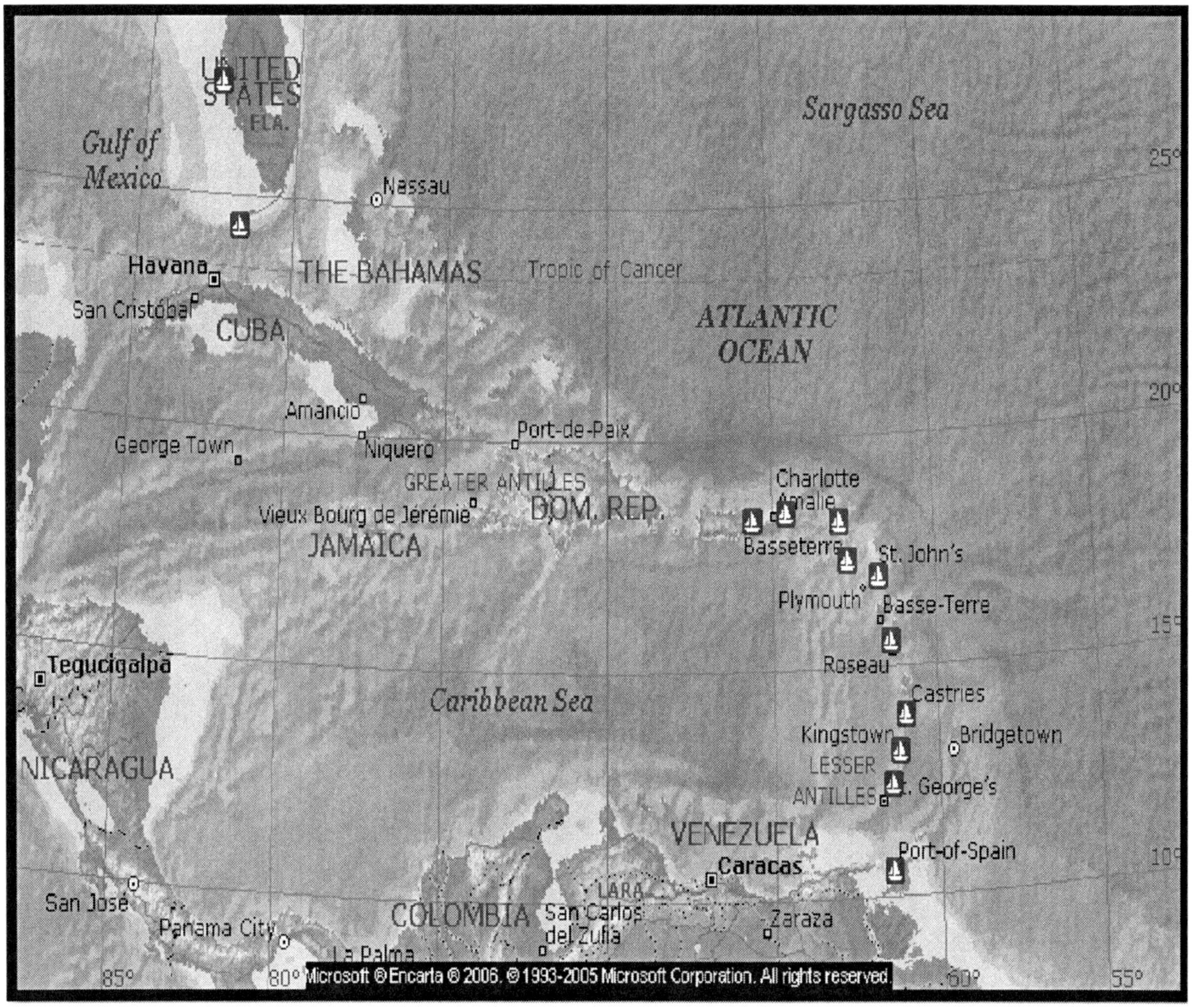

ROUTE OF *OUR PLEASURE* THROUGH THE CARIBBEAN

The relaxed, comfortable, and contented living in Trinidad for two cruising seasons was going to end soon. Instead, we would start the 1,800 mile journey through the Caribbean and into Florida. Pat and I were thinking about our leisurely Trinidad living as Peake's yard crew lowered ***Our Pleasure*** into the water. It was Feb. 6, 2006, and we had a lot of work ahead of us before ***Our Pleasure*** would be ready to sail to Florida. I had already installed a new engine heat exchanger, rebuilt the electric and manual heads, replaced all the head hoses, and replaced all the zincs. Sharvon, our Trinidad boat care person, had washed the boat and the Peake's crew polished the hull before our arrival. Seattle friends, Myrlis and Howard from *Midnight Rambler*, helped move ***Our Pleasure*** across the bay to Crews Inn. We unpacked our travel clothes, put everything away then had Pam and Bruce (*Aquabi*), over to celebrate their round-the-world sailing completion. Then we all sauntered over to meet old friends at the weekly, Thursday evening BBQ on the lawn of Crews Inn.

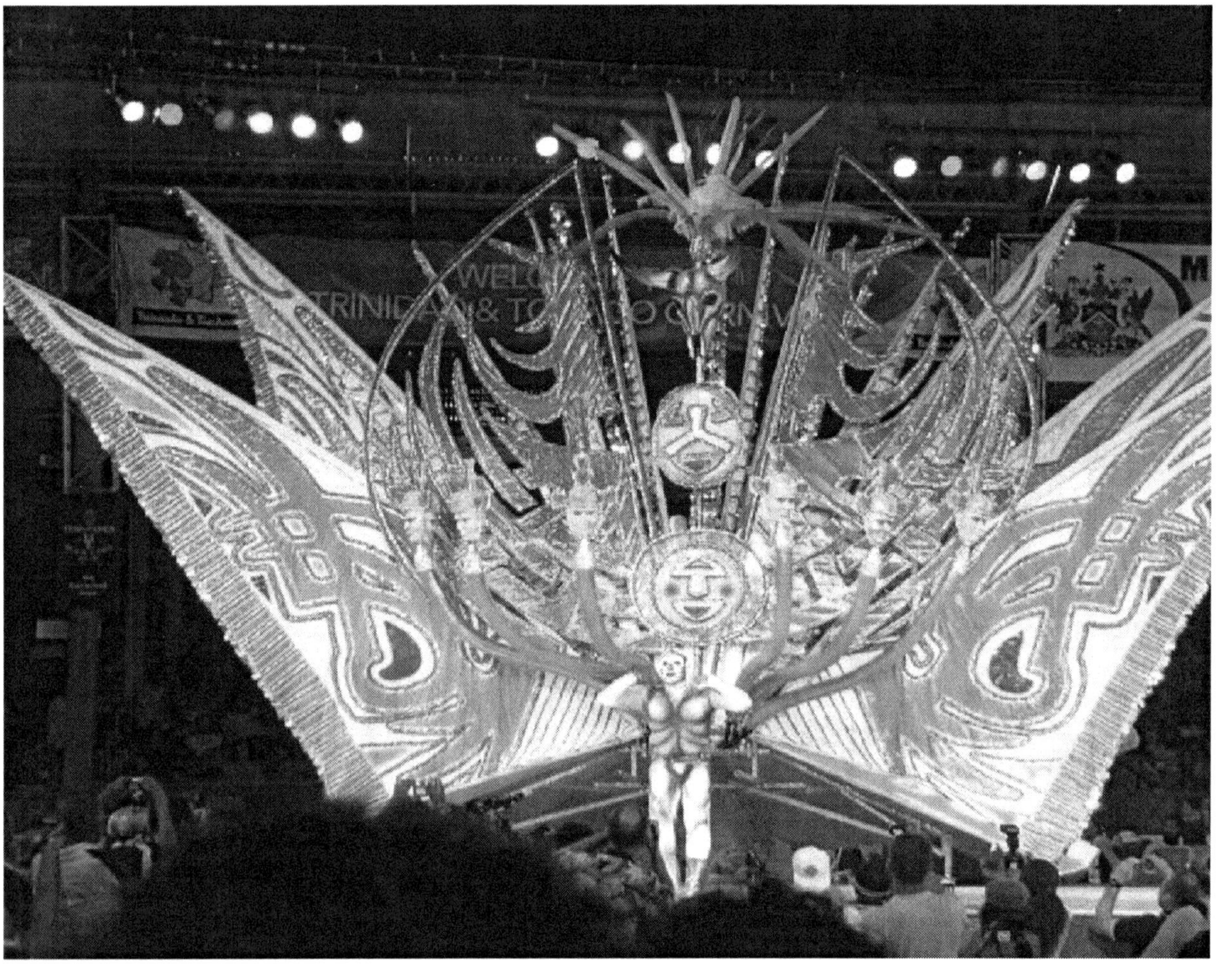

QUEEN'S SEMI-FINALS, CARNIVAL WEEK, PORT OF SPAIN, TRINIDAD

Pat's sister, Mona Jean, arrived around 11 p.m. on Feb. 16 to find out what all the excitement was about, referring to Trinidad's Carnival. We stayed up quite late that night to catch-up on both our family's comings and goings. The next evening, we went into Port of Spain for the King and Queen's semi-final competitions. Everyone marveled at the elaborate costumes. Nevertheless, with 41 queens and 41 kings in the competition, we had had-it after the queens finished sashaying across the stage to the beat of loud, ear jarring, calypso music.

The Kings were just starting their competition and it was 11:30 p.m. Jesse's early bus was ready to take any tired yachties back to the marina and we were beyond ready. We heard the king's competition did not finish until 2:30 a.m.; we made the right choice. A few days later our son, David arrived. We all had a great time together. David put in a good days work helping me remove the cockpit's vinyl dodger and side windows for a much needed scrubbing. We did many touristy things all over Trinidad and thoroughly enjoyed ourselves. On one excursion to Maracus Beach, a shark and bake stand called "Mona's," provided a good laugh for Pat's sister. Shark and bake is a popular meal in Trinidad; a generous piece of flame-grilled shark, in a deep-fried bun. The bun ingredients are from a traditional Trinidad dough recipe. The finished product is a wonderful tasting sandwich, which is right next to Kentucky fried chicken in Trinidad's popularity.

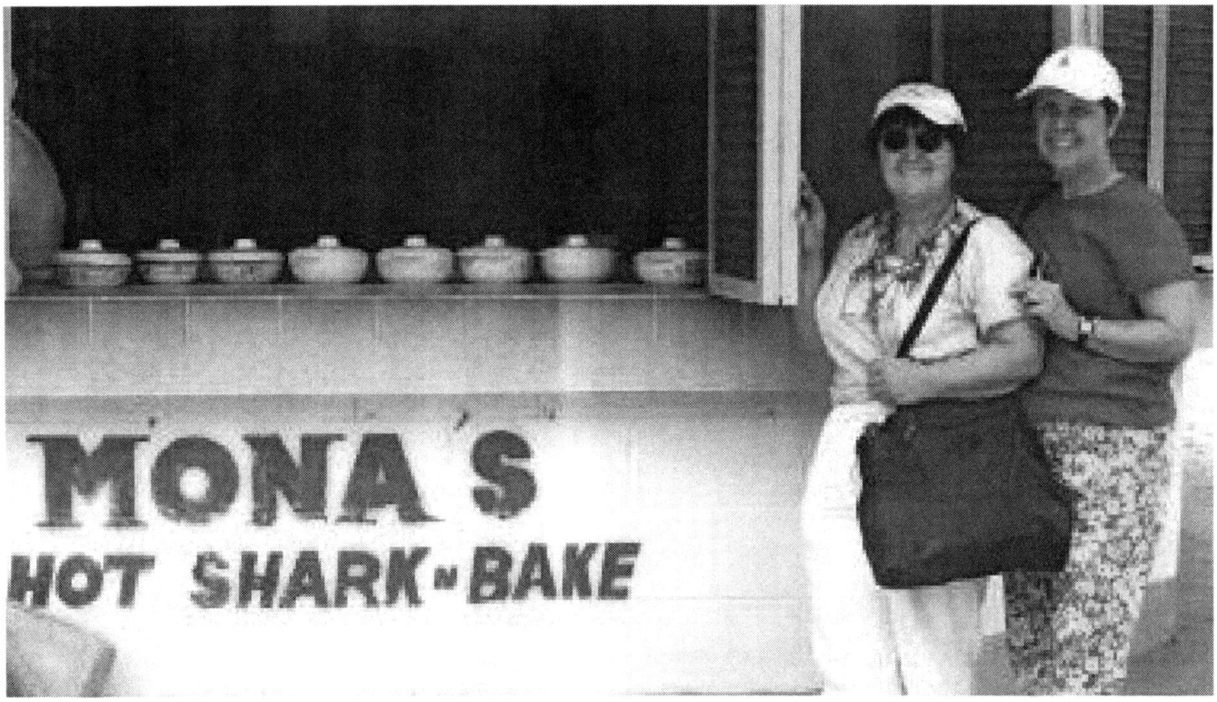

MONA AND PAT AT MARACAS BEACH, TRINIDAD

Of course, we all went to see the carnival parade, except David and I watched the parade from the streets while Mona and Pat watched from the Queen's Park Savannah Stadium. It was a hot day on the street, but with hundreds of cold drink and food stands, everyone could cool off. You can see the costumes and beautiful women up-close and take all the pictures you want. Whereas, picture taking in the stadium is difficult because of the high stage and fast pace of the competition. Also, we were told that picture taking without buying a pass was illegal and our cameras might be confiscated. The real drawback of buying a pass was the outrageous cost, T and T $1,000. A real rip-off, which we found out later, only the professional photographers bothered to buy, whereas many amateurs brought cameras in with no consequences and no fees.

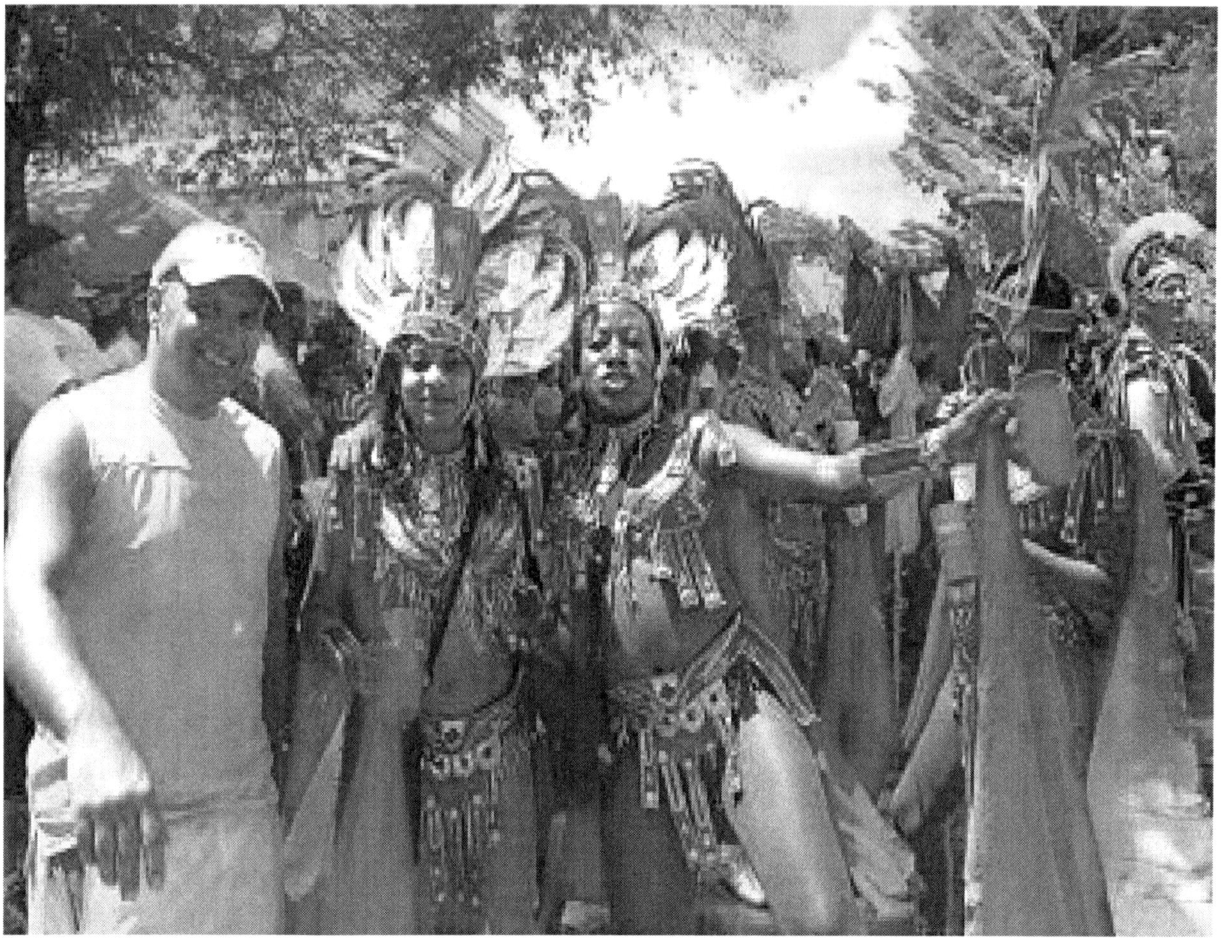

SON DAVID AT THE STREET PARADE WITH TWO CUTE REVELERS

On Mar. 2 we flew over to the island of Tobago. I rented a car to drive to the Blue Water Inn at the northeastern tip of the island at the town of Spayside. No one warned us about the long drive over some of the narrowest and curvy roads in the world. Yipes, I don't think there was a straight road of over 100 yards on the whole island. Meeting a wide truck on the narrow parts of the road is a fingernail biting experience. Many people double park, storefronts and homes are built right up to the edge of the road and sidewalks are nonexistent except in the large towns.

The resort is popular with yachties for its nice rooms and the resort's view of beautiful Tyrrel's Bay. Two islands in the bay with live reefs draw lots of divers and snorkelers. These popular islands are promoted as the dive capital of Tobago. One island, Little Tobago, is also a bird sanctuary and draws many bird watchers, but you have to be a billy goat to hike over the rocky hillsides. David and I took a snorkeling tour on one of the glass bottom boats and had a good time. I thought the fish life a little incongruous and Angel Reef was not as colorful as promoted, but the water was warm and snorkeling is always fun.

The resort had a nice bar about 10 feet from the water's edge and open to sea breezes. We thought the food at the restaurant was especially good and the décor, pleasant and relaxing. On Saturday, we drove back to the airport at Crown Point along the Caribbean side of the island. The highest point of the island contains a large rain forest and even though it was a hot and sunny day on the rest of the island, it rained in the rain forest. It seems silly, but we were amazed by the rain and lush green forest while the rest of the island was sweltering in a cloudless, hot sunny day.

As usual, readying our little ship for the 1,800 mile passage to Florida brings to mind all the hurdles that we will have to jump over first. The frustrations of customs and immigration visits, paying bills, refueling, chart/cruising guide research and worst of all, saying our goodbyes to close friends. People that have not lived in Trinidad would be surprised to learn just how many people spend the hurricane season there living on their boats. The area, to this point in time, has enjoyed a reputation as a safe boat refuge for hurricanes.

Trinidad certainly has many contrasts, but for us, concerts, theater, movies and restaurants are important. If one prefers peace, quite and solitude as many do, you can fade into the woodwork and no one will bother you. Trinidad is an important cruising destination as good Diesel fuel and services are available at reasonable prices. It is common knowledge that when going up-island toward the U.S., everything except rum gets more expensive (almost every island in the Caribbean has several rum distilleries).

All our boat hardware and systems checked out with the exception of the water heater. I disconnected the water heater as it decided to leak sometime while we were off the boat visiting in Seattle. There is a superstition popular with boaters that claims, boat stuff will break down if it is not used — maybe so. Anyway, ***Our Pleasure*** is equipped with a backup, on-demand, propane water heater so I put off replacing the electric one. Boats under 70 feet are usually short on storage space so installed equipment is not always accessible. In this case, it would take a few days just to remove all the pumps and copper tubing hindering the removal of the water heater. In addition, the ocean water temperature in the tropics heats the water stored in the water tanks to somewhere in the mid-eighties — who needs water hotter than that? Usually we shower to cool off.

Our biggest frustration however, was our 4 years old, 15 horsepower Yamaha outboard. With David and Mona visiting, we thought it would be good fun to launch the dinghy to see some local Trinidad sights. Well, the outboard would not start. I took the carburetor off and gave it a thorough cleaning, but that was not the problem. I started looking at the electrical system and did not see a spark. My voltmeter does not respond fast enough to measure a sparks momentary spike, so I fell back on a tried and true method of touching a sparkplug terminal while turning the flywheel slowly. Well, the jolt just about knocked me on my ear — not a good test for weak hearts. In my younger days, I used that test when I was building hot rods, but I don't think those sparks were that intense back then. A whopping jolt, but was the spark was strong enough? I still couldn't see a spark jump across the plug's gap. I questioned the potted electronic module known as the "brain."

In the meantime, David and Mona left on Mar. 6. I called the local Yamaha dealer located in the Port of Spain on the 8th and they said they would send out a technician. Well, the technician did not show up, so after the third day of no-shows I started calling to find out what was going on. "He would be coming," was the response. While waiting for the technician to arrive, I tried again to get it working to no avail.

At this point, the delay in leaving Trinidad was not a timing problem for our planned rendezvous with longtime Seattle boating friends Karl and Deane House. They arranged to fly into Antigua for the 19th running of the "Classic Yacht Regatta." This race is one of the Caribbean's premiere classic events with about 50 of the world's best classic yachts entered. Since this regatta does not start until April 20 and Antigua is only a few hundred miles from Trinidad, I thought we had plenty of time.

Each time I called, I heard the technician was on the way, just like, "The check is in the mail." On the sixth day, he called me to say he would be there in the afternoon. Guess what? No technician after I waited all day. The next day, through friends, I found a local mechanic with a good reputation for fixing outboards. After he picked up the outboard, I called the dealer and told them how I felt about their worthless promises and lousy service — not a good idea I was to find out. The new local mechanic on the case did a few tests and agreed with my assessment that it was the "brain." However, the "brain" was only available through the non-performing dealer in Port of Spain and he claimed not to have one. He said my outboard was a model they did not sell and parts would require shipment into Trinidad. So here we go again, with this lousy unmotivated dealer. Well, after 3 weeks of endless phone calls and pulling out what little hair I have left, Pat talked me into leaving Trinidad and finding someone along the way to fix it — reasonable logic at this point. Therefore, we decided to leave Trinidad without a working outboard.

In the mean time, Crews Inn was hosting another big gala event and we had to go. It was to benefit the Cotton Tree Foundation, a charity organization that helps children. It was a dressy affair with wonderful hors d'oeuvres prepared by the Crews Inn restaurant staff. Two open bars provided all the cool refreshments anyone could want. After the socializing, everyone took his or her seats in front of the stage for the entertainment. The most memorable act for us was Trinidad's most revered calypsonian, Denise Plummer. Calypso songs can be such fun. Diverse lyrics and timely, right-on thoughts, address everyone's concerns from the environment to the government.

English friends, Elliot and Marianne, on the yacht *Ostrica*, filled us in with lots of good information about cruising through the Caribbean. *Ostrica* is Italian for oyster, which is the manufacturer's name of their 55 foot yacht. Sailing from England, several times, they have visited most of the Caribbean islands. They gave us firsthand knowledge of names, phone numbers, and e-mail addresses of many good places to stay through the island chain.

Finally, on April 1, 2006, we paid our moorage tax (government tax apart from marina charges) and had our clearance papers officially signed and stamped. We left our comfy moorage and headed for the fuel dock to take on 200 gallons of Diesel. By 2:30 in the afternoon, we headed out the pass and into the Atlantic Ocean and sailed all night. Without our knowledge, something caught in the prop, most likely a plastic bag. When the wind died, we powered up the engine. It took a couple of hours to realize our small forward gain was not the result of an adverse current. Things seemed perfectly normal, but we were not going anywhere fast and wasting a lot of fuel. By reversing the engine, whatever was caught in the prop was freed and we were back to normal speeds.

While we were furling the main sail, one of the slides lodged sideways in the track, which caused enough friction to snap the furling line. We anchored in Tyrell Bay, Carricou to fix the furling line. The line wraps around the furling tube in a series of coils between two narrow plates. The visibility is limited and there is no room for hands or fingers. I had to work with tools I concocted from metal coat hangers. I worked until it was so dark I couldn't see any more. We had a late dinner; I told Pat I planned to get up at first light to finish installing the furling line. For some odd reason, everything went together in the morning and I restrung the line in no time. Carricou is part of the independent country of Grenada in the windward islands of the eastern Caribbean. By 7 a.m., we had the anchor up and headed for the Grenadine island of Bequia. Bequia is one of the 600 islands in the northern Grenadines, part of the independent country of Saint Vincent. We left on a 12 knot breeze, a perfect, Caribbean day.

BEQUIA

We sailed into Bequia's Admiralty Bay and picked up a mooring buoy provided by an outfit called Daffodil Marine. Of course, Elliot and Marianne recommended a different set of buoys closer to the beach and all the action. However, the buoys belonging to the company they recommended were not seen until we later took a walk along the beach. It probably was more convenient than Daffodil's location, but Daffodil's big sign at the bay's entrance got our attention. Fees in Bequia were reasonable as the mooring buoy was $15, the water taxi was $4 for two people each way, and customs and immigration set us back just $21. The monetary unit in this part of the world is the Eastern Caribbean (EC) dollar. EC $2.70 is equivalent to U.S. one dollar. However, everyone wants U.S. dollars making money transactions painless. Cruising sailboats filled most of the bay and the town's colorful buildings lined their main road.

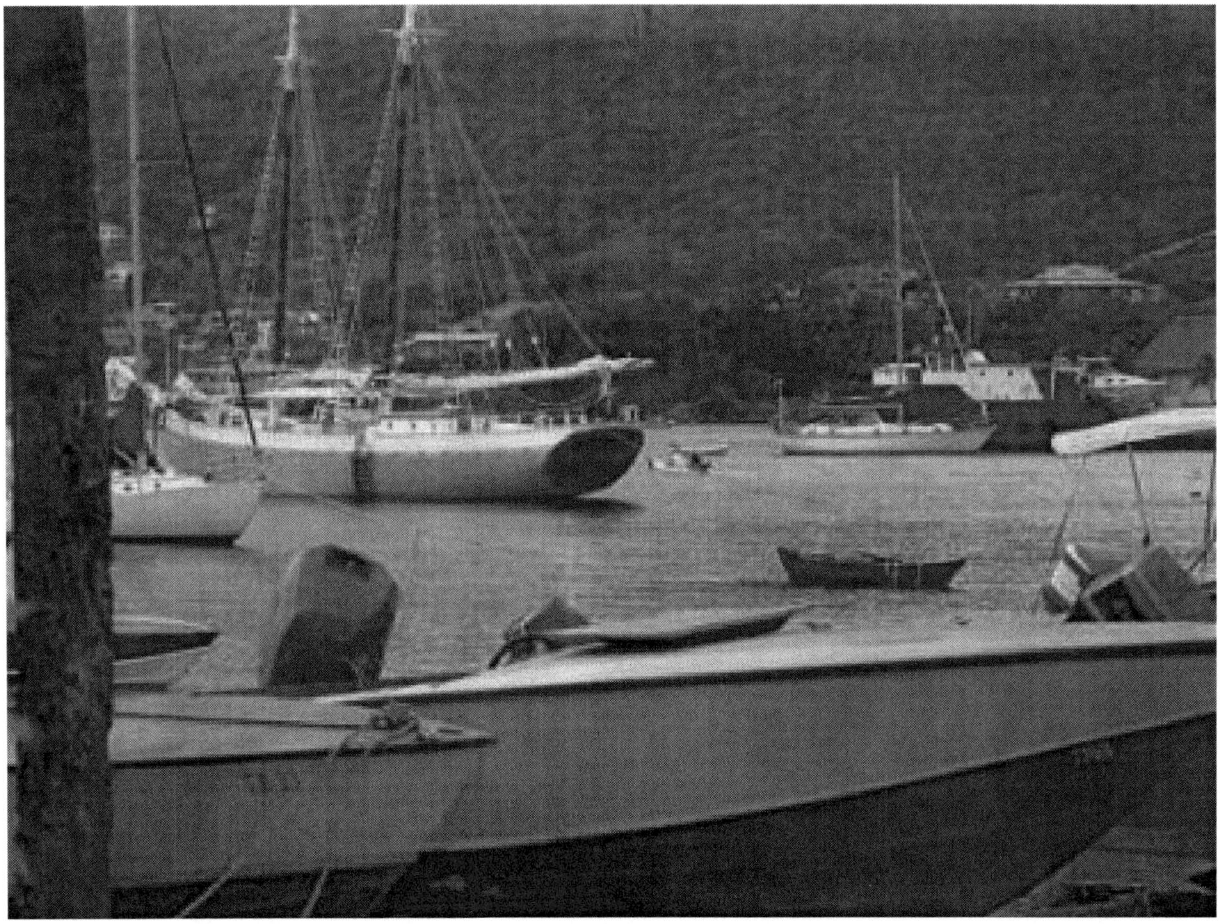

ADMIRALTY BAY, BEQUIA — FULL OF COLOR

We stayed in Bequia for three days and thoroughly enjoyed ourselves. Bourbon was the skipper of our favorite water taxi. We have no idea how that name works in the land of rum, but it is a name easily recognized by everyone using their VHF radios. In shorter time than it takes Pat to get ready to leave ***Our Pleasure***, he was at our boat. He, like everyone else we met in Bequia, was friendly and spoke understandable English. After checking in with customs and immigration, we went window-shopping through the town. We bought a Grenadine courtesy flag to fly on our flag halyard, stopped for cool refreshments at the Whale Bone restaurant and Pat sent e-mails to our family. The next morning we were happily surprised by an entrepreneur selling freshly baked baguettes and banana bread from his runabout — what a wonderful treat!

In town again, we asked a bank security guard if she could recommend a tour guide. Without hesitation, she pointed out Oliverre sitting across the street in his shiny pickup truck — probably her boy friend. His truck bed had a canvas canopy for shade and bench seats along both sides. The island is not big so two and a half hours is plenty of time to see the best sites the island has to offer. At the first stop, we met Sally, an artist from England, who along with her potter friend and his daughter was slowly restoring an old sugar mill into an art studio.

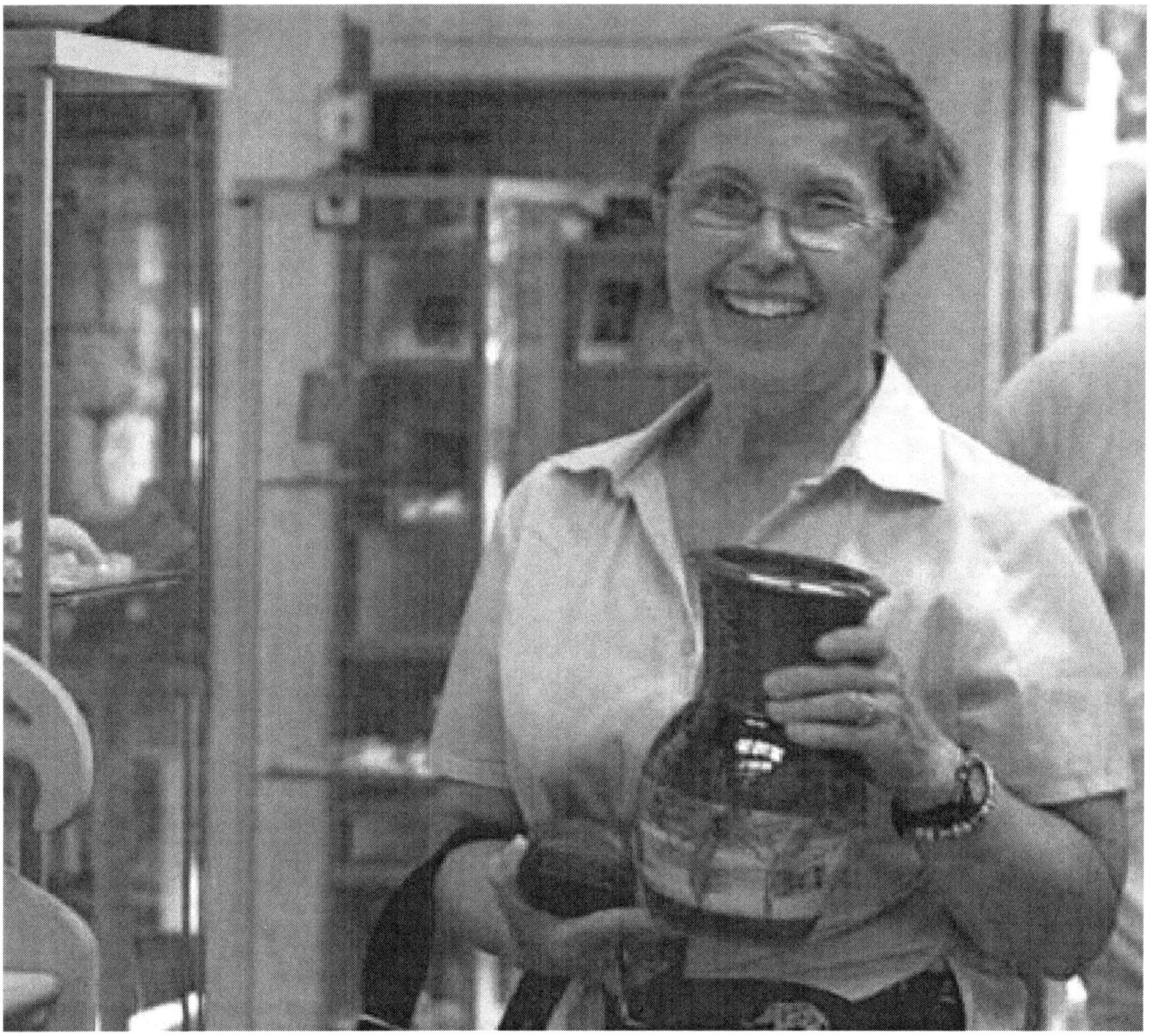

PAT'S NEW VASE AT THE "SPRING SUGAR MILL STUDIO," BEQUIA

Bequia is an attractive island with many lush areas. Several viewpoints featured old cannons guarding the bay. One other stop of note was the Oldhegg Turtle Sanctuary. Rescuing turtles must be an innate motivation driving this sanctuaries owner. He conceded to us what a rough road his undertaking had become. The government provides no help or incentives so he depends on contributions from visitors and the sale of T-shirts and knick-knacks. Newly hatched sea and land turtles are fed and nourished until they are old enough to survive on own their own.

Bequia has a number of good model boat builders that will build models from pictures, but like to visit the actual boat before starting a model project. The one Oliverre recommended was Mauvin Hutchins. He had some detailed and beautiful models on display. I was disappointed when he quoted a price of $1,600 as I thought the price would be more reasonable and I lost interest. I found out later in Seattle that good models made in the U.S. are at least twice that much.

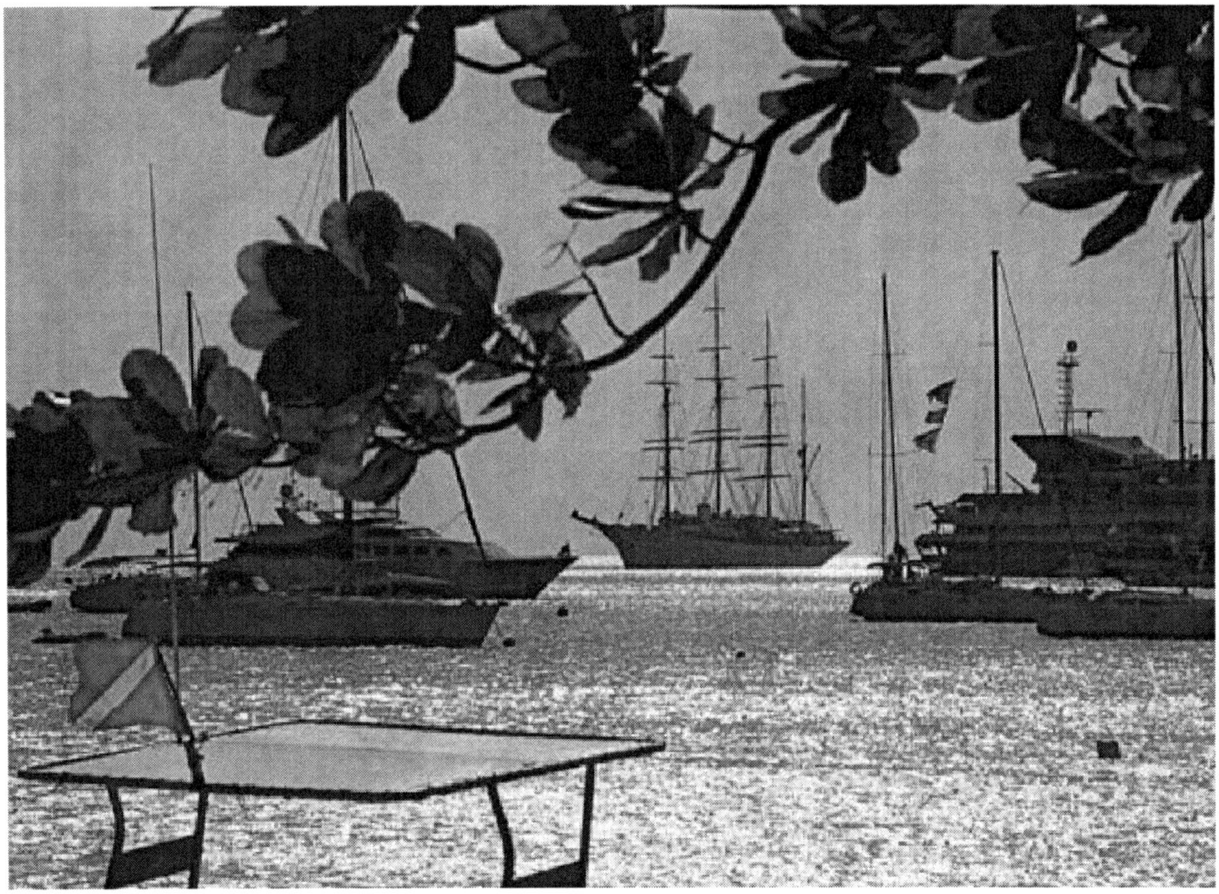

***SEA CLOUD*, ADMIRALTY BAY, BEQUIA**

I called around and found an electronic "brain" for my Yamaha outboard was available at KP Marine in St. Vincent. Pat and I jumped on a ferry and one hour later, we were in St. Vincent. Alex, from the 100 foot, U.S. power yacht, *Quiet Place*, rode along with us as he needed a hydraulic hose. The city was busy with traffic and people. Pat found a nice young Bequia woman named Joanne who led us over to the bus stand and the right bus. The white-knuckle ride to KP Marine in the town of Calliqua took about 20 minutes. The bus was a 12 passenger minivan. The driver stayed-put at the bus stop until his bus was fully packed. Of course, the scorching sunshine was pushing our deodorant to its limit.

Soon after leaving St. Vincent, the driver pulled out a bottle of Guinness® beer. The soca music was turned up to eardrum pain level and off we went in a cloud of dust. I put my hat over the loud speaker next to me, but he turned the music up louder. We squealed to a stop across from KP Marine and he kindly took the time to point out the store and showed us where to stand to catch a bus back to town. We said thanks, stepped out gladly, and under our breath, prayed we would hook-up with a non-drinking driver on the way back. Which did happen, the return driver was cautious and drove at the speed limit.

Back in Bequia, we were surprised to see the legendary *Sea Cloud*, a 353 foot four-masted barque of elegance. Wall Street tycoon, E. F. Hutton, had this magnificent ship built for his wife and cereal heiress, Marjorie Meriwether Post, as a wedding present. It was launched in 1931 in Kiel, Germany. Built by the Krupp-Germania Shipyard and designed by New York architectural firm, Stevens and Cox. When launched as *Hussar*, she was the largest private yacht in the U.S. She is now chartered in the Caribbean and maintained to the highest standards by a 60 person crew. *Star Clipper*, a smaller four-masted schooner, also paid a visit to the harbor. She also is a charter boat and was quite busy ferrying people back and forth aboard their two inboard powered launches. We walked down the beach and stopped at "Maranne's" for the best homemade ice cream on the island. We just made it to customs before they closed. Checkout was simple and no more fees were required.

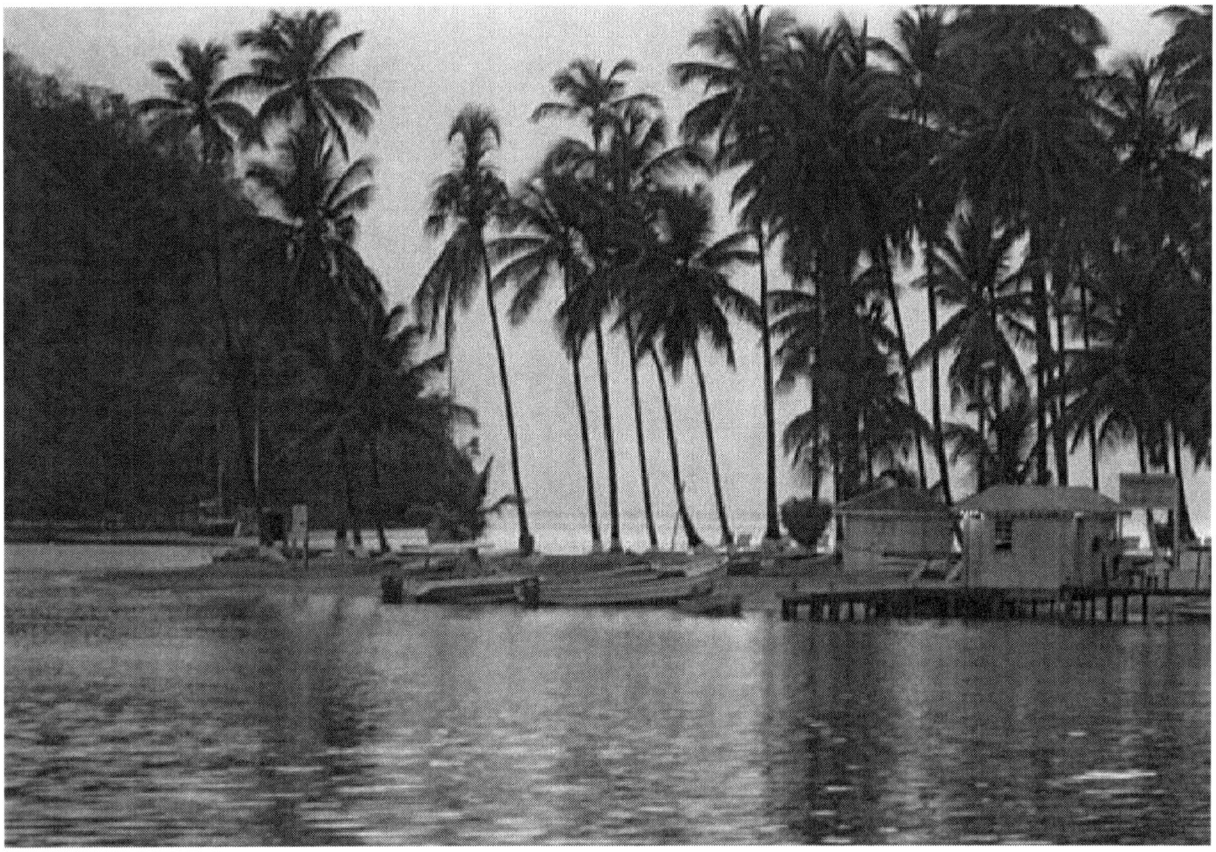

INNER HARBOR, MARIGOT BAY, ST. LUCIA

ST. LUCIA

We left Bequia at 6:30 a.m. on April 6 so we could make St. Lucia before dark. In light winds, we arrived at Marigot Bay, St. Lucia around 6 p.m. A boat boy led us into the quiet inner harbor and handed us a line from a buoy. The bay is quite picturesque with a charter agency, many new condominiums in various stages of construction, a resort, a few restaurants, and mangroves around half the bay. Check-in and out were allowed on the same form — progressive. We rowed over (no working outboard yet) to the upscale Margot Beach Club the next day. Neat and tidy with a nice beach, is a good description of this resort. I did not see many people around, however, there were three young families with small children enjoying the beach. Pat used the resort's phone system to call daughter Leslie with info about our latest travels and location.

MARTINIQUE

We left St. Lucia at about 11 a.m. for the short sail over to the French island of Martinique. We sailed into Marin Harbor on Martinique about 5:30 in the afternoon. On the way into the narrow and somewhat shallow entrance, we were stopped by a French naval patrol boat, complete with deck guns. A French officer standing at the bow and about 10 feet from our stern asked us a few minor questions. I think they were just curious and mainly wanted to know what ports we had visited. They were quite pleasant and may have needed an event for their log to show some usefulness. Once inside the harbor we found it crowded and were surprised at just how big this harbor is. There are 6 boat charter agencies, good docking space for 600 boats, many boats on harbor buoys and hundreds more at anchor. We moved through the harbor slowly to look for areas with plenty of room.

We looked for an empty dock, but on the VHF radio, a boat undertow was told the dock space was full. He was given an option of docking at the fuel dock until morning, which he took. That answered any questions we had about dock availability. We eventually found anchoring space with room to swing. However, the depth kept bouncing around in a strange manner. I saw readings on our cockpit depth sounder bounce around from zero to 8 feet below the keel. It was not until after we were well anchored that I discovered both depth sounders were on. Both being on at the same time is a real error in navigation. They interfere with each other and invalidate all readings. Normally I would have recognized the problem right away, but not moving the boat for two years one forgets about the little idiosyncrasies.

It took three attempts to set the anchor because I thought we were in shallow water. On the third try, I put out around 150 feet of chain and that worked. Finding the sounder problem established that we were in 28 feet of water, not six. After we knew, the anchor was firmly set, Pat made some drinks, and we relaxed looking at the fascinating Marin Harbor. Pat got all excited when she realized we were anchored next to old friends from Trinidad, Jim and Alli on *Kindred Spirit.* I said, "No it couldn't be the *Kindred Spirit* folks, they went to Venezuela." Well, Jim and Alli emerged from their cabin and waved to us in response to Pat's yelling. They were on the way to Venezuela; they were just taking their time.

The next day they came over in their dinghy (their outboard was working). We said we were going to row over to customs and they laughed. They reckoned we would be worn to a frazzle after rowing against the wind and chop over to the inner harbor. That info made it easy to accept their offer to ferry us over in their dinghy. They were unbelievably helpful over the next several days taking us to the supermarket, showing us the town, the boat yard and church. Check-in was informal, one official, a one-page government form and no money was required. Besides good wines, cheeses and baguettes, the French really know how to minimize bureaucratic nonsense.

Jim grew up in a French speaking part of Canada and got around very well in French speaking Martinique. He helped us find an outboard mechanic, Roby Mécanique, who was able to solve the mysterious outboard problem in just 3 hours. He found the "brain" was not a problem it was the interfacing flange surfaces between the carburetor and the engine. It came from the factory with some brown gunk between the surfaces. I added black gasket sealer after cleaning the carburetor to enhance the seal. Well, all that stuff resulted in a bad seal between the two flanges. It took Roby 3 hours to clean and polish the mating surfaces, which was mainly due to the factories hard, brown gunk. It was as simple as that and the spark, although almost an invisible blue was fine. At times, things just need that professional touch.

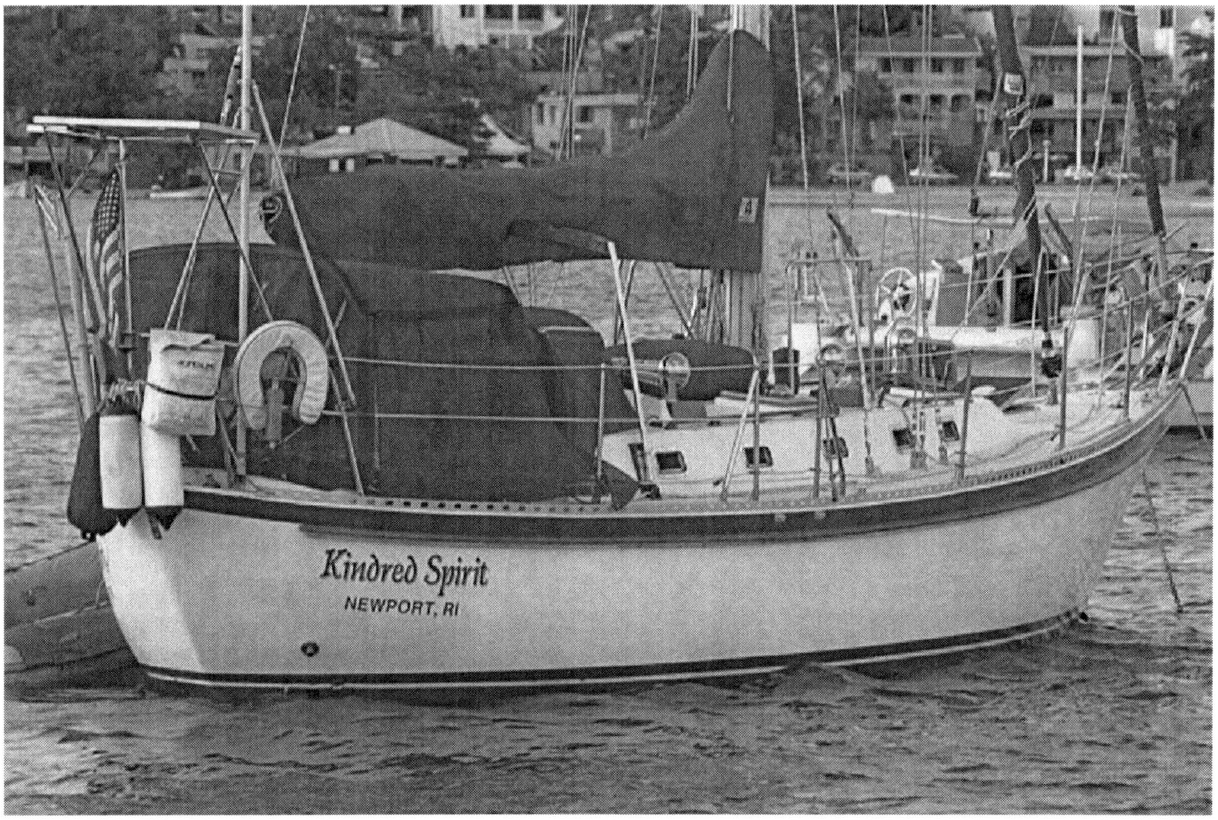

JIM & ALLI'S *KINDRED SPIRIT*, MARIN HARBOR, MARTINIQUE

The next big problem was to get the generator working again, which was now refusing to start. I spent a lot of time concentrating on the fuel system, changing the filter, checking the pump output and the injector nozzle output. Everything I looked at seemed okay. After a couple of days with no progress, Jim helped me find an engine mechanic. His name was Louis Pouget, but his nickname was "Louis the dirty." His nickname recognizes the obvious that his clothes are full of grease and his work ethics are not all that neat. There is another mechanic named Louis in Martinique, but he is neat. So, to make things easier it is either "Louis the dirty" or "Louis the clean."

Jim brought him out to the boat and it took him about 5 minutes to figure out there was no compression — how embarrassing, I thought I was losing my powers of logical thinking. He removed the air intake filter and put his hand over the air inlet, then a rag — no suction, so simple. Off came the head and there it was, a small piece of the intake valve was missing, but no pieces. Louis pondered over the missing piece for about 2 seconds, shrugged his shoulders and kept working. After Louis the dirty left, it took a couple of hours to clean up the Diesel fuel he spilled while checking the system. I called Dave right away at Entec, the generator manufacturer in Portland, Oregon and ordered new valves and a new head gasket. I made a special point to have them sent via DHL.

The next day, April 11, 2006, Pat and I celebrated our 47th wedding anniversary. Jim and Alli brought over an anniversary card — we were pleased. They also took our laundry as they were going into shore to take Nicole, their new kitten, to a Vet. That afternoon, they picked us up for a ride into town. We treated them to a delicious lunch and dessert at Ti Toqués. To enhance the celebration, we ordered an expensive bottle of wonderful French Champagne. During lunch, we planned a more adventuresome celebration the next day by renting a car to see more of Martinique.

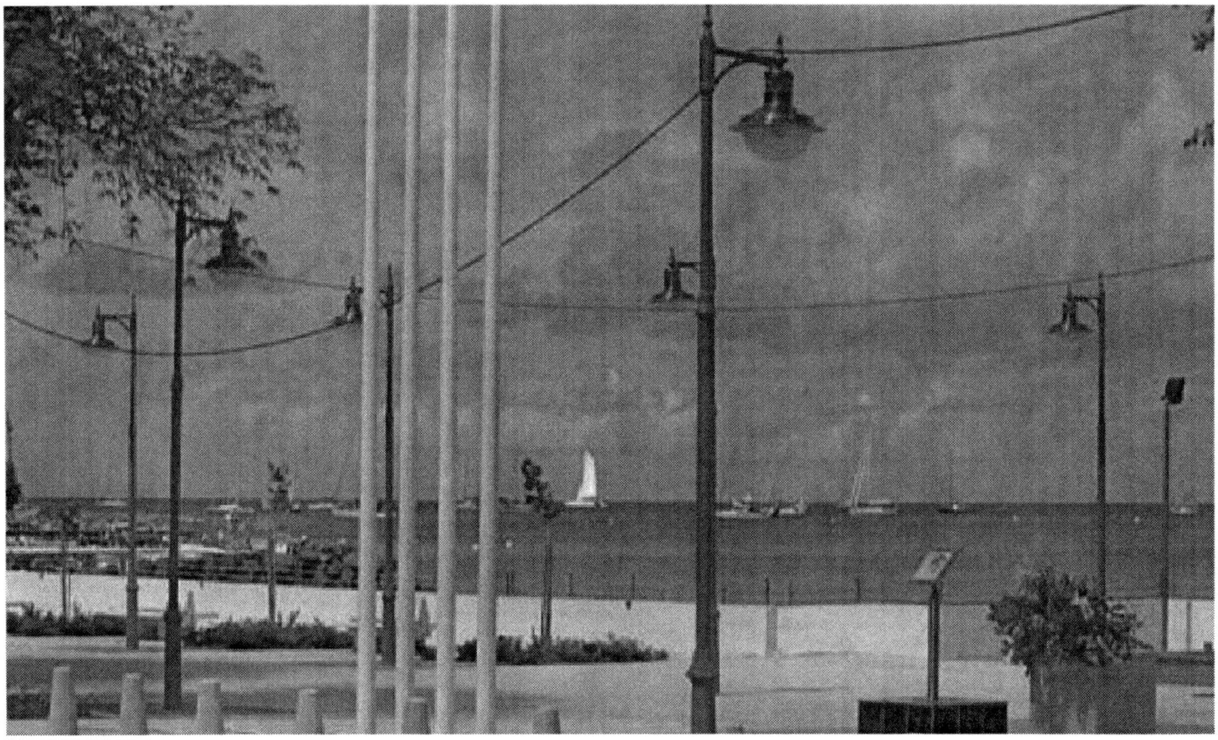

WATERFRONT PARK, SAINT ANNE, MARTINIQUE

Jim and Alli had become good friends with Michael who runs the fuel dock and grocery store at the boatyard. He also rents cars and provides space for the laundry facility, that all the yachties use. So we rented a boxy, squashed-up looking, Peugeot station wagon from Michael. Jim and Alli had driven around the island once before so they were familiar with all the good places to see. The next town up the bay, St. Anne, has a beautiful waterfront and white sandy beach. Many yachts were anchored in the bay, but a little wind could turn the exposed harbor into a rolly anchorage. The timeworn Catholic Church facing the town square was going through an extensive renovation, as were most of the public places. There were many nicely decorated French shops along narrow streets. We looked at a few of them and with more time, exploration would have been fun.

From St. Anne we went to probably the most popular beach on Martinique at Grande Anse des Salines. Which I think means, great bay of salt-water. The beach is several miles long, with sand that is fine and a beautiful light color.

Of course, there were a few topless French women walking the beach who would have looked a whole lot better dressed. This is a family beach, but no one seemed to care or even look at the few exposed women. A waterfront town called Le Robert, looked like a good stop for lunch. The local patisserie was featuring ham and cheese sandwiches on a baguette — they were excellent. Driving on further we saw the small French towns of La Trinite, Le Marigot, Le Lorrain, and the mountains of Martinique.

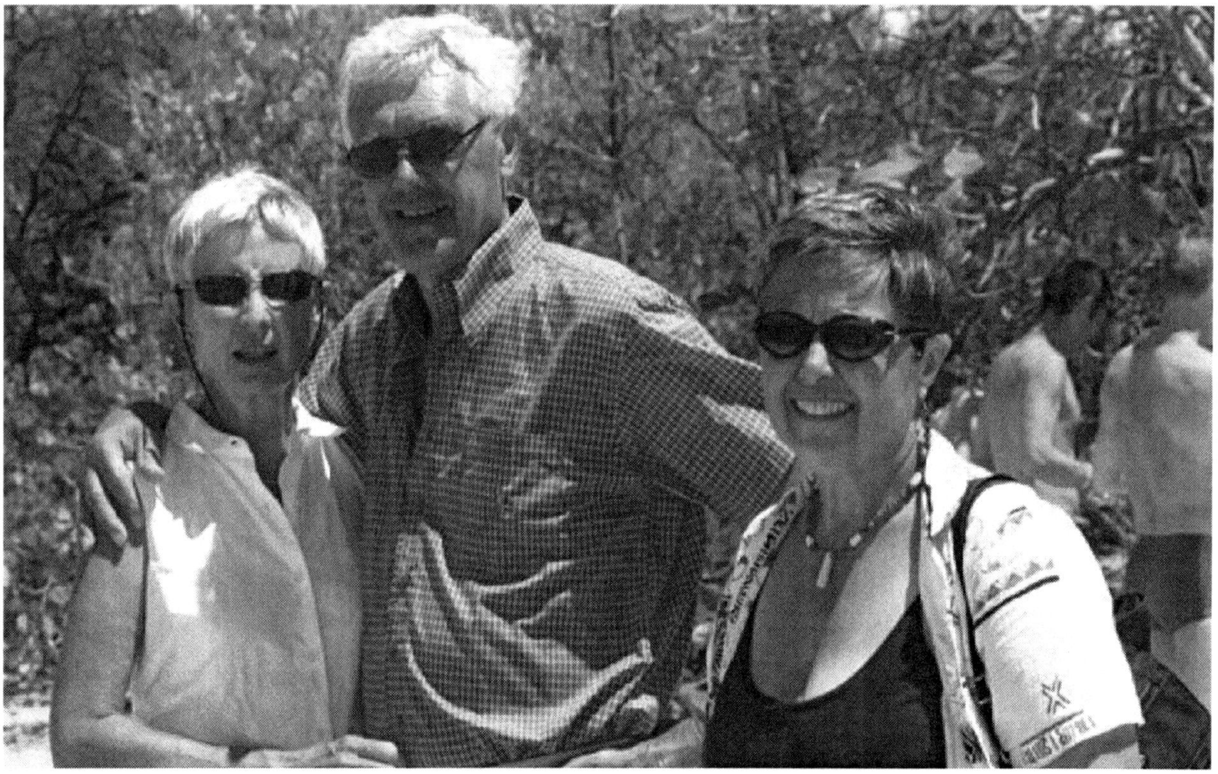

ALLI, JIM AND PAT AT GRANDE ANSE des SALINES

Our road trip took us near the rather infamous mountain, Mt. Pelée. It's a sure bet you probably weren't around when she erupted on Ascension Day, May 8, 1902. Some natives are positive that the eruption consummated the Carib natives' curse during the time they were being slaughtered by the Europeans in 1658. The eruption completely covered the city of St. Pierre, which then had a population of about 30,000. At that time, St. Pierre was the beautiful capital city of Martinique, in fact, it was known as the "Paris of the Caribbean." The people looked on Montagne Pelèe with pride because of its beautiful forests, pretty sculpturing and its beautiful resort around Crater Lake at the summit. St. Pierre was the commercial, cultural and social center of Martinique. I found the story fascinating with its curse and the ensuing eruption in which an estimated 29,933 people were burned or smothered to death. Only 2 people survived in St. Pierre, a cobbler working in his cellar and a man imprisoned in a stone jail cell for murder. Twelve ships anchored in the harbor were also destroyed when their wooden structures were set ablaze by the showering of flaming lava. The museum in town tells the story that signs of the pending eruption started around the end of April. As early as April 23, shocks from the mountain threw dishes from cabinets and shook houses. Small explosions and clouds of smoke had been seen and heard for weeks. Ash particles increased steadily and affected the people in the city with eye and breathing problems. The explosions that accompanied each eruption could be heard hundreds of miles away. Martinique officials were telling people the eruptions would subside. They were afraid that if the people left, with no one to work the sugar mill, rum factory or plantations, there would be an economic disaster. Even when molten lava was raining down the mountainside and explosions were heard as far away as St. Thomas, people were told to sit tight, not to worry — sounds like our government and our debt crisis. The governor of Martinique and his wife even went to St. Pierre with a detachment of soldiers to calm the situation and prevent people from leaving — they perished.

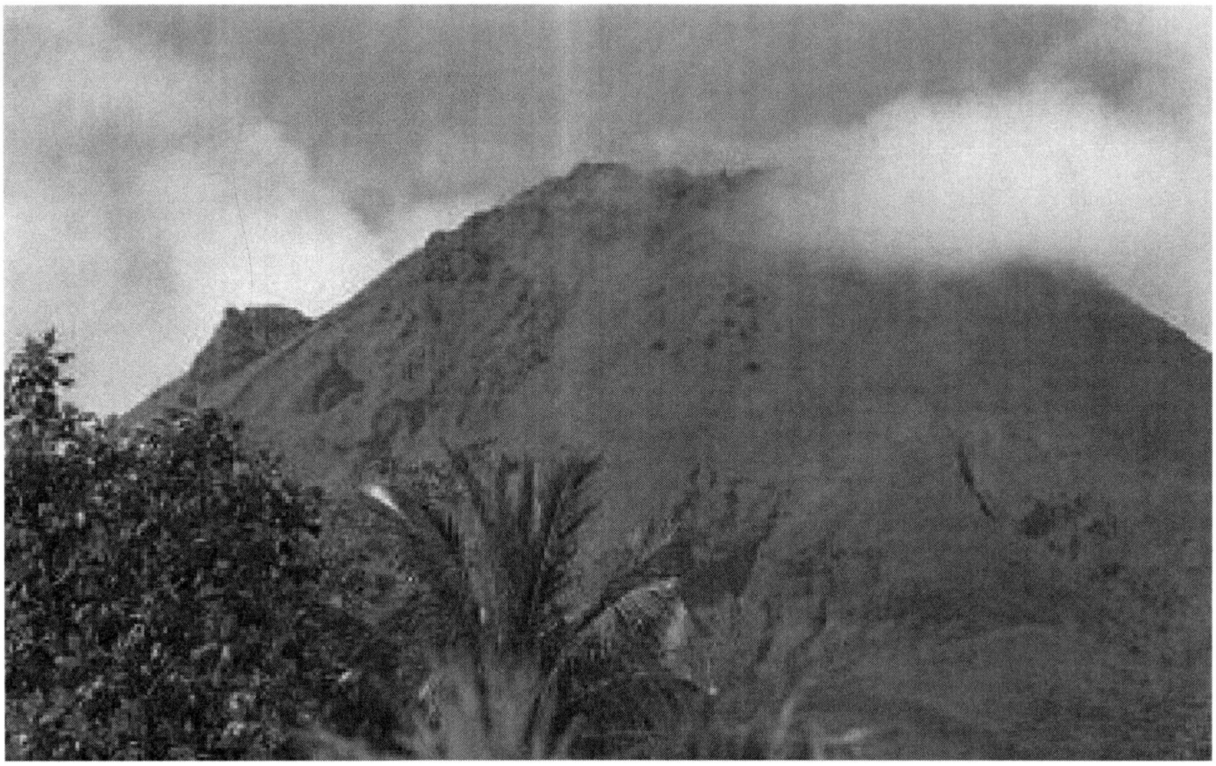

MT. PELÉE FROM THE CITY OF ST. PIERRE

In time, the capital was moved to Fort de France, which is now the capital city of Martinique. Since many of the people who now live in St. Pierre, moved into rebuilt remnants of the original buildings, we did not find the city inviting or attractive.

To add yet another chapter to Napoleon's life story, we wondered around the town of Trois Islets to find the museum dedicated to Empress, Josephine Bonaparte. She was born and raised outside the town on a 200 acre plantation. When the plantation was active, they had 150 slaves to work the cane fields. The empress's maiden name was Marie-Josephine Rose Tascher de la Pagerie, born July 27, 1763. Because of heavy car traffic through the capital city of Fort de France, we arrived 15 minutes past closing at the museum. I guess we should have traveled clockwise around Martinique instead of counterclockwise to see the museum. We took several pictures of the plantation's beautiful flowers and saw from a distance, the only original building, an open-air kitchen.

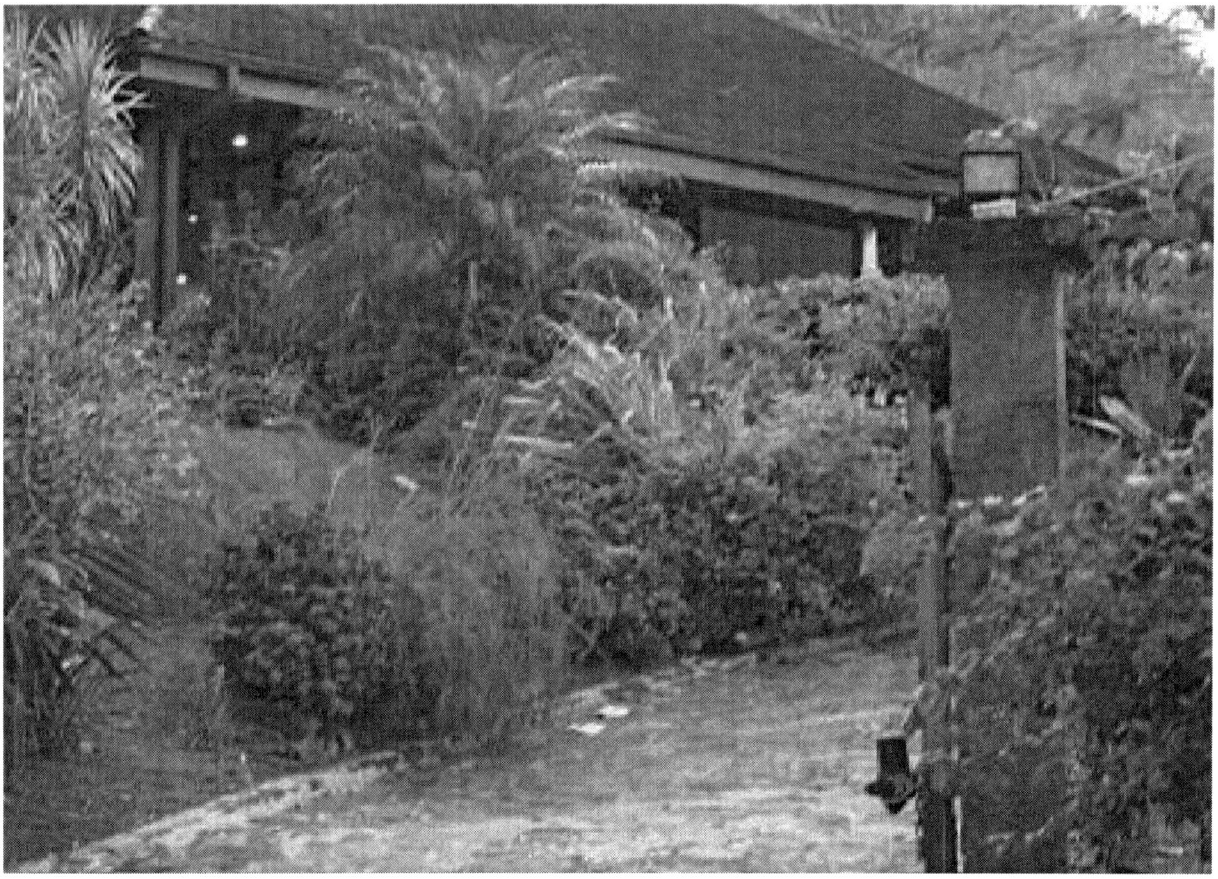

BIRTHPLACE OF EMPRESS JOSEPHINE BONAPARTE

The next day was rather normal for Martinique, cappuccinos and chocolate croissants at the Mango Bay restaurant, e-mailing, lunch and grocery shopping. April 14 was Good Friday and most of Martinique was closed. We phoned Seattle talked to Leslie and told grandchildren Mia and Mitchell we loved them. We went to the local Catholic Church, St. Etienne and Pat said the Stations of the Cross. I was interested in the construction of the church, which must have been built by shipwrights. The entire ceiling was constructed of huge timbers in the form of a ship's hull, but upside down. The church had a beautiful altar made of white marble dating back to 1766 when the church was completed. Within the face of the altar, is an impressive inlay relief of the last supper. The cost of the sculpture was said to have been 6,000 pounds, a huge amount of money in those days. The façade is cut stone and the walls are about 2 feet thick. Guarding the church entrance is a statue of St. Stephen just above the doors.

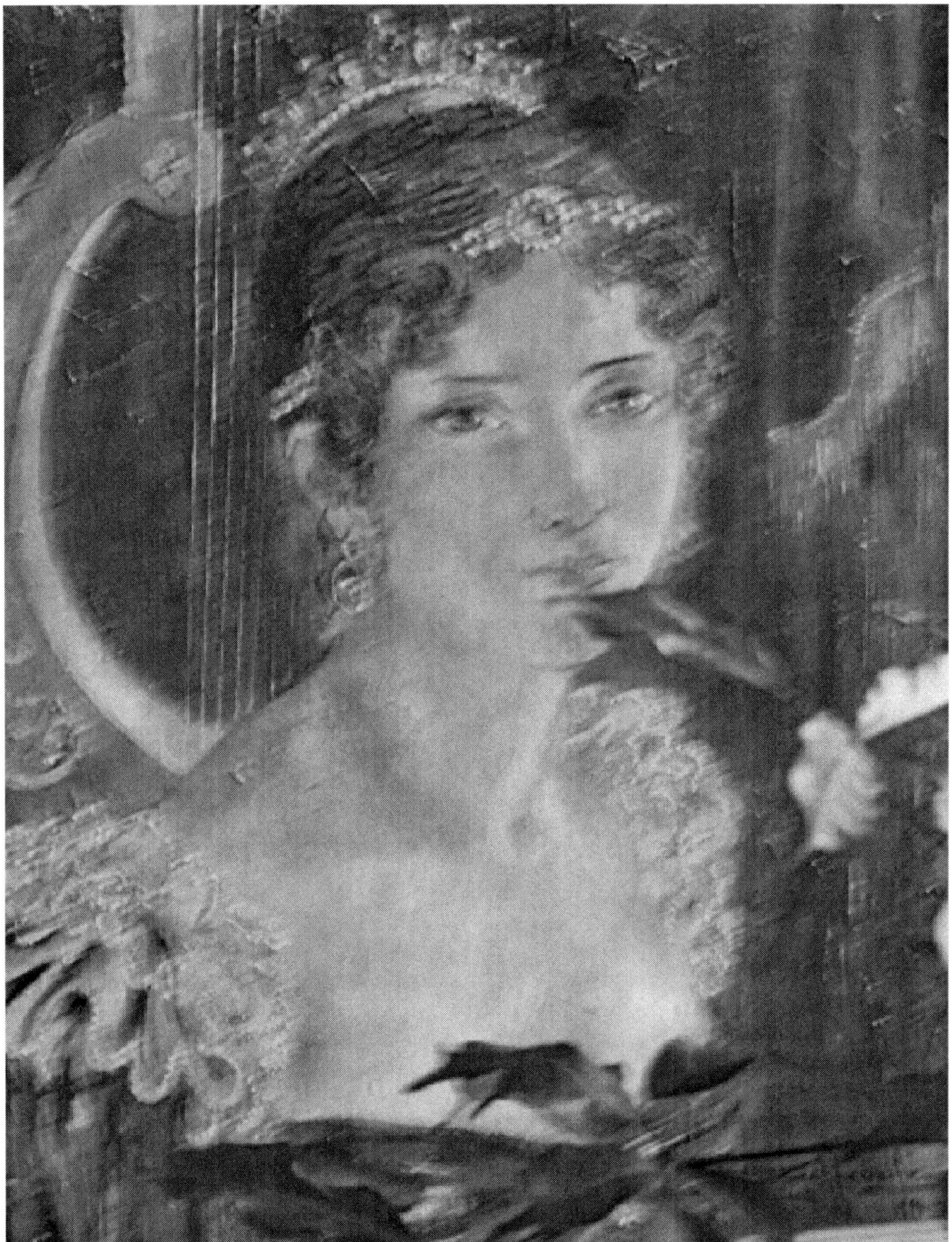

THE BEAUTIFUL EMPRESS, JOSEPHINE PAGERIE BONAPARTE, MUSÉE de la PAGERIE

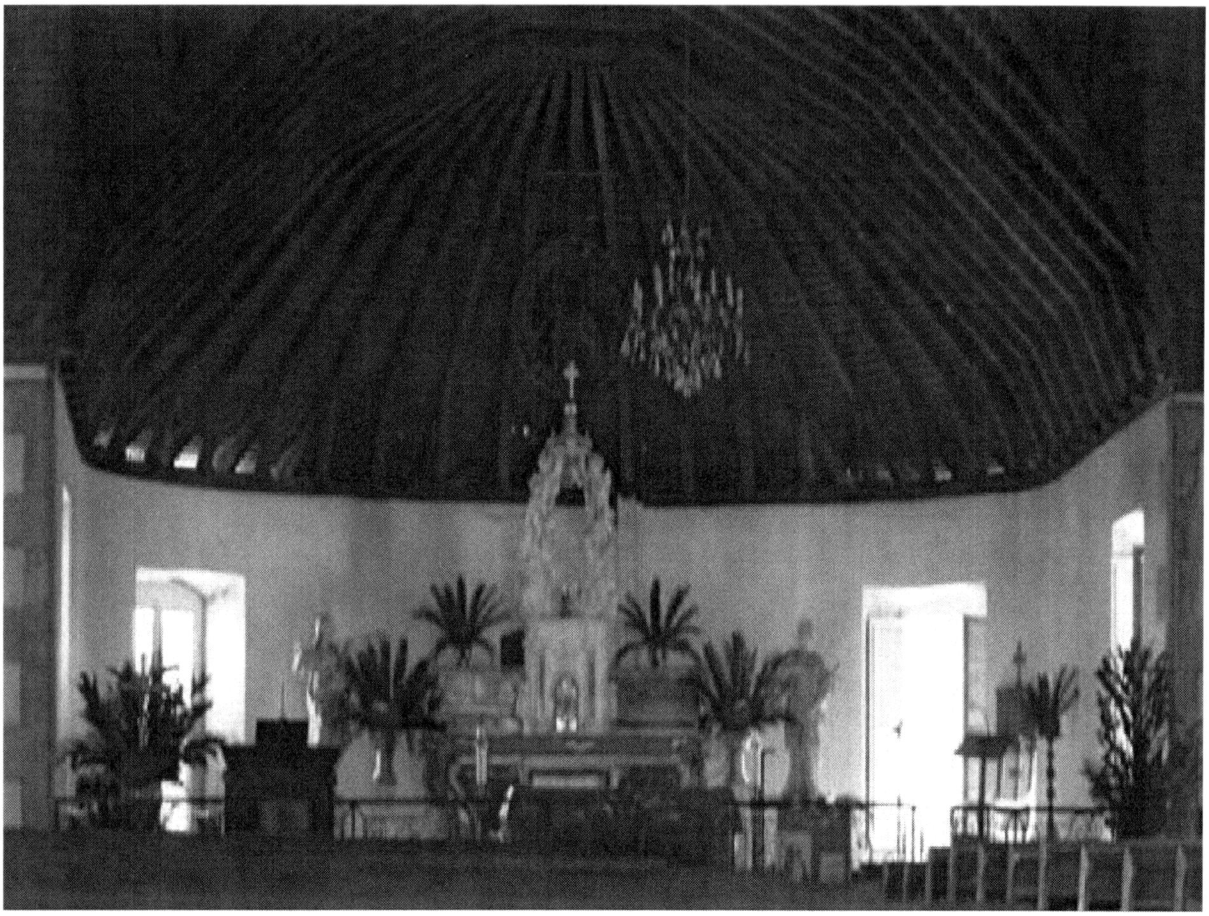

REMARKABLE CEILING OF ST. ETIENNE'S CATHOLIC CHURCH

I tried tracking our generator shipment from Entec with the UPS number Dave gave me over the phone. I was a little perturbed that he did not use DHL as I asked him to. The response indicated the parts were in St. John the capital of Antigua. It looked like the parts were moving along so I did not think to question the answer.

April 16, Easter Sunday, we took the dinghy over to town for the 9:30 a.m. Mass. When we walked into the church, it was 8:45 a.m. and the seats were filling up fast. By 9 a.m., there might have been 24 open seats. By 9:20 a.m., all the seats were filled, but the ushers kept packing people in. By time Mass started we were packed in like sardines and having a hard time breathing. Finally, the church bells rang and then the procession started with the bishop of Martinique and Guadalupe who was saying Mass. The whole Mass was also televised which seemed a little odd. The camera operators were not dressed correctly for Easter Sunday, as they looked sloppy, as if they were at a soccer game. There were only a handful of white French people at the Mass, which was odd since the majority of folks in the city were white. I have noticed the absence of whites at churches in other French countries even though they profess Catholicism. The black natives of the country seem to have the deepest religious faith.

Jim and Alli came over for an exceptional Easter Sunday dinner that Pat put together. Pat's contribution was chicken chutney served over rice and pineapple upside down cake. Alli and Jim brought the salad and ice for our drinks.

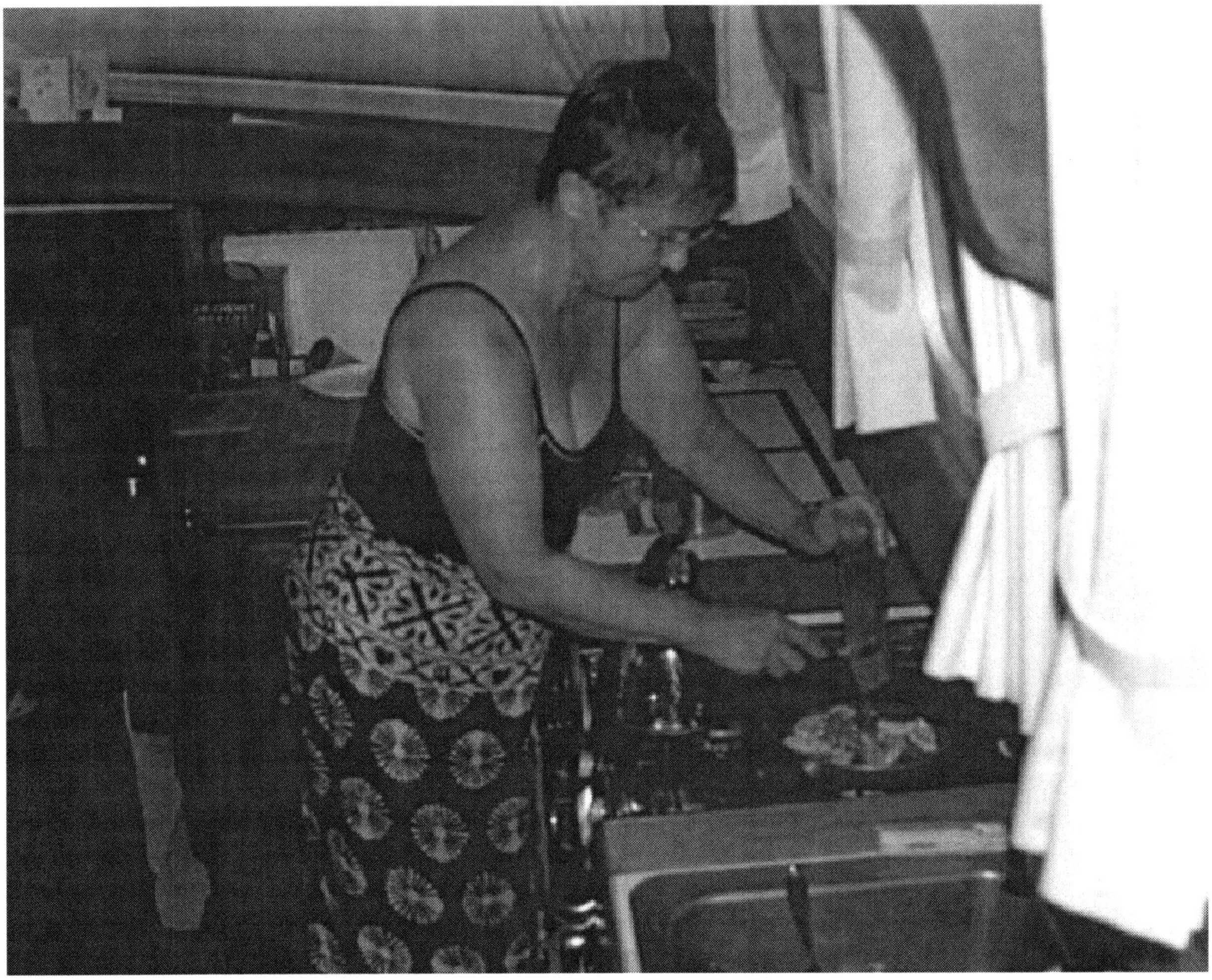

PAT'S GALLEY, EASTER SUNDAY, La MARIN, MARTINIQUE, APRIL 16, 2006

The next day Jim and Alli, pulled up their anchor, left Martinique and headed for Puerto La Cruz, Venezuela at 9 in the morning. Monday was a national holiday in Martinique so everything was closed with the exception of some restaurants. Not much to do, but be lazy. On Tuesday, everything was back to normal and our favorite internet café was open again. We checked on our gen-set parts again and they were still shown in transit, apparently stuck in St. John. This was the sixth day since they were shipped and UPS cannot un-stick them. I e-mailed Entec again and called them on the phone to see if Dave could do something from his end. Not much could be done was the answer. It did not sound right that they were stuck in Antigua since officials there should not be involved in the processing. The real block should be French customs in Martinique.

We were stuck so we took a tour of the local reefs on the *Aqua Belle.* The boat was rather odd looking on top, but inside, the boat had an air conditioned, underwater, viewing room that could seat about 80 people. The viewing was through large, thick, picture windows. It took about 30 minutes to motor out of the harbor to the reef site. The guide said we could expect to see around 15 types of fish and a variety of sponges and coral. The fish population was colorful and more interesting compared to several other reefs we have visited. We saw lots of parrotfish, sergeant majors, blue tang, blue chromis, and yellow-edge chromis. There was a smattering of spotlight parrotfish and butterfly fish. The old growth coral was not colorful, but it did not show signs of damage. It was too bad this excursion was unplanned as a number of impressive picture opportunities were missed. We figured the 2 hour trip was a good value, 22 euro per person. Afterwards, we had lunch at Ti Toqués (I think the name has something to do with "Ti's" hat), a nice French restaurant with a veal special that day, veal is one of my favorites.

No generator parts yet and it is April 20. I found on the internet a local UPS phone number for the Fort de France office, but no one there spoke English. I told our problem to the nice young woman at the internet café who did speak both French and English. She called UPS and found the parts had been there since April 13, not in Antigua as UPS tracking info said. Now, it made more sense that the parts were held up in French customs. In addition, that is why in foreign countries, DHL is superior to shippers like UPS and Federal Express. DHL maintains bonded agents in almost every country around the world and parts don't get stuck in customs. Our friendly internet young lady was also able to get the deliveryman, Willy, on his cell phone and found out the parts were in his truck. He was driving on the other side of the island.

I went over to talk to "Louis the dirty," but he was not in his workshop. The yard manager called him for me and said he would be back soon. He was doing his favorite thing, drinking beer with his buddies at the Mango Restaurant. It only took him 10 minutes to get back. I gave him Willy's number and he called, but Willy was too far away to make it to the yard that afternoon. So he arranged for the driver to deliver the parts to his house tomorrow. Pat and I were frustrated now so we went to the Mango to drown our sorrows in a cappuccino Chantilly (whipped cream on top of the cappuccino). Sure enough, his wife was not home for the delivery so we lost another day and we were missing the start of the Antigua Yacht Classic Regatta. Now Louis had to drive into Fort de France to pick up the parts.

Once we had the parts, it was only about 45 minutes to get everything back together. Louis only made one mistake. He put the new head gasket on the block and torqued down the head. That misaligned the gasket and it could not be salvaged. I saved the old gasket, matched the groves in the head, torqued the head down and crossed our fingers. The compression was good and the faithful Ferryman Diesel started right away. However, before we could pull anchor, Pat wanted to do some last minute grocery shopping. By the time I cleaned up the engine compartment, put the floorboards back and all the tools away, it was 3:30 p.m. The fuel dock closes at 5:30 and when we got there about 5 p.m., we had to wait for two big catamarans to finish fueling. After we filled up with Diesel, water, outboard fuel and ice, sunset was approaching. We decided to leave anyway since we could make Antigua in time for Karl and Deanne's arrival if we left immediately.

When we got about half way out the channel, doing 4 knots, we ran up on a sand bar. What I thought was a distant green channel buoy was actually a tiny sailboat with a dark green sail and we were out of the ship channel — not good. I was not paying attention and I wasn't watching the depth sounder. I tried to back off and turn the boat in a different direction with the bow thruster, but the boat was firmly stuck. The tide was going down, there was no wind, and daylight was fading fast. The good news was it was only sand and no rocks. I tried a "PAN-PAN" call on the radio to the French Coast Guard for assistance, but no response. Where was that patrol boat when we needed them? Pat and I were looking at each other like what else could go wrong. Then we heard an American voice say he would come over to see if he could help. His name was Dave and he had just anchored his Dashshew designed yacht, *Resolute*, a few hours before. In a few minutes, he was maneuvering a big inflatable with a 40 horsepower outboard alongside ***Our Pleasure***.

We discussed our options and decided to use Dave's inflatable to heel our boat over on its side and back out of the sand bar's grasp. We fed Dave 300 feet of our floating orange polypropylene line and attached our end to the main sail halyard. The first try nothing happened, but the second time he healed the boat far enough over to lift the keel off the bottom. We backed out easily to deeper water. Pat and I were congratulating each other when a fishing pirogue, traveling at high speed, ran between Dave's inflatable and us. Of course, they did not notice our polypropylene line floating on the water. Our frantic waving finally caught their attention, but too late. They managed to pull out the chain Dave had attached to his end of the line and that in turn broke his fuel line. So after rescuing us from the clutches of the sand bar, he was left dead in the water and we really felt bad for our Good Samaritan.

We were going to throw him a towing line to get him back to his *Resolute* when another pirogue came along and towed him back. We called him on the VHF channel we were using and offered to pay for his damaged hardware. He replied with a firm, "No." On the way out of the harbor, we called *Resolute* again on the VHF. His wife responded because Dave was in his inflatable trying to fix the broken fuel line. We asked for their e-mail address and tried a couple of times, but could not sort out the whole address. We heard Dave call us later, but by that time, he was unable to hear us. We really felt sad about the whole affair and hoped our paths would cross again so we could thank him properly.

We sailed on through the night past the remaining part of Martinique, past Dominica and past the Saints. These three islands are still in the Windward group of islands of the West Indies. The next island, Guadeloupe, is the northern most island of the Windward Island group, which extends south, all the way south to Venezuela. The British, because of their position relative to the trade winds, named them Windward Islands. Therefore, sailboats in the windward group would generally have to sail into the wind, a particularly difficult sailing angle for square-riggers.

GUADELOUPE

The next day we arrived at the French island of Guadeloupe around 4 p.m. At the northwestern end of the island is the pretty town of Deshales. Deshales has a nice bay with protection from most wind directions. We anchored at the western most part of the bay where we could get a good view of the town. Like most French towns, this one was also well cared for and inviting. There was a tall church tower with a red roof and many other interesting looking red-roofed buildings. It was getting late though and we were both tired. We took the pork roast Barbara and John (the yacht *Emerald*), gave us in Trinidad, set up the BBQ, and just hung out. It was a perfect evening to relax in the cockpit, breathe in the clean salt air, and take in the stars and lights of the town.

Antigua, the first Leeward Island of the West Indies archipelago was only 40 miles away now so we hit the sack early. Leeward means "away from the wind" because of their position relative to the northeast trade winds. In our case, as we head farther north, the trades will move closer to our starboard beam, a much better point of sail.

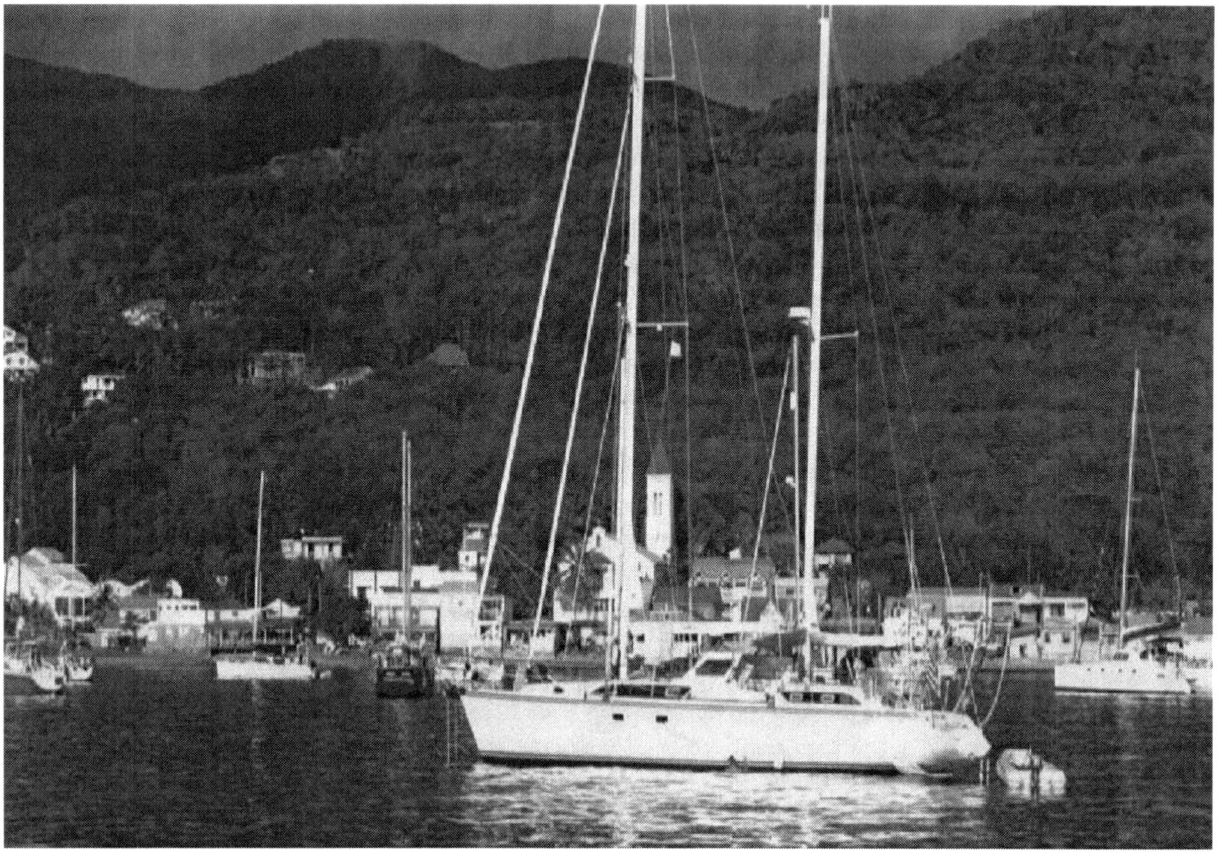

DESHALES BAY ON THE FRENCH ISLAND OF GUADELOUPE, APRIL 22, 2006

West Indies refers to all the islands included in the arc that extends from southern Florida to Venezuela. This archipelago contains hundreds of small and large islands that form a division between the Atlantic Ocean and the Caribbean Sea. The length of this arc of islands is roughly 2,000 miles. Christopher Columbus incorrectly named the island group, West Indies, because he thought they were close to India — what a difference a GPS would have made.

We left the next day right after breakfast to sail into Antigua at a reasonable time. From Deshales Bay, we could sail into Antigua just one day ahead of Karl and Deane's arrival. Keeping a time schedule in a sailboat is so difficult. You never know what problems will throw a monkey wrench into the best of plans. Even if no mechanical problems cause a delay, the weather can throw in an unforeseeable delay for days or even weeks. Along the South African coast, it took us 2 months to harbor-hop down the East Coast waiting for good weather to Cape Town.

ANTIGUA

We were pleased to arrive at Falmouth Harbor, Antigua around 3 p.m. on April 23. Of course, we were about a week and a half later than we had planned. The weather was glorious, but the wind angle required some motor sailing to stay on our course. We managed to arrive on the last day of the weeklong Classic Boats Regatta. Approaching Antigua we could see the big, highly varnished classic yachts on the racecourse. I got the camera out and waited until I had enough time to cross over the course without interfering in the race and close enough to take pictures. We only got honked at once. It was an unforgettable sight to witness all those beautifully maintained old classics racing under full sail. All the yachts had big crews dressed in nautical clothing hiking out along their rails. Those oversized sails generate lots of power.

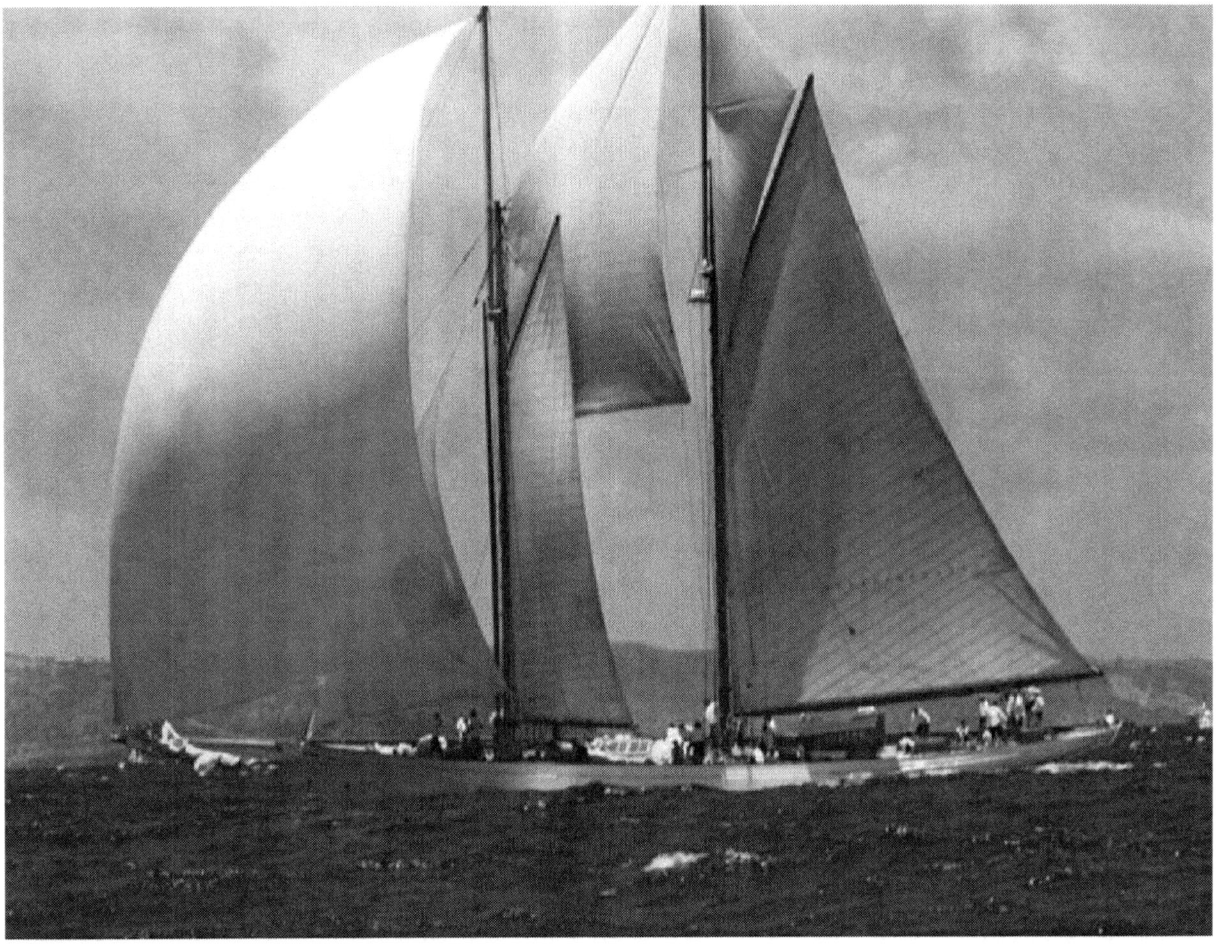

***ELEONORA*, 161 FEET OF CLASSIC ELEGANCE, ANTIGUA REGATTA 2006**

As soon as we anchored, we launched our dinghy and headed for customs and immigration. Their office was in the next bay, English Harbor, but they had left work early and we had rushed for naught. It was Sunday and we heard the thing to do on Sunday evenings, was to visit Shirley Heights. Sunday evenings brings everyone out for the views, the food, the drinks; socializing and to watch the sun go down. So we joined the crowd of probably 600 people, had a couple of rum drinks and BBQ chicken. There were 2 large bars and a couple of big 50 gallon drums cut in half for the BBQ'ing. Shirley Heights overlooks both English and Falmouth Harbors with views to Montserrat and Guadeloupe islands. We called Karl and Deane in Seattle to let them know we had made it to Antigua. They would be arriving late Monday so they made arrangements to stay overnight at an Antigua resort and meet up with us late Tuesday morning.

Monday we found all the officials at work. Customs and immigration costs were free, but the one-week port fee cost $66. We stocked up on groceries and talked to the folks at Falmouth Harbor Marina for a Tuesday morning berth. Next, we bought a pay-as-you-go SIM card from the local cell phone provider, Cable and Wireless. That was enough activity for one day. Tuesday morning we raised our anchor and motored over to the marina. The dock master, David, was there with two other line handlers to grab our lines. It was an easy transition.

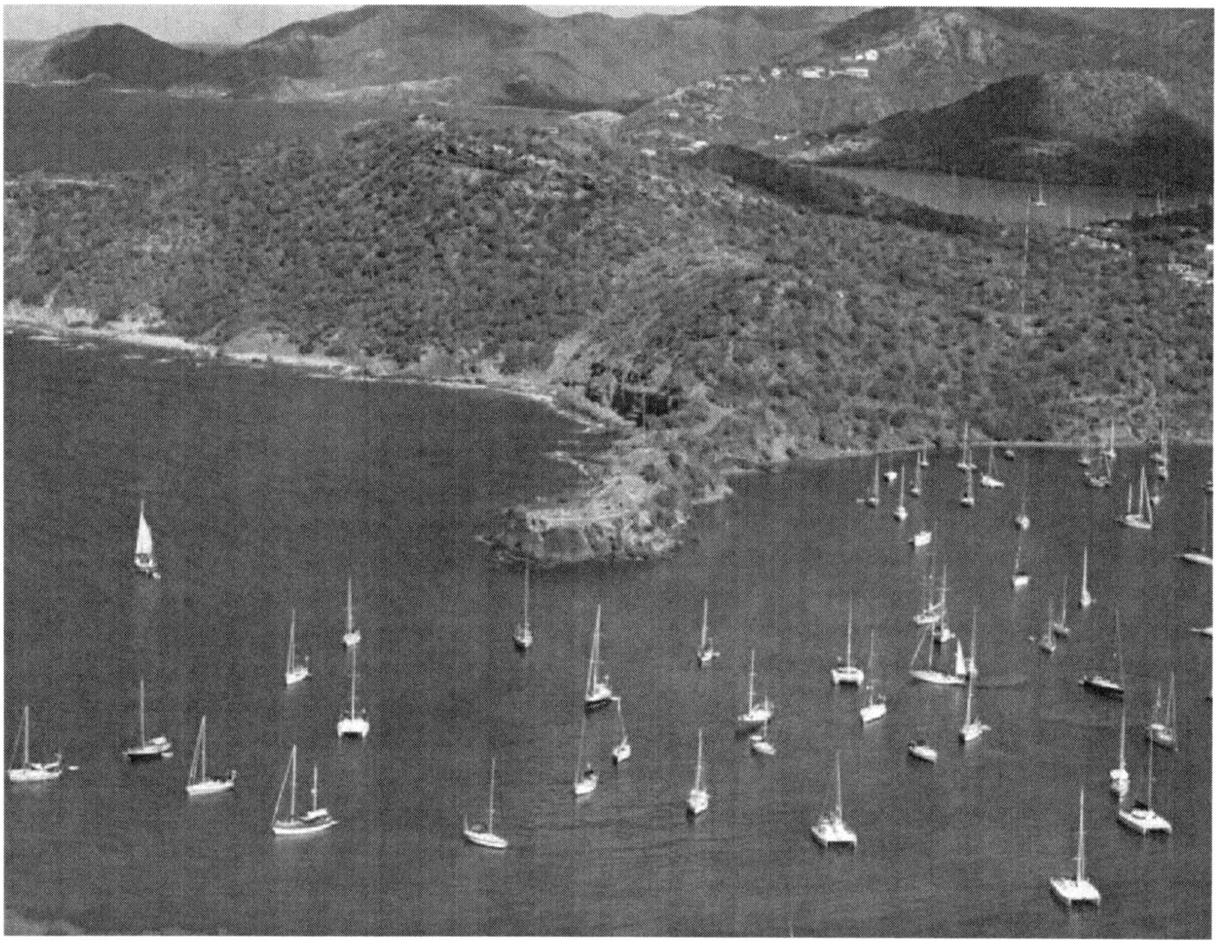

OUTER ENGLISH HARBOR FROM SHIRLEY HEIGHTS, ANTIGUA

The docks were recently built, ruggedly designed and perfect for super yachts. They were constructed of reinforced concrete on fixed concrete pilings. I don't think they would even shudder if run into by a super yacht. Designing these docks had been well planned as they were wide enough for commercial vehicles to deliver people, food, and fuel. The dock power available met U.S. standards and probably European standards as well. One of my Hubble® power connectors had to be replaced as it decided this would be a good time to quit. We thought the moorage costs were a bit steep at $100 a night and looking around we could see why. All our neighbors were multimillion-dollar yachts with big crews and equally big expense accounts. To them a few hundred dollars a night was all part of showing off your mega-yacht.

Karl and Deane found us at the marina around 11 a.m. They had run into officialdom problems though at the airport. Since they had flown in on one-way tickets, immigration wanted an official letter to say that they would be leaving Antigua as crew aboard ***Our Pleasure***. Karl had already drafted the one page document so all I had to do was sign it and stamp it with our ships seal. I felt sorry for Karl, as he had to taxi all the way back to the airport and taxi back to the marina. The taxi ride between the airport and Falmouth is about an hour. We were aware there could be a problem, but our timing uncertainties caused us to delay sending a definitive letter to Karl and Deane. Immigration would require an original letter and with my printer inoperative, I knew my letter would be late, but I knew Karl would be fast on his feet.

Well, unfortunately they got a young immigration officer who went by the book and wanted to send them back to Seattle. Only a senior officer's intervention found a reasonable compromise, which required Karl to deliver a crew letter to immigration by Tuesday. Luckily, with a little fancy footwork, we reached an acceptable conclusion.

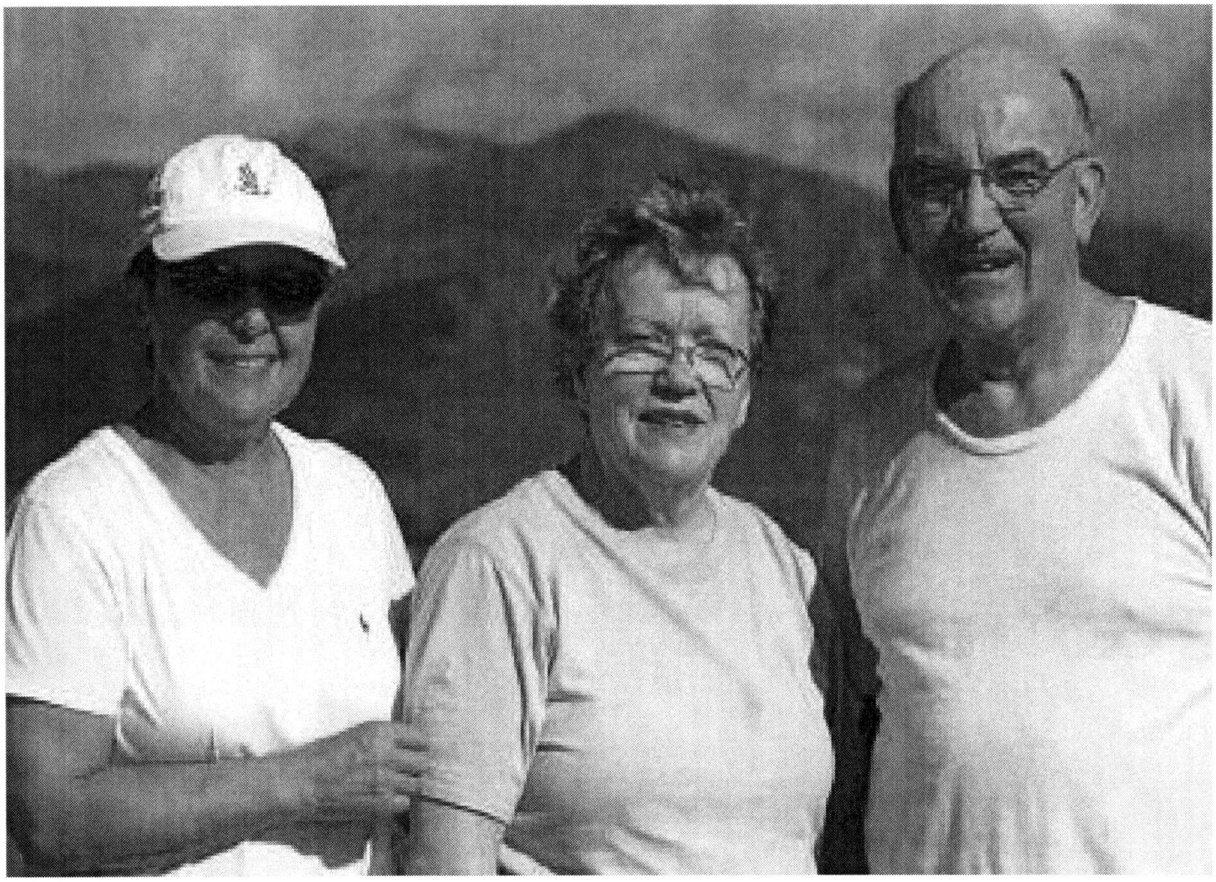

PAT, DEANE AND KARL ENJOYING SHIRLEY HEIGHTS

We spent the rest of the day wandering around Falmouth Harbor and Nelson's Dockyard over in English Bay. We poked around Nelson's Museum and thoroughly enjoyed looking at all the beautiful classic yachts moored at English Harbor. Nelson's Dock Yard at English Harbor is interesting for its old brick buildings where men worked to repair England's war ships in the 17th and 18th centuries. The buildings used for sail repairing and woodworking, all performed by skilled craftsmen, are still evident. Capstans that were turned by men, most likely slaves, to haul the ships up on the ways for repair, are still on the site. Horatio Nelson was stationed at English Harbor for three years when he was just a young naval officer. He is credited with molding the yard into a formidable repair facility. The area is also unique due to the land geography, which provides a natural protection for both bays. It would have been suicide for French ships to sail past the gun emplacements at Shirley Heights into the well-fortified bay.

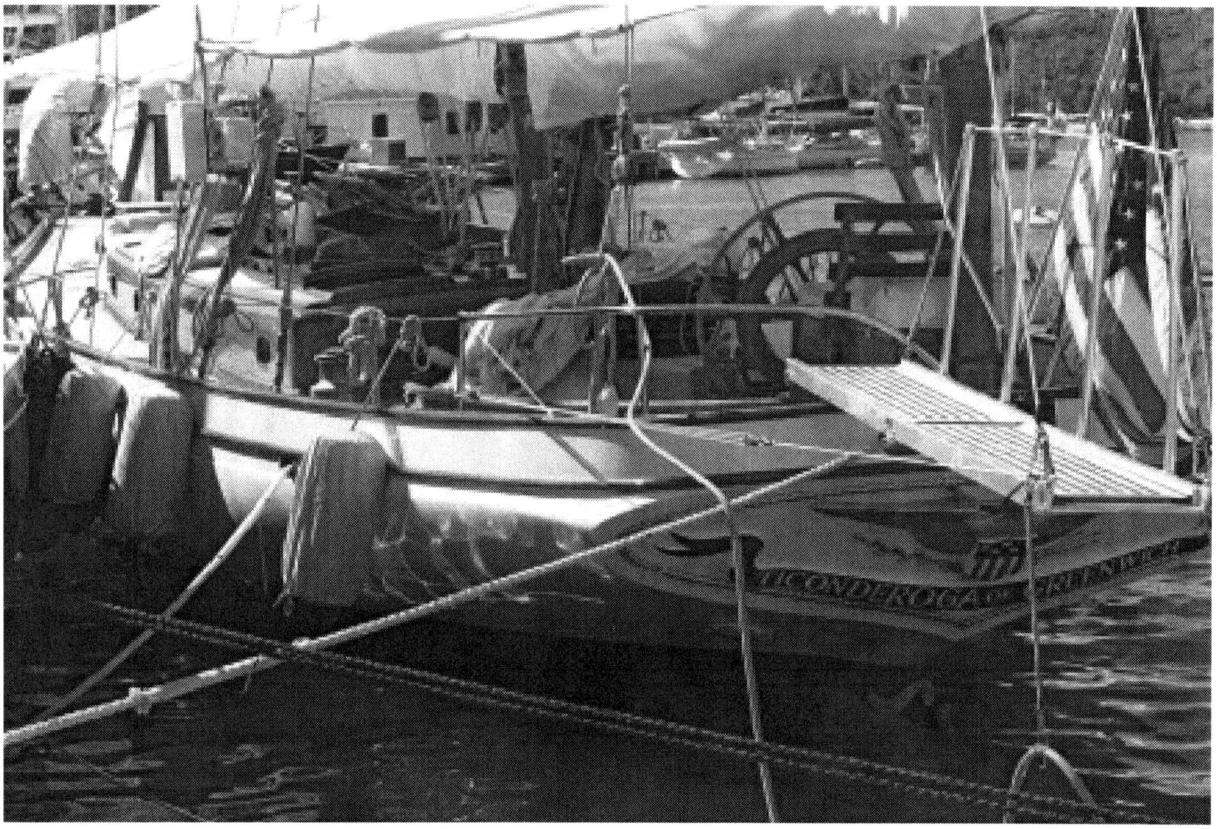

THE FAMOUS *TICONDEROGA* AT ENGLISH HARBOR, ANTIGUA

Our friends from Seattle brought us a fresh supply of coffee beans just as our Starbucks® supply was about to bottom out — it's a terrible thing to run out of coffee, especially when you are from Seattle. April 27 had rolled around again and it was time to celebrate another birthday. This time it was my 71st, which probably seems old to most young people, but I didn't feel old. Karl and Deane treated us to dinner that night. We got a good restaurant recommendation from a middle-aged English couple who were frequent Antigua visitors. So, off we went to the Galleon Beach Resort restaurant at English Harbor. The food was exceptionally good and fresh. I had my favorite, veal, the others "porked out" on shrimp and mahi-mahi. The English owner of the restaurant came over after dinner to chat with us for about 20 minutes. We complemented him on the fine dinner and he extolled the virtues of his experienced, black female chef. He was a likable friendly guy, full of interesting stories and tidbits about island life. The evening was picture perfect with hundreds of visible stars and boats in the harbor with their lights glimmering on the water — another great birthday celebration!

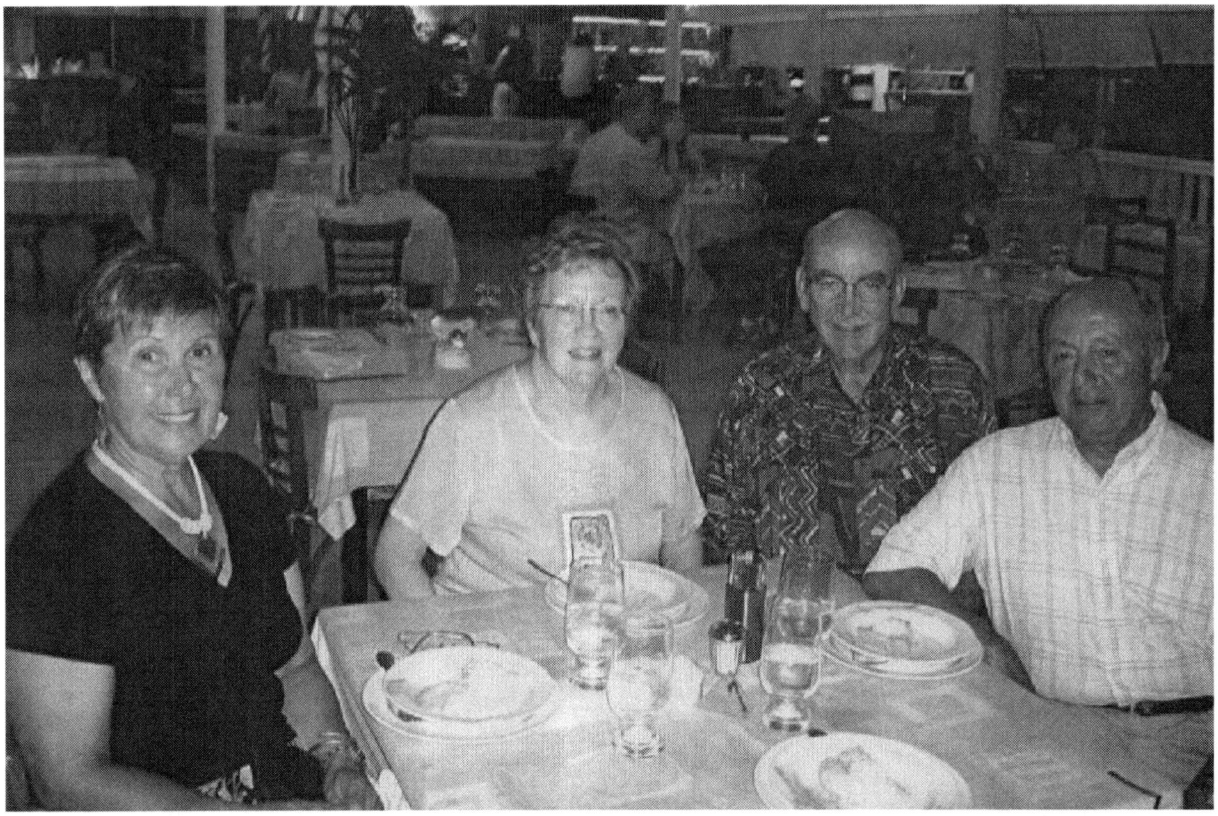

GALLEON BEACH RESTAURANT, PAT, DEANE, KARL AND CAPTAIN DICK

After 3 days in the marina, we checked out and moved into the anchorage at Falmouth Harbor. Anchoring for a day would give Deane and Karl more adjustment time to learn about our boat's systems used away from land. The next morning I started the engine about 5 a.m. to get an early start on the day. Karl also got up and watched the helm so I could operate the anchor windless. As soon as the chain tensioned up on the anchor I knew something was malfunctioning. The windless was straining to pull the anchor and the bow was being pulled down deeper into the water. The chain jumped on the gypsy a couple of times, peering into the water, I saw the problem. Wedged between the stock of the anchor and the anchor's plow type fluke was the largest collection of rocks, mud, shells, and coral I have ever seen on an anchor.

I don't know how much it weighed, but the windless is capable of lifting 1,800 pounds and it must have been close to its limit. We were actually lucky that the windless could get that mass close to the bow pulpit. I banged on the glob repeatedly with a hammer and crow bar, but that debris from the deep wasn't having any of it. Oddly enough, in my tool collection, I have carried a sledgehammer, but I had never used it during our 9 years of cruising. At first, nothing happened after hitting it as hard as I could. I was starting to doubt whether I could ever break it loose. Repeated blows finally dislodged small chunks, and then the pieces got larger. After several minutes of pounding, the massive collection of bottom debris finally cleared. That little tête-à-tête between the glob and me cost us at least an hour delay in our leaving time.

ST. KITTS

Our next port of call in the West Indies was to be the leeward island of St. Kitts about 60 nautical miles away. St. Kitts is short for St. Christopher as Columbus named her. St. Kitts has a pretty sister island named Nevis. These 2 islands make up the smallest country in the Western Hemisphere. They became independent of the UK in 1983 and have a mostly black population of fewer than 40,000. The original natives, the Carib Indians, defended their land against early French and English settlers, but some died from disease and the rest were mostly slaughtered. In the early years, the islands saw cannon balls exchanged between the French, British, and Spanish occupiers. The 1783 Treaty of Paris finally ended the fighting and the islands were ceded to Great Britain. The country is now a popular tourist destination because of its sandy beaches, green rainforests, plants and animals.

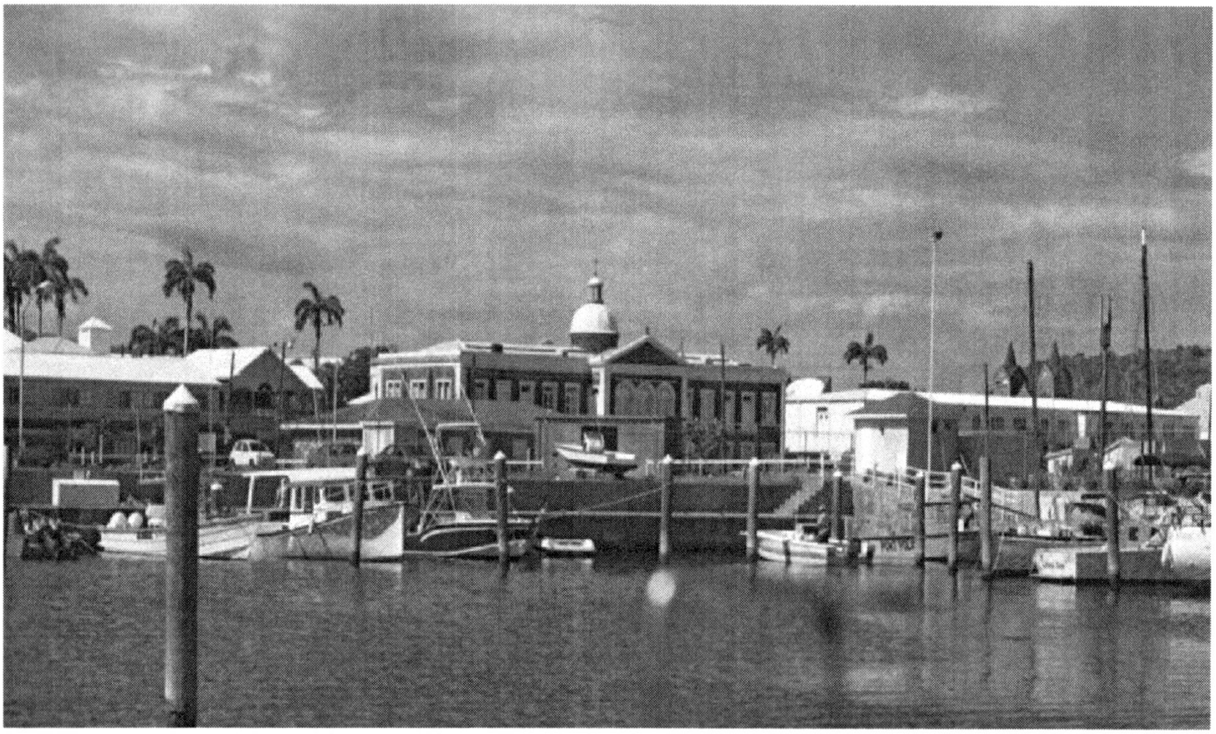

PRETTY TOWN OF BASSETERRE AS SEEN FROM PORT ZANTE, ST. KITTS

Under sunny skies and gentle breezes, we sailed into Port Zante at St. Kitts main town of Basseterre (French influence). The assistant marina manager met us at the dock and helped with our lines. We arrived late Saturday afternoon so everything was closed. The manager thought we could check into the country at the cruise ship terminal, which is next to the marina. When I got there, I heard singing to loud boom-box music. The singing was coming from a big black security guard. He yelled back to my inquiry: "The cruise ship terminal is closed for the hurricane season." With no one around and everything closed, I was in a quandary of what to do about immigration. That's when Basil of the Spice Island Taxi Service popped up and offered to take us on a tour of the island. We decided that would be a good thing to do on Sunday. He told us that customs and immigration could be taken care of at the airport — problem solved.

The showers at the marina were the best we had seen anywhere except they were not air-conditioned and there were no mirrors. The marina itself had limited space for visiting yachts and could handle about 6 more yachts. We were lucky to get a side tie along the heavy concrete breakwater. The slips with Mediterranean type moorings used wood pilings that had deteriorated below the water line. The pilings were not coated with antifouling materials and sea boring creatures had reduced their diameters by about 20%. The marina's new, massive stone breakwater, which was at least 10 feet above sea level, blocked our view of the ocean, but reduced wave action in the marina to zero. We heard that a small, earlier breakwater was destroyed in a hurricane a couple of years ago damaging boats in the harbor.

Sunday, we piled into Basil's taxi along with two other couples. They were sailing on *Happy Hour*, a yacht from the UK. Basil said the tour would take around three hours and the cost per person would be $12.50 — a good value. Off we went to the airport for customs and immigration. I was allowed to check-in and out at the same time using a few simple forms and no cash was needed. I got to their office just as an international flight arrived so it seemed like chaos everywhere. However, when I told them, I was off a yacht and wanted to check-in; I was ushered into a semi-quiet office. I was given one of the few chairs available and the corner of a desk to write on — nothing like preferential treatment.

The airport is located on the Atlantic side of the island near a good-looking Marriott Resort. The homes nearby that overlook the ocean, are large and ostentatious, so there is obviously wealthy people living or visiting the island. The islands adult literacy rate is among the highest in the Western Hemisphere at 97%. Basil explained they have a good education system and a mandatory schooling requirement for years 5 through 17. For higher education, the University of the West Indies has a nice campus on the island overlooking the Atlantic Ocean.

We drove by the Brimstone Hill Fortress on the northwestern coast, which is famous for repelling several attacks from France and Spain. At one point, France briefly regained St Kitts in 1782 after a month long siege of the fort. Some of our party didn't want to stop there, but from the road it was evident the fort had thick walls and was massively constructed. The forts location gave it such a commanding position that it was nicknamed, "The Gibraltar of the West Indies."

As we drove around St. Kitts, we saw remnants of the sugar mill industry, which the Government had shut down six months before we arrived. They were in the process of deciding how to best use their fertile land in the future. Coffee was mentioned as a good possibility. The country's gross domestic product averaged around $7,400 per person. For a West Indies country, they are doing pretty well. We saw some ancient hieroglyphs and stopped to talk to a man holding a green vervet monkey. Of course, he was looking for a donation. Our tour guide then took us to Ottley's, a restored 18th century sugar plantation. It is now a beautiful 35 acre resort, attractively restored with green lawns, royal palms and stone cottages. The Great House is beautiful, sitting high on a hill with encircling verandas and a vast expanse of manicured green lawns. The resorts restaurant looked inviting, but all everyone wanted was a cool drink on the big veranda. We stared at the calming ocean and swaying palm trees for a long time.

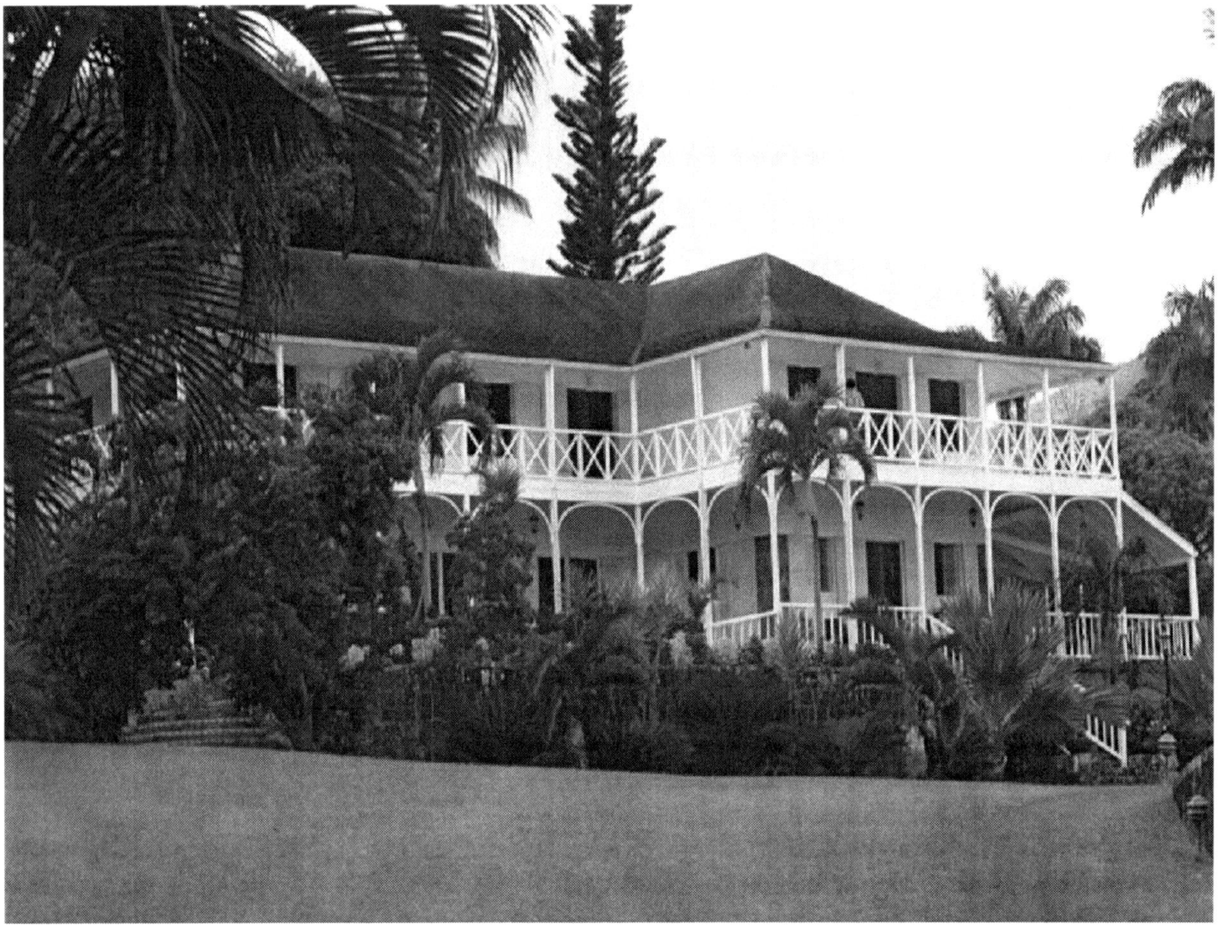

THE GREAT HOUSE AT OTTLEY'S RESORT, ST. KITTS

On May 1st, we took our early morning showers and found the marina guard was able to work out our bill and take our money. Our two night stay cost $105, which we thought seemed a little high. However, no fees were posted at the guard shack and the office was still closed. Sometimes, assumed trust is an important ingredient in foreign countries. We left St. Kitts and headed for St. Bart's (St. Barthélemy) about 47 nautical miles away.

ST. BARTS

There was not enough wind to sail so we used the ships engine. Pat baked a batch of tasty muffins around mid-morning, which were quickly devoured. We arrived about 4 p.m. and anchored as close to the harbor as we could, but still outside the harbor's breakwater protection. An international sailboat race had just ended at St. Barts and the inside harbor was full of boats. Our anchor spot was a little rolly when the wind was blowing, but tolerable. Karl and I launched the dinghy and headed for customs and immigration. St. Barts is a French island with lots of good-looking red-roofed buildings, well maintained and clean. One friendly and well-spoken young man handled customs and immigration. Check-in and checkout was only $5 and no moorage fees.

We were in the capital of St. Barts, Gustavia. It seems the French ceded St. Barts to Sweden back in 1784 so they could establish an entry at Göteborg for French goods. France got it back around 1877. Some of the street signs are still in Swedish a reminder of the islands history. St. Barts has many nice sandy beaches, hence, a good tourist industry. That probably accounts for all the expensive boutiques and up-scale restaurants. It was hot in town so the ice cream parlor became the destination of choice. The island is small at 8 square miles and with all the interesting shops in town to visit, touring other parts of the island lost its allure. We had lunch at a nice restaurant, picked up some fresh French bread, cheese, and groceries and headed back to ***Our Pleasure*** for happy hour. We planned to leave the next morning for Road Town on Tortola Island, the main island in the British Virgin Island group.

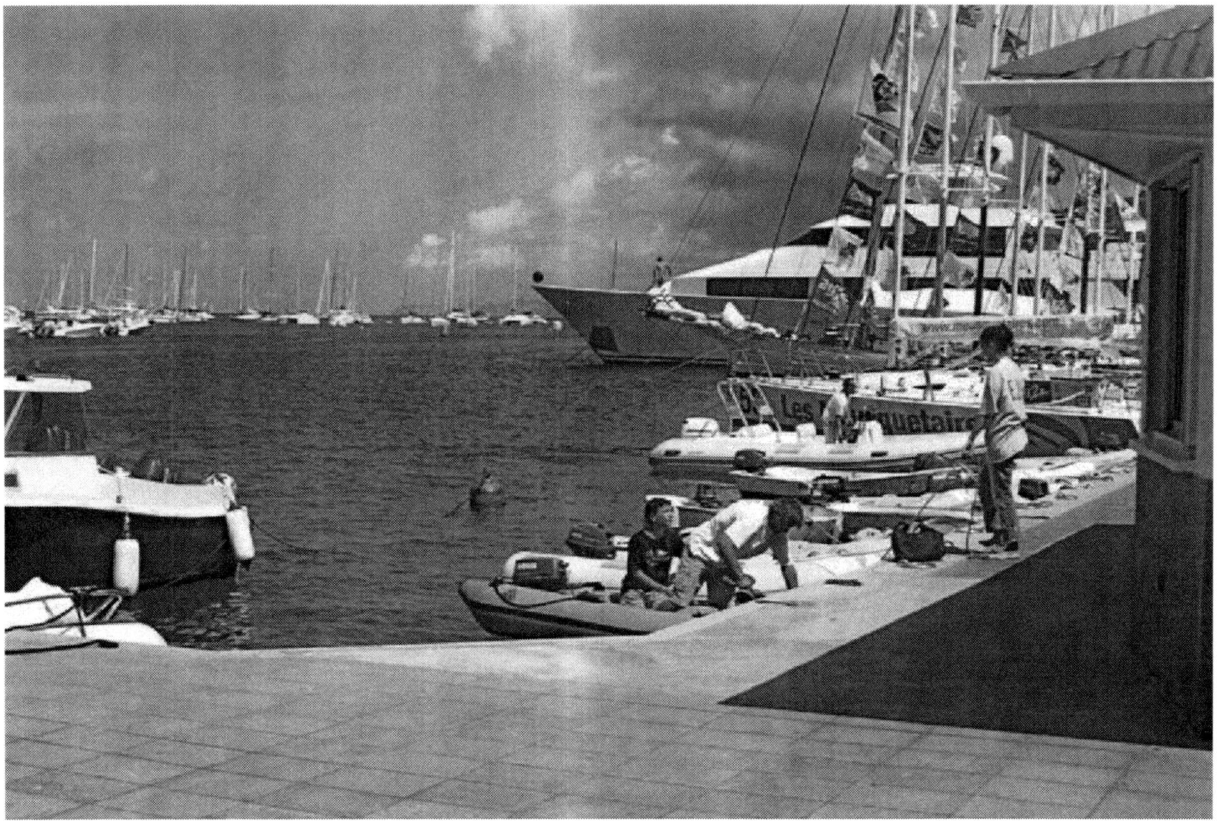

GUSTAVIA HARBOR, ST. BARTS

We left St. Barts harbor a little after 7 a.m. and headed for Tortola in light winds and a little chop. Road Town was about 120 miles away so we prepared for one overnight passage. Pat fixed a great lunch using French bread and ham from St. Barts. A heavy swell stayed with us all night and made sleeping difficult. We sailed into rain and stronger winds out of the SSE until the wind died around 11 p.m. Then a squall arrived, which kindly pushed us along at over 7 knots for an hour. In the morning, we found the wind blowing on our starboard bow and a westerly setting current. Those two tried to push us more west than we wanted to go. Pat and Deane were on watch during that time and noticed the boat was not staying on course. They woke up Karl and Karl got me up rather early in the morning. I checked the instrumentation against our backup GPS and verified that our navigation electronics were working correctly. Slight corrections to our heading and help from the engine put us back on course.

BRITISH VIRGIN ISLANDS (BVI)

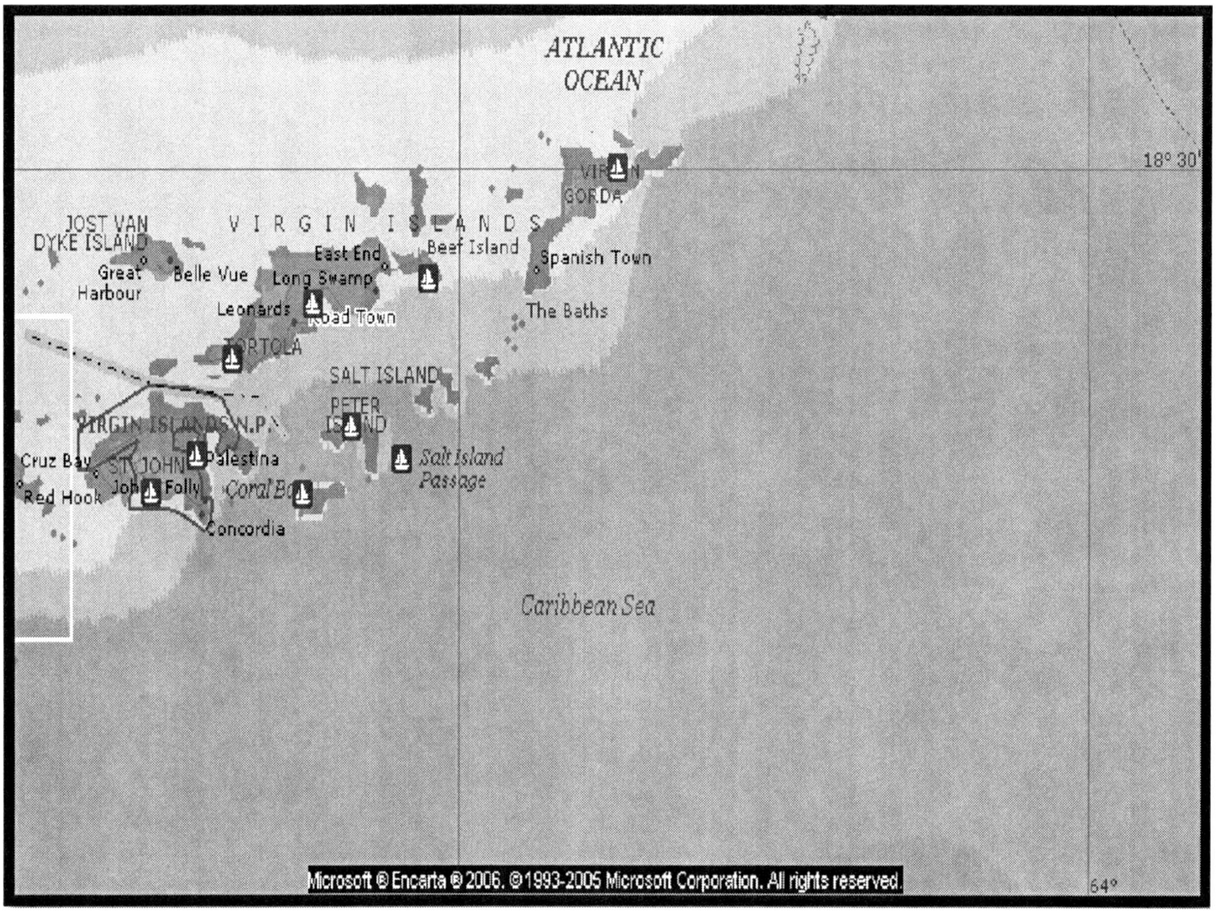

BRITISH VIRGIN ISLANDS ANCHORAGES

We passed Salt Island, BVI at dawn and sailed into the harbor at Road Town at 6:45 a.m. The location of customs and immigration was not obvious so we motored slowly around looking for a government building. I looked briefly at the depth sounder and mentioned to Karl that it was getting shallow. Karl noted that a ferry dock was right in front of us so it probably was deep enough for us. Well, we found out that the channel to the ferry dock was different from the channel we were following and up we went on a sand bar. This is too much, in all my years of sailing I have never been in intimate contact with a sand bar. Now, in just a month I managed to run up on two of them and boy, we were stuck. I couldn't go backwards, forwards, or move the bow off with the bow thruster.

We were deciding our next move when a nice young man from a local charter agency came alongside with a 160 horsepower inflatable. I made up a bridle and gave him a towing line. He pulled hard for several minutes, but no movement. He had another appointment and apologized, but he had to leave. I don't think the boat budged an inch. Karl and I were discussing how his prop would have been more efficient if his boat were facing forward instead of pulling backwards. Then a bigger boat from the Husky Towing Co. came along side. His boat was powered by two 250 horsepower outboards. We gave him the towlines and he pulled us off easily. However, his effort was not gratis, so Karl and I split the $150 charge. The towboat operator pointed out the customs office and the best place to anchor. Naturally, it was at the opposite end of the bay and their dock was in shallow water so we had to anchor in the bay. The entering procedure was simple and the officers were friendly.

The women went into town to do the laundry and Karl and I found a nice air-conditioned restaurant for lunch. The restaurant was also a Pusser's Rum store with many good-looking clothes and knick-knacks with the Pusser logo. Pusser's naval rum decanters with narrow necks and non-tipping wide bases were impressive. The restaurant featured a big variety of unusual rum drinks so I had to try a couple — I wasn't disappointed and the food was good.

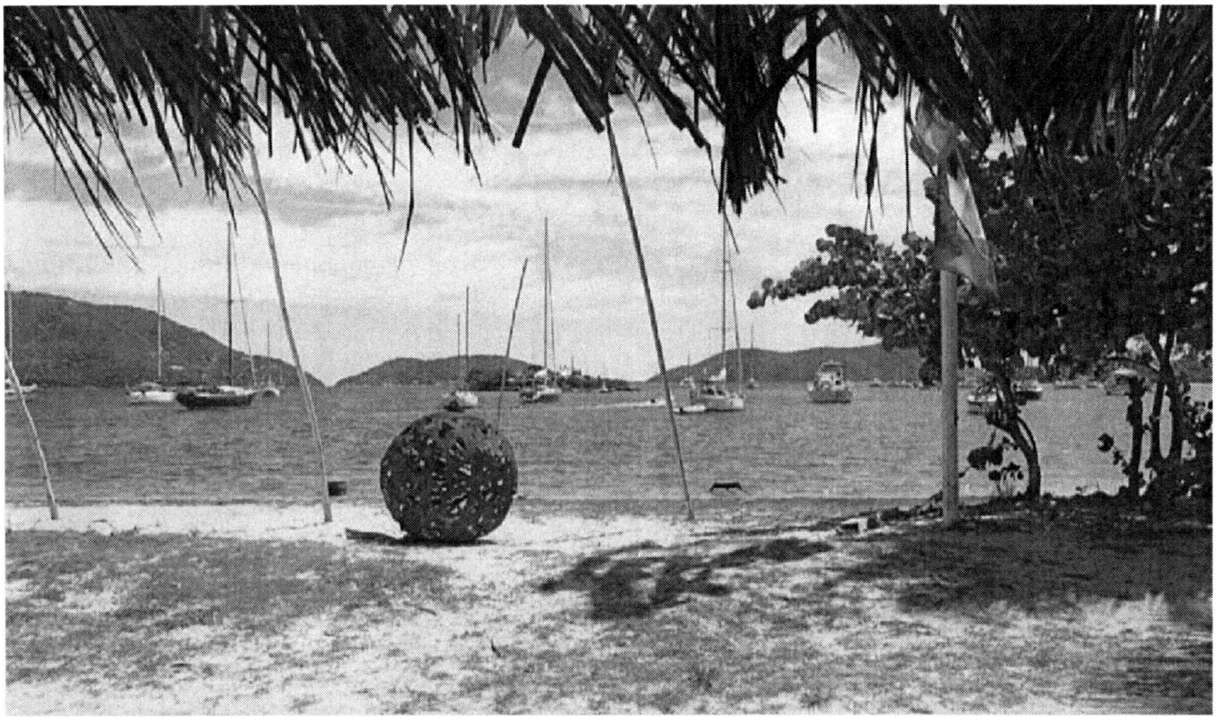

TRELLIS BAY ANCHORAGE AND AN ARTISTIC MOORING BUOY

Pusser's Rum was the official rum of the British navy when the British provided their square-rigger crews with rum rations. The men called these drinks of rum and water "grog." The word itself is interesting as it originated with an 18th century English naval man, Admiral Edward Vernon. His men nicknamed him "Old Grogram," which was shortened to become "grog." Now, George Washington's home, Mount Vernon, was named by George's half brother, Lawrence, who built the house. Lawrence happened to have served under Admiral Vernon for a while, hence the name "Mount Vernon."

The day passed by rather quickly so we stayed overnight in the harbor without moving our location. In the morning, we took our garbage ashore and I called my sister in Florida who was celebrating her birthday. Karl found a bag of ice cubes and we motored over to Trellis Bay at the west end of Tortola.

Trellis Bay was a nicely protected bay next to the Tortola airport. At the end of the bay, there were assorted art shops and restaurants. The next morning we dinghied over to the end of the bay and had breakfast at one of the restaurants along with a good cappuccino. After breakfast, Pat and I went for a walk along the beach while Karl and Deane walked over to the airport. They planned to leave ***Our Pleasure*** in Puerto Rico and needed information on flights from PR to Seattle. We tried to make flight reservations at an internet café, but all the price info on Expedia's web page was for round trips.

One of the local artists has collected old rusted sea buoys that are about four feet in diameter and cut holes in them. The holes though are clever design images of people, animals and objects found in the sea or on the beach. There were quite a few of these modified buoys all over the beach. Before leaving the bay, we had to find the people who owned the buoy where ***Our Pleasure*** was moored. There were lots of buoys in the bay with several different markings. It turned out ours belonged to one of the beach cafés and the cashier gladly accepted our $25 for one days use. From Trellis Bay, we were in a good position to visit another British island, Virgin Gouda and the Bitter End Yacht Club. The British Virgin Islands are better maintained and clean compared to the American Virgin Islands. Virgin Gouda was not very far away, so we did some sailing and arrived around 2:30 in the afternoon. The Bitter End Yacht Club is a delightful place with good-looking bungalows on the hillside, a hotel, a grocery store, lounge, beautiful restaurant, swimming pool, fuel dock and limited dock moorage, but many mooring buoys.

The water in the bay looked clean enough to run the water maker and keep our supply topped up. The water maker ran all right, but there was a smallish stream of water coming out one of the high-pressure end fittings. I turned off the water maker and while unscrewing the leaking, quarter inch diameter, brass nipple, it broke off. Apparently, the material differences between the stainless steel end fitting and the brass nipple caused an electrolysis problem. The threads of the brass nipple were paper-thin. I was lucky to have an easy-out tool that fit the brass piece broken inside the stainless plate. Then, I felt really lucky to find another nipple to replace the one that broke. With everything back in place, we were again making water without leaks. Good drinking water is so vital that I go to great lengths to make sure it is not wasted. We have often witnessed the hardship of poor water quality forcing islanders to boil their well water when their stored rainwater runs out.

Sunday morning, Pat called the hotel reception desk to see if there was a church service on the island — nope. So we jumped in the dinghy to investigate a nearby island called Saba Rock. Saba Rock is in the north sound of Virgin Gouda where the snorkeling is said to be quite good. It is not a very large island, but big enough for a few small docks, a ferry service and a small resort with a good-looking restaurant. We wondered around their gift shop and Pat found another unusual charm for her world-travel, charm bracelet. The charm features a piece of silver encased in a gold jacket in the shape of a fish. The silver is from the Spanish treasure ship, Nuestra Senora de Atocha and is a reproduction of a Spanish treasure coin. The ship was on her way to Spain when she was sunk by a hurricane in 1622, west of Key West Florida. Mel Fisher found the ship in 1985 after 20 years of searching. The ship had quite a load of gold, silver, and precious gems valued at hundreds of millions of dollars — Mel and his treasure hunters sure had a lot of patience. Oh, a stay at the Saba Rock resort costs $150 off-season and $550 in season.

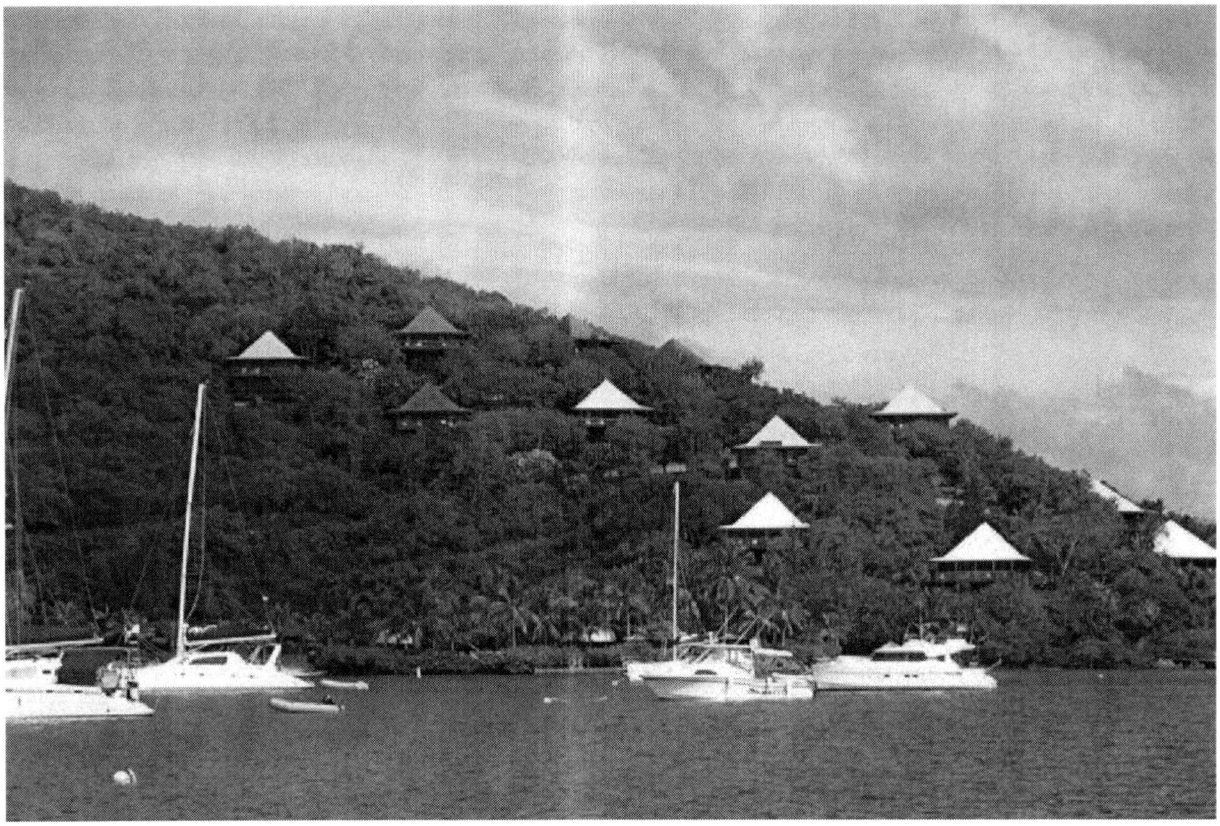

BITTER END YACHT CLUB, VIRGIN GOUDA, BVI

Back at the Bitter End Yacht Club, we dodged the little carts carrying tourists back and forth from the bungalows to make it unscathed to the restaurant. Dinner was a bit pricey at $125 per couple, but for an English restaurant, the food was very good. However, it is hard to ruin a good cut of prime rib. The dinner included a freshly baked loaf of bread, vegetables, salad, Yorkshire pudding (of course), dessert and good coffee. Everyone was impressed with the restaurants décor. There was a lot of rich mahogany paneling, big heavy beams on the ceiling and slowly moving fans reminiscent of an old Bogart movie. The chairs were quite comfortable padded rattan chairs. The lighting had an East Indian theme and all together, the restaurant was the kind of place everyone felt comfortable enough to linger well into the evening. We did some good thinking ahead by using the resort's water taxi service. After dinner, the wind had risen and getting back to ***Our Pleasure*** in our inflatable would have been a totally butt soaking experience.

We left the Bitter End on May 8 and headed for Little Harbor on Peter Island, BVI. The wind was blowing 12 knots over our starboard side, which made for a slow, but easy sail to Peter Island. The harbor was small, well protected, and quiet with only a couple of other boats. We all tried a little snorkeling in the harbor, the coral was sparse, but we found many colorful small fish. After breakfast the next day, we moved over to Norman Island and Bight Bay another island in the BVI group. Norman Island was a short trip, only three nautical miles.

We picked up a moorage buoy near the old lumber trading schooner, *William Thornton*. The *William Thornton* has been anchored is this harbor for years and has been converted into a popular restaurant and bar. Dr.

Thornton, in 1792, designed the original U.S. capital building. He was also a medical doctor, but how the American named schooner became moored in a British territory is unknown. We arrived late in the morning and not much was happening in the bay or on the schooner. Soon the runabout *Deliverance* was alongside and rafted to our starboard side. The crew was a young couple operating a marine delivery service for boaters. They stopped at all the boats in Bight Bay and other islands to sell drinks, fresh baked goods, and ice cream. It was a much-needed service, as many of the islands do not have stores. One appreciated service was the collection of our garbage, which gets smelly fast in hot latitudes.

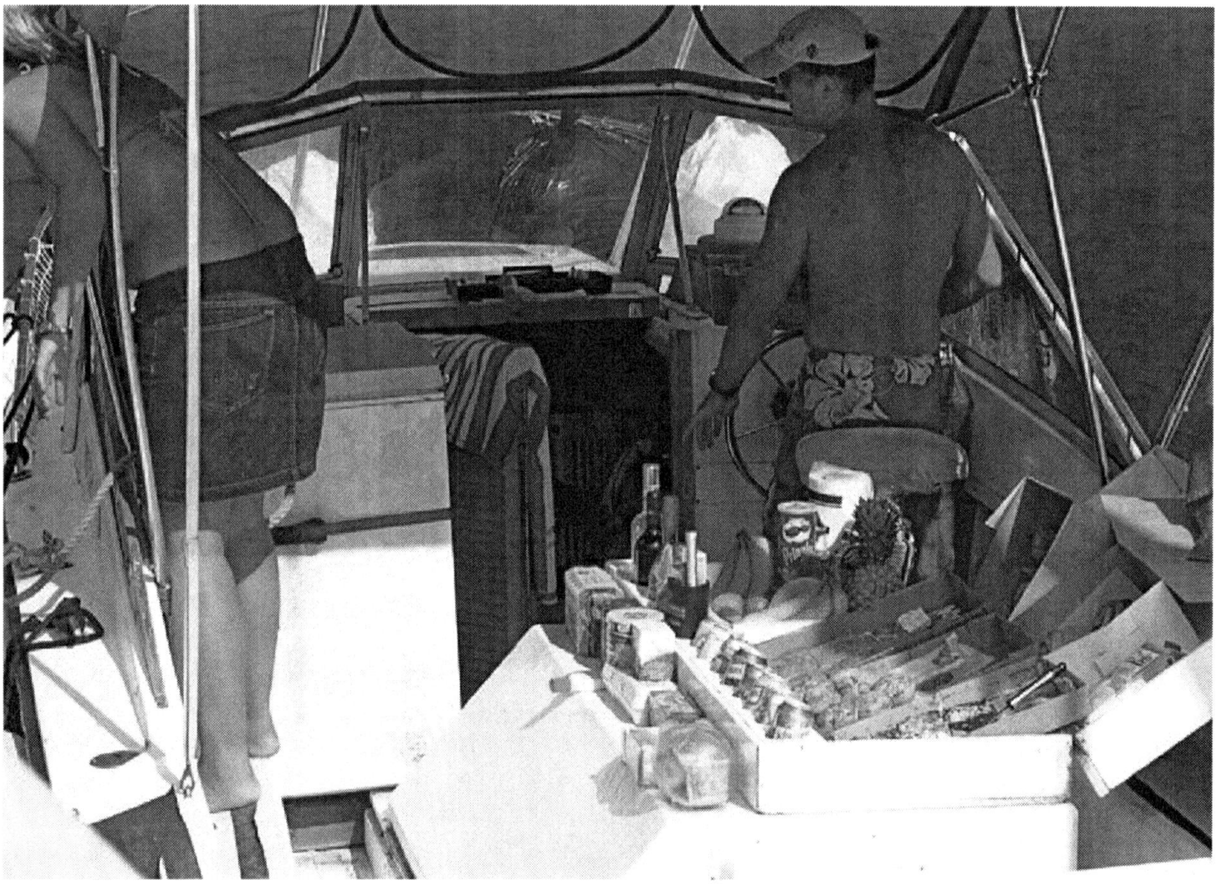

***DELIVERANCE*, A FLOATING MINI-MART, MAKING THE ISLAND ROUNDS, BVI**

We took the dinghy over to the *Thornton* for lunch. We ordered the normal stuff like cheeseburgers, fish and chips, and chicken burgers. There was only one other couple there so we thought it was probably not very popular. Well, that changed fast when the dive boats started arriving for lunch with loads of scuba divers. We went back to ***Our Pleasure*** to watch all the activity. Soon, many dive boats rafted alongside the *Thornton*, a young crowd dressed in bathing suits, and skimpy bikinis filled her decks. Their galley grill was polluting the bay with white smoke from the throng of meat eating athletic type bodies and the hullabaloo could surly be heard all the way to Tortola. The lunch bunch must have been consuming liberal quantities of beer with their hamburgers because throngs of them were diving, jumping and milling around the upper deck of the *Thornton's* stern. In no time, merrymakers were jumping off the stern sans clothing. Our moorage location close to the *Thornton* was perfectly suited to capture all the levity on video camera. When we were onboard the *Thornton*, a poster promised a free T-shirt for jumping into the water full-Monty — with courage from alcohol, many were up to that challenge.

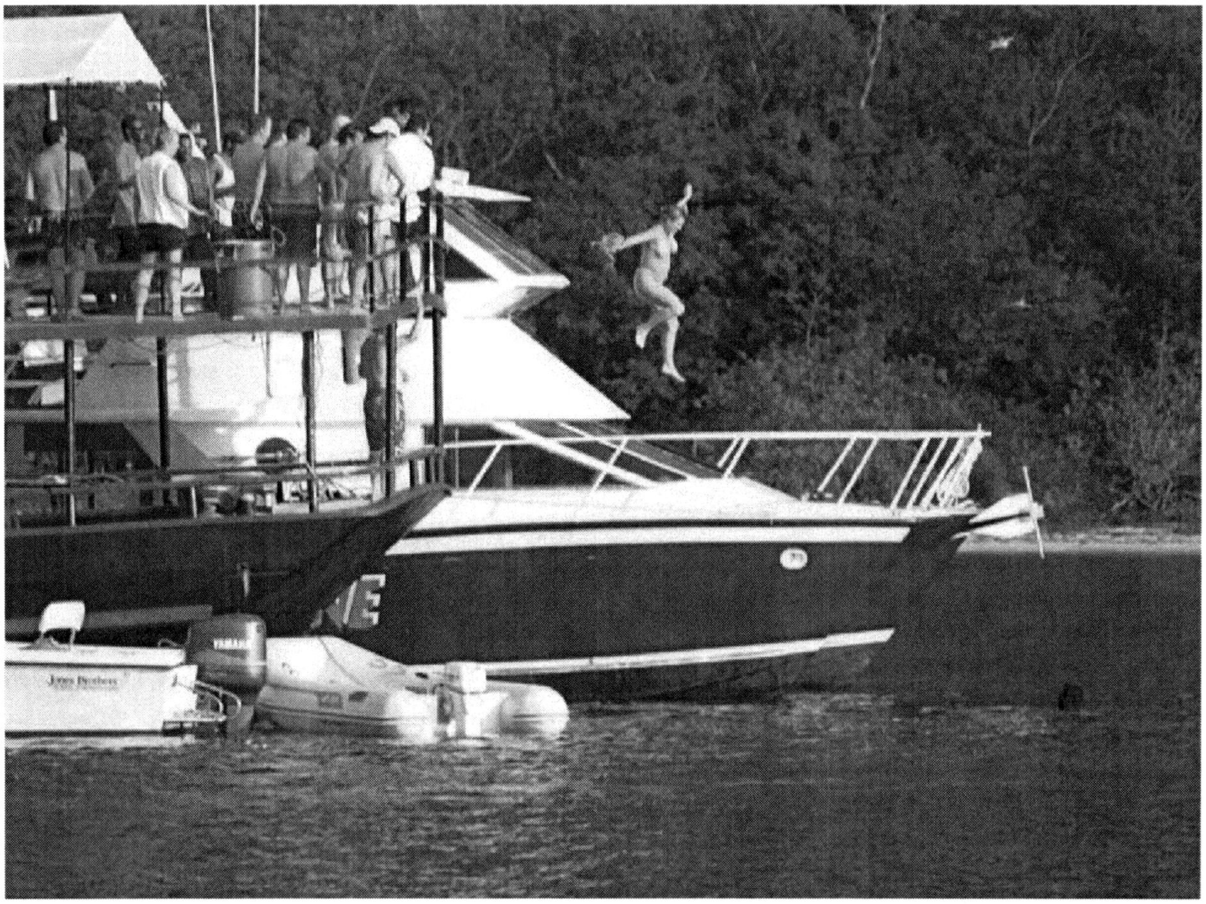

JUMPING OFF THE *WILLIAM THORNTON*, FULL-MONTY

The entertainment went on for hours. I doubt if many divers did any scuba stuff after that lunch. Pat pulled me away from my camera to take our dinghy over to the caves near the entrance to the bay. The caves are setup for snorkeling or scuba diving with mooring buoys and floats to tie up small boats and dinghies. One cave went a long way into the rock and the other cave was rather small. By dinnertime, most of the party types had left the *Thornton* and the bay was peaceful once more. We enjoyed tuna fish sandwiches on ***Our Pleasure*** for dinner and relaxed in the fading light.

To clear out of the British Virgin Islands we had to go to Sopa Bay at the west end of Tortola Island. Sopa Bay is a nice, well-protected, deep-water bay. The British government has placed plenty of mooring buoys there that are boating friendly for customs and immigration services. Once the anchor was firmly set and the dinghy launched, we rowed over to their office. There was a crowd in the office, but they handled the paper work quickly and efficiently. After checking out, we all rowed over to the small, attractive looking town at the other end of the bay. We completed our grocery shopping at a market and ate lunch at another Pusser's rum store and restaurant. I found a colorful shirt in the store with the names and flags of all the Islands of the West Indies, a little tacky, but fun.

AMERICAN VIRGIN ISLANDS

It was only a hop, skip, and jump over to the next group of islands, the American Virgin Islands. This group of three islands and 50 islets was purchased from Denmark in 1917 to establish a naval base to protect the Panama Canal. They are in the Lesser Antilles chain of the West Indies. The closest island was St. John and we arrived in the late afternoon while customs and immigration were at their peak levels. St John's harbor is small and busy and of course, there is nothing helpful in this American island like a dock or buoys for check-in. We had to anchor at the edge of a small boat anchorage with our stern slightly in the boat channel.

At their office, it was a madhouse. Every tourist coming back from the British islands by ferryboat had to check-in. I wasn't allowed to break into a tour group, I had to sandwich myself in between groups. After they determined I was checking back in to the U.S. after 9 years of cruising they found a private space for me to fill out their four page questionnaire. The form had questions like name all the ports visited, as if I carry my logbook around with me. I must have looked perplexed because one of the young immigration officers came over to help. I must say, she was quite nice. She shortened the form's questions to a pertinent few and I was out of there in no time. Leave it to the U.S. government to put out the longest form with the most questions we have ever seen.

Back on ***Our Pleasure***, the wind or tide had changed and our stern was now well into the boat channel. The channel is neither deep nor wide. Ferryboats leaving the harbor, to avoid hitting our stern, had to move to shallower parts of the channel. Well, that did not make them happy and I was getting the finger and hearing some bad language with attitude — ah, we must be back in America. I tried shouting back that they should complain to the government about the objectionable harbor conditions. I'm sure they ran with that cause.

After putting up with all the dissension, we retrieved our anchor and motored along the south coast of St. John to Caneel Bay. This bay is full of well-maintained U.S. Park's Department buoys thanks to the generosity of Laurance S. Rockefeller, son of John D. Rockefeller. Back in 1956, this philanthropist gifted the U.S. government 5,000 acres of St. John for a national park. The government then established the Virgin Island State Park, which now claims three quarters of the island (14,689 acres). Rockefeller's gift was contingent on preserving the coves, hills, tropical vegetation, and scenic beaches. By the looks of things, the Park's Department has done an outstanding job. Most of the hilly island is lush and green with beautiful beaches and clear water.

The weather was turning dark and overcast when we dinghied into the resort to pay the $15 moorage fee. The Caneel Resort is a beautiful place with manicured lawns and vibrant flowers everywhere. The resort started life from the restoration of a Danish colonial sugar plantation and mill. One of their restaurants is further up a hill that overlooks the main grounds and hotel. The windows are open frames of heavy stone and dark wood.

The breathtaking views are never ending all the way to St. Thomas. We looked around their gift shop, but it was very pricey. During the night, we witnessed intense lightning storms followed by a tropical downpour. It was muggy and hot enough that Karl had to find his way to the cockpit to get a little shuteye.

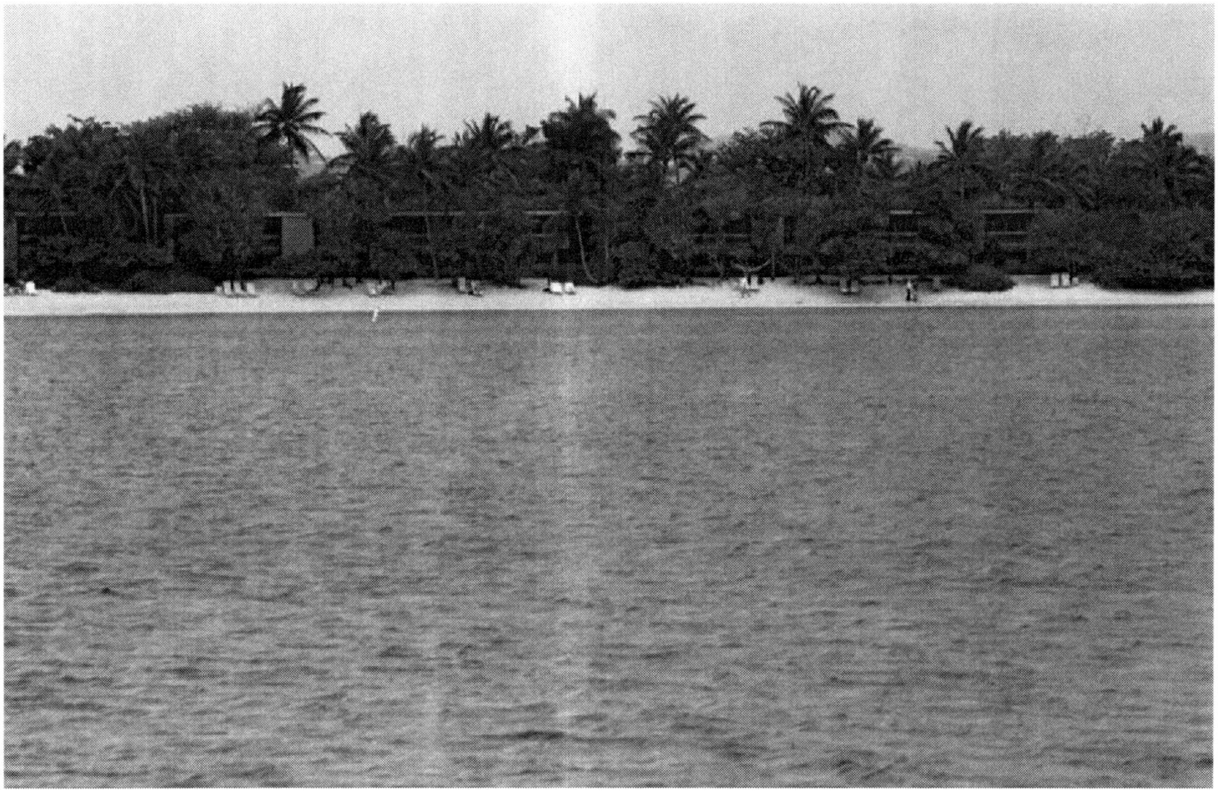

CANEEL BAY RESORT AND ITS BEAUTIFUL WHITE SANDY BEACHES

The next bay same island, Webster's Bay, was another perfect spot with plenty of mooring buoys and sandy beaches. The weather had improved significantly now and we went over to the beach to swim and pay our moorage fee. Well, we almost gave up on paying the moorage fee, as we couldn't find the deposit box. We walked from one end of the beach to the other. A man talking with friends saw Karl with the envelope and asked him if he was looking for the deposit box. Problem solved. Overgrown shrubs obscured it. When we got back to the boat, we found a bunch of sharks wanting a handout. I think they were probably nurse sharks because of all the serrations near their head. They looked like they were having the time of their lives going after our stale bread. We had a great time feeding and watching them. After running out of bread, Pat found some stale Jacob's Bran Crackers. There were probably about six sharks; including small ones that might have been newly born. The largest were around four feet long.

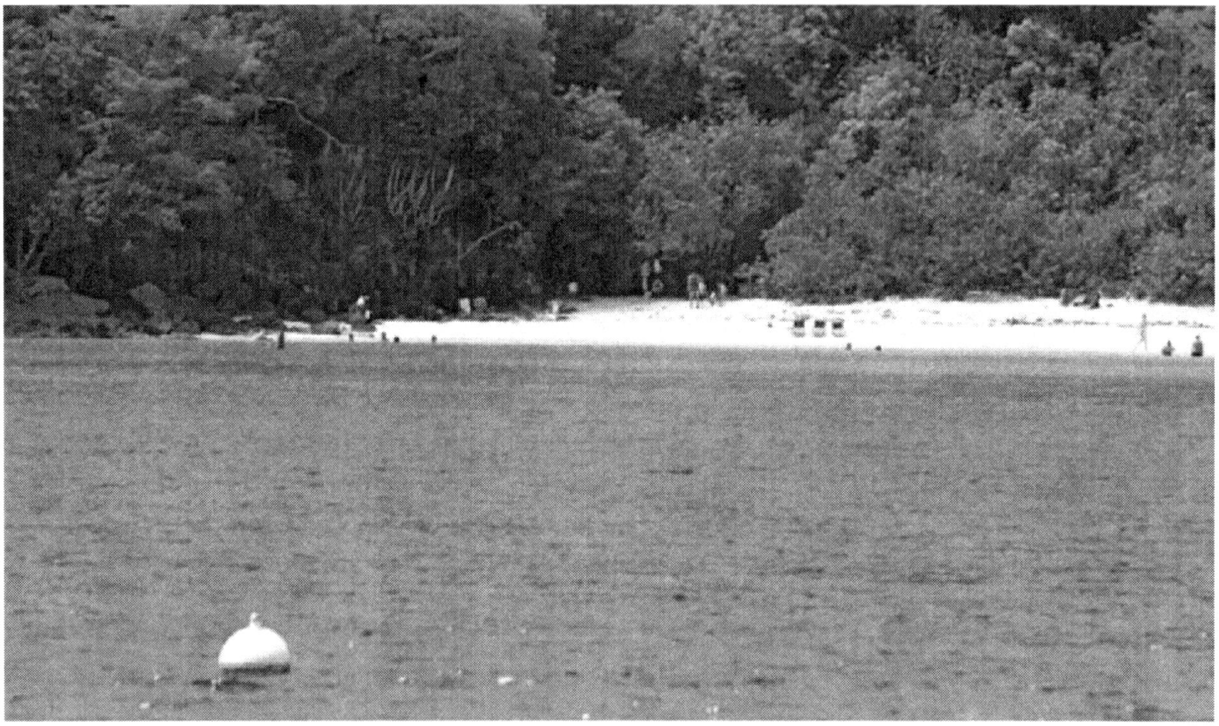

WEBSTER'S BAY, ANOTHER PART OF ST. JOHN'S PARK SYSTEM

From Webster's Bay we motored over to the main American Virgin Island, St. Thomas. The Danes first colonized St. Thomas back in 1666. With slave help, the plantations on the island flourished during the 17th and 18th centuries. However, a slave revolt on another island, St. Croix, led to their emancipation in1848. But without slaves, the economy of these islands took a nosedive. These islands changed hands several times between Denmark and Britton until the U.S. paid Denmark 25 million dollars in 1917. Since then, tourism has been the most vital part of their economy. Tourism provides employment for a population of fewer than 12,000 in retail sales and services for recreation, motels, hotels, and restaurants. Cruise ships stopping at St. Thomas bring close to 2 million people each year. Our first stop was supposed to be the chief port of the American Virgin Islands, St. Thomas Harbor. The island's capital city is named for a 17th century Danish queen. Now with an English derivation the spelling has changed slightly to Charlotte Amalie. But yachties and others have a nickname for this harbor city, "Charlotte's Armpit." If you have visited Charlotte Amalie, you probably get the connection.

According to our cruising guide, a new super yacht marina was to open in Jan. of 2006 and that was our intended destination. Well, we saw concrete pilings and dock foundations, floats for debris containment and construction equipment, but no yachts or people and it was Saturday. Seeing this marina was many months or maybe years from completion, we started looking for alternatives. There were other yachts anchored around the harbor, but I was not looking for another anchorage. We moved slowly west through a narrow, but shallow channel looking for another marina when we found the Crown Bay Marina. We did not know it was there as the chart didn't show it and neither did our guide book. We could see sailboat masts behind the massive breakwater.

I moved closer to the breakwater so I could read their entrance sign with the marina's name and the radio channel number they monitor. When I called to ask for a slip, it took the manager a few minutes to assign a berth for me. They told me to call back when I was at the entrance so they could make sure the narrow entry was clear of boat traffic. I informed them we were already there and the entrance was clear.

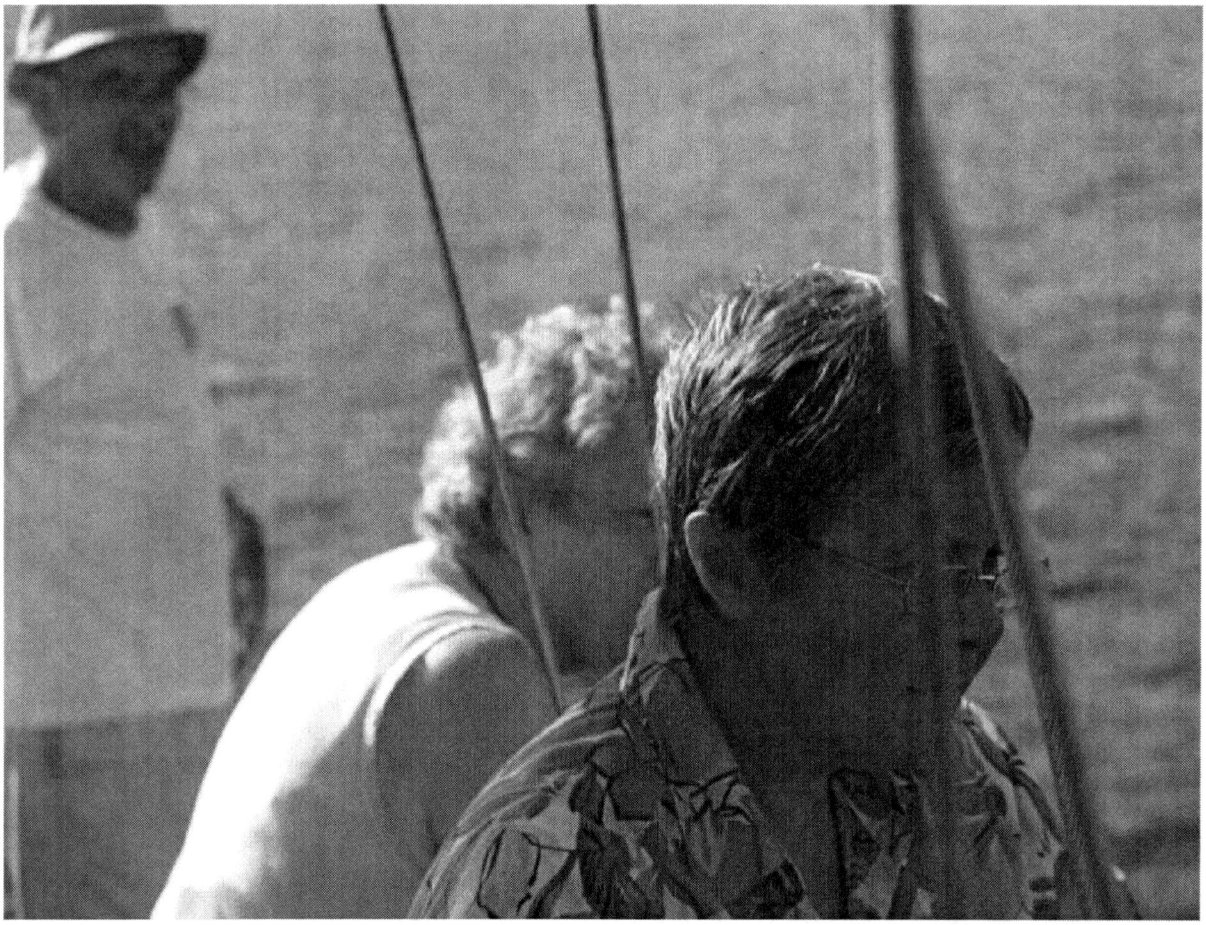

FEEDING FRENZY, WE'RE DOWN TO STALE JACOB'S BRAN CRACKERS

When we motored in, the manager was at our slip to help with the lines. The slips were high, fixed, unprotected, concrete docks, perfect for gouging newly painted fiberglass. All went well; the crew carefully positioned our fenders to protect the hull as we motored inn. The Pat and Deane took care of the laundry, Karl and I tidied up ***Our Pleasure***, then we all walked over to the marina restaurant, Tickles, for lunch. The restaurant was surprisingly nice with its openness, nautical motif and two salty characters sitting at the bar to give the place a complete nautical flavor. This restaurant turned out to be popular, always busy and featured a nice menu with a varied selection of food. The grocery store next to the restaurant, Gourmet Gallery, was similar to a small Metropolitan Market popular in Seattle. The great selection of brands was a surprise with prices ranging from out-of-sight to normal.

Back on the boat, I used the marina's Wi-Fi system to update our Seattle families. I also contacted David Dynes who was on schedule to meet us in Puerto Rico after Karl and Deane leave ***Our Pleasure*** for Seattle.

Sunday we all piled into a taxi to find Charlotte Amalie's Catholic Cathedral, St. Peter and Paul. The ride was short, through mostly quiet, closed commercial areas giving Sunday a little reverence. The cathedral, however, was full of people; standing room only. The native island priest who delivered his enthusiastic homily on "love," was full of energy and charisma. He was also the school principal with a lofty motto, "No Catholic child will be left behind." A little play on words, but this popular school is high on academics, sports, and sought after by parents desiring a good Christian education for their children. He promised not to turn away a child who wanted to attend his school. He also made it clear to parents with little or no income that the church would find a way to take care of the tuition. In addition, any child achieving a first or second academic place in their class would not pay a tuition fee. At the time, I was trying to imagine all the screaming and yelling that would take place if our church council in Seattle proposed a similar economic plan.

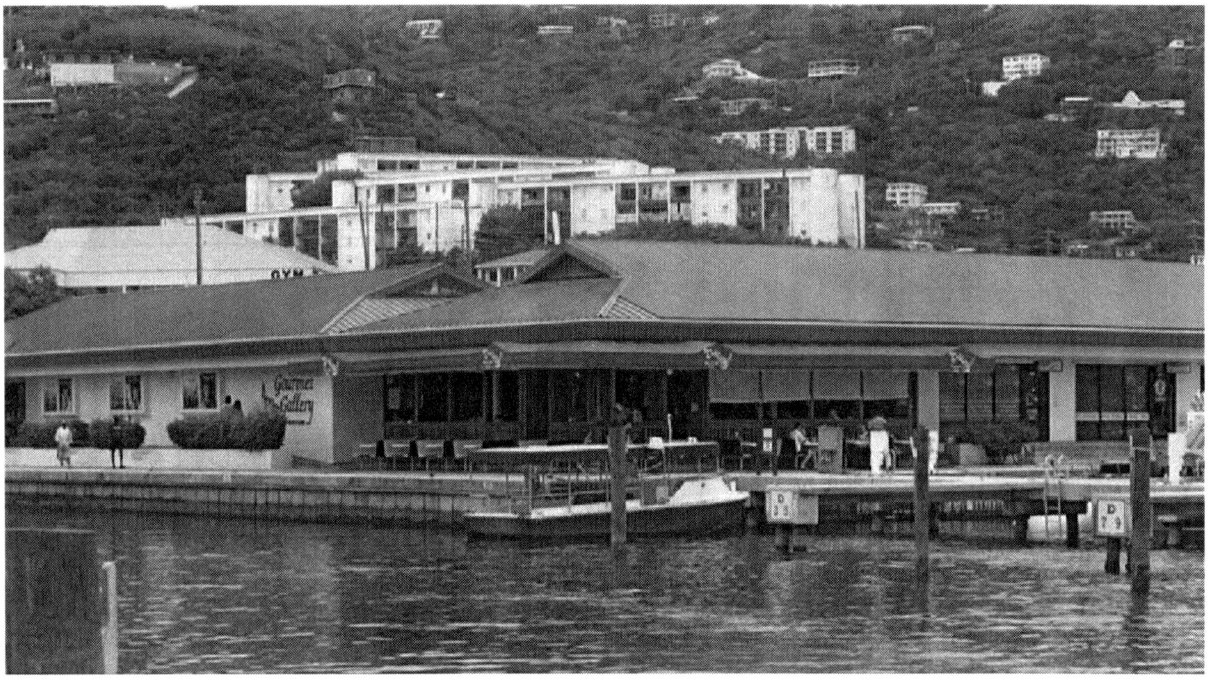

CROWN POINT MARINA, GROCERY STORE AND TICKLES RESTAURANT

Sunday was also Mother's Day so we enjoyed a fine breakfast at Tickles. After breakfast, we paid our bills and moved over to the fuel dock. We took on board 70 gallons of expensive Diesel fuel, but no taxes in the Virgin Islands. The marina charges 14 cents a gallon for potable water, which is becoming a common practice in some countries. Good drinking water is now scarce in many areas of the world and several marinas have begun charging for it. We obtained permission to pass through the marina entrance and headed in the direction of Puerto Rico.

SPANISH VIRGINS AND PUERTO RICO

We left Crown Bay around 2 p.m. and mostly motored until 4 p.m. when we found a small Spanish island. The island of Isla de Culebrita had a beautiful protected bay of white sandy beaches and a clear sandy bottom. One sailboat was anchored in the bay when we arrived and he left late that night. The island has a lighthouse, but no other structures or people. The water temperature was like a bathtub. We did a little beach exploring, but the signs indicated the island was a natural preserve and we were not supposed to disturb any of the plants or animals.

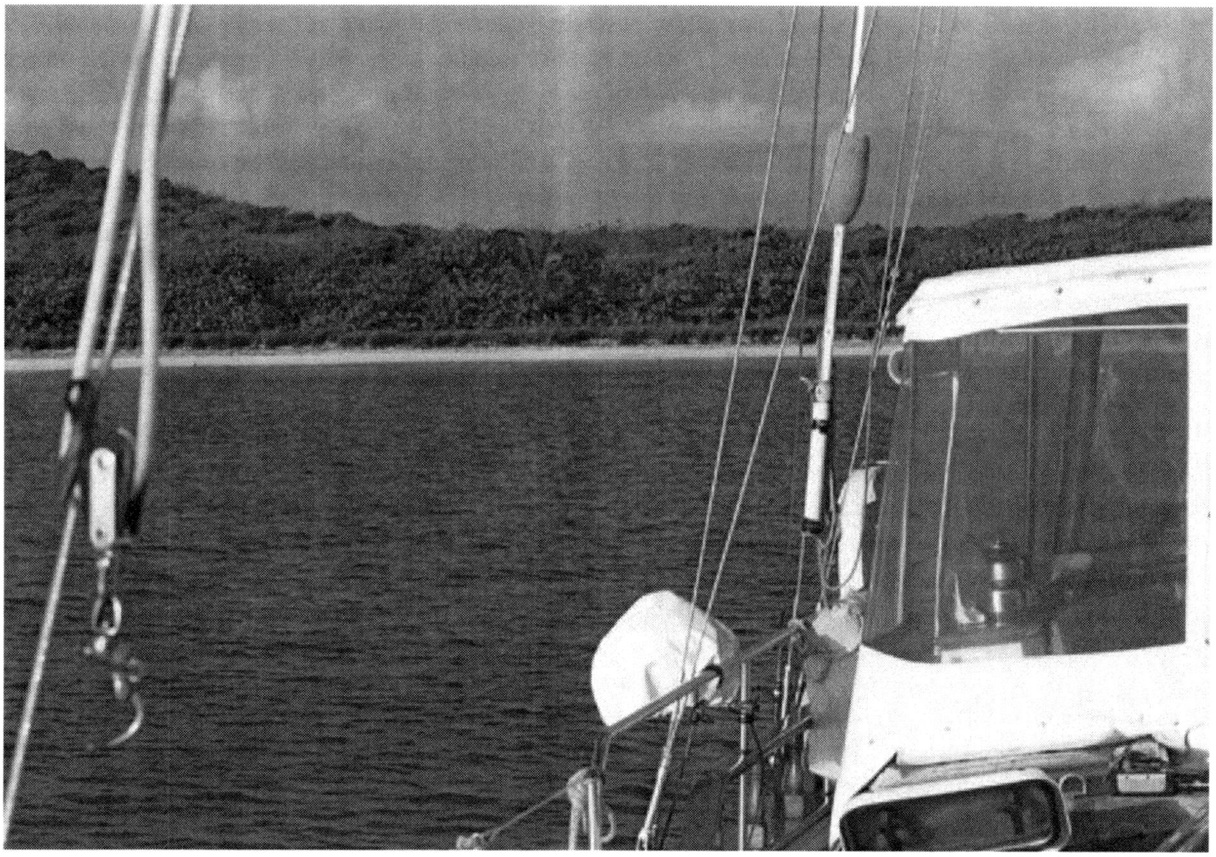

THE BAY AT ISLA de CULEBRITA, SPANISH VIRGIN ISLANDS

We left Isla de Culebrita the next morning and headed for Puerto Rico with no planned stops. Puerto Rico is a commonwealth of the U.S. composed of one large island and some minor islands. One of the minor islands, Mona Vieques, has been in the news lately. It is the preferred destination for people from the nearby Dominican Republic seeking asylum in the U.S. However, the Mona Passage, in between DR and PR can be a dangerous body of water in a small boat and has claimed many lives.

Puerto Rico was ceded to the U.S. after the Spanish American war in 1898. Spanish is still the primary language and the Catholic religion is claimed by 75% of the population. The population of four million relies mostly on tourism. An agreeable tropical climate and beautiful white sandy beaches attract tourists. The island is about 110 miles long and 40 miles wide at the west end. Tax-free incentives have attracted a few U.S. commercial ventures and some manufactures. People in St. Thomas advised us to avoid the harbor at San Juan, Puerto Rico as a destination. Not only is it crowded, but it also has a reputation of being unfriendly to yachts. Case in point, Tiger Woods aboard his 155 foot mega-yacht, *Privacy*, was turned away from the harbor just before we arrived in the area.

We were advised to try the Villa Marina at the northeast end of the island at the city of Fajardo. Well, I called the marina on the radio, but no answer. I found a phone number in the cruising guide and called on my cell phone. That worked, but they were full and advised me to try Isleta Marina on a nearby island of the same name. No one responded there either so I pulled into the only large, vacant slip available. I asked a small boat coming in for fuel if they would tell the manager about us. Well, they did and he said we could stay where we were. He had just started as manager that day and was operating at slow speed.

The island was interesting because its developers planned the offshore island as a by-boat only destination for condominium living. The condominium development included the marina, a fuel dock, and a small café. A small passenger ferry carries passengers on a five minute ride over to the mainland every half-hour. I don't know when the place was built, but it definitely had seen better days. On a positive note, the water and electricity were included in the moorage fee. The slip location was at the very beginning of the marina docks and provided good views of the mainland.

Safely tied to a dock, our next major obstacle would be to clear customs in town. Getting our papers together was a slow process and we missed the ferry to town. Karl and I launched the dinghy and motored over to customs hoping to get there before they closed. Finding a place to moor the dinghy in town was not possible. The docks were in such poor repair with broken concrete and sharp protrusions that our rubber dinghy would have been destroyed. Karl found a semi-smooth spot to drop me off and motored around until I returned. A high steel fence enclosed the government building and an armed guard was stationed at the entrance. My thought was, this area must be a sorry place to live. The guard was very cordial, asked me a few questions, and held the door open for me. The young woman officer asked me the pertinent questions and entered the answers on her computer right at the window. That was a big switch for me, as I generally have to fill in forms longhand, often using several carbon papers. In a matter of minutes, I was officially checked into the United States computer system — perfect.

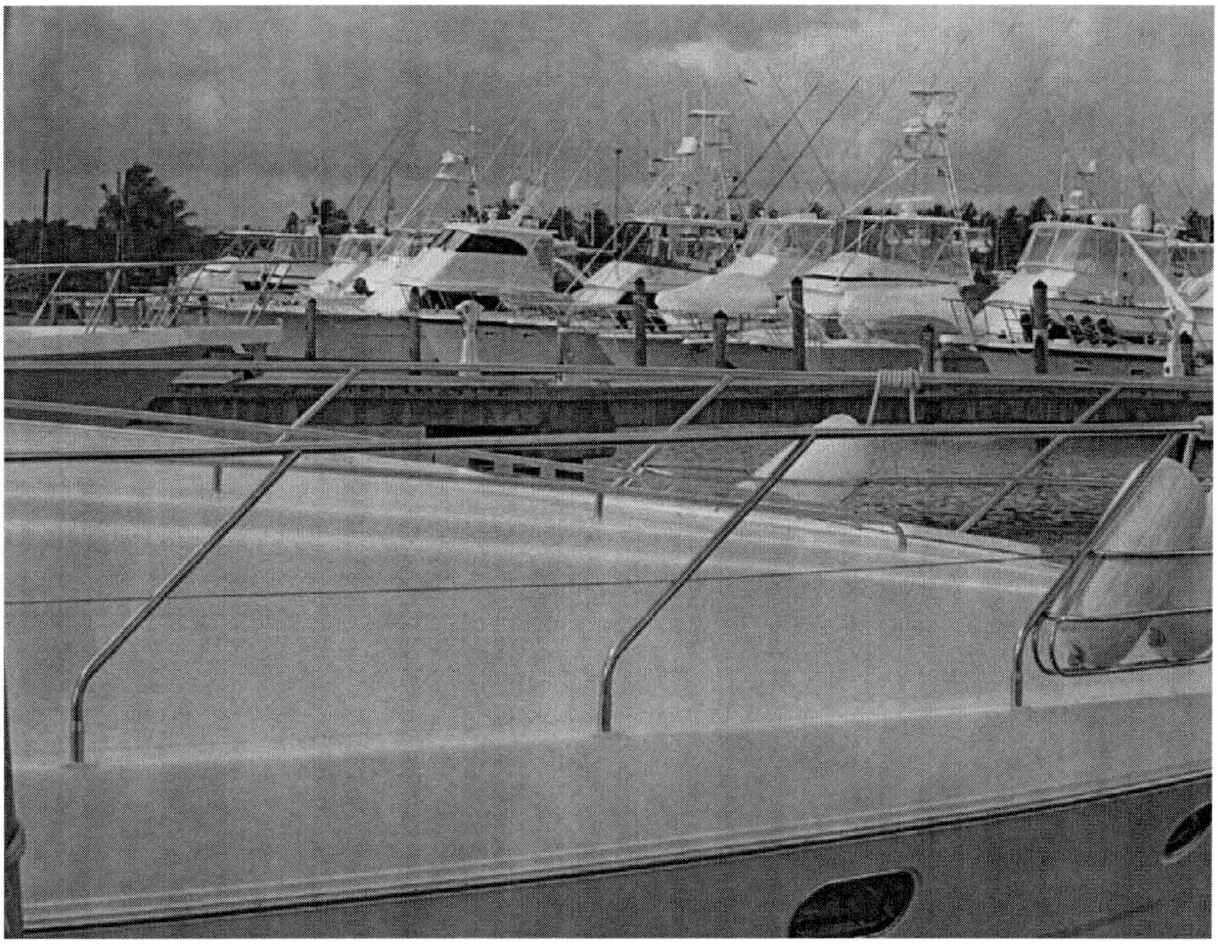

A SEA OF SPORT FISHERMEN, MARINA DEL REY, CEIBA, PUERTO RICO

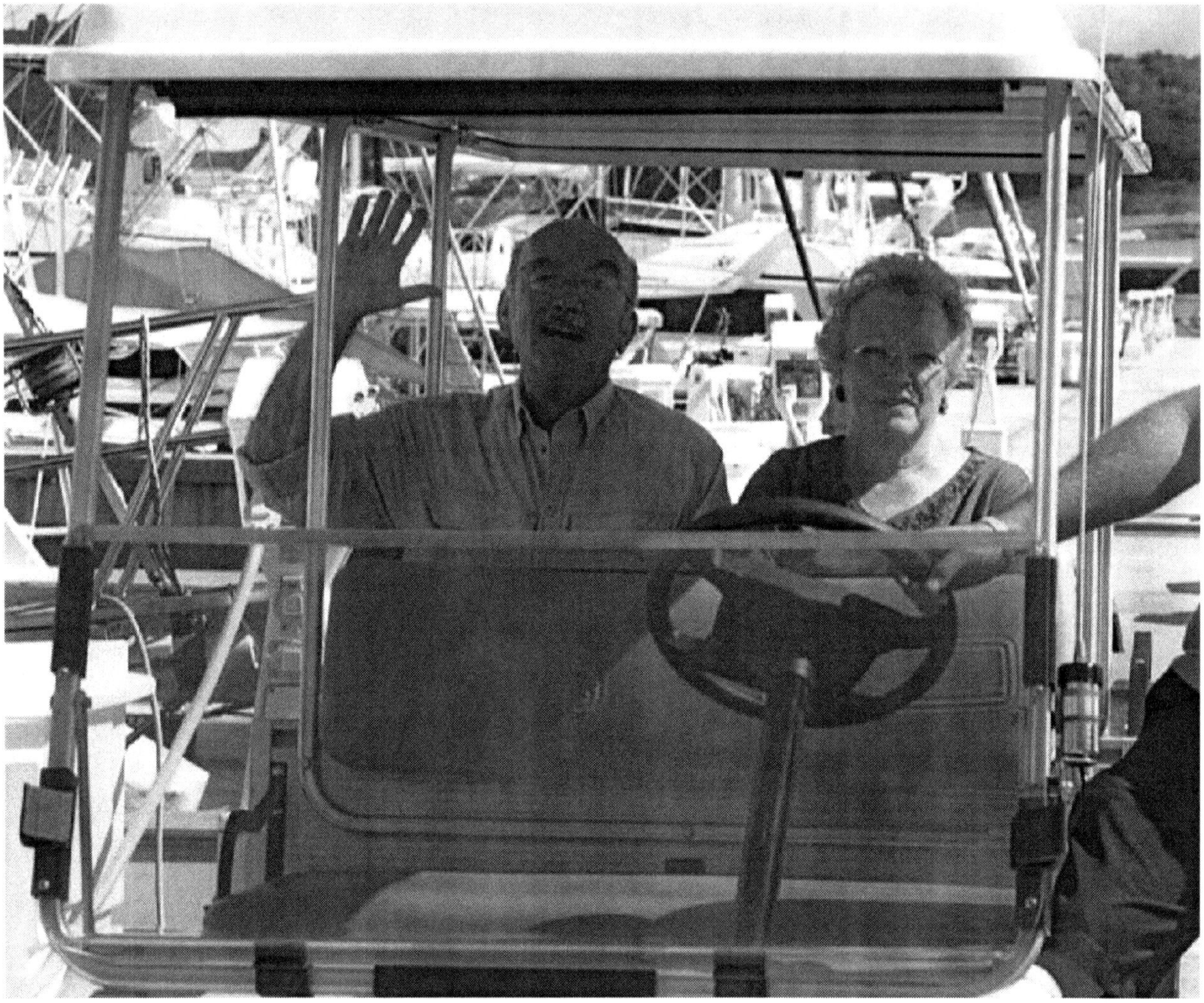

KARL AND DEANE HEADING BACK TO THE STATES, MAY 16, 2006

Back at the boat, the crew was lamenting over the poor condition of everything and thought we should look for a better moorage. The next morning we all had coffee at the sad looking café and Karl bought a bag of always-important ice cubes. Several people from the island marina and condominium were running to catch the ferry into town. This definitely was a blue-collar working class neighborhood. It was probably my imagination, but those people we saw in the morning seemed to be staring unduly at us. I thought they must not see many strangers on their island. Pat was the first to petition that we try the big marina we had heard was about that was five miles down the coast. We went back to the boat, washed everything, filled the water tanks, paid the $60 moorage fee, and headed down the coast. Sailing in the shallow waters of this area can be problematic. In the direct route was a graveyard of several boats that went aground on what looked like open water. Looks are sometimes deceiving and without good charts, sailing is a risky business. Instead of a direct route, we sailed a much safer route, but added several miles to what appeared to be a short trip.

Marina Del Rey was a big surprise. A beautiful marina with over 1,100 slips, the biggest in the West Indies. This marina has the most sport fisherman boats I have ever seen. Dock boys met us at our slip, #1411, and helped with our lines. Again, the docks were massive concrete structures designed to put up a good fight in a hurricane. The marina is so big that small-motorized carts taxis people back and forth between their boats and the marina entrance. It was Karl and Deane's last night with us so I lit up the barbeque and we had a multi-course dinner featuring tender steaks from our favorite market back in Trinidad.

Karl and Deane took a local taxi to the San Juan, Puerto Rico airport, a trip of about 60 minutes. The taxi cost was a bit outrageous at $70, whereas the marina only cost $60 a night. We called for a driver and cart on the radio and took our laundry into the marina's big self-serve Laundromat. After the laundry and a few boat projects, it was another dock ride to the marina's nice restaurant, the Mariner. It was off-season in PR as most Americans have already gone back to the states with the hurricane season looming just around the corner. Thus, the restaurant was empty except for two men eating dinner at the bar and watching a Spanish soap opera. At first, we thought maybe the food wasn't good and that we made a mistake, but the food was excellent. Everything about this marina was top drawer including the restroom facilities, which were very clean and spacious.

We rented a car for the next 2 days to explore San Juan and pick up our new crewmember, David Dynes. Our connection to David is through our daughter Leslie and David's wife — they were Kappa Kappa Gamma sorority sisters together when attending Washington State University. Several years before our cruise started, David asked me to keep a berth open for him if we ever needed another crew person. It just so happened this was the time. David wanted to experience offshore sailing before he took his family on their own offshore sail. His plane was not due until 7:10 p.m. so we had plenty of time to look around San Juan. We spent most of our time in Old Town, which has a lot of nice shops, restaurants, restored buildings, and old forts. Finding the freeway turn off for the airport was a little tricky, but we found it after the second try.

The mean airport police were just like Seattle's: "Keep moving, no stopping," they blared over loud speakers — quite unfriendly. I dropped Pat off to find David while I drove around the loop three times. David's flight went well and he arrived in good spirits. We decided to stay at the marina another day to give David more time to get familiar with ***Our Pleasure***. The next day we turned in the rental car, paid the marina bill, took one more shower, and motored out into the Caribbean around noon. Our planned course would take us about 1,500 nautical miles to Bradenton, FL. We would be sailing along the north coasts of three of the Greater Antilles islands, Puerto Rico, Hispaniola (Dominican Republic and Haiti) and Cuba.

KEY WEST

During the first 24 hours after leaving Marina Del Rey, the winds were on the light side. We did a little sailing, but mostly relied on our engine. We passed by the city of San Juan late in the afternoon. There are almost no bays for shelter on either the north or south side of the island. The next day the wind was blowing hard enough to move us along at over 5 knots. Dave and I poled out the 100% jib and sailed along nicely in light trade winds. The days were clear and sunny, the sunsets were wonderful, and the nights were full of stars. We were averaging around 125 nautical miles a day. Occasionally dolphins came to play in our bow wake entertaining us to no end. Passing the islands of the Greater Antilles would take us about 1,100 nautical miles toward the northwest. Another 200 northerly miles and we would be in Key West.

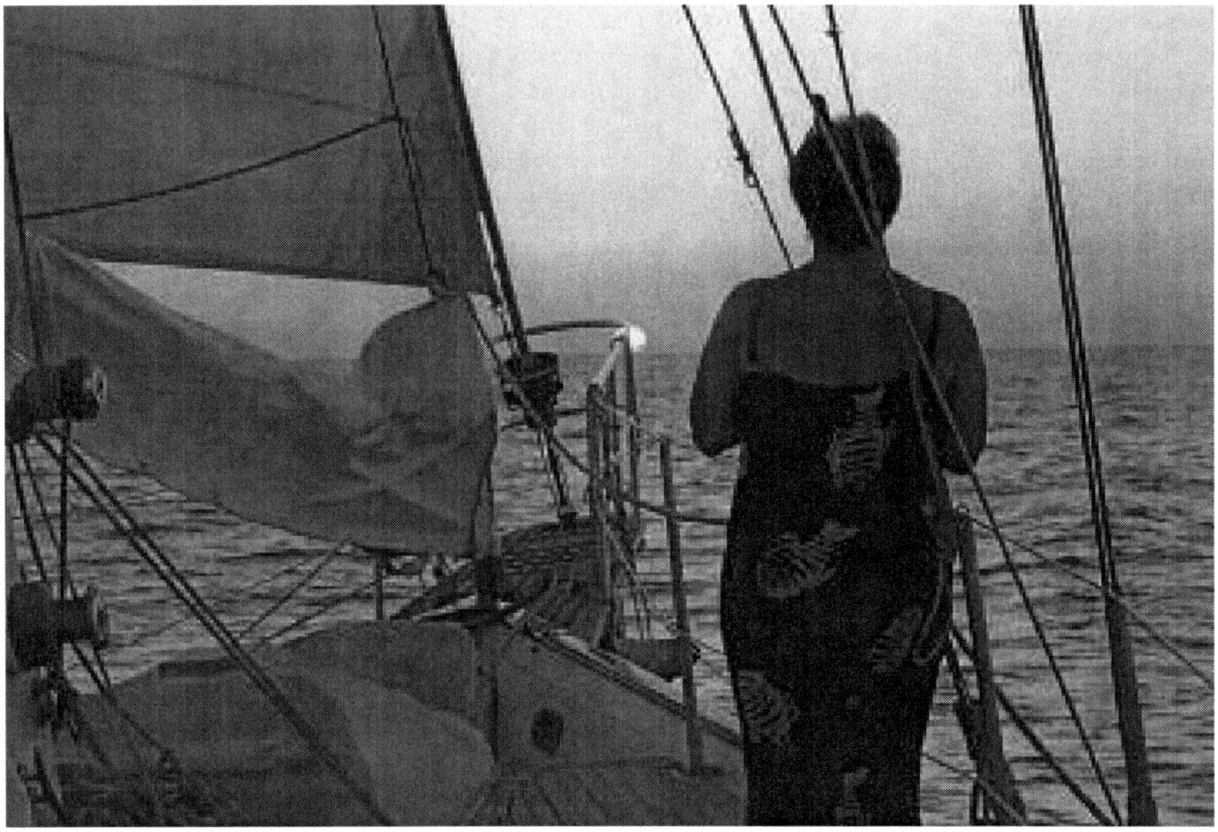

OFF THE DOMINICAN REPUBLIC — PAT AND ONE MORE BEAUTIFUL SUNSET

The trip was mundane until we reached the southern tip of Cuba and about the same latitude as the U.S. base at Guantánamo. A U.S. Coast Guard helicopter suddenly flew in low and circled around us in a close circular pattern. No questions were asked of us on the radio, just the observation and a lot of wash from the rotating blades. I wondered where he came from as it was around 100 nautical miles to Guantánamo and he came from a northerly direction. Well, a few miles further west along Cuba's coast we got our answer. Our curious helicopter had landed on a large U.S. Coast Guard ship. The ship sported a big deck cannon and probably a few other weapons we could not see.

We were certain the ship would launch a bunch of guardsmen to board us. Other yachts sailing along this coast have reported being boarded regularly, some up to three times. It is funny, we had the anticipation that we would be boarded, but it never happened. I guess they were satisfied with the flyover. They probably also had computer data from our U.S. check-in's at the U.S. Virgins and Puerto Rico. We kept our eyes on the boat until we sailed out of their sight and finally relaxed knowing they were not going to board us.

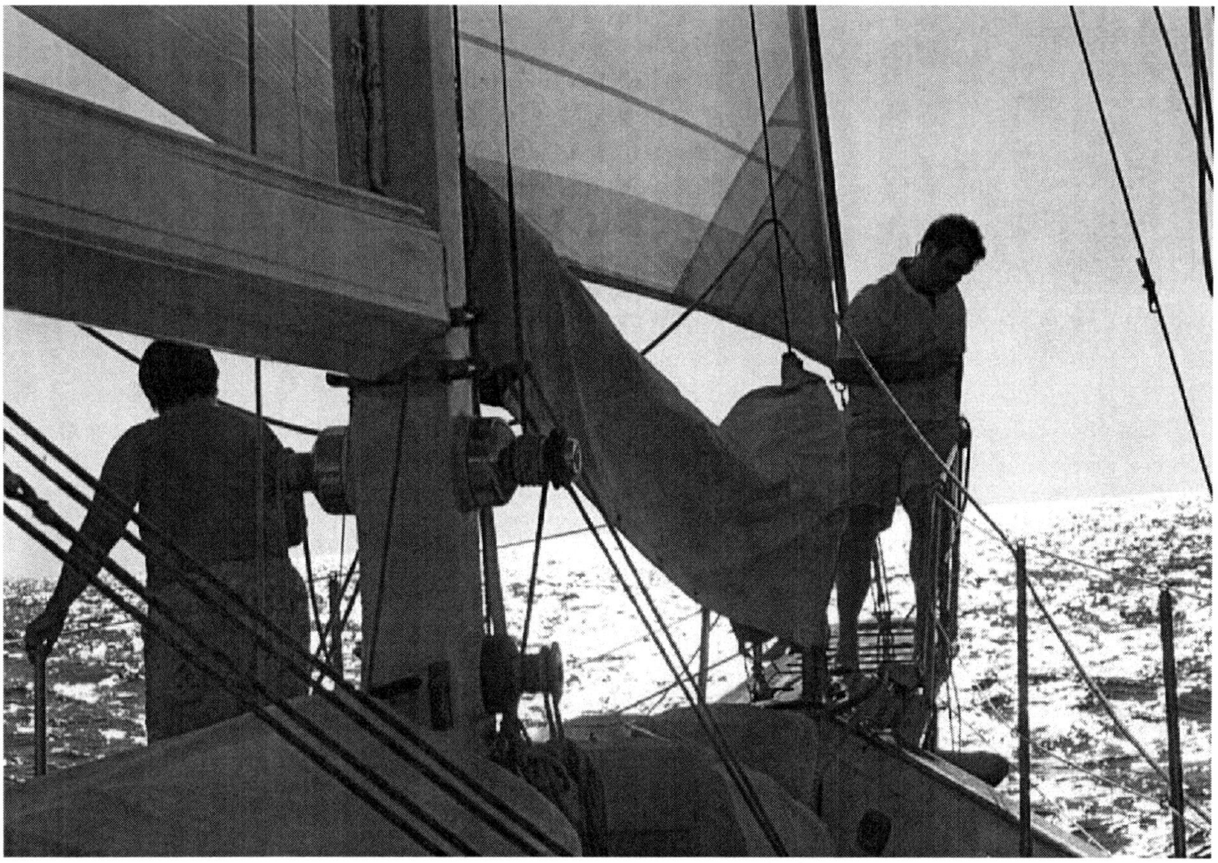

PAT AND DAVID WATCHING DOLPHINS

Another unusual circumstance happened when we were 273 nautical miles from Key West. One minute we were in 6,000 feet of water and next time we looked down we could see bottom. The watercolor changed to a light blue from a dark gray. A check of the charts verified we were sailing over the southern end of the Bahamas' Banks. The banks peak to the south in this area and in a few more miles, we would be in deep water again.

Sunday, Pat prepared a wonderful breakfast of sausages, eggs and blueberry muffins. The wind had died and we were motoring along at 5 knots. Tomorrow was Labor Day and we thought we would be entering Key West. However, about 37 miles from Key West we ran into an unexpected 2 knot negative current. I thought we were far enough from the Gulf Stream current along the east coast that it would not affect us. As the Gulf Stream races north the current apparently forms a back eddy that reaches west past the Florida Keys. For us it meant we could only make 3 knots towards Key West. Instead of arriving during daylight, we arrived at entrance buoy #1 close to midnight. To enter the narrow channel safely, we decided to wait until daylight.

We did not have a list of marinas at Key West so while David was on watch he called "information" on his cell phone. He asked for phone numbers of Key West marinas and the operator connected him with a marina and their night watchman. However, the watchman's understanding of English was quite limited so he asked David to call George. George's shift started at midnight, which would be my watch time. I called George who spoke excellent English, but he was not at a Key West marina. He was a security guard at the Stock Island Marina to the east of Key West. He tried to convince me to come into their marina as it was a nice marina, quiet, less crowded, and less expensive than Key West. He was super talkative and did not want to say goodbye. Finally, after I said goodbye five times I was able to hang-up. He did say we probably should try the Galleon Marina if he could not talk us out of our Key West destination.

Daylight poked through around 6:15 a.m. As we started to move in, a giant cruise ship overtook us and headed into Key West. We followed behind him in the channel, but his terminal came before our destination. Without a deep draft ship to follow, we had to move carefully over shallow areas into Key West Bight. By that time it was sunny and the crew at the Galleon Marina was hard at work. When I called, I was directed to a slip where a marina dockhand helped us with our lines. After ***Our Pleasure*** was squared away, we hit the showers.

The marina is part of a resort/hotel complex and we were invited to use all the facilities including the beautiful pool. However, we planned to stay only one night and there was a lot of stuff to see. First stop was, Peppies, a well-known Key West restaurant for breakfast. We started with mimosas and the rest of the day just fell into place. Of course, we toured Earnest Hemingway's Key West Home and Museum. Hemingway (1899-1961), lived all over the world including Paris, Spain, Italy, Africa, and Cuba and in Ketchum, Idaho where he committed suicide. I'm sure his travels, his jobs (reporter, ambulance driver in Italy during WWI, Italian soldier, and WWII war correspondent) and sporting interests (hunting, fishing and bull fighting) all contributed to his unique writing style. He won the Pulitzer Prize in 1953 for *The Old Man and the Sea* and the Nobel Prize for literature in 1954. His plain, expressive style is said to have moved writers away from the previous elaborate prose popular with 20th century American writers.

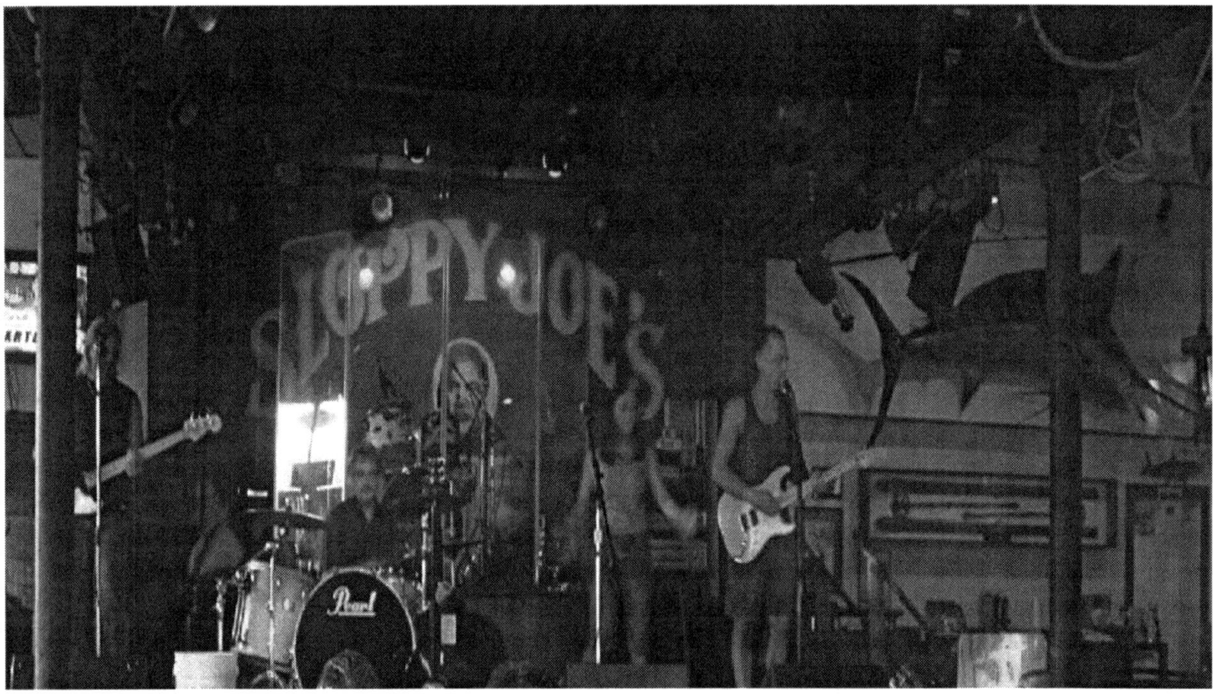

SLOPPY JOE'S, HEMINGWAY'S FAVORITE BAR, KEY WEST, FLORIDA

Anyway, we found the home and the stories about Hemingway quite interesting. His office and writing studio was over the garage with a bridge to the house. The office was full of books and original furnishings including his old manual typewriter. One story relates to the nearby 1846 lighthouse and how its bright light enabled Hemingway to find his way home from his favorite watering hole, Sloppy Joe's. The original Sloppy Joe's was closer to his house. However, when the owner of the property raised the rent by one dollar, the manager of the tavern was so upset he moved. All the bar's patrons moved the furnishings by hand to the present location in one evening. Sloppy Joe's opened for business the next day. We had a drink at Sloppy Joe's, an interesting place, but the loud, tasteless, so called music, drove us out quickly.

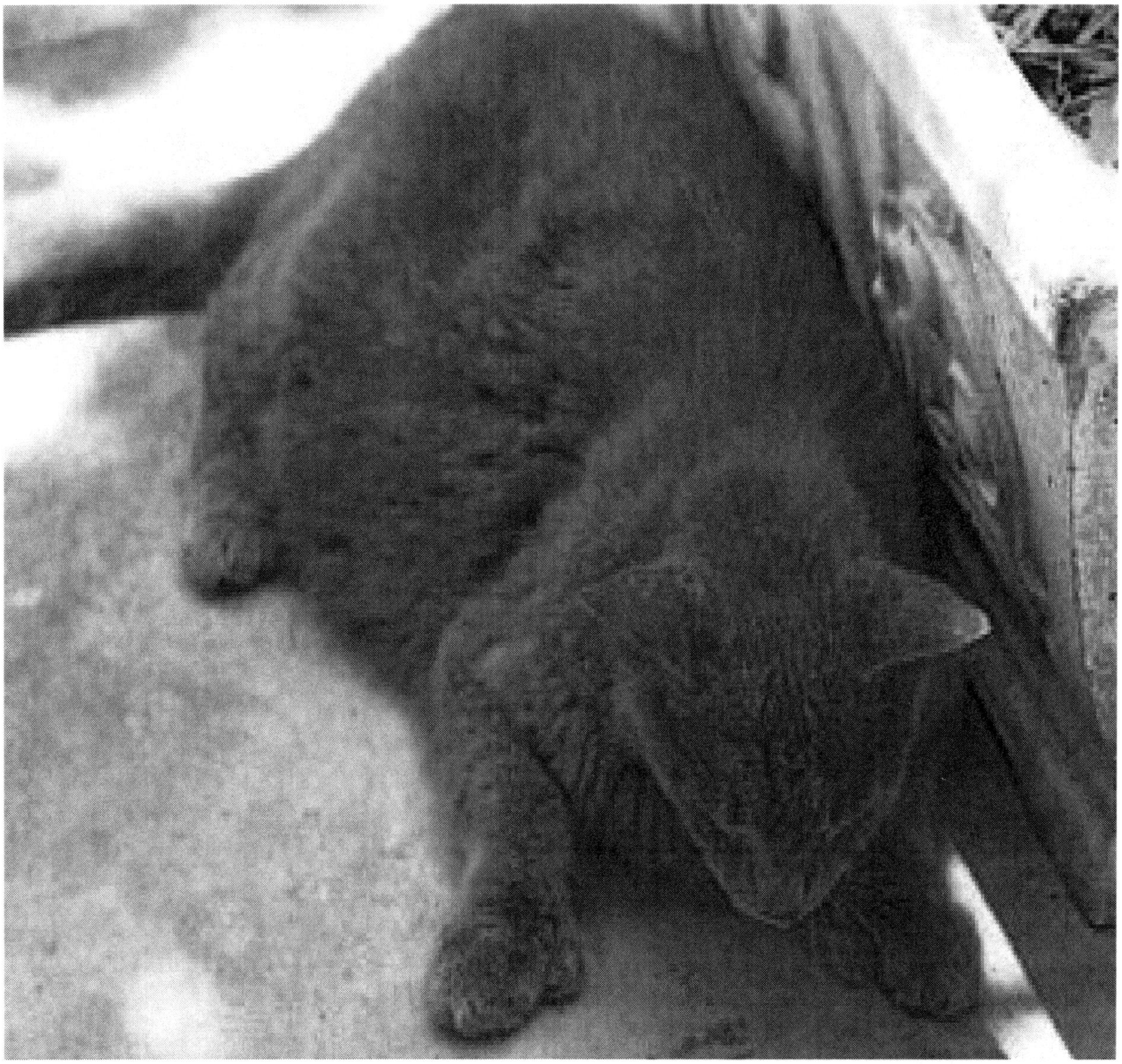

A HEMINGWAY CAT DESCENDENT WITH SIX-FRONT TOES

Around the grounds of Hemingway's house are a scattered bunch of unusual cats. There are least 50 cats mostly lazing around the spacious grounds. About half the cats are descendents of the original cat given to Hemingway by a ship's captain. The unusual thing about the cats are their front paws, they have 6 toes instead of the normal 5. They have quite an attitude toward the other cats in the compound that have only 5 toes — the normal cats get the cold shoulder, completely ignored. The many-toed cats are known as polydactyl cats. They are not of a particular breed, but look like a combination of several breeds. The caretakers have names for each cat and they respond when called by their names. Almost all names are famous movie stars or famous people — lots of fun.

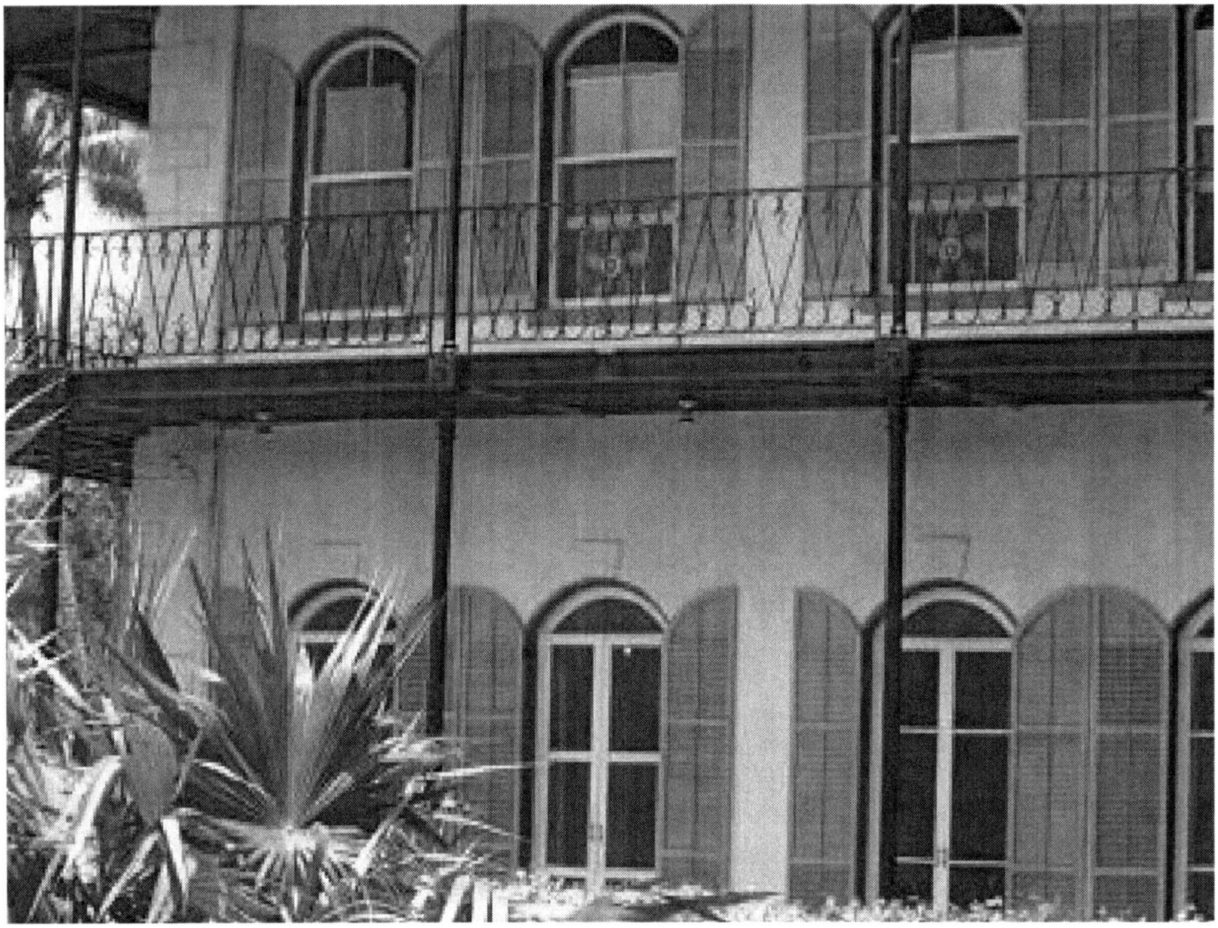

EARNEST HEMINGWAY'S HISTORIC HOME, KEY WEST, FLORIDA

We took a 90 minute tour of Key West on a rubber tired trolley and loved the old architectural styles. The Keys were incorporated in 1828 and now about 25,000 people call Key West their home. A large Cuban colony was established in Key West by 1830 because of economic hardship and persecution in Cuba. Many Cubans came later to escape Spanish rule in Cuba. The area has become somewhat of a haven for artists probably because of the huge tourism factor. There were tourists everywhere we went. The restaurants, ice cream parlors, the key lime factories and streets were crowded. Even the marinas had many small power boats that came from nearby Keys and cities of Florida.

Many of the homes have that old shuttered, weathered look of homes darkened by time and wood bleached by salt air. Others have been restored to their original beauty. Besides tourism, there is a big commercial fishing industry and military bases for the U.S. Navy and Coast Guard. I understand that naturalist John J. Audubon's house is in Key West, but we did not see it. Of course, food is a very important subject in Key West and we wanted to find a good restaurant to celebrate our arrival in Florida. David asked several people and the one name that popped up the most was Michael's. Michael's was so popular it was a no-brainer. So off we went with general directions, but nothing specific. Asking a few people along the way we were able to find it, but it was a long walk from the marina. We were lucky they were able to seat us without reservations. The seating was limited, the decor was elegant, and the food, at least my tenderloin, was wonderful.

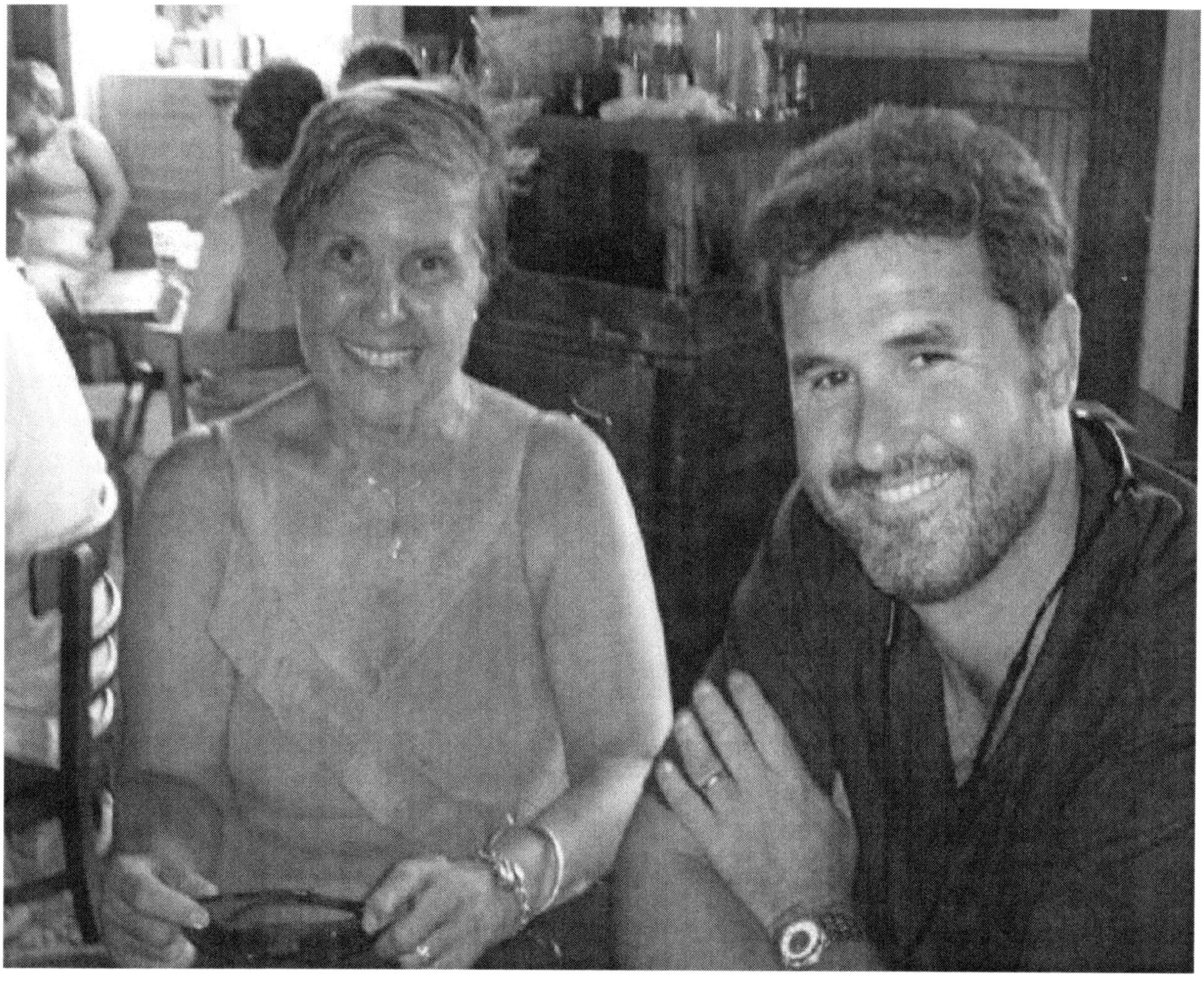

MICHAEL'S RESTAURANT, KEY WEST, PAT AND DAVID DYNES

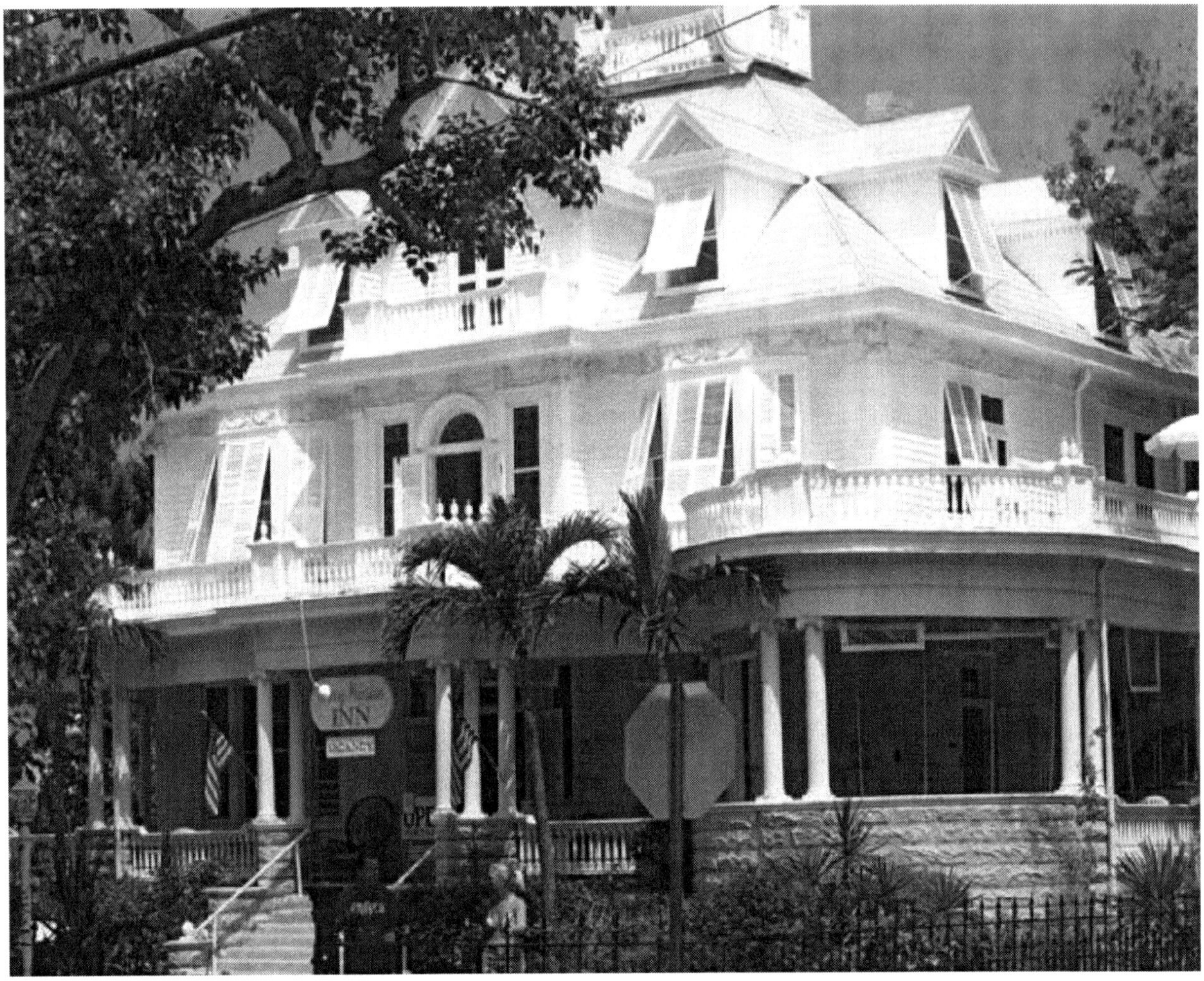

RESTORED MANSION CONVERTED TO A B&B, KEY WEST

KEY WEST TO BRADENTON FLORIDA

The next day Pat did some last minute grocery shopping. I filled the water tanks and gave the boat a scrubbing. David must have been worn out as he slept until 9 a.m. We were surprised at the marina bill for one night. At $220 a day, this marina is the most expensive marina we have ever stayed at during 9 years of offshore cruising. We should have at least walked away with a few shares of stock in the resort. We headed ***Our Pleasure*** north to follow Florida's west coastline. I was surprised at the shallowness of the Gulf of Mexico along the west Florida coast. We stayed about 50 miles off the coast and the water depth was always around 60 feet. Winds were light and not much going on. We saw a couple of other sailboats and some shrimpers, but not much else.

The southwest coast of Florida is reputed to have thousands of beautiful islands that make for extraordinary cruising. The problem is accessibility, too shallow. Almost all boat channels are 3 feet or less restricting navigation to very shallow draft vessels. We draw 6.5 feet and cannot go into most of the west coast cities. We can probably get into Cape Coral and Fort Meyers, but that's about it. I was surprised to read that even the waters around the Sarasota Yacht Club are rather shallow because of silting.

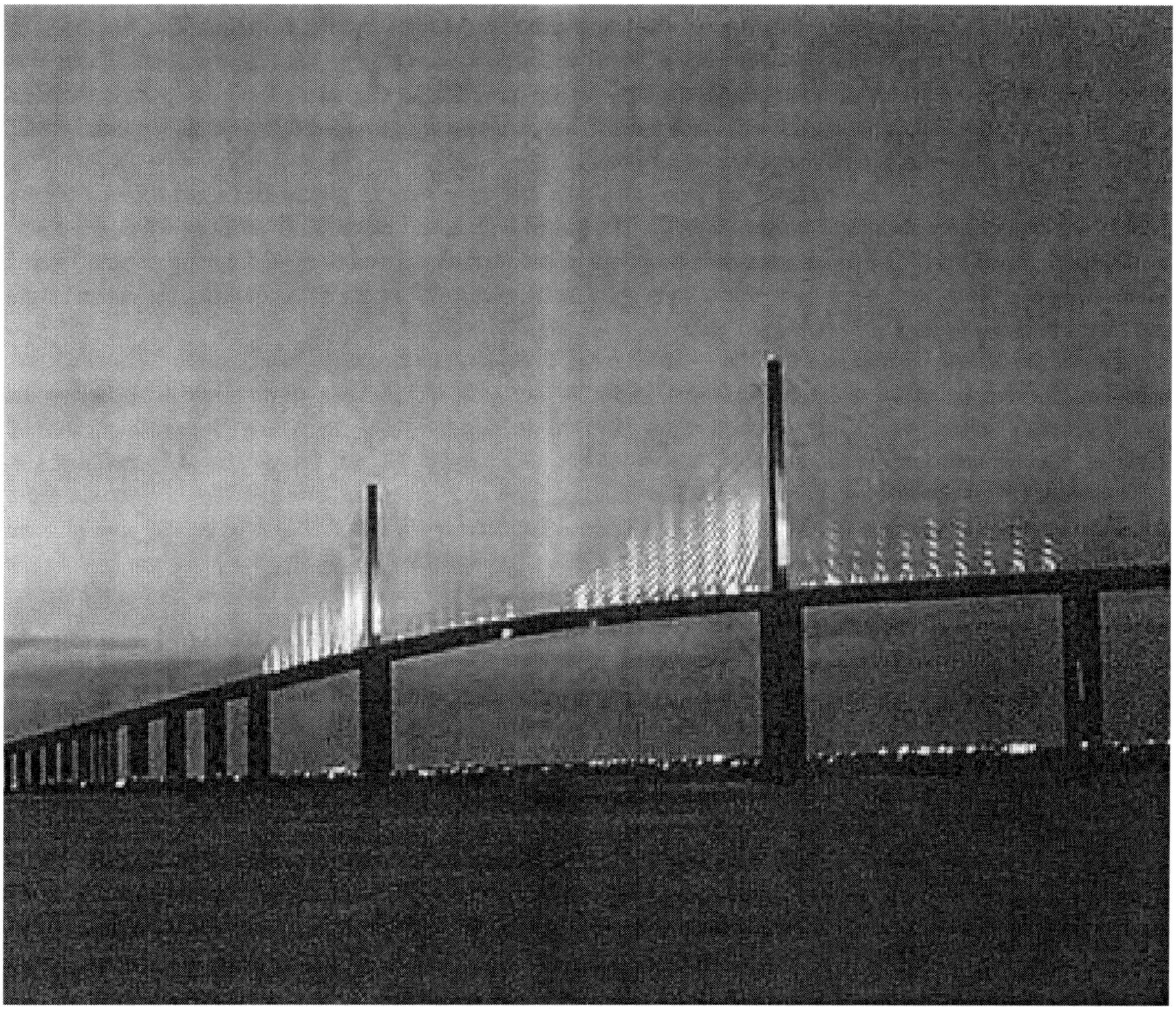

Photo courtesy of Wikipedia
SUNSHINE SKYWAY BRIDGE AFTER SUNSET

After a couple of days, we entered the big ship channel into Tampa Bay at 4 a.m. on June 3. The channel is well lit with green and red markers set close together. The buoy locations were spot-on their charted locations as verified by our GPS. This is the main shipping channel into Tampa Bay and is used by ocean going freighters. So I was quite surprised to find it was only about 100 yards wide and 35 feet deep. To follow the channel all the way into Tampa Bay you have to pass under the beautiful Sunshine Skyway Bridge. This bridge is a cable-stayed bridge completed in 1987 at a cost of $245 million. Its longest span is 1,200 feet and its vertical clearance is 193 feet. The total length of the bridge is 5.5 miles. We have often driven over this bridge when my parents lived in Clearwater, Florida and my sister lived south on Longboat Key, Florida. The bridge connects St. Petersburg to Bradenton, Florida and is a visual delight to see. At night, the 9 inch diameter tubes housing the cables are lighted to highlight the bridge's cable suspension design.

You may remember the original bridge of the same name, but a steel cantilever design. The freighter, SS Summit Venture running into a pylon during a storm in 1980, destroyed the southbound span. Thirty-five people died when several cars and one Greyhound bus on the span fell into the water. Only one person survived the span failure. His pickup truck fell and bounced off the freighter first then into the water. He successfully sued the freighter's owners, but lived only 9 more years.

When we first entered the channel we were all alone, but soon two freighters and a large Coast Guard patrol boat caught up with us and passed close by. The patrol boat called us via VHF radio to tell us what side he would be passing on. The freighters never bothered to call, but we moved over to the edge of the channel when they got close. I don't know how much water the freighter needed, but the 35 feet we saw the entire length must have been enough.

Before the Skyway Bridge, we left the main channel, turned to starboard to head for the Manatee River entrance. The channel at the rivers mouth is only about 30 feet wide and shallow; we saw only 6 feet under our keel. The sandy bottom was clearly visible, but you can't tell the depth by looking. As we got past the mouth of the river, the channel widened and the depth below the keel increased to 12 feet. The river is wide, well marked, and charted. The shallowness outside the marked channel, however, precludes any sailing. We motored the 5 miles up the Manatee River to the Twin Dolphin Marina at Bradenton, Florida. We arrived at 8:30 a.m. on June 3, 2006, 33,000 miles after leaving Seattle on Sept. 3, 1997. Charlie Price, the marina manager, was glad to see us and gave us a choice of 3 slips. My sister Barbara came down to see us and we all had a celebration lunch at the marina's restaurant, Twin Dolphin.

The end of our journey seemed too ordinary, no cheering crowd, no emotional celebrations. Our children wanted to meet us when we arrived in Florida, but the need to work, the cost of travel, schedule problems and the care of their children put a damper on that idea. The celebration for us came from within. It came from silent, emotional, feelings of accomplishment. An internal warm glow like the feeling one gets from a crackling fireplace on a snowy day. Also, there was sadness, this wonderful adventure was ending and what could replace it?

Sailing the Seven Seas in a small boat is risky and is fraught with many dangers and challenges. The 9 years of mostly good and a few bad experiences, heightened the gratification of completion. Navigating safely around 95% of the world is not a simple feat. The decisions made, right or wrong, are your own; no one can take responsibility, but the skipper. The freedom away from world problems and the lack of programming from the media reduces one's internal pressures. Away from land, you are free to think about yourself, your life and the people you love. Daydreaming on star filled nights just comes naturally. No matter where we looked, we saw the beautiful, natural order of the universe. Our sailing adventure reinforced and secured mine and Pat's belief of a loving, supreme being.

Many people have sailed around the world now so it has lost its luster with the public. It is no longer news worthy for newspapers, radio, or TV. However, meeting the people we have met, visiting the places that we have been and making friends around the world made our journey a beautiful, worthwhile experience. Two thousand miles between islands is hard to think about these days. The thought of making long passages has lost its allure. Day trips, sailing a couple of nights or a few hundred miles seems more like the right kind of cruise now.

We arrived in Florida at the peak of the June bug (known here as love bugs) season. The still air was thick with the annoying, black, slow flying, bugs. Everyone and everything outside became their landing field. They are harmless, don't bite or sting, but boy do they become annoying fast. Swatting doesn't work because there are so many of them. Kill a hundred and there will be a hundred more. It's a good thing my sister and brother-in-law invited us to stay with them at their new home in Bradenton. If we stayed inside the boat with everything closed up, we would have expired without a working air-conditioner. Their new home with pool and spa was just what the doctor ordered. Barbara even loaned us her new Honda SUV to take care of miscellaneous items until we left for Seattle.

We sailed into to Bradenton in time for our crewmember, David Dynes, to catch his scheduled flight from Sarasota to Seattle on June 5, 2006. Pat left for Seattle on the same day that Barbara and husband Jack left to visit children in Philadelphia, June 12. I stayed at their house to work on the boat until July 6, and then I left for Seattle.

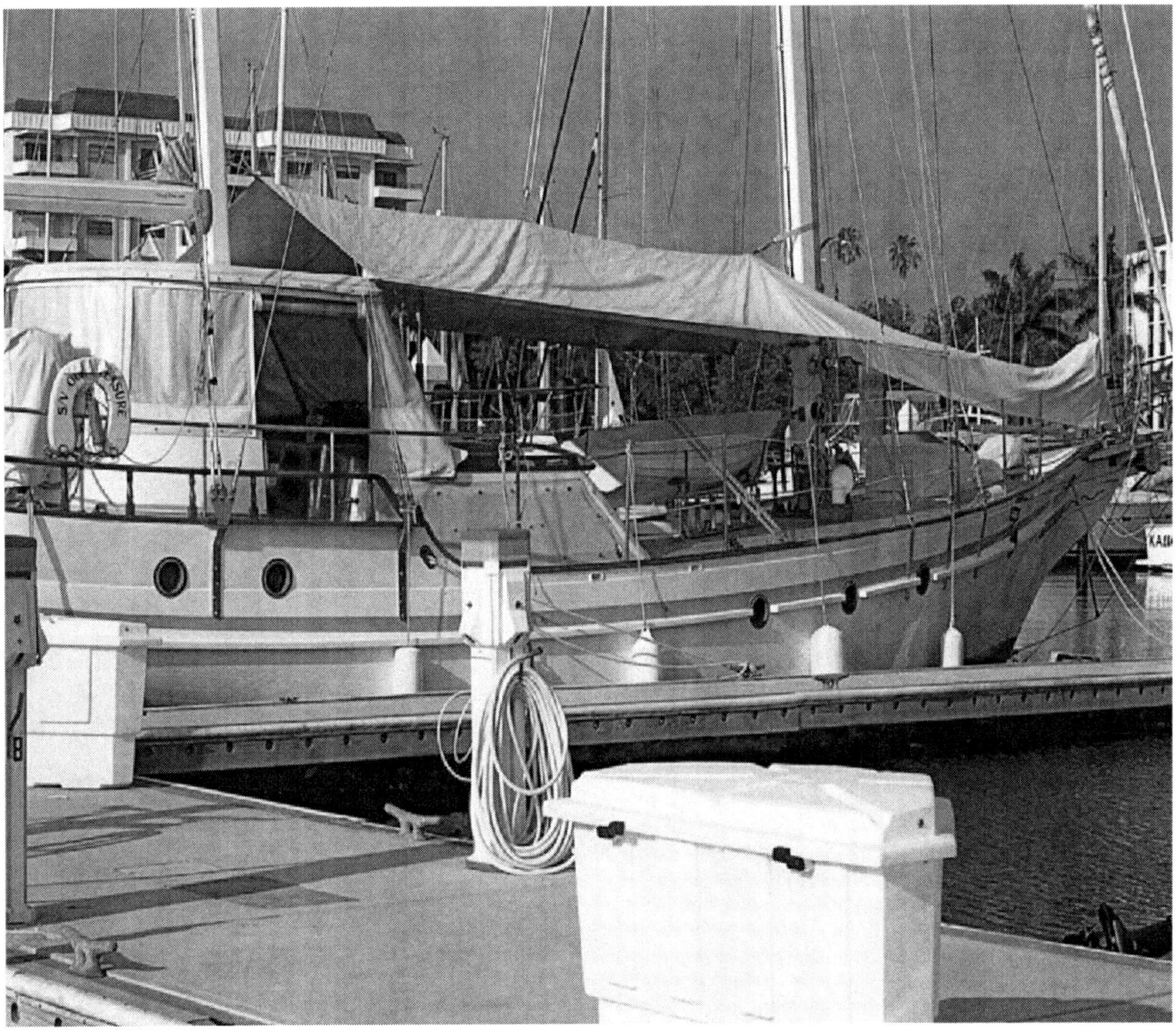

***OUR PLEASURE*, TWIN DOLPHIN MARINA, BRADENTON, FL**

ABOUT THE AUTHOR

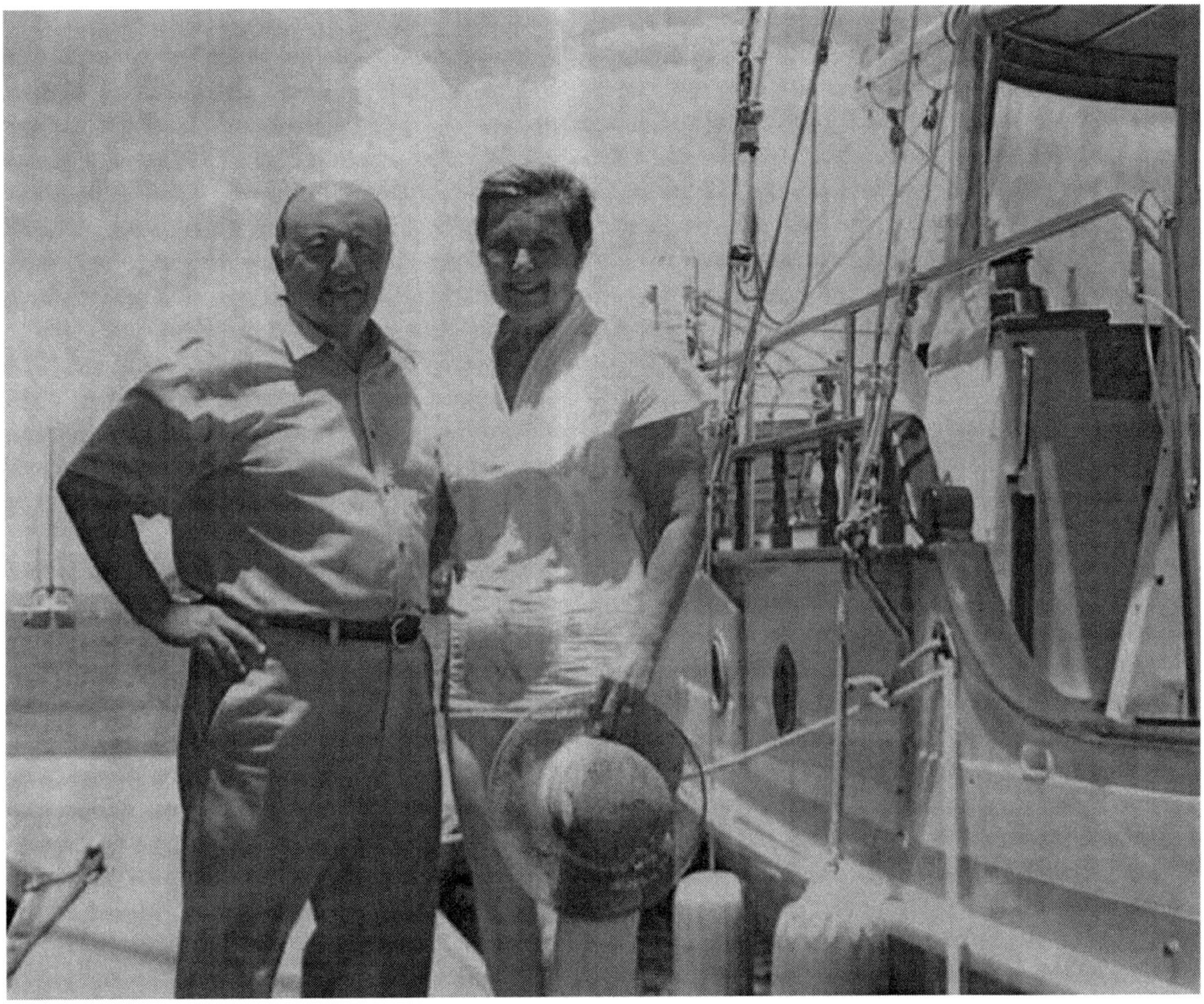

DICK AND PAT BENNETT

The author, Richard Bennett, was born to Italian parents Vincent J. and Mame Bennett in Brooklyn, NY on April 27, 1935. My father's employer, American Telephone and Telegraph Company, transferred Dad to Buffalo, NY from the Manhattan, NY office when I was about 5 years old. In Buffalo, Dad assumed the management responsibility of long distance telephone communications in the Western NY region for AT&T.

We lived in a suburb of Buffalo, Kenmore, NY where I went to St. Paul's grammar school and St. Joseph's Collegiate Institute for high school.

Some of my father's coworkers at AT&T were radio amateur operators and helped spur my interest in amateur radio and all things electrical from about 10 years of age. My parents let me fix up two unused rooms in the basement. A short wave radio, amplifiers, speakers, electronic hardware, and radio parts went in one room. In the other small room, I had a big chemistry set and glassblowing equipment. I also liked to experiment with shortwave radio using experimental long-wire antennas, strung across our backyard and sometimes our neighbors.

On April 27, 1951, my Aunt Lee and her husband, Eddy Stewart, drove into my parent's driveway, loudly blowing the horn, of a 1933 Plymouth coupe; it was my 16th year birthday present. I turned off my Bunsen burner and put away most other projects to turn this coupe into a souped-up street rod. At that time, one of my longtime school friends, Jack Domster and I were working after school at Dunn's Collision, a garage that repaired cars. Their business ran the full gamut from customizing cars, weld damaged frames to hand-rubbed lacquer paint jobs. In the back of that garage, the owner's brother fabricated small motor powered rides for children. Initially we did not have much responsibility, but learned how to sweep the garage really well. Eventually we worked with the real mechanics and learned metalworking, arc welding, gas welding, car frame straitening and spray painting. In those days, garages were one-stop-shopping for every problem.

I managed to use my garage experience and money to buy a used Chrysler engine from a junk yard ($30) for my first hotrod project. I had the head milled .040" and installed high performance engine parts from Edelbrock®. Edelbrock® was one of the few companies manufacturing high performance engine parts in those days. I built a dual exhaust manifold, chopped the top 3 inches and changed the front suspension system to a suicide front end. I never finished the hotrod because of studies, work, and lack of funds. But I was on my way toward the enjoyment of electronics and mechanical design.

My second car, a 1950 black Ford convertible, was transformed into a, souped-up speedster. At the time, I think my family thought I was consuming more than my share of the family car's time and they put up the $500 purchase price. I really modified this car down to 13 coats of hand-rubbed lacquer, electric radiator cooling fans, racing pistons, bored-out cylinders, high compression heads, machined a half-race cam, dual pipes and lots of engine chrome. This car was nice to look at and fast.

In college, I studied electrical engineering at the University of Detroit. During summer vacations, I worked at the Bell Aircraft rocket engine test facility in Wheatfield, NY. Bell was building and test flying the first U.S. manned rocket ship the Bell X-1. An Air Force bomber flying at high altitudes deployed the rocket ship from underneath the bomber's belly. Four liquid fueled rocket engines powered the rocket ship. Piloted by Captain "Chuck" Yeager, this plane was the first to break the sonic barrier in level flight. I worked with the rocket test engineers on that program and got to see each engine test fired before their installation. Besides all the excitement of engine testing, I did get to design a welded steel support structure for fuel tank storage.

Our neighbor across the street, "Sandy" Sandstrom, at that time was the vice president of engineering at Bell Aircraft. He took an interest in my hotrod and helped me land that great job for two summers supporting the Bell rocket ship project. Unfortunately, a Bell X-2 suddenly exploded under its mother ship, a EB-50A, on a test flight over Lake Ontario in 1953, killing Bell test pilot, Jean "Skip" Ziegler and an observer. Sandy had to tell the families the tragic news — that tragedy upset many residents of Buffalo and Bell's remaining flight test program was returned to the Air Force.

I met my future wife, Pat, in Buffalo. That romance started in the summer after my second year at the University of Detroit. When everyone was going back to school, my parents invited me to tour the U.S. When

I got back to Buffalo I worked on my Ford convertible and got a job rebuilding and repairing gas station gas pumps with another longtime friend from grammar school, Dick Schuster. Around that time Bell lost a big air-to-ground production missile contract called the Rascal Missile and some of the laid off employees went to work for Boeing in Seattle. One of those former Bell employees offered me a job at Boeing working in the Pilotless Aircraft Division, a job that was to be rewarding, exciting, and challenging.

Pat and I married and honeymooned along route 66 to the west coast and then up to Seattle. I first worked as an engineering aide on the Bomarc ground-to-air missile designing and testing instrumentation hardware. When the Minuteman Intercontinental Missile program contract award went to Boeing, I was transferred to that program with an engineering promotion a few years later. Working and taking advantage of Boeing's university study program, I graduated with a BS in Electrical Engineering from the University of Washington in 1976. Pat and I bought our first sailboat in partnership with Boeing manager, Dick Russell around 1965. That partnership developed into a wonderful long-term friendship. The *Jasmine Isle* was a Cheoy Lee Offshore 31.

Our second sailboat boat, *Mardalee*, was a Landfall 39. I helped United Airline pilot Ralph Warren import these sailboats from Taiwan. I did the custom interior designs, helped with marketing at boat shows and did the commissioning with Ralph. Pat and I chartered the *Mardalee* for 10 years at many locations all over Puget Sound and Canada. We bought our third sailboat, ***Our Pleasure***, in 1988. Her original designer was Bill Garden with later design changes by Mickelson. Modifications and equipment installation for long range cruising were started and added slowly over the next 9 years. We spent every summer and many weekends sailing with our children, their friends, and our friends. Seattle is blessed with hundreds of miles of protected, deep-water sailing destinations, but with one drawback, the water is always cold.

I finished my remaining 31 years on the Minuteman Intercontinental Ballistic Missile Program designing instrumentation systems for testing operational and test missiles. I retired from Boeing in 1995 as the Senior Minuteman Project Design Engineer. We raised our three children, David, Marjorie and Leslie in the Seattle suburb of Queen Anne. Pat and I, along with Leslie and her husband Bob, left Seattle on Sept. 3, 1997, being confident that our children remaining in Seattle had married good spouses, were financially independent and could manage well on their own.

CPSIA information can be obtained at www.ICGtesting.com
Printed in the USA
BVOW052152180613

323688BV00001B/1/P

9 781606 931752